Lecture Notes in Comput          5

Edited by G. Goos, J. Hartmanis and

Advisory Board: W. Brauer   D. Gries   J. Stoer

## Springer
Berlin
Heidelberg
New York
Barcelona
Budapest
Hong Kong
London
Milan
Paris
Santa Clara
Singapore
Tokyo

Keith G. Jeffery   Jaroslav Král
Miroslav Bartošek   (Eds.)

# SOFSEM '96:
# Theory and Practice
# of Informatics

23rd Seminar on Current Trends
in Theory and Practice of Informatics
Milovy, Czech Republic,
November 23-30, 1996
Proceedings

Springer

Series Editors

Gerhard Goos, Karlsruhe University, Germany

Juris Hartmanis, Cornell University, NY, USA

Jan van Leeuwen, Utrecht University, The Netherlands


Volume Editors

Keith G. Jeffery
CLRC Rutherford Appleton Laboratory
Chilton, Didcot, OX11 0QX Oxfordshire, United Kingdom
E-mail: kgj@inf.rl.ac.uk

Jaroslav Král
Charles University, Department of Software Engineering
Malostranské nám. 25, 118 00 Prague, Czech Republic
E-mail: kral@kki.mff.cuni.cz

Miroslav Bartošek
Masaryk University, Institute of Computer Science
Botanická 68a, 602 00 Brno, Czech Republic
E-mail: bartosek@ics.muni.cz

Cataloging-in-Publication data applied for

Die Deutsche Bibliothek - CIP-Einheitsaufnahme

**Theory and practice of informatics ; proceedings** / SOFSEM
'96, 23rd Seminar on Current Trends in Theory and Practice of
Informatics, Milovy, Czech Republic, November 23 - 30, 1996 /
Keith G. Jeffery ... (ed.). - Berlin ; Heidelberg ; New York ;
Barcelona ; Budapest ; Hong Kong ; London ; Milan ; Paris ;
Santa Clara ; Singapore ; Tokyo : Springer, 1996
  (Lecture notes in computer science ; Vol. 1175)
  ISBN 3-540-61994-1
NE: Jeffery, Keith G. [Hrsg.]; SOFSEM <23, 1996, Milovice>; GT

CR Subject Classification (1991): C.2, D, F, H.2, H.5, I.2, G.1-2, I.3

ISSN 0302-9743
ISBN 3-540-61994-1 Springer-Verlag Berlin Heidelberg New York

Typesetting: Camera-ready by author
SPIN 10549129    06/3142 – 5 4 3 2 1 0    Printed on acid-free paper

# Foreword

SOFSEM is special. This SOFSEM Conference, the 23rd in the series, is pivotal in the evolution of the conference. From the basis of a winter school with invited (local) speakers it has evolved to its present state, an international conference with international invited speakers and international refereed submitted papers (known as contributed talks). The history of SOFSEM was documented in the Foreword to the Proceedings of SOFSEM'95. It can also be found – together with all current information on the conference – under the general SOFSEM WWW page: http://www.ics.muni.cz/sofsem/sofsem.html.

Last year SOFSEM'95 achieved the distinction of having the proceedings published by Springer-Verlag in the Lecture Notes in Computer Science (LNCS) series. I am pleased that this fruitful association continues for this year and into the future. Also the duration was shortened – in response to results of a questionnaire at SOFSEM'94 – to one week from two, without significant loss of conference session time. Finally, there was some grouping of invited talks into themes.

This year the evolution continues; the PC chair and OC chair are elected by the Endowment Board and are then given responsibility and authority. The grouping of invited talks into themes has been strengthened by grouping the themes into certain days of the conference and ensuring session chairs have experience and knowledge of the theme. The themes this year are *Fundamentals, Distributed and Parallel Computing, AI and Control Systems, Databases and Electronic Documents, Scientific Computing and Visualization, Programming and Software Engineering.* These themes are reinforced in the contributed talks. The small, hard-working, and long-standing local programme committee (PC) of previous years was replaced by a PC of 33 people, approximately half of whom were local (Czech/Slovak) and half from 10 other countries. In many cases the non-local referees were invited speakers at previous SOFSEM conferences. This ensured in-depth international standard reviewing of the submitted papers (from 16 countries) and the result is seen in the quality of those chosen (approximately 1 in 3) from those submitted. Strict and documented PC refereeing practices ensured probity. In another evolutionary step the refereeing was done using WWW forms and a spreadsheet/database system at MU-ICS which provided the information for final decision-making at the PC meeting.

The SOFSEM'96 proceedings include papers from 19 invited talks and 22 contributed talks. I am pleased to welcome for the Opening Talk IFIP President K. Bauknecht. The excellent quality and interesting topics should ensure that this volume is of great interest both to academics and practitioners, from advanced students to very experienced professionals. Additionally there are posters and flash communications. While the invited speakers and presenters of accepted papers are the core of the conference, I would like to thank all who submitted papers to SOFSEM for their interest.

A conference such as this does not just happen. It is my pleasure to record my thanks to the Advisory Board for their guidance, to the Endowment Board for their work on invited talks and conference strategy, to the PC for their time and excellent refereeing work, and to the Organizing Committee (OC) whose members actually made it all happen. I am grateful to our sponsors whose support assists with invited speakers and advanced students, the organizing institutions for their support, the cooperating institutions for their efforts and the LNCS editors and Springer-Verlag for their trust, help and wisdom. The names are recorded elsewhere in this volume. The new management structure for SOFSEM conferences introduced this year worked smoothly; I would like to acknowledge the excellent cooperation I received from Jan Staudek as OC Chair and the *hands-off* attitude of the Endowment Board.

I would like to record some special thanks: to Jaroslav Král as a most supportive PC Vice-Chair, to Lenka Motyčková as secretary to the PC, and to Miroslav Bartošek as technical editor of the proceedings. I would like to thank especially Lukáš Hurník who composed an anthem for SOFSEM which is premiered this year, thus re-emphasizing the cultural as well as technical dimension of the conference.

On a personal note, I owe a special debt to Jan Pavelka. Following a visit to RAL in 1991, it was he who proposed that I should give an invited talk at SOFSEM'92 and thus initiated the formation of lasting professional links with friends in the Czech and Slovak Republics realized through joint projects, lectures, and seminars, technical discussions and participation in SOFSEM management. I was pleased to bring CRCIM (Czech Research Consortium for Informatics and Mathematics) representing the Czech Community into ERCIM (European Research Consortium for Informatics and Mathematics) this year, so strengthening informatics R&D in Europe and, I hope, partly repaying the debt.

As a member of the Advisory Board, more recently a member of the Endowment Board, and now as Programme Committee Chair for SOFSEM'96, I am proud to have been permitted (as an outsider) to be associated with the evolution of SOFSEM. I would like to take this opportunity to thank all my colleagues (attenders just as much as committee members) for their friendship and trust and their thoughtful comments on the future of the conference. Verily, SOFSEM is now fully international – in scope and standard – and with active management extended from a small dedicated group to a larger, local and international, no less dedicated representation. I shall continue to work for SOFSEM only as long as my contribution is useful and required.

CLRC RAL, September 1996                                    Keith G. Jeffery

# SOFSEM '96

## Advisory Board

## Endowment Board

## Program Committee

# SOFSEM '96

## Organized by

Czech Society for Computer Science
Slovak Society for Computer Science
Czech ACM Chapter
Czech Research Consortium for Informatics and Mathematics

## In cooperation with

Faculty of Informatics, Masaryk University Brno
Institute of Computer Science, Masaryk University Brno
Institute of Computer Science, Academy of Sciences Prague
Department of Computer Science, Comenius University Bratislava
CLRC Rutherford Appleton Laboratory, Oxon, UK

## Sponsored by

ApS Brno s.r.o.
Digital Equipment s.r.o.
European Research Consortium for Informatics and Mathematics
Help Service s.r.o.
Hewlett Packard s.r.o.
IBM Czech Republic s.r.o.
Oracle Czech s.r.o.
Prington a.s., financial leasing

## Organizing Committee

J. Staudek, *chair*          M. Bartošek, *vice-chair*
Z. Walletzká, *secretary*    P. Přikryl
P. Hanáček                   J. Sochor
Z. Malčík                    P. Sojka
T. Pitner                    T. Staudek

# Contents

## Invited Papers

SCIENTIFIC COMPUTING AND VISUALIZATION

PROGRAMMING AND SOFTWARE ENGINEERING

# Contributed Papers

# A Unified View to String Matching Algorithms[*]

Ricardo Baeza-Yates

Dept. de Ciencias de la Computación
Universidad de Chile
Blanco Encalada 2120
Santiago, Chile
E-mail: rbaeza@dcc.uchile.cl

**Abstract.** We present a unified view to sequential algorithms for many pattern matching problems, using a finite automaton built from the pattern which uses the text as input. We show the limitations of deterministic finite automata (DFA) and the advantages of using a bitwise simulation of non-deterministic finite automata (NFA). This approach gives very fast practical algorithms which have good complexity for small patterns on a RAM machine with word length $O(\log n)$, where $n$ is the size of the text. For generalized string matching the time complexity is $O(mn/\log n)$ which for small patterns is linear. For approximate string matching we show that the two main known approaches to the problem are variations of the NFA simulation. For this case we present a different simulation technique which gives a running time of $O(n)$ independently of the maximum number of errors allowed, $k$, for small patterns. This algorithm improves the best bit-wise or comparison based algorithms of running time $O(kn)$ and can be used as a basic block for algorithms with good average case behavior. We also formalize previous bit-wise simulation of general NFAs achieving $O(mn \log \log n/\log n)$ time.

## 1 Introduction

Pattern matching is an important problem in many different areas. The solutions to this problem differ if the algorithm has to be on-line (that is, the text is not known in advance) or off-line (the text can be preprocessed). In this paper we are interested in the first kind of algorithms. The most simple case is exact matching, which can be generalized to allow don't care characters, wildcards or a maximum number of errors (mismatches, deletions or insertions). All these variations can be described using a regular expression. In this case, the most simple searching algorithm is to construct a NFA from the regular expression and then run the NFA using the text as input [Tho68]. If the size of the regular expression is $m$, the NFA is built in $O(m)$ time and the NFA simulation requires $O(nm)$ time, being $n$ the size of the text. The algorithm at any stage keeps track of all the active states of the NFA, which in the worst case are $O(m)$.

[*] This work was partially funded by Fondecyt Chilean Grant 95-0622.

An efficient way to speed up the NFA simulation is to use a bit vector to keep track of all the NFA states. Assuming a RAM machine with word size $w \geq \log n$, we could expect to speed up the simulation to at most $O(mn/\log n)$ time. However, this is not always possible if we want limited extra space or if the regular expression is arbitrary. NFA simulations of exact string matching are implicit in [BYG92], don't care characters in [Pin85, Abr87, BYG92, WM92], approximate string matching and general regular expressions in [WM92, WMM95]. The first cases achieve the $O(mn/\log n)$ running time, but for approximate pattern matching the running time is $O(kmn/\log n)$ where $k$ is the maximum number of errors allowed, which could be $O(m)$. In all these cases, the simulation is done by just using bit-wise operations like shifts, and/ors, additions, etc, where comparisons are used only in the preprocessing phase (NFA construction).

There are other techniques for designing fast pattern matching algorithms. Instead of using a NFA, we can convert it to a DFA, and run a DFA using the text as input. For a finite size alphabet, the running time is $O(n)$. However, the NFA to DFA conversion requires in some cases $O(2^m)$ time, where $m$ is the size of the pattern. Therefore, even for small patterns of size $O(\log n)$ the total running time could be non-linear. In particular, for approximate string matching, the best upper bound for the maximum number of states of the DFA is exponential in the size of the pattern [Ukk85b]. We discuss this issue later.

In this paper we present the advantages of NFA with respect to DFA, and unify all the problems already mentioned in basically three cases: linear NFAs for generalized string matching, approximate string matching NFAs and general NFAs. For the second case, we show that it is possible to achieve running time $O(mn \log k/\log n)$ where $k$ is the maximum number of errors in a variation of the RAM model and $O(n)$ for small patterns. This should be compared with the previous best algorithms of $O(kn)$ [Ukk85a, LV88, GP90]. Also, in this case the number of states is $O(mk)$, but we reduce it to $O(m \log k)$ space by using the regularity of the NFA structure. For the generic case we formalize the approach presented in [WM92] to show that using $O(m)$ space, it is possible to achieve $O(mn \log m/\log n)$ running time. In all these cases we assume a finite alphabet, and the extension to arbitrary alphabets multiplies the complexity by an $O(\log m)$ factor. These results show that the comparison based model might not be the best for some problems and that we can use the intrinsic bit parallelism of the RAM model [BY92, WMM95], similarly to improvements achieved for sorting [FW93, AHNR95].

## 2 Preliminaries

There are ad-hoc comparison based algorithms for string matching with or without errors. Classical algorithms include Knuth-Morris-Pratt and Boyer-Moore for exact matching and dynamic programming for the case with errors. We refer the reader to [GBY91, Chapter 7] for more details. For string matching problems, non-comparison based algorithms include the use of matrix multiplication [FP74, Kar93], or bit-wise techniques as in this paper [Abr87, Der95, Wri94, WMM95].

The approach taken here tries to use the same technique for different problems.

We use a RAM machine with word size $w \geq \log_2 n$, for any text size $n$. We use the uniform cost model for a restricted set of operations including comparisons, additions, subtractions, bitwise AND and OR's, and unrestricted bit shifts (that is, the number of bits to shift is a parameter of the operation) [AHNR95]. Thus, all operations on $w$ bits take constant time, which is the case in the normal underlying hardware. This is the same assumption used for comparison-based algorithms in a RAM, so we can compare the time and space complexity. All these operations are in $AC^0$, that is, they can be implemented through constant-depth, polynomial-size circuits with unbounded fan-in.

In the following we use $\Sigma$ as a finite size alphabet. This is the usual case in practice. Some common examples of $\Sigma$ are ASCII (128 or 256), proteins (20) and DNA (4). If we need to handle arbitrary alphabets, we use the so called *effective alphabet*, which is the set of different symbols present in the pattern (which are at most $m$). For this we build a sorted table of size $m$ where we map the effective alphabet to a given index, having an extra index for symbols not in the pattern. By using binary search in this table, we can handle arbitrary alphabets. This technique increases the searching time by a factor of $O(\log_2 m)$ by using $O(m)$ extra space and $O(m \log m)$ preprocessing time. This can be reduced to a constant factor on the worst case by using perfect hashing, increasing the preprocessing time, but still depending only on $m$.

Finally, we use $x^i$ to denote the symbol $x$ concatenated $i$ times.

## 3 Deterministic Finite Automata

DFA have been related to string matching starting with the Knuth-Morris-Pratt algorithm [KMP77]. Figure 1 shows the DFA to find all occurrences of the pattern *aba*, where all the trivial transitions that go to the first state (any other character) have been removed. A straight-forward implementation of the DFA will require $O(m|\Sigma|)$ space achieving $O(n)$ running time. The space can be reduced to $O(m^2)$ if $|\Sigma| > m$ by using the effective alphabet mentioned in the previous section, at the cost of increasing the running time to $O(n \log m)$.

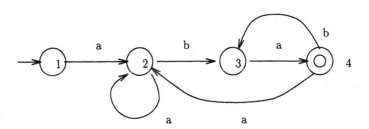

**Fig. 1.** DFA for finding *aba*.

We can distinguish forward matching edges and backward edges where we advance the pattern in the text. In fact, the famous failure function of the KMP algorithm can be defined as the state preceeding the shortest backward transition. For example, $next[4] = 2$. For the case of $next = 0$, we add one state with a forward transition on any character going to state 1. In [Sim93] it is shown that there are at most $m$ nontrivial backward edges and that the space complexity of a smart implementation of the DFA is $O(m)$ while keeping $O(n)$ running time. The construction of the DFA can also be done in linear time on the pattern size. Even more, Hancart [Han93] has proven that the searching time is $2n - 1$ in the worst case, which is the same as the KMP worst case time.

On the other hand, Knuth *et al.* [KMP77] also suggested an extension of the Boyer-Moore algorithm [BM77] to a Boyer-Moore automata (BMA) that keeps all the characters already known in the current pattern position. Figure 2 shows the BMA for the pattern *aba*, where there are forward matching transitions and backward transition that have a pattern shift associated. The problem of the maximum number of states of BMA for patterns of length $m$ is still unknown. A lower bound of $\Omega(m^3)$ is known [BYCG94] and there is clear evidence that this bound is not tight and a $\Omega(m^5)$ lower bound is conjectured in [BBYDS96]. So, for this case, DFA might be too large for most practical purposes.

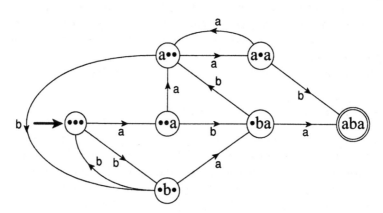

**Fig. 2.** Boyer-Moore automaton for finding the first occurrence of *aba*.

For approximate string matching with at most $k$ errors, we have that from the dynamic programming solution it is possible to compute the DFA directly using a recursive construction [Ukk85b]. The first idea is to ignore exact values larger than $k$, and replace them by a unique value (say $k + 1$). Each distinct column of the dynamic programming is a state of the DFA.

Given a pattern $p$ of length $m$, the construction starts from the state (column of $m$ elements) $(0, \ldots, k, *, \ldots, *)$ where $*$ denotes a value larger than $k$. From this state we compute the transitions for all the different symbols in the pattern, plus a default transition representing a symbol that does not appear in the pattern. Therefore, each state has at most $m + 1$ transitions. This process continues until all possible states are generated. Figure 3 shows this automaton for the pattern *aba* with $k = 1$. Final states are shown by a double box, and they are the ones where the $m$-st element of the column is less or equal than $k$. The $x$ symbol denotes any symbol except $a$ and $b$.

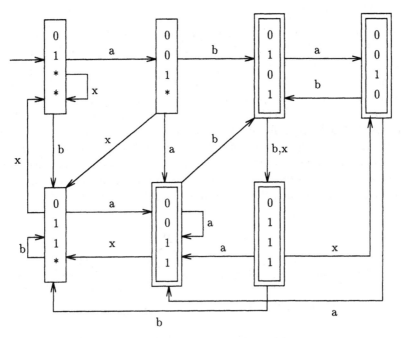

**Fig. 3.** DFA for the pattern $aba$ and $k = 1$.

Let $Q$ be the number of states. The total space is $O(mQ)$ because of having at most $m+1$ transitions per state. The preprocessing time to build this automaton is $O(mQ \log Q)$ where the $\log Q$ term is to find for each transition, the next state. The searching time depends on how the transitions are handled, but this may be done in $O(n)$. Ukkonen [Ukk85b] obtained the following upper bound for $Q$

$$Q \leq \min(3^m, 2^k |\Sigma|^k m^{k+1}).$$

This bound does not seem to be tight. For example, for $k = 1$, the maximum number of states is obtained for the pattern $baca^{m-3}$ with $m^2+1$ states. Recently, Melichar [Mel95] improved the previous bound for some ranges of $k$ to

$$O((k + 2)^{m-k}(k + 1)! \min(|\Sigma|, m + 1))$$

## 4 Generalized String Matching

In this section we unify several known results in a single problem and solution, where the NFA has size proportional to the length of the pattern. Let the pattern be a sequence of elements, each element being:

- A set or class of characters, complemented or not, including $\Sigma$ (don't care case).
- Any class, repeated zero or more times (Kleene or star closure), denoted by * (class wildcards).

For example, the pattern [Tt] [^aeiou] $\Sigma$ [0-9] * finds all sequences starting with $T$ or $t$, not followed by a vowel, followed by any character and then a sequence of 0 or more digits.

Almost the same problem is considered in [WM92], where the wildcards are always of the form $\Sigma^*$. This problem includes exact string matching, generalized string matching [Abr87, BYG92], don't care characters [Pin85, MBY91, BYG92], wildcards [WM92], the followed-by problem (one string followed by another) [MBY91] and subsequence searching [BY91]. The NFA for this problem is very simple, consisting of $m+1$ states, where $m$ is the number of non-starred elements. Figure 4 shows some examples, where we use $P_i$ for the non-starred elements and $S_i$ for the starred elements. We use $M$ to denote the total length of the pattern.

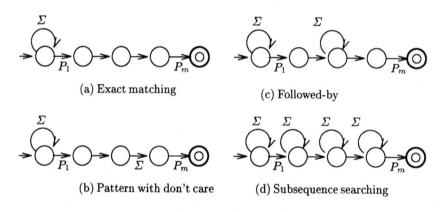

(a) Exact matching      (c) Followed-by

(b) Pattern with don't care      (d) Subsequence searching

**Fig. 4.** NFA examples of generalized string matching.

The NFA simulation is a generalization of the shift-or/and algorithm [BYG92, WM92]. Here we use the shift-and variant. Every state is one bit in a bit vector, using the enumeration induced by the automaton. So, a non-starred transition is simulated by shifting and AND-ing the vector with the entry for the current symbol $x$ in the text in a table $T_1$. $T_1$ has $\Sigma$ entries, each with $m$ bits. The entry $T_1[x]$ has a bit 1 in position $i$ if $x \in P_i$. Similarly, the starred transitions are handled by just and-ing the vector with an entry in a similar table $T_2$, where a bit is set to 1 if $x \in S_i$. The final algorithm is shown in C-like pseudocode in Figure 5, where we apply a bitwise or to both cases. Note that the initial state will always have a $\Sigma$ transition to itself, to allow finding the pattern in all possible positions of the text. A match is reported if the $(m + 1)$-st bit is a one.

If $m \geq w$, we use multiple words concatenating them, taken care of the inter-word transitions. On average it is better to apply the algorithm only on the first

$T_1$, $T_2 \leftarrow Preprocess(pattern)$
$s \leftarrow 1; mask \leftarrow 10^m$
for all characters $x$ of the text
{

      $s \leftarrow ((\text{shift left } s \text{ by } 1) \text{ and } T_1[x]) \text{ or } (s \text{ and } T_2[x]))$
      if $s$ and $mask$ then Report match

}

**Fig. 5.** Algorithm for Generalized String Matching.

word, storing the second only when needed [WM92]. The preprocessing time and total space needed is $O((\Sigma + M)m/w) = O((\Sigma + M)m/\log n)$. The running time is $O(mn/w) = O(mn/\log n)$. For patterns with $m = O(\log n)$, the time complexity is linear.

# 5 Approximate String Matching

In this section we present fast NFA simulations for approximate string matching using a NFA of size $O(m^2)$. Approximate string matching is one of the main problems in classical string algorithms. Given a text of length $n$, a pattern of length $m$, and a maximum number of errors allowed, $k$, we want to find all text positions where the pattern matches the text up to $k$ errors. Errors can be substitution, deletion or insertion of a character. We distinguish the case of only mismatches (just substitutions), and the case where we also allow insertion and deletions. In both cases the NFA has $O(mk)$ states and is very regular. This regularity allows the use of only $O(m \log k)$ bits to describe the automaton. We consider occurrences starting with a match and finishing as soon as there are at least $m - k$ matches.

## 5.1 String Matching with Mismatches

Consider the NFA for searching $p_1p_2p_3p_4$ with at most $k = 2$ mismatches, shown in Figure 6. Every row denotes the number of errors seen. The first 0, the second 1, and so on. Solid horizontal arrows represent matching a character. Solid diagonal arrows represent replacing the character of the text by the corresponding character in the pattern (that is, a mismatch). This NFA has clearly $O(mk)$ states and can be easily built in $O(mk)$ time given its highly regular structure.

This problem was considered in [BYG92], and here we summarize that solution. Instead of using one bit per state, we count the number of mismatches seen per column. Because we have at most $k$ mismatches, we need just $B = \lceil \log(k+1) \rceil$ bits per counter. Then, the new value of the counter for column $i$ is what the column $i - 1$ had before, plus zero if we had a match on that position or one otherwise. We can add these counters in parallel by concatenated in a single bit vector and having an extra bit between counters to avoid trespassing

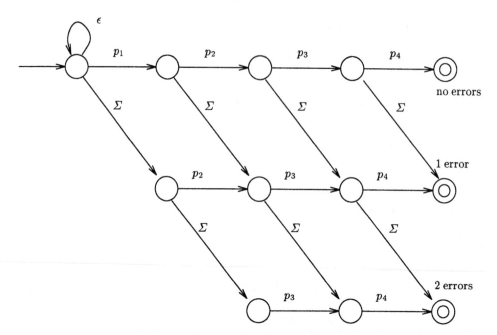

**Fig. 6.** NFA for string matching with mismatches.

carries from one counter to the next. This can be easily extended to classes of characters (mismatch implies $x \notin P_i$). The algorithm is shown in Figure 7 where $T_1[x]$ has a 1 in position $i$ if $x \neq p_i$. The extra space and preprocessing time is $O((\Sigma + m) \log k / \log n)$. The running time is $O(mn \log k / \log n)$ which is $O(n)$ for patterns of size up to $m = O(\log n / \log \log n)$.

```
B, T₁, mask₂ ← Preprocess(pattern, k)
s ← 0; mask₁ ← (01ᴮ)ᵐ
for all characters x in the text
}
        s ← ((shift left s by (B+1)) + T₁[x]) and mask₁
        if s and mask₂ then Report match
}
```

**Fig. 7.** Algorithm for Generalized String Matching with Mismatches (no wildcards).

A different bitwise simulation that requires $O(kn)$ time for small patterns is given by Dermouche [Der95]. We can combine the problem of mismatches and generalized patterns with wildcards, computing for every column the minimum of two values. Thus, using the same notation as for generalized string matching, we have for every counter

$$C_i = \min(C_{i-1} + (text \notin P_{i-1}), C_i \text{ if } text \in S_i, k+1)$$

To achieve the same time complexity as before we need to do parallel min operations. This can be done in $O(1)$ time by using several bit manipulation tricks in about ten machine instructions. With a different simulation technique we can have wildcards without using this parallel min technique, but the searching time increases [WM92].

This algorithm can also be used to count the number of mismatches between the pattern and all possible positions of the text. This is considered in [Abr87, Kos87] where a time complexity of $O(n\sqrt{m}\log m\sqrt{\log\log m})$ is given. Karloff [Kar93] improves this result to $O((n/\epsilon^2)\log^3 m)$ time for any $\epsilon > 0$, where $\epsilon$ is the maximum error tolerated (that is, the occurrences are also approximated). He also presents randomized algorithms that are better on average, but all these algorithms use matrix operations. Our algorithm requires in this case $O(mn\log m/\log n)$ which is better for patterns up to size $O(\log n(\log\log n)^2)$ and makes no mistakes ($\epsilon = 0$).

## 5.2 String Matching with Errors

Consider now the NFA for searching $p_1 p_2 p_3 p_4$ with at most $k = 2$ errors shown in Figure 8. As for the case of only mismatches, every row denotes the number of errors seen. The structure of the automaton is similar to the case of mismatches adding two additional transitions per state. Dashed diagonal arrows represent deleting a character of the pattern (empty transition), while dashed vertical arrows represent inserting a character. Let $s_{i,j}$ be true if the state on row $i$ (number of errors) and column $j$ (position in the pattern) is active. Then, after reading a new character, the new state values, $s'$, are given by

$$s'_{i,j} = (s_{i,j-1} \text{ if } p_{j-1} = text) \mid s_{i-1,j} \mid s_{i-1,j-1} \mid s'_{i-1,j-1}$$

where the first term represents a match, the second when we insert a character, the third when we substitute a character and the last, when we delete a character. Note that because we can delete a character in the text at any time, we have to use the current value of $s$, that is $s'$, instead of the previous value.

First, note that every row by itself matches the pattern. So, we can simulate every row using the technique shown for generalized string matching. By computing the dependences between rows, we obtain Wu & Manber's algorithm for approximate string matching[WM92]. In this case, the bit vectors $R_k$, being $k$ the corresponding row, are updated to $R'_k$ using the following formula

$$R'_k = (shift(R_k) \text{ \& } T[text[j]]) \text{ or } R_{k-1} \text{ or } shift(R_{k-1} \text{ or } R'_{k-1})$$

where the terms are written in the same order as before. Initially $R_k = 1^k 0^{m-k}$ ($k$ ones meaning up to $k$ deletions). The main drawback is the dependency on $R'_{k-1}$, due to the empty diagonal transitions, which does not allow us to compute

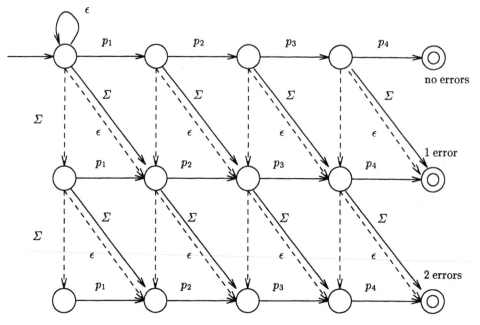

**Fig. 8.** NFA for approximate string matching.

the updated values of $R$ in parallel. The time complexity of this algorithm is $O(kmn/\log n)$ using $O((k + \Sigma)m/\log n)$ space for a RAM machine of word length $O(\log n)$.

Another possibility is to simulate the NFA by columns as for mismatches. Let us define the *value* of a column as the smallest active state level per column (or equivalently, the smallest error valid in each column). Then, the state of the search are $m$ numbers $C_i$ on the range $0...k + 1$. To update every column to $C_i'$ after we read a new text character we use

$$C_i' = \min( C_{i-1} + (text[j] \neq patt[i - 1]), \ C_i + 1, \ C_{i-1}' + 1 )$$

where the first term is either a match or a substitution, the second an insertion and the last one a deletion. Initially $C_0 = 0$ and $C_0' = C_0$. Readers familiar with the problem will recognize immediately this solution as a variation of the well known dynamic programming approach to approximate string matching. The time complexity is $O(nm)$. Smarter versions of this approach run in worst-case time $O(kn)$. This simulation is also related to Ukkonen's automata approach [Ukk85b]. The main disadvantage of this approach is again the dependency on $C_{i-1}'$ which does not allow a computation of $C'$ in parallel.

The dependency on both cases is due to the empty transitions along the diagonals. The solution is to simulate the automaton using diagonals, such that each diagonal captures the $\epsilon$-closure [BY95]. A similar idea is used to decrease the number of states of the associated DFA by Melichar [Mel95]. This idea is used next to design a faster algorithm.

Suppose we use just the diagonals of length $k + 1$ of the automaton. Let $D_i$ be the highest row value (smallest error) active per diagonal. Then, $D_1$ is always 0 (starting point). The new values for $D_i$ after we read a new text character are given by

$$D_i' = \min(D_i + 1, D_{i+1} + 1, g(D_{i-1}, text))$$

where $g(D_{i-1}, text)$ takes the value $D_{i-1}$ if there is a position $j$ such that $j \geq D_i$ and $p_{i+j} = text$; otherwise it takes the value $k + 1$. This later value is used if there are no active states in the diagonal. The first term of the min expression represents a substitution which follows the same diagonal. The second term represents the insertion of a character coming from the next diagonal above. Finally, the last term represents matching the character in previous diagonals above the current level (more than one when there are characters repeated in the pattern). This simulation has the advantage that it can be computed in parallel for all $i$. The function $g$, considering that the alphabet is finite and that $D_i$ can take only $k + 2$ values, can be precomputed based solely in the pattern. So, we would like to use bitwise parallelism to simulate the automaton. However, the drawback now is that although we can compute in parallel several minima, it is not possible to evaluate the function $g$ in parallel (each argument has $O(\log k)$ bits) without using exponential space. However, implementing $g$ by hardware (still in $AC^0$) and preprocessing the valid values of pairs $(j, text)$ in a table, the time complexity for this algorithm is $O(mn \log k / \log n)$ which is $O(n)$ for patterns of size up to $O(\log n / \log \log n)$.

A different bitwise parallelism is considered by Wright [Wri94], which packs three diagonals of the dynamic programming matrix in one word (the diagonals perpendicular to ours); Wright's approach also has the dependency problem. In [BYN96b] we show how to represent $D_i$ using $O(k)$ bits in the usual RAM model and evaluating the recurrence in $O(1)$ operations, obtaining the fastest known algorithm for approximate string matching when $(m - k)(k + 2) \leq w$. We can extend this problem to allow a generalized pattern with errors. For that we just include another function $h$ that is equivalent to $T_2$, such that

$$R_i' = \min(R_i + 1, R_{i+1} + 1, g(R_{i-1}, text), h(R_i, text))$$

with $h(R_i, text)$ being $R_i$ if $text \in S_i$ or $k + 1$ otherwise.

## 6 Regular Expressions

In this section we address general automata, where the NFA size is proportional to the length of the regular expression to be searched. The standard algorithm [Tho68] requires $O(mn)$ time in the worst case. The first sublinear algorithm is given by Myers [Mye92] which uses a four russians approach. In [WM92] a bitwise simulation for a generic NFA built using the standard Thompson's algorithm is given. By construction, all states either have one deterministic transition or two non-deterministic $\epsilon$-transitions. So, the deterministic transitions are handled by shifting left by one bit the state vector and $and$-ing it with the entry of a table $T_1$ as in previous cases. Each entry in $T_1$ also cancels all states with non-deterministic transitions. To handle all the $\epsilon$-transitions, they use tables to map one or two bytes of the new state vector into a new vector. In practice they use two bytes, which can be considered as a constant or $w/2$ for 32-bit words.

The above result can be understood better by using as a parameter the maximum space $S$ to be used. Then, we can use blocks of size $\log S$ bits to divide the bit vector of size $m$, where $m$ is the size of the NFA. Using the previous algorithm, the time complexity is $O(mn \log S/\log n)$. Using $S$ of $O(\log n)$, which means a constant number of words, we get time complexity $O(mn \log \log n/\log n)$. Any polylog number of words only decreases the searching time on a constant. The complexity can be improved if a parallel mapping operation in blocks of bits is available (easily implemented by hardware and also in $AC^0$).

This algorithm can be improved in several ways. One of them is to reduce the number of $\epsilon$-transitions based on states with out-degree greater than 1. This leads to an interesting optimization problem which is being studied. This algorithm can be extended to consider errors as is mentioned also in [WM92, WMM95] (see also [MM89]).

## 7 Concluding Remarks

In this paper we have unified several algorithms using a single technique: bitwise simulation of NFAs. We have also shown that many algorithms for approximate string matching, including dynamic programming, can be seen as specialized bitwise simulations. An additional result is the relevance of the machine model to be used. In an augmented RAM model, the new algorithm presented for string matching with errors can be a factor of $O(m/\log m)$ faster, which is another example where the traditional RAM comparison model does not seem to be the best choice.

Another issue is related to the effective use of the intrinsic bit-parallelism of the RAM model. Several new parallelism models which try to improve upon the classic PRAM model, do not address well the fact that many operations can be executed in constant time on $O(\log n)$ bits or that less memory is needed in practice. For example, our new algorithm can be considered as a parallel algorithm for $m$ processors, each one using only $O(\log k)$ bits. Then, we would like to compare this algorithm using the fact that the operations are over small words and not over $O(\log n)$ size words.

There are several extensions to the basic NFA simulations shown here. They can be extended to more general cases and used as building blocks to handle other types of patterns or to devise fast expected time algorithms. We address briefly these ideas.

First, we can extend all the simulations to handle multiple patterns by simulating all NFAs at the same time (multiplying the time complexity by the number of patterns). For large patterns we can partition the automata in several words. For approximate string matching, another possibility is to divide the pattern in $\ell$ pieces of length $m/\ell$ where up to $k/\ell$ errors are allowed, searching all pieces at once and checking the whole pattern if a piece is found. This idea is a generalization of techniques presented in [WM92, BYP92, Mye94] and together with automata partition and other ideas is used in [BYN96b, BYN96a] to design a fast expected time algorithm for approximate string matching.

## Acknowledgements

We acknowledge the helpful discussions and comments of Ricardo Dahab, Gaston Gonnet, Udi Manber and Gonzalo Navarro.

# References

[Abr87]     K. Abrahamson. Generalized string matching. *SIAM J on Computing*, 16:1039–1051, 1987.

[AHNR95]    A. Anderson, T. Hagerup, S. Nilsson, and R. Rajeev. Sorting in linear time? In *STOC'95*, pages 427–436, Las Vegas, NE, 1995.

[BY91]      R. Baeza-Yates. Searching subsequences (note). *Theoretical Computer Science*, 78:363–376, 1991.

[BYG92]     R. Baeza-Yates and G.H. Gonnet. A new approach to text searching. *Communications of the ACM*, 35:74–82, Oct 1992.

[BYP92]     R.A. Baeza-Yates and C.H. Perleberg. Fast and practical approximate pattern matching. In A. Apostolico, M. Crochemore, Z. Galil, and U. Manber, editors, *Combinatorial Pattern Matching*, Lecture Notes in Computer Science 644, pages 185–192, Tucson, AZ, April/May 1992. Springer Verlag.

[BY92]      R. Baeza-Yates. Text retrieval: Theory and practice. In J. van Leeuwen, editor, *12th IFIP World Computer Congress, Volume I*, volume Algorithms, Software, Architecture, pages 465–476, Madrid, Spain, September 1992. Elsevier Science.

[BYCG94]    R.A. Baeza-Yates, C. Choffrut, and G.H. Gonnet. On Boyer-Moore automata. *Algorithmica*, 12:268–292, 1994.

[BY95]      R. Baeza-Yates. A unified view of pattern matching problems. Technical report, Dept. of Computer Science, Univ. of Chile, 1995.

[BYN96b]    R. Baeza-Yates and G. Navarro. A faster algorithm for approximate string matching. In *Combinatorial Pattern Matching (CPM'96)*, Irvine, CA, Jun 1996. ftp//sunsite.dcc.uchile.cl/-pub/users/gnavarro/cpm96.ps.gz.

[BYN96a]    R. Baeza-Yates and G. Navarro. A fast heuristic for approximate string matching. In *Third South American Workshop on String Processing*, pages 47–63, Recife, Brazil, August 1996. ftp//-sunsite.dcc.uchile.cl/pub/users/gnavarro/wsp96.2.ps.gz.

[BM77]      R. Boyer and S. Moore. A fast string searching algorithm. *C.ACM*, 20:762–772, 1977.

[BBYDS96]   V. Bruyere, R. Baeza-Yates, O. Delgrange, and R. Scheihing. On the size of Boyer-Moore automata. In *Third South American Workshop on String Processing*, pages 31–46, Recife, Brazil, August 1996.

[Der95]    A Dermouche. A fast algorithm for string matching with mismatches. *Information Processing Letters*, 55(1):105–110, July 1995.

[FP74]    M. Fischer and M. Paterson. String matching and other products. In R. Karp, editor, *Complexity of Computation (SIAM-AMS Proceedings 7)*, volume 7, pages 113–125. American Mathematical Society, Providence, RI, 1974.

[FW93]    M. Fredman and D. Willard. Surpassing the information theoretic bound with fusion trees. *J. Comput. System Sci.*, 47:424–436, 1993.

[GBY91]    G.H. Gonnet and R. Baeza-Yates. *Handbook of Algorithms and Data Structures - In Pascal and C.* Addison-Wesley, Wokingham, UK, 1991. (second edition).

[GP90]    Z. Galil and K. Park. An improved algorithm for approximate string matching. *SIAM J. on Computing*, 19(6):989–999, 1990.

[Han93]    C Hancart. *Analyse Exacte et en Moyenne d'Algorithmes de Recherche d'un Mot dans un Texte*. PhD thesis, Universite Paris 7, Paris, France, 1993.

[Kar93]    H. Karloff. Fast algorithms for approximately counting mismatches. *Information Processing Letters*, 48:53–60, 1993.

[KMP77]    D.E. Knuth, J. Morris, and V. Pratt. Fast pattern matching in strings. *SIAM J on Computing*, 6:323–350, 1977.

[Kos87]    S.R. Kosaraju. Efficient string matching. Manuscript, Johns Hopkins University, 1987.

[LV88]    G. Landau and U. Vishkin. Fast string matching with k differences. *JCSS*, 37:63–78, 1988.

[MBY91]    U. Manber and R. Baeza-Yates. An algorithm for string matching with a sequence of don't cares. *Information Processing Letters*, 37:133–136, February 1991.

[Mel95]    B. Melichar. Approximate string matching by finite automata. In *Conf. on Analysis of Images and Patterns*, number 970 in LNCS, pages 342–349, Prague, Check Republic, 1995. Springer-Verlag.

[MM89]    E. Myers and W. Miller. Approximate matching of regular expressions. *Bulletin of Mathematical Biology*, 51(1):5–37, 1989.

[Mye92]    E. Myers. A four-russians algorithm for regular expression pattern matching. *JACM*, 39(2):430–448, 1992.

[Mye94]    E. Myers. A sublinear algorithm for approximate keyword searching. *Algorithmica*, 12(4/5):345–374, Oct/Nov 1994.

[Pin85]    R. Pinter. Efficient string matching with don't-care patterns. In A. Apostolico and Z. Galil, editors, *Combinatorial Algorithms on Words*, volume F12 of *NATO ASI Series*, pages 11–29. Springer-Verlag, 1985.

[Sim93]    I. Simon. String matching algorithms and automata. In *First South American Workshop on String Processing*, pages 151–157, Belo Horizonte, Brazil, 1993.

[Tho68]    K. Thompson. Regular expression search algorithm. *C.ACM*, 11:419–422, 1968.

[Ukk85a]    E. Ukkonen. Algorithms for approximate string matching. *Information and Control*, 64:100–118, 1985.

[Ukk85b]    E. Ukkonen. Finding approximate patterns in strings. *J. of Algorithms*, 6:132–137, 1985.

[WM92]      S. Wu and U. Manber. Fast text searching allowing errors. *Communications of the ACM*, 35:83–91, Oct 1992.

[WMM95]     S. Wu, U. Manber, and E. Myers. A subquadratic algorithm for approximate regular expression matching. *Journal of Algorithms*, 19:346–360, 1995.

[Wri94]     A. Wright. Approximate string matching using within-word parallelism. *Software Practice and Experience*, 24(4):337–362, April 1994.

# Communication in Parallel Systems

Friedhelm Meyer auf der Heide and Christian Scheideler*

Department of Mathematics and Computer Science
and Heinz Nixdorf Institute
University of Paderborn
33095 Paderborn, Germany

**Abstract.** Efficient communication in networks is a prerequisite to exploit the performance of large parallel systems. For this reason much effort has been done in recent years to develop efficient communication mechanisms. In this paper we survey the foundations and recent developments in designing and analyzing efficient packet routing algorithms.

## 1 Introduction

Communication among the processors of a parallel computer usually requires a large portion of the runtime of a parallel algorithm. These computers are often realized as sparse networks of a large number of processors such that each processor can directly communicate with a few neighbours only. Thus, most of the communication must proceed through intermediate processors. One of the basic problems in this context is to route simultaneously many messages through the network. Telecommunicaton networks, computer networks in companies and universities, or the internet are examples for networks that have to process many communication requests in parallel (e.g., telephone calls, emails, money transfers between banks). In this paper we want to describe recent developments in the field of *universal* routing algorithms, that is, algorithms that can be used in any communication network. Universal algorithms have the advantage that, in addition to providing a unified approach to routing in standard networks, they are ideally suited to routing in irregular networks that are used in wide-area networks and that arise when standard networks develop faults. Furthermore, universal routing algorithms can be used for arbitrary patterns of communication.

In this survey paper, we focus on comparing the routing time needed by distributed routing protocols to the worst case routing time of a best offline routing protocol, the so-called *routing number*. It turns out that online protocols, even deterministic protocols, can get very close to this efficiency bound under various assumptions about the topology, bandwidth, and buffer size of the underlying network.

---
* email:{fmadh,chrsch}@uni-paderborn.de, fax: +49-5251-606482, http://www.uni-paderborn.de/cs/{fmadh,chrsch}.html. Supported in part by DFG-Sonderforschungsbereich 376 "Massive Parallelität: Algorithmen, Entwurfsmethoden, Anwendungen", by DFG Leibniz Grant Me872/6-1, and by EU ESPRIT Long Term Research Project 20244 (ALCOM-IT).

## Organization of the Paper

In the following chapter we introduce the basic notation about networks, messages, and protocols for routing. In Chapter 3 we introduce the routing number of a network, and relate it to the dilation and congestion of path systems. Chapter 4 contains an overview of oblivious routing protocols, and Chapter 5 describes efficient adaptive routing protocols.

# 2 Networks, Messages, Protocols

In this chapter we introduce the basic notions used in routing theory. In particular, we describe a typically used hardware model and message passing model, define the routing problem, and describe different classes of strategies to solve routing problems.

## 2.1 The Hardware Model

We model the topology of a network as an undirected graph $G = (V, E)$. $V$ represents the computers or processors, and $E$ represents the communication links. We assume the communication links to work bidirectional, that is, each edge represents two *links*, one in each direction. The *bandwidth* of a link is defined as the number of messages it can forward in one time step. Unless explicitly mentioned we assume that the bandwidth is 1. The *size* $N$ of $G$ is defined as the number of nodes $G$ contains.

Each node in $V$ contains an *injection buffer* and a *delivery buffer*. The task of the injection buffer of a node $v$ is to store all messages $v$ wants to send out, and the task of the delivery buffer is to store all messages arriving at $v$ whose destination is $v$. Further we assume that each link has a *link buffer* (or *buffer* for short). The *size* of a buffer is defined as the maximal number of messages a buffer can store. In the *multi-port* model each link can forward at most one message per step, whereas in the *single-port* model each node can forward at most one message in one step. We only consider the multi-port model in the following, since it has become most common for packet routing in the last years.

### Network Topologies

The most commonly used network topologies in the routing literature and in parallel computers are meshes, tori and butterflies. These classes are defined in the following. (For any $k \in \mathbb{N}$, $[k]$ denotes the set $\{0, \ldots, k-1\}$.)

**Definition 1 (Butterfly).** Let $d \in \mathbb{N}$. The *d-dimensional butterfly* $BF(d)$ is defined as an undirected graph with node set $V = [d+1] \times [2]^d$ and an edge set $E = E_1 \cup E_2$ with

$$E_1 = \{\{(i, \alpha), (i+1, \alpha)\} \mid i \in [d], \ \alpha \in [2]^d\}$$

and

$$E_2 = \{\{(i, \alpha), (i+1, \beta)\} \mid i \in [d], \ \alpha, \beta \in [2]^d, \ \alpha \text{ and } \beta \text{ differ only at the } i\text{th position}\}.$$

The *d-dimensional wrap-around butterfly* W-BF$(d)$ is derived from the $BF(d)$ by identifying level $d$ with level 0.

**Definition 2 (Torus, Mesh).** Let $m, d \in \mathbf{N}$. The $(m,d)$-mesh $M(m,d)$ is a graph with node set $V = [m]^d$ and edge set

$$E = \left\{ \{(a_{d-1} \ldots a_0), (b_{d-1} \ldots b_0)\} \mid a_i, b_i \in [m], \sum_{i=0}^{d-1} |a_i - b_i| = 1 \right\} .$$

The $(m,d)$-torus $T(m,d)$ consists of an $(m,d)$-mesh and additionally the edges

$$\{\{(a_{d-1} \ldots a_{i+1} 0 a_{i-1} \ldots a_0), (a_{d-1} \ldots a_{i+1} (m-1) a_{i-1} \ldots a_0)\} \mid i \in [d], \, a_j \in [m]\} .$$

$M(m,1)$ is also called *linear array*, $T(m,1)$ *cycle*, and $M(2,d) = T(2,d)$ *d-dimensional hypercube.*

A very general class form the node-symmetric graphs.

**Definition 3 (Node-Symmetric Graph).** A graph $G = (V, E)$ is called node-symmetric if for any pair of nodes $u, v \in V$ there exists an isomorphism $\varphi : V \to V$ with $\varphi(u) = v$ such that the graph $G_\varphi = (V, E_\varphi)$ with $E_\varphi = \{\{\varphi(x), \varphi(y)\} \mid \{x, y\} \in E\}$ is isomorphic to $G$.

Intuitively, node-symmetry means that a graph looks the same from any node. Node-symmetric graphs form a very general class and include most of the standard networks such as the $d$-dimensional torus, the wrap-around butterfly, the hypercube, etc. An important subclass of the node-symmetric graphs are the edge-symmetric graphs.

**Definition 4 (Edge-Symmetric Graph).** A graph $G = (V, E)$ is called edge-symmetric if for any pair of edges $\{u, v\}, \{u', v'\} \in E$ there exists an isomorphism $\varphi : V \to V$ with $\{\varphi(u), \varphi(v)\} = \{u', v'\}$ such that the graph $G_\varphi = (V, E_\varphi)$ with $E_\varphi = \{\{\varphi(u), \varphi(v)\} \mid \{u, v\} \in E\}$ is isomorphic to $G$.

The $d$-dimensional torus, for instance, is edge-symmetric.

**Definition 5 (Leveled Graph).** A graph $G = (V, E)$ is called *leveled* with *depth D* if the nodes of $G$ can be partitioned into $D$ *levels* $L_0, \ldots, L_D$ such that every edge in $E$ connects nodes of consecutive levels. Nodes in level 0 are called *inputs*, and nodes in level $D$ are called *outputs*. If, in addition, $|L_0| = |L_D|$ and $L_1$ is identified with $L_D$, then $G$ is called a *wrapped leveled* graph with depth $D$.

The $d$-dimensional butterfly, for instance, is a leveled graph with depth $d$, and the $d$-dimensional wrap-around butterfly is a wrapped leveled graph with depth $d$.

## 2.2 The Routing Problem

Consider an arbitrary network $G$ with node set $[N]$. Let $v$ and $w$ be two nodes in $G$. We say that a message is *routed* from $v$ to $w$ if it is sent along a path in $G$ from $v$ to $w$. An instance of the routing problem is defined by a multi-set of source-destination pairs

$$\mathcal{R} = \{(v_1, w_1), \ldots, (v_n, w_n)\} .$$

Each pair $(v_i, w_i) \in [N]^2$ represents a message that has to be sent from $v_i$ to $w_i$. The following routing problems are usually studied.

- *Permutation routing*: Let $S_N$ be the set of all permutations $\pi : [N] \to [N]$. Given a permutation $\pi \in S_N$, route a message from node $i$ to node $\pi(i)$ for all $i \in [N]$.
- *h-function routing*: Let $F_{h,N}$ be the set of all $h$-functions $f : [h] \times [N] \to [N]$. Given an $h$-function $f \in F_{h,N}$, route a message from node $i$ to nodes $f(1,i), \ldots, f(h,i)$ for all $i \in [N]$. A 1-function is simply called function.
- *h-relation routing*: An $h$-relation is defined as an $h$-function $f \in F_{h,N}$ with $|f^{-1}(i)| = h$ for all $i \in [N]$. Given an $h$-relation $f \in F_{h,N}$, route a message from node $i$ to nodes $f(1,i), \ldots, f(h,i)$ for all $i \in [N]$.
- *Broadcasting*: Given a node $i \in [N]$, route a message from $i$ to all nodes $j \in [N]$.
- *Gossiping*: For every node $i \in [N]$, route a message from $i$ to all nodes $j \in [N]$.

The solution to a routing problem is called *routing protocol*. It determines for each time step, which message to choose from a buffer and which edge to use. Its basic component is the *contention resolution rule* that decides which message wins if more than one message try to use the same link at the same time.

A routing protocol is called *deterministic* if all decisions during the routing are deterministic, and *randomized* otherwise.

## 2.3 Routing Strategies

We distinguish between two kinds of protocols: *Offline* protocols and *online* protocols. In case of offline protocols we allow the system to compute, for a given routing problem $\mathcal{R}$, a routing schedule for $\mathcal{R}$ before sending out the messages. The time an offline protocol needs is defined as the time needed to route the messages according to the schedule. This implies that the time for computing that schedule does *not* count. In case of online protocols the time for computing a schedule counts.

There are basically two classes of online protocols. In order to send a message from node $v$ to $w$ in $G$ it has to traverse a contiguous sequence of links called *routing path*. Given a source-destination pair a message may either have to traverse a path specified in advance or is able to choose among several alternative paths depending on the source-destination pairs of other messages or other events. The first case is called *oblivious routing* and the second case *adaptive routing*.

**Oblivious Routing**

In case of oblivious routing the path a message uses only depends on its source and destination. Let $p_{v,w}$ denote the path from $v$ to $w$ in $G$ that has to be taken by every message that wants to travel from $v$ to $w$. Then $\mathcal{P} = \{p_{v,w} \mid v, w \in V\}$ is called *path system* of size $|V|$. In this case any routing problem $\mathcal{R}$ can be defined by specifying a *path collection* $\mathcal{P}_\mathcal{R}$ of size $|\mathcal{R}|$ that contains the path $p_{v,w}$ for every pair $(v, w)$ in $\mathcal{R}$. A path collection is called

- *simple* if no path contains the same edge more than once,
- *shortcut-free* if no piece of a path in $\mathcal{P}$ can be shortcut by any combination of other pieces of paths in $\mathcal{P}$,
- *shortest* if all paths are shortest paths in $G$, and
- *leveled* if the nodes can be arranged in levels such that every edge leads from level $i$ to level $i + 1$ for some $i \geq 0$.

The following relationship holds for these types of path collections.

$$\text{leveled} \Rightarrow \text{shortest} \Rightarrow \text{shortcut-free} \Rightarrow \text{simple}$$

Important parameters for the runtime are

- the *size n* of $\mathcal{P}_\mathcal{R}$, that is, the number of paths $\mathcal{P}_\mathcal{R}$ contains,
- the *congestion C* of $\mathcal{P}_\mathcal{R}$, that is, the maximal number of paths in $\mathcal{P}_\mathcal{R}$ that contain the same edge in $G$, and
- the *dilation D* of $\mathcal{P}_\mathcal{R}$, that is, the length of a longest path in $\mathcal{P}_\mathcal{R}$.

In case that we want to route random functions, we often use the notion of expected congestion that is defined as follows. For an edge $e$ and a path system $\mathcal{P}$, let the expected congestion $\bar{C}_e$ of $e$ be defined as the expected number of messages that traverse $e$ using paths in $\mathcal{P}$ during the routing of a randomly chosen function. The *expected congestion* of $\mathcal{P}$ is then defined as $\bar{C} = \max_{e \in E} \bar{C}_e$.

In case of bounded buffers, *deadlocks* can arise during the routing. Packets are defined to run into a deadlock if they prevent each other from moving forward because of full buffers.

**Adaptive Routing**

In case of adaptive routing the path a message uses is not predetermined. There are several parameters that are used to measure the performance of adaptive routing protocols: The bisection width, expansion [9], flux [13], or routing number (see Section 3) of a network.

In adaptive protocols that do not restrict the messages to approach their destinations via shortest paths, *livelocks* can happen. Packets run into a livelock if they run infinitely often along the same cycle in the network.

## 2.4 The Message Passing Model

The most commonly used and well understood routing model in the literature is the *packet routing model*. In this model time is partitioned into synchronous *steps*. One step is defined as the time a message needs to be sent along an edge. (It is usually assumed that every edge needs the same amount of time to forward a packet.) A node must store an entire message before it can forward any part of the message along the next edge on its route. Hence, messages can be viewed as atomic objects called *packets*. A packet has the following format.

| message | routing information | source | destination |

In a network with $N$ nodes the source and destination need $\lfloor \log N \rfloor + 1$ bits, each. Throughout this paper we restrict the routing information to be very small, namely of length at most $O(\log N)$. It is usually needed to store information about the path a packet has to follow or the priority level of a packet. We assume the messages to have uniform length.

Packet routing algorithms are used on machines such as the NCube, NASA MPP, Intel Hypercube, and Transputer-based machines. Since the packet model does not make assumptions about packet lengths, it is the easiest and therefore the most studied model in the literature.

## 3 The Routing Number

The aim of this paper is to survey results on relating the routing time needed by online routing protocols to the worst case routing time of a best offline routing algorithm, the so-called *routing number*. This number is defined as follows (see, e.g., [2]):

Consider an arbitrary network $G$ with $N$ nodes and bandwidth one. For a permutation $\pi \in S_N$, let $R(G, \pi)$ be the minimum possible number of steps required to route messages offline in $G$ according to $\pi$ using the multi-port model with unbounded buffers. Then the *routing number* $R(G)$ of $G$ is defined by

$$R(G) = \max_{\pi \in S_N} R(G, \pi) \ .$$

In case that there is no risk of confusion about the network $G$ we will write $R$ instead of $R(G)$. The routing number has the following nice property.

**Theorem 6.** *For any network $G$ with routing number $R$, the average number of steps to route a permutation in $G$ is bounded by $\Theta(R)$.*

**Proof.** Let $\bar{R} = \frac{1}{|S_N|} \sum_{\pi \in S_N} R(G, \pi)$ denote the average number of steps to route a permutation in $G$. Consider any fixed permutation $\pi$. In order to bound the minimum number of steps to route $\pi$ we will use a probabilistic argument based on Valiant's trick (see [24]) by first sending the packets to random intermediate destinations before sending them to the destinations prescribed by $\pi$. Let $X$ be a random variable denoting the minimum number of steps necessary to route a randomly chosen permutation. According to the Markov Inequality it holds:

$$\text{Prob}(X \geq 3\bar{R}) \leq \tfrac{1}{3} \ .$$

Therefore, for a randomly chosen permutation $\varphi$ for the intermediate destinations, it holds that with probability at most $\tfrac{1}{3} + \tfrac{1}{3} < 1$ the minimum number of steps to route first according to $\varphi$ and then according to $\pi$ exceeds $6\bar{R}$. Therefore there exists an offline protocol that routes $\pi$ in at most $6\bar{R}$ steps. Thus $R \leq 6\bar{R}$, which completes the proof. ∎

Hence asymptotically the routing number is not only an upper bound, but also a lower bound for the average permutation routing time using optimal routing strategies in $G$.

Note that the routing number might be defined by some protocol which uses specific routing paths tailored to the permutation to be routed. This implies the following result.

**Remark 7** *For any network $G$ of size $N$ with routing number $R$, there exists a collection of simple paths for any permutation routing problem $\pi \in S_N$ with congestion at most $R$ and dilation at most $R$.*

The question is whether it is possible to find such a path collection in an efficient way for every permutation routing problem. This will be answered by the following two sections. The first section deals with the problem of choosing a path system with low dilation and expected congestion, and the second section shows how to choose path collections out of such a system in a distributed way such that the dilation and congestion bounds in Remark 7 can be reached up to constant factors for any permutation routing problem.

## 3.1 Relationship to Dilation and Expected Congestion

A necessary prerequisite for efficient oblivious routing is a path system with low dilation and low expected congestion. In this section we construct path systems that have dilation and expected congestion close to the routing number for arbitrary networks. The main result of this section is formulated in the next theorem.

**Theorem 8.** *For any network $G$ of size $N$ with routing number $R$ there is a simple path system with dilation at most $R$ and expected congestion at most $R$. Furthermore, for random functions the congestion is bounded by $R + O(\sqrt{\max\{R, \log N\} \cdot \log N})$, w.h.p.* [*]

**Proof.** Let $G$ be a network of size $N$ with routing number $R$. Then for any permutation $\pi_i : [N] \to [N]$ with $\pi_i(x) = (x + i) \bmod N$ for all $i, x \in [N]$ there is a path collection $\mathcal{P}_i$ along which packets can be routed in at most $R$ time steps. Therefore the congestion and dilation of $\mathcal{P}_i$ is at most $R$. We then choose $\mathcal{P} = \bigcup_{i=0}^{N-1} \mathcal{P}_i$ to be the path system for $G$. Clearly, this path system has congestion at most $N \cdot R$ and dilation at most $R$. It remains to bound the expected congestion and the congestion that holds w.h.p. for routing a random function in $G$ using paths in $\mathcal{P}$.

Consider any edge $e$ in $G$. Let the random variable $X$ denote the number of paths that cross $e$ and are used by a packet. Since each node in $G$ chooses a destination for its packet uniformly and independently at random, the probability that a path crossing $e$ is used by a packet is $1/N$. Therefore the expected congestion is at most $R$.

For any node $v$ in $G$, let the binary random variable $X_v$ be one if and only if the packet with source $v$ contains $e$ in its routing path. Then $X = \sum_{v \in V} X_v$. Since we consider routing a random function, the probabilities of all $X_v$ are independent. As $E(X) \leq R$, the Chernoff bounds (see [7]) therefore yield that

$$\text{Prob}(X \geq (1 + \epsilon)R) \leq \begin{cases} e^{-\epsilon^2 R/3} & : \text{ if } 0 \leq \epsilon \leq 1 \\ e^{-\epsilon \cdot R/2} & : \text{ if } \epsilon \geq 2 \end{cases}$$

This probability is polynomially small in $N$ for $\epsilon = O(\max\{\sqrt{\frac{\log N}{R}}, \frac{\log N}{R}\})$ sufficiently large. Hence w.h.p. there exists no edge with a congestion greater than $R + O(\sqrt{\max\{R, \log N\} \cdot \log N})$. ∎

For node-symmetric networks we can strengthen Theorem 8 by showing that the path system may even be assumed to consist of shortest paths. This is important, because some oblivious routing protocols are especially good for shortest path systems, see Chapter 4. Since the diameter of a network is a lower bound for its routing number, we use the diameter instead of the routing number in the following theorem.

**Theorem 9.** *Let $G$ be a node-symmetric network with $N$ nodes and diameter $D$. Then there exists a shortest path system that has an expected congestion of $D + O(\sqrt{\frac{D \log N}{N}})$.*

**Proof.** Consider the problem of gossiping in $G$. Perform the random experiment of choosing at random shortest path for all source-destionation pairs $(u, w) \in V^2$ independently from all other source-destionation pairs. For every node $v$ in $G$, let the binary random variable $X_{u,w}^v$ be one if and only if the path chosen from $u$ to $w$ traverses $v$ and $p_{u,w}^v = \text{Prob}(X_{u,w}^v = 1)$. Further let the random variable $C_v$ denote the number of paths traversing $v$. Then it holds

$$C_v = \sum_{(u,w) \in V^2} X_{u,w}^v .$$

---

[*] By "with high probability" (or w.h.p. for short) we mean a probability of at least $1 - 1/N^k$ for any constant $k > 0$.

Since $G$ is node-symmetric there exists for any fixed node $v'$ in $G$ an automorphism $\varphi$ that maps $v$ to $v'$. Thus it holds

$$E(C_v) = \sum_{(u,w)\in V^2} p_{u,w}^v = \sum_{(u,w)\in V^2} p_{\varphi(u),\varphi(w)}^{\varphi(v)}$$

$$= \sum_{(u,w)\in V^2} p_{u,w}^{v'} = E(C_{v'})$$

Hence, $E(C_v)$ is the same for every node in $G$, namely at most $N \cdot D$. Since the paths are chosen independently at random, applying Chernoff bounds yields that $C_v = N \cdot D + O(\sqrt{D \cdot N \log N})$, w.h.p. Thus there exists a path system in $G$ with such a congestion. Since, for a randomly chosen function, each of the paths has a probability of $\frac{1}{N}$ to be chosen, Theorem 9 follows. ∎

Theorem 9 implies, for instance, that there exists a shortest path system in a butterfly of size $N$ with expected congestion at most $\log N + 1$. Similarly, the following result holds for edge-symmetric networks.

**Theorem 10.** *Let $G$ be a edge-symmetric network with $N$ nodes, degree $d$, and diameter $D$. Then there exists a shortest path system that has expected congestion $\frac{D}{d} + O(\frac{1}{N}\sqrt{\max\{\frac{N \cdot D}{d}, \log N\} \cdot \log N})$.*

## 3.2 Valiant's Trick

In Section 3.1 we have seen that for any network with routing number $R$ there is a fixed path system that yields asymptotically optimal parameters $C$ and $D$ for almost all functions. However, Borodin and Hopcroft [4] could prove a very high lower bound for the maximal congestion that can be reached by a permutation routing problem in a network using a fixed path system. Their result has been improved by Kaklamanis *et al.* [8]. Together with an extension by Parberry [18] we obtain the following theorem.

**Theorem 11.** *Let $G$ be an arbitrary network of size $N$ with degree $d$, and let $\mathcal{P}$ be an arbitrary path system in $G$. Let $n$ nodes in $G$ be determined as sources and destinations. Then there is a permutation $\pi \in S_n$ that has a congestion $C_\pi$ of $\Omega(\frac{n}{d\sqrt{N}})$.*

Hence, if $G$ has constant degree and all nodes in $G$ are source and destination, that is $n = N$, then there exists a permutation with congestion $\Omega(\sqrt{N})$. Therefore the congestion might be much higher than the dilation since networks of bounded degree can have a diameter of $O(\log N)$.

For the $d$-dimensional hypercube $M(2, d)$ Theorem 11 implies a worst case congestion of $C = \Omega(\sqrt{2^d}/d)$. Kaklamanis *et al.* present a path system in [8] that reaches this bound.

In case that messages have to be sent from the top level to the top level of a $d$-dimensional wrap-around butterfly according to some arbitrary permutation, Bock [3] presents a path system that reaches the lower bound $C = \Omega(\sqrt{2^d}/d)$.

According to Theorem 11, oblivious routing might perform very poorly for some functions. Thus, in order to get close to the routing number, we have to turn to non-oblivious strategies. A beautiful, simple idea was presented in [24].

**Valiant's trick:**
Consider routing an arbitrary $h$-relation. Route the packets first to intermediate destinations according to a randomly chosen $h$-function, before routing
them to their true destinations.

Applying this trick to a fixed path system $\mathcal{P}$ yields the following strategy:
Each node first chooses random intermediate destinations for its packets. Then
each packet is first sent to this intermediate destination, and from there to its final
destination, both times using the path prescribed in $\mathcal{P}$.

With this strategy, the congestion of *every* permutation routing problem can be
brought close to the expected congestion of $\mathcal{P}$, w.h.p. In particular, the following theorem holds.

**Theorem 12.** *Let $\mathcal{P}$ be an arbitrary path system of size $n$ with dilation $D$ and expected
congestion $\bar{C}$. Then every $h$-relation can be routed along paths in $\mathcal{P}$ using Valiant's trick
with dilation at most $2D$ and congestion at most $2h \cdot \bar{C} + O(\sqrt{\max\{h \cdot \bar{C}, \log n\} \cdot \log n})$,
w.h.p.*

**Proof.** Let $V$ be the set of sources in $\mathcal{P}$. Consider an arbitrary edge $e$ in $\mathcal{P}$. For every
$v \in V$ and $i \in \{1, \dots, h\}$, let the binary random variable $X_{v,i}$ be one if and only if
the $i$th packet in $v$ traverses $e$. Further let the random variable $X$ denote the number
of packets that traverse $e$. Then $X = \sum_{v \in V} \sum_{i=1}^{h} X_{v,i}$. According to the definition of
the expected congestion, $E(X) \le h \cdot \bar{C}$ holds. If we choose a random $h$-function, then
the probablities for all $X_{v,i}$ are independent. Hence the Chernoff bounds yield that

$$\text{Prob}(X \ge (1 + \epsilon)h\bar{C}) \le \begin{cases} e^{-\epsilon^2 h\bar{C}/3} & : \text{ if } 0 \le \epsilon \le 1 \\ e^{-\epsilon \cdot h\bar{C}/2} & : \text{ if } \epsilon \ge 2 \end{cases}$$

which is polynomially small in $n$ for sufficiently large $\epsilon = O(\max\{\sqrt{\frac{\log n}{h \cdot \bar{C}}}, \frac{\log n}{h \cdot \bar{C}}\})$. Therefore the collection of paths in $\mathcal{P}$ used for routing packets from their sources to interme-
diate destinations and from the intermediate destinations to their destinations has a
congestion of at most $2h \cdot \bar{C} + O(\sqrt{\max\{h \cdot \bar{C}, \log n\} \cdot \log n})$, w.h.p., if the intermediate
destinations are chosen according to a random $h$-function. Further, the dilation of the
resulting paths is at most $2D$. ∎

Theorems 8 and 12 yield the following result.

**Corollary 13.** *For any network $G$ of size $N$ with routing number $R$ there exists a
simple path system $\mathcal{P}$, such that routing any $h$-relation along paths in $\mathcal{P}$ using Valiant's
trick has dilation at most $2R$ and congestion $2h \cdot R + O(\sqrt{\max\{h \cdot R, \log n\} \cdot \log n})$,
w.h.p.*

This result implies that if there is an oblivious protocol that can route packets
along an arbitrary simple path collection with dilation $D$ and congestion $C$ in time
$O(D + C)$ then a combination of the path selection strategy in Corollary 13 and this
protocol would yield a routing protocol that reaches the optimal routing performance
of permutation routing in arbitrary networks. Unfortunately, no oblivious protocol is
known so far that reaches this bound for arbitrary simple path collections. However,
the following result shown in [11, 12] lets us hope that such a protocol may exist.

**Theorem 14.** *For any simple path collection $\mathcal{P}$ with congestion $C$ and dilation $D$ there exists an offline protocol that finishes routing in $\mathcal{P}$ in $O(C + D)$ steps, using only constant size buffers.*

In the next chapter we summarize what kind of online oblivious protocols have already been found.

# 4 Oblivious Routing Protocols

In the previous chapter we have seen that oblivious routing has the potential to achieve an efficiency that is close to the routing number, because the dilation and expected congestion are essentially of the same order of magnitude as the routing number. Hence what we need are oblivious routing protocols with runtime close to $O$(dilation+congestion). In this chapter we present some universal oblivious routing protocols that (nearly) reach this time bound for different classes of path collections.

## 4.1 The Random Rank Protocol

The *random rank protocol* has its origin in a paper by Aleliunas [1] and Upfal [23], and has been extended to constant size buffers in [19] (see also [9] and [10]). It routes packets along an arbitrary leveled path collection of size $n$ with congestion $C$ and depth $D$ in $O(C + D + \log n)$ steps, w.h.p., using edge buffers of size at least one. In the following we only describe the protocol for unbounded buffers. (See [17] for an easy proof of the runtime bound.)

At the beginning, every packet $p$ gets a random rank denoted by rank$(p)$ that is stored in its routing information. We require rank$(p)$ to be chosen uniformly and independent from the choices of the other packets from some fixed range $[K]$ ($K = O(C + D + \log n)$ is chosen sufficiently large). Additionally, each packet stores an identification number id$(p) \in [n]$ in its routing information that is different from all identification numbers of the other packets. The random rank protocol uses the following contention resolution rule.

> **Priority rule:**
> It two or more packets contend to use the same link at the same time then the one with minimal rank is chosen.

If two packets have the same rank then, in order to break ties, the one with the lowest id wins. The protocol then works as follows in each time step

> For each link with nonempty buffer, select a packet according to the priority rule and send it along that link.

Consider an arbitrary leveled network with $N$ input and $N$ output nodes. Let the routing number be defined as the worst case time needed by the best offline protocol to send packets from the inputs to the outputs according to an arbitrary permutation. Then the random rank protocol and Corollary 13 together yield the following result.

**Theorem 15.** *Any wrapped leveled network with $N$ inputs, $N$ outputs, and routing number $R$ can route any h-relation from the inputs to the outputs in time $O(h \cdot R + \log N)$, w.h.p., using constant size buffers.*

## 4.2 The Growing Rank Protocol

Now we present a protocol that routes packets along an arbitrary shortcut-free path collection of size $n$ with congestion $C$ and dilation $D$ in $O(C + D + \log n)$ steps, w.h.p., using buffers of size $C$. It is called *growing-rank protocol* [15] and works as follows.

Initially, each packet is assigned an integer rank chosen randomly, independently, and uniformly from $[K]$ ($K = O(C + D + \log n)$ is chosen sufficiently large). For each step, the protocol works as follows.

For each link with nonempty buffer,

- choose a packet $p$ according to the priority rule,
- increase the rank of $p$ by $K/D$, and
- move $p$ forward along the link.

This protocol together with Valiant's trick yields the following result.

**Theorem 16.** *For any shortcut-free path system of size $n$ with dilation $D$ and expected congestion $\bar{C}$, any permutation can be routed using the growing rank protocol in time $O(\bar{C} + D + \log n)$, w.h.p.*

This theorem applied to node-symmetric networks yields the following result together with Theorem 9.

**Corollary 17.** *Let $G$ be a node-symmetric network of size $N$ with diameter $D$. Then the growing rank protocol routes packets according to an arbitrary h-relation in time $O(h \cdot D + \log N)$, w.h.p.*

This result is optimal for permutation routing in arbitrary node-symmetric networks with diameter $D = \Omega(\log N)$, since Theorem 9 together with Theorem 12 and Theorem 14 implies that the routing number of any node-symmetric network with diameter $D = \Omega(\log N)$ is bounded by $\Theta(D)$.

Unfortunately, it has been shown in [16] that the growing rank protocol can not be efficiently applied to arbitrary simple path collections. Furthermore, it is not clear yet whether efficient shurtcut-free path systems exist for any network. In case of shortest path systems, however, networks exist such that any shortest path system has a much higher expected congestion then the best simple path system.

## 4.3 The Trial-and-Failure Protocol

In the following we present a protocol that routes packets along an arbitrary simple path collection of size $n$ with link bandwidth $B \leq \log n$, congestion $C$, and dilation $D$ in time

$$O\left(\frac{C \cdot D^{1/B} + D \log n}{B}\right)$$

w.h.p., without buffering. This protocol is called *trial-and-failure protocol* and has been presented in [6]. The idea of the trial-and-failure protocol is that once a packet leaves its source it has to move along the edges of its path without waiting until it reaches its destination. If too many packets want to use the same link at the same time then some are discarded (and therefore have to be rerouted).

Initially, each packet $p_i$ chooses uniformly and independently from the other packets a random rank $r_i \in [K]$ ($K = O(C \cdot D^{-1+1/B} + \log n)$ is chosen sufficiently large) and a random delay $d_i \in [D]$. Additionally, $p_i$ stores an identification number $\mathrm{id}(p_i) \in [n]$ in its routing information that is different from all identification numbers of the other packets. Let us define the following contention resolution rule.

**B-priority rule:**
If more than $B$ packets attempt to use the same link during the same time step, then those $B$ with lowest rank win.

If two or more packets have the same rank then, in order to break ties, the ones with the lowest id's win. Then the protocol works as follows.

**repeat**

- **forward pass**: Each active packet $p_i$ waits for $d_i$ steps. Then it is routed along its path, obeying the $B$-priority rule.
- **backward pass**: For each packet that reached its destination during the forward pass, an acknowledgment is sent back to the source. Upon receipt of the acknowledgment, the source declares the packet inactive.

**until** no packet is active

Clearly, the forward pass needs $2D$ steps to be sure that every packet that has not been discarded during the routing reaches its destination. In the backward pass, the forward pass is run in reverse order. Therefore, no collisions can occur in the backward pass, and $2D$ steps suffice to send all acknowledgments back.

The trial-and-failure protocol has several applications. If we simulate link bandwidth by buffers we arrive at the following result.

**Corollary 18.** *Given any simple path collection with buffer size $B$, congestion $C$, and dilation $D$, the trial-and-failure protocol requires $O(C \cdot D^{1/B} + D \log n)$ time to route all packets, w.h.p.*

This result is optimal if $C \geq D \log n$ and $B \geq \log D$. Together with Valiant's trick it yields the following result.

**Corollary 19.** *Let $G$ be an arbitrary network of size $N$ with buffer size $B$ and routing number $R$. Then the trial-and-failure protocol routes packets according to an arbitrary $h$-relation in time $O((h \cdot R^{1/B} + \log n)R)$, w.h.p.*

In the case of shortest path collections, the trial-and-failure protocol can be combined with the growing rank protocol to yield the following tradeoff between routing time and buffer size for oblivious routing.

**Theorem 20.** *Given any shortest path collection of size $n$ with buffer size $B$, congestion $C$, and dilation $D$ there exists an on-line routing protocol that requires*

$$O\left(\frac{C \cdot D^{1/B} + \log n}{B} \cdot (C + D + \log n)\right)$$

*time to route all packets, w.h.p.*

Together with Theorem 9 and Valiant's trick we get the following result.

**Corollary 21.** *Let $G$ be an arbitrary node-symmetric network of size $N$ with buffer size $B$ and diameter $D$. Then the trial-and-failure protocol routes packets according to an arbitrary $h$-relation in time*

$$O\left(\frac{h \cdot D^{1+1/B} + \log n}{B} \cdot (h \cdot D + \log N)\right) ,$$

*w.h.p.*

## 4.4 The Duplication Protocol

In [6] a protocol is presented that routes packets along an arbitrary simple path collection of size $n$ with congestion $C$, dilation $D$, and bandwidth $\Theta(\log(C \cdot D)/\log\log(C \cdot D))$ in

$$O\left(D \log\log n + C + \frac{\log n \cdot \log\log n}{\log\log(C \cdot D)}\right)$$

time steps, w.h.p., without buffering. It is called *duplication protocol*. The structure of the duplication protocol is similar to that of the trial-and-failure protocol with the difference that each new trial the number of copies sent out for a packet is duplicated. This significantly increases the chance that finally one of the copies will be able to reach the destination. The protocol uses the following rule in case of collisions between packets:

**$B$-collision rule:**
If more than $B$ packets attempt to use the same link during the same time step, then *all* of them are discarded.

If we simulate bandwidth by buffer size, we arrive at the following result.

**Corollary 22.** *Given any simple path collection $\mathcal{P}$ of size $n$ with congestion $C$ and dilation $D$, there exists a routing protocol that requires*

$$O\left(\left(D \log\log n + C + \frac{\log n \cdot \log\log n}{\log\log(C \cdot D)}\right) \cdot \frac{\log(C \cdot D)}{\log\log(C \cdot D)}\right)$$

*time, w.h.p., and uses buffers of size $O(\log(C \cdot D)/\log\log(C \cdot D))$.*

Together with Corollary 13 this protocol yields the following result.

**Corollary 23.** *For any network $G$ of size $N$ with routing number $R = \Omega(\log N)$ and buffer size $O(\log R/\log\log R)$, the duplication protocol can be used to route any permutation in time*

$$O\left(\frac{\log R \cdot \log\log N}{\log\log R} \cdot R\right) ,$$

*w.h.p.*

## 4.5 The Protocol by Rabani and Tardos

In [20], Rabani and Tardos present a protocol that routes packets along an arbitrary simple path system with congestion $C$ and dilation $D$ in

$$O(C) + (\log^* n)^{O(\log^* n)} D + poly(\log n)$$

time, w.h.p., using buffers of size $C$. Together with Corollary 13 their protocol yields the following result.

**Corollary 24.** *For any network $G$ of size $N$ with routing number $R \geq \log^k N$, $k \geq 0$ sufficiently large, there exists an oblivious routing protocol for routing any $h$-relation in time $(h + (\log^* N)^{O(\log^* N)})R$, w.h.p.*

## 4.6 Open Problems

In the following we state some important open questions. Is there an online protocol that can route packets along an arbitrary simple (not necessarily shortcut-free) path system of size $N$ with congestion $C$ and dilation $D$ in time $O(C + D + \log N)$ ? If this is true then, in case of unbounded buffers, randomized oblivious routing can asymptotically reach the performance of offline protocols. How do bounded buffers influence the runtime of oblivious routing strategies ? Are ghost packets (see [10]) necessary for efficient routing with bounded buffers in leveled networks ?

# 5 Adaptive Routing Protocols

Adaptive protocols are very appealing compared to oblivious protocols, since they allow a parallel system to react more flexibly in case of faulty or overloaded communication links or processors. Another motivation for adaptive routing is that bounded buffers are difficult to handle for oblivious routing strategies. Usually, the only way to avoid deadlocks using oblivious routing strategies is simply to delete the packets in case of full buffers and restart them again from the source (see,i.e., the trial-and-failure protocol). However, in case of unbounded buffers we know from Corollary 13 and Theorem 14 that randomized oblivious routing strategies have at least a chance to be as efficient as randomized adaptive routing strategies. This, of course, crucially depends on whether it is possible to design an efficient protocol for routing packets along an arbitrary simple path collection.

In the deterministic case, however, adaptive routing protocols are usually far superior against oblivious routing protocols, since the worst case congestion for routing an arbitrary permutation using a fixed path system can be fairly large (see Theorem 11). But even if the congestion is small, deterministic oblivious routing strategies might still perform very poorly as will be shown in the following theorem.

We investigate the behavior of non-predictive routing protocols in which all scheduling decisions have to be independent from the future routing paths of the packets. Note that the growing rank protocol is not deterministic and hence not nonpredictive. However, for any fixed setting of the initial ranks it is nonpredictive. The same holds for the random rank protocol and its extensions [21, 9, 10]. The following example shows that all these protocols perform poorly in a deterministic setting even on leveled networks. The proof can be found in [16].

**Theorem 25.** *Suppose we are given any deterministic non-predictive routing protocol Q for routing on the D-dimensional butterfly. Then, for any C, there is a routing problem with congestion C for which Q takes time $\Omega(C \cdot D)$.*

Therefore in case of deterministic routing, efficient adaptive routing protocols are highly needed. In the following section we present a network for which an efficient deterministic adaptive routing protocol is already known. This result will be used in Section 5.2 to develop, for any network, a deterministic adaptive routing protocol that has a performance close to the routing number of that network.

## 5.1 Deterministic Routing in the Multibutterfly

In this section describe a network in which deterministic routing can be done efficiently. It is called the (elementary) *s-ary multibutterfly*.

The basic building block of the *s*-ary multibutterfly is an *s-ary m-splitter* (see [5]).

The *s*-ary *m*-splitter (or $(s, m)$-splitter) is a bipartite graph with $m$ input nodes and $m$ output nodes. In this graph the output nodes are partitioned into $\sqrt{s}$ output sets, each with $m/\sqrt{s}$ nodes. Every input node has $\frac{\sqrt{s}}{2}$ edges to each of the $\sqrt{s}$ output sets. The edges connecting the input set to each of the output sets define an expander graph with properties described in [5].

The *s-ary d-dimensional multibutterfly* $(s, d)$-MBF has $d$ levels. The vertices at level $0 \le i \le d - 1$ are partitioned into $\sqrt{s}^i$ sets of $m_i = \sqrt{s}^{d-i}$ consecutive nodes. Each of these sets in level $i$ is an input set of an *s*-ary $m_i$-splitter. The output sets of that splitter are $\sqrt{s}$ sets of size $m_{i+1}$ in level $i + 1$. Thus each node in the $(s, d)$-MBF is the endpoint of at most $2 \cdot \sqrt{s}(\sqrt{s}/2) = s$ edges.

For this network the following result can be shown. It's proof can be found in [5].

**Theorem 26.** *For sufficiently large s, the s-ary multibutterfly of size N can route any permutation from the top level to the bottom level in time $O(\log_s N)$.*

This result has recently been improved in [14] for an extended version of the $(s, d)$-MBF that has a degree of $O(s)$.

**Theorem 27.** *Given an extended s-ary multibutterfly of size N with $s \ge 2$, $s \cdot N$ packets, s per node, can be routed deterministically according to some arbitrary s-relation in time $O(\log_s N)$.*

## 5.2 Routing via Simulation

In this section we present an efficient deterministic adaptive routing protocol for arbitrary networks, as it is described in [14]. Let $H$ be an arbitrary network of size $N$ with routing number $R$. The idea is that, in order to route packets in $H$ deterministically according to an arbitrary permutation, a suitably chosen multibutterfly is embedded in $H$, and $H$ simulates the routing steps of the multibutterfly.

Consider first the more general problem of simulating one routing step of an arbitrary network $G$ by a network $H$. We start with describing how to embed $G$ in $H$. In order to simplify the construction, let $H$ be a network of size $N$, and $G$ be a network of size $M$ with at most $N/2$ edges. Let $d_1, \ldots, d_M$ be the degree sequence of $G$, i.e., $d_i$ is the degree of node $i$ in $G$. Then $\sum_{i=1}^{M} d_i \le N$. Our strategy is to partition the nodes of $H$ into clusters $C_1, \ldots, C_M$ such that for all $i \in \{1, \ldots, M\}$ cluster $C_i$ consists of $d_i$ nodes simulating the $d_i$ endpoints of node $i$ in $G$. For this we choose an arbitrary spanning tree $T$ in $H$. Let $r$ be an arbitrary node in $T$. We mark the nodes in $T$ with numbers in $\{1, \ldots, M\}$ starting with $r$ by calling Mark$(1, true, r)$:

**Algorithm Mark$(i, m, v)$:**

$i$: number of nodes already marked
$m$: boolean variable indicating whether father has been marked
$v$: actual node to be considered

if $m = false$ then
    mark $v$ with the number $\ell$ obeying $\sum_{j=1}^{\ell-1} d_j < i \leq \sum_{j=1}^{\ell} d_j$
    $i = i + 1$
    for every son $w$ of $v$: call Mark$(i, true, w)$
else
    for every son $w$ of $v$: call Mark$(i, false, w)$
    mark $v$ with the number $\ell$ obeying $\sum_{j=1}^{\ell-1} d_j < i \leq \sum_{j=1}^{\ell} d_j$
    $i = i + 1$
return the value of $i$

Basically, the algorithm ensures that on a pass downwards through the tree only every second node is marked such that afterwards on a pass upwards the other half of the nodes can be marked. Hence it is easy to see that the following two results hold.

(a) cluster $i$ has diameter at most $3d_i$ for all $i \in \{1, \ldots, M\}$, and
(b) the maximal number of clusters that share the same link is constant.

Let the nodes of each cluster be connected by an Euler tour along edges in $T$. (An Euler tour in a tree is defined as a directed cycle that uses any edge in $T$ in any direction at most once.) Because of (a) this tour can have a length of at most $6d_i$.

Further we want to simulate every edge in $G$ by a path in $H$ that connects the nodes simulating its endpoints. Let $R$ be the routing number of $H$. Since our clustering allows the endpoints of edges in $G$ to be distributed in $H$ such that every node in $H$ has to simulate at most one endpoint, there is a path collection in $H$ for simulating the edges in $G$ with congestion at most $R$ and dilation at most $R$.

Consider now the problem of simulating an arbitrary routing step in $G$. Clearly, any routing step can be extended to the situation that along every edge in $G$ a packet has to be sent. This event can be simulated in the following way by $H$.

- Moving the packets to the nodes simulating the endpoints of the edges they want to use in $G$: This can be done by sending the packets along an Euler tour connecting the nodes of the respective cluster in $T$. Because of (b) this can be coordinated among the clusters deterministically in time $O(\max_i d_i)$ using only constant size buffers.
- Moving the packets along an edge in $G$: This can be done by sending the packets along the paths simulating edges in $G$. Since these paths have congestion at most $R$ and dilation at most $R$, this can be done deterministically in time $O(R)$ using only constant size buffers (see Theorem 14).

If we restrict the maximum degree in $G$ to be $O(R)$, we get the following result.

**Theorem 28.** *Any network $H$ of size $N$ with routing number $R$ can simulate any routing step in a network $G$ with degree $O(R)$ and $O(N)$ edges in $O(R)$ steps using only constant size buffers.*

Theorem 28 and Theorem 27 together yield the following result.

**Theorem 29.** *Let $H$ be an arbitrary network of size $N$ with routing number $R$. Then there is a deterministic online protocol that routes any permutation in time $O(\log_R N \cdot R)$, using constant size buffers.*

Theorem 29 has the following implications.

**Corollary 30.** *For any network $H$ of size $N$ with routing number $R = \Omega(N^\epsilon)$ for some constant $\epsilon > 0$ there exists a deterministic routing strategy that routes any permutation in $H$ in $O(R)$ steps.*

$R = \Omega(N^\epsilon)$ holds, for instance, for all networks with diameter $\Omega(N^\epsilon)$ or bisection width $O(N^{1-\epsilon})$. According to [22], every $N$-node graph of genus $g$ and maximal degree $d$ has bisection width $O(\sqrt{gdN})$. Thus the following result is true.

**Corollary 31.** *For any network $H$ of size $N$ with genus $g$ and degree $d$ such that $g \cdot d = O(N^{1-\epsilon})$, $\epsilon > 0$ constant, there exists a deterministic routing strategy that routes any permutation in $H$ in $O(R)$ steps.*

This result implies that for any planar network with degree $O(N^{1-\epsilon})$ there is an asymptotically optimal deterministic permutation routing strategy.

## 5.3 Open Problems

The results above only yield asymptotically optimal routing strategies if the routing number is large enough. How efficient is deterministic online routing for networks with small routing number ? No non-trivial lower bounds are known so far.

# References

1. R. Aleliunas. Randomized Parallel Communication. In *Proc. of the ACM SIGACT-SIGOPS Symp. on Principles of Distributed Computing*, pp. 60-72, 1982.
2. N. Alon, F.R.K. Chung, R.L. Graham. Routing Permutations on Graphs via Matchings. *SIAM J. Discrete Math.* 7(3), pp. 513-530, 1994.
3. S. Bock. Optimales Wormhole Routing im hochdimensionalen Torus. Diploma thesis, Paderborn University, March 1996.
4. A. Borodin, J.E. Hopcroft. Routing, merging, and sorting on parallel models of computation. *Journal of Computer and System Sciences* 30, pp. 130-145, 1985.
5. A. Borodin, P. Raghavan, B. Schieber, E. Upfal. How much can hardware help routing? In *Proc. of the 25th Ann. ACM Symposium on Theory of Computing*, pp. 573-582, 1993.
6. R. Cypher, F. Meyer auf der Heide, C. Scheideler, B. Vöcking. Universal Algorithms for Store-and-Forward and Wormhole Routing. In *28th Ann. ACM Symp. on Theory of Computing*, pp. 356-365, 1996.

7. T. Hagerup, C. Rüb. A Guided Tour of Chernoff Bounds. *Information Processing Letters* 33, pp. 305-308, 1989/90.

8. C. Kaklamanis, D. Krizanc, T. Tsantilas. Tigth Bounds for Oblivious Routing in the Hypercube. *Mathematical Systems Theory* 24, pp. 223-232, 1991.

9. F.T. Leighton. *Introduction to Parallel Algorithms and Architectures: Arrays, Trees, Hypercubes.* Morgan Kaufmann, San Mateo, CA, 1992.

10. F.T. Leighton, B.M. Maggs, A.G. Ranade, S.B. Rao. Randomized Routing and Sorting on Fixed-Connection Networks. *Journal of Algorithms* 17, pp. 157-205, 1994.

11. F.T. Leighton, B.M. Maggs, S.B. Rao. Universal Packet Routing Algorithms. In *Proc. of the 29th Ann. Symp. on Foudations of Computer Science*, pp. 256-271, 1988.

12. F.T. Leighton, B.M. Maggs, S.B. Rao. Packet Routing and Job-Shop Scheduling in O(Congestion + Dilation) Steps. *Combinatorica* 14, pp. 167-186, 1994.

13. T. Leighton, S. Rao. An Approximate Max-Flow Min-Cut Theorem for Uniform Multicommodity Flow Problems with Applications to Approximation Algorithms. In *Proc. of the 29th Ann. IEEE Symp. on Foundations of Computer Science*, pp. 422-431, 1988.

14. F. Meyer auf der Heide, C. Scheideler. Deterministic Routing with Bounded Buffers: Turning Offline into Online Protocols. To appear at *Proc. of the 37th Ann. IEEE Symp. on Foundations of Computer Science*, 1996.

15. F. Meyer auf der Heide, B. Vöcking. A Packet Routing Protocol for Arbitrary Networks. In *12th Symp. on Theoretical Aspects of Computer Science* (STACS 95), pp. 291-302, 1995.

16. F. Meyer auf der Heide, B. Vöcking. Universal Store-and-Forward Routing. Technical Report, Paderborn University, 1996.

17. F. Meyer auf der Heide , R. Wanka. Kommunikation in parallelen Rechnernetzen (in German). In *Highlights aus der Informatik*, I. Wegener (editor), Springer Verlag, pp. 177-198, 1996.

18. I. Parberry. An Optimal Time Bound for Oblivious Routing. *Algorithmica* 5, pp. 243-250, 1990.

19. N. Pippenger. Parallel Communication with Limited Buffers. In *Proc. of the 25th IEEE Symp. on Foundations of Computer Science*, pp. 127-136, 1984.

20. Y. Rabani, É. Tardos. Distributed Packet Switching in Arbitrary Networks. In *28th Ann. ACM Symp. on Theory of Computing*, pp. 366-375, 1996.

21. A.G. Ranade. How to Emulate Shared Memory. *Journal of Computer and System Sciences* 42, pp. 307-326, 1991.

22. O. Sýkora, I. Vrťo. Edge Seperators for Graphs of Bounded Genus with Applications. *Theoretical Computer Science* 112, pp. 419-429, 1993.

23. E. Upfal. Efficient Schemes for Parallel Communication. In *Proc. of the ACM SIGACT-SIGOPS Symp. on Principles of Distributed Computing*, pp. 241-250, 1982.

24. L.G. Valiant. A Scheme for Fast Parallel Communication. *SIAM Journal of Computing* 11(2), pp. 350-361, 1982.

# An Overview of the Tigger Object-Support Operating System Framework

Vinny Cahill*

Distributed Systems Group
Department of Computer Science
Trinity College Dublin
Ireland
http://www.dsg.cs.tcd.ie/

**Abstract.** This paper describes the motivations for and main features of Tigger – a framework for the construction of a family of object-support operating systems that can be tailored for use in a variety of different application domains. An important goal of the design of Tigger is that instantiations of the framework should be able to support (a number of) different object models in order to allow a range of object-oriented languages for distributed or persistent programming to be supported without unnecessary duplication of effort. A further goal of the design is that instantiations of the framework should be able to support the same object model in different ways depending on the requirements of the applications to be supported by those instantiations. This paper describes the main features of the Tigger framework that allow these goals to be realised.

## 1  Introduction

While the use of object-support operating systems – supporting distributed or persistent objects – has been advocated for many application domains [5], research within the Distributed Systems Group (DSG) at Trinity College has recently been considering their deployment in two specific areas: support for Concurrent Engineering (CE) environments[1]; and support for the development and execution environments of next-generation, multi-user/distributed, arcade and personal-computer (PC) video games [15].

These application domains are similar at one level in that they are fundamentally concerned with multiple distributed users interacting via shared distributed and persistent objects. Moreover, these two application domains are not necessarily distinct; game development is inherently a CE activity involving game designers, artists, musicians, and software developers. Furthermore, the

---

* Email: vinny.cahill@dsg.cs.tcd.ie
[1] By "environment" is really meant what is known in the CE community as a "framework", i.e., a system encapsulating a set of tools, together with the data used by those tools, under a common design management protocol.

technologies being deployed in both domains, for example, real-time video and audio or three-dimensional graphics, overlap.

Despite these similarities, there are many differences that must be accommodated. At the highest level, the object models appropriate to each application domain differ. CE environments often employ what may be described as a *shared data object model* in which objects are passive and accessed by active threads of control. In contrast, the game execution environment described in [15] employs a *reactive object model* with event-based communication, i.e., objects representing game entities are autonomous but react to events raised by other objects. Objects receive notifications of events of interest determined by reference to parameters of those events. While these particular models represent different positions along a continuum of possible object models, the key observation is that an important feature of any flexible object-support operating system should be the ability to support a number of different object models without duplication of effort, if not necessarily simultaneously.

While these application domains exhibit similar functional requirements, their non-functional requirements vary considerably from application to application and installation to installation. Requirements in areas such as support for security, heterogeneity, reliability and fault tolerance, allowable memory usage, and real-time behaviour vary considerably. For example, the requirements for supporting the *same* video game on a stand-alone arcade machine or PC, in a private network of arcade machines, or across the public telephone network vary considerable but must be supported by a common system interface. Likewise the requirements imposed by supporting a concurrent software engineering environment in a traditional workstation/server environment are different from those of any of the above scenarios. Nevertheless, the game developer still needs easy access to the game execution system during testing and debugging and, more importantly, the game designer needs immediate access to the execution system during the game tuning phase when the "playability" of the game is being improved. The key observation here is that any flexible object-support operating system should be capable of supporting the same object model in different ways depending on the way in which the applications supported by the system are to be deployed.

In keeping with these observations, the Tigger project[2] undertook the design, not of a single object-support operating system, but of a family of object-support operating systems whose members can be customised for use in a variety of different application domains. The two primary goals of this design were:

1. to allow members of the family to support (a number of) different object models in order to allow a range of different object-oriented programming languages for distributed and persistent programming to be supported without unnecessary duplication of effort; and

2. to allow the same object model to be supported in different ways subject to differing non-functional requirements.

---

[2] which was named after A.A. Milne's famously bouncy character!

To support customisability, the design is captured as a framework that can be instantiated to implement the individual members of the family. The Tigger framework can be instantiated to implement particular object-support operating systems meeting particular functional and non-functional requirements. Instantiations of the Tigger framework can be layered above bare hardware, (real-time) microkernels, or conventional operating systems. The Tigger framework is sufficiently general so as to allow a set of possible instantiations that is capable of supporting a wide range of object-oriented programming languages for distributed or persistent programming and that is suitable for use in a wide range of application areas exhibiting different non-functional requirements. In addition, the Tigger framework has been designed to be extensible so that new functionality can be supported when required.

The major abstractions supported by the Tigger framework are distributed or persistent objects, threads, and extents (i.e., protected collections of objects). A given Tigger instantiation may support only distributed objects, only persistent objects, or both. Of course, different instantiations will support these abstractions in different ways (for example, in order to accommodate different object models) by employing different mechanisms and policies.

Individual Tigger instantiations may support additional abstractions, such as activities (i.e., distributed threads) and object clusters as required. Moreover, all of these abstractions are based on lower-level abstractions such as contexts (i.e., address spaces) and endpoints (i.e., communication channels) that are not normally expected to be used directly by supported languages or individual applications.

The simplest object-support operating system that can be instantiated from the framework is one supporting a single user and a single object model providing either distributed or persistent objects. Other instantiations of the framework may support additional abstractions, multiple users, or multiple object models.

The remaider of this paper gives an overview of the Tigger framework, concentrating on the way in which it provides support for distributed and persistent programming languages. For a complete description of the framework see [3].

## 2   Related Work

This section introduces a number of previous systems that have particularly influenced Tigger: the Amadeus object-support operating system, which was developed by DSG, and the Choices and PEACE object-oriented operating systems.

Amadeus [9] was a general-purpose object-support operating system that supported distributed and persistent programming in multi-user distributed systems. Amadeus was targeted for use in what may broadly be described as cooperative applications concerned with access to shared data in domains such as computer-aided design (CAD), office automation, and software engineering.

A major feature of Amadeus was that it was designed to support the use of a range of existing object-oriented programming languages. A language could be extended to support a set of (inter-related) properties including distribution, persistence, and atomicity for its objects by using the services of the Amadeus Generic Runtime Library (GRT), while maintaining its own native object reference format and invocation mechanism [4]. The Amadeus GRT provided a range of mechanisms from which the language designer could choose those appropriate for the intended use of the extended language. Extended versions of C++ and Eiffel, which were known as C** [7] and Eiffel** [13] respectively, and an implementation of the E persistent programming language [12] were supported by Amadeus.

Other major features of Amadeus included language-independent support for atomic objects and transactions [14, 24] based on the use of the RELAX transaction manager and libraries [11], and a novel security model supporting access control for objects at the level of individual operations as well as isolation of untrustworthy code [17].

Experience with the design and implementation of Amadeus has obviously had a major influence on Tigger. Tigger shares the goal of language independence and has adopted several of the key features of Amadeus including the idea of a GRT and the basic security model. However, the goal of Tigger is to allow the implementation of a variety of object-support operating systems providing more or less functionality as required, rather than a single general-purpose system as was the goal of Amadeus.

Apart from Amadeus, Tigger has been most influenced by Choices [6], which developed a C++ framework for the construction of operating systems for distributed and shared memory multiprocessors, and PEACE [19], which addressed the use of object-oriented techniques in the construction of a family of operating systems for massively parallel computers. The PEACE family encompasses a number of different members ranging from one supporting a single thread of control per node to one supporting multiple processes per node.

In some sense, Tigger may be seen as combining these two research areas to develop a family of *object-oriented object-support operating systems*. The development of an object-oriented object-support operating system, to be known as Soul, was proposed previously by Shapiro in [20]. Shapiro envisaged developing a "hierarchy of object-support object types and classes" that could "be re-used, parameterized, and combined together, in order to build specific object-support functions". This is indeed a reasonable description of the Tigger framework! A later paper on Soul, [21], elaborated on the original proposal and described a "preliminary design" for the interface that should be provided by a microkernel suitable for hosting the Soul class hierarchy. However, no other description of the Soul object-oriented object-support operating system appears to be available in the literature. The Soul project has apparently instead concentrated on the development of specific mechanisms for object reference management and garbage collection in distributed systems.

# 3   Overview

Tigger is a framework for the construction of a family of object-support operating systems. Every instantiation of the framework is an object-support operating system to which one or more object-oriented programming languages are bound in order to provide an application programming interface. Like other object-support operating systems, Tigger instantiations will typically provide support for features such as creation of distributed or persistent objects; access to remote objects; object migration; access to stored persistent objects; dynamic loading of objects on demand; dynamic loading and linking of class code; and protection of objects.

In fact, the heart of any Tigger instantiation is a generalised object-access mechanism that allows local, remote, stored, protected, or unprotected objects to be accessed in a uniform manner. This mechanism provides support for all aspects of locating the target object, mapping the object and its class into memory, and forwarding the access request to the object as required. In fact, this basic mechanism subsumes much of the functionality provided by the Tigger framework and provides the basis for supporting a high degree of network transparency for object access. Of course, the details of what this mechanism does, and how it does it, are subject to customisation and will differ from one Tigger instantiation to another.

It is important to understand two points about the nature of the functionality provided by a Tigger instantiation. First, a Tigger instantiation, in cooperation with the runtime libraries of supported languages, *only* provides the necessary support for the use of objects by applications, i.e., a Tigger instantiation is *an object-support system*. The semantics and function of the objects that they support are opaque to Tigger instantiations. A particular object might implement a spreadsheet, one cell in a spreadsheet, a file, or a file server. The distinction is not visible to Tigger instantiations. While some objects will implement (parts of) particular applications (such as the "spreadsheet cell" object above), other objects may provide common services including those that are usually thought of as being part of an operating system (such as the "file server" object above).

The second major point to be understood is that a Tigger instantiation is *a language-support system* – the functionality provided by a Tigger instantiation is intended to be used by object-oriented programming languages to provide programming models based on distributed or persistent objects to their application programmers. Thus, the main interface provided by a Tigger instantiation is that provided for the language implementer. The interface used by an application developer is that provided by a supported language. Moreover, a Tigger instantiation provides only basic support for distribution or persistence that is intended to be supplemented by each language's runtime library in order to implement the programming model of the language. How support for distribution or persistence is made available in any language – whether transparently to application programmers, via a class library, or even via the use of particular language constructs – is not mandated by the Tigger framework. Likewise, the degree of network transparency provided by the language is a function of the programming model supported by the language. Of course, the Tigger framework has been designed to support languages that provide a high degree of network transparency.

# 4 Software Architecture

Tigger instantiations are intended to support both conventional object-oriented programming languages that have been extended to support distributed or persistent programming as well as object-oriented languages originally designed for that purpose. Moreover, this is intended to be done in a way that does not impose particular constructs and models on the language and, where an existing language is being extended, that does not necessarily require changes to its compiler nor to its native object reference format or local invocation mechanism. In this way, the language designer is free to choose the object model to be provided to application programmers independently. Supporting existing (local) object reference formats and invocation mechanisms allows the common case of local object invocation to be optimised. Finally, where an existing language is to be supported, this approach facilitates the reuse and porting of its existing compiler and runtime libraries.

In order to achieve these goals, every Tigger instantiation provides one or more GRTs providing common runtime support for one or more languages supporting distributed or persistent programming that have similar requirements on their runtime support. A more precise characterisation of a GRT is given in [3]. Suffice it to say here that a GRT is *generic* in the sense that it provides only that part of the support for distribution or persistence that is independent of any language. Every GRT is bound to a *Language Specific Runtime Library* (LSRT) for each language to be supported. The LSRT provides language-dependent runtime support. Each GRT provides an interface to the language implementer that has been designed to interface directly and easily to an LSRT. Thus, the interface to a Tigger instantiation seen by a language implementer is that of one of the GRTs that it provides.

This basic approach to language support is derived from the Amadeus project. Unlike Amadeus, which provided a single GRT supporting a (fairly limited) range of mechanisms that could be used by supported languages, the Tigger framework allows GRTs to be customised depending on the object model and intended use of the language(s) to be supported. For example, GRTs supporting remote object invocation (ROI) and/or distributed shared memory (DSM) style access to distributed objects, GRTs supporting the use of different object fault detection or avoidance schemes, and GRTs supporting the use of eager, lazy, or no swizzling can all be instantiated from the framework. A given Tigger instantiation can support one language or several similar languages with one GRT, or a number of different languages with several GRTs. For example, figure 1 shows one possible scenario in which one Tigger instantiation provides two different GRTs: one GRT is being used to support the C** and Eiffel** programming languages while the other is being used to support the E programming language. Both C** and

Eiffel** support distributed and persistent objects using ROI and eager swizzling respectively, while E is a non-swizzling persistent programming language. The figure depicts a scenario in which one application is written using some combination of two supported languages. While such interworking between languages may be facilitated when the languages involved have some of their runtime support in common, it should be noted that it cannot be implemented completely at this level – additional mechanisms are still required at higher levels to, for example, support inter-language type checking.

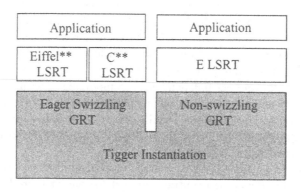

**Fig. 1.** A Tigger instantiation.

Amadeus supported exactly the set of languages depicted in figure 1 but with a single GRT. However, the Amadeus GRT was both complex and large, and hence penalised languages and applications that typically only required a subset of the features that it provided. The Tigger approach allows the GRT to be customised according to the specific requirements of the language implementer.

## 4.1 Logical Model

The classes making up the Tigger framework are divided into five main class categories [2]. Essentially, each of these class categories is responsible for supporting some subset of the fundamental abstractions provided by the Tigger framework as follows:

- the GRT class category – known as Owl[3] – supports distributed and persistent objects and optionally clusters, and provides the main interface to supported languages. An instantiation of Owl corresponds to a GRT as described above and, a single Tigger instantiation may include multiple Owl instantiations.

---

[3] Yes, you've guessed it! All the class categories are called after characters from A.A. Milne's books.

- the threads class category – known as Roo – supports threads and related synchronisation mechanisms, and may support activities and jobs. Supported languages (i.e., their LSRTs) and applications may use Roo directly.
- the communications class category – known as Kanga – supports endpoints. Again, supported languages and applications may use Kanga directly.
- the storage class category – known as Eeyore – supports containers and storage objects. Supported languages are not expected to use Eeyore directly and hence its main client is Owl.
- the protection class category – known as Robin – supports extents and related abstractions.

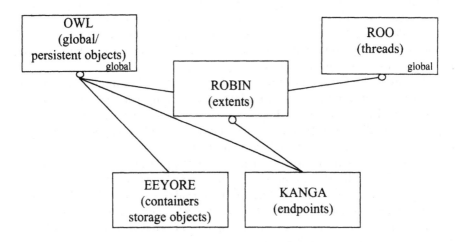

**Fig. 2.** Tigger class categories.

Figure 2 is a top-level class diagram for the Tigger framework showing the class categories introduced above and their using relationships. Note that both Owl and Roo are labelled as **global** meaning that they may be used by all the other class categories. In the case of Roo, this reflects the fact that all the components of a Tigger instantiation are expected to be thread-aware. In the case of Owl, this reflects the fact that components of a Tigger instantiation may use distributed or persistent objects.

While Owl is specialised depending primarily on the needs of the language(s) to be supported, the other class categories can also be specialised to support different mechanisms and policies. In particular, different instantiations of Robin determine whether the Tigger instantiation of which it is a part supports only a single extent or multiple extents, as well as whether it supports one or more contexts. Other responsibilities of Robin include supporting cross-extent object invocation and unique object identification. Decisions made about the implementation of Robin are therefore of fundamental importance for the overall structure of a Tigger instantiation.

The Robin and Owl class categories are described in detail in [3]. For descriptions of early versions of Roo and Kanga see [8]. Eeyore is based on the Amadeus persistent object store (POS) framework described in [16]. The remainder of this paper gives an overview of the Owl class category.

# 5   Object-Support Functionality

This section considers how the functionality required to support distributed and persistent objects can be divided between an LSRT and a GRT. Given this separation of responsibilities, the major services supported by Owl, as well as the main options for implementing those services, are then identified. An important goal of Tigger was that Owl should provide as much of the required functionality as possible. Only where a service is clearly language-specific or is intimately connected with the code that is generated by the language's compilation system is that service assigned to the LSRT.

In reading the following sections, it should be borne in mind that a particular Owl instantiation (i.e., GRT) might support only persistent objects, only distributed objects, or both. Hence, not all of these services will need to be supported by all Owl instantiations. Furthermore, the list presented here is not exhaustive; Owl can be extended to support other services.

**Object layout and naming**: Unless the compilation system is to be seriously constrained by the use of a GRT, the LSRT should be able to dictate the layout of objects in memory, the format of internal/local references used by such objects, and the mapping from such an object reference to the address of a collocated object. To reflect this fact, internal/local references are referred to as *language references* or lREFs from here on.

A GRT, on the other hand, should be responsible for the provision of globally unique object identifiers (OIDs) suitable for identifying every object in the system[4] A GRT should also be responsible for the provision of external/global references (referred to simply as global references or gREFs from here on). A GRT should also implement the mapping from a gREF for an object to the location of that object in the system.

Where the language to be supported already supports distribution or persistence, its LSRT will already support its own form of OID and gREF. Moreover, its lREFs and gREFs may be the same. Owl does not support all possible existing gREF formats but only those that support an Owl-defined protocol. Owl instantiations may however use (virtual) addresses as gREFs. Owl also supports languages in which gREFs and lREFs are the same as long as the gREFs support the appropriate protocol.

**Object access, binding, and dispatching**: Each language is free to determine how objects may be accessed by their clients. However, it is important

---

[4] In the Tigger framework, responsibility for the format and allocation of OIDs actually rests with Robin rather than Owl.

to realise that this decision has important repercussions for the choice of object fault avoidance or detection mechanisms that are available and for the ways in which object faults can be resolved. Typically, the choice of possible object fault avoidance, detection, or resolution mechanisms is constrained by the form of access to objects allowed. For example, the use of proxies to represent absent objects is not appropriate where direct access to the instance data of an object by its clients is allowed.

Since the means of binding code to objects and of dispatching invocations (including the layout of parameter frames) is usually intrinsic to the compilation system, these must continue to be implemented in the LSRT. Thus, a GRT need not be involved in local object invocation. However, this also means that when ROI is used to access remote distributed objects, the marshalling and unmarshalling of ROI requests, as well as the dispatching of incoming requests to their target objects, must be done by or in cooperation with the LSRT.

**Object allocation and garbage collection**: Owl only supports allocation of objects on the heap or embedded in other (heap-allocated) objects. Moreover, Owl is responsible for management of the heap and hence provides the routines to allocate (and where supported, deallocate) objects.

When necessary, Owl supports garbage collection of distributed or persistent objects both within memory and within the POS as required.

**Object fault detection and avoidance**: Detection or avoidance of object faults is the responsibility of the LSRT since it depends on the type of access to objects supported and the mechanisms used may need to be tightly integrated with the compilation system. For example, if presence tests are used to detect absent objects, the language compiler or preprocessor will usually be required to generate the code necessary to perform these tests before any access to an object proceeds.

Owl does however provide underlying support for a number of common object fault detection mechanisms (for example, presence tests and proxies) as well as support for object fault avoidance. Other object fault detection mechanisms may be implemented entirely at the language level.

**Object fault resolution**: Where object fault detection is used, Owl provides the underlying means of resolving object faults including locating the target objects, mapping objects, transferring ROI requests to objects, and/or migrating threads as appropriate. The choice of object fault resolution policy is however constrained by the LSRT.

In the case of ROI requests, the formatting of the request must however be carried out by the LSRT since only it understands the format of parameter frames. Owl does however support the marshalling and unmarshalling of lREFs and values of basic types. The translation of lREFs to the corresponding gREFs and vice versa must be carried out in cooperation with the LSRT. Similar comments apply to migration of objects. On the remote side, the LSRT must be prepared to accept incoming ROI requests from the GRT, unmarshal the parameters, dispatch the request in the language-specific manner, and, once the request has been completed, to marshal the reply. Note that the dispatching of the request must be carried out by the LSRT since only it understands the dispatching mechanism to be used.

**Mapping, unmapping, and migration**: Owl provides the basic support for the mapping and unmapping of persistent objects as well as the migration of distributed objects.

During mapping or migration, Owl supports the conversion of objects to local format where heterogeneity is supported; no, lazy, and eager swizzling of references as required; and binding of code to mapped objects. In each case, these actions require language- (and indeed type-) specific information. Hence, while Owl supports each of these, it does so in cooperation with the LSRTs of supported languages.

Where swizzling is used, the GRT must be able to translate a gREF to the appropriate lREF (whether or not the target object is mapped into the current address space). This again requires cooperation with the LSRT depending on the object faulting strategy in use.

Likewise, binding of code to a recently-mapped object must be done in a language-specific way. However, Owl provides the underlying support for dynamic linking where this is required including supporting the storage and retrieval of class code.

Determining which objects can be unmapped or migrated also depends on the object faulting strategy in use. Nevertheless, Owl supports both anchored and non-anchored code.

**Clustering**: Owl supports the use of both application-directed and transparent clustering as required.

**Directory Services**: Finally, Owl provides a (persistent) name service (NS) that can be used to attach symbolic names to object references.

# 6 An Overview of the Owl Class Category

Just as the overall Tigger framework describes the architecture of a family of object-support operating systems, Owl may be said to describe the architecture of a family of GRTs. A GRT supporting one or more specific languages is instantiated by providing appropriate implementations of (a subset of) the classes that constitute the Owl class category. The process of instantiating a GRT from Owl is obviously driven by the requirements of the language(s) to be supported but is also constrained by the model of a GRT and of GRT–LSRT interaction embodied in the design of Owl. This section describes the abstract model of a GRT, and of its interaction with an LSRT, that underpins the design of Owl. The next section describes the organisation of the Owl class category in more detail.

## 6.1 GRT Model

A GRT provides runtime support for distribution or persistence in cooperation with the LSRTs of the languages that it supports and the other components of the Tigger instantiation of which it is a part. Some GRTs support only distributed objects, others only persistent objects, while some support both. Whether a GRT supports distributed or persistent objects is determined by the way in which it is instantiated. Thus, distributed or persistent objects can be seen as specialisations of abstract *GRT objects* supported by Owl. Every GRT supports at least the following services for GRT objects[5]:

- object creation;
- location-independent object naming;
- object faulting;
- object mapping and unmapping;
- directory services.

Together these services constitute the basic runtime support that must be provided for any distributed or persistent programming language. Depending on how each is implemented, the resulting GRT can support distributed or persistent objects using various policies and mechanisms. A given GRT can also provide additional services such as object deletion or garbage collection, object clustering, or marshalling and unmarshalling of ROI requests. The Owl class category described in the remainder of this paper includes classes providing a number of these additional services. Moreover, Owl has been designed to be extensible so that support for further services, for example, transaction management, can be provided in the future.

Typically, each of these services is invoked by a *downcall* from the LSRT to the GRT and makes use of *upcalls* from the GRT to the LSRT when a language-specific action has to be performed or language-specific information obtained.

Every GRT provides exactly one form of gREF and one swizzling policy as dictated by the language(s) to be supported. A GRT may support either object fault avoidance or object fault detection. In the case of object fault detection, the actual detection of object faults is the responsibility of the LSRT. A given GRT may support the LSRT in using a number of different techniques for object fault detection or the object fault detection technique used may be completely transparent to the GRT. A GRT supporting object fault detection may provide a number of different interfaces for object fault reporting. Each object fault reporting interface implies a set of allowable object fault resolution techniques that the GRT can apply. In addition, a GRT for use in a multi-extent Tigger instantiation always provides interfaces supporting cross-extent object invocation and object migration between extents.

## 6.2 Object Model

Abstractly, at the language level, an *object* is an entity with identity, state, and behaviour [2]. Every language object is assumed to have an associated *type* that specifies the interface to the object available to its clients.

---

[5] In the following, the term *"object"* is used as a synonym for "GRT *object*" unless otherwise noted.

On the other hand, a GRT object can be viewed as being essentially a container for one or more language objects that can be uniquely identified and to which code implementing the interface to the contained object(s) can be bound dynamically by the appropriate LSRT. Distributed or persistent language objects must be mapped, in a way specific to their language, onto appropriate GRT objects. The most obvious mapping is to use a single GRT object for each dynamically allocated language object. Other mappings are also possible. For example, an array of language objects could be contained within a single GRT object or a language object might be embedded within another language object that is contained within a GRT object. The main consequence of supporting arrays of language objects or embedded language objects is that lREFs may map to arbitrary addresses within a GRT object rather than just the start address of the object.

In any case, both the internal structure of a particular GRT object and the semantics implemented by the contained language objects are dictated by the language level. Such information can be acquired by the GRT if necessary only by making upcalls to the LSRT. In particular, a set of upcall methods, which are implemented by the appropriate LSRT and which the GRT can call when required, must be bound to every GRT object in a way defined by Owl.

**Object Allocation and Layout** New GRT objects are created dynamically in the GRT's heap by explicitly calling the GRT. Neither static allocation of GRT objects in some per-context data segment nor stack allocation of GRT objects is supported.

Every GRT object has a header that is used to store information required by the GRT to manage the object. Depending on the GRT instantiation, this header may be allocated contiguously with the GRT object in memory or separately (perhaps to allow GRT objects to be moved within memory while mapped). In normal operation, an object's GRT header is transparent to the language level although it may be accessed by upcall code provided by the LSRT.

Language objects are expected to be contiguous in memory but may have contiguous or non-contiguous headers containing information required by their LSRTs. In order to support LSRTs that use non-contiguous object headers, a GRT may be specialised to allow GRT objects to be split into (at most) two memory regions resulting in the four possible GRT object layouts being supported

**Object Naming** GRT objects are uniquely identified by Robin OIDs. GRTs may assign OIDs to objects either eagerly, i.e., when they are created, or lazily, i.e., at least some time before they become visible outside of their cradle extent, i.e., the extent in which they were created. A GRT that supports lazy OID allocation may for example allocate OIDs to objects only when they become known outside of their cradle extent, when they become known outside of the context in which they were created, or, if clustering is supported, when they become known outside of their initial cluster.

Supporting lazy OID allocation requires that the GRT can detect when an object reference is about to be exported from an extent, context, or cluster as appropriate. This means that lazy OID allocation is only possible if the GRT supports swizzling and may additionally require an address space scan [22].

A GRT object to which no OID has been allocated is known as an *immature* object. By definition immature objects exist and are known only within the extent in which they were created. When allocated an OID, an object is said to be *promoted* to being a *mature* object.

The gREFs provided by a GRT serve not only to allow the referenced object to be located but are also used to support object fault handling mechanisms. For example, as well as providing the target object's OID or storage identifier, a gREF might contain information to allow a proxy for the object to be created when required.

In addition, since most GRTs will support embedded language objects within a GRT object, a gREF may refer to a particular offset within a GRT object. This is useful where a gREF is to be converted to an lREF referring to such an embedded language object rather than its enclosing language object.

**Code Management** The code to be bound to each language object is provided by its LSRT as a *class*. A given type may be represented by one or more classes. For example, if the LSRT uses proxies for object fault detection, then every type may be represented by a real class bound to language objects of that type and a proxy class bound to proxies for objects of that type. Each class consists of *application code*, which implements the methods required by the object's type, and *upcall code*, which implements the upcall methods to be bound to GRT objects containing objects of that type[6]. As mentioned previously, the upcall code is bound to the appropriate GRT object by the GRT while the application code is bound to the language object in a language-specific way by its LSRT, usually in response to an upcall from the GRT. Note however that only a single set of upcall methods can be associated with each GRT object.

Each class is represented by a *class descriptor* and named by a *class identifier* that acts as an index for the class descriptor in the GRT's *class register* (CR).

**Objects and Representatives** A distributed or persistent language object can have *representatives* in many contexts. The representatives of an object might be used to implement an object and its proxies, the replicas of a replicated object, or the fragments of a fragmented object. The mapping of a distributed or persistent language object onto a set of representatives is thus language-specific. Moreover, depending on the object model supported by the language, the existence of multiple representatives of an object in the system may or may not be transparent to application programmers.

To support this model, a GRT object can likewise have representatives in many contexts. The representatives of a GRT object share its identity. However,

---

[6] Upcall code may be specific to one type or shared between different types, for example, Eiffel** uses the same upcall code for all types.

the representatives may be different sizes and may or may not have application code bound to them. Moreover, the code bound to each representative may be the same or different. All representatives of a GRT object do however have GRT object headers and all have (possibly different) upcall code bound to them. If, when, and how representatives for GRT objects are created depends on the GRT instantiation. For example, to support a language that uses proxies for object fault detection, a GRT might be instantiated that creates representatives for absent GRT objects that are the same size as the real object and have proxy application code bound to them. If the language uses descriptors to represent absent objects, the GRT instantiation might create representatives for absent objects that are smaller that the actual object and have no application code bound to them.

When the GRT creates or maps an object or a representative for an object, such as a proxy, the GRT will ask the LSRT to *prepare* the object/representative for possible accesses by its clients by making an upcall to the object/representative. This upcall allows the LSRT to carry out any appropriate language-specific actions necessary to make the object/representative ready to be accessed. Typically, this will include binding application code to the object/representative but may also involve initiating swizzling or doing other format conversions which are necessary prior to the object/representative being accessed. Thus, initiating swizzling is the responsibility of the LSRT and not the GRT. When exactly the GRT makes this upcall depends on the particular GRT instantiation.

# 7  The Organisation of the Owl Class Category

A GRT consists of a number of major functional components that can be individually customised to implement a GRT providing some required set of object-support mechanisms and policies. The seven major components of all GRTs are illustrated in figure 3 along with one optional component. These major components are implemented by instances of classes derived from the major class hierarchies that make up the Owl class category. Other Owl class hierarchies describe GRT objects, clusters, and various support classes used by the major components of a GRT.

The main interface between an LSRT and a GRT is provided by an instance of $OwlGRT_{sc}$[7]. Subclasses of OwlGRT provide the major GRT methods related to object (and cluster) management callable from LSRTs and are also responsible for the translation between lREFs and gREFs that takes place at the LSRT/GRT interface.

Every GRT has a heap in which objects are created and mapped as required. A GRT's heap is implemented by an instance of $OwlHeap_{sc}$ that provides the methods to allocate and deallocate memory from the heap. Higher-level methods, such as those to create objects and clusters within the heap or those to map and unmap objects and clusters into and out of the heap, are provided by

---

[7] The notation "$ClassName_{sc}$" is used to denote subclasses of ClassName, i.e., "ClassName$_{sc}$" can be read as "one of the subclasses of ClassName".

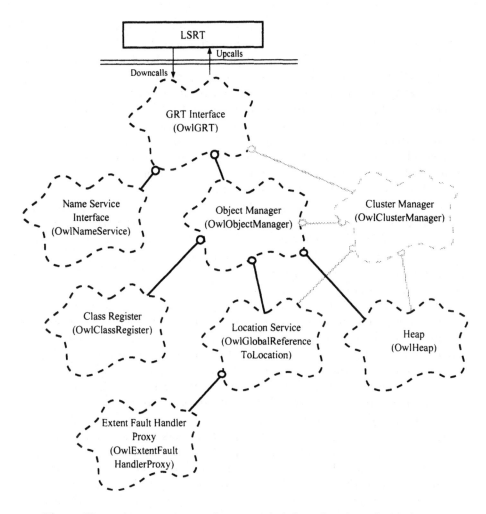

**Fig. 3.** The major components of a GRT and their main using relationships.

a heap manager – an instance of **OwlManager**$_{sc}$. Heap managers come in two varieties: object managers (OMs) and cluster managers (CLMs). OMs – instances of **OwlObjectManager**$_{sc}$ – provide methods related to the creation, mapping, and unmapping of objects, while CLMs – instances of **OwlClusterManager**$_{sc}$ – provide methods related to the creation, mapping, and unmapping of clusters. Every GRT has an OM. A GRT that supports application-directed clustering will also have a CLM. Thus, as indicated by the shaded lines in figure 3, a CLM is an optional component of a GRT. The OM or CLM is also the component of the GRT that interacts with Eeyore – the storage class category – to store and retrieve objects or clusters respectively when required.

While heap managers are responsible for control of the heap, the location of, and, where necessary, forwarding of access requests to absent objects (be they persistent objects stored in the POS, distributed objects located on another node, or objects belonging to a different extent) is encapsulated within the location service (LS) component of the GRT, which is implemented by an instance of **OwlGlobalReferenceToLocation**$_{sc}$. The LS implements the GRT's mapping from the gREF for an object to its current location in the (possibly distributed) system. Since an absent object reported to the LS may actually be non-existent or, in a multi-extent Tigger instantiation, belong to a different extent, the LS is also responsible for raising extent faults. In a GRT supporting distribution, the LS is a distributed component and uses Kanga – the communications class category – for communication between its distributed parts.

Every GRT has a proxy for its local EFH, which is an instance of **OwlExtentFaultHandlerProxy**$_{sc}$. Thus, instances of **OwlExtentFaultHandlerProxy**$_{sc}$ are kernel-aware objects that allow cross-extent object invocation to be implemented.

A CR is a repository for class descriptors and code. Every GRT uses a CR – an instance of **OwlClassRegister**$_{sc}$ – to obtain the class code for new and recently mapped objects when required. A CR is normally persistent and may also be remotely accessible. Likewise, the objects that it uses to store classes and their code would normally be expected to be persistent. Thus, a CR represents a good example of a service provided by the Tigger framework that is itself implemented using distributed and persistent objects. The design of the Tigger framework assumes that there is a single CR in each system, which is shared between all the GRTs (and all the extents) in that system. It is worth noting that although the CR is a trusted service, it can belong to any desired extent.

Finally, every GRT also provides a NS to supported languages via an instance of **OwlNameService**$_{sc}$. Although instances of **OwlNameService**$_{sc}$ are local volatile objects that are private to one GRT, the directories to which they refer are typically implemented by distributed persistent objects. Thus the NS as a whole can be seen as another example of a service provided by the Tigger framework that is itself implemented using distributed and persistent objects. Moreover, individual directories may belong to different extents.

In addition to the class hierarchies describing the main components of the GRT, further class hierarchies describe objects and clusters. The **OwlObject** class hierarchy describes the methods supported by GRT objects and the structure of GRT object headers. The **OwlObject** hierarchy also describes the upcalls that must be provided for each object by the LSRT and provides the means of binding the upcall code to a GRT object/representative. Similarly, the **OwlCluster** class hierarchy describes the methods supported by clusters. In addition, Owl includes a number of other important class hierarchies that are introduced briefly here.

- **OwlLanguageReference** Describes the protocol to be supported by lREFs.
- **OwlGlobalReference** Describes the protocols supported by gREFs.
- **OwlGlobalReferenceToAddress** Describes the GRT's mapping from a gREF for an object to its address in the current context.
- **OwlClusterIdentifier** Describes the protocol for cluster identifiers.

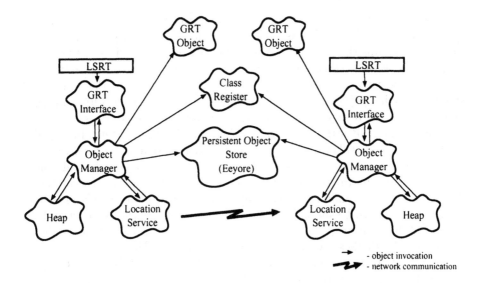

**Fig. 4.** The interactions between the major components of a GRT.

- **OwlClusterIdentifierToAddress** Describes the GRT's mapping from the identifier of a cluster to its address in the current context.
- **OwlMarshalStream** Provides methods for constructing messages including ROI request messages and replies.
- **OwlRequestDescriptor, OwlRPCDescriptor,** and **OwlMigrationDescriptor** describe messages sent by GRT components that are constructed by LSRTs.
- **OwlDirectory** Describes the interface to an NS directory.
- **OwlDirectoryEntry** Describes an entry in an NS directory.
- **OwlCode** Describes objects used to store executable code.
- **OwlClassDescriptor** Describes a class descriptor.

It should be understood that above list is not exhaustive and that other classes are required to implement a GRT. Those presented typically use the services of other simpler classes describing their internal data structures or providing "house-keeping" functionality.

**Interactions Between GRT Components** Figure 4 shows the main interactions that occur between the major components of a GRT. For the sake of generality, the GRT in question is assumed to support both distribution and persistence and is hence distributed over multiple nodes and makes use of a POS instantiated from Eeyore.

The LSRTs of supported languages usually invoke methods provided by the GRT interface. This will typically result in the GRT interface invoking one of the other components of the GRT, normally the NS interface or OM. In the case where the request from the LSRT is related to object management (for example, requests to create or delete objects and requests related to object faulting), the GRT interface calls the OM. The OM will typically use the services of the LS, the heap, or the POS to carry out the request. During object fault handling, the request is typically forwarded to the LS. The LS may indicate that the object should be retrieved from the POS and mapped locally, return the object immediately, forward the request to the OM at the node where the object is located, or raise an extent fault if the object may belong to a different extent. In handling the request, the LS will typically communicate with its remote peers who may, in turn, need to upcall their local OMs. Thus, an OM typically provides a downcall interface for use by the GRT interface and an upcall interface for use by the LS during object fault handling. Like the interface to the GRT, the interfaces to both the OM and LS must be specialised depending on the approach to object faulting supported. In addition, as a heap manager, the OM also provides an upcall interface for use by the heap when heap space is exhausted. This interface typically causes the OM to try to unmap some objects. The OM may use the CR to load class code for newly created objects or objects that have been mapped recently and is also the component that most commonly makes upcalls to GRT objects. Finally, the OM may upcall the GRT interface – usually to convert a gREF to an lREF or vice versa.

Both the CR and POS are potentially shared by different GRTs in different extents including GRTs of different types. Moreover, they are typically implemented by distributed objects and are accessible from multiple GRTs using location-transparent object invocation.

Figure 5 shows the interactions that occur between the major components of a GRT that supports application-directed clustering. Such a GRT has an additional component, its CLM, that is interposed between the OM and other components such as the heap, LS, and POS. Requests related to clusters (for example, requests to create or delete clusters) are passed by the GRT interface directly to the CLM while requests related to objects are still passed to the OM. A request concerning some object might result in the OM making a corresponding request to the CLM for that object's cluster. Since the unit of location, mapping, and unmapping is a cluster rather than an individual object, the CLM is responsible for interacting with the LS, POS, and heap to resolve the request in much the same way as the the OM is in a GRT that does not support application-directed clustering. Resolving the request might require that a CLM make an upcall to its local OM. Like the interfaces to the GRT interface, OM, and LS, the interface to the CLM is also specialised depending on the approach to object faulting supported.

# 8 Status

At the current time, the design of the first complete version of the framework has been completed and a number of instantiations are being implemented. [23] describes the first Tigger instantiation implemented. The so-called T1 instantiation supports an extension to C++ for distributed and persistent programming

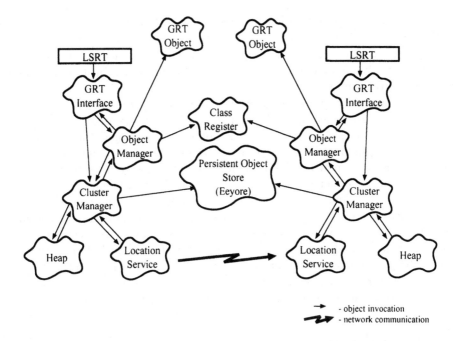

**Fig. 5.** Interactions between parts of a GRT supporting application-directed clustering.

inspired by PANDA/C++ [1]. T1 is a single-extent Tigger instantiation layered above UNIX that implements a single distributed and persistent address space and supports DSM-style access to global and persistent objects. Object faults are detected as memory protection faults. No swizzling is employed and virtual addresses are used as gREFs. In addition, T1 supports application-directed clustering.

Another Tigger instantiation is currently being implemented to support a novel object model providing application-consistent DSM [10].

## 9   Summary and Conclusions

An object-support operating system may be described as one that has been designed specifically to support object-oriented applications, especially distributed applications or those that manipulate persistent data. Unfortunately, most existing object-support operating systems can support only a single language or else severely constrain the way in which different languages can be supported, in particular, by supporting only a single object model. In contrast, the Tigger project undertook the design, not of a single object-support operating system, but of a family of object-support operating systems whose members can be customised for use in a variety of different application domains. The two primary goals of this design were to allow members of the family to support (a number of) different object models and to allow the same object model to be supported in different ways subject to differing non-functional requirements. This design is captured as a framework that can be instantiated to implement the individual members of the family.

While framework technology is well-established and the use of frameworks to implement customised operating systems is not new, the use of a framework as the basis for implementing customised object-support operating systems is novel. The Tigger framework provides a common basis for the implementation of both single and multi-user object-support operating systems that support a range of object-oriented programming languages for distributed and persistent programming and encompass different non-functional requirements such as heterogeneity or protection. While traditional operating system architectures emphasise the distinction between the operating system kernel, which runs in supervisor mode, and user-level servers and applications, which do not, the design of Tigger emphasises the orthogonality between protection and operating system structure. Thus, the resulting framework encompasses both single-user systems with no kernel and multi-user systems having a distinguished kernel.

## Acknowlegdements

Thanks to Brendan Tangney, Neville Harris, Paul Taylor, and Alan Judge for their many and varied contributions to the work described in this paper.

## References

1. Holger Assenmacher, Thomas Breitbach, Peter Buhler, Volker Huebsch, and Reinhard Schwarz. PANDA - supporting distributed programming in C++. In Oscar M. Nierstrasz, editor, *Proceedings of the 7th European Conference on Object-Oriented Programming*, volume 707 of *Lecture Notes in Computer Science*, pages 361–383. Springer-Verlag, 1993.
2. Grady Booch. *Object-Oriented Analysis and Design with Applications*. Benjamin/Cummings, Redwood City, CA, 1994.
3. Vinny Cahill. On The Architecture of a Family of Object-Support Operating Systems. Ph.D. thesis, Department of Computer Science, Trinity College Dublin, September 1996.
4. Vinny Cahill, Seán Baker, Gradimir Starovic, and Chris Horn. Generic runtime support for distributed persistent programming. In Paepcke [18], pages 144–161.
5. Vinny Cahill, Roland Balter, Xavier Rousset de Pina, and Neville Harris, editors. *The COMANDOS Distributed Application Platform*. ESPRIT Research Reports Series. Springer-Verlag, 1993.
6. Roy H. Campbell, Nayeem Islam, and Peter Madany. *Choices*, Frameworks and Refinement. *Computing Systems*, 5(3):217–257, Summer 1992.
7. Distributed Systems Group. C** programmer's guide (Amadeus v2.0). Technical Report TCD-CS-92-03, Department of Computer Science, Trinity College Dublin, February 1992.

8. Christine Hogan. The Tigger Cub Nucleus. Master's thesis, Department of Computer Science, Trinity College Dublin, September 1994.

9. Chris Horn and Vinny Cahill. Supporting distributed applications in the Amadeus environment. *Computer Communications*, 14(6):358–365, July/August 1991.

10. Alan Judge. *Supporting Application-Consistent Distributed Shared Objects*. PhD thesis, Department of Computer Science, Trinity College Dublin, 1996. In preparation.

11. Reinhold Kröeger, Michael Mock, Ralf Schumann, and Frank Lange. RelaX - an extensible architecture supporting reliable distributed applications. In *Proceedings of the $9^{th}$ Symposium on Reliable Distributed Systems*, pages 156–165. IEEE Computer Society Press, 1990.

12. John McEvoy. E**: Porting the E database language to Amadeus. Master's thesis, Department of Computer Science, Trinity College Dublin, 1993.

13. Colm McHugh and Vinny Cahill. Eiffel**: An implementation of Eiffel on Amadeus, a persistent, distributed applications support environment. In Boris Magnusson, Bertrand Meyer, and Jean-Francois Perot, editors, *Technology of Object-Oriented Languages and Systems (TOOLS 10)*, pages 47–62. Prentice Hall, 1993.

14. Michael Mock, Reinhold Kroeger, and Vinny Cahill. Implementing atomic objects with the RelaX transaction facility. *Computing Systems*, 5(3):259–304, 1992.

15. Karl O'Connell, Vinny Cahill, Andrew Condon, Stephen McGerty, Gradimir Starovic, and Brendan Tangney. The VOID shell: A toolkit for the development of distributed video games and virtual worlds. In *Proceedings of the Workshop on Simulation and Interaction in Virtual Environments*, 1995.

16. Darragh O'Grady. An extensible, high-performance, distributed persistent store for Amadeus. Master's thesis, Department of Computer Science, Trinity College Dublin, September 1994.

17. Joo Li Ooi. Access control for an object-oriented distributed platform. Master's thesis, Department of Computer Science, Trinity College Dublin, August 1993.

18. Andreas Paepcke, editor. *Proceedings of the 1993 Conference on Object-Oriented Programming Systems, Languages and Applications*. ACM Press, September 1993. Also SIGPLAN Notices 28(10), October 1993.

19. Wolfgang Schröder-Preikschat. *The Logical Design of Parallel Operating Systems*. Prentice Hall, London, 1994.

20. Marc Shapiro. Object-support operating systems. *IEEE Technical Committee on Operating Systems and Application Environments Newsletter*, 5(1):39–42, Spring 1991.

21. Marc Shapiro. Soul: An object-oriented OS framework for object support. In A. Karshmer and J. Nehmer, editors, *Operating Systems of the 90s and Beyond*, volume 563 of *Lecture Notes in Computer Science*. Springer-Verlag, July 1991.

22. Pedro Sousa, Manuel Sequeira, André Zúquete, Paulo Ferreira, Cristina Lopes, José Pereira, Paulo Guedes, and José Alves Marques. Distribution and persistence in the IK platform: Overview and evaluation. *Computing Systems*, 6(4):391–424, Fall 1993.

23. Paul Taylor. The T1 cub. Tigger document T16-94, Distributed Systems Group, Department of Computer Science, Trinity College Dublin, November 1994.

24. Paul Taylor, Vinny Cahill, and Michael Mock. Combining object-oriented systems and open transaction processing. *The Computer Journal*, 37(6), August 1994.

# The Arias Distributed Shared Memory: An Overview

P. Dechamboux[1], D. Hagimont[2], J. Mossière[3] and X. Rousset de Pina[3]

[1] GIE Dyade (Bull-INRIA)
[2] Institut National de Recherche en Informatique et Automatique (INRIA)
[3] Institut National Polytechnique de Grenoble (INPG)

Unité de Recherche INRIA Rhône-Alpes 655, avenue de l'Europe
38330 Montbonnot St Martin - France

**Abstract.** Arias is a system serviceee for distributed information systems, which provides low-level support for applications that make an intensive use of sharing and persistence. Arias is based on a persistent distributed shared memory that can be tailored and tuned according to the needs of the supported environment. This paper summarizes the basic design choices and describes the implementation of the first prototype.

## 1 Introduction

Most current information computing environments operate on local or wide area networks. Such distributed environments are mainly used because they enable and enhance the cooperation of multiple users through specific distributed applications. Typical examples of such applications are large hypertext or hypermedia information management systems in areas like CAD and software engineering, or object-oriented databases. More precisely, this class of applications has the following characteristics:

– Large size of data, due to the world-wide spread of information bases.
– Persistence of processed data.
– Highly interconnected information, through multiple links.
– A high sharing rate among cooperating users.
– Data access from distributed workstations.

Information management systems must be based on current standards. One of such standards is Unix, despite the fact that this system is not adapted to provide support for these applications for the following reasons:

– Primitive mechanisms for information sharing.
– No integrated support for distribution, and particularly for naming.
– Persistence management by users.

The advent of 64-bit address processors and high speed networks allows us to reconsider the solutions currently proposed for applications implementation.

With fast networks, solutions based on distributed virtual memory become feasible and wide addressing spaces facilitate the management of a unique virtual space.

The goal of the Arias project is to design and to implement a set of system services which are characterized by the following points:

- Services should provide an appropriate support for sharing of complex and persistent data. They should meet the requirements of both cooperative applications and database managers.
- Compatibility with current standards must be preserved, specially with the Unix system.
- Services should benefit from recent technical evolutions in order to be efficient.

A large spectrum of existing runtime frameworks can benefit from these services (examples are given in section 7). Our main goal is not to implement applications directly above these services. We are rather aiming at providing services designed to support frameworks, each framework being dedicated to a class of applications with similar behavior. Already known examples are frameworks for distributed applications development and DBMS, which hide the low-level features of the system interface. In the following, we use the term *application* to describe client entities (frameworks or final applications).

After a general presentation of the provided services (section 2), we present respectively our proposition for memory management (section 3), consistency and synchronization (section 4), permanence (section 5) and protection (section 6). Section 7 presents our current experiments in using these services, section 8 contains a comparison with similar projects and section 9 concludes this paper.

## 2 General presentation

We want to provide a service which allows sharing of persistent data between Unix processes executing on homogeneous interconnected workstations. Three types of problems have to be addressed :

- Data sharing and consistency of shared data.
  If sharing is implemented by copying shared data on different machines, then we need to address the issue of the type of consistency to ensure between these copies.
- Resistance to node failures.
  Shared data is persistent, which means that its lifetime does not depend on that of the process which creates it. However, this property is not sufficient to resist node failures. For that purpose, we must provide a stable storage for permanent segment (for example on a disk). As a consequence, the system must also enable coherent (atomic) updates of the permanent image of segments.

– Access control.

We should allow access to shared data with different access rights according to processes or users; we therefore need to provide a protection service for shared data.

One of the basic design choices is to provide mechanisms which allow users to implement the policy which best fits the needs of their applications, rather than enforcing a system-defined policy. For example, the system does not enforce a consistency model, but provides the tools and the mechanisms which allow the implementation of different consistency policies. Application designers may also decide to use predefined policies which are provided.

Users may adapt the behaviour of the Arias system to the specific requirements of their applications by writing what we call a *specialized protocol*, and plugging it into Arias. In this way, they can parameterize the behaviour of consistency and synchronization (i.e., the management of the coherence of distributed execution memory) as well as of permanence (i.e., the management of the consistency of permanent memory with respect to execution memory).

The remaining of this section describes the service which handles data sharing, the service which implements permanence and the protection service.

## 2.1 Data sharing service

The service which handles data sharing is composed of two parts: shared memory management and consistency management.

**Shared memory management**

The main design choice for memory management is the use of 64 bit addressing for managing a single address space. In our system, shared memory is built out of a block of $2^{63}$ bytes reserved at the same virtual address in all Unix processes which use it. Therefore, virtual addresses may be freely exchanged between processes as system-wide unique identifiers.

The allocation unit within this memory is a segment, a sequence of contiguous pages. The segment size is fixed at creation time. Segments are persistent (i.e., their lifetime does not depend on that of the process which created them). A segment is designated by its base virtual address which remains unchanged during its whole life. Segments need to be explicitly destroyed. The system ensures that the range of address space occupied by a destroyed segment is never reallocated and that each attempt to access a destroyed segment generates an exception. The implementation of a garbage collector is left to the care of applications which are able to interpret the contents of segments.

During execution, shared memory management relies on the paging mechanisms of the machines. Due to segment sharing, concurrent accesses at the same page may occur simultaneously on several hosts, as pages can be replicated in the memory of each host. The system does not handle consistency among different copies of the same page, but it provides the mechanisms which allow applications to implement their own consistency policy.

## Consistency management

The supplied mechanisms rely on the following observations:

- Most of the time, the segment and even the page have a granularity which is too coarse to be chosen as the synchronization and consistency unit. Hence, it is necessary to provide a finer grain unit if we want to avoid problems due to false sharing (processes accessing disjoint areas of the same page).
- Applications synchronize their access to potentially shareable data. It is therefore possible to link synchronization and data consistency enforcement, and specifically to postpone the application of consistency on a data zone to synchronization time (e.g. the request of a lock on this zone).

Mechanisms which implement consistency manage zones which are sequences of contiguous bytes. Each zone has a particular copy called the *master copy*. The system knows how to find the master copy of a zone at any moment; the system also provides primitives which allow updating zone copies from the master copy and conversely, or to change the ownership of the master copy. This set of primitives may be used to implement usual policies for consistency management (section 4). A number of "standard" protocols are provided, e.g. entry consistency protocol (strong consistency is only enforced at lock acquisition on zones) combined with a synchronization policy of readers/writer style and with a pessimistic transactional scheme.

## 2.2 Permanence service

A segment of memory may be made permanent (have an image on a permanent physical support, e.g. a disk), which permits failure resistance. Non permanent segments are called volatile. We provide two mechanisms for permanence management: permanent copy (make a segment permanent) and logging. Client applications can log a set of modifications of different segments as a list of records on disk. Validation of this log ensures that these modifications are atomic. In case of failure, the log allows a consistent image of the permanent memory to be rebuilt.

The format of modification records and the processing of these modifications are handled under applications' control. Actually, application control the format and the semantics of records written into the log, along with the use of the log upon error recovery. An application can therefore manage a "before" log (store old validated values) or an "after" log (store validated modifications). The application also controls the updates of permanent images of segments which can be modified implicitly in an asynchronous way, or explicitly in a synchronous way.

In our system, we distinguish between two levels of memory: the execution memory where segments are manipulated by applications, and the permanent memory. This distinction allows us to always maintain, even during execution, a consistent version of segments in permanent memory.

To facilitate their management, permanent images of segments are grouped into logical storage units called volumes. A volume is managed by a single server at a given moment. It can be transferred to another server during its existence.

## 2.3 Protection service

The protection service provides facilities for controlling accesses to segments. The protection service is based on two concepts: protection domains and capabilities. A protection domain defines a set of accessible segments along with the available operations for each of them. A system mechanism ensures that processes executing within a domain access its segments according to the specified rights. A capability is a data structure which defines an access right on a segment. It integrates a segment name (virtual address) and a set of access rights to this segment, expressed in terms of read, write and execute operations.

At a given moment, a Unix process using the protection service runs within a protection domain which defines its current addressing context. Two different protection domains can share segments with the same or different rights. At the first access to a segment within a domain, the system checks if the domain owns a capability for this segment, and if so, authorizes the mapping of the segment with the specified rights.

A domain can export capabilities of a special type to other domains. Such capabilities are called *domain capabilities* and define the entry points of the domain. A domain capability is associated with a procedure to be executed in another domain. When such a procedure cannot be executed locally because the segment to which it belongs cannot be mapped locally, the domain capability is searched for and a cross-domain procedure call is performed if it was found.

A domain change generally includes a transfer of capabilities from the caller to the callee for input parameters and conversely for the output ones. The protection service provides an interface description language (IDL) which allows the transferred capabilities to be specified. Capability transfers are specified by the domain which exports its entry points and must be accepted by the caller (cf. section 6). The advantage of this approach is that the executed code can be rendered totally independent of protection.

In the following, we essentially study the four basic concepts necessary for the implementation of the memory service which we have designed. These are segment management, consistency and synchronization, permanence, and protection.

## 3 Segment management

Persistent memory is composed of segments. A segment keeps its base virtual address unchanged during its whole lifetime and also keeps the same size, fixed at creation time.

## 3.1 Manipulation of segments

**Creation.** In order to create a segment, an application provides the size of the segment to allocate, and obtains in return its base address. Only virtual space is allocated at creation. Data pages which physically compose the segment are created only when accessed by applications.

**Destruction.** The destruction of a segment is always explicit. An application can make it implicit at its level by providing a garbage collector. Segments manipulated by the protection service are destroyed when the capabilities which designate them disappear from the system. Explicit destruction of a segment is immediate and irrevocable, but it may require special rights if the segment is protected.

Destruction of a segment implies the destruction of all of its associated structures, including its permanent image, if such an image exists. After the destruction of the segment, the range of virtual space it occupied becomes invalid. Some applications may keep pointers which point into this address interval, or certain segments may contain such pointers. Attempts to access a destroyed segment raise an exception in the calling application.

**Access.** First access to a page by an application triggers a page fault. To process this fault, the system first identifies the segment to which the missing page belongs. If the system discovers that this page does not belong to any segment (a segment which has not been allocated yet, or an already destroyed one), an exception is raised. Otherwise, the segment is mapped at the host (if not already mapped), and a copy of the page is loaded on the faulting node (see section 4).

Since specific protocols are managing data consistency (more precisely zone updates), the system pager is not responsible for loading consistent data in physical memory (it mainly allocate pages).

## 3.2 Location

We consider here the problem of locating segments in virtual memory. Recall that we distinguish two levels of memory: execution memory and permanent memory. A segment is in execution memory if it is used by at least one process. If a permanent segment is not in execution memory, the system must locate it in permanent memory, and then create the data structure which represents it in execution memory. A volatile segment exists only in execution memory.

A segment is represented in execution memory by a segment descriptor, which contains the necessary information for data consistency management. The initial assumption is that this descriptor is managed in a single version at a single host, called *primary host* of the segment. All the hosts which use the same segment should communicate with its primary host to access the descriptor. We show later that we can avoid systematic communication with the primary host through caching mechanisms.

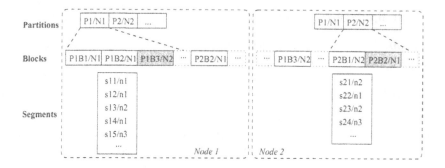

**Fig. 1.** Location scheme

In order to locate the descriptors (and thus the segments) that are not present locally, we implement the mechanisms depicted in Fig. 1. On each node, there is a table which allows to locate the primary host of a set of segments (the segment level in the figure). This association is defined on a unique node for each segment. Arias uses a two-level decoding scheme in order to locate this node:

- Partition Table.
  The global virtual space is sliced into partitions of equal size that can be dynamically allocated when more virtual space is needed. They have a "location host" which is responsible for locating directly or indirectly the table containing the primary host of the segments belonging to its virtual address range. The partition table is replicated on all sites and is maintained strictly consistent.
- Partition Blocks.
  In order to improve segment allocation (see section 3.3), partitions are sliced into blocks of equal size. A block of a partition can be managed either by the partition host or by any other host. The blocks table of a partition, located at the partition host, gives the host that manages a block. This host always contains the table entry which defines the primary host of each segment belonging to this block address range. Thus, finding this entry costs at most two messages: one to the partition host and one to the block manager host. Finally, each host which uses a segment but which is not the primary host of this segment owns a *descriptor cache*. This cache contains the location of the primary descriptor along with other information.

The segment descriptor can be moved for efficiency or administration reasons. In this case, the location host is notified, along with all the hosts which carry a descriptor of this segment in their cache. This systematic update is usable because the displacement of a descriptor is a rare event compared to the cost of these notifications.

## 3.3 Allocation of segments

When a segment is created, it is necessary to carefully choose its base address because this address is immutable, and because it identifies the segment and allows the location host to be located.

When the creation of a segment is requested, the application can optionally specify in which partition it wants the segment to be created. If such a constraint is not expressed, the system chooses a partition according to the load of the location hosts.

The simplest solution to perform allocation is to maintain an allocation cursor for each partition and to send allocation requests when partitions are remote. To avoid messages, we use a two-level allocation scheme (Fig. 1): at the partition level, we allocate *allocation blocks*; then, inside these blocks, we allocate segments. Allocation blocks are address intervals of intermediate size between that of partitions and that of segments. Each host owns an allocation block belonging to each of the existent partitions of the system. It allocates segments in the blocks belonging to the relevant partitions, without the need to contact the location hosts of the concerned partitions. When a block is exhausted, it is returned to its home location host and a new block is taken.

By using this technique, we reduce communications between the host which wants to create the segment and the location host of the partition in which the segment needs to be created. This allows a very fast creation of segments and also allows using Arias for data which has a very short lifetime.

# 4 Consistency and synchronization

Shared virtual memory systems generally impose on applications a unique service for consistency and synchronization, which may not be appropriate for their needs. As no universal model for consistency and synchronization (C&S) has emerged, applications must support the cost of an unadapted service. With Arias [11], applications have the possibility to define their own model, or to choose one among several available models.

In this section, we present this approach and its rationale, then we describe the architecture of our service of C&S and the functions it offers.

## 4.1 The Arias approach

We realize the C&S service in two layers: a "generic" layer which implements the functions of a C&S service which are independent of any particular model, and a "specific" layer which implements a particular C&S protocol. A specific C&S protocol is implemented using the functions of the generic layer. In the generic layer, we find the definition of the consistency and synchronization units and their location in the system. The C&S unit which we manage is the *zone*. A zone is a sequence of contiguous bytes, without limits on its size, but included in a segment (see section 3). A zone is designated by its initial address and specified by its address and its size.

Each zone has a master copy which resides on a particular host called the *zone master*. The master host makes all decisions concerning the aspects of the zone (number of copies, mobility, etc.). At a given moment, each zone has a master host; this master host can change dynamically. The location of a zone in the system is handled by the zone master.

When an application wants to access a zone, it asks the specific C&S protocol associated with its segment; if the protocol sees that the host which has issued the request is the zone master, it handles the request locally. Otherwise, the demand is forwarded to the master host, the location of this master being the responsibility of the generic layer.

The principal function of the generic C&S layer is to provide an association between a zone and its master in a transparent way for specific protocols. The interface of the generic layer is the same as that of a message passing layer. The generic layer allows the emission of a message to the master of a determined zone and the reception of the answer. Elements of the generic layer and its architecture are detailed in the next section.

## 4.2 General architecture of the C&S service

The generic C&S layer is implemented on each host. Above it, we implement the specialized protocols layer. The generic layer routes C&S messages to the concerned zone master and route answer messages. These messages contain two types of information.

- C&S information to be interpreted by the specialized protocol.
  It can be a synchronization request, but also the contents of a zone when managing data consistency.
- Information which concerns exclusively the generic layer.
  This information includes the zone concerned by the message, the specialized protocol involved and information about the message nature (displacement of the master copy, emission of a copy of the zone, answer to a message).

In order to reach the zone master, the generic layer asks the segment location service (section 3) for the primary host of the segment to which the zone belongs. On the primary host, the segment descriptor keeps the association between a zone and its zone master which allows the generic layer to know where it must route the message. On each host, there is a cache which contains the identity of zone masters that have been accessed recently. These caches are fragments of the descriptors of mapped segments. They are lazily updated on cache misses. With each specialized protocol is associated a message handler. This handler is activated upon the reception by the generic layer of a message concerning this protocol. The handler interprets the message and executes appropriate actions. The generic layer allows the registration of new protocols. It associates a unique identifier and keeps the association handler-identifier of the protocol.

# 5 Permanence

Some of the segments of the distributed virtual memory can be made fault re-
sistant. This fault resistance is obtained through managing a permanent image
of the segments on a stable support like a disk. In this section, we study interaction between the segment image in execution memory and the one in storage
memory. Like other Arias services, the goal is to provide applications with a
set of mechanisms allowing to build different storage policies. The interest of
having several policies is that they can provide different levels of reliability and
of efficiency.

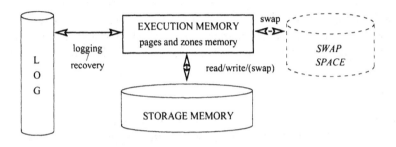

**Fig. 2.** Architecture of the storage sub-system

Fig. 2 displays the different elements which compose the storage service. This
figure gives a purely centralized vision of the storage service; distribution will
be considered later. Our system manages two disjoint and independent storage
spaces: the storage memory and the log.

We now provide a detailed description for each of these elements and explain
how the execution memory needs to interact with them (e.g., optimization of
the paging process).

## 5.1 Storage memory

The storage memory contains the permanent images of segments. It is composed
of the storage memories of the hosts participating in the implementation of the
system. Each storage memory is divided into volumes in which permanent images
of segments are stored. A permanent image of a segment is fully contained within
a volume. Manipulations which can be done on the storage memory of a host
are very limited:

- Creating and deleting volumes and permanent images of segments on disks.
- Reading and writing a page, or a part of a page in a segment.
- Making a permanent segment unavailable (it cannot be mapped into the
  virtual memory anymore).

The only properties guaranteed by the permanent memory are atomic creation or destruction of the permanent image of a segment, along with the atomicity of the modifications of a page which belongs to a segment. However, atomicity for the modifications of a segment relatively to a set of modifications is not guaranteed. If an application requires such a property, it should implement it through the logging mechanism described in section 5.2.

The storage memory service can be used by applications in order to explicitly copy modified parts of permanent segments. This service is also used by other components of our system. For instance, an asynchronous copier uses it to copy zones of permanent segments with validated modifications (i.e., modifications which have been previously registered into a log).

In principle, we manage two levels of independent memory: execution memory and storage memory. Theoretically, no cooperation is needed between the managers of these two memory levels. However, for efficiency reasons and to spare paging space, the paging manager relies on the storage memory manager to store permanent segments pages. This cooperation is described in section 5.3.

## 5.2 The log

The system provides a logging service which ensures the atomicity of a set of modifications that have been done on permanent segments. This service allows applications to register data into a log so they can repair permanent segments after a failure.

The logging service is expandable as it allows the use of several recovery protocols. These protocols are used upon a node failure to repair the part of permanent memory managed by that host. During the failure recovery, the logging service is able to determine whether a log has been validated or not. It then applies the appropriate recovery procedure from a particular protocol, the records of a log being related to one of these recovery protocols.

The actions associated with the logs are log creation, log records registration and log validation or abortion.

A log is a set of ordered records, all related to one application. These records are written in sequential order by an application; the order of writes defines the order of records. They are composed of a header whose structure is known by the logging service followed by information dedicated to a particular recovery protocol. The structure and the semantics of the second part of information are not known by the logging service. It is only processed upon failure by the relevant recovery protocol.

It is possible to consider two implementations of logs. Both have an influence on the efficiency of logging and the availability of permanent segments upon failure. We present these implementations below:

**Centralized.** In the first implementation, a log is stored on a single host. This provides a total order for operations to be executed at error recovery.

**Distributed.** The second implementation, which has been chosen, manages distributed logs. Such a log is partitioned, and therefore it becomes necessary to define the ordering conditions. The partition is done in such a way that each log partition is stored at the node where the concerned segments reside. Therefore, such a node can recover almost autonomously. In this solution, a total order is ensured for a log partition. At the global level, only a partial order is ensured but it is sufficient.

The logging service must be very efficient. The handling of I/O operations (mainly updates under normal conditions) constitutes the major source of performance hits. It is obvious that sequential access to the disk reduces the I/O cost as it limits the movement of the disk head. The solution that we suggest is therefore to realize logical logs over a physical log. This physical log is stored on a dedicated disk if we want to keep a maximum efficiency, or on a special partition of a general-use disk. Each host which participates in the implementation of the permanent memory owns therefore a physical log.

Finally, an asynchronous copying service is implemented so that updates on permanent images of segments can be saved on the permanent image without provoking a performance hit. A mechanism which manages the consumption of the physical log is coupled to the asynchronous copier. This coupling allows the elimination of obsolete logs from the physical log so the storage space they occupy can be reused.

## 5.3 Paging strategy

An objective of Arias is to adapt the paging strategy applied at each node to the requirements of the system. This strategy does not take into account the distributed context of Arias. Decisions are always made locally and aim at minimizing expensive disk I/Os and swap space consumption.

**Strategy for volatile segments.** Pages belonging to volatile segments have always an associated image reserved in swap space. The only optimization that can be applied here is to avoid to copy the page at swap out time if both copies are already equal.

**Strategy for permanent segments.** An associated image is reserved in swap space for pages belonging to permanent segments only when the page is modified on the site. At swap out time, nothing is done for unmodified pages as they can be reloaded from storage memory. For other pages, if the page is valid with respect to modifications (i.e., all local modifications have been validated), the page is copied to the storage memory and swap space can be released. In other cases, the page is copied to swap space.

# 6 Protection

The protection mechanisms that we propose must allow different protection policies to be implemented. In particular, we do not want to be restricted to a hierarchical protection model. Given that, we decided to use protection mechanisms based on software capabilities.

Our protection service [7] is based on the classical concepts of capabilities and protection domains. A capability represents rights allowing either to access a segment or to change the protection domain. A protection domain is defined as a set of capabilities.

We also decided also to separate the definition of protection policy from the application development. This means that capabilities are transparent to the code which uses Arias services. Solutions where cooperating protection domains exchange capabilities explicitly to allow this cooperation were also excluded. Domain changes are transparent for the code which triggered them, so that the code does not need to manipulate other things than virtual addresses. Domain changes are performed implicitly when required. It allows an existing application to be protected without any modification on the application code.

To implement this transparency, capabilities are managed only by the system. When an application program addresses a non-mapped segment, the process traps into the kernel where a capability associated with that segment is searched for in the current domain. This capability can authorize the segment to be mapped within the domain, or it can allow the execution to be transferred to another protection domain. This way, the program manipulates only virtual addresses and its execution depends only on the content of the protection domains.

In the remaining of this section, we present the implementation of the protection domains, capability management, and the implementation of domain changes.

## 6.1 Implementation of domains

A domain is a protection space which can be shared by several Unix processes that have the same rights on the domain segments.

In order to make domain management more flexible, we found essential to allow the management of capability lists. A capability list can represent a set of rights to a service. These rights can be given by providing simple access to the list, which implicitly gives the rights defined in the list. Access to these lists is also controlled through a capability.

A capability can therefore give rights on a segment, on a domain (domain change) or on a capability list. An addressing fault on a segment triggers a look up for a capability asociated with it in the current domain.

As explained before, each user level Unix process initially executes within a protection domain. However, such a process may change its protection domain. Thus, the execution flow of control (also called activity) needs to migrate to another addressing space, associated with the target domain, in which only authorized segment will be made available. This addressing space is implemented with a Unix process which behaves as a server for that domain. This domain server is dynamically created if it does not exist yet on the site where the domain is invoked.

Notice that protection and distribution are orthogonal since a domain change can always be performed locally.

## 6.2 Capability management

Capabilities are managed by the system. This means that it is not possible for a program to forge a capability. All capabilities are registered by the system and a new capability is created at segment creation time.

The system handles three types of capabilities:

- Capabilities on segments.
  They allow a segment to be mapped in the domain which contains the capability. The capability also specifies the mode of the authorized mapping (read-only, read-write, or execution).
  When an activity tries to access a segment which has not been mapped or which has been mapped with a non compatible mode, the system looks for a capability on the segment with the appropriate mode. If such a capability is found, the segment is mapped in this mode; otherwise, it is a protection violation and an exception is sent to the activity which has triggered the fault. A capability on a segment is composed of the segment address and of the authorized mapping mode.
- Capabilities on capability lists.
  Capability lists are designated by means of unique identifiers. They provide the rights specified by the capabilities they contain. These capabilities can be on their turn placed into lists, allowing the construction of capability trees. Trees and lists are used to specify the content of a protection domain. A capability on a list defines rights to read (gives the rights specified by the capabilities contained in the list), to write (allows addition or removal of capabilities) or to copy (allows the copying of a capability from the list).
- Domain capabilities.
  A domain capability is a capability associated with a procedure call. It is used when a code segment (a segment that contains procedures) cannot be mapped into the current protection domain. The capability allows the activity to be transferred into another domain where it can call the procedure. A domain capability is composed of a domain identifier, of an entry point address (procedure) and of the specification of parameters transfer rules.

## 6.3 Domain changes

When a program changes its domain on a procedure call, the procedure's actual parameters are passed to the target domain. The execution of the procedure in the domain might need capabilities associated with these parameters, in particular when parameters are pointers to shared segments. The problem is that of the transfer of these capabilities without any modification on the application code.

In order to solve this problem, we associate with a domain capability the specification of the corresponding procedure call. This specification describes the parameters and the control over associated capability transfers between domains.

To specify these domain entry points, we use an IDL (Interface Description Language) extended with clauses related to protection. This language allows the definition of PPI (Protected Procedure Interfaces). A PPI defines the signature of a procedure, and for each parameter it defines the manipulation rules for capabilities to be applied when a call to this procedure triggers a domain change.

The protection rules should permit the control of both entering and leaving rights for the caller and the callee domains, and upon the call and the return of the procedure:

- The server specifies the capabilities required to perform the call and the capabilities which it can give on return of the call. Our extended IDL also allows to specify where incoming capabilities should be placed in the domain capability tree.
- The client specifies if it accepts to give the required capabilities and if capabilities returned are sufficient (Actually, the client accepts or refuses the PPI of the server); it also specifies the place for the returned capabilities to the caller domain.

When a server creates a domain capability, it associates with it a PPI which corresponds to its service. A client can either accept the capability as is, or copy the domain capability to overload the PPI definition (to change the place for received capabilities).

The extended IDL allows the specification of the capabilities that must be passed along with pointer parameters, the type and attributes of the capabilities (r/w/x) and the placement of the capabilities. Below is an example of PPI:

```
procedure Biblio_Register (
  in capa_seg_read TDOC *doc
     install BIB_DOC_LIST,
  out String[10] refbib
  );

procedure Biblio_LookUp (
  in String[10] keywords,
  out capa_seg_read TLISTREF *listref
  );
```

With the first PPI, a read capability is passed with the *doc* parameter. This capability is to be installed in the *BIB_DOC_LIST* capability list in the target domain. With the second one, a read capability is returned. If the client accepts the domain capability with this PPI, the returned capability will be added to a temporary list associated with the activity. However, the client may copy the domain capability and overload the PPI associated with the new capability:

```
procedure Biblio_LookUp (
  in String[10] keywords,
  out capa_seg_read TLISTREF *listref
     install BIB_LIST_REF
  );
```

This way, the returned capability will be installed in the capability list designated by *BIB_LIST_REF*. The IDL also provides the possibility to specify the transfer of a set of capabilities associated with a complex data structure. For example, the following PPI allows a set of capabilities associated with an array to be passed in parameter:

```
procedure Proc (
  in (capa_seg_read char *)tab[10]
  );
```

A similar PPI can be defined for a link list structure.

# 7 Experiments

As we have already emphasized, the integration with the Unix system is a key design choice of the project. We have implemented our platform over the AIX system, a version of Unix running on IBM RS-6000 and Bull Escala Machines. We are currently experimenting with our prototype with the following applications:

- A Clustered File System (CFS).
  We have implemented a distributed file system based on our distributed shared memory. This file system uses distributed shared segments in order to share files between the workstations of multiple users. We have implemented several consistency protocols in order to evaluate the advantage of tailoring specific protocols according to the application needs. Our results show that CFS out-performs the native NFS implementation on our platform.
- An object database system (O2).
  We are currently experimenting with object-oriented databases. More precisely, we are implementing a new version of the O2 [4] Store database system based on the Arias distributed shared memory. Such database systems are often implemented above Unix, which means that they must develop persistence and data sharing services on their own. Preliminary results show that we can reduce the overhead of these services in a sensitive way.
- CAD tools.
  A very promising experiment is the implementation of distributed cooperative CAD tools on top of a distributed shared memory system. We are currently involved in a European project in which CAD tools from the building industry should be ported on a platform similar to Arias built out of the technology provided by the project partners.

# 8 Comparison with existent models

In this section, we compare our works with projects of the same field. For this comparison, we consider the four work axis we described in sections 3, 4, 5 and 6.

**Management of a single virtual space** Several research projects are considering the use of 64-bit processors to manage a single virtual space in a distributed system. This is the case of Opal [3], Mungi [8], and Angel[10]. The use of virtual addresses as a unique name is widely recognized, but very few solutions have been proposed for address allocation, and for the location or the migration of segments inside this space. This is one aspect where we intend to provide new solutions. Besides, these projects provide solution which are not compatible with Unix as processes cannot directly address their private data.

**Consistency and synchronization** The strong coupling between consistency and synchronization is inspired from the work done on cache consistency maintenance in distributed DBMS [5] and in the Midway project [1], where Entry Consistency is used.

Management of different consistency protocols has already been addressed in research projects like Munin [2], but no current system allows applications to specify their own protocol for consistency management. Munin allows only a limited choice among a set of protocols implemented as a part of the system.

**Permanence** As for consistency, current systems [9] do not allow applications to specialize the management of logs in function of their particular needs. We provide applications with the possibility to ensure the permanence of their segments the implementation of an optimal logging policy.

**Protection** Most systems based on the use of a single virtual address space provide protection through software capabilities and protection domains (Opal [3], Mungi [8]). However, these systems impose on users the direct manipulation of capabilities and use encrypted capabilities. Therefore, application programmers are responsible for a part of capability management. We suggest that capabilities should be handled in a transparent way for users, which makes applications code independent of the protection.

## 9 Conclusion

In this paper, we have presented the objectives and the overall design of the Arias distributed shared memory system.

The Arias system manages persistent shared data in a unique address space, thus allowing pointers to be shared between distributed cooperating processes.

The system provides a service which allows these data to be managed on a stable storage and to be updated atomicaly, thus resisting node failures.

Arias also provides a protection service based on software capabilities for access control on shared data.

The main rationale behind those services is not to implement policies, but rather to provide generic services from which the most adequate policy can be delivered.

The evaluation of the current prototype is not yet completed, but preliminary results have validated most of our design choices. The perpectives of continuation of this work is first to pursue the experiments with the distributed environements described above. Also, we found that most of the ideas applied in our framework could be applied to other existing systems. In particular, the protection model have already been implemented in a CORBA architecture and in the Java environement [6].

**Acknowledgments.** T. Han, T. Jacquin, A. Knaff,E. Pérez-Cortés and F. Saunier contributed to the design and implementation of the Arias system. We also would like to thank S. Krakowiak for reviewing this paper.

This work was partially supported by CNET (France Télécom).

# References

1. B. Bershad and M. Zekauskas, "The Midway Distributed Shared Memory System" COMPCON'93 Conference, pp. 528-537, February 1993.
2. J. Carter, J. Bennett and W. Zwaenepoel, "Implementation and performance of Munin", *13th ACM Symposium on Operating Systems Principles (SOSP'91)*, pp. 152-164, October 1991.
3. J. S. Chase, H. M. Levy, M. J. Feeley and E. D. Lazowska, "Sharing and Protection in a Single-Address-Space Operating System", *ACM Transactions on Computer Systems,* vol. 12, num. 4, pp. 271-307, November 1994.
4. O. Deux et al., "The O2 System", Communication of the ACM, 34(10), October 1991.
5. M. Franklin and M. Carey, "Client-Server Caching Revisited", Proceedings of the International Workshop on Distributed Object Management, Edmonton, Canada, August 1992.
6. D. Hagimont, J. Mossière and X. Rousset de Pina, "Hidden Capabilities: Towards a Flexible Protection Utility", Proceedings of the 7th SIGOPS European Workshop, September 1996.
7. D. Hagimont, J. Mossière, X. Rousset de Pina and F. Saunier, "Hidden Software Capabilities", proceedings of the 16th International Conference on Distributed Computing Systems, May 1996.
8. G. Heiser, K. Elphinstone, S. Russell and J. Vochteloo, "Mungi: a distributed single address-space operating system", Proceedings of the 17th Australasian Computer Science Conference, pp 271-280, January 1994.
9. C. Mohan, D. Haederle, B. Lindsay, H. Pirahesh and P. Schwarz, "ARIES: A Transaction Recovery Method Supporting Fine-Granularity Locking and Partial Rollbacks Using Write-Ahead Logging", ACM Transaction on Database Systems, 17(1), March 1992.
10. K. Murray, A. Saulsbury, T. Stiemerling, T. Wilkinson, P. Kelly and P. Osmon, "Design and implementation of an object-orientated 64-bit single address space microkernel", Proceedings of the 2nd USENIX Symposium on Microkernels and other Kernel Architectures, pp. 31-43, September 1993.
11. E. Pérez-Cortés, P. Dechamboux, T. Han, "Generic Support for Consistency in Arias", Proceedings of the 5th Workshop on Hot Topics in Operating Systems (HOTOS-V), pages 221-226, Rosario, Washington, May 1995.

# CORBA and Object Services

## Jan Kleindienst[2], František Plášil[1,2], Petr Tůma[1]

[1]*Charles University, Faculty of Mathematics and Physics,*
*Department of Software Engineering*
*Malostranské náměstí 25, 118 00 Prague 1, Czech Republic*
*e-mail: {plasil, tuma}@kki.ms.mff.cuni.cz*

[2]*Institute of Computer Science, Czech Academy of Sciences*
*Pod vodárenskou věží, 180 00 Prague, Czech Republic*
*e-mail: {kleindie, plasil}@uivt.cas.cz*

**Abstract.** The paper provides an overview of the basic concepts of OMG CORBA. It summarizes the main ideas behind the OMG Reference Model Architecture and the components it defines. Particular attention is paid to the Object Request Broker and Object Services. An evolving example is used to illustrate the CORBA philosophy. The authors draw on their long-term practical experience with CORBA, particularly with implementing the Persistent Object Service [KPT96].

## 1 About OMG

The Object Management Group, Inc. (OMG), founded in 1989, is an international organization grouping system vendors, software developers, and end-users. OMG is currently supported by more than 500 members, including market giants such as DEC, HP, IBM, Microsoft, and SUN. The main goal of OMG is to promote object-oriented technology by defining "*a living, evolving standard with realized parts, so that application developers can deliver their applications with off-the-shelf components for commons facilities like object storage, class structure, peripheral interface, user interface, etc.*" [OMG95c]. To achieve this goal, OMG has defined the Object Management Architecture (OMA) characterized by definition of two models: the *Core Object Model* (and its extensions called *profiles*) and the *OMA Reference Model*. An application conforming to the OMA Reference Model implicitly meets the key OMG objectives of *portability, interoperability,* and *reusability* that are considered a "holy grail" of the software industry.

## 1.1 OMG Structure and Technology Adoption Process

The heart of OMG is its board of directors (BOD) that votes upon all documents to be adopted by OMG. Technical issues are dealt with by the Technical Committee (TC). The TC guarantees that the proposed software components comply with the spirit of the OMA Reference Model in which case it recommends them to the BOD. The TC spans several working groups, e.g. Task Forces (TFs), Special Interest Groups (SIGs), and subcommittees. A TF is responsible for generating Requests for Information (RFIs), and, subsequently, Requests for Proposals (RFPs). A RFI should gather information and suggestions on a particular technical issue both from the OMG and non-OMG software communities. A RFI encourages proposals for solving the technical issue that it addresses. Typically, proposals are not adopted on the first attempt, but they must undergo several revisions. To ensure that proposals are feasible and backed up by the respondent's intention to make them commercially available, each proposal must contain a "proof of concept" section describing the steps already taken by the submitter towards implementation. Proposals are then usually combined into a joint submission(s). At this stage, the TF recommends this submission(s) to the TC which consequently votes upon recommending it to the BOD. Through its approval by the BOD, the proposed technology is officially adopted by OMG. The time of the adoption phase may vary from six months to several years.

## 1.2 OMG Object Model and OMA Reference Model

OMG's understanding of the object-oriented paradigm is reflected in the Core 92 Object Model (Core92) [OMG95c]. Core92 defines such concepts as object, inheritance, subtyping, operations, signatures, etc. Additional concepts can be added to Core92 to create an extension (*component*). A component should not replace, duplicate, and remove concepts. Components should be orthogonal to each other. A *profile* is a combination of Core92 and one or more components. Typical examples of profiles are the CORBA profile (Section 2), the Common Object Model, the ODP Reference Model, and the (proposed) Core 95 Object Model [OMG95e]. With the intention to provide a broad object-oriented architectural framework for the development of object technology, OMG defined the OMA Reference Model [OMG95c], published in 1992. The OMA Reference Model is comprised of the following four components:

The *Object Request Broker* component serves as a means for delivering requests and responses among objects. It is a backbone of the OMA Reference Model, interconnecting all the remaining components.

The *Object Services* component provides a standardized functionality (defined in the form of object interfaces), e.g. for class and instance management, storage, integrity, security, query, and versioning.

The *Common Facilities* component uses Object Services and defines a collection of facilities (such as a common mail facility) that a group of applications is likely to have in common.

The *Application Objects* component is not standardized by OMG. Application Objects use Common Facilities and Object Services via the Object Request Broker.

## 1.3    CORBA Evolution

The Common Object Request Broker Architecture (CORBA) is a common framework that separates requesters of services (clients) from providers of services (object implementations) and, via ORB, allows for sending messages between them. The CORBA architecture is based on CORBA/OM derived from OMG/OM. CORBA/OM is a *concrete* object model that deals with the format of requests being delivered from clients to object implementations, operations upon objects, objects' interfaces and attributes, objects' data types, and objects' implementation.

CORBA was adopted by OMG in December 1991 as a joint submission of DEC, HP, etc. The first version was denoted as CORBA 1.1 and was, in 1994, replaced by CORBA 1.2 which brought more or less "cosmetic changes" with respect to CORBA 1.1. A much more important development step was CORBA 2.0, which was adopted in December 1994 and which overcomes the drawbacks of CORBA 1.2 by specifying ways for interconnecting different ORBs, and also by suggesting means for establishing interoperability between CORBA-based and non-CORBA-based environments, such as Microsoft's COM/OLE. Since the difference between CORBA 1.2 and 2.0 is quite dramatic, we will distinguish these two versions when necessary. Throughout the paper, wherever we use *CORBA* we mean CORBA 2.0 [OMG95a].

## 1.4    Common Facilities

Common Facilities (CF) provide a higher-level functionality than Object Services; informally, they are application oriented, while Object Services are "system oriented". A major expected advantage of Common Facilities (they are still in the stage of RFP) is that if properly designed, they may reduce the amount of code being written from scratch and become shared among CORBA-based applications. Common facilities, with interfaces defined in an object-oriented manner, are divided into two categories: *horizontal CF* and *vertical CF*. Horizontal CF are intended for cooperation among typical specialized applications, e.g. document editing, graphical user interface. To reflect this intention, they are divided into four groups: *User interface* (e.g. similar to those provided by OLE and OpenDoc), *information management* (e.g. Compound document storage, data interchange), *system management* (e.g. configuring, installing distributed object components), and *task management* (e.g. workflow, e-mail). Vertical CF provide object-oriented interfaces for vertical market segments (finance, insurance, etc.).

# 2  CORBA

## 2.1  Principles

According to the OMA Reference Model, the role of an ORB is to provide means for communication between objects and their clients. For the purposes of defining concepts specific to ORB functionality, CORBA has introduced the *CORBA Object Model* as an extension to the OMG Core Object Model.

The CORBA Object Model defines an *object* as an encapsulated entity that provides requestable services and a *client* as an entity that requests these services. It should, however, be noted, that being a client is not a static property - an entity is referred to as a client only at the moment when a service is requested. A *request* for a service is associated with a requested operation, a target object and, optionally, *parameters* and a *context*. As an outcome of the service, a result can be returned to the client. Should an abnormal condition occur, an *exception* can be returned, possibly with additional return parameters characteristic for the exception. Requestable services are available as *operations*. An operation is identified by its name and *operation signature*, consisting of a specification of the request parameters (types and information flow direction), a specification of the operation result, a specification of possible exceptions together with accompanying parameters, a specification of additional contextual information, and a specification of the execution semantics (either *at-most-once* or *best-effort*).

The set of operations requestable from an object is determined by its interfaces. An *interface* is a collection of operation signatures.

## 2.2  Interface Definition Language

Object interfaces are defined using the OMG Interface Definition Language (IDL) introduced in the CORBA specification [OMG95a]. The definition written in IDL completely specifies an interface and provides all information needed by the client to request services via the interface.

IDL is based on ANSI C++ grammar with several extensions. An IDL specification consists of one or more module, interface, exception, constant or type definitions.

Throughout the text, we will demonstrate several features of a CORBA environment through an evolving example. In this example, we introduce the interface *Book* providing the operation *Find()* for searching the text of the book and the readonly attribute *sName()* for retrieving the book's name. The example is based on the Orbix, a CORBA implementation done by IONA Technologies [ORBIXa, ORBIXb].

In our example, the IDL definition of a book's interface could be as follows:

*interface Book {*
  *readonly attribute string sName;*

```
unsigned short Find (in string sWhat);
};
```

An interface of an object can also contain an *attribute*. This syntactical construct implies generating two operations, one for getting and the second one for setting the attribute's value; a readonly attribute implies generating only the operation for getting the attribute's value.

Being a purely descriptive language, IDL is not used to request the specified services. Instead, the IDL definitions are mapped to the client's programming language to be used by its standard constructs. CORBA 2.0 standardizes the IDL mapping to C, C++ and Smalltalk, standard mappings to other languages either already exist (e.g. Java), or are expected to follow (e.g. COBOL).

Suppose that in our example both the client and the implementation of the *Book* interface use C++. In the C++ environment, the *Book* interface is mapped to a Book class with corresponding methods:

```
class Book: public virtual CORBA::Object {
public:
  virtual char *sName (ENV env);
  virtual unsigned short Find (const char *sWhat, ENV env);
};
```

The parameter env servers mainly for registering exceptions.

## 2.3   The Structure of a CORBA ORB

The structure of a CORBA ORB is depicted on Fig. 1. The OMG standard defines the structure in terms of interfaces and their semantics. In an actual implementation, however, there is no obligation to reflect the structure; it is only necessary to preserve the interfaces and their semantics.

### 2.3.1  Client Side (Stubs, DII, Interface Repository)

To request a service from an object, the client can use either static or dynamic invocation (Fig. 2). The static invocation mechanism requires the client to know the IDL definition of the requested service at compile time. The definition is used to automatically generate *stubs* for all requestable operations. To request an operation, the client calls the appropriate stub which passes the request to the ORB Core for delivery.

As opposed to static invocation, the dynamic invocation mechanism requires the client to know the IDL definition of a requested service at run time. To request an operation, the client specifies the target object, the name of the operation, and the parameters of the operation via a series of calls to the standardized *Dynamic Invocation Interface*.

Again, the request is then passed to the ORB Core for delivery. The semantics of the operation remains the same regardless of the invocation mechanism used. To obtain an IDL interface definition at run time, the client can use the *Interface Repository*. The repository makes IDL definitions (e.g. module, interface, constant and type definitions) available in form of persistent objects accessible via standardized interfaces. The ORB is responsible for finding the target implementation, preparing it to receive the request, and communicating the data of the request. The client need not care about the location of the object, language of the implementation, or other things not described in the interface.

On the client side, a target object is usually represented as a proxy (object) supporting the same interface as the target object. In the case of static invocation of an operation *m*, the proxy's method m calls the stub associated with m; the stub is responsible for

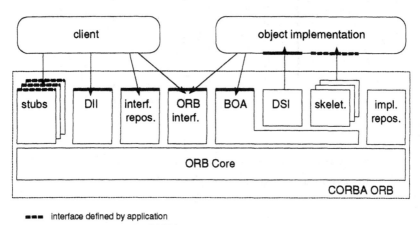

**Figure 1** Structure of a CORBA ORB

creating the request and passing it to the ORB Core for delivery to the target object. In case of dynamic invocation, the client's code creates the request dynamically by calling the DII interface; in principle, no proxy and stub are necessary.

On the client side in our example, a book is represented by a proxy referenced via MyBook. Static invocation might take the form:

```
iLineNr = MyBook->Find ("keyword",env);        // static invocation
```

Dynamic invocation with the same effect could be:

```
Req = MyBook->_request ("Find");               // dynamic invocation
*(Req->arguments ()->add(ARG_IN)->
   value ()) <<= "keyword";
Req->invoke ();
*(Req->result ()->value ()) >>= iLineNr;
```

Note that in Orbix, a proxy supports also the DII interface.

## 2.3.2 Implementation Side (Skeletons, DSI, Implementation Repository, Object Adapters)

Again, either the static or the dynamic mechanism can be used to convey the request to the actual service implementation (Fig. 3). The static mechanism requires the IDL definition of the requested service to be available at compile time. An automatically generated operation-specific *skeleton* is then used by the ORB to call the implementation of the requested service.

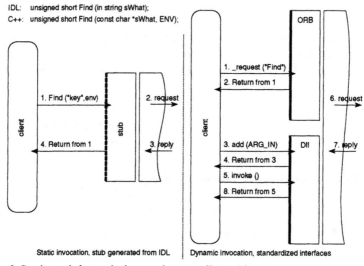

Static invocation, stub generated from IDL | Dynamic invocation, standardized interfaces

**Figure 2** Static and dynamic invocation on client side

The dynamic request delivery mechanism expects the implementation to conform to the standardized *Dynamic Skeleton Interface*. Through this interface, the ORB dispatches the request to the target object (to the service implementation). In analogy to the dynamic invocation mechanism on the client side, no compile time information about the interfaces is needed. The information necessary to locate and activate implementations of requested services is stored in the *Implementation Repository*. The implementation repository is specific to a particular ORB and environment and is not standardized by CORBA. To access services provided by the ORB itself, an implementation uses the *Object Adapter*. To satisfy the needs of diverse environments, the ORB can be equipped with several different object adapters. Each ORB, however, must provide the standardized *Basic Object Adapter* (BOA) interface. The operations of BOA include generation and interpretation of object references, authentication of clients, and activation and deactivation of target objects.

In the implementation, in our example, the static and dynamic request delivery mechanisms might take the forms:

```
class StaticBookImpl : public BookSkeleton {
public:
  char *sName (ENV) {return (sMyName);};
  unsigned short Find (const char *sWhat,ENV env)
    {return (FindInText (sMyText,sWhat));};
private:
  char *sMyName;
  char *sMyText;
};


class DynamicBookImpl : public DynamicImplementation {
public:
  void invoke (REQ Req, ENV env) {
    if (Req->op_name () == "Find") then {
      MyParams = new NVList ();
      *(MyParams->add(ARG_IN)->value ()) <<= (char *) NULL;
      Req->params (MyParams);
      Req->result
        (FindInText (sMyText,MyParams->item (0)->value ()) ;
    } else ...
// the rest omitted for sake of brevity
```

### 2.3.3 ORB Interface

For accessing the general services provided by an ORB, both client and implementation use the *ORB* interface. The operations of this interface include converting object references to strings and vice-versa, determining the object implementation and interface, duplicating and releasing copies of object references, testing object references for equivalence, and ORB initialization.

### 2.3.4 ORB Core, Interoperability

CORBA 1.1 left the implementation of the ORB Core totally to the ORB vendor. It was hence almost impossible to interconnect two or more CORBA-compliant ORBs released by different vendors. This lack is remedied by the CORBA 2.0 specification that defines two approaches for achieving interoperability: the *General Inter-ORB Protocol* (GIOP) and *Inter-ORB bridging*.

The General Inter-ORB Protocol specifies a set of low-level data representations and message formats for communication between ORBs. It is designed to be simple enough to work on top of any underlying connection-oriented transport protocol, such as TCP/IP and IPX/SPX. The GIOP based on TCP/IP is called the *Internet Inter-ORB Protocol* (IIOP). CORBA 2.0 requires GIOP as the mandatory protocol. To allow "out of the box" interoperability, CORBA 2.0 specifies the optional *Environment Specific Inter-ORB Protocol* (ESIOP) as an alternative to the GIOP. It has been mainly specified to allow integration of DCE [DCEwww] with CORBA (DCE/ESIOP).

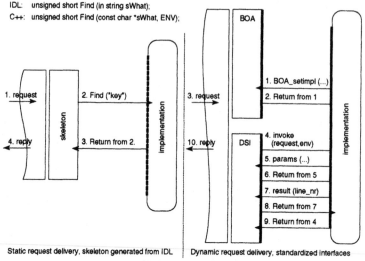

**Figure 3** Static and dynamic request delivery on implementation side

The main idea of bridging lies in mapping requests from one vendor's format to another when crossing ORB boundaries. Bridging can be performed either at the ORB Core level as an ad hoc solution for every $ORB_i$-$ORB_j$ pair (*in-line bridging*), or at the application level (*request-level bridging*). Request-level bridges mediate requests by utilizing DII and DSI mechanisms (Sections 2.3.1 and 2.3.2) to dynamically create and dispatch requests. Bridges are currently mainly used for connecting CORBA with non CORBA-compliant platforms, such as COM/OLE.

Compared to CORBA 1.0, by demanding either the presence of the IIOP protocol or a "half-bridge" that translates an ORB's native request format into the standardized IIOP request format and vice versa, CORBA 2.0 extends the requirements for fulfilling CORBA compliancy.

# 3 Object Services

The collection of Object Services is one of the fundamental components introduced by the OMA Reference Model. It provides functionality a CORBA-based application may use to increase its portability. One may consider it as a high-level library with standardized interfaces specified in IDL. The design and specification of Object Services have been guided and supervised by the Object Service Task Force (OSTF) that, during the years 1992-1996, issued five RFPs, each dealing with a different set of Object Services. The specification of the adopted Object Services was published by OMG in the manual entitled "CORBAservices: Common Object Services Specification" [OMG95f]. This is perhaps the reason why in some publications Object Services are also called *CORBA Object Services*.

## 3.1 Architecture and Design Principles

The key design principle, introduced by the OSTF [OMG95b] and denoted as the Bauhaus principle, reads: "*Minimize duplication of functionality. Functionality should belong to the most appropriate service. Each service should build on previous services when appropriate.*" This principle somewhat contradicts with another design principle stated in the same document: "*It should be possible to separately specify and implement each object service.*" In the paper [KPT96], we showed that complying with the both principles at the same time is not a trivial task.

## 3.2 Basic Set of Object Services

In the document [OMG95d] published in 1992, OSTF identified twenty-five Object Services and their mutual dependencies. The first four services were subject of RFP1 issued that year: the Naming, Event Notification, Lifecycle, and Persistence Services. Other RFPs followed, each dealing with a different subset of services: RFP2 - Concurrency, Externalization, Relationship, Transaction; RFP3 - Time, Security; RFP4 - Licensing, Properties, Query; RFP5 - Change Management, Collections, Trader. The document [OMG95b] also identifies other candidates that may, in the future, enrich the collection of the original twenty-five services, e.g. Narrowing, Index, or Recovery/Fault Management.

With respect to the limited size of this paper, we focus, in Sections 3.3 through 3.6, upon the Lifecycle, Events, Persistence, and Relationship Services, particularly as they are in our opinion of fundamental importance and also as we have practical experience with their implementation [KPT96].

## 3.3 Life Cycle Service

The Life Cycle Service provides its client with means to create, delete, copy, and move objects. Objects are created by *object factories*. These are simply other objects capable of creating and returning an object as a result of some sort of *create()* request. As the parameters required to create an object may vary among different object types, the factory interface is not standardized. A *generic factory* can be used to dispatch or coordinate calls to several object factories. Generic factories can be hierarchically organized. As it is not possible to dispatch calls to factories with potentially different proprietary interfaces (provided by different vendors), the generic factory can only dispatch calls to factories that inherit the standardized *GenericFactory* interface. Additional request parameters are passed in a form of *criteria* list, each parameter being stored as a named value.

An object is deleted by issuing a *remove()* request on its *LifeCycleObject* interface. Objects can make themselves unremovable; this property is signaled by returning an appropriate exception as a result of the *remove()* request. An object can be moved or copied to another location using the *move()* or *copy()* requests of its *LifeCycleObject* interface. To find a target location of the operation, the Life Cycle Service uses a *factory finder*. By issuing the *find_factories()* request, the client can ask a factory finder to return a set of factories capable of creating a new copy of the object in a target location. The specification does not standardize any mechanism for transferring the object state from one location to another.

## 3.4    Events Service

In some cases, synchronous communication provided by an ORB may not be suitable for an application. For such applications, the Events Service provides a decoupled inter-object communication model.

The Events Service defines the roles of event *suppliers* and event *consumers* for objects which generate and process events, respectively. Two approaches are defined depending upon who is active in the communication process - in the *push* model, a supplier calls its consumer to deliver data, whereas in the *pull* model, a consumer calls its supplier to request data. Although in principal possible, neither supplier nor consumer is expected to call the other communicating object directly. Instead, all events are passed through an *event channel*. From the supplier's point of view, the event channel acts as a consumer; from the consumer's point of view, the event channel acts as a supplier. The event channel also provides operations to register both suppliers and consumers. Subject to the quality of service, the event channel can provide one-to-one, one-to-many, or many-to-many communication, and other additional features.

Communication among objects can be either *generic* or *typed*. Generic communication relies on suppliers and consumers having a standardized interface capable of passing an object of the class *any* as event data. With typed communication, suppliers and consumers are expected to agree on a proprietary one-way operation to pass event data in a suitable format.

## 3.5    Persistent Object Service

In a slight discrepancy with its name, one of the goals of the Persistent Object Service (POS) specification was to avoid defining the internals of the Persistent Object Service as much as possible. Therefore, the POS specification aims at providing a common interface to define a general enough framework for all potential persistent service implementations without assuming much about their internal functionality.

The core of the service functionality is encapsulated within a component called the *Persistent Data Service* (PDS). A PDS is responsible for carrying out the basic persistent operations, such as *store()* and *restore()*, on persistent objects. These operations hide all communication between a PDS, persistent objects and, a *Datastore* behind a standardized interface. Internally, a PDS communicates with persistent objects via a proprietary *protocol*. Another proprietary mechanism is used to communicate with a Datastore. While neither of these two mechanisms is standardized, the specification contains examples of both the protocol and the Datastore interface.

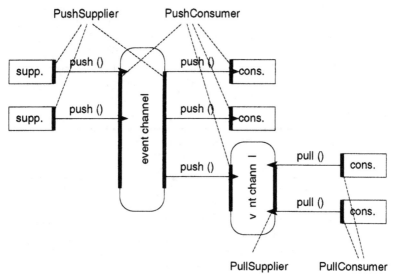

**Figure 4** An example of an Events Service application

A *Persistent Identifier* (PID) is used to describe the location of an object's persistent data in a Datastore. With the exception of the mandatory string attribute specifying a target Datastore type, the PID structure is not standardized. To facilitate use of several PDSs with possibly different protocols and underlying Datastores, the POS specification introduces the notion of the *Persistent Object Manager* (POM). The POM has a standardized interface similar to that of a PDS; its role is to dispatch incoming requests to the appropriate PDS. The behavior of the dispatch mechanism is not standardized.

The POS specification demands very little of persistent objects themselves. Apart from the obvious need to support an appropriate protocol, an object may inherit the standardized *SynchronizedData* interface. Through this interface, the POM notifies the object of operations on its persistent state. To allow external control of its persistency, a persistent object may also inherit the standardized *PersistentObject* interface, similar in functionality to both the POM and PDS interfaces.

## 3.6 Relationship Service

The Relationship Service serves as a tool for expressing inter-object relations in a similar way as E-R diagrams do. The service specification is divided into three levels. Level one concentrates on support for describing relationships among "regular" objects (called here related objects); level two provides support for manipulating graphs of related objects, and finally level three adds support for commonly used special cases of relationships.

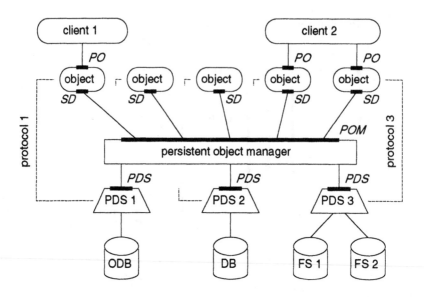

**Figure 5** An example of a Persistent Object Service architecture

A related object participates in a relationship indirectly, via a *Role* object (role for short). While a role is associated with exactly one related object, the related object can have several roles representing it in relationship(s). A role can put constraints on the type of the related object it is associated with and on the number of relationships it is participating in. A relationship among roles is represented by a *Relationship* object. A relationship is characterized by its degree (arity) and the names of the participating roles; additional constraints can limit the types of roles that can participate in the relationship. Once created, a relationship is immutable. Both the *Role* and *Relationship* interfaces are standardized. A role can be queried for its associated object, a list of relationships in which it participates, and a list of related roles and objects. It is also possible to destroy all relationships in which a particular role participates. Similarly, the *Relationship* interface can be used to get a list of participating roles.

Related objects can be involved in a graph. The basic building block of a graph is *Node* object. Either a Node object can be associated with its related object via reference, or the related object can inherit the *Node* interface. Unlike related objects in general, a node is aware of its roles and can be queried to return a list of them. Furthermore, nodes impose additional constraints on the type of the associated roles.

Given a starting node, a graph can be traversed according to a given *Traversal* object. A *Traversal* object produces a sequence of *directed edges* of a graph. A directed edge indicates whether the traversal should continue to an adjacent node. The traversal object can use three different strategies to traverse a graph, i.e. breadth first, depth first and best first. To determine the relevant nodes and edges, *Traversal* object queries a user-supplied *TraversalCriteria* object. Given a node, traversal criteria tells the *Traversal* object which of the associated relationships and related objects to visit. The specification also introduces the concept of *propagation value* to be used in conjunction with standardized traversal criteria in situations where it is not suitable or feasible to use a *TraversalCriteria* object provided by the client.

In many applications, one-to-many containment relations and one-to-one reference relations will be used. A definition of roles and relationships specialized to form these relations is included in level three of the Relationship Service specification.

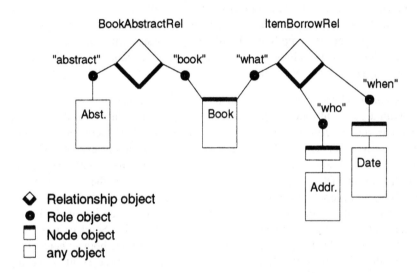

**Figure 6** An example of a Relationship Service application

# 4 Relation to Other Standards and Environments

## 4.1 Relation to DCE

In this section, we identify the similarities of the both CORBA and DCE platforms, and, on the other hand, emphasize their differences.

### 4.1.1 Similarities

Promoted by the OSF organization, Distributed Computing Environment (DCE) [DCEwww] is similar to CORBA in its main goal - providing means for building distributed applications. Both environments export server functionality via an architecture-neutral collection of IDL interfaces. Both come with an IDL compiler that generates stubs and skeletons responsible for marshalling and unmarshalling data from the IDL source. Both platforms provide communication transparency and for both platforms the semantics of local calls differs from that of remote calls, since the latter do not have to be completed due to a network failure.

### 4.1.2 Differences

DCE is procedure-oriented (neither object-oriented nor object-based). DCE's IDL is based on C and does not support inheritance. However, the IDL compiler of DCE 1.2 should have an option of compiling IDL into C++ classes while supporting single inheritance. While CORBA allows the dynamic creation of requests via DII and DSI (Section 2.3.2), DCE does not provide such a feature.

The collection of Object Services, a fundamental component of OMA, furnishes CORBA with a powerful functionality. DCE does not have its functionality stratified into a similar set of services. On the other hand, many DCE facilities have their analogies in some of the OMG Object Services and vice versa. For example, OMG's Naming Service is an analogue of DCE's Directory Service that strictly defines the responsibility of the DCE cells for resolving local names via the Cell Directory Service (CDS) and global names via a collection of CDS servers. Another example might be the analogy of OMG's Concurrency Control Service with DCE's standardized POSIX thread implementation. OMG's Security Service is a good example showing how DCE's powerful Security Service providing both authentication and authorization inspired the CORBA designers during the process of proposing OMG's Security Service. Compared to DCE, the approach to security is generally believed to be the major disadvantage of the contemporary CORBA (OMG Security Service is still being worked on by the OMG Object Services TF). For some OMG services, such as the Transaction and the Event Notification Services, there is no analogy as DCE does not provide any facility for handling transactions or sending events.

### 4.1.3 Issues of Building CORBA upon DCE

At the time when the CORBA 2.0 specification was being prepared, most DCE supporters believed that the CORBA ORB Core would be built merely upon DCE, or that at least the DCE/ESIOP protocol would be required as a mandatory protocol. It did not happen. Instead, CORBA 2.0 ORBs are built upon the mandatory IIOP and the DCE/ESIOP protocol is only optional, even though the DCE/ESIOP protocol, compared to IIOP, includes advanced features such as Kerberos security, authenticated RPC, and an option to choose from connection-oriented or connectionless protocols. In our view, the main reason why the IIOP protocol was given a priority over

DCE/ESIOP is the OMG idea of using the Internet as a backbone for the ORB-to-ORB communication. The authors of our currently favorite book [OHE96] even claim that "*IIOP will eventually transform the Internet into a CORBA bus.*"

## 4.2 Relation to Java

This section compares the CORBA and Java computational models and the underlying communication protocols IIOP and HTTP, and illustrates the complementary character of both platforms.

### 4.2.1 Different Computational Models

The main characteristic of the CORBA computational model is locating most of the available system functionality encapsulated in objects on the implementation (server) side. As a CORBA application can actually contain many CORBA objects distributed on various machines with possibly different hardware and operating systems, the CORBA computational model is characterized by *distributed objects*.

Java facilitates a different computational model. At runtime, all remote objects required by a Java application are downloaded to the client and dynamically bound to become part of the application. Thus, in general, the application grows in time if it downloads objects from the remote server(s). The Java Virtual Machine (JVM) provides a platform-independent environment in which the precompiled code of the Java application (*bytecode*), together with the downloaded bytecode of the remote objects used by this application, is interpreted. It is worth emphasizing that this computational model does not facilitate any remote invocation from the client to the implementation (server) side as is done in the CORBA computational model. In Java, only the bytecode of the objects is distributed, not the object state. Thus, the Java computational model is characterized by *distributed code*. A more detailed comparison of CORBA and Java can be found in [JKW96].

### 4.2.2 Complementary Character of both Platforms

The above discussion shows that Java complements CORBA rather than competing with it. The are also serious attempts to implement the CORBA architecture using the Java language. As typical examples let us mention HORB [Hir96] and BlackWidow [BlackW]. Even though some implementations perform rather slowly, some current releases of JVM bytecode interpreters furnished with automatically invoked compilers (*just-in-time* compilers) allow for efficient implementations of CORBA in Java, thus drastically improving the odds against more common C++ implementations of CORBA. While taking advantage of the both platforms, a rational marriage of CORBA and Java may result in the advent of the new era of distributed computing.

To illustrate the complementary character of both platforms, we focus briefly on developing Java environments, such as OrbixWeb [OWeb], BlackWidow [BlackW], and Joe/NEO [NEO95]. Typically, in these environments a Java *applet*, i.e. a Java application running under a WWW browser, located on a client provides a lightweight front end to an ORB running on a remote server. Downloadable by any Java-enabled WWW browser, the applet may interact with the user by taking advantage of the standard Java library with built-in multimedia capabilities, thus providing a visually appealing graphical interface. The communication between the applet and the ORB is done via a classical CORBA stub-request-skeleton mechanism, usually through the IIOP protocol. The presence of this additional communication link between the client and the server relieves the burden of the HTTP daemon running at the server, since the applet requests and the ORB responses are routed via IIOP. In case of OrbixWeb, the ORB called Orbix is implemented in C++. BlackWidow has both components implemented in Java. Joe is implemented in Java and the ORB called NEO in C++.

### 4.2.3 Java Security Restrictions

Unfortunately, there is one significant restriction as an outcome of the Java tight security policy: a Java applet can open a communication link only to the server from which it has been downloaded (although this feature is not built-in in the language). Applied to the communication triangle - applet, HTTP daemon, ORB, this means that if an applet has been downloaded via a HTTP daemon from an imaginary server `applet.source.com`, it can open an IIOP connection to this server only. An attempt by the applet to connect to any other server would result in a Java security violation exception. Hence the ORB must reside on the same machine that runs the HTTP daemon. This may become an unjustifiable restriction for some applications. One ad hoc (and rather hacky) solution to this problem is to modify the *SecurityManager* class in the Java standard library. This class implements the Java security policy. For example, in case of running the Netscape browser with an appropriately tampered *SecurityManager* class in its *moz3_0.zip* file containing the Java standard library, the applet downloaded from `applet.source.com` could open a connection not only to this server running the HTTP daemon but also to another one, called for example `corba.server.com`, running the ORB. It is expected that in the future the user will be allowed to give up this restriction via a cleaner mechanism, e.g. an environment variable similar to the CLASSPATH environment variable which contains the directories accessible from a Java application.

### 4.2.4 IIOP versus HTTP

The IIOP protocol is used by CORBA as a user-transparent TCP/IP-based protocol for delivering requests. The HTTP protocol [HTTPwww], also built upon TCP/IP, is used by WWW browsers for downloading HTML documents as well as Java applets from WWW servers. CORBA's IIOP protocol overcomes the limitations of HTTP in the following way: first by allowing a client applet to use a wide range of data types supported by IIOP as opposed to HTTP which does not standardize data types allowed for transmission. Second, the combined power of simple HTTP operations (downloading a HTML document, a picture, sound, and an applet) and CGI scripts (scripts performed on the WWW server whose output is redirected to the WWW client) is now fundamentally expanded by allowing the client to call objects residing on a server directly without starting a CGI process upon every request. Third, the HTTP protocol opens a socket connection for every client request. The IIOP protocol, on the other hand, leaves the connection opened during the entire session, thus reducing the socket initialization overhead. However, the recently specified HTTP 1.1 protocol allows persistent connections.

## 5 On the near future of CORBA (instead of conclusion)

In the paper, we have presented an overview of OMG's role, CORBA basic concepts and structure, Object Services, and CORBA's relations to other standards and environments (particularly DCE and Java). In this concluding section, we emphasize and illustrate the dynamics of CORBA's evolution and provide the reader with landmarks which, in our view, frame the picture of CORBA's near future. The current trends in the evolution are clearly reflected in the OMG Task Force names (and SIG names in some cases) and particularly in the RFPs issued by the TFs recently.

As its name suggests, the **ORB and Object Services Platform TF** is involved in evolution of ORB and Object Services. The ORB interface is being improved, IDL type extensions and object multiple interfaces are being discussed, secure IIOP RFP has been issued, and the COM/CORBA interoperability is being considered. Work upon the following Object Services is in progress: the Startup, Trader, Collection, Time, and, especially, Security Services. The **Analysis and Design Platform TF** issued RFP1 with the intention to define common Object Analysis and Design (OA&D) meta-models (static, behavior, usage, and architectural models) and IDL specifications for model interchange among OA&D tools.

A lot of current OMG attention is paid to Common Facilities which are now being split into two OMA components: Common Facilities (originally Horizontal Common Facilities) and Domain Interfaces (originally Vertical Common Facilities) [OMG96]. The **Common Facilities Platform TF** is concerned particularly with the Financial, Internationalization and Time, Data Interchange and Mobile Agent, Printing, and System Management Facilities. The **Domain Technology Committee** has appointed TFs for specifying domain interfaces, e.g. for the following fields: asset and content management, telecommunication, manufacturing, and business objects. A great deal of OMG effort is directed towards the integration of CORBA and the Internet. The **Internet Special Interest Group** has been appointed by OMG to foster this integration.

All in all, CORBA-related activity has accelerated enormously, and it is becoming hard to follow the field in its entirety. Just for illustration, during the first six months of 1996, OMG produced roughly 300 documents, mostly proposals and responses from major software companies. This fact indicates the magnitude of OMG's impact on the software industry.

## Acknowledgements

The authors of this paper would like to express their thanks to Adam Dingle for proofreading the text and for valuable comments on contents of the Section 4.

## References

[Ben95] R. Ben-Nathar: CORBA: A guide to Common Object Request Broker Architecture. McGraw-Hill. 1995.

[BlackW] BlackWidow, PostModern Computing. URL: http://www.pomoco.com

[DCEwww] Object Software Foundation, URL: http://www.omg.org

[Hir96] S. Hirano: HORB Home Page. Work in Progress at Japan's Electrotechnical Laboratory (ETL), URL: http://ring.etl.go.jp/openlab/horb

[HP95] HP ORB Plus 2.0, URL: http//www.hp.com

[HTTPwww] Basic HTTP,http://www.w3.org/pub/WWW/Protocols/HTTP/HTTP2.html

[IBM94a] IBM Corp. SOMobjects Developer Toolkit Users Guide, Version 2.1, 1994.

[IBM94b] IBM Corp. SOMobjects Developer Toolkit Programmers Reference Manual Version 2.1, 1994.

[JKW96] J. Kiniry, A. Johnson, M.Weiss: Distributed Computing: Java, CORBA, and DCE, Version 1.2, URL: http://www.osf.org, Feb 1996

[KPT95] J. Kleindienst, F. Plášil, P. Tůma: Implementing CORBA Persistence Service, TR 117, Charles University Prague, Dept. of Software Engineering, 1995.

[KPT96] J. Kleindienst, F. Plášil, P. Tůma: Lessons Learned from Implementing the CORBA Persistence Service, In Proceedings of OOPSLA'96, San Jose, Oct 1996

[MoZa95] T.J. Mowbray, R. Zahavi: The Essential CORBA, J. Wiley & Sons, 1995.

[NEO96] Solaris NEO Operating Environment, Product Overview, Part No. 95392-003, Sunsoft Inc, March 96.

[OHE96] R. Orfali, D. Harkey, J. Edwards: The Essential Distributed Objects. Survival Guide. John Wiley & Sons, 1996

[OMG92] Object Service Architecture, OMG 92-8-4, 1992.

[OMG94a] Common Object Services Volume I, OMG 94-1-1, 1994.

[OMG94b] Persistent Object Service Specification, OMG 94-10-7, 1994.

[OMG94c] Relationship Service Specification, Joint Object Services Submission, OMG 94-5-5, 1994.

[OMG94d] Compound LifeCycle Addendum. Joint Object Services Submission. OMG 94-5-6, 1994.

[OMG94e] Object Externalization Service. OMG 94-9-15, 1995.

[OMG95a] Common Object Request Broker Architecture and Specification Revision 2.0, OMG 96-3-4, 1995.

[OMG95b] Object Services RFP 5. OMG TC Document 95-3-25, 1995.

[OMG95c] Object Management Architecture Guide, 3rd Edition, R.M. Soley (Editor), John Wiley & Sons, 1990.

[OMG95d] Object Services Architecture, Revision 8.1, OMG 95-1-47, 1995.

[OMG95e] Object Models, Draft 0.3, OMG 95-1-13, 1995.

[OMG95f] CORBAservices: Common Object Services Specification, OMG 1995

[OMG96] Description of New OMA Reference model, OMG 96-05-02, 1996

[ORBIXa] Orbix, Programmer's Guide. IONA Technologies Ltd. Dublin, 1994

[ORBIXb] Orbix, Advanced Programmer's Guide. IONA Technologies Ltd. Dublin, 1994.

[OWeb] IONA Home Page, URL: http://www.iona.com

[Sie96] J. Siegel: CORBA. Fundamentals and Programming. J. Wiley & Sons, 1996

# Decision-Theoretic Reasoning and the Human-Computer Interface: Advances in Embedded Intelligent Agents

Eric Horvitz

Microsoft Research, Redmond Washington, USA
horvitz@MICROSOFT.com

**Abstract.** Advances in the use of automated decision-theoretic reasoning to enhance the human-computer interface will be presented. Following a brief survey of research on Bayesian networks and influence diagrams, principles of embedded decision-theoretic agents will be discussed. Key concepts will be highlighted within the contexts of work on the Vista and Lumiere projects. The Vista project centered on building an intelligent interface to assist NASA Mission Control flight engineers with managing the complexity of information about Space Shuttle propulsion systems in time-critical contexts. Moving from aerospace to personal computing, related work on the Lumiere project at Microsoft Research will be presented. The goal of Lumiere is to develop more responsive interfaces for personal computers.

# Probabilistic Approaches to Motion Planning

Mark H. Overmars and Petr Švestka

Department of Computer Science, Utrecht University
P.O.Box 80.089, 3508 TB Utrecht, the Netherlands
e-mail: markov@cs.ruu.nl, petr@cs.ruu.nl

**Abstract.** The motion planning problem asks for computing a collision-free path for a robot amidst a collection of obstacles. In this paper we discuss a recently developed probabilistic paradigm for robot motion planning, which has been applied successfully to a wide range of motion planning problems. The motion planning process is split into two phases: the learning phase and the query phase. In the learning phase a roadmap is constructed, capturing the possible motions of the robot. This roadmap is a graph with nodes corresponding to randomly chosen robot configurations and edges corresponding to simple collision-free motions between the nodes. In the query phase this roadmap is used to find paths connecting different pairs of robot configurations. We give an overview of the approach and present some experimental results for problems involving various types of robots, including robot arms and car-like robots. These demonstrate the power of the paradigm. Also, we briefly describe an extension for solving coordinated motion planning for multiple robots.

## 1 Introduction

In a general formulation, the motion planning problem asks for computing a feasible path for some robot in a workspace with obstacles for moving from an initial position to a goal position. Many variations and extensions of the motion planning problem can be defined, based on the geometry of the robot and restrictions on its motions (like the restriction that a car cannot move sideways), based on the workspace and the obstacles (like whether the obstacles are known in advance), and based on the type of solution required (e.g., do we want to solve one single path question, or do we want to preprocess the workspace for multiple path queries).

Many different approaches to motion planning have been suggested. Let us briefly describe some of them. See the book of Latombe [12] and the references mentioned there for more details.

The *potential field* approach builds an artificial potential field in the workspace. The goal configuration attracts the robot while the obstacles push the robot away. In this way a number of forces work on the robot. The resulting force determines the direction for the robot to move in. The approach is easy to implement because only local calculations are required. The main problem is that the robot might get stuck in a local minimum where the forces add up to 0. Additional techniques are required to escape from such minima. For example, simple Brownian (random) motion can be applied to the robot until it is far enough away from the minimum. Alternatively, one can try to model the potentials in such a way that no local minima occur, but this is only possible in restricted situations.

Potential field approaches do not necessarily find a solution when one exists. To design exact solutions one often considers the *configuration space* of the robot. The position and orientation of a robot is defined by a number of parameters, the configuration. The configuration space is the space of all possible configurations. Its dimension depends on the number of parameters that define the configurations, the degree of freedom. For example, a planar robot that can move arbitrarily (also called a free-flying robot) has three degrees of freedom and, hence, the configuration space is 3-dimensional. Part of the configuration space is forbidden. When the robot is in such a configuration it intersects an obstacle. The remaining part is called the *free configuration space.* A motion for the robot is only possible when a path exists in this free configuration space.

To find such a path one can compute the free configuration space. It is then divided into a number of simple cells. These cells become nodes in a graph and nodes are connected with edges when the corresponding cells are neighbours. A path for the robot is now computed by determining the cells that contain the start and goal configuration of the path and then following a path in the graph connecting these cells. Such a path in the graph can be transformed into a path for the robot. This approach is referred to as the *(exact) cell decomposition approach.* Even though this is possible for most robots the complexity of the algorithms is very high. Alternatively one can compute only an approximation of the free space, for example using a collection of rectangular blocks.

Another approach is the *roadmap approach.* Here one computes a collection of roads through the free configuration space, capturing the connectivity of the space. This roadmap is stored as a graph. For example, Voronoi diagrams can be used for this. To compute a path for the robot between a start and goal configuration we first compute paths from the start and goal to nearby points on the roadmap. These are called the *retractions* of the start and goal configurations. Next we use the graph to compute a path between the two retractions along the roadmap. Such roadmaps can be complete in the sense that any possible motion can be found using the roadmap, or approximate. The probabilistic approach described in this paper can be considered as a roadmap approach.

Recently there has been a renewed interest in developing heuristic, but practical motion planners. This was motivated by the fact that previous methods, although often practical for simple problems involving robots with few degrees of freedom, fail to solve efficiently more challenging (but practical) problems involving robots with many degrees of freedom (high-dof) or robots with nonholonomic constraints, that is, constraints on the type of motion that is allowed.

Among the most successful planners has been RPP [3], a potential field based method that uses Brownian motion for escaping from local minima. It has successfully been applied to articulated robots with many degrees of freedom. Also,

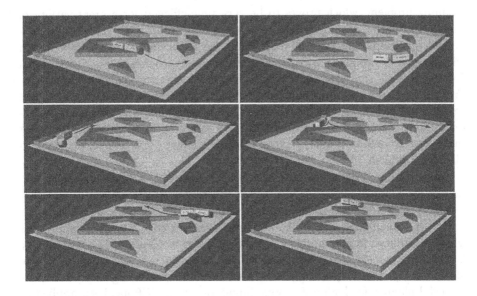

**Fig. 1.** A path for a tractor with two trailers, computed with the Probabilistic Path Planner.

it has been used in practise for checking whether parts can be removed from air-craft engines for inspection and maintenance, and for automatically synthesising a video clip with graphically simulated human and robot characters entailing 78 degrees of freedom. In [11] the probabilistic convergence of the planner is proven, and a finite estimate of the expected complexity is given. It has however some drawbacks. For example, since the planner is potential field based, it does not maintain any knowledge about the configuration space after having solved a particular problem, and, for this reason, each new problem requires a whole new search. In other words, it is a single shot approach. Furthermore, it turns out to be easy to create seemingly simple problems for which the planner consumes a more than reasonable amount of time, due to very low transition probabilities between certain basins in the potential field. Also, the method does not directly apply to nonholonomic robots.

Genetic algorithms are utilised in [1] for guiding path searches in high-dimensional configuration spaces, and, for certain problems, this approach proves to be very efficient. A heuristic learning approach using a cell-decomposition of the configuration space is presented in [4]. For robots with up to 6 degrees of freedom fairly good results where obtained. In [10] a potential field approach is described that uses heuristics to limit the configuration space portion that is explored.

In this paper we give a survey of a probabilistic paradigm for the motion planning problem, which proves to be very time-efficient for a great variety of robots, including high-dof articulated robots and robots with various nonholonomic constraints. We refer to it as *PPP* (the *Probabilistic Path Planner*). An advantage over the above mentioned methods is its generality. There are only a few components that are robot specific, and these are easy to define/implement. Furthermore, it is a learning approach, that is, it builds data structures that, once constructed, can be used for retrieving arbitrary paths quasi-instantaneously. Potential field methods inherently do not have this property, due to the fact that the potential field always depends on the goal configuration of a particular path planning problem.

Many planners based on *PPP* have been developed. A first single-shot version of the planner for free-flying planar robots was described in [13] and subsequently expanded into a general learning approach, for various robot types, in [14]. Independently, "*PPP*-like" preprocessing schemes for holonomic robots where introduced in [8] and [5]. These schemes also build probabilistic roadmaps in the configuration space, but focus on the case of many-dof robots. In [9] the ideas developed in [14] and [8] have been combined, resulting in a even more powerful planner for high-dof robots. Simultaneously, *PPP* has been applied to nonholonomic robots. Planners for car-like robots that can move both forwards and backwards as well as such that can only move forwards are described in [19]. *PPP* applied to tractor-trailer robots is the topic of [21]. Probabilistic completeness of the planners for nonholonomic robots is proven in [19, 17]. Recently some first results on the expected running times of *PPP*, under certain geometric assumptions on the free configuration space, have been obtained [2]. For a thorough survey of probabilistic path planning for holonomic robots we also refer to the thesis of Kavraki [7]. Finally, extensions of *PPP* addressing multi-robot path planning problems have been presented in [20].

Here we will give a global overview of the results in some of these papers. For more detail we refer the reader to the original publications.

## 2   The probabilistic paradigm *PPP*

*PPP* can be described in general terms, without focusing on any specific robot type. The idea is that during the *learning phase* a data structure is incrementally constructed in a probabilistic way, and that this data structure is later, in the *query phase*, used for solving individual motion planning problems.

The data structure constructed during the learning phase is an undirected graph $G = (V, E)$, where the nodes $V$ are probabilistically generated free configurations (that is, configurations of the robot where it does not intersect any obstacle) and the edges $E$ correspond to (simple) feasible paths. These simple paths, which we refer to as *local paths*, are constructed by a *local planner*. A local planner $L$ is a symmetric function that takes two configurations as arguments, and returns a path connecting them that is feasible in absence of obstacles (that is, the path respects the constraints of the robot). If, given two configurations $a$

and $b$, the path $L(a, b)$ is collision-free, then we will say that $L$ connects from $a$ to $b$.

In the query phase, given a start configuration $s$ and a goal configuration $g$, we try to connect $s$ and $g$ to suitable nodes $\tilde{s}$ and $\tilde{g}$ in $V$. Then we perform a graph search to find a sequence of edges in $E$ connecting $\tilde{s}$ to $\tilde{g}$, and we transform this sequence into a feasible path for the robot.

## 2.1 The learning phase

We assume that we are dealing with a robot $\mathcal{A}$, and that $L$ is a local planner that constructs paths feasible for $\mathcal{A}$. As mentioned above, in the learning phase a probabilistic roadmap is constructed, and stored in an undirected graph $G = (V, E)$. The construction of the roadmap is performed incrementally in a probabilistic way. Repeatedly a random free configuration $c$ is generated and added to $V$. Heuristics however are used for generating more nodes in "difficult" areas of the free configuration space. We try to connect each generated node $c$ to the graph by adding a number of edges $(c, n)$ to $E$, such that the local planner can connect from $c$ to $n$.

This edge adding is done as follows: First, a set $N_c$ of neighbours is chosen from $V$. This set consists of nodes lying within a certain distance from $c$, with respect to some distance measure $D$. Then, in order of increasing distance from $c$, we pick nodes from $N_c$. We try to connect $c$ to each of the selected nodes if it is not already graph-connected to $c$. Hence, no cycles will be created and the resulting graph is a forest, i.e., a collection of trees. The motivation for preventing cycles is that no query would ever succeed *thanks to* an edge that is part of a cycle.

Let $\mathcal{C}$ denote the configuration space of the robot (from now on called its C-space), and $\mathcal{C}_f$ the free portion of $\mathcal{C}$ (i.e., the free C-space). To describe the roadmap construction algorithm formally, we need a function $D \in \mathcal{C} \times \mathcal{C} \to \mathbf{R}^+$. It defines the distance measure used, and should give a suitable notion of distance for arbitrary pairs of configurations, taking the properties of the robot $\mathcal{A}$ into account. We assume that $D$ is symmetric. The graph $G = (V, E) \in \mathcal{C}_f \times \mathcal{C}_f^2$ is constructed as follows:

**The learning algorithm:**

> $V = \emptyset$, $E = \emptyset$
> **loop**
>     $c =$ a "randomly" chosen free configuration
>     $V = V \cup \{c\}$
>     $N_c =$ a set of neighbours of $c$ chosen from $V$
>     **forall** $n \in N_c$, in order of increasing $D(c, n)$
>         **if** $\neg graph\text{-}connected(c, n) \wedge L(c, n) \subset \mathcal{C}_f$
>         **then** $E = E \cup \{(c, n)\}$

The learning method, as described above, leaves a number of choices to be made: A local planner must be chosen, a distance measure must be defined, and it must be defined what the neighbours of a node are. Furthermore, heuristics for generating more nodes in interesting C-space areas can be defined. See below for the choices made for various robot types.

## 2.2 The query phase

During the query phase, paths are to be found between arbitrary start and goal configurations, using the graph $G$ computed in the learning phase. The idea is that, given a start configuration $s$ and a goal configuration $g$, we try to find feasible paths $P_s$ and $P_g$, such that $P_s$ connects $s$ to a graph node $\tilde{s}$, and $P_g$ connects g to a graph node $\tilde{g}$, with $\tilde{s}$ graph-connected to $\tilde{g}$ (that is, they lie in the same connected component of $G$). If this succeeds, we perform a graph search to obtain a path $P_G$ in $G$ connecting $\tilde{s}$ to $\tilde{g}$. A feasible path (in C-space) from $s$ to $g$ is then constructed by concatenating $P_s$, the subpaths constructed by the local planner when applied to pairs of consecutive nodes in $P_G$, and $P_g$ reversed. Otherwise, the query fails. The queries should preferably terminate 'instantaneously', so no expensive algorithm is allowed for computing $P_s$ and $P_g$.

For finding the nodes $\tilde{s}$ and $\tilde{g}$ we use the function $query\_mapping \in \mathcal{C} \times \mathcal{C} \to V \times V$, which maps a configuration pair $(a, b)$ to the nearest pair of graph-connected nodes $(\tilde{a}, \tilde{b})$ in $G$. We refer to $\tilde{a}$ as $a$'s graph retraction, and to $\tilde{b}$ as $b$'s graph retraction.

The most straightforward way for performing a query with start configuration $s$ and goal configuration $g$ is to compute $(\tilde{s}, \tilde{g}) = query\_mapping(s, g)$, and to try to connect with the local planner from $s$ to $\tilde{s}$ and from $\tilde{g}$ to $g$. However, since no obstacle avoidance is incorporated in the local planner, it may, in unlucky cases, fail to find the connections even if the graph captures the connectivity of free C-space well.

Experiments with different robot types indicated that simple probabilistic methods that (repeatedly) perform short random walks from $s$ and $g$, and try to connect to the graph retractions of the end-points of those walks with the local planner, achieve significantly better results. For many robots very good performance is obtained by what we refer to as the *random bounce walk* (see also [9]). The idea is that repeatedly a random direction (in C-space) is chosen, and the robot is moved in this direction until a collision occurs (or time runs out). When a collision occurs, a new random direction is chosen. This method performs much better than for example Brownian motion in C-space. For nonholonomic robots walks of a similar nature can be performed, but care must of course be taken to respect the nonholonomic constraints.

## 2.3 Smoothing the paths

Paths computed in the query phase can be quite ugly and unnecessarily long. This is due to the probabilistic nature of the algorithm, and to the fact that cycle-creating edges are never added.

To improve this, one can apply some path smoothing techniques on these 'ugly' paths. The smoothing routine that we use is very simple. It repeatedly picks a pair of random configurations $(c_1, c_2)$ on the "to be smoothed" path $P_C$, tries to connect these with a feasible path $Q_{new}$ using the local planner. If this succeeds and $Q_{new}$ is shorter than the path segment $Q_{old}$ in $P_C$ from $c_1$ to $c_2$, then it replaces $Q_{old}$ by $Q_{new}$ (in $P_C$). So basically, randomly picked segments of the path are replaced, when possible, by shorter ones, constructed by the local planner. The longer this is done, the shorter (and nicer) the path gets. Typically, this method smoothes a path very well in less than a second for low-dof robots, and in a few seconds for high-dof robots.

# 3 Application to holonomic robots

In this section an application of the probabilistic paradigm to two types of holonomic robots is described: free-flying robots and articulated robots.

We consider here only planar holonomic robots (that is, robots without non-holonomic constraints). A free-flying robot is represented as a polygon that can rotate and translate freely in the plane among a set of polygonal obstacles. Its C-space is represented by $R^2 \times [0, 2\pi[$. A planar articulated robot consists of $n$ *links* $L_1, \ldots, L_n$, which are some solid planar bodies (we use polygons), connected to each other by $n - 1$ *joints* $J_2, \ldots, J_n$. Furthermore, the first link $L_1$ is connected to some *base point* in the workspace by a joint $J_1$. At joint $J_i$, link $L_i$ can rotate around some point which is fixed to link $L_{i-1}$ (or to the workspace, if $i = 1$). The range of the possible rotations of each link $L_i$ is constrained by $J_i$'s *joint bounds*, consisting of a lower bound $low_i$ and an upper bound $up_i$. The C-space of a $n$-linked planar articulated robot can, hence, be represented by $[low_1, up_1] \times [low_2, up_2] \times \ldots \times [low_n, up_n]$.

A very general local planner exists, that is directly applicable to all holonomic robots. Given two configurations, it connects them by a straight line segment in C-space and checks the motion along this line segment for collision and joint limits (if any). We refer to this planner as *the general holonomic local planner*. The distance between two configurations $a$ and $b$ is defined as the length (in C-space) of the local path connecting $a$ and $b$. For both the free-flying robots and the articulated robots, we utilise the structure of $G$ to identify "difficult" areas in which more "random" nodes are to be added than in others. We increase the chances for node generation in areas (of C-space) where the graph shows disconnectivities (that is, where there are a number of separate connected components present).

We have implemented the method for planar free-flying and articulated robots in the way described above, and we present some experimental results obtained with the resulting planners. The implementations are in C++ and the experiments were performed on a Silicon Graphics Indigo[2] workstation with an R4400 processor running at 150 MHZ. This machine is rated with 96.5 SPECfp92 and 90.4 SPECint92.

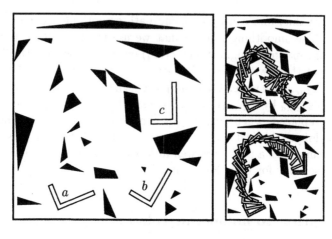

|       | 0.25 sec. | 0.5sec. | 0.75 sec. | 1.0 sec. | 1.25 sec. |
|-------|-----------|---------|-----------|----------|-----------|
| (a,b) | 35%       | 55%     | 85%       | 95%      | 100%      |
| (a,c) | 20%       | 90%     | 100%      | 100%     | 100%      |
| (b,c) | 15%       | 75%     | 85%       | 100%     | 100%      |

**Fig. 2.** An L-shaped free-flying robot and its test configurations are shown. At the top right, we see two paths computed by the planner and smoothed in 1 second. The table gives the results.

In the test scenes used, the coordinates of all workspace obstacles lie in the unit square. Furthermore, in all scenes we have added an obstacle boundary around the unit square, hence no part of the robot can ever move outside this square.

The experiments are aimed at measuring the "knowledge" acquired by the method after having learned for certain periods of time. This is done by testing how well the method solves certain (interesting) queries. For each scene we define a *query test set* $T_Q = \{(s_1, s_1), (s_2, g_2), \ldots, (s_m, g_m)\}$, consisting of a number of configuration pairs (that is, queries). Then, we repeatedly build a graph by learning for some specified time $t$, and we count how many of these graphs solve the different queries in $T_Q$. This experiment is repeated for a number of different learning times $t$. The time spent per query is bounded by 0.3 seconds (on our machine). The results are summerized in a table, showing for each of the test queries the percentage of runs, learning for a particular amount of time, that solve the query. The darker the box, the better the result.

In the scene in Figure 2 we have a free flying L-shaped robot, placed at the configurations $a$, $b$, and $c$. Experimental results are shown for the three corresponding queries, and two paths are shown, both smoothed in 1 second. We see that around 1 second of learning is required for obtaining roadmaps that solve the queries.

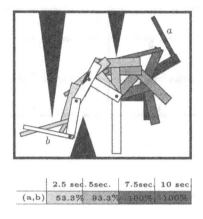

| | 2.5 sec. | 5sec. | 7.5sec. | 10 sec |
|---|---|---|---|---|
| (a,b) | 53.3% | 93.3% | 100% | 100% |

**Fig. 3.** A four-dof articulated robot, and a path.

In Figures 3 to 5 results are given for articulated robots.

In the first two scenes, just one query is tested. In both figures, several robot configurations along a path solving the query are displayed using various grey levels. The results of the experiments are given in the two tables. We see that the query in Figure 3 is solved in all cases after having learned for 10 seconds. Learning for 5 seconds however suffices to successfully answer the query in more than 90% of the cases. In Figure 4 we observe similar behaviour.

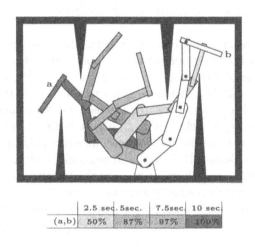

| | 2.5 sec. | 5sec. | 7.5sec. | 10 sec |
|---|---|---|---|---|
| (a,b) | 50% | 87% | 97% | 100% |

**Fig. 4.** A five-dof articulated robot, and a path.

Figure 5 shows a very difficult scene. We have a seven dof robot in a very

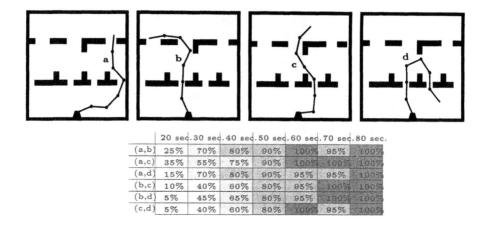

| | 20 sec. | 30 sec. | 40 sec. | 50 sec. | 60 sec. | 70 sec. | 80 sec. |
|-------|------|------|------|------|------|------|------|
| (a,b) | 25% | 70% | 80% | 90% | 100% | 95% | 100% |
| (a,c) | 35% | 55% | 75% | 90% | 100% | 100% | 100% |
| (a,d) | 15% | 70% | 80% | 90% | 95% | 95% | 100% |
| (b,c) | 10% | 40% | 60% | 80% | 95% | 100% | 100% |
| (b,d) | 5% | 45% | 65% | 80% | 95% | 100% | 100% |
| (c,d) | 5% | 40% | 60% | 80% | 100% | 95% | 100% |

**Fig. 5.** A seven-dof articulated robot in a very constrained environment and the query test set.

constrained environment. The configurations $a$, $b$, $c$, and $d$ define 6 different queries, for which the results are shown. These where obtained by a customised implementation by Kavraki and Latombe [9]. In this implementation, optimised collision checking routines are used, as well as a robot-specific local planner. Furthermore, "difficult" nodes are heuristically identified during the learning phase, and "expanded" subsequently.

## 4 Application to nonholonomic robots

We now consider nonholonomic mobile robots. More specifically, we apply the Probabilistic Path Planner to car-like robots and tractor-trailer robots.

We model a car-like robot as a polygon moving in $R^2$, and its C-space is represented by $R^2 \times [0, 2\pi[$. The motions it can perform are subject to nonholonomic constraints. It can move forwards and backwards, and perform curves with a turning radius bounded below by $r_{min}$, like an ordinary car. A tractor-trailer robot is modelled as a car-like one, but with an extra polygon attached to it by a revolute joint. Its C-space is (hence) 4-dimensional, and can be represented by $R^2 \times [0, 2\pi] \times [-\alpha_{max}, \alpha_{max}]$, where $\alpha_{max}$ is the (symmetric) joint bound. The car-like part (the *tractor*) is exactly a car-like robot. The extra part (the *trailer*) is subject to further nonholonomic constraints. Its motions are (physically) dictated by the motions of the tractor (For details, see for example [12]).

### 4.1 Car-like robots

A *RTR path* is defined as the concatenation of an rotational path (circle arc), a translational path (straight line segment), and another rotational path (circle arc). With this path construct we define the *RTR local planner*. Given two argument configurations $a$ and $b$, this local planner constructs the shortest RTR path connecting $a$ to $b$. The RTR construct allows for very efficient collision checking. We use a distance measure that is induced by the RTR local planner: The distance between two configurations is defined as the length (in workspace) of the shortest RTR path connecting them. Regarding the node adding heuristics, we use the geometry of the workspace obstacles to identify areas in which is advantageous to add some extra, geometrically derived, non-random nodes. Particular obstacle edges and (convex) obstacle corners define such geometric nodes (See [19] for more details). Furthermore, as for free-flying robots, we use the structure of the graph $G$ to guide the node generation.

We have implemented the planner as described above, and some experimental results are presented in this section. The planner was run on a machine as described in Section 3. Again the presented scenes correspond to the unit square with an obstacle boundary. The simulation results are presented in the same form as for the holonomic robots (in Section 3). That is, for different learning times we count how often graphs are obtained which solve particular, predefined, queries.

Figure 6 shows a relatively easy scene. The topology is simple and there are only a few narrow passages that can cause problems. As query test set $T_Q$ we use $\{(a,b),(a,d),(b,e),(c,e),(d,e)\}$. (At the top-right of Figure 6 paths solving the queries $(a,d)$ and $(b,e)$, smoothed in 1 second, are shown.) The minimal turning radius $r_{min}$ used in the experiments is 0.1. We see that after only 0.3 seconds of learning, the constructed networks solve each of the queries in most cases (but not all). Half a second of learning is sufficient for solving each of the queries, in all trials.

Figure 7 is a completely different type of scene. It contains many (small) obstacles and is not at all "corridor-like". Although many individual motion planning problems in this scene are quite simple, the topology of the free C-space is quite complicated, and can only be captured well in relatively complicated graphs. As query test set $T_Q$ we use $\{(a,b),(a,c),(a,d),(c,d)\}$. Furthermore, as in the previous scene, $r_{min} = 0.1$. Again, we show two (smoothed) paths computed by our planner (solving the queries $(a,b)$ and $(c,d)$). We see that about 2 seconds of learning are required to obtain networks which are (almost) guaranteed to solve each of the queries.

## 4.2  Tractor-trailer robots

As a last example of nonholonomic robots, we now briefly consider tractor-trailer robots. Again, we will not go into many details (we refer to [16] for a more thorough discussion of the topic). We use a local planner, by Sekhavat and Laumond [15], which transforms its configuration coordinates into the chained form, and uses sinusoidal inputs. As distance measure we use a (cheap) approximations of the workspace lengths of the local paths.

See Figure 8 for two feasible paths computed by the Probabilistic Path Planner. The computation time of the roadmap from which the paths where retrieved

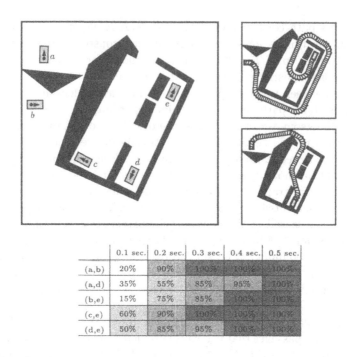

| | 0.1 sec. | 0.2 sec. | 0.3 sec. | 0.4 sec. | 0.5 sec. |
|---|---|---|---|---|---|
| (a,b) | 20% | 90% | 100% | 100% | 100% |
| (a,d) | 35% | 55% | 85% | 95% | 100% |
| (b,e) | 15% | 75% | 85% | 100% | 100% |
| (c,e) | 60% | 90% | 100% | 100% | 100% |
| (d,e) | 50% | 85% | 95% | 100% | 100% |

**Fig. 6.** A scene with a car-like robot, and its test configurations. At the top right, two paths computed by the planner and smoothed in 1 second are shown.

took about 10 seconds (on the average).

## 5   A multi-robot extension

We conclude this paper with an extension of *PPP* for solving multi-robot path planning problems. That is, problems involving a number of robots, present in the same workspace, that are to change their positions while avoiding (mutual) collisions. For overviews of previous work on this topic we refer to [12] and [6].

Most previous successful multi-robot planners fall into the class of *decoupled planners*, that is, planners that first plan separate paths for the individual robots more or less independently, and only in a later stage, in case of collisions among the robots, try to adapt the paths locally to prevent the collisions. This however inherently leads to planners that are not complete, that is, that can lead to deadlocks. To obtain some form of completeness, one must consider the separate robots as one composite system, and perform the planning for this entire system. However, this tends to be very expensive, since the composite C-space is typically of high dimension, and the constraints of all separate robots add up.

For example, multi-robot problems could be tackled by direct application of *PPP*. The robot considered would be composed of the separate "simple" robots,

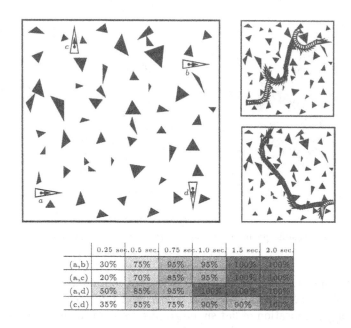

| | 0.25 sec. | 0.5 sec. | 0.75 sec. | 1.0 sec. | 1.5 sec. | 2.0 sec. |
|---|---|---|---|---|---|---|
| (a,b) | 30% | 75% | 95% | 95% | 100% | 100% |
| (a,c) | 20% | 70% | 85% | 95% | 100% | 100% |
| (a,d) | 50% | 85% | 95% | 100% | 100% | 100% |
| (c,d) | 35% | 55% | 75% | 90% | 90% | 100% |

**Fig. 7.** Another scene with a car-like robot, and its test configurations. At the top right, two paths computed by the planner and smoothed in 1 second are shown.

and the local planner would construct paths for this composite robot. This is a very simple way of obtaining multi-robot planners. However, as mentioned above, a drawback is the high dimension of the configuration space, which, in non-trivial scenes, will force *PPP* to construct very large roadmaps for capturing the structure of $C_f$. Moreover, each local path in such a roadmap will consist of a number of local paths for the simple robots, causing the collision checking to be rather expensive.

In this section we briefly describe a scheme where a roadmap for the composite robot is constructed only after a discretisation step, that allows for disregarding the actual C-space of the composite robot.

We refer to the separate robots $\mathcal{A}_1, \ldots, \mathcal{A}_n$ as the *simple robots*. One can also consider the simple robots together to be one robot (with many degrees of freedom), the so-called *composite robot*. A feasible path for the composite robot we refer to as a *coordinated path*. We assume that the simple robots are identical, although, with minor adaptions, the presented concepts are applicable to problems involving non-identical robots as well.

A roadmap for the composite robot is constructed in two steps. First, a *simple roadmap* is constructed for just one robot with *PPP*. Then $n$ of such roadmaps are combined into a roadmap for the composite robot (consisting of $n$ simple robots). We will refer to such a composite roadmap as a *super-graph*. After such a super-graph has been constructed, which needs to be done just once for a given

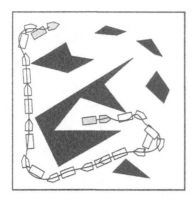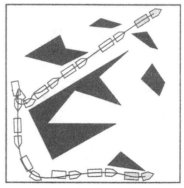

**Fig. 8.** Two feasible paths for a tractor-trailer robot, obtained in 10 seconds.

static environment, it can be used for retrieval of coordinated paths. We present two super-graph structures: *flat super-graphs* and *multi-level super-graphs*. The latter are a generalisation of flat super-graphs, that consume much less memory for problems involving more than 3 robots.

The scheme is a flexible one, in the sense that it is easily applicable to various robot types, provided that one is able to construct simple roadmaps for one such robot.

### 5.1 Discretisation of the multi-robot planning problem

Given a graph $G = (V, E)$ storing a simple roadmap for robot $\mathcal{A}$, we are interested in solving multi-robot problems using $G$. We say a node *blocks* a local path, if the volume occupied by $\mathcal{A}$ when placed at the node intersects the volume swept by $\mathcal{A}$ when moving along the local path.

The idea now is that we seek paths in $G$ along which the robots can go from their start configurations to their goal configurations, but we disallow simultaneous motions, and we also disallow motions along local paths which are blocked by the nodes at which the other robots are stationary. We refer to such paths as $G$-discretised paths. It can be proven that restricting the motions in this way does not limit the power of the approach. That is, any solvable multi-robot path planning problem can be solved using $G$-discretised paths, assuming $G$ is large enough.

### 5.2 Using super-graphs

The question now is, given a simple roadmap $G = (V, E)$ for a robot $\mathcal{A}$, how to compute $G$-discretised paths for the composite robot $(\mathcal{A}_1, \ldots, \mathcal{A}_n)$ (with $\forall i : \mathcal{A}_i = \mathcal{A}$). For this we introduce the notion of *super-graphs*, that is, roadmaps for the composite robots obtained by combining $n$ simple roadmaps. We discuss two types of super-graphs. For more details on both data structures we refer to [20].

*The flat super-graph method.* In a flat super-graph $F_G$, each node corresponds to a feasible placement of the $n$ simple robots at nodes of $G$, and each edge corresponds to a motion of one simple robot along a non-blocked local path of $G$. Any path in the $G$-induced super-graph describes a $G$-discretised path (for the composite robot), and vice-versa. Hence, the problem of finding $G$-discretised paths for our composite robot reduces to graph searches in $F_G$. In order to obtain nice and smooth multi-robot paths (with robots performing simultaneous motions), we apply certain smoothing techniques. A drawback of flat super-graphs is their size, which is exponential in $n$ (the number of robots).

*The multi-level super-graph method.* The multi-level super-graph method aims at size reduction of the multi-robot data structure, by combining multiple node-tuples into single super-nodes. While a node in a flat super-graph corresponds to a statement that each robot $\mathcal{A}_i$ is located at some particular node of $G$, a node in a multi-level super-graph corresponds to a statement that each robot $\mathcal{A}_i$ is located in some *subgraph* of $G$. But only subgraphs that do not *interfere* with each other are combined. We say that a subgraph $A$ interferes with a subgraph $B$ if a node of $A$ blocks a local path in $B$, or vice versa. For obtaining suitable subgraphs, we compute a recursive subdivision of $G$, a so-called *G-subdivision tree*.

## 5.3   Application to car-like robots

We have applied both the flat super-graph method as well as the multi-level super-graph method to *car-like* robots. The resulting planners (in C++) have been tested for a number of problems, involving multiple cars in the same environment. The simple roadmaps have been computed by *PPP*. Both resulting planners are quite time-efficient for up to three robots. For more robots the flat super-graph methods consumes too much memory. The multi-level method give good results for up to 5 robots. We show here just two problems solved, in Figures 9 and 10. The problems were solved (by the multi-level super-graph method) in, respectively, 30 and 15 seconds. The super-graphs had about 20000 nodes in both cases.

# 6   Conclusions

A general probabilistic technique for path planning has been described in this paper. It consists of two phases. In the learning phase a probabilistic roadmap is incrementally constructed, which can subsequently, in the query phase, be used for solving individual motion planning problems in the given scene. It is a fast and flexible method. In order to apply it to some particular robot type, all one needs to define (and implement) is a local method which computes paths feasible

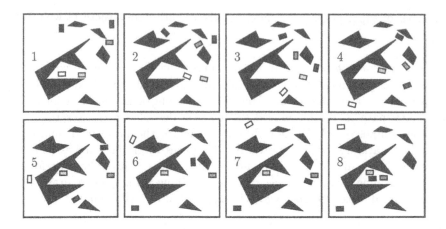

**Fig. 9.** Snapshots of a coordinated path for 5 car-like robots.

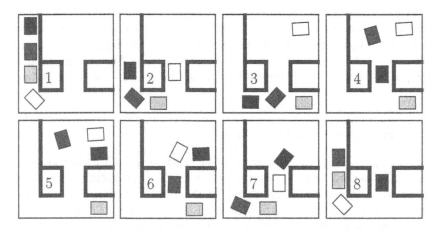

**Fig. 10.** Snapshots of a coordinated path for 4 car-like robots.

for this robot type, and some (induced) distance measure. It can be shown that proper choice of the local method guarantees probabilistic completeness, that is, any solvable problem will, with probability going to 1, be solved in finite time [17]. Various extensions of the approach have been developed. One such extension has been described in this paper, dealing with the multi-robot path planning problem. Another extension deals with robots that have non-symmetric control system, like for example car-like robots that can only move forwards. Here, directed graphs are used for storing the roadmaps. Path planning amidst movable obstacles is another problem to which *PPP*-like planners have recently been applied.

# References

1. J. M. Ahuactzin, E.-G. Talbi, P. Bessiere, and E. Mazer. Using genetic algorithms for robot motion planning. In *10th Europ. Conf. Artific. Intell.*, pages 671–675, London, England, 1992. John Wiley and Sons, Ltd.
2. J. Barraquand, L. Kavraki, J.-C. Latombe, T.-Y. Li, R. Motwani, and P. Raghavan. A random sampling scheme for path planning. *Intern. Journal of Rob. Research*, 1995, submitted.
3. J. Barraquand and J.-C. Latombe. Robot motion planning: A distributed representation approach. *Internat. Journal Robotics Research.*, 10(6):628–649, 1991.
4. B. Faverjon and P. Tournassoud. A practical approach to motion planning for manipulators with many degrees of freedom. In *Proc. 5th Intern. Symp. on Robotics Research*, pages 65–73, Cincinnati, OH, USA, 1990.
5. Th. Horsch, F. Schwarz, and H. Tolle. Motion planning for many degrees of freedom - random reflections at C-space obstacles. In *Proc. IEEE Internat. Conf. on Robotics and Automation*, pages 3318–3323, San Diego, USA, 1994.
6. Y. Hwang and N. Ahuja. Gross motion planning—a survey. *ACM Comput. Surv.*, 24(3):219–291, 1992.
7. L. Kavraki. *Random networks in configuration space for fast path planning*. Ph.D. thesis, Department of Computer Science, Stanford University, Stanford, California, USA, January 1995.
8. L. Kavraki and J.-C. Latombe. Randomized preprocessing of configuration space for fast path planning. In *Proc. IEEE Internat. Conf. on Robotics and Automation*, pages 2138–2145, San Diego, USA, 1994.
9. L. Kavraki, P. Švestka, J.-C. Latombe, and M.H. Overmars. Probabilistic roadmaps for path planning in high dimensional configuration spaces. *To appear in IEEE Trans. Robot. Autom.*, 1996.
10. K. Kondo. Motion planning with six degrees of freedom by multistrategic bidirectional heuristic free-space enumeration. *IEEE Transactions on Robotics and Automation*, 7(3):267–277, 1991.
11. F. Lamiraux and J.-P. Laumond. On the expected complexity of random path planning. Technical Report 95087, LAAS, Toulouse, France, March 1995.
12. J.-C. Latombe. *Robot Motion Planning*. Kluwer Academic Publishers, Boston, USA, 1991.
13. M.H. Overmars. A random approach to motion planning. Technical Report RUU-CS-92-32, Dept. Comput. Sci., Utrecht Univ., Utrecht, the Netherlands, October 1992.
14. M.H. Overmars and P. Švestka. A probabilistic learning approach to motion planning. In *Algorithmic Foundations of Robotics*, pages 19–37. A. K. Peters, Boston, MA, 1994.
15. S. Sekhavat and J.-P. Laumond. Topological property of trajectories computed from sinusoidal inputs for nonholonomic chained form systems. In *Proc. IEEE Internat. Conf. on Robotics and Automation*, April 1996.
16. S. Sekhavat, P. Švestka, J.-P. Laumond, and M.H. Overmars. Multi-level path planning for nonholonomic robots using semi-holonomic subsystems. In *Algorithmic Foundations of Robotics*, Toulouse, France, July 1996.
17. P. Švestka. On probabilistic completeness and expected complexity of probabilistic path planning. Technical Report UU-CS-96-20, Dept. Comput. Sci., Utrecht Univ., Utrecht, the Netherlands, May 1996.

18. P. Švestka and M.H. Overmars. Coordinated motion planning for multiple car-like robots using probabilistic roadmaps. In *Proc. IEEE Internat. Conf. on Robotics and Automation*, pages 1631–1636, Nagoya, Japan, 1995.
19. P. Švestka and M.H. Overmars. Motion planning for car-like robots using a probabilistic learning approach. *To appear in Intern. Journal of Rob. Research*, 1996.
20. P. Švestka and M.H. Overmars. Multi-robot path planning with super-graphs. In *Proc. CESA'96 IMACS Multiconference*, pages 482–487, Lille, France, July 1996.
21. P. Švestka and J. Vleugels. Exact motion planning for tractor-trailer robots. In *Proc. IEEE Internat. Conf. on Robotics and Automation*, pages 2445–2450, Nagoya, Japan, 1995.

# Learning in Order to Reason: The Approach

Dan Roth[1]

Dept. of Appl. Math. & CS,
Weizmann Institute of Science
Rehovot 76100
Israel
danr@wisdom.weizmann.ac.il
http://www.wisdom.weizmann.ac.il/~danr

## Abstract

Any theory aimed at understanding *commonsense* reasoning, the process that humans use to cope with the mundane but complex aspects of the world in evaluating everyday situations, should account for its flexibility, its adaptability, and the speed with which it is performed. Current theories of reasoning, however, do not satisfy these requirements, a fact we attribute, at least partly, to their separation from learning.

While the central role of learning in cognition is widely acknowledged, most lines of research nevertheless study the phenomenon of "learning" separately from that of "reasoning". The work presented here is motivated by the belief that learning is at the core of any attempt at understanding high level cognitive tasks. A formal model for the study of reasoning is developed in which a learning component has a principal role, and its advantages over traditional formalisms for the study of reasoning are shown.

This paper presents an integrated theory of learning, knowledge representation and reasoning within a unified framework called *Learning to Reason*. The Learning to Reason framework combines the interfaces to the world used by known learning models with a reasoning task and a performance criterion suitable for it. It is shown that the framework efficiently supports "more reasoning" than traditional approaches and at the same time matches our expectations of plausible patterns of reasoning. Several results are presented to substantiate this claim, presenting cases where learning to reason about the world is feasible but either reasoning from a given representation of the world or learning representations of the world do not have efficient solutions.

Overall, this framework suggests an "operational" approach to reasoning, that is nevertheless rigorous and amenable to analysis. As such, it may be a step toward a rigorous large-scale empirical study of learning and reasoning.

The paper presents work originally introduced by Khardon and Roth [KR94a] and surveys further developments made within this framework in more recent works.

# 1 Introduction

Consider a baby robot, starting out its life. If it were a human being, nature would have provided for the infant a safe environment in which it can spend an initial period of time. In this period the robot adapts to its environment and learns about the structures, rules, meta-rules, superstitions and other information the environment provides. In the meantime, the environment protects it from fatal events. Only after this "grace period", is the robot expected to have "full functionality" in the environment, but naturally, its performance depends on this environment and reflects the amount of interaction it has had with it.

While the central role of learning in cognition is widely acknowledged, early theories of intelligent systems have assumed that cognition (namely, computational processes like reasoning, language understanding, object recognition and other "high level" cognitive tasks) can be studied separately from learning, or as phrased by Kirsh [Kir91], that "learning can be added later".

This paper presents a new framework for the study of Reasoning. In contrast to earlier approaches to reasoning, the *Learning to Reason* framework views learning as an integral part of the process, and suggests to study the entire process of *learning* some knowledge representation and *reasoning* with it.

In this framework an agent is given access to its favorite learning interface, and is also given a grace period in which it can interact with this interface and construct a representation KB of the world $W$. The reasoning performance is measured only after this period, when the agent is presented with its reasoning task. A related scenario in which the agent learns and reasons in an on-line fashion is also studied and sometimes yields a more natural view of the learning and reasoning process.

In the Learning to Reason framework it is not assumed that the knowledge representation describing the "world" is *given* to the agent. Instead, the agent constructs the knowledge representation while interacting with the world. In this way the reasoning task is no longer a "stand alone" process, and the agent does not need to reason from a previously defined "general purpose" knowledge representation. Rather, it can choose a knowledge representation that facilitates the reasoning task at hand. Moreover, we take the view that a reasoner need not answer efficiently *all* possible queries, but only those that are "relevant", or "common", in a well defined sense. This relaxation can be used by the agent in selecting its knowledge representation. In addition, by viewing the interaction of the agent with the environment while learning and reasoning in a unified way the performance of the agent can be measured relative to the environment it interacts with. Thus, while in the Learning to Reason framework the knowledge representation used by the agent is still a crucial ingredient, its effectiveness now depends on whether it is efficiently learnable and, at the same time, supports efficient reasoning performance relative to the environment.

We prove the usefulness of the Learning to Reason approach by showing that through interaction with the world, the agent truly gains additional reasoning power, over what is possible in the traditional setting. Several results are presented to substantiate this claim, presenting cases where learning to reason about the world is feasible but either (1) reasoning from a given representation of the world or (2) learning representations of the world do not have efficient solutions.

In this paper we present a high level survey of the theoretical work within the Learning to Reason framework. The work on this framework started by Khardon and Roth in [KR94a], and many of the works discussed here are extensions of this paper in various directions. No technical details are given in this presentation. Rather, we motivate the framework, present its high level principles and briefly discuss how they can be implemented and what results they yield. For preliminaries on reasoning, learning and rigorous definitions for the material presented here, consult [KR94a].

## 1.1 Motivation

The generally accepted framework for the study of reasoning in intelligent systems is the knowledge-based system approach [McC58, Nil91]. It is assumed that the knowledge is given to the system, stored in some *representation language* with a well defined meaning assigned to its sentences. The sentences are stored in a Knowledge Base (KB) which is combined with a reasoning mechanism, used to determine what can be inferred from the sentences in the KB. Many knowledge representations can be used to represent the knowledge in a knowledge-based system. Different representation systems (e.g., a set of logical rules, a probabilistic network) are associated with corresponding reasoning mechanisms, each with its own merits and range of applications. The question of how this knowledge might be acquired and whether this should influence how the performance of the reasoning system is measured is normally not considered. The intuition behind this approach is based on the following observation:

**Observation:** *If there is a learning procedure that can learn an exact description of the world in representation R, and there is a procedure that can reason exactly using R, then there is a complete system that can learn to produce "intelligent behavior" using R.*

We believe that the separate study of learning and the rest of cognition is, at least partly, motivated by the assumption that the converse of the above observation also holds. Namely, that if there is a system that can Learn to Reason, then there is a learning procedure that can learn a representation of the world, and a reasoning procedure that can reason with it.

Computational considerations, however, render the traditional self-contained reasoning approach as well as other variants of it not adequate for common-sense reasoning. This is true not only for the task of deduction, but also for many other forms of reasoning which have been developed, partly in order to avoid the computational difficulties in exact deduction and partly to meet some (psychological and other) plausibility requirements. All those were shown to be even harder to compute than the original formulation [Sel90, Pap91, Rot96]. As a consequence, a lot of recent work in reasoning aims at identifying classes of limited expressiveness, with which one can perform some sort of reasoning efficiently [LB85, Cad95, Lev92, Sel90]. However, none of these works meet the strong tractability requirements for common-sense reasoning (as described, for example, in [Sha93]), even though, (as argued, for example, in [DP91]) the inference is sometimes restricted in implausible ways.

Very few works have considered the question of integrating theories of reasoning and learning in any formal way. In fact, results in these two fields are in a fairly disconnected state. The current emphasis of the research in learning is on the study of inductive learning (from examples) of concepts (binary classifications of examples). In this framework the performance of the learner is measured when classifying future examples. Perhaps the most important open question in learning theory today is concerned with the learnability of DNF or CNF formulas (the problems are equivalent in the current framework). However, even if one had a positive result for the learnability of these classes, this would be relevant only for classification tasks, and cannot be used for reasoning. The reason is that if the output of the learning algorithm is a CNF expression, then it cannot be used for reasoning, since this problem is computationally hard. From a traditional reasoning point of view, on the other hand, learning a DNF is not considered interesting, since it does not relate easily to a rule based representation. Alternative representations studied in learning theory are also not geared towards supporting the reasoning task, and are thus not directly usable. Other problems that exist in the interface between a learning algorithm and a reasoning algorithm are discussed later in this paper.

In this work, therefore, while we build on the framework and some of the results of computational learning theory, we distinguish the traditional learning task which we call here *Learning to Classify* (L2C) from the new learning task, *Learning to Reason*.

The Learning to Reason approach should also be contrasted with various knowledge compilation studies [SK96, MT93]. There, a theory (KB) is given to the system designer who is trying to compile it, off line, into a more tractable knowledge representation, to facilitate the answering of future queries. In our approach, a world representation is not given to the agent, but instead, it is assumed that the agent can access the world itself via some reasonable interface and acquire information that, later on, will support query answering correctly and efficiently.

This work is similar in nature to the Neuroidal model developed by Valiant [Val94]. The model developed there provides a more comprehensive approach to cognition, and akin to our approach it views learning as an integral and crucial part of the process. There, the agent reasons from a learned knowledge base, a complex circuit, and thus can be modeled by our framework. Indeed reasoning in the Neuroidal model shares many properties with the Learning to Reason framework. One difference is that in some instances of the Learning to Reason framework, though not all, in an effort to give a more formal treatment of a reasoner that has learned its knowledge base, we restrict our discussion to a fixed, consistent world.

# 2 Learning to Reason

Motivated by the abovementioned computational considerations we argue that a central question to consider, if one wants to develop computational models for commonsense reasoning, is how the intelligent system acquires its knowledge and how this process of interaction with its environment influences the performance of the reasoning system. Thus the Learning to Reason theory is concerned with studying the entire process of *learning* some knowledge representation and *reasoning* with it. In its most abstract form the Learning to Reason approach has the following principles:

- Intelligent agents are not omniscient:
  The view of commonsense reasoning taken here is that the agent has to function in a very complex world that may be hard to represent exactly. Luckily, the agent need not be omniscient, but rather has to perform well on a fairly wide, but restricted, set of tasks. Thus, the requirements from the reasoning stage may be relaxed.

- The goal of the learning stage depends on the required functionality:
  The learning stage is not evaluated by how well its output models the world, but rather by how well it supports the required functionality. Given, for example, that the agent is only required to perform well on a restricted[1] class of tasks, there may not be a need for the agent to learn a complete description of the world. A partial or approximate representation may be sufficient to support the relaxed reasoning requirements.

- Interaction with the world is a key issue:
  The interaction of the agent with its environment during the learning stage is an important aspect of this view. The type of interaction assumed depends on the task the agent is to perform and may range from observing examples, actively studying the environment using membership queries, interacting with a teacher or "being told" some facts. Naturally, there may be a tradeoff between the strength of this interaction and the resulting functionality.

- The knowledge representation used may depend on the functionality:
  The notion of knowledge representation is as important in the Learning to Reason framework as in the more traditional KBS framework. However, the effectiveness of the knowledge representation here depends on its learnability and on how well it supports inference, rather than on its comprehensibility. In this way, there may not exist a "general purpose" knowledge representation on which a "general purpose" inference engine can act. Instead, various

---

[1] This should not be taken too narrowly. The intention is not to perform well a single mission, but rather learn in order to perform well on a fairly wide collection of tasks, which share some commonality. This is the way it has been used in the cases already studied.

different knowledge representations should learned in order to support various tasks.

- The performance of the agent is measured with respect to the world it functions in, and not in any absolute terms:
  The world in which the agent performs its task is the same world that supplies the agent the information when learning. One interpretation of this principle may be that the performance of the agent is measured only on a collection of tasks that are "relevant" or "common" in the environment.Another may be that the same arbitrary "world" that supplies the information in the learning phase is used to measure the agent's performance later. In its general form this principle induces a unified way to view the interaction of the agent with its environment during the learning and reasoning stages, and suggests that both should be governed by the same distribution.
  In general, there may not be a need to appeal to a notion of a "world" at all (e.g., by not making any assumptions on the world the agent functions in) when the performance of the agent on the required functionality can be measured with respect to the functionality observed while learning.

- Rigor and efficiency:
  The aim was to define the framework in a way that is rigorous and amenable to analysis. For this purpose the interaction of the agent with its world is defined in a formal way (as in Computational Learning Theory), as are the tasks to be performed and any assumptions made on the world the agent functions in. In addition, it is usually required that Learning to Reason is done in time that is polynomial in the natural complexity parameters.

## 3   Results

Reasoning, as the term is used in AI, is viewed as having a major role in several high level cognitive tasks, including language understanding, high level vision and planning, tasks which rely on performing some sort of *inference*. A basic inference task considered in this context, that of *deductive inference*, is the focus of this presentation. In the first part of this section we concentrate on the ideas as presented by Khardon and Roth in the original paper on this framework, and discuss some of the results proved there. Later, we briefly survey some other results proved within this framework. The results are presented at a high level and without any of the technical details. Consult the relevant papers for those.

### 3.1   General Framework

Several general questions regarding the relation of the Learning to Reason (L2R) framework to the two existing ones, the traditional reasoning framework and the traditional learning framework have been considered [KR94a]. Most of these were considered for the task of deductive reasoning. First, it was shown that when the class of queries is not restricted, L2R implies L2C. However, the interesting aspect of this is that this property does not hold if the class of queries is restricted in some natural way (see next section). A second basic question to consider concerns the possibility of Learning to Reason by putting together existing learning and reasoning algorithms. As pointed out earlier, this approach has a problem whenever the output of the learning algorithm does not support efficient reasoning, as happens in many of the commonly used knowledge representations. Even when this is not a problem, it turns out that the straightforward approach that builds a L2R system by reasoning from the output of a (PAC or mistake bound) L2C algorithm, has some shortcomings. In particular, it is shown that a PAC learning algorithm, provided that it has an additional property ("learning from below"), can be combined with a reasoning algorithm to yield a PAC-Learn to Reason algorithm. The significance of this result, however, is that it exhibits the *limitations* of L2R by combining reasoning and learning algorithms: relaxing the requirement that the algorithm learns from below is not possible. Similar behavior is shown for mistake-bound algorithms.

## 3.2 Deductive Reasoning

The most striking evidence to the usefulness of this approach is given in the context of deductive reasoning. It is shown that the new framework allows for efficient solutions even in cases where the separate learning and reasoning tasks are not tractable. The following results are shown for Learning to Reason algorithms that use a set of models (satisfying assignments) as their knowledge representation. The results build on a characterization of reasoning with models developed in [KR94b] (based on ideas from [Bsh95]).

- **Learning to Reason without Reasoning:**
  Consider the reasoning problem $W \models \alpha$, where $W$ is some CNF formula and $\alpha$ is a $\log n$CNF (i.e., a CNF formula with at most $\log n$ literals in each clause). Then, when $W$ has a polynomial size DNF[2] there is an exact and efficient Learning to Reason algorithm for this problem, while the traditional reasoning problem (with a CNF representation as the input) is NP-Hard.

- **Learning to Reason without Learning to Classify:**
  Consider the reasoning problem $W \models \alpha$, where $W$ is any Boolean formula with a polynomial size DNF and $\alpha$ is a $\log n$CNF. Then, there is an exact and efficient Learning to Reason algorithm for this problem, while the class of Boolean formulas with polynomial size DNF is not known to be learnable in the traditional (Learning to Classify) sense.

Learning to Reason algorithms that use formulas as their knowledge representation are also considered and results of the same nature can be shown there too.

---

[2] The DNF representation is not given to the reasoner. Its existence is essential, since the algorithm is polynomial in its size.

Of course, these algorithms do not solve NP-hard problems. Rather, the additional reasoning power is gained through the interaction with the world. In the first instance, examples from the world are used to construct the model-based representation. In the second instance the queries presented by the interface are used to construct the approximation of $W$. An additional crucial observation used is that in order to reason with respect to $W$ one need not learn $W$ exactly. Instead, it is sufficient to use the least upper bound approximation of $W$. (The least upper bound approximation is, in some sense, [SK96, KR94b] the function closest to $W$ in the class of queries we reason about). These approximations are shown to be learnable in a form that supports the reasoning task efficiently, and this is used to prove the Learning to Reason results.

These results show that neither a traditional reasoning algorithm (from the CNF representation) nor a traditional learning algorithm (that can "classify" the world) is necessary for Learning to Reason. Moreover, the results exemplify the phrase "intelligence is in the eye of the beholder" [Bro91], since our agent seems to behave logically, even though its knowledge representation need not be a logical formula and it does not use any logic or "theorem proving".

To summarize, the new positive results are made possible by a combination of several features, which can be viewed as a direct application of the general principles listed above to the current instantiation. First, we relax the inference problems by restricting the classes of queries considered[3], while, at the same time, using different knowledge representations (that may not be in the traditional comprehensible form) in which this can be exploited. Second, we represent in our KB the least upper bounds of the "world" function rather than the exact representation. Third, and perhaps conceptually most important, our formal framework for the study of reasoning is different from previous ones since we allow the agent to interact with the world, and can therefore measure its performance relative to the world.

# 4 Other Learning to Reason Results

As mentioned above, the framework should be seen in a more general context and can be applied in a variety of tasks. We briefly point to results which have be recently developed for other, related, reasoning tasks within this framework. We discuss in the following only theoretical results within this framework, and do not consider more applied work that is influenced by this framework [GR96].

## 4.1 Abductive Reasoning

The results cited above are based on learnability results for model-based representations. Together with the results in [KR94b], which show how model-based

---

[3] Notice that restricting the classes of queries considered does not change the intractability of the deduction problem, if the world is represented traditionally, as a CNF formula.

representations can be used for efficient abductive reasoning (see there for details on the abduction formalisms used) this yields an algorithm for Learning to Reason abductively. Moreover, as in the deductive case, the result obtained can be phrased as a "Learning to Reason without Reasoning" result.

## 4.2   Default Reasoning

As in the case of abductive reasoning, learnability results for model-based representations, together with the results in [KR95a], which show how model-based representations can be used for efficient default reasoning, yield an algorithm for Learning to Reason with defaults. In particular, the results provide a "Learning to Reason without Reasoning" result to fragments of Reiter's default logic.

## 4.3   Reasoning with Partial Assignments

The deductive reasoning approach presented above has been extended in [KR95b] to handle partial assignments in the input. Several interpretations for partial information in the interface with the environment are discussed there and the work on model-based representations is extended to deal with partially observable worlds. Then, learning to reason algorithms that cope with partial information are presented. These results exhibit a tradeoff between learnability, the strength of the oracles used in the interface and the expressiveness of the queries asked. As in the cases above, it is shown that one can learn to reason with respect to expressive worlds, that cannot be learned efficiently in the traditional learning framework, and do not support efficient reasoning in the traditional reasoning framework. In addition, this work suggests another important motivation for the study of reasoning (and in particular, deductive reasoning) and for integrating it with learning. It is shown that when dealing with partial information in the interface, classification problems become deductive reasoning problems.

## 4.4   Non-Monotonic Reasoning

In [Rot95, Val95] a different view of reasoning in the presence of partial assignments is developed. The approach presented there implements in its general form the L2R principle that the performance of an agent is measured with respect to the world it functions in. Namely, the interaction of an agent with its environment during the learning and reasoning stages are defined in a unified way, via the notion of an *observation*.

This is used to formalize the intuition that incomplete information may actually help to support efficient and plausible reasoning; the underlying assumption is that missing information in the interaction of the agent with its environment may be as informative for future interactions as observed information.

Formally, [Rot95] shows that the problem of reasoning from incomplete information can be presented as a problem of learning attribute functions over a generalized domain. Several examples, which have been used over the years as "bench-marks" for various formalisms and that illustrate various aspects of the non-monotonic reasoning phenomena, are considered and translated into Learning to Reason problems. It is then demonstrated that these have concise representations over the generalized domain and it is shown that these representations can be learned efficiently, yielding Learning to Reason algorithm that learn to reason non-monotonically.

## 4.5 Learning to Take Action

[Kha96] extends the framework in another direction and studies planning problems. As in other instances of the Learning to Reason framework, the problem of learning to take actions is viewed as a supervised learning problem. In this case, the learning problem is in a dynamic stochastic domain; the agent receives observations (a teacher acting in the world) and learns from it an acting strategy. This model implements the L2R principles and, in particular, the performance of the agent is measured with respect to the world it functions in with very few assumptions made on the world. The knowledge representation selected in this case is that of production rule systems and it is shown that action strategies based on this representation can be learned. The most significant addition to the framework developed there is that the agent *acts* in the world, and there by changes it. Other works in planning which can be viewed within the Learning to Reason framework include, for example, [Bau96].

## 4.6 Learning Active Classifiers

Many classification algorithms are "passive", in that they assign a class-label to each instance based only on the description given, even if that description is incomplete. In contrast, an *active* classifier can, at some cost, obtain the values of missing attributes, before deciding upon a class label. The problem of learning active classifiers is formalized and studied in [GGR96]. It is shown there that while the "learn then optimize" approach to this problem is certainly sufficient (in principle) to determine active classifiers, it can fail (for complexity reasons) in various ways. Perhaps the main point made there is that one may be better off learning the active classifier directly. The basic idea implements some of the L2R principles, in that it is suggested to learn just enough to perform some particular task, in a representation tailored to this task, rather than trying to learn everything.

## 5 Conclusions

We have presented the *Learning to Reason* framework, a recently introduced framework for the study of reasoning in intelligent systems, and surveyed some of the recent results shown within it.

The *Learning to Reason* approach is intended to overcome some of the fundamental problems in earlier approaches to reasoning. This framework differs from existing ones in that it sees learning as an integral part of the process, it avoids enforcing rigid syntactic restrictions on the intermediate knowledge representation, and it makes explicit the dependence of the reasoning performance on the input from the environment.

The usefulness of the Learning to Reason approach is shown by exhibiting few interesting results, that are not possible in the traditional setting. For the problem of deductive reasoning we have shown cases in which the new framework allows for successful Learning to Reason algorithms, but stated separately, either the reasoning problem or the learning problem are not (or not known to be) tractable. Results of the same nature have been shown also for other inference problems including various reasoning and planning formalisms.

We have made explicit the main principles of the approach and have demonstrated that these can implemented in various ways in many inference problems. In all these cases we have shown that the Learning to Reason approach efficiently supports "more reasoning" than traditional approaches and at the same time matches our expectations of plausible patterns of reasoning.

Certainly, these are not the only works which can be viewed as implementations of the L2R principles. Some practitioners have argued before, as is argued here, for an "operational" approach to the study of reasoning. One of the contributions of this line of research is that it shows, in a formal sense, that an operational approach is not a "necessary evil" but rather a well justified path and moreover, that an "operational" approach to reasoning can be developed, that is rigorous and amenable to analysis.

We believe that this framework is a step toward constructing an adequate computational theory of reasoning. One major difference between the traditional, knowledge-based system approach to intelligent inference and the L2R approach is that the latter approach suggests that for large scale reasoning to work in practice, reasoning systems need to be trained over a large number of examples. Integrating the knowledge acquisition stage with the reasoning stage in a plausible manner, as suggested here, may thus be an important step toward a rigorous large-scale empirical study of learning and reasoning.

# References

[Bau96]  E. Baum. Toward a model of mind as a laissez-faire economy of idiots. In *Proc. of the International Conference on Machine Learning*, 1996.

[Bro91]  R. A. Brooks. Intelligence without representation. *Artificial Intelligence*, 47:139–159, 1991.

[Bsh95]  N. H. Bshouty. Exact learning via the monotone theory. *Information and Computation*, 123(1):146–153, 1995.

[Cad95]  M. Cadoli. *Tractable Reasoning in Artificial Intelligence*. Springer-verlag, 1995. Lecture notes in Artificial Intelligence, vol. 941.

[DP91]  J. Doyle and R. Patil. Two theses of knowledge representation: language restrictions, taxonomic classification, and the utility of representation services. *Artificial Intelligence*, 48:261–297, 1991.

[GGR96] R. Greiner, A. Grove, and D. Roth. Learning active classifiers. In *Proc. of the International Conference on Machine Learning*, 1996.

[GR96] A. R. Golding and D. Roth. Applying winnow to context-sensitive spelling correction. In *Proc. of the International Conference on Machine Learning*, 1996.

[Kha96] R. Khardon. Learning to take actions. In *Proc. of the National Conference on Artificial Intelligence*, pages 787–792, 1996.

[Kir91] D. Kirsh. Foundations of AI: the big issues. *Artificial Intelligence*, 47:3–30, 1991.

[KR94a] R. Khardon and D. Roth. Learning to reason. In *Proc. of the National Conference on Artificial Intelligence*, pages 682–687, 1994.

[KR94b] R. Khardon and D. Roth. Reasoning with models. In *Proc. of the National Conference on Artificial Intelligence*, pages 1148–1153, 1994. To appear in Artificial Intelligence Journal.

[KR95a] R. Khardon and D. Roth. Default-reasoning with models. In *Proc. of the International Joint Conference of Artificial Intelligence*, pages 319–325, August 1995. To appear in Artificial Intelligence Journal.

[KR95b] R. Khardon and D. Roth. Learning to reason with a restricted view. In *Workshop on Computational Learning Theory*, pages 301–310, July 1995.

[LB85] H. Levesque and R. Brachman. A fundamental tradeoff in knowledge representation and reasoning. In R. Brachman and H. Levesque, editors, *Readings in Knowledge Representation*. Morgan Kaufman, 1985.

[Lev92] H. Levesque. Is reasoning too hard ? In *Proceeding of the 3rd NEC research Symposium*. 1992.

[McC58] J. McCarthy. Programs with common sense. In R. Brachman and H. Levesque, editors, *Readings in Knowledge Representation, 1985*. Morgan-Kaufmann, 1958.

[MT93] Y. Moses and M. Tennenholtz. Off-line reasoning for on-line efficiency. In *Proc. of the International Joint Conference of Artificial Intelligence*, pages 490–495, August 1993.

[Nil91] N. J. Nilsson. Logic and artificial intelligence. *Artificial Intelligence*, 47:31–56, 1991.

[Pap91] C. H. Papadimitriou. On selecting a satisfying truth assignment. In *Proc. 32nd Ann. IEEE Symp. on Foundations of Computer Science*, 1991.

[Rot95] D. Roth. Learning to reason: The non-monotonic case. In *Proc. of the International Joint Conference of Artificial Intelligence*, pages 1178–1184, 1995.

[Rot96] D. Roth. On the hardness of approximate reasoning. *Artificial Intelligence*, 82(1-2):273–302, April 1996.

[Sel90] B. Selman. *Tractable Default Reasoning*. PhD thesis, Department of Computer Science, University of Toronto, 1990.

[Sha93] L. Shastri. A computational model of tractable reasoning - taking inspiration from cognition. In *Proc. of the International Joint Conference of Artificial Intelligence*, pages 202–207, August 1993.

[SK96] B. Selman and H. Kautz. Knowledge compilation and theory approximation. *Journal of the ACM*, 43(2):193–224, March 1996.

[Val94] L. G. Valiant. *Circuits of the Mind*. Oxford University Press, Nov. 1994.

[Val95] L. G. Valiant. Rationality. In *Workshop on Computational Learning Theory*, pages 3–14, July 1995.

# Database Semantics in Heterogeneous Environment

Jaroslav Pokorný

Charles University, Department of Software Engineering,
Faculty of Mathematics and Physics, Malostranské nám. 25
118 00 Praha 1, Czech Republic

**Abstract.** The notion of attribute is presented as a universal construct for describing conceptual and database models. Unifying tools based on the typed lambda calculus give possibilities to define appropriate notions for expressing an equivalency of schemes in different models. Moreover, the expressiveness of conceptual and data models is defined an compared to the recent approaches. A taxonomy of conceptual and database models based on these notions is proposed. particular models will be compared with respect to their expressiveness. Practical consequences of the theory developed could help in constructing so called co-operative information systems as well as in transforming user requirements between two different kinds of information environment.

## 1 Introduction

For a reasonable supply of information it is necessary to access external databases. The main problem of their common manipulation is the design autonomy of them, the using different data models, model different aspects of the real world and a natural consequence of human understanding - the semantic relativism appearing in modeling the same situation [BMN93].

Speaking more generally, one of the largest information systems (ISs) challenges is semantic interoperability (e.g., integrating or co-ordinating semantically similar but separately developed databases such as all those containing customer information). Similar observations are now identified in approaching WWW data. Particularly, the problem occurs when heterogeneous information resources are considered and there is requirement to access them in an unified way. The reason, why no sufficiently successful solution of the problems given above exists, lies in a weakness of formal models applied in our database world. There is the need for enriching, modifying or replacing the current data/conceptual models. Partially expressed semantics offered by well-known database models does not reflect exactly the semantics of the real world.

On the other hand, the database theory has its own sources appropriate for expressing database meaning. Usually, he notion of conceptual schema plays a significant role. It serves not only as a design stage in a top-down approach supporting IS development, but it can be used as a tool for explaining database meaning. Since database schemes arise from conceptual schemes by a transformation, it is clear that the corner stone for database semantics studying lies there.

The paper is focused on a database theory based on the notion of attribute. In Section 2 some issues concerning database semantics are summarized. Section 3 is devoted to fundamentals of attribute theory based on a functional type system, a typed lambda calculus, and an intensional logic. In Section 4 some key notions of the database theory are specified. Various measures for comparing of information contained in attributes are discussed. Section 5 contributes to solving problems of expressiveness of different database models. Section 6 comparises our approach with related works. Finally, some conclusions are shortly mentioned.

## 2 Database Semantics - General Ideas

The fundamental question appearing in connection with data semantics is „what is data semantics". For our goal, we will discuss these questions in Section 2.1. In Section 2.2, we briefly summarize well-known ISO approach to database semantics. It will serve to us as the referential one for further considerations. In Section 2.3 , we identify a collection of goals that arise in the using of database semantics in practice.

### 2.1 What, Where, How

In [Sh95], where Sheth summarizes interesting issues from the panel of the DS-6 conference, several perspectives are offered. One of them, typical for the IS context, says that semantics can be viewed as a mapping between an object modelled, represented and/or stored in an IS (e.g. an „object" in a database) and the real-world object(s) it represents. Intuitively, data semantics is a connection from a database to the real-world outside the database.

Another issue is to distinguish between „data semantics" and „data application semantics", i.e. the latter view emphasizes that applications provide the context of the use of the data. Database designers should remark that the context is given by the conceptual schema. Each conceptual schema should support some form of agreement between the agents observing the real world. It is useless to talk about semantics without an agreement. Speaking in more software engineering terms, we can look for semantics of a database in the results of analysis and design of IS, e.g. not only in conceptual structures but also in functional descriptions (what) and, perhaps procedural ones (how). Certainly, one could ask for semantics of the conceptual structures. Obviously, the problems with their semantics are the same. The only difference is that conceptual structures are more closed to the application domain than database ones. Any other movement up in these levels of abstraction stops in the natural language. An agreement of agents on the level of natural language should be supposed as an axiom.

According to [Sh95] we can formulate the following basic issue:

- there is no semantics without an interpretation agent to determine/derive the „meaning" associated with data.

Thus semantics lie in the what people interact with, communicate, interpret, and use knowledge of application domain. The conceptual schema could at least partly solve this problem. One could think that the successful approach to data semantics depends strongly on possibilities of conceptual models and, consequently, modeling methods of application domain.

After outlining what is data semantics and where to find it, further associated question is how to represent it. The database history offers many approaches to reach it. We could recall again conceptual models or semantic networks (in better cases).

Unfortunately, these tools are very simple to express an often complex essence of objects in application domain. Most approaches deals with so called „weak semantics", i.e. with simple structural formalisms supported usually by some fragments of the 1st order logic. In contrary, „deep semantics" involves the issues of human cognition, perception, or interpretation. Associated theories are rather informal and intuitive (see, e.g. [ISO82], [SCS91], [LNE89]) in comparing to approaches to semantics of e.g. value-oriented database schemes ([Hu86], [HY84]). We remind that the latter approaches usually do not use the conceptual level at all.

## 2.2 The ISO Approach to Database Semantics

In early 80ties, the group of experts formulated quite sound theory of conceptual schemes and information bases [ISO82]. The notion of proposition was used. *Necessary propositions* hold in all object worlds and, naturally, sentences denoting these propositions belong to the *conceptual schema*. The set of object worlds expresses here the (time-variable) application domain. All other (logically consistent) propositions are denoted by sentences belonging to so called *information base*. For example, the proposition expressed by the sentence "Films are shown in theatres" belongs to the conceptual schema, "The Stargate is shown in Metro" belongs into the information base. Thus, conceptual schema and information base are expressions of a language. These ideas result into the schema on Figure 1.

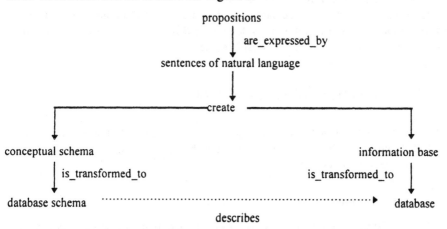

**Fig. 1.** Traditional schema of database semantics

The using of a natural language as the language of sentences to enhance the expressiveness of this approach is possible, but it is not developed in [ISO82] in detail. Moreover, a conceptual schema expressed by necessary propositions is not symmetrical in comparing to the (e.g. relational) database schema that expresses a type of certain data structures. We could remind e.g. the theory described in [Hu86], where database schema bears an information given by its instances. Thus, a schema and its instances are clearly separated. Returning to the ISO's conceptual level, there is no straightforward connection of a necessary proposition described in the conceptual schema with any "related" sentences - propositions from the information base.

The second critical aspect of the above approach concerns integrity constraints (ICs). To describe the database semantics it is not necessary to support the traditional approach resulting in formulating database IC used as filters separating false data. This idea could be justified by the following consideration. Some necessary propositions model ICs. But they are redundant in the conceptual schema, since they are logical consequences of the information base. Semantics of a database is given by TRUE-propositions to which instances of the database correspond. Thus, we do not need any conceptual equivalents for ICs used on the database level.

Obviously, "right" data must be assumed in the above approach. ICs provide a useful information in a process of analysis and design in a traditional IS development life-cycle. Thus, we will consider them only occasionally.

### 2.3 Using Database Semantics

Suppose two (conceptual/database) schemes $S_1$ and $S_2$. Understanding database semantics can help to solve at least the following tasks:
- *accessing problem*: quering through $S_1$ database stored under $S_2$ (and vice-versa),
- *viewing problem*: viewing through $S_1$ databases stored under $S_2$,
- *data exchange problem*: transforming data stored under $S_1$ into a database stored under $S_2$,
- *design problem:* transforming schema $S_1$ into $S_2$.

We will discuss rather structural semantics of data, i.e. we omit an important aspect of databases - their behaviour. Approaches devoted to this problem are associated rather to object-oriented world and are not considered here.

## 3 Database Semantics through Attributes

A more natural approach for conceptual modeling is based on the notion of *attribute* viewed as an empirical function that is described by an expression of a natural language. Moreover, the function is typed.

### 3.1 Types and Domains

A hierarchy of types is constructed as follows. The existence of some (*elementary*) types $S_1,...,S_k$ ($k \geq 1$) is assumed. They constitute a *base* **B**. More complex types are obtained in the following way.

If $S,R_1,...,R_n$ ($n \geq 1$) are types, then
(i) $(S:R_1,...,R_n)$ is a (*functional*) type,
(ii) $(R_1,...,R_n)$ is a (*tuple*) type.
The set of *types* **T** over **B** is the least set containing types from **B** and those given by (i)-(ii).

*Remark:* The notation $(\beta{:}\alpha)$ is equivalent to $F\alpha\beta$ (Curry) and $(\alpha\rightarrow\beta)$ (Church).

When $S_i$ in **B** are interpreted as non-empty sets, then $(S{:}R_1,...,R_n)$ denotes the set of all (total or partial) functions from $R_1\times...\times R_n$ into S, $(R_1,...,R_n)$ denotes the Cartesian product $R_1\times...\times R_n$.

An important elementary type is Bool defined as the set {TRUE, FALSE}. The type Bool allows to type such objects as sets and relations. Sets and relations are modelled as unary and n-ary characteristic functions, respectively.

The fact that X is an object of type $R \in$ **T** will be written alternatively X/R, or "X is the R-object". For each typed object o the function type returns type(o) $\in$ **T** of o. For example, mathematical functions may be easily typed. Arithmetic operations +, -, *, / are examples of (Number:Number,Number)-objects. Logical connectives, quantifiers and predicates are also typed functions: e.g., **and**/(Bool:Bool,Bool), R-identity $=_R$ is (Bool:R,R)-object, universal R-quantifier $\Pi_R$, and existential R-quantifiers $\Sigma_R$ are (Bool:(Bool:R))-objects. R-singularizer $I_R$ /(R:(Bool:R)) denotes the function whose value is the only member of an R-singleton and in all other cases the application of $I_R$ is undefined. In the conceptual modeling, each base of elementary types consists of descriptive and entity sorts.

We emphasize that **T** described above gives a powerful tool for our approach. It is possible to type functions of functions etc. Since the characteristic function of a set models a set, the notion of set is redundant here.

### 3.2 Attributes

Some expressions of a natural language denote very natural "object structures" usable in building a database.

For example, "the film which they are showing at a given theatre at a given date" (abbr. FDT) is a (Film:Theatre,Date)-object, i.e. FDT is conceived as a (partial) function f:Theatre $\times$ Date $\rightarrow$ Film, where theatre, date, and film are appropriate sorts. Actually, this function - attribute is moreover parametrized by possible worlds and time moments. The notion of possible world is inspired by intensional logic (IL) (see, e.g. [Ti78]). In IL thinkable (logically consistent) states-of-affairs relative to the given language L constitute the logical space of L and are called *possible worlds*.

In a usual possible world, films are shown in theatres, and, moreover, one film in a given date. On the other hand, they are some possible worlds where they have not theatres or where there is more films in each theatre which they are showing in a given date. The timing in the attribute definition supports the life of object associations expressed by the attribute. Since FDT is not the typical case (time is included explicitly there), suppose the attribute "the director of a given theatre" (DT). DT provides different directors for a fixed theatre as they are changing with time.

More formally, *attributes* are functions of type ((S:T):W), where W is the logical space (possible worlds), T contains time moments, and S is from **T**. By $M_w$ we denote the application of the attribute M to $W/W$, $M_{WT}$ denotes the application of $M_W$ to the time moment $T$. We will often omit parameters W and T in type(M).

Objects - functions can be constructed in a more complicated way. For example, "the departments in a company" could be viewed as an attribute DC of type ((Bool:(Bool:Employee)):Company), i.e. the departments are classes of employees and the DC gives a class of classes (of peoples) for a given company.

### 3.3 Intensions and Extensions

Considering attributes as functions, we explore a lot of other functions that do not need possible world. For example, even numbers, COUNT, + (adding) provide such functions. They have the same behaviour in all possible worlds.

Thus, we can distinguish between two categories of functions: empirical (e.g. attributes) and analytical. The former are called *intensions*. They are conceived as partial functions from the logical space. Range of these functions are again functions (defined on the time moments). The latter functions are called *extensions*. Generally, extensions are of type R, where R is not (V:W) for any type V. Arithmetic operations, Boolean connectives, quantifiers, and aggregate functions are typical extensions. Analogously, FDT, DT, and DC applied to the possible world $W$ provide extensions.

### 3.4 Manipulating Functions

A manipulating tool for functions is a typed lambda calculus. Thus, we have obtained a cheap and powerful language for formulating schema transformation, queries etc.

Our version of the typed lambda calculus uses tuple types and it directly supports manipulating objects typed by **T**. Starting with a collection **Func** of constants, each having a fixed type, and denumerable many variables of each type, the *language of (lambda) terms* LT is defined as follows:

Let types R, S, $R_1$,..., $R_n$ (n≥1) are elements of **T**.

(1) Every variable of type R is a term of type R.

(2) Every constant (a member of F) of type R is a term of type R.

(3) If M is a term of type (S:$R_1$,..., $R_n$), and $N_1$,...,$N_n$ are terms of types $R_1$,..., $R_n$, respectively, then M($N_1$,...,$N_n$) is a term of type S.          */application/*

(4) If $x_1$,...,$x_n$ are different variables of the respective types $R_1$,..., $R_n$ and M is a term of type S, then **lambda** $x_1$,...,$x_n$(M) is a term of type (S:$R_1$,..., $R_n$)
          */lambda abstraction/*

(5) If $N_1$,...,$N_n$ are terms of types $R_1$,..., $R_n$, respectively, then
($N_1$,...,$N_n$) is a term of type ($R_1$,..., $R_n$).          */tuple/*

(6) If M is a term of type ($R_1$,..., $R_n$), then
M[1],...,M[n] are terms of respective types $R_1$,..., $R_n$.          */components/*

Terms can be interpreted in a standard manner by means of an interpretation assigning to each function symbol from **Func** an object of the same type, and by a semantic mapping [ ] from LT into all functions given by the type system **T**.

Speaking briefly, an application is evaluated as the application of an associated function to given arguments, a lambda abstraction "constructs" a new function. In the conventional approach a valuation δ used. This mapping allows to assign objects to every variable occurring in a term. Practically, we can consider e.g. [+(3,x)] as a parametrized function which gives 3 + x for given x (more precisely, for every δ).

For example, DC(IBM)(NETWORKS) is TRUE, if there is the department Networks in the company IBM (NETWORKS is a constant of type (Bool:Employee)). Certainly, it is true while NETWORK contains all employees of the department Network. Consequently, a discussion like this one is associated to a possible world, usually the actual one.

Assuming $W,T \in \mathbf{B}$, each attribute A (A is its identifier) can be specified by term **lambda** w (**lambda** t (A(w)(t)) where the symbol A (variable of LT of the same name) has the unique "consistent" valuation - the attribute A itself.

According to the semantics of the quantifiers and the singularizer, we can write simply **foreach** x(M) instead of $\Pi$(**lambda** x(M)). Similarly, **forsome** x(M) replaces $\Sigma$(**lambda** x(M)). Finally, we write I(**lambda** x(M)) shortly as **onlyone** x(M) and read "the only x such as M". (Naturally, M/Bool.)

Similarly, some aggregation operators as

$$COUNT_S/Number:(Bool:S), SUM_S/Number:(Bool:Number) \text{ etc.}$$

can be defined with usual meaning.

The deductive power of LT is generally given by ß-reduction. The main rule of the such system is so-called ß-rule **lambda** $x_1,...,x_n(M)(N) = M[x_i \leftarrow N[i]]$ where the right side of equality represents substitution of N[i] for $x_i$ in M. The typed lambda calculus has some useful properties. For example, ß-reduction is strongly normalizing, i.e. there is always the normal form for each term of LT, and this form is unique (Church-Rosser property).

### 3.5 Querying with Functions

The lambda calculus can be used as a theoretical tool for building a functional database language [Pok89],[Be94]. A *query* is expressed by a term of LT. For example

**lambda** z, n (n=COUNT(**lambda** f (**forsome** d (f=FDT(z,d)))) )

denotes the query "Give a class of couples associating to each theatre the number of films showing there". We note that the defining term can be more "structured", i.e. its type is generally an arbitrary type of **T**. The above query could be also reformulated as **lambda** z (**lambda** n (...). In our conceptual framework, each query is an attribute. In fact, attributes used in the query term are applied to a possible world, i.e. the defining term needs **lambda** w (**lambda** t ... in its head.

We remind here also the high-order function *map*, a well-known concept o functional programming. Suppose f/(R:S). Then *map*/(((Bool:R):(Bool:S)):(R:S)).

Let us now consider an example. The lambda term

$$\text{**lambda** f,t **lambda** d (f=FDT(t,d))} \qquad (1)$$

of type ((Bool:Date):Film,Theatre) defines the attribute "The dates in which they are showing a given film at a given theatre" (abbr. DFT). Suppose the *map* function for type(DFT). Its value is of type ((Bool:(Bool:Date)):(Bool:Film,Theatre)). Then *map*(DFT) gives the function associating with a class (relation) C(FILM,THEATRE) a class of classes. Each such class contains classes of dates. For example, for the class {(STARGATE,METRO),(STARGATE,OLYMPUS)} we could obtain the class {{03/08/96,03/09/96}, {03/04/96}}. Sometimes the set-collapse operation may follow. Its effect provides a simplification of the above result, i.e. the class {03/08/95,03/09/95,03/04/95} is obtained.

There are at least two possibilities how include *map* into LT. One direction is to add typed constants $map_R$ into **Func** (since our LT has no type polymorphism). A similar solution offers the language MC mentioned in [Be94]. This language, unfortunately, does not allow to use lambda abstraction to create higher-order function.

Due to a flexibility of LT, the second approach is allowed. There is a straightforward possibility to define a term simulating $map_R$.

Finally, we mention the version of the functional language of Shipman's Functional Data Model [Gr92]. The language only allows nested applications of functions. The functional *map* is hidden in context-oriented semantics of multivalued functions.

We will consider the attribute FT/((Bool:Film):Theatre), i.e. FT(OLYMPUS) returns a class of films. Let NAME_OF_FILM be the attribute assigning to films their names. Thus, NAME_OF_FILM is single-valued. Its application to a class of films, i.e. NAME_OF_FILM(FT(OLYMPUS)) returns a class of names, i.e. the result that is not too close to our strongly typed apparatus.

The language LT makes it possible to increase its computational power by adding new built-in functions into **Func**. Thus, it is not computationally complete. There are other approaches based on lambda calculus providing a computationally complete language. We refer to [PK90] for details about FDL language in which functions are "programmed" by multiple equations rather than by an external language (as e.g. constants in **Func**).

### 3.6 Attributes and Propositions, Information Capability

Attributes are "containers" of information. Given the extension of the attribute A in a possible world $W$ and time moment $T$ (shortly $WT$) it is possible to generate the set of *basic propositions*; they are denoted by sentences such as "they are showing the film Stargate at the Metro on March 8th". These propositions are, obviously, expressible by LT and they contribute to the information base (in the similar sense as in Section 2.2). Propositions are ((Bool:T):W))-objects, i.e. intensions in IL. Then the above proposition is specified by term

$$\textbf{lambda } w \textbf{ (lambda } t \text{ (FDT}_{wt}(\text{METRO},03/08/95) = \text{STARGATE}))$$

By $BP_{A,WT}$ we will denote the set of basic propositions generated by A in $W$ and $T$. With propositions the notion of logical implication is naturally connected. Let P, Q be two sets of propositions. Then P *logically implies* Q iff in all $WT$ in which all the members of P are true, the members of Q are true as well. For any class of propositions P the function *entailment* Cn associates to P all its logical consequences. It is easy to prove that P logically implies Q iff Cn(Q) is subset of Cn(P).

The *information capability* of the attribute A in $WT$ is defined as Cn($BP_{A,WT}$) in [Du92]. To extend the notion to include more attributes is straightforward.

### 3.7 Definability of Attributes

The lambda calculus provides an appropriate tool for defining new attributes from a set of attributes. For the purposes of formal defining of basic database notions, we won't require an arbitrary language LT. We call a language LT *database-applicable*

iff it has the following properties:
1. Bool, Real (or T) and W are among the types of **B**.
2. There is a distinguished binary predicate $=_R$ for any type R among constants of **Func**.
3. There are logical connectives, R-quantifiers and R-singularizer (for any R) among constants of **Func**.

In the remainder of the paper, we will consider database-applicable languages LTs only. All other LTs may be considered as an extension of a given database-applicable language LT. We will assume a fixed interpretation assigning to symbols of **Func** in LT their intended interpretation.

Similarly to database schemes (or view schemes), attributes need not be mutually independent. For example the attributes DFT and FT can be expressed by FDT. Generally, an attribute A is *definable* over attributes $A_1,...,A_n$ iff there is a term M of LT such that
1. M is composed from $A_1,...,A_n$, and at most from function symbols from **Func** and variables,
2. no subterm of M is logically true or false formula,
3. $A_w = M_w$ for all possible worlds.

(Recall that equality in the point 3. is a partial function.) The term M is called a *defining term* for A.

Again, it is straightforward to extend the notion of definability to a relation between two sets of attributes. For example, the term (1) parametrized by w and t is the defining term for DFT. The attribute FT is expressible as

**lambda w(lambda t(lambda h(lambda f (exists d (f=FDT$_{wt}$(h,d))) )))**

A special case is offered by two attributes A, B sharing the same domain. Then A is *strong definable from* B, if there is a function $f$ giving for each possible world

$$A_w(x) = f(B_w(x))$$

for all x. Comparing this condition to the condition 3. from definition of definability, the difference is essential. The former concerns a transformation $f$ of values of extension B applied to x, the latter involves a transformation $f$ (obtainable using M) of extension of B as the whole. For example, "Ancestors of a person" (abbr. AP) and "Predecessor of a person" (abbr. PP) are defined on Person and they are mutually definable. On the other hand, they are not strongly mutually definable. The set of ancestors of x cannot be computed from the $PP_w(x)$ alone. More of the PP extension is necessary. Strong definability implies definability but not vice versa.

In [DKMS86] the notion of definability is studied in connection to the notion of informational equivalence of attributes. Two sets A, B of attributes are *informationally equivalent* iff for every possible world the respective information capabilities of A and B are the same. Furthermore, in [DKMS86], it is shown that the notions of informational equivalence and definability are interchangeable, i.e. A, B are informationally equivalent iff A and B are mutually definable.

## 4. Modeling Databases

In this section we redefine well-known database notions which create building stones for a hierarchy of schemes usually used in designing a database. Our hierarchy of abstractions divides the conceptual level into four sublevels:

(C1) expressions of a natural language,

(C2) abstract constructions (attributes)

(C3) description of attributes in LT (conceptual schema)

(C4) description of data structures (database schema).

Certainly, attributes exactly model an application realm. They include all necessary information for information base generating. On the conceptual schema level it is mostly appropriate to add usual ICs that provide a guide for an implementation of an associate database. Their patterns on (C2) level are propositions called often *consistency constraints* (CCs) [Zla85].

Let LT be a database-applicable language. Then a *conceptual schema* (with respect to LT) is a couple $S_{LT} = (A,I)$ where $A$ is a tuple $(A_1,...,A_n)$ of typed variables of LT called *attribute identifiers* and $I$ is a tuple of other terms of LT representing CCs. In [Du92], analytical and empirical CCs are distinguished. The former give TRUE in all possible worlds, the latter depend on the logical space.

Note that each conceptual schema $S_{LT}$ is a term of LT. It is reasonable to restrict ICs to terms with attribute identifiers as the only ones free variables.

Let $A = (A_1,...,A_K)$ ($K \geq 1$) and $\delta$ be a valuation. Since $\delta(A)$ returns the attribute A, we can obtain the set $\{\delta(A_1),..., \delta(A_K)\}$ of attributes and create its information capability $P_W$ for the given possible world $W$. The set $P_W$ of propositions might be called an *information base* of $S_{LT}$ for $W$. We denote it $S^*$ whenever we assume a fixed language LT and a fixed world $W$. Often $W$ is the actual world. Trivially, propositions described by $I$ must be contained in $P_W$.

On the other hand, the above construction is quite abstract. We need "data-bearers" that are storable in a database. When is $A_{WT}$ representable? For example, while type($A_{WT}$) is built from user defined sorts from $B$. The database level is dependent on the database model chosen. Usually, we can easily omit parametrizing by W and T in type($A$) in most of cases. The conceptual ICs are transformed to sentences of a formal language (usually they are expressed as closed formulas of the predicate calculus). Possibly, other ICs will appear. They correspond to so called inherent ICs (e.g. the functionality of LT may cause generating functional dependencies in RDM). The revised schema of database semantics is depicted in Figure 2.

Finally, what is the appropriate generalization of the notion of model from that of conceptual and database modeling? One observation is that it is sufficient to consider only the set of generic types chosen to characterize a model.

**Definition 1.** Let **Sorts** be a countable set of *sort variables* ranging possible (entity and descriptive) sorts. Replacing the base $B$ by the set of sort variables in the definition of type system $T$, we obtain *parametrized types* $T_{Par}$. Then any subset of $T_{Par}$ is said to be a *modeling tool*. Its members are called *constructs*.

**Definition 2.** If the only types allowed as valuations of sort variables are descriptive sorts, then each defined modeling tool is called a *value-oriented* (or *database*) *model*.

If a modeling tool is not value-oriented model, then it is called a *conceptual model* (or *object-oriented model*).

*Remark:* Today, the notion object-oriented is rather applied in object-oriented approach, where objects have methods etc.

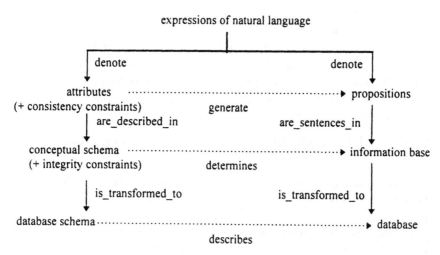

**Fig. 2.** Revised schema of database semantics

## 4.1 Taxonomy of Modeling Tools

We present now above notions by examples. By $E$ we will denote variables valuated by entity sorts, $D$ will be used for descriptive sorts, $C$ denotes either $E$ or $D$. The following modeling tools cover some well-known database and conceptual models:

- $E_1,...,E_n,D_1,...,D_m$ (m,n $\geq$ 1)          *sortalization*

- (Bool:$D_1,...,D_m$) (m$\geq$1)          *relational data model*

- (Bool:$E_1,...,E_m$) (m$\geq$2)          *Chen's E-R model*

  ($D:E_1,...,E_m$) (m$\geq$1)

- (Bool:$E_1,E_2$), (Bool:$E,D$), (Bool:$D,E$)          *Binary E-R model without functionality*

- ($D:E$), ($E:D$), ($E_1,E_2$)          *Binary E-R model with functionality*

- (Bool:$E_1,...,E_m$) (m$\geq$1)          *Chen's E-R model with class construct*

  ($D:E_1,...,E_m$) (m$\geq$1)

- (Bool:$E_1,...,E_m$)          *Chen's E-R model with*

  ($D:E_1,...,E_m$)          *multivalued attributes*

  ((Bool:$D$):$E_1,...,E_m$) (m$\geq$1)

- (Bool:$E_1,...,E_m$)          *Chen's E-R model with class construct*

$(D:E_1,...,E_m)$ (m>1)        *and class attribute*

$(D:(\text{Bool}:E))$

- $((\text{Bool}:C_1,...,C_n):(C_{n+1},...,C_m))$     *HIT data model(simple types)*

$((C_1,...,C_n):(C_{n+1},...,C_m))$

$(n \geq 1, m \geq 2)$ and at least one $C$ is $E$

- Consider $D_1,...,D_m$ $(m \geq 1)$ We call them *parametrized simple types*. A *parametrized nested type* is defined recursively as follows:
  - A parametrized simple type is a parametrized nested type.
  - If $T_1,...,T_k$ $(k \geq 1)$ are parametrized nested types, then $(\text{Bool}:T_1,...,T_k)$ is a parametrized nested type.     *nested relations*

- $(D:(\text{Bool}:(\text{Bool}(E),\text{Bool}(E))))$     *relationships among classes*

*Remarks*:
◊ The last modeling construct is of higher-level. Its application is required e.g. in the modeling statistical data [Pok96b]. Subtyping (ISA-hierarchies) is also possible [Pok96a].
◊ Allowing $E$ variables among parametrized simple types results in construct that are supported in modeling tools known as complex objects.
◊ Parametrized types containing the Bool type are interpreted usually as total functions in practice. For example, Codd's relations contain only „positive" tuples and no negative information. This is equivalent to assume the Closed World Assumption (e.g., [Ull88]). Generally, above constructs make it possible to distinguish that a function is non-defined or returns the empty set.


## 4.2 Semantic Information

Using attributes to enhance the possibilities of conceptual and data modeling has been studied intensively in 80ties [MP81], [Zla85], [DKMS86], [Mat87], [Pok89] on the HIT Data Model. A predominant theme in much of this work has been to explain most of well-known database problems in the functional approach. It has been shown that query languages, schema transformations etc., can be expressed in a powerful and effective way.

More general discussion concerning informational capability of attributes is studied in [DM90], [Du92]. Two mutually non-comparable measures for attributes comparing are proposed there.

The first is based on so called distinguishing capability of attributes. Two attributes A,B (having the same domain of their extension) have the same *distinguishing capability* iff for every possible world there exists a function $f$ (bijection) providing an appropriate transformation of the B extension on the A extension. One direction in comparison of A and B supposes a function surjection only. B has *greater distinguishing capability* than A if for each possible world there is a function $f$ (surjection) such that

$$A_w(x) = f(B_w(x))$$

for all x. We emphasize that the $f$ is generally different in different possible worlds. This contrasts to definability attributes where a "universal" function $f$ is required. There is shown in [Du92] that definability implies distinguishing but not vice versa.

Consider, e.g., the assigning of ZIPs to towns. TOWN_IN_ADDRESS and ZIP_OF_ADDRESS are both defined on addresses. There is a function $f$ assigning to each town its ZIP. That is, ZIP_OF_ADDRESS has greater distinguishing capability than TOWN_IN_ADDRESS. The attribute TOWN_IN_ADDRESS is neither strong definable nor definable from ZIP_OF_ADDRESS. The function $f$ is not analytical, but empirical.

A partly positive result associates strong definability to distinguishing capability in one direction. If A has greater distinguishing capability than B, then B is strongly definable from A.

The second relation between attributes studied in [Du92] is connected with the amount of information generated from attributes, i.e. with cardinality of the set of different values that $A_w(x)$ returns for different values of x. This is called a *comparison based on cardinality*. For example, BOOK_NUMBER and ISBN_OF_BOOK (both defined for copies of books) could be compared in this sense. Obviously, BOOK_NUMBER is greater with respect its cardinality than ISBN_OF_BOOK. The comparison based on cardinality is not in any relationship to the distinguishing capability. The overview of all notions is depicted on Figure 3.

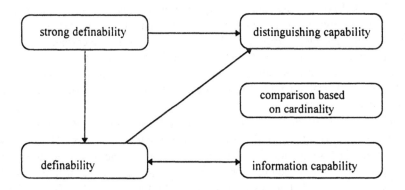

**Fig. 3.** Relationships of notions

We shortly mention the notion of information capacity studied in [Hu86], [HY84], and others. Their results are based on various classes of mappings between instances of two relational databases schemes. The information capacity of some relational schema S determines its set of instances (compare with the notion of information capability in Section 3.6). Unfortunately, any semantic correspondence between these schemes is not required there. None of the classes of mappings has been shown to guarantee this.

# 5. Comparing Modeling Tools

It is often claimed that the possibilities of all E-R approaches are approximately the same. However, diversity of all entity-oriented approaches does not give a unique decomposition of object system. The works [Pok89], [Pok93] are focused on a formalization of the notion of expressiveness of modeling tools. It is shown that this expressiveness depends on basic objects given in the conceptual realm (a certain "similarity" of elementary types) and on basic constructs allowing to construct conceptual bridges between notions in different conceptual realms.

We omit here expressiveness of value-oriented models because their information bases are databases, i.e. data structures without underlying conceptual schemes. Associated existing theories rely rather on data dependencies than on information that data structures represent.

## 5.1 Unification of Bases

Ensuring such "compatibility" of two possible worlds is partly achieved by a *unification* of bases of elementary types and with the help of so called *integration attributes*. To be of the same expressive power, two conceptual/database models must guarantee that every conceptual schema in the former model must be expressible in the latter model and vice versa.

We extend the notion of informationally equivalent attribute sets to schemes. Schemes $S_i = (A_i, I_i)$ (i=1,2) are said to be *informationally equivalent* iff $A_1$ and $A_2$ are informationally equivalent and $I_1$ may be converted into $I_2$ by appropriate substitutions of attributes and vice versa. The substitutions are made in accordance with mutual definability of the respective attribute sets. This is correct, if one assumes certain "compatibility" of types in $B_1$ and $B_2$, since a common LT can not be assumed. At least, the types in $B_1$ that are not in $B_2$ must be expressible by means of substitution as types of $B_2$ and vice versa.

Formally, a *substitution*, $\Theta_{ij}$, is a finite mapping from $B_i$ to $T_j$ (i ≠ j). $B_i \Theta_{ij}$ stands for the result of applying $\Theta_{ij}$ to $B_i$. Thus, we can assign a new base of elementary types, $B_i'$, to $B_i$. Each substitution can be written as a set of bindings enclosed in curly braces. A particular case is adding elementary types allowed by substitutions of the form $\{\leftarrow S\}$, where $S \in B_j$. For example, let $B_1 = \{Bool, S_1, S_2, S_3\}$, $B_2 = \{Bool, R_1, R_2\}$, and $\Theta_{12} = \{S_3 \leftarrow (Bool:(Bool:R_1))\}$, $\Theta_{21} = \{R_2 \leftarrow (S_1, S_2)\}$. After applying these substitutions we obtain bases $B_1'$ and $B_2'$. It is easy to verify that $B_1' = B_2'$.

If there are substitutions $\Theta_{12}$ and $\Theta_{21}$ such that $B_1' = B_2'$, then $B_1$ and $B_2$ are said to be *unifiable*. According to unifiability, $B_1'$ and $B_2'$ are said to be *unified*. Results of particular substitutions results in B-unifiability. We say that $B_i'$ is $B_j$-*unified* (i≠j). Obviously, two identical bases are unifiable.

In practice, we specify the substitution by a set of bindings. For example, bases specified in example are unifiable. It implies, that a notion denoting an object of type $R_2$ is expressible by a couple of notions of type $(S_1, S_2)$.

The substitution $\Theta_{ij}$ is not only a formal construction as should be to seem from the above considerations. Let us to consider, for a moment, the base

$$B_3 = \{Bool, S_1, S_2, S_3, R_1, R_2\},$$

i.e. $B_3 = B_1 \cup B_2$. Then, e.g., $S_3$ given by the binding $S_3 \leftarrow (Bool:(Bool:R_1))$ has one possible interpretation expressing an association (a bijection) of objects o/$S_3$ to objects o'/Bool:(Bool:$R_1$). On an intuitive level, the base $B_3$ makes an integration environment for "miniworlds" given by bases $B_1$, $B_2$. In other words, there is a so called *integration attribute* Is-explained-as of type $((Bool:(Bool:R_1)):S_3)$. The reversed attribute to it can be called Is-covered-by/ $(S_3:(Bool:(Bool:R_1)))$. Notice that Is-explained-as and Is-covered-by are rather generic names for expressing these semantic connections. Thus, a unification of bases is designer-oriented (empirical) process. The above integration attributes are in a good accordance with our intuition. They express a deepness of our notions used in modeling the object system.

As a more realistic example, we assume that the object system is defined over the base $B_1 = \{Theatre, Bool, Actor, Street, House\#\}$. Another possibility how to model the same starts with basic sorts given by the base $B_2 = \{Bool, Actor, Address\}$. In this case, theatres are modelled, e.g., as classes of actor groups which are playing in particular plays. So, we can specify these facts by the attribute

$$\text{is-explained-as}_{Theatre}/((Bool:(Bool:Actor)):Theatre),$$

i.e. to each theatre a class of actor groups is assigned. Similarly, the sort Address can be conceived as the couple (House#, Street), the attribute

$$\text{is-explained-as}_{Address}/((House\#, Street):Address)$$

describes this fact. Certainly, not all substitutions are useful. Given a couple of substitutions $\Theta_{12}$ and $\Theta_{21}$, we draw a *dependency graph* DEP, where nodes are sort symbols from $B_1$, $B_2$. There is an arc from x to y if there is a member of substitution $\Theta_{12}$ or $\Theta_{21}$ of form y $\leftarrow$ ...x... .The couple of substitutions is *well-formed* if their dependency graph has no cycle. We will suppose this property in all considerations that follow.
*Remark:* Remind that the cycle checking algorithm runs in O(k) where k is the number of arcs in DEP. Finding out all cycles is computational hard (exponential time).

## 5.2 Expressiveness of Conceptual Models

To formalize the idea of "the same expressiveness" of two modeling tools, a definition were proposed in [POK89] requiring the unifiability of bases of respective environments LTs. Informally, what is conceptually expressible in the first modeling tool must be expressible in the second and vice verse. But simple examples show that the unifiability of base is not enough. A priori given unifiable bases are too weak requirement. Even unified bases do not give the full possibility to construct information equivalent conceptual schemes, since information "compatibility" depend on concrete conceptual relationships built from sorts of **B**.

We propose a modified definition. First, a connection of conceptual models to LTs must be specified. We say that a conceptual model $\Gamma$ is *applied w.r.t. a language* LT, if sort variables of $\Gamma$ are valuated by sorts of LT.

**Definition 3.** Let $\Gamma_1$ and $\Gamma_2$ be two conceptual models applied w.r.t. $LT_1$ and $LT_2$, respectively, that differ mutually in $B_1$ and $B_2$ only. Then $\Gamma_2$ *dominates* $\Gamma_1$, if for each conceptual schema $S_1$ in $\Gamma_1$ there is $B_2'$ and a conceptual schema $S_2$ in $\Gamma_2$ applied w.r.t $LT_2'$ (i.e. $LT_2$ with the base $B_2'$) such that $S_1$ and $S_2$ are informationally equivalent. We say that $\Gamma_1$ and $\Gamma_2$ have the *same expressive power* if each of them dominates the other.

It is easy to prove that $B_2'$ in the definition 3 is $B_1$-unified. Each two $B_1$ and $B_2$ associated with respective conceptual models having the same expressive power are unifiable. In [Pok89] the equivalence of Binary model with functionality and Chen's E-R model was briefly proved. Also a statistical classification (class of classes) was proved to be redundant as a modeling construct added to the Chen's E-R model. The paper [Pok93] includes the proof of equivalance of Binary model without functionality and Chen's E-R model as well as that Chen's E-R model dominates Chen's E-R model with class construct.

## 5.3 Conceptual vs. Database

Considering real problems with the database semantics, the notions of information capability on the conceptual level (C3) should be in a relationship with information capacity in the sense of [Hu86] on the database level (C4). Databases in our approach are only approximations of information bases. This fact follows from impossibility to design all ICs. With the assumption of correct data it is possible to find schema transformations from level C3 (conceptual schema) into level C4 (e.g. relational schema) that induce correct mapping between sets of instances of the schemes (definition on the sense of [MIR94]). Various E-R models have been successfully studied in the past (e.g. [MM90]), HIT [DKMS86], and the others. Particularly, there are correct implementations a set of attribute extensions. In such cases, e.g. information equivalence on the level C2 (in the sense of Section 3.7) can imply the information equivalence in the level C4 (in the sense [Hu86]).

## 6 Related work

The problem associating of similar objects has been previously solved e.g. by Sheth and Kashyap in [SK93]. They introduce so called semantic proximity between object $O_1$ and $O_2$ by the 4-tuple semPro$(O_1,O_2) = $ <Context, Abstraction, $(S_1, S_2)$, $(St_1,St_2)$)> where $S_i$ are types of $O_i$ and $St_i$ is an extension of $O_i$ (as a value in some w and t). Note that authors distinguish so called real world semantics (compare to our notion of attribute) and model world semantics (compare to implementation of $A_{wt}$ in a database). Clearly, two objects having different extensions in the databases can have the same extensions in the application domain. The term Context refers here to the context in which a particular similarity holds.

Speaking by our terms, the Context is given by two environments (perhaps two possible worlds) based on bases $B_1$ and $B_2$, respectively. The term abstraction refers to a mechanism used to map the types of objects to each other. Some of the more useful abstractions include: a total bijection of type (S2:S2), a partial function of type

(S2:S2), generalization, functional dependencies. The last two abstractions are also expressible with our notion of integration attribute.

Authors of [DHS93] define also the Context for resolving semantic heterogeneity. Their Context is defined as a data structure that gives the meaning and the environmental information of the database extension. The environment here means the scope of the data, the constraints and rules that the data need to follow. The proposed model unifies databases extension and its schema with an appropriate context. The result reminds a semantic network using four abstractions: subsumption, aggregation, association, and membership. A query mechanism is given which modifies queries from one context into queries in other context.

For example, the query „Give conductors of films which they are showing at Olympus" can not be answered from the database about theatres (conductors are not stored in this context), but in the context of the database belonging to the Film institute it is possible. Other form of the context is used in [SSR94].

## 7 Other Research

It is now widely recognized in the database research community that modeling evaluation of conceptual structures is as important as dealing with static aspects of the conceptual schema. In [Pok94], the functional approach extended to three-level description of behaviour is described. Due to a very close relationship between conceptual modeling and object-oriented technology, the strategy used in [Pok96a] to specify typed objects, and data functions (attributes) in object-oriented environment, follows the above database philosophy.

## References

[Be94] Beeri, C.: Query Languages for Models with Object-Oriented features. In: Advances in Object-Oriented Database Systems, A.Dogac, Springer-Verlag, 1994.

[BMN93] Busse,R., Müller,A., E.J.Neuhold: Information Handling - A Challenge for Databases and Expert Systems. Proc. of DEXA'93, Springer-Verlag, 1993.

[DKMS86] Duží,M., Krejčí,F., Materna,P., Staníček,Z.: HIT Method of Data Base Design (a Functional Approach to Information Representation). Res. Rep., Technical Univ. Brno, 1986.

[DM90] Duží,M., Materna,P.: Attributes: Distinguishing Capability versus Information Capability. Computers and AI, Vol. 9., 1990, No. 2, pp. 169-185.

[DHS93] Duong, T., Hiller, J., Srinivasan, U.: A Unifying Model of Data, Metadata and Context. Proc. of DEXA '93, Springer-Verlag, 1993.

[Du92] Duží,M.: Semantic Information Connected with Data. Proc. of ICDT'92, Springer-Verlag, 1992, pp.376-390.

[Gr92] Gray,P.M.D.: Combining Functional and Logic Programming in Expert Database Systems. In: Expert Database Systems, K. Jeffery (ed.), Academic Press, 1992.

[Hu86] Hull, R.: Relative information capacity of simple relational database schemata. SIAM J. of Comput., 15,3,1986, pp. 856-886.

[HY84] Hull, R., Yap, C.K.: A format model: A theory of database organization. Journal of ACM, 31 (3), 1984, pp. 518-537.

[ISO82] van Griethuysen (ed.): Concepts and Terminology of the Conceptual Schema and Information Base. ISO/TC97/SC5/N695/,1982.

[LNE89] Larson, J.A., Navathe, S.B., Elmasri, R.: A Theory of Attribute Equivalence in Databases with Application to Schema Integration. IEE Trans. on Software Engineering, Vol. 15, No. 4, 1989, pp. 469-463.

[Mat87] Materna,P.: Entity Sorts: What are They ?. Computers and AI,6,4,1987.

[MIR94] Miller, R.J., et al: Schema Equivalence in Heterogeneous Systems: Bridging Theory and Practice. Proc. of 4th Int. Conf. on Extending Database Technology, M. Jarke, J. Bubenko, K. Jeffery (Eds.), Springer-Verlag, 1994.

[MM90] Markowitz, V.M., Makowsky, J.A.: Identifying Extended Entity-Relational Object Structures in Relational Schemas. IEEE Transactions on Software Engineering, Vol. 16, No. 8, 1990.

[MP81] Materna,P., Pokorný,J.: Applying Simple Theory of Types to Databases. Information Systems,6,4,1981, pp.283-300.

[PK90] Poulocassilis,A., King,P.: Extending the functional data model to computational completeness. Proc. of EDBT-90, Springer Verlag, LNCS 4/6, pp. 75-91.

[Pok89] Pokorný, J.: A function: unifying mechanism for entity-oriented database models. Entity-Relationship Approach, C.Batini (ed.), Elsevier Science Publishers B.V. (North-Holland), 1989, pp. 165-181.

[Pok93] Pokorný, J.: Semantic relativism in conceptual modeling. Proc. of Int. Conf. DEXA' 93, Springer-Verlag, 1993, pp. 48-55.

[Pok94] Pokorný,J.: On Behaviour Modeling Using a Functional Approach. Proc. of the 4th Int. Conf. ISD'94, Bled, 1994, pp. 73-82.

[Pok96a] Pokorný,J.: Functional information modeling in an object-oriented environment. Proc. of the Fifth International Conference Information Systems Development - ISD'96, Gdansk, 1996 (in press).

[Pok96b] Pokorný,J.: Conceptual modeling of statistical data. Proc. of Int. Conf. DEXA'96, Zurich, 1996 (in press).

[SCS91] Saltor, F., Castellanos, M., García-Solaco: Suitability of data models as canonical models for federated databases. ACM SIGMOD Rec., (Special isssue: Semantic issues in Multidatabase Systems), Vol. 20, No.4, pp. 4-48

[Sh95] Sheth, A.: Data Semantics: what, where and how? Summary of the Panel discussion of DS-6 Conference, 1995

[SK93] Sheth, A., Kashyap. V.: So far (schematically) yet So Near (Semantically). Proc. of the DS-5 Conf. on Semantics of Interoperable Database Systems, Hsiao, D., Neuhold, E., Sacks-Davis R. (eds.), IFIP Transactions A-25, North-Holland, 1993.

[SSR94] Sciore, E., Siegel, M., Rosenthal, A.: Using Semantic Values to Facilitate interoperability Among Heterogeneous Information Systems. ACM TODS, 19, 2, 1994, pp. 254-290.

[Ti78] Tichý,P.: Two Kind of Intensional Logic, Epistemilogie, 1, 1978, pp. 143-146.

[Ull88] Ullman, J.: Principles of Database and Knowledge-Base Systems. Vol. 1, Computer Science Press, 1988.

[Zla85] Zlatuška,J.: HIT Data Model. Database from the Functional Point of View. VLDB'85, Stockholm, 1985.

# Business Case Processing - Rationale, Survey and Trends

Kenneth Robinson and Damian Mac Randal

User Interface Design Group Leader, Information Systems Engineering, Department for Computation and Information, Rutherford Appleton Laboratory, Chilton, Didcot, Oxon OX11 0QX, UK

**Abstract.** Modern businesses are increasingly under pressure to improve competitiveness. In recent years, it has been realised that a significant way to improve effectiveness is to identify and optimise the key *processes* that organisations undertake to achieve their business objectives. One element of business processes that is often important is IT support, and a significant aspect of modern IT support is business case processing (often called workflow). This paper will cover:

- Why processes are important to organisations.
- An overview of business case processing/workflow systems, highlighting those features which are most significant.
- A description of the results of a recent European project to develop a state of the art business case processing system.

## 1  Introduction

In this paper the role of business processes in keeping organisations effective through a period of great change is addressed. Firstly, the concept and importance of business processes, especially with respect to conventionally-structured organisations, is discussed. An overview of a popular approach by which organisations can investigate their own processes, re-design them, and then implement them is presented, illustrated by some real examples.

Business case processing (also called workflow) systems are increasingly used to provide IT support for business process execution. Many workflow systems are now available, and the capabilities and attributes of such systems are described. Criteria for choosing between them are also given, along with a select list of systems which are available in the marketplace. A brief summary of outstanding issues in the area is also provided, together with references to further information.

The paper concludes with a description of HICOS, a European Community project, which developed a state of the art business case processing system.

## 2  Business Processes and Re-engineering

In recent years, the importance of a process view on organisational operations and effectiveness has been realised. This section begins by providing a definition of business process, followed by an illustration of how the process view can impact organisational activities in fundamental ways. A brief description of business process re-engineering, a popular methodology for re-defining organisations from a business process viewpoint, is then given.

## 2.1 Background

Hammer and Champy's definition of process is "a group of related activities that takes one or more inputs and creates an output that is of value to a customer" [1]. An example process might be the set of activities involved in an insurance company when a client sends in a claim for repair to their car under a car insurance policy, following an accident. In many companies, the claim will be passed between several departments within the organisation. The net effect is that the elapsed time to handle the claim is often weeks; however, studies have shown that the actual *staff time* spent on the claim is often of the order of twenty minutes in total. The extra time has gone in passing information from one person to another, and waiting for the information receiver to start handling the next phase of the claim process.

>From the customer's point of view, the delay is time-consuming, expensive (a car may have to be hired in the interim), and frustrating. In today's world, customers are much more fickle in their allegiances to companies and products, and therefore retaining customer satisfaction is vital. In addition, competition from other insurance companies is intensifying with special policies appearing for various groups; as a result, change is now the norm. Flexibility is increasingly important.

Many companies still organise on a functional department basis, with a strict management hierarchy. This type of organisational structure has several problems, including a focus on structure, not process, so that management is overly concerned with retaining or increasing their own personal domains. Managers make decisions and give staff instructions, so the focus is on management, not the customer. As a result, many staff are under-motivated: they feel they are just another cog in a large system. No single person is responsible for the claim process; it may not even be recognised as a process as such. This type of process is said to be *fragmented*. Curiously, only the bureaucracy of the system actually achieves process completion. As a result, customers have difficulty in even finding out where their claim is in the system, increasing their frustration. Since the company focus is on organisational structure, the system is slow to respond to change, potentially lethal in today's marketplace.

How can the organisation improve the situation? By taking a process view, the whole claims process can be re-worked, via a process known as business process re-engineering. An overview of how this is approached, and some possible results, are described below.

## 2.2 Business Process Re-engineering (BPR)

Hammer and Champy's [1] definition of re-engineering is: "Re-engineering is the fundamental rethinking and radical re-design of business processes to achieve dramatic improvements in critical, contemporary, measures of performance, such as cost, quality, service, and speed."

The aim is to make order of magnitude improvements, so the key words in BPR are *fundamental/radical/dramatic*. [It should be noted that many companies feel the risks involved in BPR are too high, and aim to incrementally improve individual business processes; this activity is known as textitbusiness process improvement or BPI.]

It is important to set up a high quality team, with senior management backing, to undertake the reengineering exercise. This team needs to ask fundamental questions such as:

- Why do we do what we do?
- Why do we do it the way we do it?

bearing in mind the need to:

- Ignore what *is*, concentrate on what *should be*.

The first step in this process-oriented approach is to identify and analyse the current processes, typically defined by their inputs and outputs. The next stage is to identify what the new processes should be: a successful BPR exercise needs to look at the organisation overall to discover what the new process set might be. In many ways this is the hardest part of the exercise, as it is fatally easy to select current processes, not realising that the boundaries of the new processes may well differ markedly from the old.

Having chosen the new processes, one of these should be selected for redesign or improvement. It is important at this stage to be innovative and creative; this is where the major gains are to be made, as many existing processes contain redundant steps, heavyweight checking procedures, etc, which mitigate against an efficient and effective process.

Two examples serve to illustrate the sorts of approach that has proved useful:
*Car insurance claim procedures*

In the old model, the insurance company would send an assessor to estimate the likely cost of repair, and if the vehicle was deemed repairable, the customer would contact a number of garages, getting quotes, and following approval by the company, arrange the repair. Garage costs are kept down by selecting the lowest quote.

One new model is to *franchise* garages to do repair work. The customer is given a list of authorised repair agents, covering the country in reasonable density, to whom the car can be taken in the event of an accident. This simplifies markedly the process for both the customer and the insurance company. Garage costs are kept down by post facto checks; the occasional element of malpractice is easily spotted and the franchise removed if necessary. Note both the insurance company and the garage gain - the insurance company by reducing the amount of work to be done in processing the claim, the garage by getting guaranteed business. The customer is happier as the time to get the vehicle back on the road is much reduced, and the part of the process handled by the customer much simpler.

*Supermarket chain and suppliers*

In the old process, suppliers are informed by the supermarket chain of what and how much should be delivered, which branches should receive the deliveries, and when. In one new scenario, suppliers are given access to the supermarket chain database to decide when to resupply merchandise. The supermarket chain gains by not having to manage the inventory, do warehousing etc; the supplier gains by having guaranteed sales. In addition, advance knowledge of stock requirements is obtained, which means use of production lines can be optimised.

Note that in both cases the borderlines between organisations are becoming blurred - the process actually spans a number of organisations/people.

There are many examples of re-engineered processes that can be cited. An analysis of these shows that a number of *characteristics* emerge. Typically, several jobs are combined, and the workers themselves make decisions, rather than management. Process steps are performed in a natural order, with work being performed where it makes most sense. Processes often have multiple versions, so that the majority of cases, simple in nature, can be processed quickly. Checks and controls are reduced, and reconciliation is minimised. Customer satisfaction is improved by providing a single point of contact, as IT support enables data to be centralised and made available to decentralised users. In the organisation, hybrid centralised/decentralised operations become normal: IT support enables data to be centralised and made available to decentralised users.

Significant *culture* changes also take place. The new work unit is the *process team* (case teams, virtual teams, and so on), with multidimensional jobs becoming the norm (complex tasks for smart people, not simple tasks for simple people). Staff are empowered - they make the rules, not obey them, and authority is devolved. There are significant implications for staff recruitment and career development, as job preparation exercises move from a training focus to education. Performance and award systems also have to change, as results, not activity, are important, and advancement is a change, not a reward. Pay becomes dependent on performance, and promotion on ability. Performance itself may be measured by contacting customers to see how happy they are. pay on performance, promote on ability)

Inevitably, the *Organisation* changes. Staff values change, as work is productive, not protective. Staff work for *customers*, not bosses; are aware of their value to the organisation, and get paid for value created. As a result, they accept ownership of problems; feel they belong to a team; and are constantly learning. Management also changes; managers become coaches, and executives become leaders. Overall, organisational hierarchies flatten, improving communications within the organisation.

**Implications of IT developments** One of the critical drivers for process improvement is often the innovative impulse following from changes in information technologies. Blind application of IT to existing processes often, however, gives only a small, even negligible, gain. IT often produces major gains by changing the *rules* of the process game; the following table shows some of the ways in which this can take place.

| Old Rule | Disruptive Technology | New Rule |
|---|---|---|
| correct information in only one place | shared databases | information can appear where needed |
| only experts do complex work | expert systems | generalists can do work of expert |
| businesses centralise or decentralise | telecommunications | both possible |
| managers make all decisions | decision support tools | all jobs include decision-taking |
| field staff need offices for information | wireless-based data communications | data available everywhere |
| best contact with buyer is personal | online videodisc | best contact with buyer is effective |
| need to find out where things are | automatic identification/tracking | things tell you where they are |
| plans get revised periodically | high performance computing | plans automatically revised |

Due to limitations of space, this has necessarily been an overview. More detail on the re-engineering exercise can be found in [1], [2]. Further BPR references can be found in the WWW pages in [7], [8].

## 3  Workflow Management Systems (WfMS)

In this section the focus is on the characteristics and attributes of workflow systems, rather than individual workflow products themselves. Some criteria are presented for choosing between different workflow systems.

One definition of a workflow system is: "Workflow software is designed to improve business processes by providing the technology enabler for automating these aspects of the workflow: routing work in the proper sequence, providing access to the data and documents required by the individual work performers, and tracking all aspects of the process execution". One feature of a workflow tool is to allow the process logic to be modified separately from the task logic embedded in the user applications which the workflow links.

The market for workflow systems is immense; sales in the USA and western Europe in 1995 totalled $1B. Unsurprisingly, there are many vendors trying to sell their wares, but in some ways products are still immature, as we shall see. Customers are still cautious - the following data arises from a survey of Gartner Group clients:

| Status | Percentage |
|---|---|
| not planning | 8% |
| evaluate in 12 months | 27% |
| evaluating | 40% |
| pilot | 17% |
| wide use | 8% |

There are three main aspects to workflow:

− the processes which the WfMS is to support;
− the relationship of the workflow system to the organisation
  * modelling of staff relationships and organisational units
  * specific versus generic staff assignment
  * static and dynamic role resolution
  * predefined versus dynamically defined roles
− infrastructure - the IT platforms to be used, the storage of process definitions, and the introduction of the WfMS.

## 3.1 Attributes of WfMSs

At least four classes of WfMS can be identified:

**Production** designed to automate business-critical transaction-oriented processes (eg loan arranging, insurance claims, accounting).

**Collaborative** for business-critical processes that are not transaction-oriented (eg technical document production, software development).

**Administrative** desktop software to automate administrative work driven by paper forms (eg expense claims, purchasing, budgetting).

**Ad hoc** routing and tracking of routine office work that is based on unstructured information (eg information distribution, review/approval).

Improvements in information flow and integration are often results of installation of a WfMS. Productivity (and the ability to estimate it) and throughput are also improved. Other benefits include monitoring of operations and increased flexibility. A frequent benefit is that customer satisfaction is greater as a consequence. Other organisational benefits are reduced cost and staff time for a process, and improvement in staff morale by the automation of repetitive tasks. Those WfMSs with some BPR support obviously provide a powerful business tool.

The picture is not uniformly rosy, however. Unsatisfactory aspects include interoperability, scalability, and reliability problems. Cost, both in terms of purchase price and organisational investment (eg installation and maintenance) can be inhibiting. It also needs to be borne in mind that not all processes can be automated, and subjective events can define the workflow, causing problems.

## 3.2 Criteria in WfMS Choice

Given the complexity of these systems, a wide range of criteria needs to be considered before even piloting of a WfMS is sensible, let alone production use. The first question is - what is the basic model of product (ie, will it model the processes necessary?). There is little point in investing time in a system which cannot represent the types of process in the organisation.

The next major issue is the way in which the workflow definitions are created. Basically, these can be developed either using a graphical user interface tool, or via a scripting language. The former, if well-designed, is to be preferred, but it should be checked that the workflow definition is generated automatically from the graphical tool - some suppliers' tools merely offer the capability of drawing the process graphically, as an aid to visualisation, with no automatic definition generation for the execution engines. The skill required to use the tools should also be assessed - does the user have to be a programmer, or is it usable by, say, a business manager? In addition, some systems allow changing the workflow definition during process execution, which can be a considerable benefit if something unusual happens, unconsidered during the process design phase. However, this is a two-edged sword; there may be loss of process integrity as a consequence, so that auditing, legal, or quality requirements may be compromised.

Other features that are desirable include rule-based branching using a workflow variable value; parallel routing and rendezvous; event-driven routing; and queue sorting and filtering.

Document integration can also be critical. The document support system needs to handle all the document types required, and document index data should be easily accessible. Various strengths of coupling are possible between the WfMS and the document system, ranging from built-in, through tight, to loose coupling.

On the standards front, it is necessary to consider which standards are essential to the business. DDE, OLE, host data/SQL are favourites; APIs for system programmers are also needed.

Workflow standards are now emerging in the market sector. The Workflow Management Consortium was set up in 1993, and currently has some 175 members. They support five working groups, which are aiming to define workflow standards in the following areas:

- process definition model and interchange APIs
- client APIs
- application invocation interface
- workflow interoperability
- administration and monitoring

(More information can be found via the Workflow Management Consortium's WWW page at [10].)

## 3.3 Sources

A shortlist of some of the more well-known WfMSs is given here, followed by
supplier names:

FlowMark *IBM*

Cimage WorkflowCimage *Enterprise Systems*

1View:Workflow *Dorotech*

Dataflo *DataWorks*

Documentum *ECS*

Visual WorkFlo *FileNet*

Lava 4.3 *Lava Systems*

Staffware *MDIS*

MD&A Complete Process *Parallax Works*

Memo *Verimation*

Viewstar System *View Star UK*

Action Workflow System *Action Technology*

FloWare *Plexus*

InConcert *XSoft*

TeamWARE Flow *ICL*

Other sources of information can be found in references [3] [4] [5], and via
the WWW pages given in [6], [7], [9].

# 4  State of the Art Business Case Processing System - HICOS

## 4.1  Introduction

In trying to enhance competitive advantage, one major problem facing large European user organizations in sectors such as banking and insurance is the need
for an effective and efficient means for improving their work procedures. As an integrated business case processing system, HICOS provides effective mechanisms
to enable this. By focusing on the business process, rather than discrete tasks, it
provides improved internal structures for business case processing, more transparent and secure processes, and the ability to respond rapidly to a changing
business environment. It achieves this by providing a suite of modules covering
the complete process lifecycle, from business requirements identification through
to enactment in a production environment, covering:

**Case analysis:** analysing, scoping and outline (re-)design of a new or existing
case.

**Case design:** high level and detailed design or re-design of an existing case by
a domain expert (not an IT specialist).

**Case execution:** provision of the necessary information to case workers to enable them to decide which steps of the case should be undertaken next. A
range of platforms must be supported. In addition, support for disconnection
and reconnection is required for portable machines.

As part of this analysis, design and execution process lifecycle, HICOS directly tackles several issues that raise particular problems for organizations involved in BPR:

**Relation to existing systems:** the vast software investment in existing organisations means that it is totally impractical to suggest that these be replaced. Instead HICOS offers object-oriented "wrapping" for these legacy systems, allowing use of the already installed software. At the same time, this also provides a mechanism for migration to future technology bases, critical to the long-term future of the company. Examples of current systems that can be exploited by HICOS include mainframe based legacy software (via an object-oriented encapsulation), organisation models, and existing database systems.

**Distributed processes:** increasingly, companies are structured as semi-autonomous business units that interwork closely, and potentially have independent IT provision. Fully independent organisations now cooperate on specific initiatives by forming *virtual enterprises* with similar requirements. HICOS allows processes to be distributed across multiple execution platforms, the Case Processors, running on one or more machines. Current platforms include mainframes, Unix client-server systems and PC networks. Since the Case Processors are self-contained, it is possible to detach part of a case and execute it on a standalone PC. Thus mobile workers such as agents/brokers can be integrated into the process.

**Management of change:** since business processes are subject to a rapidly changing environment, it is important that process definitions can be easily modified without sacrificing the high level of rigour and quality demanded for business critical processes. The HICOS Case Builder Tool not only offers a graphical process editing capability, but also provides simulation/reasoning capabilities to enhance confidence in the correctness of the proposed process. The resulting definition can then be output in a form that is directly executable by the Case Processors.

The key issues for organisations using Business Case Processing Systems include:

- the correct identification of business processes
- support for (re-) engineering these processes in a user-natural way
- high confidence in the correctness of implemented processes (for auditing)
- evaluation and optimization of the processes before they go "live"
- integration with existing organisation models
- data management facilities
- easy phased migration from old technology to new

These features require support for identifying coherent business processes and then analysing, describing, modelling and defining them. Process definition, ideally, should be in a language that has some formal semantics, thus enhancing confidence that the case will operate as intended. Following definition, support is required for testing, execution, monitoring and adaptation of the business process. These captured processes may involve more than one organisation to achieve desired results, increasing the need for flexibility and robustness as well as interoperability with other automated or manual case processing systems.

These modules have been developed as part of the HICOS ESPRIT project, and showcases demonstrating the capabilities of the complete system have been completed in both insurance and banking areas. The following section will describe the HICOS system in more detail, concentrating on the process analysis and design features.

## 4.2   HICOS System Description

The HICOS system comprises three modules, corresponding to the analysis, design and execution phases of the process lifecycle. The first two phases embody the development system; the latter, the runtime system. The development system comprises of a methodology to identify, scope, design and optimize a process; tools to aid the capture of the results obtained from using the methodology; and a design tool to capture, design, evaluate and specify the process. The "output" from the development system is a specification of the business case in a formal language. The runtime system then supports instances of this case running on and across different platforms, including handling inter- and intra-organisational interworking and detached working on parts of processes. Each step of the case is passed to a case worker with the necessary role specification for that step, migrating the case to another Case Processor if necessary. The runtime system also handles invocation of the necessary software to carry out the primitive actions specified in the process. These "Application Objects" may carry out the task themselves, use existing legacy software, or merely pass on the request to a case worker - a manual action. The structure of the HICOS system is shown in in Figure 1. It should be noted that the AOs use client-server technology, so can run on any platform accessible to the HICOS system.

The development system "modules" have been designed to operate independently, so that alternative design tools could be used in conjunction with the BeCAMe methodology, and vice versa; or indeed one of the components could be used alone to support just part of the complete case design process. However together they provide integrated support for the development of a process from its conception through to its specification in a formal language suitable for execution.

Process design is a collaborative effort between the Business Analyst/ Case Architect, with the overview of the organisation necessary to identify and scope the process; the Case Designer who understands the details of both the process and how the organization works; and the IT specialist, who is responsible for the application software used by the process and indeed for the Case Processors that will run the process. Recognising this, the HICOS development system provides support for these three levels of user, and for communication between users within and between levels. It also provides mechanisms to encourage end user (case worker) involvement at all stages of the design process, an essential prerequisite for successful adoption of the resulting case.

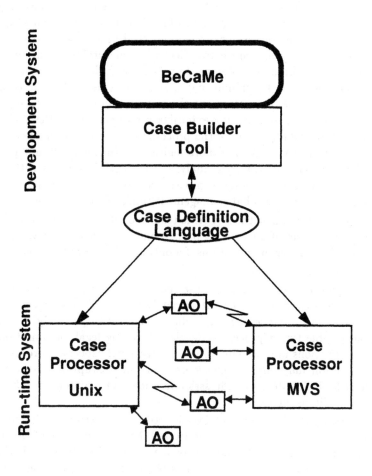

*Figure 1: HICOS System Structure*

**BeCAMe** The analysis phase is supported by the Business Case Analysis Methodology (BeCAMe). Targeted at BPR personnel, the methodology provides a structured set of issues to be considered and information to be gathered before embarking on process definition. There are four stages to BeCAMe:

*Process Selection:*

The process being considered must be strategically relevant, for example it is a process that occurs often, is time and cost consuming and/or is critically important for clients. This process identification can be done as part of a complete re-engineering exercise, or may be part of a continuous programme of process improvement.

*Status Quo Analysis:*

This is an important step, even if the process is being re-engineered from scratch. Not only does it help create a common understanding of the process within the design team, but it also helps highlight the more obscure complexities in the organization or task that the redesigned process will have to handle. The main objective of this stage is to collect the structural information that can be used as the basis for later modelling. In parallel with this, the collection of performance data, such as throughput, costs, etc, can be useful later in comparing possible target designs. By setting out the information that has to be captured in a series of modules and making extensive use of checklists, BeCAMe allows the scope and overall objectives of the process to be captured, independently of the process design, thus ensuring more logical and business-relevant processes. A critical component of status quo analysis is in-depth interviews with the case workers currently carrying out the process, ie capture what is actually done, warts and all, rather than what management thinks should be done.

By the end of this stage, the BeCAMe team should have a good feeling for the strengths/ weaknesses of the existing process and have identified several possible alternative solutions (or modifications if a only small scale redesign is intended).

*Target Process Design:*

Once the process is understood, the real business of (re-)design can begin. Firstly an "ideal concept" is generated, partly to act as a long term objective, partly to break any mind-set generated during the status-quo analysis. From this a more achievable target process is developed, taking legal, organisational and practical restrictions into account. The organizational aspects of process testing and introduction must also be considered, so that disruption to the business is minimized. (BeCAMe also addresses operation and maintenance phases, but these are not discussed here.)

During this phase, the methodology identifies those strategic design and organisational issues that ought to be addressed. For example, one of the modules deals with where to set the boundaries of the process. Firstly, there is the question of where the process starts and ends, which tasks properly belong in this process and which really belong in a precursor process. For example, does the case begin in the mailroom or only when a query reaches the appropriate person?; is archiving of the case results a separate process?; and so on. Secondly, how far down is the process design taken, what is the granularity of the primitive steps? Being too prescriptive may make the case too rigid or reduce job satisfaction in the personnel processing the cases; similarly, underspecification must be avoided. Thirdly, how extensive should the process be, how many special cases should be covered? - at some point the extra design effort and process complexity outweigh the benefits from handling yet another exception explicitly rather than relying on a general exception mechanism and case worker's common sense. Other modules deal with how the process is initiated, what actors are involved and where handoffs occur, what external contacts, documents or information are needed, and so on.

Throughout the design phase, the emphasis is on the enterprise wide view required to ensure effective and efficient processes. The Case Builder Tool (described below), can be used to capture quickly the outline process design(s), so that feedback can be obtained from as many people in the organization as desired.

*Detailed Design:*

Once a target design has been established, further BeCAMe modules contain advice on what optimizations could be applied. The first, and most critical, is to carry out a value-added assessment, ie to examine each component task and decide whether it provides something of value to a customer, provides something of (real) value to the business, or actually contributes very little to the case. A typical example of this would be making a copy of a document when all that is required later is confirmation of its existence. These non-value-adding steps should be eliminated. The second major optimization aspect is to look for ways to compress the design: *horizontally* by reducing the number of people involved, the number of hand-offs required, etc; and *vertically* by merging tasks, exploiting concurrency, etc. Other optimization modules look at the potential for automation or semi-automation, reuse of existing procedures/cases, and so on.

Finally, the structural and performance information captured earlier also allows more informed evaluation of alternative proposals, including simulation to check for errors, anomalies, bottlenecks, etc. The net result of applying BeCAMe during this target case design is better, more effective processes.

The BeCAMe methodology is supported with two specific information capture tools, a form based manual and a hypertext system. Both tools cover the entire spectrum of BeCAMe in complementary ways. The manual is intended to assist primarily in the earlier stages, facilitating note taking during interviewing and providing checklists to ensure completeness of captured data. The hypertext system provides good detailed support for analysis of the data, and can provide useful overviews of what data has been collected so far and what parts of the methodology have still to be tackled.

As mentioned above, BeCAMe consists of modules and sub-modules addressing specific aspects of business case analysis and design. Each module is independent and can be applied alone or in a subset of the complete methodology to explore one or more aspects of a case. Each module specifies not only how it relates to other modules, including its prerequisites and deliverables, but also what analysis/design skills and tools are required for its execution. As well as the modules, BeCAMe provides an introduction and tutorial to case analysis and design, help with planning the re-engineering project, advice on interviewing techniques and data capture and, of course, guidance on how to exploit the facilities of the Case Builder Tool.

**Case Builder Tool** The Case Builder Tool (CBT) supports both high-level and detailed design phases. The primary function of the CBT is to offer designers a user-natural graphical way to describe their process, using concepts and constructs that are familiar to them, and to explore the performance and behaviour of the designed case.

*Canvases:*

The basic mechanism provided by the CBT is a Canvas or drawing area on which symbols selected from a palette can be placed to create a diagram or flowchart of the process. Figure 2 shows a typical CBT screen. Symbols represent either tasks to be carried out or process structuring constructs such as decisions, parallelism, loops, etc. Task symbols can represent either primitive actions to be carried out (manually or by software), or higher level tasks which contain other structure/task symbols. Thus parts of the diagram can be closed down inside a single high level task, making it much easier to both obtain and maintain an overview of the overall process. Placing the symbols on the Canvas builds up an internal representation of the process, and the CBT ensures that symbols can only be placed in valid positions on the diagram, i.e. on appropriate existing flowlines. Not only does this ensure that the underlying process is always "valid", but it encourages the designer to think of the process at all times rather than merely cataloguing a sequence of activities. Thus activities are considered to be constituents of the process, rather than the process being a consequence of the activity sequence.

Unfortunately, business processes are almost invariably complex, both in terms of the relationships between the process steps and in terms of the factors that have to be taken into account at each step. To help the designer cope with this surfeit of information, rather than overload one diagram (visually or via dialogue boxes) the CBT provides alternative Canvases, each one giving a different view on the underlying process. These views are tied together, so changes in one view are instantly reflected in the others.

As an example, consider the specification of who should carry out each task. Adding role labels to a standard flowchart does not help the designer to see where transfers between roles occur, or to get a feel for how much of the process is done by the various case workers. A better mechanism, as adopted by the CBT, is to provide a separate Canvas displaying a Role Activity Diagram (RAD) on which the tasks are shown in columns corresponding to the role of the person who is to carry them out. While this sort of layout gives a poor idea of the structure of the process - consecutive actions are not necessarily adjacent - it clearly shows what tasks each *person* is expected to do and where the processing has to be handed on to someone else - a major source of delay, if not error, in case processing.

This multi-Canvas concept goes further than just offering different views of the process design. It also permits different approaches to the design production. For example, specification of an existing process is probably best done using the RAD Canvas, capturing the tasks done by each person in turn. Design from scratch is probably best done by capturing an outline of the high level tasks and then successively refining these until the design is complete. The system is extensible, so that other canvases can be added as required.

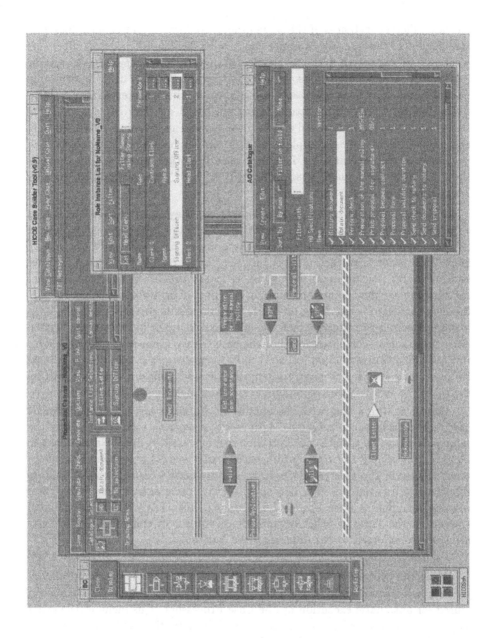

*Figure 2: Typical CBT Screen*

*Roles:*

The roles mentioned above identify the characteristics of the personnel that will carry out the tasks specified in the process. Since the actual individuals concerned cannot be known at design time, abstract roles are used and the case processor maps these to specific actors at runtime. For a small organization, a simple role label is probably sufficient. Larger organizations, however, frequently allocate different instances of the same process to different individuals, based on the specifics of the case - for example a particular clerk would deal with all clients whose name starts with A-D, or a particular engineer would specialize in marine engines. To accommodate this, roles can be parameterized using information from the case. The Case Processor, in conjunction with an external organization model, selects the required actor at runtime based on their current values of these parameters. This external organization model can be a simple table of roles and names, or could be a complex, existing competence/security database used elsewhere in the organization. In either case, the organization model provides the CBT with the available (parameterized) roles for the case designer to use.

*Events:*

Business processes are rarely self-contained; they must respond to events occurring in the external world - orders arriving, the financial year ending, a customer query, and so on. Generally, these events have associated with them more information than their mere occurrence, eg the item ordered, the customer name, etc. By placing event-wait symbols in the process design, the designer can indicate at what point this information is to be incorporated into the case, the case waiting for the event if it has not already occurred. The event-wait is parameterized to identify which specific event instance(s) is expected and to fetch the associated information into the case. Every event-wait must specify a timeout and a timeout action (possibly null) to ensure a case cannot stall waiting for something that is not going to happen. Naturally, since a case can itself be the source of events, a corresponding event-raise mechanism is provided.

As well as interacting with the outside world, the event mechanism can be used to synchronize/control separate processes or separate parallel strands of the same process. In fact, since case initiation can be considered to be a response to an event containing the startup information and process termination to be an event returning the case results back to the "outside", case invocation can be thought of as an event activity. This opens up the potential for interworking cases running in different Case Processors, including both HICOS and non-HICOS systems in the same or other organizations, subject of course to the security mechanisms enforced by the different event handlers.

*Application Objects:*

When the overall structure has been captured, the designer, usually in conjunction with someone from the IT department, has to specify the details required for automatic execution by the Case Processors. This includes the exact software to be invoked to carry out the desired activities, and the data to be passed to/from this software. Some of this software may be built-in to the Case Processors, eg simple forms to present some information and request the case worker to make a decision based on it. Alternatively, it could be a wrapper or an interface into a pre-existing system. In all cases, the interface for the designer is the same, the actual details of what, how and where to call being handled by the Case Processor (and the IT department). this frees the process design from the changes in the IT underpinnings, easing IT system migration.

To assist the above detailed design steps, the CBT offers a set of Catalogues describing the IT facilities available. Simple cut-and-paste/drag-and-drop enables the design to be quickly fleshed out to a fully executable specification.

*Building confidence in the design:*

At this stage, the design is "complete". But is it correct? With an IT system that is going to be actually carrying out a business's core processes, rather than just supporting part of them, it is *essential* that the designer is given the utmost confidence that the process as specified will perform as intended. To achieve this, the CBT provides three levels of analysis. The first merely checks that the specification is complete and syntactically correct, and could be executed by the Case Processors. Following this, the designer can simulate the case execution, stepping through the process one task at a time. At each step the designer is presented with the data that would be made available to the task and prompted for return values. This enables the designer to check that:

- the data provided to the task is sufficient for the case worker/software to generate the required return data;
- case workers are not asked to carry out tasks in a non-intuitive order;
- the different case workers are only asked to perform tasks appropriate to their position/ competence.

The simulation can also give information about case worker workload and case timings. Unfortunately, at best, simulation can only give an indication of possible case performance for those paths the designer actually simulates, and even then, unless the data/timings used are based on real/realistic information, the results could be misleading. As a result, any simulation output reporting timings, resource requirements, workloads or the like, whether from the CBT or from any other tool, should be treated with informed caution.

In a large or complex process the number of possible (and sensible) paths would be too large for the designer to do much more than try the few most common cases. What is possible in the CBT, because of its formal basis, is to apply some simple formal reasoning to the case design. The CBT reasoning module can prove properties about the case that will hold no matter what data is presented at runtime (excluding cataclysmic events such as power failure etc). Generally these are of a templated form such as "No cheque will be issued without having been authorized"; "If an acceptance letter is sent, a policy is always issued" or "the client database is always updated". Most organizations have such business rules or procedures that must be obeyed by all cases running in the organization, and the reasoner provides a simple way to gain confidence of the compliance of a new process, no matter how complex.

Finally, once the designer is satisfied with the process design, the complete process specification is written out in a form that can be directly input to the Case Processors, avoiding the introduction of any errors during installation or instantiation of the case.

## 4.3   Current Status

The HICOS project described here was an ESPRIT III project, No 6657 which ended in January 1996. The HICOS system is currently being deployed within an ESPRIT IV Business Best Practice Pilot, "We-Do-IT", No 20317. Further details can be obtained from the authors, or from the WWW URL http://www.bonn-service.de/empirica/hicos.htm. The system is also being marketed commercially.

# References

1. Hammer, M., Champy, J.: Reengineering the Corporation: A Manifesto for Business Revolution. Nicholas Brealey Publishing Ltd, London, 1993.
2. Hammer, M., Stanton, S. A.: The Reengineering Revolution: The Handbook HarperBusiness, 1995
3. Tramell, K.: Work Flow without Fear Byte (April 1996)
4. Thé, L.: Workflow tackles the productivity paradox Datamation (15 Aug 1995)
5. Thé, L.: Getting into the Workflow Datamation (1 Oct 1994)
6. comp.groupware          FAQ:          http://www.cis.ohio-state.edu:80/hypertext/faq/usenet/comp.groupware-FAQ/top.html
7. Workflow And Reengineering International Association (WARIA): http://www.waria.com/waria/
8. The BPR Homepage: http://ls0020.fee.uva.nl/people/wim/bre.htm
9. Concordium: Workflow on the Web http://www.cityscape.co.uk/users/ef48/
10. Workflow Management Coalition: http://www.aiai.ed.ac.uk/WfMC/

# Data Mining and the KESO Project

Arno Siebes*

CWI, P.O. Box 94079, 1090 GB Amsterdam, The Netherlands
e-mail: arno@cwi.nl

**Abstract.** Data Mining and Knowledge Discovery is a young but vigorously growing research area. Its aim is to discover structure or knowledge in databases. It comprises a wide variety of algorithms and techniques for towards this goal.

One of the main challenges in building a data mining system is the flexibility necessary both to support the current variety of algorithms and to extend it easily with new kinds of data mining algorithms. In the KESO project this challenge is met by basing the system on an *Inductive Query Language*.

## 1 Introduction

Knowledge Discovery and Data Mining is a rapidly growing research (and application!) area. There are books reporting the state of the art in 1991 and 1996 [25, 10]. It has its own workshops and conferences, such as KDD'95 and KDD'96 [11, 31]. It has its own home on the web, *The Knowledge Discovery Mine* at http://info.gte.com/~kdd with an associated mailing list, (nick)named "Nuggets". Moreover, from 1997 it will have its own journal, viz., "Data Mining and Knowledge Discovery", to be published by Kluwer Academic Publishers.

True to the spirit of the SOFSEM conferences, this paper aims to give both an introduction to this fascinating area and to highlight one of its current research directions. This paper is, however, *not* a survey paper. Many interesting and important topics are mentioned only briefly if at all. Rather, this paper focusses on one type of data mining problem, viz., *classification* and one data mining system, viz., the KESO system[2].

In more detail, this paper is organised as follows. Section 2 gives a broad introduction to knowledge discovery in databases in general and data mining in particular. The terminology is defined and the most important problem areas are indicated. Next, in Section 3, one particular data mining problem, *classification* is discussed in more detail. Classification is chosen because it illustrates some of the important recurrent problems of data mining and because it has many different

---

* This research is supported by ESPRIT under contract 20.596

[2] Restricting the scope allows for a more detailled discussion and by this I hope to convey the spirit (and fun) of data mining research. The interested reader is urged to consult the references to learn more about other data mining problems, algorithms and systems.

(algorithmic) approaches. I'll focus on one such approach, viz., *classification trees*.

Then the focus of the paper shifts from data mining problems and algorithms to data mining systems. In particular to the KESO system. In Section 4 the rationale for KESO is given. Section 5 explains the underlying concepts and Section 6 sketches (part of) its architecture. The KESO system shares many aspects with other Data Mining systems, such as Explora ([18]), Kefir ([23]), and others (see, e.g., [10]). Its high modularisation and the fact that it can be programmed makes it, however, unique in this field.

The programming (inductive query language) aspect of KESO is illustrated in Section 7. Here it is shown how the discovery of classification trees can be programmed in KESO.

## 2 Data Mining and Knowledge Discovery in Databases

### 2.1 Terminology

There has been quite some confusion concerning the proper terminology in the area of Knowledge Discovery and Data Mining. In [13], *Knowledge Discovery in Databases* was defined as "the non-trivial process of identifying valid, novel, potentially usefull, and ultimately understandable patterns in data." However, this was almost exactly what other authors would use as a definition for Data Mining. Later, in [9], a clear distinction between Knowledge Discovery and Data Mining was made. Paraphrasing we get the following "definitions":

**Knowledge Discovery in Databases** (KDD) refers to the complete process. Besides Data Mining, it encompasses pre-processing steps such as the cleaning and integration of data, as well as post-processing steps such as the interpretation of results and the consolidation of discovered knowledge.
**Data Mining** refers to *one step* in the KDD process, viz., that step in which the patterns are discovered (semi-)automatically.

In practice Data Mining and KDD cannot (and should not) not be separated. The (almost) universal experience is that Data Mining requires only between 10% and 20% of the total effort. However, despite the importance of the other steps of the KDD process, I'll restrict myself to Data Mining, more information on the other steps in the KDD-process can, e.g., be found in [10].

I often rephrase this definition of Data Mining as: *the induction of a model from a database*. In other words in Data Mining we have initially a large (possibly infinite) collection of possible models (patterns) and a (finite) database. Data Mining should result in those models that describe the database best (those patterns that fit the database best).

I like this definition so much, because it highlights some of the most important problems associated with Data Mining, viz., *induction*, *database*, and *model*.

Induction as an inference scheme means that we generalise from a *finite* number of facts (the database). The finite basis of facts on which we base our conclusions leads to the *problem of induction:* there is no absolute guarantee of correctnes. For example, before the discovery of Australia, Europeans had seen millions of swans, all of them white. The generalisation *Swans are white* seemed more than reasonable. However, Australia provided examples of *black* swans.

Moreover, given a finite number of facts there are, in general, infinitely models that describe the database exactly. However, such absolutely correct models often perform badly on new facts. This problem is often called *overfitting.* Since the whole point of Data Mining is often to use the induced models to predict in new situations this is bad news. It means that good fits are not exact fits.

Databases are not very often random samples from a population. For example, banks only have credit histories of those clients that they gave credit. In other words, a credit model induced from the credit database cannot be used automatically for those clients one would reject under the old credit-regime. This problem is called *reject inference.*

Finally, reject inference is a problem of "tuples missing in the database." Similarly, there are quite often attributes missing in the database. Corporate databases are in general maintained for reasons other than data mining. That means that information that could of vital importance for the data mining task at hand is simply not present. Thus, even if absolute models could exist in theory, in Data Mining one often finds statistical (or probabilistic) models.

The Data Mining community approaches these problems pragmatically. On the one hand one can take statistical safety measures against overfitting and there is some literature on reject inference [12]. On the other hand, there is "the Human in the cycle". That is, at the end of the day the data miner decides how good a result is. This pragmatic approach is, by the way, is one of the prime motivations for insisting on understandable results.

## 2.2 Models

**What Models?** As discussed above, Data Mining is the induction of a model. But what kind of model? Answering this question on a rather abstract level is relatively easy. The model one is after can always be seen as a function (or, more general as a relation).

On a more concrete level, it is probably impossible to give a comprehensive answer. The kind of model one tries to induce depends on at least on the question one tries to solve and on what kind of data one has in the database. So, rather than aiming at a comprehensive answer I list some classes of models that have receiced much attention in the Data Mining community; the reader is urged to consult e.g., [10] to get a more detailled picture.

**Functional Models** when one of the attributes is a (real-valued) function of the other attributes, the aim is to discover this function.

**Dependencies** where one tries to discover significant dependencies between attributes. Examples are Association Rules ([2]) and, of course, functional dependencies ([21]). An example of an association rule is, e.g., the discovery that if a customer buys diapers he will often buy a sixpack.

**Classification** learning a function that maps tuples into one of several predefined classes. This topic will be discussed in more detail in the next subsection.

**Clustering** which is somewhat similar to classification, only the classes are not pre-defined. It is both the most interesting and the hardest kind of Data Mining problem.

As already stated above, what kind of model class one uses depends on the kind of *mining question* one tries to answer as well as on the kind of data one has. For example, classification models are a special type of functions, and so are functional dependencies. But functional models are not always the best choice. One criterium is the representation of the model. In the next section we discuss this question for classification models.

**Discovering Models** When one has decided on what kind of model one is after, the best (relative to the database) model has to be discovered. There are many kinds of techniques. In fact, the reader should note that model induction is not only a problem studied in Computer Science, but has also received much attention in Statistics. Many of the techniques that can be found under such headings as *Exploratory Data Analysis* [32] and *Multivariate Analysis* [22] can be seen as a kind of data mining algorithms. Especialy modern techniques in these areas, such as *Projection Pursuit* [14, 17] are very close in spirit to current Data Mining research.

What technique should be used depends on what kind of model one is after, the type of data in the database, and the domain knowledge one has on the problem at hand. For example, if the model should be a function, the data is all numerical and one knows the function expression except some parameters one should use *regression*. However, if one does not know the function expression, techniques such as Neural Networks [15] and Genetic Programming [19, 20] can be used. Similarly, for cluster models, techniques range from simple cluster analysis techniques [6] to Bayesian classification [5].

In some cases, such as regression, there are techniques that allow one to compute the best (defined in a formal way) model directly. In others, such as association rules, one can effectively enumerate all possibilities and choose those that are good enough (as defined by the user). In still other cases, there are no known direct computations and an exhaustive search is prohibitively expensive. In such latter cases *heuristics* are used that yield a reasonable (not necessarily best) model. Examples in this class are (again) Neural Networks and Genetic Programming.

Quite often there is more than one technique available for the problem at hand. One of the aims of the ESPRIT-III project STATLOG was to find out which algorithms performed best for some of these problems, depending on, a.o., database characteristics. The result in this respect was: there are no clear cut winners, see [24]. In other words, the data miner should try some different techniques and pick the best result. How to do this in the case of classification problems is discussed in the next section.

# 3  Classification

## 3.1  The Problem and Approaches

For the classification problem, we assume that our database has $n$ regular attributes, say $A_1, \ldots, A_n$. Moreover, there is an extra attribute $A_{n+1}$ that assigns one of the pre-defined classes $C_1, \ldots, C_k$ to each of the tuples in the database. The goal is to device a procedure that assigns the correct (or better, most likely) class to a *new* tuple $(v - 1, \ldots, v_n)$.

There are various ways in which one can approach this problem. First of all, one could device a technique that compares the new tuple with the tuples in the database and picks the most likely class on the basis of these comparisons. *Naive Bayes* and *k-Nearest Neighbours* are examples of this approach [28]. For naive Bayes, one assumes that the attributes are conditional independently distributed given the class and computes the most likely class using Bayes rule and the marginal distributions found in the database. For $k$-Nearest Neighbour one needs a distance function. Using this function one computes the $k$ tuples in the database that are closest to the new tuple. The class $C_j$ that occurs most frequently among these $k$ nearest neighbours is the class that is assigned to the new tuple.

Another approach is to induce a model that allows one to assign a class to a new tuple without consulting the database. Within this approach, there are two sub-approaches possible. Either one induces what distinguishes one class from another or one induces what characterises each class. An example of the former approach is *Discriminant Analysis* and of the latter *Classification Trees* are a prime example.

Discriminant analysis is easiest understood if we assume that we just two (regular) real valued attributes and two classes. Then we simply plot the points in the database, label all points with their class and draw the line that distinguishes the two classes best. See [28] for more details. Classification trees are the topic of the remainder of this section.

A final approach is to consider functions as models for classification problems. That is, induce a function that assigns the correct class to a tuple. In that approach, one could, e.g., employ Neural Networks. This option is discussed in depth in [3] and [28].

## 3.2  Classification Trees: ID3

One of the most popular approaches to classification problems is classification by *trees*. These trees are often called *Decision Trees* in the Computer Science literature, whereas statisticians often call them *Classification Trees*. In this paper, I'll use the latter term. These trees are models of the form as in Figure 1.

This tree should be read as follows. If the outlook is sunny and the humidity is normal, we will play golf. However, if the outlook is sunny and the humidity is high, we won't play golf.

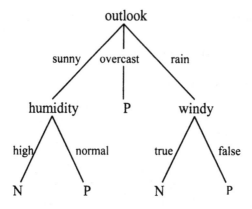

**Fig. 1.** A Classification Tree for Golf

Clearly, such a model is far easier to understand than a Neural Network. The question now is, of course, how do we induce such a tree from a database? The number of possible trees prohibits an evaluation of all possible trees to pick out the best. For example, the largest possible tree would have all attributes on all paths from the root to a leaf and would have branches for all relevant attribute values at each node. The smallest possible tree would have no splits at all. And each tree in between is also possible. In other words, heuristics have to be employed.

Most algorithms that build classification trees have the same simple underlying algorithm; they differ, of course, in the heuristics employed. In its description, I'll use $\mathcal{A}$ to denote the set of regular attributes $A_1, \ldots, A_n$.

1. Set-up the tree $T$ with one node $N$ that represents the complete database.
2. If node $N$ covers one of the classes $C_i$ *good enough*, lable that node with class $C_i$ and stop.
3. Otherwise, *pick an attribute $A \in \mathcal{A}$* and partition the set of objects covered by $N$ on the values they take for $A$ in the sets $N_1, \ldots, N_m$. Create a branch for each of the $N_i$.
4. Apply the procedure recursively to each of the child nodes.

The algorithms differ in what *good enough* means, what attribute $A$ is chosen, and how the set of objects is partitioned. In ID3 [26] *good enough* is interpreted as saying "all nodes covered by $N$ belong to the same class", the choice of attribute $A$ is explained below and $N$ is partitioned using all distinct values used for attribute $A$.

For the choice of attribute $A$, assume that node $N$ covers a subset $S$ of the database. If we denote by $P(C_i, S)$ the fraction of tuples in $S$ that belong to class $C_i$, the class-entropy of $N$ is given by:

$$Ent(N) = -\sum_{i=1}^{i=k} P(C_i, S)log(P(C_i, S))$$

If we split $N$ on the attribute values taken for attribute $A$, we get, say, nodes $N_1, \cdots, N_r$ which cover the partitioning $S_1, \cdots S_r$ of $S$. The resulting class-entropy after this split is given by:

$$E(N, A) = -\sum_{j=1}^{r} \frac{|S_j|}{|S|} Ent(S_j)$$

The *quality* of this split, called the *information gain* is defined as *Gain(N, A) = Ent(N) - E(N, A)*. ID3 makes the split that gives the greatest gain.

## 3.3 Variations

It should be clear that ID3 is but one of the (many) possibilities to flesh out the skeletom algorithm presented in the previous subsection. First, one could use different criteria to decide which attribute is taken next. Quinlan used a different *Gain-criterium* for the C4 family of algorithms [27].

In CART [4], the choice of the splitting attribute is based on *impurity measures*. Such an impurity measure quantifies how the tuples covered by a node are distributed over the classes. Using the impurity measure, gains are computed using, e.g., an information theoretic approach (like ID3) or the Gini index.

Similarly, one could decide not to split a node with all possible attribute values. Especially in the case of continuous attributes this leads to very fat trees. For example, both C4.5 [27] and CART [4] handle such cases differently. Moreover, both CART [4] and GID3* [8] don't necessarily split discrete attributes on all values.

Finally, I should note that growing the tree is but on aspect of tree induction. The second step is to *prune* the resulting tree, e.g., to avoid overfitting. The reader should consult, e.g., [4] for more details.

## 3.4 Scoring Trees

Different classification tree algorithms will yield different trees. As mentioned before, the *StatLog* project showed that there is no single best algorithm. Rather, one should compare the different results on a given database and pick the best.

The simplest way to gauge the quality of a classification model is *train and test*. The database is randomely divided in two parts. The model is induced on one part and its performance is scored on the other part.

Slightly more elaborate is $k$-fold cross-validation. The database is randomely divided in $k$ parts. Each of the $k$ parts is used as a test set once, while the model is then induced from the remainder of the database. This yields $k$ point estimates of the correctness. The average of these point estimates is then taken as a point estimate of the model induced from the *complete database.*

An even more elaborate estimation procedure is *bootstrapping.* In this case, we make a large number of *bootstrap samples* of the original database; a bootstrap sample is a sample of the same size as the database, which is (of course) sampled with replacement. Performing train and test on each of the bootstrap samples gives a distribution of the correctness for the model induced from the original database.

There is no easy rule that states which technique should be used in which case. A rule of thumb is that the larger the database is wrt the complexity of the model, the simpler the scoring method we can use. See [24] and [7] for more details on these techniques.

## 4  KESO: **The Project**

Now that some insight in what data mining is and how it can be done, the attention is shifted to Data Mining systems. One of the main challenges in building such a data mining system is the flexibility necessary both to support the current variety of algorithms and to extend it easily with new kinds of data mining algorithms. In the KESO project this challenge is met by basing the system on an *Inductive Query Language.*

That is, we base our system on the communality of many of the current data mining algorithms.

## 5  KESO: **The Concepts**

Without loss of generality ([1]) we assume that our database consists of one *Universal* relation $DB$, with schema $\mathcal{A} = \{A_1, \ldots, A_n\}$, with associated domains $D_i$. The set of all possible databases over $\mathcal{A}$ is denoted by $inst(DB)$.

### 5.1  Description Languages

In [29] Data Surveying has been introduced as the discovery of interesting subsets, e.g., the discovery of groups of clients with a highly deviating probability of filing a claim in an car-insurance database. Actually, not the groups are discoverd, but *descriptions* of these group. If a description is interpreted as a selection query on the database, the resulting selection is the subgroup described by the description. For example, the discovery of the description

$$sex = male \wedge age \in [16, 21]$$

would indicate that young male drivers are a (positive or negative) risk-group for the insurance company.

Descriptions only as selection queries is, however, too narrow a definition. Often one is interested in some (structured) set of simple descriptions. For example, the set of descriptions that partitions the database best according to some quality measure. Another example is the induction of classification trees later in this paper, where descriptions should represent complete classification trees. Since sets of descriptions suffice for the purposes of this paper, I'll limit (although it is (slightly) more general than in [29]) the definition to:

**Definition 1 Description Language.** A *simple description* $\phi$ for $DB$ is a selection query[3] on $DB$. A *simple description language* $\Phi$ for $DB$ is a set of simple selections.

A subset $\Psi$ of $\mathcal{P}\Phi$ is a *set description language* for $DB$. An element $\psi \in \Psi$, i.e., a set of elements of $\Phi$ is a *set description*.

"Description" will be used for both simple and set descriptions, if only one of the two kinds is meant it will be stated explicitly. This paper uses simple descriptions of the form:

$$A_1 = v_1 \wedge \cdots \wedge A_j = v_j; \{A_1, \ldots, A_j\} \subseteq \mathcal{A} \wedge v_j \in D_j$$

and the obvious set descriptions.

## 5.2 Quality Functions

The "interestingness" of a description is measured with a *quality function*, which is based on *cross-tables*. Two notational conventions used in the definition of cross-tables are:

**Definition 2 Cover and Support.** Let $\Phi$ be a simple description language for $DB$ and $\phi \in \Phi$ a simple description:

1. the *cover* of $\phi$, denoted by $\langle \phi \rangle$, is the subset of all tuples in $db$ that satisfy $\phi$;
2. the *support* of $\phi$, denoted by $\lfloor \phi \rfloor$ is the projection of $\langle \phi \rangle$ on the domain of the attributes used in $\phi$.

The cover of $age = 25 \wedge sex = male$ is the set of all 25 year old males in the database. Its support is simply $(age = 25, gender = male)$, if there is at least one in the database.

I will slightly abuse notation and write $\lfloor t \rfloor_\phi$ to denote the projection of a tuple $t \in \langle \phi \rangle$ on the domain of the attributes used in $\phi$. Using these conventions, *cross-tables* are defined as follows:

**Definition 3 Cross-table.** Let $\phi, \psi \in \Phi$ be two simple descriptions, the *cross-table* of $\phi$ with regard to $\psi$, denoted by $C(\phi|\psi)$, is defined by:

$$C(\phi|\psi) = \{(x,y)| \ x \in \lfloor \phi \rfloor \wedge y = |\{t \in db| \ t \in \langle \phi \rangle \cap \langle \psi \rangle \wedge x = \lfloor t \rfloor_\phi\}|\}$$

For set descriptions $\phi = \{\phi_1, \ldots, \phi_k\}$ and $\psi = \{\psi_1, \ldots, \psi_l\}$ the cross-table is defined by:

$$C(\phi|\psi) = \{C(\phi_i|\psi_j)| \ 1 \leq i \leq k \wedge 1 \leq j \leq l\}.$$

The cross-tables for mixed cases are defined analogously.

---

[3] For a precise definition of a *query*, consult, e.g., [1]. A selection query is a query whose result is a subset of the original table.

For example, $C(\{age = 16, age = 17\}|\{damage = yes, damage = no\})$ evaluates to the familiar kind of table (on some hypothetical database):

|  | damage = yes | damage = no |
|---|---|---|
| age = 16 | 54 | 16 |
| age = 17 | 54 | 36 |

Quality functions simply take such cross-tables as input and yield, e.g., some real number as output. In fact, all that is needed is that the quality of two descriptions can be compared:

**Definition 4 Quality function.** A quality function $Q$ for a description language $\Phi$ is a pair $(\psi, f)$, in which $\psi \in \Phi$ is the *target descriptions* and $f$ a computable function whose co-domain is some ordered set $D$. The quality of a description $\phi \in \Phi$ is defined by:

$$Q(\phi) = f(C(\phi|\psi))$$

We use the generality of ordered sets as co-domains in KESO since the user can interactively influence the discovery process. In this paper, however, user interaction is not taken into account and the quality functions will be real-valued.

The inductive queries, or better *survey tasks* in KESO could now be specified by a pair $(\Phi, Q)$, in which $\Phi$ is a description language and $Q$ a quality function. The intuitive result of such a survey task is given by (a set of) description(s) that maximizes the quality function.

## 5.3   Search Algorithms and Operators

However, such survey tasks specify *what* has to be discovered, but not *how* it should be discovered. A key observation in [29] is that, given a database state, the quality function defines a "quality landscape" over the description language. Moreover, well-known search algorithms, such as the Hill-Climber and Simulated Annealing, only need operators such as "neighbour" on the description language to find the peaks in this landscape.

By defining operators on the quality language, it turns into an *algebra*:

**Definition 5 Description Algebra.** A description algebra is specified by a pair $(\Phi, \mathcal{O})$, in which $\Phi$ is a description language and $\mathcal{O}$ a set of operators on $\Phi$.

The final part of the specification task is, of course, the search algorithm that finds the descriptions of maximal quality using the operators in $\mathcal{O}$.

Defining what exactly constitutes a search algorithm is outside the scope of this paper[4]. However, what we require is firstly that the algorithm reports a local maximum of the quality landscape and and secondly that the algorithm is *polymorphic* in the description algebra and the database under the assumption that the algebra offers the operators needed by the algorithm.

To make this second point slightly more precise, let an *abstract operator* be a *(operator name, arity)* pair. If $\mathcal{O}_1$ is a set of abstract operators, and $\mathcal{O}_2$ a set

---

[4] See, e.g., [33] for definitions of search algorithms and some remarkable results.

of concrete operators of a description algebra $\Phi$, $\mathcal{O}_1 \subseteq \mathcal{O}_2$ denotes that $\mathcal{O}_2$ has a concrete operator for every abstract operator in $\mathcal{O}_1$; i.e., one with the same name and arity.

Let $\mathcal{O}$ be a set of abstract operators, the type of a *discovery algorithm D for* $\mathcal{O}$ is given by:

$$D : \forall \tau[\tau = ((\Phi, \mathcal{O}_\tau), Q) : \mathcal{O} \subseteq \mathcal{O}_\tau]$$
$$\forall DB \text{ for which } \Phi \text{ is a description language}$$
$$\forall db \in inst(DB) : (\tau, DB, db) \rightarrow \Phi$$

The definition of a survey task is now given by:

**Definition 6 Survey task.** Let $db \in inst(DB)$ be a database, a survey task for $db$ is a triple $((\Phi, \mathcal{O}), Q, \mathcal{S})$, such that $(\Phi, \mathcal{O})$ is a description algebra for $DB$, $Q$ is quality function for $\Phi$ and $\mathcal{S}$ is a search algorithm for $\mathcal{O}$.

# 6 KESO: The Architecture

## 6.1 Components and Modules

The components of a survey task are faithfully reflected in the architecture of the KESO system. In particular, $S$ is mirrored by the *Search Manager*, $\mathcal{O}$ by the *Description Generator*, and $Q$ by the *Quality Computer*. Obviously, there is not one component that embodies the description language $\Phi$, since this is the "hypothesis language" shared by the components.

**The Search Manager** The Search Manager contains a number of Search Modules, each of which implements a search algorithm[5]. That is, each of these modules can orchestrate a search process, but it does not manipulate descriptions nor does it compute qualities. It relies on other components to perform these tasks. It uses the results of these tasks to decide what the next step in the discovery process should be.

**The Description Generator** The Description Generator also consists of a number of modules. Each of these modules implements one of the operators on a specific descrition language. These modules may consult the knowledge base to determine what the result of a operation on a (set of) descriptions should be. A search component will tell the description generator what operators it should apply to which (sets of) descriptions.

---

[5] Actually, the KESO architecture does not contain a Search Manager, the Search Modules simply share a library, e.g., for communication purposes. Conceptually, it might be easier to think in terms of a Search Manager.

**The Quality Computer** The Quality Computer is the component that interfaces with KESO's mining server. Through this server it queries the database to gather statistics on a description, such that it can compute the quality of this description. It contains, modularly, a set of different quality functions. All of these sub-modules share the same interface to the dataserver.

The quality computer computes the quality of the descriptions that are newly generated by the description generator. The set of new descriptions together with their quality are handed back to the search module that bases its next step on this information.

As an aside, note that the queries on the underlying database generated by the Quality Computer are strongly connected. This fact is exploited in the mining server, which contains a *browsing optimisation* module. This module temporarily stores results from queries and re-uses these results to speed up the discovery process. The advantage of this kind of optimisation has already been shown in [16].

## 6.2 The Communication

The communication of these components is through the Search Space Manager, which persistently stores the search space[6]. The logical flow of information is as sketched above, albeit through the Search Space Manager. That is, the components store records in the Search Space Manager and request records from it. The records in the Search Space Manager, contain, a.o.,

- an *id-field*, i.e., logical name for the description,
- a field for the description itself,
- a field for the quality of this description,
- a field which contains the name of the operator using which the description is generated,
- a *parent* field which contains the id(s) of the descriptions from which the description is generated.

The parent field gives the search space a graph-structure. Each search space has a default element, called *anchor*, on which the search graph is anchoredred. If requested, the quality of anchor record is smaller than any other quality, e.g., it is $-\infty$, and it is its own parent.

Activating the correct modules, setting up the communication channels etc. is done by the *Mining Conductor*. Which executes the *mining scripts* (= survey task in KESO) issued by the user.

---

[6] One of the motivations for the persistent storage of the Search Space is that it enables the user interaction. A second motivation is that it allows the user to roll-back in a discovery session and to return to such a session at a later dat.

# 7   ID3 in KESO

## 7.1   The Tree-language

First of all, we have to define the description language. From the observation above, we see that each description has to represent a complete tree. That is, we have to use set descriptions. In fact, we use the set-descriptions given as an example in Section 4.1. Each simple description $\phi$ that is an element of such a set description $\psi$ simply denotes the slection along the path from the root of $\psi$ to a leaves. Clearly, not all such set descriptions can be interpreted as a proper tree. Hence, we have to ensure that we only construct set descriptions that do represent a proper tree.

## 7.2   Search Module: A Hill-Climber

Next, we specify a Hill-Climber algorithm as follows:

**Hill-Climber**
Create-record(parent = anker, operator = initiate)
continue := true
**While** continue **do**
    $X$ := Request-records(Leaves)
    $x$ := max-quality-record($X$)
    $y$ := Request-record(oid = $x$.parent)
    If $x$.quality > $y$.quality
    Then Create-record(parent = $x$.oid, operator = neighbour)
    Else continue := false
**od**

It first *initiates* the search space, by creating the first record (other than the *anker*. Then it starts its main cycle. First it requests the *leaves* in the search graph, i.e., the descriptions (more precisely the records) that were created in the previous cycle. It then chooses from these leaves the description $x$ with the highest quality. If the quality of this record is higher than that of its parent $y$, it requests that all *neighbours* of $x$ (including their quality) are computed and restarts the cycle. If not, the Hill-Climber terminates because $y$ is a (local) optimum.

## 7.3   Operators: Initiate and Neighbour

The Hill-Climber algorithm as specified above is not especially tailored towards the construction of decision trees. That is achieved in the specification of the operators.

The first operator is the *initiate* operator. This operator should construct a one-node tree, in which the single node represents the complete database. The selection along the empty-path is simply *true*, thus:

## Initiate

$x :=$ Request-record(description = Null, operator = initiate)

Update-record($x$.oid, description = $\{true\}$)

Note that we assume that fields have default a Null-value.

The next operator is the *neighbour* operator. It receives a tree as input and outputs all trees that have one *internal* node extra. That is, we make one split extra. In the case of ID3, the input tree is a set of simple descriptions $\Phi = \{\phi_1, \ldots, \phi_k\}$. And making a split in $\Phi$ means that we replace one of the $\phi_i$ by all selections of the form $\phi_i \wedge A_j = v_j$ such that $A_j$ is not yet "used" in $\phi_i$ and $v_j \in D_j$.

To make this slightly more precise, denote by $Att_\phi$ the attributes that are used in $\phi$. For example, if $\phi \equiv A_1 = v_1 \wedge A_2 = v_2$, then $Att_\phi = \{A_1, A_2\}$. But paths should be extended with selections on attributes *not yet* used: define $Att^\phi = A \setminus Att_\phi$. Continuing our example, $Att^\phi = \{A_1, \ldots A_n\} \setminus \{A_1, A_2\} = \{A_3, A_4, \ldots, A_n\}$. Finally, for a simple description $\phi$ and an attribute $A \in Att^\phi$, the *split* in $\phi$ on $A$ is given by:

$$split(\phi, A) = \{\phi \wedge A = v | v \in Domain(A)\}$$

With these definitions, the neighbour operator for ID3 is specified as follows:

## Neighbour-ID3

$x :=$ Request-record(description = Null, operator = Neighbour)

$y :=$ Request-record($x$.parent)

$\Phi :=$ $y$.description

**Forall** $\phi \in \Phi$

    **Forall** $A \in Att^\phi$

        Create-record(description = $(\Phi \setminus \phi) \cup split(\phi, A)$,

            operator = Neighbour, parent = $y$)

Delete-record($x$)

Note that since we replace one record $r$ with "Neighbour" in its operator field by a set of new records, one for each possible split, we create new records and destroy the "seed record" $r$.

## 7.4 Quality Functions

For the quality function, note that a node $N$ in ID3 corresponds with a description $\phi$ that belongs to the path that ends in $N$. The set $S$ covered by $N$ is thus $\langle\phi\rangle$. Clearly, the class-entropy $Ent(\phi)$ can be computed from the cross-table $C(\phi|\{C = 1, \cdots, C = k\})$.

Reinterpreting $E(N, A)$ is slightly more difficult. For, if we have a tree, we cannot see at which node it extends its parent simply by inspecting it. However, if we have such a set-description $\Phi$, we can retrieve its parent $\Psi$ from the database.

By computing $\Psi \backslash \Phi$ we get the description $\phi$ that was extended and by computing $\Phi \backslash \Psi$ we get its "offspring" $\phi_1, \ldots, \phi_r$. Since the size of $\langle \phi \rangle$ follows directly from the cross-table above, computing the Gain is simple:

**Gain-ID3**

$x := $ Request-record(quality = Null)
$y := $ Request-record($x$.parent)
$\Phi := x$.description
$\Psi := y$.description
$Cross_1 := $ Request-cross-table($\Psi \backslash \Phi | \{C = 1, \cdots, C = k\}$)
$Cross_2 := $ Request-cross-table($\Phi \backslash \Psi | \{C = 1, \cdots, C = k\}$)
$Quality := $ Gain($Cross_1, Cross_2$)
Update-record(oid = $x$.oid, quality = $Quality$)

## 7.5 Specifying ID3

And the mining script for ID3 on some database called *test* is given by:

**ID3**

database = test
description language = set-descriptions
search module = Hill-Climber
    neighbour = Neighbour-ID3
    quality = Gain-ID3

# 8 Discussion

The introduction of Data Surveying as the discovery of interesting subsets may lead the reader to believe that survey tasks are a, perhaps interesting, but rather limited view on data mining. However, selection queries form a rather expressive class and the structured descriptions even more so.

In this paper we have seen how classification trees can be expressed and discovered. Elsewhere, in [30], I have shown how modern statistical techniques such as Projection Pursuit fit in this framework. One of the goals of the KESO project is to provide solutions for the discovery of Dependencies, Classifications, and Clusterings.

It should be obvious from the discussion of ID3 and its implementation in KESO that it is fairly easy to program other classification tree algorithms in KESO. We just need to replace the quality computation, or the neighbour operator. An important aspect of the project is consequently the implementation of a sufficiently large collection of modules. However, programming the system is good for "power-users" who know (and test!) what they are doing. The project will also implement a variety of ready-to-run mining scripts for the less sophisticated user. Important examples of that latter class are, e.g., *discretization* and *refinement programs.* A pruning algorithm could, e.g., be implemented with such a refinement program .

The performance figures of Data Surveyor ([16]), in many ways a precursor of KESO, gives confidence in the performance aspects of KESO.

**Acknowledgments** The members of the KESO development team are Heikki Mannila and A. Inkeri Verkamo of the University of Helsinki, Willi Klösgen, Dietrich Wettschereck, and Stefan Wrobel from GMD, Fred and Donald Kwakkel and Marcel Holsheimer from Data Distilleries, and Sunil Choenni, Martin Kersten, (and myself) from CWI.

# References

1. S. Abiteboul, R. Hull, and V. Vianu. *Foundations of Databases.* Addison Wesley, 1994.
2. R. Agrawal, T. Imielinski, and A. Swami. Mining association rules between sets of items in large databases. In *Proceedings of the 1993 International Conference on Management of Data (SIGMOD 93)*, pages 207 – 216, May 1993.
3. C. Bishop. *Neural Networks for Pattern Recognition.* Clarendon Press, 1995.
4. L. Breiman, J. H. Friedman, R. A. Olshen, and C. J. Stone. *Classification and Regression Trees.* Wadsworth, 1984.
5. P. Cheeseman and J. Stutz. *Bayesian Classification (Autoclass): Theory and Results*, pages 153 – 180. In Fayyad et al. [10], 1996.
6. B. S. Duran and P. L. Odell. *Cluster Analysis, A Survey.* Lecture Notes in Economics and Mathematical Systems, vol 100. Springer-Verlag, 1974.
7. B. Efron and R. J. Tibshirani. *An Introduction to the Bootstrap.* Monographs on Statistics and Applied probability, vol 57. Chapman & Hall, 1993.
8. U. M. Fayyad. Branching on attribute values in decision tree generation. In *Proceedings of the 12th National Conference on Artificial Intelligence*, pages 601–606. AAAI/MIT Press, 1994.
9. U. M. Fayyad, G. Piatetsky-Shapiro, and P. Smyth. *From Data Mining to Knowledge Discovery: An Overview*, pages 1 – 34. In Fayyad et al. [10], 1996.
10. U. M. Fayyad, G. Piatetsky-Shapiro, P. Smyth, and R. Uthurusamy, editors. *Advances in Knowledge Discovery and Data Mining.* AAAI/MIT Press, 1996.
11. U. M. Fayyad and R. Uthurusamy, editors. *AAAI-95 Conference on Knowledge Discovery and Data Mining*, Montreal, Quebec, 1995.
12. A. Feelders. Learning from biased data using mixture models. In Simoudis et al. [31], pages 102 – 107.
13. W. Frawley, G. Piatetsky-Shapiro, and C. Matheus. *Knowledge Discovery in Databases: An Overview*, pages 1 – 27. In Piatetsky-Shapiro and Frawley [25], 1991.
14. J. Friedman and J. Tukey. A projection pursuit algorithm for exploratory data analysis. *IEEE Transactions on Computing*, C-23:881–889, 1974.
15. J. Hertz, A. Krogh, and R. G. Palmer. *Introduction to the Theory of Neural Networks.* Santa Fe Institute Lecture Notes vol 1. Addison-Wesley, 1991.
16. M. Holsheimer, M. Kersten, and A. Siebes. Data surveyor: Searching the nuggets in parallel. In Fayyad et al. [10].
17. P. J. Huber. Projection pursuit. *The Annals of Statistics*, 13(2):435–475, 1985.

18. W. Klösgen. Explora: A multipattern and multistrategy discovery assistent. In Fayyad et al. [10].
19. J. R. Koza. *Genetic programming*, volume 1. MIT Press, 1992.
20. J. R. Koza. *Genetic programming*, volume 2. MIT Press, 1994.
21. H. Mannila and K.-J. Räihä. Algorithms for inferring functional dependencies from relations. *Data and Knowledge Engineering*, 12:83–99, 1994.
22. K. Mardia, J. Kent, and J. Bibby. *Multivariate Analysis*. Probability and Mathematical Statistics. Academic Press, 1979.
23. C. J. Mateus, G. Piatetsky-Shapiro, and D. McNeill. Selecting and reporting what is interesting: The kefir application to healthcare data. In Fayyad et al. [10].
24. D. Michie, D. Spiegelhalter, and C. Taylor, editors. *Machine Learning, Neural and Statistical Classification*. Ellis Horwood series in Artificial Intelligence. Ellis Horwood, 1994.
25. G. Piatetsky-Shapiro and W. J. Frawley, editors. *Knowledge Discovery in Databases*. AAAI Press, Menlo Park, California, 1991.
26. J. Quinlan. Induction of decision trees. *Machine Learning*, 1:81–106, 1986.
27. J. Quinlan. Probabilistic decision trees. In Y. Kodratoff and R. Michalski, editors, *Machine Learning: An Artificial Intelligence Approach, Vol 3*. Morgan Kaufmann, 1990.
28. B. Ripley. *Pattern Recognition and Neural Networks*. Cambridge University Press, 1996.
29. A. Siebes. Data surveying, foundations of an inductive query language. In Fayyad and Uthurusamy [11], pages 269–274.
30. A. Siebes. On the inseparability of data mining and statistics. In *Proceedings of the Mlnet Familiarization Workshop: Statistics, Machine Learning and Knowledge Discovery in Databases*, 1995.
31. E. Simoudis, J. Han, U. M. Fayyad, and R. Uthurusam, editors. *AAAI-96 Conference on Knowledge Discovery and Data Mining*, Portland, Oregon, 1996.
32. J. Tukey. *Exploratory Data Analysis*. Addison-Wesley, 1977.
33. D. H. Wolpert and W. G. Macready. No free lunch theorems for search. Technical Report SFI-TR-95-02-10, The Santa Fe Institute, Februari 1996.

# Computer Visualization - Concepts, Trends and Current Research

Gitta Domik

University of Paderborn, Dept. of Computer Science, D-33095 Paderborn, Germany

## 1 Definition and History of Visualization

### 1.1 What is Computer Visualization ?

„Scientific Visualization", „Information Visualization", and „Software Visualization" are exemplifications of „Computer Visualization", describing methods and techniques to *map* from one domain of computer representation (binary numbers which we will call „data/information" to emphasize the presence of meaning within the binary numbers) to another domain of computer representations (computer generated pictures)(see Figure 1).

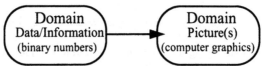

**Figure 1:** Visualization as Mapping Process

To be more explicit in defining „Computer Visualization" we should start with the roots of the word itself: to visualize means „to form a mental vision, image, or picture of (something not visible or present to sight, or of an abstraction); to make visible to the mind or imagination" [1]. In computer visualization the amount of data to be represented in pictorial form is usually large, sometimes gigantic. „Data" is the result of an initial mapping from the real world, with concrete problems to solve, to a computer represented version, usually accomplished by using (scientific) models, measurements, or other forms of (optimal) descriptions of the real world. Similarly to the mapping process „reality -> computer", there is also an additional mapping process *after* the generation of a picture on the screen or on a hardcopy: the mapping from the computer generated picture into the mind of the viewer (see Figure 2). In order to make reality visible „to the mind of the viewer", all three mapping processes (and not just one!) must be free of errors or misunderstandings: 1) the first mapping (reality -> computer) must be comprehensive/complete; 2) the second mapping (binary numbers -> pictures) must maximize human understanding; 3) the third mapping must be unambiguous. Incomplete (scientific) models or measurements, ineffective or misunderstood pictures will lead to errors in the interpretation of the viewer. The backtracking arrows in Figure 2 point to the view of and interaction with the picture (*) and the interpretation of either data or reality itself (**).

Within this context we can now present several definitions of visualization as given in key references. The first definition is taken from the first publication on „Visualization of Scientific Computing", namely the report of a workshop by the National Science Foundation that laid the foundation-stone for Scientific Visualization":

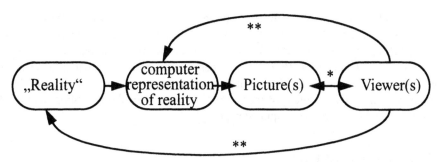

**Figure 2:** Visualization as Extended Mapping Process

„Visualization is a method of computing. It transforms the symbolic into the geometric, enabling researchers to observe their simulations and computations. Visualization offers a method for seeing the unseen. It enriches the process of scientific discovery and fosters profound and unexpected insights. In many fields it is already revolutionizing the way scientists do science." [2]

The second definition emphasizes the mapping process of visualization and points towards advanced possibilities of multi-media computers:

„A useful definition of visualization might be the binding (or mapping) of data to a representation that can be perceived. The types of binding could be visual, auditory, tactile, etc. or a combination of these." [3]

A yet third definition emphasizes the last mapping stage of Figure 2:

„Visualization is more than a method of computing. Visualization is the process of transforming information into a visual form, enabling users to observe the information. The resulting visual display enables the scientist or engineer to perceive visually features which are hidden in the data but nevertheless are needed for data exploration and analysis." [4]

### 1.2 Computer Visualization in the 80's and '90s

To be complete, a history of computer visualization must include the history of computer graphics, of visual perception, and of much more. Instead, I will treat computer visualization as the field it emerged as in the second half of the 1980's. An overwhelming need for visual representation arose from the expected increase of data rates from measuring devices, such as in the space missions, and from scientific computations on supercomputers. The gigantic masses of data that needed to be searched for patterns and anomalies were often termed „fire hose of data", to suggest a comparison between the unsuccessful attempt of drinking from a fire hose to satisfy ones thirst with the unsuccessful attempt of understanding reality by looking at the available masses of data. Parallel to this overwhelming need for new approaches to data analysis, the mid '80s brought graphical workstations, equipped with color, sufficient memory and storage on a very reasonable price tag. However, the new hardware alone did not immediately solve the problem of interpreting large amounts of data. The National Science Foundation therefore asked an Advisory Committee on „Graphics, Image Processing, and Workstations" (1986) to make recommendations to HW/SW builders to improve scientific productivity through visual display technology and methods. The committee decided to make recommendations to the research community instead to develop new concepts and techniques for „Visualization in Scientific Computing (ViSC)". ViSC has been shortened to „Scientific Visualization" and now often stands for the scientific approach to computer visualization, instead of its narrow meaning as intended in the '80s. The report of the workshop held by the advisory committee is the above quoted paper [2].

## 2 The Need for Strategy

In order to ensure visual representations that are effective for the visualization goal intended, systematic strategies for the mapping „data -> picture" are needed [5]. These strategies include novel paradigms, mapping rules, and better suited system designs to exploit available hardware and state-of-the-art computer graphics algorithms to reach the intended goals. Strategies may be made available to the user in widely differing modes: as a list of rules for the designer, in form of rules in an expert system or in the way of intelligent agents.

To give a simple example of the many choices a user has to make during a visualization process, lets look at the comparison of leaves from different trees. We restrict ourselves to comparing the lengths and width of leaves and thus perform measurements for various types of trees at certain time intervals. In this way we have mapped the „reality" (leaves) into a data set consisting of four variables: *leaf length, leaf width, leaf type, leaf age. Age* and *type* would be independent variables (dimensions), and *length* and *width* dependent variables. We are further assuming that hardware and software possibilities allow the use of positioning on a 2-d screen, and the placing of graphical symbols at various sizes at these positions. Therefore the available visual attributes are: position_x, position_y, symbol type, symbol size. The mapping process from data (four variables) to picture (four visual attributes) offers 24 possibilities: (number of variables)!/((number of variables)-(visual attributes))!, with (number of variables > number of visual attributes).

However, only some of these possibilities will offer coherent and easy to understand visuals. For instance, it will be more useful to map length and width into the screen position, than type and age, as length and width define spatial extensions also in reality. It will furthermore be more useful to map leaf type to symbol type and leaf age to symbol size than vice versa, because ordinal data types (like leaf age) are easier to be interpreted by size than by symbol. Nominal data types (like leaf type) are better distinguished by hue or by symbol type rather than by symbol size. Furthermore knowledge of the aim of the interpreter is important to chose the correct mapping function: Are the leaf lengths and widths to be compared with each other or the growth rate?

Most visualization processes are more complicated as in the example above, and most system designers or application users are not aware of abilities and limitations of human perception in any detail. Still, system designer and application user make decisions in the mapping process that may or may not lead to an expressive and effective visual result. This section and the next are aimed at reducing the manifold choices we have in the mapping stage of „data -> picture" towards the few expressive and effective mappings available. In this section we will look merely at two factors that influence the choice of mapping:

1. data (*what is to be displayed*)
2. and interpretation aims (*what is the goal of the viewer*)

## 2.1 Data modeling

A *data model* is a conceptual view of data to be displayed. It must not be confused with data format, which is a physical view of data elements and arrays. A general data model contains information of syntax and semantics about the data. It has proved to be a challenge to provide complete data models that are application independent. For scientific visualization alone, Brodlie et al. [6] and Gallop [7] have suggested elaborate classification schemes. Data models are an active area of visualization research, and progress is being made. Newest results can usually be observed at the yearly visualization conferences by IEEE.

The basic idea of a data model is to provide information on various data characteristics and then use this information to choose the best graphical elements and attributes to create expressive and effective visualizations. Data models may include information on:

• data type (e.g. nominal, ordinal, quantitative)

• data structure (e.g. point, scalar, vector)

• data continuity (continuous vs. discrete data elements)

• topology of data elements

• data reliability

• valid range of data

To elaborate on one such data characteristic and discuss its influence, lets take a closer look at „data type (e.g. nominal, ordinal, quantitative)". A data item will be classified as nominal, if it is a member of a certain class, e.g. a member of the set [Maple, Birch, Oak]. A data item will be classified as ordinal, if it has an assigned place in an arrangement of similar data items. An example is one day of the week, which has an inherent order in the arrangement of week days. A data item will be classified as quantitative, if it carries information about a precise numerical value, e.g. 2.3, or 4.56, or 2.5E-35. An example of quantitative data may be emission values from a space mission. Depending on the data type, various visual attributes are more or less suitable to express the data items(s). For nominal data items hue is a very effective attribute to distinguish between members of one set. If brightness alone were used to distinguish between various nominal data items, increasing brightness will force a (false!) order on data items and therefore invite misinterpretation. For ordinal data types brightness is a suitable attribute. For quantitative data items position in a plot proves to be the most useful visual attribute. Mackinlay [8] published a prioritized list of visual attributes for these three data types with decreasing effect for decreasing priority number (see Table I):

Table I: Priorities of Visual Attributes for Various Data Types (Excerpt) [8]

| Priority | Quantitative | Ordinal | Nominal |
|---|---|---|---|
| (highest) 9 | Position | Position | Position |
| 8 | Length | Density | Hue |
| 7 | Angle | Saturation | Density |
| 6 | Slope | Hue | Saturation |
| 5 | Area | Length | Shape |
| 4 | Density | Angle | Length |
| 3 | Saturation | Slope | Angle |
| 2 | Hue | Area | Slope |
| (lowest) 1 | Shape | Shape | Area |

## 2.2 Interpretation aims

Interpretation aims are the goals viewers pursue with their visualization results. As with data models it is also hard to provide a general classification scheme of interpretation aims. Goals are described in application dependent languages and it is misleading to the application specialists (the viewers) to be forced to use standard terms. Examples of interpretation aims in scientific visualization may be identifying objects, comparing values, distinguishing objects, or categorizing objects [9]. Goals for software visualization are distinguished by their focus on text, data structures, performance or algorithms [10]. Goals for information visualization may be to optimize the cost structure for searching information, or to optimize the amount of information to be fitted on the available screen [11]. Let us assume the goal of the viewer is to search for the cheapest flight between city A and city B. A chart showing all connecting flights using „size" of a symbol to encode „price" (the larger the symbol size, the larger the price) will quickly focus our view on the smallest symbols.

## 3 A Review of Novel Concepts

The previous section can be seen as an approach to a minimal visualization strategy. In many excellent scientific papers such and similar strategies have been developed and their implementation into a visualization system discussed. Some of these novel approaches have led to actual visualization systems, some approaches exist as ideas only. In this section I have gathered some new and interesting approaches to performing the visualization process.

### 3.1 „Renaissance teams"

Donna Cox of NCSA (National Center for Supercomputer Applications, Illinois, USA) suggests to create teams consisting of domain experts, computer graphics experts, visual design experts or other needed expertise to discuss the most optimal visual designs.

Results of work by Donna Cox and her „Renaissance teams" prove the power of this approach. The one and only disadvantage is the high cost factor of such solutions. [12]

## 3.2 Mackinlay's APT

Mackinlay [8] presented his APT (A Presentation Tool) in the mid 80's as a concept for an automatic visualization system, designed to display information stored in relational databases as 2-d business graphics. Typical displays are bar, scatter and line charts. APT uses graphics primitive such as areas (e.g. circles and bars), lines, marks (such as + or -) and visual attributes such as color, size and orientation. The primitives are organized into primitive graphical languages. The primitive graphical languages include: horizontal axis, vertical axis, line chart, bar chart, scatter plot, color, shape, size, saturation, texture, orientation, tree and network. The grammar for generating alternative representations is defined by three composition rules, which combine the primitive graphical languages into complete graphs. Double-axis composition can compose graphical sentences that have identical horizontal and vertical axes, such as showing „sales data by year" for two different divisions on the same set of axes. Single-axis composition aligns two sentences that have identical horizontal or vertical axis. For example two bar charts which are side by side, one encoding gross national product (GNP) by country and the other encoding population by country. Country is the common axis, while GNP and population are the different second axis. Mark composition uses two different attributes of the same area or mark to encode different variables, such as using the size of a circle to encode a state's population and the color of the circle to encode the average age of the state's population. Once the strategies for composing a complete graph have been defined, the graph is tested against the *expressiveness and effectiveness* criteria. A set of facts is *expressive* in a language if it contains a sentence that encodes all the facts in the set and not encodes additional information (artifacts). A presentation is *effective* when it can be interpreted accurately or quickly, or when it can be rendered in a cost-effective manner. For each generated presentation, the primitives are filtered, with their expressiveness criteria used to generate a list of candidate designs. The effectiveness criteria are used to order the candidate designs so that the most effective presentation will be the first choice.

## 3.3 SAGE by Roth and Mattis

SAGE (A System for Automatic and Graphical Explanation) by Roth and Mattis [13] is an extension of Mackinlay's work. SAGE allows a number of graphical techniques (more than APT), but is still restricted to 2-d graphics. SAGE also elaborates the characterization of data, semantics and relations. E.g. the graphical expression of

$$total\_costs = material\_costs + labor\_costs$$

would reflect the composition „+" in the graph (e.g. two bar segments for each represented interval which add to one bar segment viewed together).

In SAGE a user's immediate goal may determine the connection of different relations and will thereby affect how they should be integrated in the presentation. SAGE uses a technique of segmenting the total presentation request into sub-requests to coordinate text and graphics displays by converting a topic outline prepared by a discourse processor into a serial list of sub-requests. This indicates to the graphics system that information expressed in contiguous portions of the text should be considered more related, and therefore displayed together. More generally, this characteristic provides a vehicle for expressing two, often competing, informational goals: the need to express as much information as possible and the need for selected partitions of sets or relations to be easily and cohesively viewed.

## 3.4 Casner's BOZ

„BOZ is an automated graphic design and presentation tool that designs graphics based on an analysis of the task for which a graphic is intended to support" [14]. The same limitations as in APT and SAGE, relational database and 2-d graphics, hold for BOZ.

The initial and foremost criteria for the choice of a graphical expression in BOZ is the *task* of the user. It is formally described by logical operators, which then are mapped to perceptual operators. A graph is chosen for display that satisfies the visualization task and minimizes the cost for performing the user's task.

## 3.5 Senay and Ignatius: VISTA

VISTA (VISualization Tool Assistant) again uses a similar approach as in APT, but extends the graphical expressions to the third dimension [15]. VISTA is rule-based and uses an extensive list of rules on effective mapping strategies. VISTA's rules are twofold: (a) they support an expressive and effective visual representation of (scientific) data by analyzing known characterization of data, and (b) they are based on research in human visual perception, including treatment of illusions, preattentiveness, and psychophysics.

Another extension to the previously named concepts is the interactive modification of automatically generated displays by the user. This approach offers more possibilities for real-life design of visualization systems.

The architecture of VISTA is split into three main units:

The first phase is the *data unit*, in which the user can select a set of interactive data manipulation operators. There are some dynamically organized menus from which the user can select data sets and data variables. Furthermore s/he can obtain a data subset from the database by selecting several data variables from one or more data sets. The order of selection defines a default importance ordering, though the user can redefine it.

The second phase is the *design unit*, in which the system generates a composite visualization technique. Once VISTA generates the composite visualization technique, the user can modify it within the design unit.

The third phase is the *rendering unit*, which gets the primary input from the design unit. The rendering unit creates an image according to the design description by using appropriate rendering algorithms. At last the rendering unit displays the image resulting from this process on the user's terminal. Also the rendering unit provides interactive facilities for image manipulation, for example: the viewing operations rotation, translation, zooming and image manipulation operators, with which the user can select any component of the visualization technique corresponding to a data partition and interactively modify its attributes.

### 3.6 Robertson's Natural Scene Paradigm (NSP)

While the above discussed systems first produced graphical expressions from graphical primitives (bottom-up approach), Robertson [16] suggests a top-down approach. He satisfies his own request to the research community „... we need a methodology, based on some appropriate information theory of visualization, for choosing data representations to best achieve any specific visualization aim" by a methodology called the Natural Scene Paradigm (NSP). It is based on the idea, that humans are very capable in interpreting natural scenes. There is no problem in finding out connected patterns, distinguishing between fore- and background, recognizing whether scene properties are independent or in relation to each other and so on.

The Natural Scene Paradigm suggests to map data elements independent of their application field onto features of natural scenes, e.g. mountains and valleys, showing patterns of density and color. NSP uses three input streams to its mapping function: (a) structure and nature of each data variable, including dimensionality, parameter relationships, type of data (ordinal or nominal, discrete or continuous); (b) interpretation aims, such as importance of individual data variables (point, local, global), and their relative importance (priority ordering or weighting of these attributes); and (c) user directives, including any display constraints (for example, analyst requirements forcing particular representations). The mapping function then matches data variables to interpretation aims and user directives by choosing representations optimizing the match.

By definition, the NSP assures coherency through top-down design of complex scenes and problem-free interpretation through perceptual skills of humans.

### 3.7 Wehrend and Lewis (Catalogue of Visualizations)

The goal of Wehrend and Lewis [9] was to provide help for the visualization mapping based on previous successful examples. After looking at a series of successful examples of visualization techniques they classified each technique by two features: attribute and operation. „Attribute" describes what kind of data is to be displayed. Choices are scalar, scalar field, nominal, direction, direction field, shape, position, spatially extended region or object, and structure. „Operations" to be performed on these attributes are: identify, locate, distinguish, categorize, cluster, distribution, rank, compare within and between relations, associate, and correlate. The catalogue of visualizations is a large 2-d matrix defined over all attributes and operations. Each matrix elements contains a set of successful (expressive and effective) visualization techniques for the particular pair of (attribute/operation).

## 4 Visual Perception and the Human

In computer visualization we assume that a human interprets a computer generated visual. To create expressive and effective visual representations, knowledge of human perception is paramount. Unfortunately human perception is complex to describe because it is inherently non-linear, contains many exceptions, and is dependent on very different aspects, such as biological, psychophysical, and cognitive aspects. Therefore the approach to finding optimal visual representations is often „trial-and-error". Unfortunately a pleasing picture on the screen may be inexpressive and ineffective and therefore misleading in the interpretation, but chosen by the viewer (or graphics expert) out of lack of human perception expertise. To quote one example, the use of color tables may create unexpected color effects, e.g. color bands, that may be interpreted in a very misleading way. This effect only appears when creating visuals on a computer. To quote another example, the use of dark blue for small objects may result in not being able to see the objects in focus. This latter example is based on biological facts of the human eye. A third example is the Machband effect, an illusion that enhances borders between two fields of brightness values. Both latter examples appear on the computer screen as well as on other (e.g. printed) visuals.

To get basic information on human perception, an introductory literature, such as [17] is recommended. Information on effective color displays is discussed in a comprehensive manner in [18]. Computer visualization yet raises more complex questions about human perception than these books will answer. One such question concerns the many new possibilities offered by 3D input and output devices. While availability and request for 3D input and output devices are on the increase, little data is available on the comparison between different hardware offered on the market. In computer visualization, we have long moved away from the simple anaglyph stereo to shutter glass stereo and head mounted displays, similarly we have matching input devices, such as 3D trackballs or the data glove. But how good are the various stereo modes and does more pricey mean better? In the section „3-d Perception" below I will discuss one study on the quality of 3-d display modes and some of its interesting results.

Much of what we see and interpret is only comprehensible because we had a special education that taught us to recognize certain objects or features. Past and cultural experiences add to our understanding and ways of interpretation. Special limitations, such as color blindness, or special abilities, such as a good mental rotation ability, vary the amount of information a person can extract from a visual representation. For color blind persons, black-and-white representations may produce equivalent understanding as their colored counterparts. With interactive visualization systems, a well developed fine motor coordination is helpful. If the motor coordination is not well developed, larger buttons may be helpful. So additionally from being dependent on data characteristics, interpretation aims, general perception rules, the creation of effective visualizations seems to be also dependent on individual abilities. Visualization systems that know about individual human constraints are called 'adaptive visualization system'. Section 4.1 below discusses a way of extracting knowledge about abilities of a user in order to use this knowledge as a constraint in the mapping of data -> pictures. I would like to point out, that constraints in computer-human interaction may be limitations of a human *or* limitations of the computer device used. Color blindness can be restricting, but so can a bad monitor with aged phosphor cells. Similarly, the quality of an input device will influence the fine motor coordination of a person.

## 4.1 Adaptive Visualization Systems

Even if we understand and recognize general rules of visual perception, individual differences in the abilities of users may vary enough to produce misleading visual representations. To ensure meaningful visualizations, the visualization system needs to adapt to desires, disabilities and abilities of the user. In this section we propose the generation of a „user model" to describe collective information of a particular user (see [19]).

### 4.1.1 User modeling

User modeling denotes the generation of the user model by extracting information from the user ([20]). Information can be extracted from the user in one of three ways:

- Through explicit modeling: the user typically fills out a form and answers to direct questions.
- Through implicit modeling: the user is being observed in his/her use of the system.
- The user is asked to solve special tasks and is being observed in doing so.

A complete user model evolves in several stages, whereby each style of user modeling is being used. Typically, the extraction of information starts with explicit modeling to inquire about gender, age, or education. Subsequently, the user has to complete special tasks that reveal limitations of his/her vision and/or hand-eye coordination. By continuously observing the user in his/her use of the visualization system, the user model can be improved over time. Significant information for the user model is expected from the completion of special tasks. We have therefore focused on implementing special tests that reveal abilities and disabilities of the user. Most of the tests are currently implemented at the motivational level of educational games: users enjoy performing the tests and may call them up repeatedly. Motivation in performing these tests is important both for the purpose of user modeling as well as for training certain abilities through repetitive performance of the tests.

### 4.1.2 „Games" to test the user

The following four abilities describing the performance of a user as relevant for visualization have been investigated in more detail: color perception, color memory, color ranking and fine motor coordination. Details on user modeling of mental rotation is in

[19]. Additionally we have found several abilities that might be of influence, but have not been investigated in any detail so far: reasoning, size recognition, perceptual speed, visual versus verbal recognition, and embedded figure recognition.

Following is a description of each of the four user abilities investigated, explaining its relationship to visualization and the tests or „games" which extract information about this ability from the user. Between fifteen and twenty users were tested for each of the abilities. In two of the four abilities (perception and fine motor coordination) we were able to derive quantitative evaluations of the results. In two of the our abilities (color ranking and color memory) the test results are described in a qualitative manner.

**Color perception:** Color perception is defined as the process of distinguishing points or homogeneous patches of light by a subject. It is a cognitive ability and varies among people. Color perception depends on a person's color deficiency, gender, ethnological information, quality of monitor used and the lightening situation in the room. No general assumption of color perception for one visualization instance can therefore be made a priori.

Since color graphics workstations have become a standard equipment at scientific institutions, color coding is one of the most commonly used visualization technique to represent data. Colors used must be set to values that are easily distinguished by the viewer. Therefore the goal for the "color perception test" is to find a set of discriminatory colors. A standardized test optometrists use to determine color deficiencies, the "Farnsworth Hue 100" test ([21]), has been used as a basis. In a very similar manner, the essence of our test is to sort forty pastel (low saturation) color chips so that every chip has a minimal color difference to its neighbour. Colors that can not be distinguished would appear out of order in the test results. We use only forty colors instead of one hundred or more (in the original Farnsworth test) to keep the user motivated to perform the test. Our first results indicate that these forty colors give us enough information to eliminate colors that would cause problems for color coding.

For twenty users two parameters each were measured: a) the time it took the user to perform the color perception test, and b) an error factor describing the errors in the final arrangement of the color chips. In order to compare measured time between slow and quick users, we used the time difference between the actual timing measurement of the color perception test and similar tasks (e.g. sorting numbers, sorting angles). Figure 3 shows two test results for the color perception test, once for a non color deficient user (3a) and once for a color deficient user (3b). Besides by the increased error factors, color deficient users were also noticeable in the time it took them to perform the test.

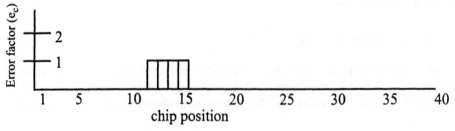

**Figure 3 (a)** Error factors of non color deficient viewer

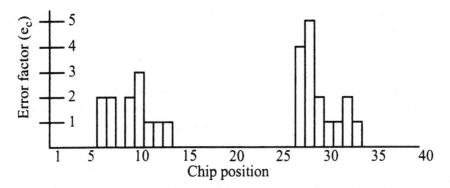

**Figure 3 (b)** Error factors of color deficient viewer

The error factor $e_c$ in Figure 3, calculated for each test result, is dependent on the misplacements of chips relative to their neighbours:

$$e_c = abs(c_c - c_l) + abs(c_r - c_c)\text{-}2,$$

with $c_c$... current chip number, $c_l$... number of left chip, $c_r$... number of right chip. Figure 3 (a) reflects the error factor for each of the forty chips for a typical non-color deficient user who misplaced one color chip. Figure 3 (b) shows the error factor for each chip for user 9 (color deficient).

**Color ranking:** Color ranking is the association of color with ordinal or quantitative data items. If a temperature scale is to be displayed, standard color mapping (low temperature mapped to blue, high temperatures mapped to red, yellow and white) may be used. If no "standard mapping" is known for specific data characteristics, an artificial ranking of colors from "low" to "high" is necessary. Because human perception has no inherent ranking of colors, the association of color with ordinal or quantitative data items is individual, depending on the problem domain as well as the viewer's education, color deficiencies and preference.

Interpreting the meaning of a color picture often involves instant recognition of low values versus high values. The presence of a color scale showing the used color range and its associations is extremely important. Still, misinterpretation can only be avoided, if the viewer is in agreement with the association. The goal of the "color ranking test" is therefore to have the viewer reveal their own intuition on color sequences. This is done by having the user match colors of an available color gamut to a number scale from one to ten. Typical color scales expected from this test were:

black (0) - purple - blue - cyan - dark.green - lt.green - yellow - orange - red - white (10)
or
black(0) - purple - blue - cyan - dark.green - lt.green - red - orange - yellow - white (10)

Results from the color ranking test proved to differ widely from one user to the next. Even though spectral scales and increasing perceptual brightness were among the fifteen test results, most users lacked a specific strategy. We are currently devising the test to receive more meaningful results. The user-chosen color scale should be used preferably for visualization of ordinal data items.

**Color memory:** Color memory is the ability of a person to recall a color from memory. Even though we are able to distinguish between numerous colors [22]), we can only do so when comparing one color to another. If color samples are not directly compared to each other we can only process a small fraction of colors (around ten). Interpreting the meaning of a color picture series often involves recognizing (and therefore remembering) the same color in several pictures. Specifically for the distinction of nominal data items, we prefer to use colors the user can easily distinguish.

The idea for the corresponding "color memory" test has been borrowed from the well known game "Memory". Nine color cards are shown to the user for ten seconds. When they are turned face-down, the user needs to pick the correct color corresponding to one color card that will be shown to him/her. The user may guess as many times as needed, but the amount of guesses is entered into a log file. The game can vary in difficulty by changing the timing allowed to view the nine cards. As in all other tests and games introduced in this paper, the results (what colors are memorized best) are not only dependent on user's abilities but also on the quality of hardware and lightning environment. For our purposes we see this as an advantage of modeling the current environment as perfectly as possible rather than a lack of separation between the content of different visualization models (e.g. user model and resource model).

**Fine motor coordination:** Fine motor coordination is the user's ability to perform precision manual tasks, demanding good eye-hand coordination and motor speed. This ability is influenced by age, gender, experience, motor (dis)abilities of the user as well as the input device used. With increasing age the ability to coordinate the interaction between eye and hand decreases ([23]). While in general men are faster in tapping a single key, women are faster in moving small objects to a specific destination. Players of computer games are an excellent example to show the increase of fine motor coordination with experience. Naturally, motor disabilities impair fine motor coordination. Additionally to these individual characteristics of a user, type and quality of the input device used plays a large role in the accuracy of fine motor coordination.

Interactive visualization requires fine motor coordination, e.g. to point at small objects or to trace structures on the screen. The "fine motor coordination test" as currently implemented determines the user's speed and error rate to trace a predefined path on the screen. Error rate, as an indicator for accuracy, is measured by counting the number of times the user leaves the predefined path.

The result of fifteen users in Figure 4 compares time and error rate: the quadrants are separated by the mean error rate and mean user's speed, respectively. Quadrant I describes the best candidates for a quick and accurate access via mouse. Quadrant IV describes users with a certain handicap for these tasks. Initial tests showed, that the type of pointing device used was a major influence to the results. In order to observe differences in the user's ability alone, the same mouse was used for all tests.

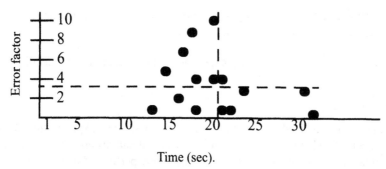

Time (sec).

**Figure 4:** Results of fine motor coordination test

## 4.2 3-d Perception

Over the past few years, 3d graphics has received a great deal of attention. While it is widely acknowledged as an opportunity for many application areas, it is also a challenge for those who seriously look at the advantages and disadvantages of the wide variety of 3-d interface products offered on the market. One issue of interest is the effectiveness of a particular 3-d display mode in comparison with „equivalent" techniques. The so far existing general discussions of 3-d perception did not lead to helpful conclusions for 3-d hardware buyers. In a team effort between Sabine Volbracht (as the M.Sc. student whose theses we are discussing here), Khatoun Shahrbabaki (at that time graduate assistant at my institute and co-advisor for the thesis), Gregor Fels (professor of Organic Chemistry, and co-advisor for the thesis), and myself (advisor of the thesis), we approached the question of „how effective are 3-d display modes": we reduced the testing environment to one application area (organic chemistry), one visualization technique (the molecule stick model, which is the preferred visual representation for the research work of Professor Fels), and three 3d display modes (perspective viewing, anaglyph stereo and shutter glass stereo). We then made observations on the effectiveness of the different display modes by measuring accuracy and time during the performance of several tasks by the user. The six tasks used for this experiment were strongly influenced by actual research tasks of Professor Fels. The three 3d display modes were implemented in the following way:

**Perspective viewing:** The molecules are projected onto a 2D plane using perspective projection and color.

**Anaglyph stereo:** Two perspective views of the molecules are generated, a right- and a left-eye perspective view with complementary colors (red/green or red/cyan). The observer uses glasses with red/green or red/cyan filters, respectively. Color can not be used for carrying information about the molecules in this mode.

**Shutter glass stereo:** Two perspective views of the molecules are generated using the same color scale as in the perspective molecules. Here the right- and left-eye views of the molecules are presented alternately on the screen with 120 Hz (60 right-eye views and 60 left-eye views alternating per second). The observer looks through Stereo-Graphics CrystalEyes® LCD shutter glasses.

The following sections describe the experiment and its result in more detail [24].

### 4.2.1 Experiment

The experiment involved 81 participants and was based on [25] and [26]. The subjects were students of chemistry or computer science and had different experiences with 3d representations of organic molecules. The tasks were performed interactively on each of the 3d display modes. The interaction was restricted to molecule rotations with the mouse. An objective comparison was based on the correct answers of the questions and measured time for answering.

Before beginning the experiment and before each task, the subjects received practice time for a few minutes to become proficient with each 3d display mode and familiar with the particular molecule. Once the subject pressed a 'Start/Ready' Button, the interviewer explained the task. After performing the task, the subject pressed the 'Start/Ready' Button again to indicate the end of the trial. At that time the response time and other necessary information were recorded.

For each task subjects saw a different molecule. In this way we avoided subjects remembering the structure of molecules. Three tasks (identifying, comparing, and positioning) were tested by providing six questions. Identifying and comparing were each tested with a simple and a complex molecule to understand the relationship between complexity and viewing. Additionally another identification task without interaction was considered. The particularity of this is the absence of hidden relevant objects. That means the difference between the first two identifying tasks and the last one is the importance of depth information for identifying. For the first two tasks depth information is very important for identifying rings, because the molecules cannot be positioned in a way that all rings can be seen clearly at the same time. Some ring are always hidden. For the third identifying task all the relevant rings can be seen clearly in the initial position. So rotations are not necessary. The six tasks were as follows:

**T1:** Identifying (simple molecule): „Count the rings in this molecule"
**T2:** Identifying (complex molecule): „Count the rings in this molecule"
**T3:** Comparing (simple molecule): „Identify the nearest and the most distant atom from the viewer"
**T4:** Comparing (complex molecule): Determine the order of benzene rings on the z-axis.
**T5:** Positioning: Position the benzene ring parallel to the screen plane
**T6:** Identifying: Count the benzene rings in this molecule.

### 4.2.2 Results of 3D Perception Experiment

Mean response time and mean response error were computed separately by a two-way Analysis of Variance with 9 experimental conditions consisting of the factorial combination of three classes of display mode and three levels of experience (students of chemistry with and without special knowledge in organic chemistry, and students of computer science). Error values were expressed as follows:

**T1 (rings):** Difference to the correct number of rings. The correct answer was 5 rings.
**T2 (rings):** Difference to the correct number of rings. The correct answer was 15 rings.
**T3 (distance):** Sum of error distances on the z-axis from the first and the last atom in angstroms. The distance between these two atoms behaved on 10.78 angstroms.
**T4 (distance):** Sum of error distances on the z-axis from the center of the benzene rings in angstroms. For evaluation of this task the rings were arranged in increasing order of z-distances and numbered. An error distance was only measured when in the order of the subject a lower number followed a higher number. So the greatest error behaved on 15.48 angstroms (computed from 6! possibilities).
**T5 (angle):** Error angle in degrees.
**T6 (rings):** Difference to the correct number of rings. The correct answer was 8 rings.

**Table II:** Main effect of display mode for P (perspective), A (anaglyph), and S (shutter glasses) averaged over 27 subjects and three experience levels. 'E' represents the mean response error, 'T' the mean response time.

|  | P | A | S |
|---|---|---|---|
| T1: E (error rings) | -0.30 | -0.04 | -0.11 |
| T1: T | 26.75 sec | 22.40 sec | 25.64 sec |
| T2: E (error rings) (variance) | 0 (10.46) | -1.96 (7.81) | -1.15 (5.90) |
| T2: T | 91.84 sec | 66.93 sec | 67.02 sec |
| T3: E (error distances in angstroms) | 4.266 | 1.374 | 1.167 |
| T3: T | 92.77 sec | 70.86 sec | 53.08 sec |
| T4: E (error distances in angstroms) | 4.380 | 0.780 | 0.953 |
| T4: T | 137.07 sec | 90.37 sec | 79.04 sec |
| T5: E (error angle in degrees) | 11.78 | 4.65 | 4.75 |
| T5: T | 78.48 sec | 58.32 sec | 76.25 sec |
| T6: E (error rings) | -0.11 | -0.67 | -0.59 |
| T6: T | 33.69 sec | 45.87 sec | 43.31 sec |

Table II summarizes the main effect of display mode for all tasks, averaged over 27 subjects and three experience levels (81 participants). In order to compare different mean times and errors, a Newman-Keuls test ($\alpha = 0.05$) was applied in each case.

In T1, significant differences occurred neither in the amount of errors nor in the measured response time between the three display modes, but rather in the response time for the various experience levels. The Newman-Keuls test indicated that chemistry students specializing in organic chemistry were significantly faster in identifying rings than students of computer science.

In T2, where molecules were more complex, the differences in both measured units were significant. The Newman-Keuls tests showed that a) identifying in shutter and anaglyph mode was better than in perspective mode and b) students of organic chemistry made significantly less errors when performing the task.

In T6, where no interaction was necessary, perspective viewing proved to be significantly better than the other two display modes. This unexpected result might be explained by the fact, that if the third dimension doesn't provide any necessary information it's appearance makes the interpretation task more difficult. We presume that in such a case a redundant visual cue decreases the effectiveness of a visualization. However, perspective viewing is often not reliable, because information needed may be hidden.

In T3 and T4, where spatial information was relevant, viewing in perspective mode was considerably worse than the stereo modes, as expected.

The analysis of the obtained data from T5 showed an interesting result, namely that positioning errors were smaller in anaglyph and shutter mode than in perspective mode, but that positioning time was only significantly better in anaglyph mode. The difference in mean time of shutter and perspective mode was not significant.

In comparing the three display modes it is an interesting outcome that shutter and anaglyph mode are not significantly different. A comparison of cost and performance of the three here discussed 3d display modes for research tasks in organic chemistry would therefore favour anaglyph stereo. This recommendation does not include an evaluation of the significance in using color. The lack of color in anaglyph stereo is a serious disadvantage.

The experiments also demonstrated that the experience level of the user to *identify* special objects is relevant. No indication was given that this is true for *positioning or comparing* tasks.

A comparison of complex and simple molecules showed that increasing complexity also increases the difference between perspective and stereo modes to favour stereo modes.

## 5 Conclusions

It is still too early to expect a solid foundation to the science of computer visualization. This paper was intended both as a review over the field and a view at two specific research ares within the field -- as seen from the perspective of a computer scientist. Further research, especially in the areas of data models, perception and intelligent agents as applied to computer visualization, will add much towards a well founded mapping process from "bits and bytes" to "understanding".

# References

1. The Oxford English Dictionary, 1989.

2. McCormick, B.H., T.A. DeFanti, M.D. Brown (ed), Visualization in Scientific Computing, Computer Graphics Vol. 21, No. 6, November 1987

3. Foley, J. and B. Ribarsky, Next-generation Data Visualiza- tion Tools, in Scientific Visualization, 1994, Advances and Challen- ges, Ed: L. Rosenblum, R.A. Earnshaw, J. Encarnacao, H. Hagen, A. Kaufman, S. Klimenko, G. Nielson, F. Post, D. Thalmann , Aca- demic Press.

4. Gershon, N., From Perception to Visualization, in Scientific Visualization, 1994, Advances and Challenges, Ed: L. Rosenblum, R.A. Earnshaw, J. Encarnacao, H. Hagen, A. Kaufman, S. Klimenko, G. Nielson, F. Post, D. Thalmann , Academic Press.

5. P. Robertson and L. De Ferrari, Systematic Approaches to Visualization: Is a Refer- ence Model Needed? in Scientific Visuali- zation, 1994, Advances and Challenges, Ed: L. Rosenblum, R.A. Earnshaw, J. Encarnacao, H. Hagen, A. Kaufman, S. Klimenko, G. Nielson, F. Post, D. Thalmann , Academic Press.

6. K.W. Brodlie, L.A. Carpenter, R.A. Earnshaw, J.R. Gallop, R.J. Hubbard, A.M. Mum- ford, C.D. Osland, P. Quarendon (eds), Scientific Visualization, Techniques and Appli- cations, 1992. Springer-Verlag.

7. Gallop, J., 1994. Underlying data models and structures for visualization, in Scientific Visualization, eds. Rosenblum et al., Academic Press, pp. 239-250.

8. Mackinlay, J., 1986, Automating the Design of Graphical Presentations of Relational Information, ACM Trans. on Graphics, Vol. 5, No. 2, April 1986, pp 110-141.

9. Wehrend, S. and C. Lewis, 1990, A Problem-oriented Classification of Visualization Techniques, Proceedings of Visualization 1990, IEEE Computer Society Press.

10. J.T. Stasko and Ch. Patterson, 1992, Understanding and Characterizing Software Visualization Systems, Proc. of 1992 IEEE Workshop on Visual Languages, IEEE Com- puter Society Press.

11. George G. Robertson, Stuart K. Card, and Jock D. Mackinlay, „Information Visuali- zation Using 3D Interactive Ani- mation", CACM, Vol. 36, No. 4, April 1993.

12. Cox, D., Using the Supercomputer to Visualize Higher Dimensions: An Artist's con- tribution to Scientific Visualization", Leonardo, Vol. 22, 1988, pp. 233-242.

13. Roth, S.F., John Kolojejchick, J.Mattis, and J. Goldstein, 1993, Interactive Graphic Design Using Automatic Presentation Knowledge. In Zahid Ahmed, Kristina Miceli, Steve Casner, and Steve Roth, editors, Workshop on Intelligent Visualization Systems. IEEE Computer Society/Visualization '93, October 1993.

14. Stephen M. Casner, A Task-Analytic Approach to the Automated Design of Graphic Presentations, ACM Trans Graphics, Vol. 10, No. 2, April 1991, Pages 111-151.

15. H. Senay and E. Ignatius, A Knowledge-Based System for Visualization Design, IEEE Computer Graphics and Applications, November 1994, pp. 36-47.

16. Robertson, P.K. , 1991, A Methodology for Choosing Data Representations. IEEE Computer Graphics and Applications, Vol. 11, No. 3, May 1991, pp. 56-68.

17. Sekuler, R. and R. Blake, 1985, Perception, published by Alfred A. Knopf.

18. Travis, D., 1991, Effective Color Displays. Academic Press.

19. Domik, G.O. and B. Gutkauf, 1994, User Modeling for Adaptive Visualization Sys- tems, Proceedings of IEEE Visualization '94, IEEE Computer Society, 1994, pp. 217- 223.

20. Fischer, G., 1991, The Importance of Models in Making Complex Systems Comprehensible, in D. Ackerman and M. Tauber (editors) Mental Models and Human Computer Communications, Elsevier Science, Amsterdam, pp. 3-36, 1991.

21. Higgins, K.E., 1975, The logic of color vision testing, a primer.

22. Hunt, R.W., 1987, Measuring Color, Ellis Horwood Limited, Market Cross House, Cooperstreet, Chichester, West Sussex, PO 191EB, England.

23. Ruff, R.M. and S.B. Parker, 1993, Gender and age-specific changes in motor speed and eye-hand coordination in adults: normative values for the finger tapping and grooved pegboard tests. Perceptual and motor skills, 76, pp. 1219-1230.

24. Volbracht, S., G. Domik, K. Shahrbabaki, G. Fels, in print, An Experimental Comparison of 3D Display Modes, IEEE Visualization 1996, San Francisco, USA

25. Eberts, R.E., 1994, User Interface Design. Prentice-Hall, Inc.

26. Conte, S.D., H.E. Donsmore and V.Y. Shen, 1986, Software engineering metrics and models. Benjamin/Cummings Publishing Company Inc.

# High Performance Computing -
# The Computational Chemistry Perspective

Luděk Matyska

Institute of Computer Science and Faculty of Informatics, Masaryk University,
Botanická 68a, CZ-602 00 Brno, Czech Republic
e-mail: ludek@ics.muni.cz

**Abstract.** This paper gives a subjective look at the high performance computing from the computational chemistry perspective. Using basic *ab initio* and molecular dynamics algorithms as examples of typical computational chemistry problems, the software engineering and architectural issues of contemporary high performance computers are discussed. The parallel computational chemistry is also presented, with a brief discussion of distributed environments used.

## 1 Introduction

While the number of computers available worldwide is rapidly increasing, the demand for computational power is increasing even faster. Almost any computer in computer centers around the globe is saturated and more purchases are planned everywhere to keep pace with the load. While a substantial amount of these computations is represented by (commercial) information processing and database operations, scientific numerically oriented computations are still the most demanding in terms of pure computing power.

The first computers were developed to do some particle physics computations, needed for the understanding of principles leading to the development of the first atomic bomb. Perhaps not surprisingly, computations of similar nature still belongs to those taking up all the computing power of computers available to scientists. As the processing power and capabilities of computers evolved, new applications were (and still are) developed along. When we look at any High Performance Computing[1] Center around the (western) world, we may find the following research areas covered

- computational fluid dynamics, from engineering applications, like wing behavior simulations, through physics (numerical simulation of fusion plasmas), to astrophysics (star formation) and other areas;
- weather and climate modeling (from some point of view this is just a specialization of computational fluid dynamics field);
- finite element analysis (constructions);

---

[1] While the name Supercomputing Center is still used more frequently, the HPC label is gaining increasing support to make evident that not only traditionally "supercomputers" are installed and used there.

- geophysics and petroleum engineering;
- Monte Carlo simulations, especially in particle and high energy physics;
- molecular biology, including Human Genome Project;
- chemistry and biochemistry.

While this list is far from complete, it covers all the main subjects[2] influenced by the contemporary high performance computing.

There are many similarities and at least as many dissimilarities between "normal" and high performance computing. New questions and problems in computer science were raised, starting at the theory side, going through software engineering and ending with architectural requirements for the high performance computing. This paper's aim is to introduce and discuss at least some of these, using two areas of computational chemistry, namely *ab initio* and molecular dynamics, as working examples. The paper is organized as follows: in the next section, the computational problem is presented, including some brief introduction to the chemistry research field. Software engineering issues are discussed in the third section, while the following one covers some requirements on the computer hardware. Parallel programming, including brief description of the most important models used, is discussed in the fifth section. The last section gives a summary with some future expectations.

## 2 The Chemical Problem

Contemporary chemistry is not imaginable without computing. None of the prestigious chemical journals accepts a paper where experiment is not supported by results of appropriate computation. Even in the bastion of experimental chemistry, the (organic) synthesis, experiments (including discovery of new synthetic pathways) must be accompanied by results of computer simulations. Moreover, majority of experimental methods is based on elaborate and complex mathematical models and the experiments themselves cannot be evaluated without computational support. In fact, computational chemistry is one of the most demanding research area in terms of computing power and memory and disk space.

The foundation of theoretical chemistry is molecular quantum mechanics, which relates molecular properties to the motion and interactions of electrons and nuclei. The properties studied covers everything, from energy, through the values of many physical and physico-chemical properties, like dipole moment or boiling point, spectral characteristics, up to such complex properties like chemical reactivity. Molecular quantum mechanics is based on Schrödinger equation, formulated in 1925. Very soon became clear, that direct quantitative prediction of most, if not all, chemical properties is possible using only values of a small number of physical constants (masses and charges of elementary particles, the velocity of light, and Planck's constant). Such a procedure is known as an *ab initio* approach, and is independent of any experiment other than determination of these constants. The exact solution of Schrödinger equation is a formidable,

---

[2] Perhaps with the notable exception of military research.

if not impossible task, and it must be replaced by approximate mathematical models. Substantial part of computational chemistry is directly connected with the search for such models and their solutions.

Recently, simulations of chemical systems using *molecular dynamics* are gaining increased interest, especially for large, biologically active systems, like proteins (enzymes) and nucleic acids. Roughly speaking, molecular dynamics is trying to quantify complex chemical properties studying time-dependent behavior of chemical systems. While individual time steps may be computed using *ab initio* methods, the very large number of these steps required for any reasonable computer simulation forces use of much simpler (and therefore much faster) methods for prediction of basic properties (i.e. energy) of chemical systems. Even with these simplifications, the computational requirements remain enormous.

## 2.1 *Ab initio* Methods

Solution of Schrödinger partial differential equation

$$\hat{H}\Psi = E\Psi \ , \tag{1}$$

leads directly to the energy and many other properties of stationary state of a molecule [1, 2]. In (1), $\hat{H}$ is the Hamiltonian, a differential operator representing the total energy, $E$ is the numerical value of energy of the state, and $\Psi$ is the wavefunction. The square of the wavefunction, $|\Psi|^2$ ($\Psi$ may be complex) is interpreted as a measure of the probability distribution of the particles within the molecule. While the general Schrödinger equation covers nuclei and electrons simultaneously, it is possible to separate nuclear and electronic motions using the Born-Oppenheimer approximation. This corresponds to new version of Schrödinger equation,

$$\hat{H}^{\text{elec}}\Psi^{\text{elec}}(\boldsymbol{r}, \boldsymbol{R}) = E^{\text{eff}}(\boldsymbol{R})\Psi^{\text{elec}}(\boldsymbol{r}, \boldsymbol{R}) \ , \tag{2}$$

where the electronic wavefunction $\Psi^{\text{elec}}$ depends on the electronic, $\boldsymbol{r}$, and the nuclear, $\boldsymbol{R}$, coordinates, the electronic Hamiltonian, $\hat{H}^{\text{elec}}$ corresponds to motion of electrons only in the field of fixed nuclei, and $E^{\text{eff}}$ is the effective electronic energy, which depends on nuclear coordinates only.

The main task of the theoretical chemistry is to solve the electronic Schrödinger equation (2). While the Born-Oppenheimer approximation is highly accurate, the properties of molecule are now described by the potential energy (hyper)surface, $E(\boldsymbol{R})$, where minima corresponds to the ground states of molecule. The exact solution of Schrödinger equation is impossible for any but the most trivial systems. Simplifying assumptions and procedures must be applied to make the solution possible for larger molecules.

The first approximation restricts the form of the wavefunction, which must be constructed from a set of one-electron functions, molecular orbitals $\phi$. For the $n$ electron system,

$$\Psi = \begin{vmatrix} \phi_1(1) & \phi_2(1) & \cdots & \phi_n(1) \\ \phi_1(2) & \phi_2(2) & \cdots & \phi_n(2) \\ & & \vdots & \\ \phi_1(n) & \phi_2(n) & \cdots & \phi_n(n) \end{vmatrix} , \tag{3}$$

where the first row corresponds to all the possible assignation of electron 1 to individual molecular orbitals, the second row holds for electron 2 and so forth.

The next approximation restricts the molecular orbitals, which are defined as linear combinations of pre-defined functions, known as basis functions (together they form the so-called basis set),

$$\psi_i = \sum_{\mu=1}^{N} c_{\mu i} \chi_\mu . \tag{4}$$

The most commonly used basis functions are of the gaussian type, and have the general form

$$g(\alpha, r) = c x^n y^m z^l e^{-\alpha r^2} , \tag{5}$$

where $r$ depends on $x$, $y$, and $z$, $\alpha$ is the constant determining the orbital size, and $c$ is such that

$$\int_{allspace} g^2 = 1 \tag{6}$$

holds.

The solution of Schrödinger equation is usually based on the variational method, which states that for any wavefunction $\Phi$, the expectation value of the corresponding energy

$$E' = \int \Phi^* \hat{H} \Phi d\tau , \tag{7}$$

is always greater than the energy of exact wavefunction $\Psi$. Thus, the solution of Schrödinger equation is equivalent to finding the set of molecular coefficient $c_{\mu i}$ fulfilling the Roothaan-Hall equations

$$\sum_{\nu=1}^{N} (F_{\mu\nu} - \epsilon_i S_{\mu\nu}) c_{\nu i} = 0 \quad \mu = 1, 2, \ldots, N . \tag{8}$$

$\epsilon_i$ is the one-electron energy of the molecular orbital, $S$ is the overlap matrix,

$$S_{\mu\nu} = \int \chi_\mu^*(1) \chi_\nu(1) dx_1 dy_1 dz_1 , \tag{9}$$

(asterix denotes complex conjugation) and $F$ is the Fock matrix,

$$F_{\mu\nu} = H_{\mu\nu}^{core} + \sum_{\lambda=1}^{N} \sum_{\sigma=1}^{N} P_{\lambda\sigma} [(\mu\nu|\lambda\sigma) - \frac{1}{2}(\mu\lambda|\nu\sigma)] . \tag{10}$$

The quantities $(\mu\nu|\lambda\sigma)$ are two-electron repulsion integrals:

$$(\mu\nu|\lambda\sigma) = \int\int \chi_\mu^*(1)\chi_\nu(1)\left(\frac{1}{r_{12}}\right)\chi_\lambda^*(2)\chi_\sigma(2)\,dx_1dy_1dz_1dx_2dy_2dz_2 \ , \qquad (11)$$

and $P$ is the one-electron density matrix,

$$P_{\lambda\sigma} = 2\sum_{i=1}^{occ} c_{\lambda i}^* c_{\sigma i} \ . \qquad (12)$$

The Roothaan-Hall equation (8) is not linear since Fock matrix and the molecular orbitals themselves depend on the molecular coefficients (whose values represent the solution to (8)). Solution is based on an iterative process, called *Self Consistent Field (SCF) theory*.

The presented treatment forms the basis of Hartree-Fock theory. While this theory was successfully used for the computation of properties of many chemical systems, the approximations used are too severe and the Hartree-Fock treatment suffers from substantial omission of electron interactions. They must be considered in order to increase the accuracy of results.

The exact wavefunction $\Psi$ cannot be expressed as a simple determinant, as assumed by the Hartree-Fock theory. The *configuration interaction (CI)* methods overcome this insufficiency by substituting some occupied molecular orbital in the Hartree-Fock determinant with a virtual (unoccupied) one and combining this new determinant with the unsubstituted one. The *Full CI* method constructs the wavefunction $\Psi$ as a linear combination of the Hartree-Fock determinant and all possible substituted determinants,

$$\Psi = b_0\Psi_0 + \sum_{s>0} b_s\Psi_s \ , \qquad (13)$$

where $s$ runs over all possible substitutions and 0 denotes the Hartree-Fock level. The $b$'s are new coefficients whose values are to be found. The full CI is the most complete non-relativistic treatment possible, it is, however, prohibitely expensive. The theoretical complexity of this approach, see Tab. 1, does not allow direct use of full CI method[3] for any but trivial system. Instead, approximations where the full expansion is truncated at some level, are used. The most popular (while still very expensive) are limitations to doubles only, CID, to singles and doubles, CISD, and up to triples, CISD(T). Quadratic variants, QCID, QCISD, and QCISD(T), while even more computationally expensive, remove size inconsistency[4] which plagues the simpler variants.

---

[3] The *ab initio* treatment of HIV protease, which is an enzyme with $\approx 1\,500$ atoms, using only modest basis set with $10\,000$ basis functions, requires evaluation of some $4\,500^{10\,000}$ configurations.

[4] The method is said to be size consistent if the properties computed for system composed from several independent subsystems are just a summation of properties of individual subsystems.

Different approach how to overcome the deficiencies of the Hartree-Fock treatment represents the Møller-Plesset perturbation theory, which treats the electron correlation through the mathematical techniques known as many body theory. The derived methods form a series, denoted by MP$n$, $n \geq 2$, with increased computational complexity. Detailed description of the Møller-Plesset theory may be found in references [1, 2].

While the theoretical complexity of *ab initio* methods may be found in Tab. 1, the actual memory and disk requirements for one of the most widely used *ab initio* computer programs, the Gaussian, are presented in Tabs. 2 and 3. The theoretical as well as actual requirements depend not only on the number of molecular orbitals (i.e., the property of the studied system), but on the number of basis functions used, i.e., the property of the method. The simplest usable basis set uses one basis function per hydrogen atom and five basis functions per each first row element (from Lithium to Fluorine). To obtain more accurate results, much larger basis sets must be used, with dozens of basis functions for first row elements and $\approx 5$ for hydrogen. For a simple hydrocarbon, $C_5H_{12}$, the smallest basis set consists of 32 basis functions, while the largest basis set in general use have some 219 basis functions. For large chemical systems of biological interest, like proteins and nucleic acids with hundreds and even thousands of atom, the basis set may have tens or even hundreds thousands basis functions.

**Table 1.** *Ab initio* Methods Complexity

| Method | CPU | Memory |
|---|---|---|
| SCF | $N^4$ | $N^2$ |
| MP2 Energies | $ON^4$ | $OVN$ |
| MP2 Gradients | $ON^4$ | $N^3$ |
| MP4, QCISD(T) | $O^3V^4$ | $N^4$ |
| Full CI | $((O+V)!/(O!V!))^2$ | |

$N$ is the number of basis functions, $O$ $(V)$ is the number of occupied (virtual) orbitals, respectively. Data taken from [2].

## 2.2 Molecular Dynamics

Many chemically and biologically interesting properties cannot be derived from the single point energy calculations. Large extents of the potential energy surface (if not the whole one) must be explored. The simplest example is the search for minima on PES, which corresponds to the more or less stable conformation of molecules. The understanding of dynamics of chemical processes requires not only knowledge of stationary points, but of their neighborhood as well. Molecular dynamics [3] methods belongs to the most popular methods used for the exploration of dynamic properties of molecules and molecular systems. hey also serve as an example of computationally very expensive non-*ab initio* methods.

The molecular dynamics simulation is based on the detailed study of motion of individual atoms with time. Atoms are approximated by points and move according to the laws of Newtonian mechanics. The simulation requires integration of Newton's equations of motion over time,

$$F_i(t) = m_i \frac{\partial^2 r_i(t)}{\partial t^2}, \qquad i = 1, N \ (N \equiv \text{number of atoms}) \ , \tag{14}$$

where $F_i(t)$ is force on atom $i$ at time $t$ and $r_i(t)$ is a position of atom $i$ at time $t$. The force on atom $i$ is computed as a negative gradient of the potential energy function,

$$F_i = -\frac{\partial}{\partial r_i} E(r_1, r_2, \ldots, r_N) \tag{15}$$

The Verlet algorithm is used for the integration,

$$r_i(t + \Delta t) = 2r_i(t) - r_i(t - \Delta t) + \frac{F_i(t)}{m_i}(\Delta t)^2 \ . \tag{16}$$

The velocities are computed by formula

$$v_i(t) = \frac{r_i(t + \Delta t) - r_i(t - \Delta t)}{2\Delta t} \ , \tag{17}$$

and are used for the computation of the temperature of the whole system[5],

$$T(t) = \frac{1}{(3N - n)k_B} \sum_{i=1}^{N} m_i |v_i|^2, \quad i = 1, N \ , \tag{18}$$

where $(3N - n)$ is the number of unconstrained degrees of freedom and $k_B$ is Boltzmann's constant.

During the molecular dynamics simulation, a trajectory (i.e., the history of the motion over a period of time) for a molecular system is generated in an iterative fashion. Molecular dynamics simulations are often performed on large biological systems, whose potential energy cannot be computed using *ab initio* methods. As with the motion equations themselves, the behavior of the molecular system is usually well described by simple laws of classical mechanics if the simulation is performed at high (room) temperatures and the detailed information regarding hydrogen atoms is not needed[6]. Thus, empirical potential functions are used to define potential energy surface. These functions usually

---

[5] Velocities are not directly needed for the integrations.

[6] The last requirement is not generally valid, as hydrogen bonds play very important role in the behavior of biologically important chemical systems in water. This drawback is usually overcome by the addition of correction terms to the equation (19).

include terms to describe bond stretch, bond and dihedral angle deformations, and nonbonded interactions. The typical potential energy function may look like

$$E(r_1, r_2, \ldots, r_N) = \sum_{\text{bonds}} \frac{1}{2} K_b (R - R_0)^2 + \sum_{\text{angles}} \frac{1}{2} K_a (\theta - \theta_0)^2 + \quad (19)$$

$$+ \sum_{\text{dihedrals}} K_d [1 + \cos(n\phi - \gamma)] +$$

$$+ \sum_{i,j} 4\varepsilon_{ij} \left[ \left( \frac{\sigma_{ij}}{r_{ij}} \right)^{12} - \left( \frac{\sigma_{ij}}{r_{ij}} \right)^6 \right] + \left( \frac{q_i q_j}{\varepsilon r_{ij}} \right) ,$$

where $K_b$, $K_a$, and $K_d$ are force constants and $R_0$, $\theta_0$, and $\gamma$ are equilibrium structural parameters for bonds, bond angles, and dihedral angles, respectively. The parameters $\sigma$, $\varepsilon_i$, and $q_i$ for the nonbonded interactions (the last term) are the Lennard-Jones radius, well depths, and partial charge for each atom, respectively.

The time step for the integration of (16) is of the order of 1 fsec ($10^{-15}$ sec). This is necessary to ensure the numerical stability of integration. Some $10^6$ integration steps are required to model processes whose duration is about 1 nsec ($10^{-9}$ sec). However, the time scale of $\mu$sec ($10^{-6}$) or even the msec ($10^{-3}$), which is required when modeling biologically interesting processes, is still unattainable.

## 3  Software

Methods of computational chemistry, like those described above, were developed with the aim to enhance the knowledge of physical and chemical properties and their foundations. It cannot be overemphasized that the computational experiment is always a complement to the "real" experiment, not its replacement. Naturally, the *number* and *complexity* of real experiments to be performed is heavily influenced by the available computational methods (and their employment). It is not worthwhile to try to replace *all* experiments by just the computation.

The complexity of the underlying algorithms and computational models and the requirement that computations have to accompany experiments, raises many interesting — and hard — questions to all the areas of software engineering. In the following, program Gaussian[7] [4] will be used as an example on which the problems and their (approximate) solutions will be demonstrated.

The development of Gaussian began in the late 70's, and the first widely used versions keep the label 1982 and 1985. The current version, dated 1994 consists of some 500 000 lines of Fortran 77 code[8] plus several thousand lines of auxiliary routines and programs written in C. The whole program is decomposed to dozens individual programs and a special program — the driver — is responsible

---

[7] Gaussian is a trademark of Gaussian, Inc.

[8] In fact, some parts are still written in Fortran 66.

for calling (linking up) the individual programs — modules — in the required sequence (which may contain cycles, like in the SCF procedure or during geometry optimizations).

As is usual with computational chemistry programs, Gaussian 94 is ported to almost any computer architecture in use. The availability ranges from high-end vector supercomputers (CRAY, NEC, Fujitsu), through workstations down to the personal computers, running either Linux or NetBSD or MS Windows. Gaussian 94 implements many *ab initio* methods, the most demanding in terms of computing power and memory space are those presented in the preceding section. The actual primary (main) memory and disk space requirements are summarized in Tabs. 2 and 3.

**Table 2.** Memory Requirements for Gaussian'92 Jobs

| Method | Units | No. of Basis Functions | | | | |
|--------|-------|------|-----|-----|-----|-----|
| | | 100 | 150 | 200 | 250 | 300 |
| SCF in-core, HF | GB | 0.1 | 0.5 | 2 | 4 | 8 |
| UHF/ROHF | GB | 0.2 | 1.0 | 3.2 | 8 | 16 |
| MP2 Direct | MB | 2 | 6 | 16 | 32 | 64 |
| MP2 Semi-direct | MB | 3 | 9 | 28 | 48 | 80 |

These are just the *minimal* RAM requirements. As much as two-fold speedup (in CPU time) may be achieved doubling the minimum numbers provided (reducing, among other, the required I/O).

To further illustrate the CPU hunger of *ab initio* methods, we computed single point energy of pentane, $C_5H_{12}$, using different methods and different basis sets. The results are presented in Tab. 4, where the sharp increase in computational demand going from ordinary Hartree-Fock and MP2 to higher order methods is easily seen. The more than 4 orders in magnitude difference between the simplest and the most sophisticated method illustrates the choice faced by each computational chemist: using the lower level treatment, even larger systems are computationally feasible, but the highest level is necessary to obtain the most precise results. This choice is even more complicated by the fact, illustrated in Tab. 5, where the actual energy computed by individual method and basis set is presented. The $C_5H_{12}$ is rather simple molecule and the differences in computed energy are very small, not justifying the more than exponential increase in CPU time. Based on his/her own experience, each user must decide where the feasibility limit for the concrete system lies.

The first Gaussian implementations used computers with small primary memory, sometimes even without the virtual memory support[9]. But even when virtual

---

[9] Perhaps surprisingly, but even contemporary vector computers don't always support paged virtual memory (cf. Sec. 4).

**Table 3.** Disk (Scratch) Storage Requirements for Gaussian'92

| Basis Functions | SCF Freq. | MP2 Direct | MP2 Freq. STINGY |
|---|---|---|---|
| 60 | 26 | 12 | 45 |
| 80 | 82 | 36 | 145 |
| 100 | 200 | 90 | 350 |
| 120 | 415 | 185 | 725 |
| 140 | 770 | 340 | 1 350 |
| 160 | 1 300 | 580 | 2 300 |
| 180 | 2 100 | 1 000 | 3 700 |
| 200 | 3 200 | 1 400 | 5 600 |
| 220 | 4 700 | 2 100 | 8 200 |
| 240 | 6 600 | 2 900 | 12 000 |
| 260 | 9 000 | 4 100 | 16 000 |
| 280 | 12 000 | 5 500 | 22 000 |
| 300 | 16 000 | 7 200 | 28 400 |
| ⋮ | | | |
| 1000 | 2 100 000 | 950 000 | 3 800 000 |

All values are in MB.

**Table 4.** Comparing Methods' Complexity

| Method | Basis Set (# basis functions) | | | |
|---|---|---|---|---|
| | 3-21G (69) | 6-31G(d) (99) | 6-31+G(d) (119) | 6-311++G(2d,p) (219) |
| RHF | 1.0[†] | 3.4 | 7.4 | 61.6 |
| MP2 | 1.8 | 11.6 | 24.8 | 218.4 |
| MP4 | 77.7 | 357.2 | 868.6 | – |
| QCISD(T) | 179.3 | 630.3 | 1645.0 | * |

[†]Job CPU time 17.2 seconds.
*Estimate $\approx$ 100 000 (i.e. 20 CPU days).

**Table 5.** Computed Energy

| Method | Basis Set (# basis functions) | | | |
|---|---|---|---|---|
| | 3-21G (69) | 6-31G(d) (99) | 6-31+G(d) (119) | 6-311++G(2d,p) (219) |
| RHF | -195.24844 | -196.32915 | -196.33083 | -196.38650 |
| MP2 | -195.70976 | -196.98843 | -196.99613 | -197.19185 |
| MP4 | -195.78058 | -197.07312 | -197.08170 | – |
| QCISD(T) | -195.78649 | -197.07637 | -197.08504 | – |

All values given in Hartrees.

memory was available, it was prohibitely expensive to rely blindly on the virtual memory support to handle large primary memory space requirements. Special computational methods were developed, based either on (i) "manual" virtualization or on (ii) reduction of memory requirements by recomputation. In the first case, the large vectors and matrices are stored explicitly on disk (using a set of scratch files) and are manipulated explicitly from inside the program. While this approach allows to "expand" the main memory, this expansion is costly paid by the overall slowdown of the program (unless very fast I/O subsystem is available[10]). The second method is based on the observation that recomputation of some quantities, especially values of many integrals used in the evaluation of Fock matrix, is much faster than their reading from secondary storage. This statement is becoming more and more valid with the fast increase in computer power which is not accompanied with the same increase in the secondary (and even primary) memory speed.

The extensive use of secondary storage in Gaussian opened another problem. Potentially, large number of files must be kept open, but all operating systems seriously limit the number of simultaneously opened files. Special file subsystem was developed, with one large (.rwf) file serving as a file depository. Gaussian is currently able to keep up to one thousand internal "files" simultaneously, these "files" are accessed by a set of procedures which mimics the ordinary **open, read,** and **write** operations [5]. The actual size of the .rwf file was a source of a different set of problems encountered when the Gaussian code was moved to fast RISC microprocessor based workstations. While the file size is not limited (at least from the practical point of view) on supercomputers, there are limits of usually 2 GB per file on workstations. When the computational power of RISC microprocessors eventually reached the supercomputing domain, this file size limitation revealed and restricted workstation use to just smaller basis set computations, even as the raw CPU power was sufficient for much larger tasks. Currently, two solutions are available — with the move to 64bit domain, the file size limits were lifted ($ge 1$ Tbyte), and the Gaussian file subsystem was enhanced to allow split of the .rwf file[11].

We run the computational experiment taken from [2], where the conventional (i.e., using the secondary disk storage) method was compared with the direct (i.e., recomputing the integrals) method for series of similar molecules with increasing complexity[12]. The results, presented in Tab. 6, indicate that for the used

---

[10] High-end post Hartree-Fock calculation may produce sustained I/O throughput on the order of more than 100 MB/s even on workstations; this throughput may be required for many hours (and even days) of CPU time. We will return to this problem in Sec. 5.

[11] This split has additional advantage that the I/O load may be distributed over several I/O channels.

[12] Unless otherwise stated, all the results presented in this book were obtained on the Silicon Graphics POWER Challenge computer equipped with 12 R10000/195 MHz processors, 2 GB of main memory and 40 GB of disk space and running an IRIX 6.2 operating system. Rev.C3 [4] of Gaussian'94 was used.

computer the conventional method is preferable for the whole range of chemi-cal systems studied, but the difference is decreased. This is due to the primary sequential character of the file access pattern, which is very efficiently buffered. For less powerful computers, like Digital's AlphaStation 600/266, starting with $n = 7$, the direct method is becoming faster [2].

**Table 6.** SCF CPU and Disk Requirements for Linear $C_nH_{2n+2}$

| n | # Basis Functions | SCF Conventional .int file (MB) | CPU (s) | SCF Direct CPU (s) |
|---|---|---|---|---|
| 1 | 23 | 2 | 6.5 | 6.4 |
| 2 | 42 | 4 | 9.0 | 8.6 |
| 3 | 61 | 16 | 17.4 | 16.1 |
| 4 | 80 | 42 | 35.8 | 75.7 |
| 5 | 99 | 92 | 68.4 | 128.6 |
| 6 | 118 | 174 | 124.2 | 203.6 |
| 7 | 137 | 290 | 206.3 | 295.8 |
| 8 | 156 | 437 | 315.9 | 406.7 |
| 9 | 175 | 620 | 452.1 | 540.9 |
| 10 | 194 | 832 | 615.1 | 692.1 |

As mentioned above, Gaussian 94 is almost entirely written in Fortran 77. Efficient compilation of this large program is a hard problem for the compilers available, even as the whole program is divided to subsystems with less than 50 000 lines of code each. Compilation of the whole program takes more than 3 CPU hours on the R10000/195 MHz processor, using the highest optimiza-tion of the SGI compiler available (-03). The compiler is stretched to its limits and internal compiler bugs are expressed sometimes in very mysterious ways. Gaussian 94 distribution contains more than 300 test input files together with the output files for comparison with actual implementation. The whole suite takes more than 1 CPU day on IBM RS/6000 model 590. While trying to re-compile the Gaussian 94, Rev.C3 (optimized for the R8000 processor) for the newest R10000 processor, we found that using native SGI Fortran 77 compiler for IRIX 6.2 (compiler version 6.2), it is not possible to produce correct program: compilation with just conservative optimization, -02 (and, in fact, compilation with no optimization at all) lead to *faster* code than the more aggressive -03 optimization level, but the code gave completely incorrect results for the DFT computations. The -03 gave correct DFT results, but failed completely in some cases of SCF calculations.

The correctness of the compiler is essential. This sounds trivial, but is far from it. Both vector and RISC processors require very complex program transfor-mations and optimizations to be performed by the compiler in order to efficiently utilize their potential [6]. In the case of large program, it is almost impossible to locate the compiler error without very time consuming debugging (compiler error cannot be discovered through program analysis itself). The debugging may not always rely on the available debuggers, as the code may be to large to fit into the internal debugger tables, and programmer has to return to the "golden age" of inserted `write` statements. In the early phase of program development, the situation is even worse. There may be nothing to compare the program results with. This is especially true with *ab initio* methods, where the directly computed quantities are not experimentally measurable. The same is also true for molecular dynamics simulations, as the fsec trajectory itself is experimentally unavailable. In these cases, the validation of results lies on (i) comparison with results of similar programs, or (ii) comparison with some experimentally available quantity, whose value may be computed from the program results. The first approach may be very dangerous especially when high precision is sought for, as small but favorable discrepancies may be ascribed to the new method while their origin may lie in some numerical instability or even the bug in program. Only large test sets may help to reveal any such problem, but this may not be always possible for immodest CPU time requirements. In the second approach, another computational level is introduced, where new bugs may be hidden. Moreover, the high precision experimental results may be scarce and not always reliable[13].

## 4 Architecture

High performance computing activities pose naturally some requirements on the usable hardware. While it is possible to do *any* computation on *any* general purpose computer, the maximal efficiency is attainable only when the problem (embedded in the program) matches the computer (its architectural design). Not so long ago, supercomputers formed a special group which was rather easily distinguishable from other computers. Since its introduction in Cray 1 (1976) the vector processing unit represented for a long time "the heart" of a supercomputer. Vector processing was thus equivalent to supercomputing and everybody knew who was who.

The situation started to change during 80's, when massively parallel computers became available on the market. The real "revolution" was, however, initiated by microprocessors, especially the RISC ones. The incredibly fast increase of raw computing power enabled, in the last few years, to build computers based on RISC (micro)processors with the theoretical computing power of vector supercomputers not far away in time. The first Cray 1 had the theoretical performance peak of $160\,\mathrm{Mflop/s}$[14], Cray Y-MP as well as Cray C90 have vector

---

[13] Some 15 years ago, when a discrepancy between theoretical computation and experiment was discovered, the computations were checked first. Currently, it is more and more often the experiment, which is in error. This is, however, not necessarily true for new computational methods and programs.

[14] Although potentially highly misleading, the number of floating point operations per second may serve as an *upper* bond for the actual computing power. In fact, there is not too much rationality in any computer comparison not based on performance values obtained with the actual application

processors with peak performance slightly under 1 Gflop/s and the most powerful contemporary vector processors of NEC and Fujitsu have peak performance of $\approx$ 2 Gflop/s. This must be compared with the recent RISC processors, like MIPS R10000, HP PA RISC 8000, and DEC Alpha EV56 (formerly 61124A) all with performance $\approx$ 400 Mflop/s. And Intel Pentium Pro processor is theoretically able to operate at at least half of this speed. These numbers means that today's highest-performance microprocessors outperform the vector machines on scalar code. Taking only the raw number crunching power of its processor is clearly not sufficient to distinguish a supercomputer from "ordinary" one.

The width of address and data path must also be taken into account. Since 1976, supercomputers used 64 bit data and address width. While microprocessors moved fast from 16 to 32 bit data and address width, the next step took longer time. However, it is not sufficient to have the required data widths without the operating and development systems support. Since 1993, 64 bit microprocessors are available, recently complemented by truly 64 bit operating system implementation (Digital UNIX and SGI IRIX 6.x may serve as typical examples). 64 bits means not only enough precision (operations working in double precision are now faster than their single precision counterpart and quad long (128 bits) operations already moved from the prohibitely expensive levels), but also much larger address space, and file size limits.

While introduced in the era of virtual memory, the first vector supercomputers (and even some recent ones) did not support it. Instead, very sophisticated memory schemes [7, 8] were used, in order to keep pace with the processors' "hunger" for data. In Cray C90, up to 1 024 memory banks may be found, which are connected to processors via multi-stage interconnect with an aggregate 246 Gbyte/sec of bandwidth. In NEC SX-4 system, single-node configuration have a maximum bandwidth of 512 GByte/sec (a multi node configuration has a theoretical maximum of 8 Tbyte/s maximum bandwidth). The memory to processor bandwidth in microprocessor based machines is much lower. The SGI POWER Challenge computer uses one bus with 1.2 Gbyte/s sustained (2 Gbyte/s burst) rate with maximum of 8 banks interleaved memory; similar values hold for the Digital's high-end computers. Just 153 million of 8 byte words may be transferred in a second on this bus — clearly insufficient value for processor capable to complete > 400 millions floating point operations per second. While some latency may be hidden by the use of primary and secondary caches, the computational chemistry codes do not always fit very well into the limited cache. According to the recent measurements of Roberto Gomperts (roberto@boston.sgi.com), CPU time for the Gaussian's test178 (single point direct SCF calculation with 300 basis functions) is 7.08 min on a R10000 processor with 1 MB secondary cache and just 5.95 min for the same processor with 2 MB cache. Additional 1 MB of secondary cache results in 19 % performance increase.

Computational chemistry programs are not only consuming a lot of memory but their disk space requirements are also notable. Again, classical supercomputers are equipped with high performance I/O subsystems. The individual I/O port on Cray C90 can provide up to 1,8 Gbyte/s of bandwidth, and NEC SX-4 has I/O ports with 1,6 Gbyte/s of bandwidth. On the other hand, the SGI POWER Challenge may be equipped with only SCSI Fast Wide channels with bandwidth of just 20 Mbyte/s[15]. While faster I/O channels are also available (Fiber channel, SSA), their bandwidth is usually in the range of 100 Mbyte/sec. However, the real bottleneck is not the capacity of I/O channel but the actual speed of secondary storage device. This is usually overcome by a hierarchy of memories, like in the NEC SX-4 vector supercomputer, where the primary memory of up to 16 Gbyte (single node configuration) may be accompanied with 32 GB of extended (slower) memory. This extended memory may be either directly mapped from the application or it may be used as large buffer pool for actual I/O disk operations.

The dependence on I/O throughput may be again exemplified by our experience with upgrade of POWER Challenge computer. The original configuration consisted of 6 R8000 processors and 1 GB 4 way interleaved RAM, with the usual run queue size of 8 (2–3 Gaussian jobs). This configuration was upgraded to 12 R10000 (theoretically 1.3 times faster in floating point operations and more than 2 times faster in integer operations) and 2 GB 8 way interleaved RAM. The operating system and the I/O subsystem were initially left unchanged. The run queue size increased to 16, with 4–5 Gaussian jobs. The R8000 configuration was balanced, with less than 1 % of time spent waiting on I/O operations. This number increased to more than 20 % after the upgrade and even values near the 50 % wait I/O were observed. The empirical "rule of thumb" says that at least 80 Mbyte/sec sustained I/O throughput is required for the usual Gaussian'94 job on an 200 Mflop/sec processor to reduce the wait I/O state to negligibility.

# 5  Parallel Computing

Parallel computing environment provides, at least in theory, an excellent opportunity for high performance computing. In the last 15 years, three phases may be recognized:

1. The first generation of massively parallel computers, with thousands of processing elements with small all moderate computing power each. Either SIMD (which may be seen as a special kind of vector computers), like Thinking Machines CM-2 or MasPar's MP-1 and MP-2 machines, or MIMD ("the" massively parallel computers), like CM-5 or KSR-1 and KSR-2, were built.
2. The symmetric multiprocessing machines, SMP (or shared memory machines) with at most dozens processors sharing the interleaved memory. Examples include multiprocessor vector machines (Cray C90, NEC) and many high-end microprocessor based computers (Digital's AlphaServers, SGI Challenges and POWER Challenges, Sun's UltraSparcs, and many other). These are probably commercially the most successful parallel computers till now.

---

[15] The internal I/O backplane speed is 320 Mbyte/sec.

3. The second generation of (almost) massively parallel computers, equipped with hundreds of powerful RISC microprocessors. Typical examples are IBM SP1 and SP2 and Cray T3D and the newest T3E machines.

Almost all the players from the first phase already vanished and these machines are no longer built for sale. On the other hand, Cray T3D belongs to the most successful model of the Cray family, at least measured by the number of machines sold. The SMP machines (both vector and RISC processor based) have very strong position on the market. What are the causes and what we may expect is discussed in the following text.

The name of the game in the parallel computing is *scalability*. This is an overloaded world, as at least two meanings may be assigned to it: (i) we call a system (an algorithm, program or computer) scalable, if the run time of a given task decreases linearly with the number of processing elements used; (ii) we may also call a system scalable, if the total time of an execution remains unchanged when both the number of processing elements and the problem size is simultaneously increased. Usually, scalability is associated with the first meaning, and accordingly much attention is given to the achievement of linear speedup. The achievable speedup is limited by the Amdahl's law, i.e., by the proportion of parallelizable to serial parts of the program. While there exists "embarrassingly parallel" problems [9], the scalability of any given problem is always limited from above[16].

As usual, computational chemistry plays an important role in the use of parallel computers [10]. The main task lies in the porting the existing sequential code (and underlying methods) to parallel machines. Several approaches are identified, based on two basic models, SPMD (single program multiple data) and MPMD (multiple programs multiple data). Within the SPMD, the data parallelism is the key word and the data replication and data distribution are the alternatives, while for MPMD, the task (and data) distribution must be used.

Data replication, while the most supported model by existing software products, is not the viable route to achieve true scalability in any of its meaning. In general, the memory requirement for data replication is in order of $N$ times memory requirement of the whole application run sequentially ($N$ is the number of processors), what is clearly intolerable.

Distributed data paradigm, on the other hand, is still too young and all the implementations are very hardware dependent. While data distribution paradigm is also supported by software development tools, notably by High Performance Fortran (HPF), these tools are still not mature and reliable enough to provide a usable development platform[17].

---

[16] In the extreme case, if the task requires $N$ operations, ideal parallelization will need $N$ processors. Increasing further the number of processors cannot decrease the computational time.

[17] The very long time needed for the development of HPF compiler for the first few hardware platforms suggests that too many research problems are not yet completely solved. The performance of codes produced by the HPF compilers still suffers when

The actual failure of HPF and other (semi)automatic parallelization tools gave raise to complementary activities of the programming toolkits and languages development. PVM [11], TCGMSG [12], and Linda [13] are the most commonly used environment for computational chemistry parallel codes. PVM and TCGMSG are based on message-passing paradigm and both provide external library routines which must be linked with the application. Linda is a memory model and a full coordination language, based on the idea of tuple space; however, there are commercially available libraries which provide Linda-like functionality for common programming languages (C and Fortran). Use of any of these tools requires a substantial redesign and recoding of the original program. PVM is currently used as the "number one" for the development of new parallel programs[18]. Linda forms the basis of the parallel Gaussian'94 implementation [4].

The above mentioned packages and systems are well suited not only for special purpose parallel hardware, but are successfully used on networks of workstations. These packages may be seen as the first steps towards large scale distributed computing, where hundreds of computers connected via network are used as a large metacomputer.

Despite increased number of users, the parallelization of *ab initio* and other molecular electronic structure codes reached at most very modest success. The effort was mainly focused to the efficient use of automatic parallelizing computers for SMP machines. The scalability is almost perfect for codes like AMBER [17], but only for few processors.

Molecular dynamics (MD) algorithms are inherently parallel [10, 18] and therefore much better suited for large scale parallelism than the *ab initio* computations. The parallelization must take care of both the evaluation of pair interactions (19) and the integration of particle motion (16). Three different approaches were used for the force calculations: (i) atom decomposition, with each processor working on a set of atoms, (ii) force decomposition, with each processor computing a subset of interatomic forces, and (iii) spatial decomposition, with each processor responsible for a fixed spatial region. A bottleneck for large systems is the long-range forces calculation (last term in (19)), which scales as $N^2$ and requires global communication; this bottleneck is currently being removed by application of new algorithms, not by better parallelization techniques. Despite all the efforts, the best codes for MD simulations are still those using just simple SMP machines. Up to 64 node MIMD computers were used with very good results; perhaps surprisingly Transputers (and occam) were extensively used for parallel MD program development.

---

compared with the performance of native Fortran 77 compilers. Only currently vendor supported Fortran 90 compiler implementations are becoming common on the market

[18] See proceedings from any conference on practical aspects of parallel programming [14, 15, 16].

# 6 Future Prospect

Where all these efforts will be in the next decade? The Teraflops and even the Petaflops computer architecture and programming models are currently discussed [19]. The computational chemistry community is eagerly looking towards new architectures which will open new possibilities for thorough theoretical study of large molecules and even molecular systems. An *ab initio* molecular dynamics study of enzyme catalysis, which requires time trajectory of tens msecs, is just an example of problem not solvable even using Petaflops computer (at least without development of completely new algorithms and methods).

How the over next generation machines may look like? There are generally three accepted categories:

1. Computer with a modest number of very powerful processors. Computers like NEC SX-4 or Fujitsu VPP-500 are the children of this road.
2. Massively parallel computer with tens thousand processing elements. Intel Paragon or CRAY T3E may be seen as prenatal versions of these future computers.
3. Embarrassingly parallel computers, with very large number (an order of millions) of hybrid chips encompassing processor and memory. Not yet commercially available.

The fourth category covers the not yet thought architectures (neural or chemical computers). In any case, the future computers will be highly parallel machines.

The large number of individual components found in any parallel system increase the probability of a fault. With the usual mean time between failures (MTBF) of 5 years, the system with 1 024 elements will experience a fault every 9 hours (for 16 384 elements this value drops to 32 minutes). Both architectural (redundancy, alternative paths between individual elements) and software (checkpointing, self-adaptation) sides of the problem are studied [20]. Understanding of key aspects of fault tolerance is essential for the efficient use of networked computers (the virtual and meta computers) where the probability of some node or link fault will always be much higher than in tightly coupled massive parallel systems [21].

Regardless of the architectural design, the software part will play the most important role in the future systems. The research in scalable parallel multi-user operating systems, scalable I/O, and especially in portable programming and debugging tools must accompany the development of new generation of high performance computers.

# 7 Conclusion

Computational chemistry is a long time established research field, well known for its hunger for computing power as well as for primary and secondary memory space. It is not an exaggeration to say that all (kinds of) computers were at least once used for the computational chemistry tasks. The experience of the development, use and maintenance of large software systems had its own influence on many aspects of practically oriented computer science, especially on field of computer architecture and software engineering. While much of the code was developed with very little knowledge of up to date software engineering practices, it may serve as an excellent example of the requirements which have the high performance computing community on the computer science. Issues like program debugging and validation are of utmost importance if the very complex algorithms are to be transformed into correct programs. Very long life cycles, accompanied with much faster changes in the original "specification" (i.e., in the formulation of theories and hypothesis, which provide the theoretical foundation of algorithms to be coded), poses problems not known (and not yet solved) in other areas of computer utilization. Contemporary available parallel and distributed environments created new challenges and problems for which, again, no definite solutions are yet known. Last but not least comes the efficiency, optimal code generation, problem very complicated in the heterogeneous environment, where the portability of program is also required. There is no widely available program development and validation methodology and programmers have to rely on their own experience and/or their own methods.

The aim of this paper was not to give definite answers but to raise the proper questions and show them in the proper context. While the presentation is given solely in terms of computational chemistry, the problems discussed are more general and apply to the whole high performance computing field.

And the last remark: the extent of future high performance computing will be much more that today coupled with the development of new algorithms, methods and software engineering methodology than with the increased raw computing power of available computers.

## 8  Acknowledgment

The computations were done using the POWER Challenge computer, located at the Supercomputing Center Brno, whose support is acknowledged. The financial support of the Grant Agency of the Czech Republic grant no. 203/94/0522 is also appreciated.

## References

1. Hehre, W. J., Radom, L., Rague Schlayer, P.von, and Pople, J. A. *Ab Initio Molecular Orbital Theory*. John Wiley & Sons, New York, 1986.
2. Foresman, J. B. and Frisch, Æ. *Exploring Chemistry with Electronic Structure Methods*. Gaussian, Inc., Pittsburgh, PA, second edition, 1996.
3. Lybrand, T. P. Computer simulation of biomolecular systems using molecular dynamics and free energy perturbation methods. In Lipkowitz, K. B. and Boyd, D. B., editors, *Reviews In Computational Chemistry*, volume I, pages 295–320, New York, 1990. VCH Publishers, Inc.

4. Frisch, M. J., Trucks, G. W., Schlegel, H. B., Gill, P. M. W., Johnosn, B. G., Robb, M. A., Cheeseman, J. R., Keith, T., Petersson, G. A., Montgomery, J. A., Raghavachari, K., Cioslowski, J., Stefanov, B. B., Nanayakkara, A., Challacombe, M., Peng, C. Y., Ayala, P. Y., Chen, W., Wong, M. W., Andres, J. L., Binkley, J. S., Defrees, D. J., Baker, J., Stewart, J. P., Head-Gordon, M., Gonzales, C., and Pople, J. A. *Gaussian 94, Revision C.3.* Gaussian, Inc., Pittsburgh, PA, 1995.

5. Frisch, M. J., Frisch, Æ., and Foresman, J. B. *Gaussian 94 Programmer's Reference.* Gaussian, Inc., Pittsburgh, PA, 1994.

6. Dowd, K. *High Performance Computing.* O'Reilly and Associates, Inc., Sebastopol, CA, 1993.

7. Lenoski, D. E. and Weber, W.-D. *Scalable Shared-Memory Multiprocessing.* Morgan Kaufmann Publishers, Inc., San Francisco, CA, 1995.

8. Fosdick, L. D., Jessup, E. R., Schaube, C. J. C., and Dominik, G. *An Introduction to High-Performance Scientific Computing*, chapter 11–14, pages 335–530. The MIT Press, Cambridge, MA, 1995.

9. Laganà, A., Gervasi, O., Baragli, R., Laforenza, D., and Perero, R. Where are embarassingly parallel problems? The atom-diatom quasiclassical reactivity. *Theoretica Chimica Acta*, 84:413– 422, 1993.

10. Kendall, R. A., Harrison, R. J., Littlefield, R. J., and Guest, M. F. High performance computing in computational chemistry: Methods and machines. In Lipkowitz, K. B. and Boyd, D. B., editors, *Reviews In Computational Chemistry*, volume VI, pages 209–316, New York, 1995. VCH Publishers, Inc.

11. Geist, G. A., Beguelin, A., Dongarra, J. J., Jiang, W., Manchek, R., and Sunderam, V. S. *PVM: A User's Guide and Tutorial for Networked Parallel Computing.* The MIT Press, Cambridge, MA, 1994.

12. Harrison, R. J. Portable tools and applications for parallel computers. *Int. J. Quant. Chem.*, 40:847, 1991. TCGMSG available from ftp.tcg.anl.gov.

13. Carriero, N. and Gelernter, D. *How to write parallel programs: A First Course.* The MIT Press, Cambridge, MA, 1990.

14. Dongarra, J., Gengler, M., Tourancheau, B., and Vigoroux, X., editors. *EuroPVM'95*, Paris, 1995. Hermès.

15. Dongarra, J. J., Madsen, K., and Wasniewski, J., editors. *Applied Parallel Computing*, Heidelberg, 1995. Springer Verlag.

16. Liddell, H., Colbook, A., Hertzberger, B., and Sloot, P., editors. *High-Performance Computing and Networking*, Heidelberg, 1996. Springer Verlag.

17. Pearlman, D. A., Case, D. A., Caldwell, J. W., Ross, W. S., III, T. E. C., Ferguson, D. M., Seibel, G. L., Singh, U. C., Weiner, P. K., and Kollman, P. A. Amber 4.1. Technical report, University of California, San Francisco, 1995.

18. Smith, W. Molecular dynamics on distributed memory (MIMD) parallel computers. *Theoretica Chimica Acta*, 84:385–398, 1993.

19. Sterling, T. L., Messina, P. C., and Smith, P. H. *Enabling Technologies for Petaflops Computing.* The MIT Press, Cambridge, MA, 1994.

20. *Integrating Fault Tolerance in off-the-shelf Massively Parallel Systems*, Brussels, 1996. ESPRIT Workshop within HPCN Europe'96.

21. Lamotte, J.-L. A tool for the numerical validation of parallel code programming with Fortran 77 and PVM. In Dongarra et al. [14], pages 173–178.

# Iterative Methods for Unsymmetric Linear Systems

Henk A. Van der Vorst

Mathematical Institute, University of Utrecht
PO Box 80.010, NL-3508 TA Utrecht, the Netherlands
vorst@math.ruu.nl

**Abstract.** We will present an overview of a number of related modern iterative methods for the solution of unsymmetric linear systems of equations. We will show how these methods can be derived from simple basic iteration formulas, and how they are related to each other.

Special attention will be given to hybrid methods, such as Bi-CGSTAB, Bi-CGSTAB($\ell$), and GMRESR. We will emphasize implementation aspects, in particular in view of parallel processing. In general, preconditioning poses additional problems with respect to parallel processing, and we will discuss this aspect as well.

## 1 Introduction

We will discuss a number of related modern iterative methods for the solution of linear systems of equations

$$Ax = b,$$

in which $A$ is an $n$ by $n$ nonsingular unsymmetric matrix. These methods are so-called Krylov projection type methods and they include popular methods as Bi-Conjugate Gradients, CGS, Bi-CGSTAB, QMR, and GMRES. We will show how these methods can be derived from simple basic iteration formulas. Only algorithmic aspects of the methods will be discussed, for more theoretical background the reader is referred to literature.

For the application of the iterative schemes one usually thinks of special classes of linear sparse systems, for instance, those arising in finite element or finite difference approximations of (systems of) partial differential equations. However, the structure of the operator plays no explicit role in any of these schemes, and these schemes may also successfully be used to solve certain large dense linear systems. Depending on the situation that can be attractive in terms of numbers of floating point operations.

Iterative methods form an alternative for direct methods if the matrix of the system is large and sparse, since the amount of memory space for iterative schemes is limited, and also the amount of computational work can be significantly less, but that depends very much on, often a priori unknown, properties of the given system.

It turns out that all described iterative methods are parallelizable in a rather straight forward manner. However, especially for computers with a memory hierarchy (i.e., cache or vector registers), and for distributed memory computers, the performance can often be improved significantly through rescheduling of the operations.

Iterative methods are often used in combination with so-called preconditioning operators (approximations for the inverses of the operator of the system to be solved). These preconditioners help to reduce the total computational work, but unfortunately they are often not very well parallelizable. We will give an overview of some approaches for improving parallelism on a coarse-grained level.

## 2  Basic iteration method

A very basic idea, that leads to many effective iterative solvers, is to to write the matrix $A$ of a given linear system as the sum of two matrices, one of which a matrix that would have led to a system that can easily be solved. The most simple splitting we can think of is $A = I - (I - A)$. Given the linear system $Ax = b$, this splitting leads to the well-known Richardson iteration:

$$x_i = b + (I - A)x_{i-1} = x_{i-1} + r_{i-1}. \tag{1}$$

In many cases better approximations $K$ to the given matrix $A$ are available, which define the splitting $A = K - R$, with $R = K - A$. The corresponding iterative method then reads as

$$Kx_i = b + Rx_{i-1} = Kx_{i-1} + b - Ax_{i-1}.$$

Solving for $x_i$ leads formally to

$$x_i = x_{i-1} + K^{-1}(b - Ax_{i-1}).$$

If we define $B \equiv K^{-1}A$ and $c = K^{-1}b$, then the $K$–splitting is equivalent to the standard splitting for $Bx = c$. Therefore, it is no loss of generality if we further restrict ourselves to the standard splitting. Any other splitting can be incorporated easily in the different schemes by replacing the quantities $A$ and $b$, by $B$ and $c$, respectively.

From now on we will also assume that $x_0 = 0$. This too does not mean a loss of generality, for the situation $x_0 \neq 0$ can, through a simple linear transformation $z = x - x_0$, be transformed to the system

$$Az = b - Ax_0 = \tilde{b},$$

for which obviously $z_0 = 0$.

Multiplication of the standard iteration formula (1) by $-A$ and adding $b$ gives

$$b - Ax_i = b - Ax_{i-1} - Ar_{i-1}$$

or

$$r_i = (I - A)r_{i-1} = (I - A)^i r_0.$$

Hence, it follows that

$$x_{i+1} = r_0 + r_1 + r_2 + \cdots + r_i = \sum_{j=0}^{i}(I - A)^j r_0$$

$$\in \{r_0, Ar_0, \ldots, A^i r_0\} \equiv K_{i+1}(A; r_0).$$

The subspace $K_{i+1}(A; r_0)$ is called the *Krylov subspace* of dimension $i + 1$, generated by $A$ *and* $r_0$. Apparently, the Richardson iteration delivers elements of Krylov subspaces of increasing dimension. By including iteration parameters in the iteration (1), we obtain other elements of the same Krylov subspaces.

In order to identify better solutions in the Krylov subspace we need a suitable basis for this subspace, one that can be extended in an efficient way for subspaces of increasing dimension. The obvious basis $r_0$, $Ar_0$, ..., $A^{i-1}r_0$, for $K^i(A; r_0)$, is not very attractive from a numerical point of view, since the vectors $A^j r_0$ are increasingly in the direction of the dominant eigenvector for increasing values of $j$ (the power method !), and hence the basis vectors become dependent in finite precision arithmetic.

Instead of the standard basis, one usually prefers an orthonormal basis and Arnoldi [1] suggested to compute this basis as follows. Start with $v_1 \equiv r_0/\|r_0\|_2$. Assume that we have already an orthonormal basis $v_1, \ldots, v_j$ for $K^j(A; r_0)$, then this basis is expanded by computing $t = Av_j$, and by orthonormalizing $t$ with respect to $v_1, \ldots, v_j$. In principle, the orthonormalization process can be carried out in different ways, but the most commonly used approach is a modified Gram-Schmidt procedure [22]. In Section 3, we will see how this is done, in the context of the GMRES algorithm.

## 2.1 Optimal Krylov subspace methods

Suppose that we have an orthonormal basis $v_1, v_2, \ldots, v_k$, for the k-dimensional Krylov subspace $K^k(A; r_0)$, and let us define $V_k$ as the matrix with $k$ columns $v_1$ to $v_k$. Since we are looking for a solution $x_k$ in $K^k(A; r_0)$, that vector can be written as a combination of the basis vectors of the Krylov subspace, and hence

$$x_k = V_k y.$$

Note that $y$ has $k$ components.

There are three successful approaches for constructing a suitable approximation $x_k$:

1. The minimum residual approach: require $\|b - Ax_k\|_2$ to be minimal over $K^k(A; r_0)$.

2. The Ritz-Galerkin approach: require that $b - Ax_k \perp K^k(A; r_0)$.

3. The Petrov-Galerkin approach: require that $b - Ax_k$ is orthogonal to some other suitable $k$-dimensional subspace.

The minimum residual approach leads to methods like GMRES, MINRES, and ORTHODIR. The Ritz-Galerkin approach leads to such popular and well-known methods as Conjugate Gradients, the Lanczos method, and FOM.

If we select the $k$-dimensional subspace in the third approach as $K^k(A^T; s_0)$, then we obtain the methods Bi-CG and QMR. More recently, hybrids of the three approaches have been proposed, like CGS, Bi-CGSTAB, BiCGSTAB($\ell$), TFQMR, FGMRES, and GMRESR.

## 3    The minimum residual approach: GMRES

The orthogonal basis-vectors $\{v_j\}$, for the Krylov subspace, are related, and these relations can be expressed in matrix formulation as

$$AV_k = V_{k+1}H_{k+1,k}. \tag{2}$$

The matrix $H_{k+1,k}$ is a $(k + 1)$ by $k$ upper Hessenberg matrix of which the elements $h_{i,j}$ are defined in Algorithm 1. Also expression (2) will be clear from that algorithm.

We look for an $x_k \in K^k(A; r_0)$, that is $x_k = V_k y$, for which $\|b - Ax_k\|_2$ is minimal. This norm can be rewritten as

$$\|b - Ax_k\|_2 = \|b - AV_k y\|_2 = \|b - V_{k+1}H_{k+1,k}y\|_2.$$

Now we exploit the fact that $V_{k+1}$ is an orthonormal transformation with respect to the Krylov subspace $K^{k+1}(A; r_0)$, and that $b = \|r_0\|_2 V_{k+1}e_1$:

$$\|b - Ax_k\|_2 = \|\|r_0\|_2 e_1 - H_{k+1,k}y\|_2,$$

and this final norm can be minimized by solving the minimum norm least squares problem:

$$H_{k+1,k}y = \|r_0\|_2 e_1.$$

In GMRES [31] this is done with Givens rotations, that annihilate the subdiagonal elements in the upper Hessenberg matrix $H_{k+1,k}$.

In order to avoid excessive storage requirements and computational costs for the orthogonalization, GMRES is usually restarted after each $m$ iteration steps. This algorithm is referred to as GMRES($m$); the not-restarted version is often called 'full' GMRES. In Fig. 1, we give a scheme for GMRES($m$), that solves $Ax = b$, with a given preconditioner $K$.

It can be verified that the vectors $v_j$ satisfy the relation (2).

There are various different implementations of GMRES. Among those are: Orthomin [39], Orthodir [23], Axelsson's method [2], and GENCR [16]. These methods are often more expensive than GMRES per iteration step, or less robust.

```
x_0 is an initial guess;
for j = 1, 2, ....
    r = b - Ax_0;
    v_1 = r/||r||_2;
    s := ||r||_2 e_1;
    for i = 1, 2, ..., m
        w = Av_i;
        for k = 1, ..., i
            h_{k,i} = v_k^T w;
            w = w - h_{k,i} v_k;
        end k;
        h_{i+1,i} = ||w||_2;
        v_{i+1} = w/h_{i+1,i};
    Solve "||H_{m+1,m} y_m - s||_2 is minimal";
    x = x_0 + sum_{k=1}^{m} y_k v_k
    if ||b - Ax||_2 small enough then exit
        else x_0 = x
```

**Fig. 1.** Sketch of GMRES(m)

Orthomin seems to be still popular, possibly since this variant can be easily truncated, in contrast to GMRES. We will discuss another variant, GMRESR, that can be truncated as well. The truncated and restarted versions of these algorithms are not necessarily mathematically equivalent.

A good overview of all these methods and their relations is given in [30].

## 3.1 GMRESR and GMRES⋆

In [38] it has been shown how each step of the GMRES-method can be combined with other iterative schemes. The iteration steps of GMRES (or GCR) are called outer iteration steps, while the iteration steps of the other iterative method are referred to as inner iterations. The combined method is called GMRES⋆, where ⋆ stands for any given iterative scheme. When GMRES is used as the inner iteration method, the combined scheme is called GMRESR[38]. The GMRES⋆ algorithm is given in Fig. 2.

Similar schemes have been proposed by others as well, see for instance [29, 3].

For the approximation of the solution of $Az = r_i$, we may select any appropriate solver, for instance, one cycle of GMRES($m$), since then we have also locally an optimal method, or some other iteration scheme. In the approximation step, we may also exploit possibilities for more parallelism. For instance, in the context of the solution of discretized partial differential equations, we may approximate parts of the solution vector by solving a number of subproblems over uncou-

```
x_0 is an initial guess; r_0 = b - Ax_0;
for i = 0, 1, 2, 3, ...
    Let z^appr be an approximate solution of Az = r_i.
    c = Az^appr (often available from the
        approximation procedure)
    for k = 0, ..., i - 1
        α = c_k^T c
        c = c - αc_k
        z^(m) = z^(m) - αu_k
    c_i = c/||c||_2; u_i = z^(m)/||c||_2
    x_{i+1} = x_i + (c_i^T r_i)u_i
    r_{i+1} = r_i - (c_i^T r_i)c_i
    if x_{i+1} is accurate enough then quit
end
```

**Fig. 2.** The GMRES$\star$ algorithm

pled subdomains. The costs of the approximation step help to amortize in part the costs for the construction of the $c_i$, which, as we will see, may lead to a performance bottle-neck on distributed parallel computers.

## 4 The Ritz-Galerkin approach: FOM

The Ritz-Galerkin conditions imply that $r_k \perp K^k(A; r_0)$, and this is equivalent to

$$V_k^T(b - Ax_k) = 0.$$

Since $b = r_0 = ||r_0||_2 v_1$, it follows that $V_k^T b = ||r_0||_2 e_1$, with $e_1$ the first canonical unit vector in $\mathbb{R}^k$. With $x_k = V_k y$ we obtain

$$V_k^T A V_k y = ||r_0||_2 e_1.$$

This system can be interpreted as the system $Ax = b$ projected onto $K^k(A; r_0)$.

Obviously, we have to construct the $k \times k$ matrix $V_k^T A V_k$, but this is, as we have seen readily available from the orthogonalization process:

$$V_k^T A V_k = H_{k,k},$$

so that $x_k$, for which $r_k \perp K^k(A; r_0)$, can be inexpensively computed by solving $H_{k,k} y = ||r_0||_2 e_1$, and then $x_k = V_k y$. This algorithm is known as FOM or GENCG.

It will not come as a surprise that there is a strong relation between GMRES and FOM. Nevertheless, it was shown only very recently that there is a nice relation between the GRMRES residual $r_k^G$ and the FOM residual $r_k^F$ (for the unrestarted methods):

$$\|r_k^F\|_2 = \frac{\|r_k^G\|_2}{\sqrt{1 - (\|r_k^G\|_2/\|r_{k-1}^G\|_2)^2}}, \tag{3}$$

([10]: theorem 3.1). From this relation, we see that when GMRES has a significant reduction at step $k$, in the norm of the residual, then FOM gives about the same result as GMRES. On the other hand when GMRES locally stagnates (i.e., when $\|r_k^G\|_2 = \|r_{k-1}^G\|_2$), then FOM has a break down. This shows that GMRES is a more robust approach.

Also from a parallel point of view, GMRES and FOM behave very much the same, since the dominating computational costs are in the construction of the basis vectors $v_j$ for the Krylov subspace. Since GMRES(m) is more widely used, we will concentrate our discussion on that method.

## 5  Parallel performance of GMRES(m)

In this section, we will study the performance of GMRES(m) on a distributed memory computer. We will use a simple model for the computation time and the communication cost for the main kernel in GMRES(m); for a more elaborate description and analysis of the performance of Krylov subspace methods we refer to [12].
We use the term *communication cost* to indicate all the wall clock time spent in communication that is not overlapped with useful computation (so that it really contributes to wall-clock time).
The term *communication time* refers to the wall-clock time of the entire communication. In the case of a nonoverlapped communication, the communication time and the communication cost are the same.

**Remark:** Our quantitative formulas are not meant to give very accurate predictions of the exact execution times, but they will be used to identify the bottlenecks and to evaluate improvements.
Indeed, our experiments show that our models are relatively close to reality, and thus may be used as convenient tools for understanding the negative effects of global communication.

For a processor grid with $P = p^2$ processors, we have that $p_d = \sqrt{P}$. For nearest neighbour communication, let $t_s$ denote the communication start-up time and let the transmission time associated with a single inner product computation be $t_w$. Then the global accumulation and broadcast time for 1 inner product is taken as $2p_d(t_s + t_w)$, while the global accumulation and broadcast for $k$ simultaneous inner products takes $2p_d(t_s + k\,t_w)$.

For GMRES(m) the communication time for the modified Gram-Schmidt algorithm (with $\frac{1}{2}(m^2 + 3m)$ accumulations and broadcasts) is

$$T^G_{comm} = (m^2 + 3m)p_d(t_s + t_w).\tag{4}$$

Note that for other processor configurations one only needs to select an appropriate value for $p_d$ in (4).

From (4), we conclude that the communication cost for GMRES(m) is of the order $\mathcal{O}(m^2\sqrt{P})$ and for large processor grids, and large values of $m$, this may become a bottleneck. Moreover, in the standard implementation we cannot reduce these costs by accumulating multiple inner products together, since the modified Gram-Schmidt orthogonalization of one single vector against a set of vectors and its subsequent normalization is an inherently sequential process.
However, if the modified Gram-Schmidt orthogonalization can be done for a set vectors simultaneously, then we have more possibilities for reduction of communication overhead. We will now discuss how to generate such a set of vectors.

Suppose the set of vectors $v_1, \hat{v}_2, \hat{v}_3 \ldots, \hat{v}_{m+1}$ has to be orthonormalized, where $\|v_1\|_2 = 1$. The modified Gram-Schmidt process can be implemented as is sketched in Figure 3. This reduces the number of messages to only $m$, instead

for $i = 1, 2, \ldots, m$ do
    orthogonalize $\hat{v}_{i+1}, \ldots, \hat{v}_{m+1}$ on $v_i$
    $v_{i+1} = \hat{v}_{i+1}/\|\hat{v}_{i+1}\|_2$

**Fig. 3.** Modified Gram–Schmidt orthogonalization

of $\frac{1}{2}(m^2 + 3m)$ for the usual implementation of GMRES(m), but the length of the messages has increased. In this way, start-up time is saved by packing small messages, corresponding to one block of orthogonalizations, into one larger message. Note that the computation time for this approach is equal to that for the standard modified Gram–Schmidt algorithm. We will refer to this variant of GMRES: **parGMRES(m)**.

In order to be able to use this parallel modified Gram–Schmidt algorithm in GMRES(m), a basis for the Krylov subspace has to be generated first. The idea to start with some non-orthogonal basis for the Krylov subspace, and then to orthogonalize this basis afterwards, was already suggested for the CG algorithm, in [8], for shared (hierarchical) memory parallel vector processors.
In [8] it is also reported that the s-step CG algorithm may converge slowly due to

numerical instability for $s > 5$. In the parGMRES(m) algorithm stability seems to be much less of concern, since each vector is explicitly orthogonalized against all the other vectors, and we first generate a well-conditioned polynomial basis for the Krylov subspace, see [4, 11]. Furthermore, because of the restart, rounding errors made before restart can not have an accumulated effect on iterations carried out after the restart.

The basis vectors for the Krylov subspace $\hat{v}_i$ are generated as indicated in Figure 4, where the parameters $d_i$ are chosen to keep the condition number of the

$$\hat{v}_1 = v_1 = r/\|r\|_2$$
$$\textbf{for } i = 1, 2, \ldots, m \textbf{ do}$$
$$\hat{v}_{i+1} = \hat{v}_i - d_i A \hat{v}_i$$

**Fig. 4.** Generation of a polynomial basis for the Krylov subspace

matrix $[v_1, \hat{v}_2, \ldots, \hat{v}_{m+1}]$ sufficiently small. In order to achieve this, one might start in the first cycle with a suitable Chebychev recursion, for later cycles one may then take into account the GMRES information of the previous cycle. For more details on this, see [4], and [33]: Section 6.

We present some experimental observations on the parallel performance of GMRES(m) and parGMRES(m) on a 400-processor Parsytec Supercluster. We will consider the performance of only one (par)GMRES(m) cycle.

The T800-20 transputer processors of the Parsytec are connected in a fixed $20 \times 20$ mesh, of which arbitrary submeshes can be used. The transputer supports only nearest neighbour synchronous communication; more complicated communication has to be programmed explicitly. The communication rate is fast compared with the flop rate, but to current standards the T800 is a slow processor. For further details on our testing circumstances, see [13].

We have solved a convection diffusion problem discretized by finite volumes over a $100 \times 100$ grid, resulting in the standard five-diagonal matrix with a tridiagonal block-structure, corresponding to the 5-point star. This relatively small problem size was chosen, because for processor grids of increasing size it very well shows the expected degradation of performance for GMRES(m) and the large improvements of parGMRES(m) over GMRES(m). Furthermore, the parallel behavior for this problem size on this slow machine corresponds quite well to much larger problems on more modern machines; see [13].

We give speed-ups and efficiencies in Table 1. Since the problem did not fit on a single processor, the speed-up and efficiency values were computed against

| processor grid | $m = 30$ | | | | $m = 50$ | | | |
|---|---|---|---|---|---|---|---|---|
| | GMRES(m) | | parGMRES(m) | | GMRES(m) | | parGMRES(m) | |
| | E (%) | S | E (%) | S | E (%) | S | E (%) | S |
| $10 \times 10$ | 77.2 | 77.2 | 95.9 | 95.9 | 76.8 | 76.8 | 98.2 | 98.2 |
| $14 \times 14$ | 53.9 | 106. | 88.8 | 174. | 50.9 | 99.8 | 92.1 | 181. |
| $17 \times 17$ | 40.5 | 117. | 69.4 | 201. | 39.5 | 114. | 73.6 | 213. |
| $20 \times 20$ | 28.6 | 114. | 53.4 | 214. | 27.1 | 108. | 55.7 | 223. |

**Table 1.** Efficiencies and speed-ups for GMRES(m) and parGMRES(m)

a (fairly accurately) estimated sequential runtime.

We clearly see that the performance of parGMRES(m) is much better than the performance of GMRES(m). For a more elaborate discussion, see [13].

# 6 The Petrov-Galerkin approach: Bi-CG

For unsymmetric systems we can, in general, not create an orthonormale basis by short-term recurrences (as is the case when $A$ is symmetric) [17].

However, it turns out to be possible to create bi-orthogonal basis sets $\{v_j\}$, and $\{w_j\}$, for $K^k(A; r_0)$ and $K^k(A^T, s_0)$, respectively, by three-term recurrence relations (for some arbitrary $s_0$). In matrix notation, these relations can be written as

$$AV_k = V_{k+1}T_{k+1,k}, \tag{5}$$

and

$$A^T W_k = W_{k+1}T_{k+1,k}. \tag{6}$$

The $(k + 1)$ by $k$ matrix $T_{k+1,k}$ is tridiagonal, and $w_j^T v_i = 0$, for $j \neq i$.

We may proceed in a similar way as for the Ritz-Galerkin approach, but here we use the matrix $W_k$ for the projection of the system

$$W_k^T(b - Ax_k) = 0,$$

or

$$W_k^T AV_k y - W_k^T b = 0.$$

Using (5), we find that $y$ satisfies

$$T_{k,k}y = \|r_0\|_2 e_1,$$

and $x_k = V_k y$. This method is known as the Bi-Lanczos method [24].

We have assumed that $w_i^T v_i \neq 0$. The generation of the bi-orthogonal basis breaks down if for some $i$ the value of $w_i^T v_i = 0$, this is called a *serious breakdown*. Likewise, when $w_i^T v_i \approx 0$, we have a near-breakdown. The way to get around this difficulty is to employ a *Look-ahead strategy*, which amounts to taking a number of successive basis vectors for the Krylov subspace together and to make them blockwise bi-orthogonal. This has been worked out in detail in [26, 19, 20, 21]. Another way to avoid breakdown is to restart as soon as a diagonal element gets small. Of course, this strategy is attractively simple, but one should realise that at a restart the Krylov subspace, that has been built so far, is thrown away, which destroys possibilities for faster (i.e., superlinear) convergence.

We may construct an LU-decomposition, without pivoting, of $T_{k,k}$. If this decomposition exists, then it can be updated from iteration to iteration and this leads to a recursive update of the solution vector, which avoids to save all intermediate $v$ and $w$ vectors. This variant of Bi-Lanczos is usually called Bi-Conjugate Gradients, or shortly Bi-CG [18].

Of course, one can in general not be certain that an LU decomposition (without pivoting) of the tridiagonal matrix $T_{k,k}$ exists, and if it does not then we have also a breakdown (a *breakdown of the second kind*), of the Bi-CG algorithm. Note that this breakdown can be avoided in the Bi-Lanczos formulation of the iterative solution scheme, e.g., by making an LU-decomposition with 2 by 2 block diagonal elements [5]. It is also avoided in the QMR approach (see Section 6.1). For a computational scheme for Bi-CG, see [6].

## 6.1 QMR

The QMR method [21] relates to Bi-CG in a similar way as GMRES relates to FOM. We start from the recurrence relations for the $v_j$:

$$AV_k = V_{k+1}T_{k+1,k}.$$

Similar as for GMRES, we would like to construct the $x_k$, with $x_k \in K^k(A; r_0)$, or $x_k = V_k y$, for which

$$\|b - Ax_k\|_2 = \|b - AV_k y\|_2 = \|b - V_{k+1}T_{k+1,k}y\|_2.$$

Now pretend that the columns of $V_{k+1}$ are orthogonal, then

$$\|b - Ax_k\|_2 = \|V_{k+1}(\|r_0\|_2 e_1 - T_{k+1,k}y)\|_2 = \|(\|r_0\|_2 e_1 - T_{k+1,k}y)\|_2,$$

and in [21] it is suggested to solve the projected miniminum norm least squares problem at the right-hand side. Since, in general the columns of $V_{k+1}$ are not orthogonal, the computed $x_k = V_k y$ does not solve the minimum residual problem, and therefore this approach is referred to as a Quasi-minimum residual approach [21].

This leads to the simplest form of the QMR method. A more general form arises if the least squares problem is replaced by a weighted least squares problem [21]. No strategies are yet known for optimal weights.

In [21] the QMR method is carried out on top of a look-ahead variant of the bi-orthogonal Lanczos method, which makes the method more robust.

It is tempting, but difficult, to make a comparison between GMRES and QMR. GMRES really minimizes the 2-norm of the residual, but at the cost of increasing work per iteration step for keeping all residuals orthogonal and increasing demands for memory space. QMR does not minimize this norm, but often it has a comparable fast convergence as GMRES, at the cost of twice the amount of matrix vector products per iteration step. However, the generation of the basis vectors in QMR is relatively cheap and the memory requirements are limited and modest. In view of the relation between GMRES and FOM, it will be no surprise that there is a similar relation between QMR and Bi-CG, for details of this see [10]. This relation expresses that at a significant local error reduction of QMR, Bi-CG and QMR have arrived almost at the same residual vector (similar as for GMRES and FOM). However, QMR has to be preferred in all cases because of its much smoother convergence behaviour.

Several variants of QMR, or rather Bi-CG, have been proposed, which increase the effectiveness of this class of methods in certain circumstances. Some of these variants will be discussed in coming subsections.

With respect to parallelism, it should be noted that most of the time consuming operations in Bi-CG and QMR can be carried out easily in parallel. On some systems, the communication time involved in the 4 innerproducts per iteration step may cause some delay. This problem can be relieved in very much the same way as has been suggested for the CG method, for more details and further references, see [14].

## 6.2 CGS

For the bi-conjugate gradient residual vectors it is well-known that they can be written as $r_j = P_j(A)r_0$ and $\hat{r}_j = P_j(A^T)s_0$, and because of the bi-orthogonality relation we have that

$$(r_j, s_i) = (P_j(A)r_0, P_i(A^T)s_0)$$

$$= (P_i(A)P_j(A)r_0, s_0) = 0,$$

for $i < j$.

The iteration parameters for bi-conjugate gradients are computed from innerproducts like the above. Sonneveld observed that we can also construct the vectors $\tilde{r}_j = P_j^2(A)r_0$, using only the latter form of the innerproduct for recovering the bi-conjugate gradients parameters (which implicitly define the polynomial $P_j$). By doing so, it can be avoided that the vectors $s_j$ have to be formed, and there are no operations with the matrix $A^T$.

The resulting CGS [35] method works in general very well for many unsymmetric linear problems. It converges often much faster than Bi-CG (about twice as fast in some cases) and does not have the disadvantage of having to store extra vectors like in GMRES. These three methods have been compared in many studies (see, e.g., [28, 7, 27, 25]).

## 6.3  Bi-CGSTAB

Bi-CGSTAB [37] is based on the observation that the Bi-CG vector $r_i$ is orthogonal to the entire subspace $K^i(A^T, s_0)$. As a result, we can, instead of squaring the Bi-CG polynomial, construct iteration methods by which $x_i$ are generated so that $r_i = \tilde{P}_i(A)P_i(A)r_0$ with other $i^{th}$ degree polynomials $\tilde{P}$. An obvious possibility is to take for $\tilde{P}_j$ a polynomial of the form

$$Q_i(x) = (1 - \omega_1 x)(1 - \omega_2 x)...(1 - \omega_i x), \tag{7}$$

and to select suitable constants $\omega_j$. This expression leads to an almost trivial recurrence relation for the $Q_i$.

In Bi-CGSTAB, the parameter $\omega_j$ in the $j^{th}$ iteration step is chosen as to minimize $\|r_j\|_2$, with respect to $\omega_j$, for residuals that can be written as $r_j = Q_j(A)P_j(A)r_0$.

Bi-CGSTAB can be viewed as the product of Bi-CG and GMRES(1). Of course, other product methods can be formulated as well.

## 6.4  Bi-CGSTAB($\ell$)

Because of the local minimization, Bi-CGSTAB displays a much smoother convergence behavior than CGS, and more surprisingly, it often also converges (slightly) faster. A weak point in Bi-CGSTAB is that we get a breakdown if an $\omega_j$ is equal to zero. One may equally expect negative effects when $\omega_j$ is small. In fact, BiCGSTAB can be viewed as the combined effect of Bi-CG and GCR(1), or GMRES(1), steps. As soon as the GCR(1) part of the algorithm (nearly) stagnates, then the Bi-CG part in the next iteration step cannot (or only poorly) be constructed. For an analysis, as well as for suggestions to improve the situation, see [32].

Another dubious aspect of Bi-CGSTAB is that the factor $Q_k$ has only real roots by construction. It is well-known that optimal reduction polynomials for matrices with complex eigenvalues may have complex roots as well. If, for instance, the matrix $A$ is real skew-symmetric, then GCR(1) stagnates forever, whereas a method like GCR(2) (or GMRES(2)), in which we minimize over two combined successive search directions, may lead to convergence, and this is mainly due to the fact that then complex eigenvalue components in the error can be effectively reduced.

It has been shown in [34], that the polynomial $Q$ can also be constructed as the product of $\ell$-degree factors, without the construction of the intermediate lower degree factors. The main idea is that $\ell$ successive Bi-CG steps are carried out, where, for the sake of an $A^T$-free construction, the already available part of $Q$ is expanded by simple powers of $A$. This means that after the Bi-CG part of the algorithm vectors from the Krylov subspace $s, As, A^2s, ..., A^\ell s$, with $s = P_k(A)Q_{k-\ell}(A)r_0$ are available, and it is then relatively easy to minimize the residual over that particular Krylov subspace. There are variants of this approach in which more stable bases for the Krylov subspaces are generated

[33], but for low values of $\ell$ a standard basis satisfies, together with a minimum norm solution obtained through solving the associated normal equations (which requires the solution of an $\ell$ by $\ell$ system. In most cases Bi-CGSTAB(2) will already give nice results for problems where Bi-CGSTAB may fail.

Bi-CGSTAB(2) can be represented by the following algorithm:

$$x_0 \text{ is an initial guess; } r_0 = b - Ax_0;$$
$$s_0 \text{ is an arbitrary vector, such that } s_0^T r_0 \neq 0,$$
$$\text{e.g., } s_0 = r_0$$
$$\rho_0 = 1; u = 0; \alpha = 0; \omega_2 = 1$$
$$\text{for } i = 0, 2, 4, 6, \ldots$$
$$\rho_0 = -\omega_2 \rho_0$$

even BiCG step:
$$\rho_1 = s_0^T r_i; \beta = \alpha \rho_1 / \rho_0; \rho_0 = \rho_1$$
$$u = r_i - \beta u; v = Au$$
$$\gamma = s_0^T v; \alpha = \rho_0 / \gamma;$$
$$r = r_i - \alpha v; s = Ar$$
$$x = x_i + \alpha u$$

odd BiCG step:
$$\rho_1 = s_0^T s; \beta = \alpha \rho_1 / \rho_0; \rho_0 = \rho_1$$
$$v = s - \beta v; w = Av$$
$$\gamma = s_0^T w; \alpha = \rho_0 / \gamma$$
$$u = r - \beta u; r = r - \alpha v$$
$$s = s - \alpha w; t = As$$

GCR(2)-part:
$$\omega_1 = s^T r; \mu = s^T s; \nu = s^T t; \tau = t^T t$$
$$\omega_2 = t^T r; \tau = \tau - \nu^2/\mu; \omega_2 = (\omega_2 - \nu \omega_1/\mu)/\tau$$
$$\omega_1 = (\omega_1 - \nu \omega_2)/\mu$$
$$x_{i+2} = x + \omega_1 r + \omega_2 s + \alpha u$$
$$r_{i+2} = r - \omega_1 s - \omega_2 t$$
$$\text{if } x_{i+2} \text{ accurate enough then quit}$$
$$u = u - \omega_1 v - \omega_2 w$$
$$\text{end}$$

For more general Bi-CGSTAB($\ell$) schemes, see [34, 33].
The Bi-CGSTAB(2) algorithm requires 14 vector updates, 9 innerproducts and 4 matrix vector products per full cycle. This has to be compared with two steps of Bi-CGSTAB, which require 4 matrix vector products, 8 innerproducts and 12 vector updates. With respect to memory requirements, Bi-CGSTAB(2) is also only slightly more expensive than Bi-CGSTAB: it requires 2 $n$-vectors more than Bi-CGSTAB.
It has been shown in [9], that for the related Conjugate Gradients method, on distributed memory machines the innerproducts may cause communication overhead problems. We note that the Bi-CG steps are very similar to conjugate gradient iteration steps, so that we may consider similar approaches as those suggested for Conjugate Gradients, for reducing the effects of communication overhead, caused by the 4 innerproducts in the Bi-CG parts. For an overview of these approaches see [6].

If on a specific computer it is possible to overlap communication with communication, then the Bi-CG parts can be rescheduled for creating overlap possibilities:

1. the computation of $\rho_1$ in the even Bi-CG step may be done just before the update of $u$ at the end of the GCR part.

2. The update of $x_{i+2}$ may be delayed until after the computation of $\gamma$ in the even Bi-CG step.

3. The computation of $\rho_1$ for the odd Bi-CG step can be done just before the update for $x$ at the end of the even Bi-CG step.

4. The computation of $\gamma$ in the odd Bi-CG step has already overlap possibillities with the update for $u$.

For the GCR(2) part we note that the 5 innerproducts can be handled together, in order to reduce start-up times for their global assembling. This gives Bi-CG-STAB(2) a (slight) advantage over Bi-CGSTAB. Furthermore, we note that the updates in the GCR(2) may lead to more efficient code than for BiCGSTAB, since some of them can be combined.

# 7 Parallelism in the preconditioner

The previously discussed iterative methods may be combined with preconditioning. The easiest way to explain this is the following one. Given the linear system $Ax = b$, we construct an operator $K$ that approximates $A$ but that leads to simpler to solve systems.

For instance, $K$ may be constructed so that more parallelism is obtained. An obvious way to do this is to skip certain elements in the matrix, or to replace the system by a number of smaller overlapping subsystems. In the context of solving discretized partial differential equations over a given domain, this amounts to splitting up the domain into a number of, possibly slightly overlapping, subdomains and to impose suitable boundary conditions on the boundaries that do not coincide with the boundary of the large domain. These internal boundary conditions require special attention, since their choice may dramatically influence the performance of the overal method in terms of CPU-time.

In general the approximating operator may not vary within each subdomain during the iteration process, except for GMRESR. In this method the approximations may be chosen adaptively to the situation at hand.

Since this approach leads to much flexibility in the design of software, we will discuss in it some more detail. For more conventional approaches for approximating $A$, for instance by *Incomplete LU decompositions*, and for parallelizing those, we refer to [15].

In [36] interface conditions along subdomains are studied and continuity for the solution at the interface is forced up to some degree. It has been proposed to include also mixed derivatives in these relations. The involved parameters can be determined locally by a normal mode analysis, and they can be adapted to the discretized problem. It is shown that the resulting domain decomposition method defines a standard iterative method for some splitting $A = M - N$, and the local coupling aimes at minimizing the largest eigenvalues of $I - AM^{-1}$. Of course, this method can be accelerated and impressive results for GMRES acceleration are shown in [36]. Some attention is paid to the case where the solutions for the subdomains are obtained in only modest accuracy per iteration step.

Recently, Washio and Hayami [40] employed a domain decomposition approach for a rectangular grid by which one step of SSOR [41] is done for the interior part of each subdomain. In order to make this domain-decoupled SSOR more resemble the global SSOR, the SSOR iteration matrix for each subdomain is modified by premultiplying it with a matrix $(I - X_L)^{-1}$ and postmultiplying it by $(I - X_U)^{-1}$. The matrices $X_L$ and $X_U$ depend on the couplings between adjacent subdomains. In order to further improve the parallel performance, the inverses are approximated by low-order truncated Neumann series. Experimental results have been shown for a 32-processor NEC-Cenju distributed memory computer.

Radicati and Robert [28] used an algebraic version of the domain decomposition approach by computing Incomplete LU factors within overlapping block diagonals of a given matrix $A$. When applying the preconditioner to a vector $v$, the values on the overlapped region is averaged from the two values computed from the two overlapping Incomplete LU factors. The approach of Radicati and Robert has been further perfected in [12], where the effects of overlap have been studied from the point of view of geometric domain decompositioning. Artificial mixed boundary conditions on the internal boundaries of the subdomains are introduced. In [12]:Table 5.8 experimental, results have shown for a decomposition into $20 \times 20$ slightly overlapping subdomains of a $200 \times 400$ mesh for a discretized convection-diffusion equation (5-point stencil). When taking Incomplete LU preconditioning for each subdomain, it is shown that the complete linear system can be solved by GMRES on a 400-processor distributed memory Parsytec system with an efficiency in the order of 80% (compared with $\frac{1}{400}$-th of the CPU time of a standard Incomplete LU preconditioned GMRES for the unpartitioned system on 1 single processor).

# References

1. W. E. Arnoldi. The principle of minimized iteration in the solution of the matrix eigenproblem. *Quart. Appl. Math.*, 9:17–29, 1951.
2. O. Axelsson. Conjugate gradient type methods for unsymmetric and inconsistent systems of equations. *Lin. Alg. and its Appl.*, 29:1–16, 1980.
3. O. Axelsson and P. S. Vassilevski. A black box generalized conjugate gradient solver with inner iterations and variable-step preconditioning. *SIAM J. Matrix Anal. Appl.*, 12(4):625–644, 1991.
4. Z. Bai, D. Hu, and L. Reichel. A Newton basis GMRES implementation. *IMA J. Numer. Anal.*, 14:563–581, 1991.

5. R. E. Bank and T. F. Chan. An analysis of the composite step biconjugate gradient method. *Num. Math.*, 66:295–319, 1993.

6. R. Barrett, M. Berry, T. Chan, J. Demmel, J. Donato, J. Dongarra, V. Eijkhout, R. Pozo, C. Romine, and H. van der Vorst. *Templates for the Solution of Linear Systems: Building Blocks for Iterative Methods*. SIAM, Philadelphia, PA, 1994.

7. G. Brussino and V. Sonnad. A comparison of direct and preconditioned iterative techniques for sparse unsymmetric systems of linear equations. *Int. J. for Num. Methods in Eng.*, 28:801–815, 1989.

8. A. T. Chronopoulos and C. W. Gear. s-Step iterative methods for symmetric linear systems. *J. on Comp. and Appl. Math.*, 25:153–168, 1989.

9. L. Crone and H. van der Vorst. Communication aspects of the conjugate gradient method on distributed-memory machines. *Supercomputer*, X(6):4–9, 1993.

10. J. Cullum and A. Greenbaum. Relations between Galerkin and norm-minimizing iterative methods for solving linear systems. *SIAM J. Matrix Analysis and Appl.*, 17:223–247, 1996.

11. E. de Sturler. A parallel variant of GMRES(m). In R. Miller, editor, *Proc. of the fifth Int.Symp. on Numer. Methods in Eng.*, 1991.

12. E. De Sturler. *Iterative methods on distributed memory computers*. PhD thesis, Delft University of Technology, Delft, the Netherlands, 1994.

13. E. De Sturler and H.A. Van der Vorst. Reducing the effect of global communication in GMRES(m) and CG on parallel distributed memory computers. *J. Appl. Num. Math.*, 18:441–459, 1995.

14. J. Demmel, M. Heath, and H. Van der Vorst. Parallel numerical linear algebra. In *Acta Numerica 1993*. Cambridge University Press, Cambridge, 1993.

15. J. J. Dongarra, I. S. Duff, D. C. Sorensen, and H. A. van der Vorst. *Solving Linear Systems on Vector and Shared Memory Computers*. SIAM, Philadelphia, PA, 1991.

16. H. C. Elman. *Iterative methods for large sparse nonsymmetric systems of linear equations*. PhD thesis, Yale University, New Haven, CT, 1982.

17. V. Faber and T. A. Manteuffel. Necessary and sufficient conditions for the existence of a conjugate gradient method. *SIAM J. Numer. Analysis*, 21(2):352–362, 1984.

18. R. Fletcher. *Conjugate gradient methods for indefinite systems*, volume 506 of *Lecture Notes Math.*, pages 73–89. Springer-Verlag, Berlin–Heidelberg–New York, 1976.

19. R. W. Freund, M. H. Gutknecht, and N. M. Nachtigal. An implementation of the look-ahead Lanczos algorithm for non-Hermitian matrices. *SIAM J. Sci. Comput.*, 14:137–158, 1993.

20. R. W. Freund and N. M. Nachtigal. An implementation of the look-ahead Lanczos algorithm for non-Hermitian matrices, part 2. Technical Report 90.46, RIACS, NASA Ames Research Center, 1990.

21. R. W. Freund and N. M. Nachtigal. QMR: a quasi-minimal residual method for non-Hermitian linear systems. *Num. Math.*, 60:315–339, 1991.

22. G. H. Golub and C. F. Van Loan. *Matrix Computations*. The Johns Hopkins University Press, Baltimore, 1989.

23. K. C. Jea and D. M. Young. Generalized conjugate-gradient acceleration of nonsym- metrizable iterative methods. *Lin. Algebra Appl.*, 34:159–194, 1980.

24. C. Lanczos. Solution of systems of linear equations by minimized iterations. *J. Res. Natl. Bur. Stand*, 49:33–53, 1952.

25. N. M. Nachtigal, S. C. Reddy, and L. N. Trefethen. How fast are nonsymmetric matrix iterations? *SIAM J. Matrix Anal. Appl.*, 13:778–795, 1992.

26. B. N. Parlett, D. R. Taylor, and Z. A. Liu. A look-ahead Lanczos algorithm for unsymmetric matrices. *Math. Comp.*, 44:105–124, 1985.
27. C. Pommerell and W. Fichtner. PILS: An iterative linear solver package for ill-conditioned systems. In *Supercomputing '91*, pages 588–599, Los Alamitos, CA., 1991. IEEE Computer Society.
28. G. Radicati di Brozolo and Y. Robert. Parallel conjugate gradient-like algorithms for solving sparse non-symmetric systems on a vector multiprocessor. *Parallel Computing*, 11:223–239, 1989.
29. Y. Saad. A flexible inner-outer preconditioned GMRES algorithm. *SIAM J. Sci. Comput.*, 14:461–469, 1993.
30. Y. Saad and M. H. Schultz. Conjugate Gradient-like algorithms for solving non-symmetric linear systems. *Math. of Comp.*, 44:417–424, 1985.
31. Y. Saad and M. H. Schultz. GMRES: a generalized minimal residual algorithm for solving nonsymmetric linear systems. *SIAM J. Sci. Statist. Comput.*, 7:856–869, 1986.
32. G. L. G. Sleijpen and H.A. Van der Vorst. Maintaining convergence properties of BICGSTAB methods in finite precision arithmetic. *Numerical Algorithms*, 10:203–223, 1995.
33. G. L. G. Sleijpen, H.A. Van der Vorst, and D. R. Fokkema. Bi-CGSTAB($\ell$) and other hybrid Bi-CG methods. *Numerical Algorithms*, 7:75–109, 1994.
34. G. L. G. Sleijpen and D. R. Fokkema. BICGSTAB($\ell$) for linear equations involving unsymmetric matrices with complex spectrum. *ETNA*, 1:11–32, 1993.
35. P. Sonneveld. CGS: a fast Lanczos-type solver for nonsymmetric linear systems. *SIAM J. Sci. Statist. Comput.*, 10:36–52, 1989.
36. K.H. Tan. *Local coupling in domain decomposition*. PhD thesis, Utrecht University, Utrecht, the Netherlands, 1995.
37. H. A. Van der Vorst. Bi-CGSTAB: A fast and smoothly converging variant of Bi-CG for the solution of non-symmetric linear systems. *SIAM J. Sci. Statist. Comput.*, 13:631–644, 1992.
38. H. A. Van der Vorst and C. Vuik. GMRESR: A family of nested GMRES methods. *Num. Lin. Alg. with Appl.*, 1:369–386, 1994.
39. P. K. W. Vinsome. ORTOMIN: an iterative method for solving sparse sets of simultaneous linear equations. In *Proc.Fourth Symposium on Reservoir Simulation*, pages 149–159. Society of Petroleum Engineers of AIME, 1976.
40. T. Washio and K. Hayami. Parallel block preconditioning based on SSOR and MILU. *Numer. Lin. Alg. with Applic.*, 1:533–553, 1994.
41. D. Young. *Iterative Solution of Large Linear Systems*. Academic Press, New York, 1971.

# Core Technologies for System Renovation

Mark van den Brand[1], Paul Klint[2,1], Chris Verhoef[1] *

[1] Programming Research Group, University of Amsterdam, Kruislaan 403,
NL-1098 SJ Amsterdam, The Netherlands
[2] Department of Software Technology, Centre for Mathematics and Computer
Science, P.O. Box 4079, NL-1009 AB Amsterdam, The Netherlands
e-mail: markvdb@wins.uva.nl, paulk@cwi.nl, chris@wins.uva.nl

**Abstract.** Renovation of business-critical software is becoming increasingly important. We identify fundamental notions and techniques to aid in system renovation and sketch some basic techniques: generic language technology to build analysis tools, a knowledge retrieval system to aid in program understanding, and a coordination architecture that is useful to restructure monolithic systems thus enabling their renovation. We argue that these techniques are not only essential for the renovation of old software but that they can also play an important role during the development and maintenance of new software systems.

*Categories and Subject Description:* D.2.6 [**Software Engineering**]: Programming Environments—Interactive; D.2.7 [**Software Engineering**]: Distribution and Maintenance—Restructuring; D.2.m [**Software Engineering**]: Miscellaneous—Rapid prototyping; D.3.2 [**Programming Languages**]: Language Classifications—Specialized application languages; E.2 [**Data**]: Data Storage Representations—Composite structures
*Additional Key Words and Phrases:* re-engineering, system renovation, intermediate data representation, coordination language, query algebra

## 1   Introduction

There is a constant need for updating and renovating business-critical software systems for many and diverse reasons: business requirements change, technological infrastructure is modernized, the government changes laws, or the third millennium approaches, to mention a few. So, in the area of software engineering the subjects of program understanding and system renovation become more and more important, see, for instance, [BKV96] for an annotated bibliography. The interest in such subjects originates from the difficulties that one encounters when

---

* The authors were all in part sponsored by bank ABN AMRO, software house DP-Finance, and the Dutch Ministry of Economical Affairs via the Senter Project #ITU95017 "SOS Resolver". Chris Verhoef was also supported by the Netherlands Computer Science Research Foundation (SION) with financial support from the Netherlands Organization for Scientific Research (NWO), project *Interactive tools for program understanding, 612-33-002.*

attempting to maintain large, old, software systems. It is not hard to understand that it is very difficult—if not impossible—to renovate such *legacy* systems.

The purpose of this paper is to identify core technologies for system renovation and to incorporate reverse engineering techniques in forward engineering so that the maintenance problem may become more manageable in the future. We identify the following core technologies for system renovation:

- Generic language technology.
- Techniques for extracting information from existing source code.
- Visualization of extracted information.
- Decomposition of systems into smaller components.
- Coordination of (heterogeneous) components.
- Construction techniques for components.

Why are these technologies essential for system renovation? Before the actual renovation can start it will be necessary to make an inventory of the specification and the documentation of the system to be renovated. It is our experience that either there is no documentation at all, or the original programmers that could possibly explain the functionality of parts of the system have left, or both. The only documentation that is left is the source code itself. Thus, since the vital information of the software is solely accessible via the source code, techniques are needed for understanding this code. Note that legacy systems are usually polylingual, hence generic language technology is desirable to obtain analysis tools for all these languages. Given the results of program understanding (logic) components and their relationships in the system can be identified. The latter can be used to restructure the system via coordination techniques, this creates the possibility to redesign the extracted (logic) components into physical ones.

We will briefly review some of these technologies in this paper. The presentation is largely determined by our own current research and practice in re-engineering and does not aim at completeness.

First we introduce some basic terminology in re-engineering and generic language technology.

## 1.1 Re-engineering

We briefly recall some re-engineering terminology as proposed in [CC90]. The term reverse engineering finds its origins in hardware technology and denotes the process of obtaining the specification of complex hardware systems. Now the meaning of this notion has shifted to software. While *forward engineering* moves from a high-level design to a low-level implementation, *reverse engineering* can be seen as the inverse process. It can be characterized by analyzing a software system in order to, firstly, identify the system components and their interactions, and to, secondly, make representations of the system on a different, possible higher, level of abstraction. Reverse engineering restricts itself to *investigating* and *understanding* a system, and is also called *program understanding*. Adaptation of a system is beyond reverse engineering but within the scope of system renovation. The notion *restructuring* amounts to transforming a system from one representation to another one at the same level of abstraction. An essential aspect of restructuring is that the semantic behaviour of the original system and the new one should remain the same; no modifications of the functionality is involved. The purpose of *re-engineering* or *renovation* is to study the system, by making a specification at a higher abstraction level, adding new functionality to this specification and develop a completely new system on the basis of the original one.

## 1.2 Generic Language Technology

Another issue we will encounter is to what extent various tools depend on specific programming languages. We will classify language (in)dependence in the following categories:

- We call a system *language-independent* if it has *no* built-in knowledge of a specific language. An example is the UNIX[3] tool `grep(1)`, that can be used for simple textual searches in source files.
- We call a system *language-dependent* if the knowledge of a language is hardwired in the system, e.g., a C-compiler. This knowledge can be implemented in the system by hand, via a generator, or via a combination of these approaches.
- We call a system *language parameterized* (or *generic*) if the language is a parameter of the system and upon instantiation with a language definition a language-specific system is obtained. Examples are the Synthesizer Generator [RT89] and the ASF+SDF Meta-Environment [Kli93, DHK96].

## 1.3 Related Work

There are not many scientific papers that actually discuss the re-engineering of large software systems, as we discovered during the compilation of an annotated bibliography [BKV96]. There are probably two reasons for this. First, academic software is easily put aside, because there is in general no real economic necessity to keep it running. Second, re-engineering projects carried out in industry are not frequently published for commercial reasons. This paper is based on our experiences in re-engineering a large academic software system as well as on the cooperation with a large commercial bank and a software house specialized in financial software.

We discuss a knowledge retrieval system based on a query algebra that is language parameterized and interprets queries directly. It supports multidirectional traversal of the syntax trees representing the code of legacy systems. Some related work on the topic of knowledge retrieval systems is [Ode93, PP94a, PP94b, REQ94, DRW96]. In [Ode93] a query mechanism is used for a completely different purpose than ours, namely, to define type checkers, the tree traversal

---

[3] UNIX is a registered trademark of UNIX System Laboratories

mechanism is, however, similar to ours. In [PP94a, PP94b] it is claimed that the described Source Code Algebra is language-independent, but the data base in which the source code is stored must be initialized with language specific entries. Adding a new language results in adapting the data base. The Source Code Algebra is conceptually language parameterized, but the implementation technique used required instantiation of language parameters, thus yielding a language-dependent system. All examples in [PP94b] only use top-down tree traversal. [DRW96] describes tools for analysing C/C++ programs for program understanding. These tools are generated and support a procedural mechanism to retrieve information from the C/C++ programs. So it is not based on a query algebra and is language-dependent. REQL [REQ94] is a source code query language. The syntactic notions in a language are translated to attributes in a data base and into queries to test for relationships and properties. These attributes are hard-wired in the system but can be used for more than one language. The visualization mechanism and querying mechanism are fully integrated. This is a disadvantage since it prevents the visualization of results obtained by other mechanisms. It also supports some procedural functionality to analyze programs. An implementation of the query language REQL is described that permits the connection of parsers for different languages.

We will also discuss a coordination architecture to implement the decomposition of legacy systems. A detailed overview of related work on software architectures and coordination languages can be found in [BK96b].

## 1.4 Organization of the Paper

In Section 2 we discuss a common representation format that is useful to exchange data both between components in a (legacy) system and between tools in a re-engineering environment. In Section 3 we discuss a knowledge retrieval system based on a query algebra which uses the common representation format of Section 2. In Section 4 we discuss a mechanism to decompose a legacy system into smaller components and show how the exchange of data between these components can be established via the common representation format of Section 2. In the final section we put the core technologies for re-engineering in the perspective of forward engineering.

## 2 Exchanging Data: the Annotated Term Format

How can re-engineering tools share and exchange information? How can components of a legacy system exchange information during incremental renovation?

We propose a data structure, called the *Annotated Term Format (ATF)* specially designed for the data exchange between (possibly) heterogeneous components in a software system. This data format describes terms extended with annotations and is able to accommodate the representation of *all* possible data that might be exchanged between components. The representation is such that individual components are, so to speak, immune for information that is added and manipulated by other components.

ATF can also be used as internal data structure of the components themselves. It is a powerful format in which it is possible to represent, for instance, parse trees that can be annotated with many and diverse sorts of information, such as textual coordinates, access paths, or the result of program analysis (e.g., data flow analysis).

## 2.1 Annotated Terms

Below we will give an inductive definition of terms in Annotated Term Format, we will discuss the annotation mechanism and we give examples of its use. A full formal specification of ATF is given in [BKOV] and is beyond the scope of this paper.

**Definition 1.** For each set $S$, let $S^* = \{s_1 \ldots s_n | s_i \in S, 1 \leq i \leq n\}$ be the set of words over $S$.

The set $S" = \{"s" | s \in S^*\}$ is called the set of quoted words[4]. The empty quoted word is represented as "".

Terms in Annotated Term Format are called *ATerms* and they are defined as follows:

- Let $C$ be a set of constants, then $C^+ \subseteq$ ATerms.
- Let $N$ be a set of numerals, then $N^+ \subseteq$ ATerms.
- Let $L$ be a set of literals, then $L" \subseteq$ ATerms.
- [] is an ATerm, called the *empty list*. Let $T_1, \ldots, T_n$ be ATerms, then $[T_1, \ldots, T_n]$ is an ATerm called *list*.
- Let $F$ be a set of function symbols together with their arity. Let $(f, n) \in F$, so $f$ is a function symbol of arity $n$. Let $T_1, \ldots, T_n$ be ATerms, then $f(T_1, \ldots, T_n)$ is an ATerm called *application*.
- Let $T$ be an ATerm and $T_1, \ldots, T_n$ be (distinct) ATerms with $n \geq 1$, then $T\{T_1, \ldots, T_n\}$ is an ATerm called *annotation*.

By instantiating $C$, $N$, $L$, and $F$ we can obtain various forms of annotated terms.

**Example: ATerms** Choose $C = \{a, b, c\}, N = \{1, 2, 3\}, L = C \cup N$, and $F = \{(f, 1), (g, 2), (h, 3)\}$. Examples of ATerms are then:

- *constants*: abc.
- *numerals*: 123.
- *literals*: "abc" or "123".
- *lists*: [], [1, "abc", 3], or [1, 2, [3, 2], 1].
- *functions*: f("a"), g(1,[]), or h("1", f("2"), ["a","b"]).
- *annotations*: f("a"){g(2,["a","b"])} or "1"{[1,2,3],"abc"}.

---

[4] For simplicity, we assume in this presentation that " $\notin S$.

## 2.2 Representing Parse Trees

The use of ATF can be demonstrated by showing how to represent parse trees in ATF, and by annotating them with path and visualization information, respectively. This can be done by instantiating $C$, $N$, $L$, and $F$. Note that this example will be used in Section 3.2 when we discuss a knowledge retrieval system.

Let $C$ and $N$ be the empty set, and let $L$ be $\{a, \ldots, Z, 0, \ldots, 9\}$. Let the set of function symbols $F$ consist of the following elements:

- $(\text{prod}, 1)$, e.g., $\text{prod}(T)$ represents production rule $T$.
- $(\text{appl}, 2)$, e.g., $\text{appl}(T_1, T_2)$ represents applying production rule $T_1$ to the arguments $T_2$.
- $(1, 1)$, e.g., $1(T)$ represents literal $T$.
- $(\text{sort}, 1)$, e.g., $\text{sort}(T)$ represents sort $T$.
- $(\text{lex}, 2)$, e.g., $\text{lex}(T_1, T_2)$ represents (lexical) token $T_1$ of sort $T_2$.
- $(\text{w}, 1)$, e.g., $\text{w}(T)$ represents white space $T$.

With the functions defined above we can represent simple parse trees in ATF. A complete specification of parse trees is given in [BKOV].

The following context-free syntax rules (in SDF [HHKR92]) are necessary to parse the input sentence **true and false**.

```
sort Bool
context-free syntax
   true            -> Bool
   false           -> Bool
   Bool and Bool -> Bool {left}
```

The parse tree below represents the input sentence **true and false** in ATF, in Figure 1 this parse tree is depicted.

```
appl(prod("Bool and Bool -> Bool"),
     [appl(prod("true -> Bool"),[l("true")]),
      w(" "),l("and"),w(" "),
      appl(prod("false -> Bool"),[l("false")])
     ])
```

Note that this parse tree is completely self-contained and does not depend on a separate grammar definition.

To demonstrate the annotation mechanism we extend the above definition to create pointers to trees in the form of paths. A path is a list of natural numbers $[n_0, \ldots, n_k]$ where each number $n_i$ stands for the $n_i$th son of the node $n_{i-1}$ where $1 \leq i \leq k$. The first number $n_0$ represents the root. The syntax of paths in ATF can be obtained by extending $N$ with $\{0, \ldots, 9\}$ and extending the set of functions with $\{(\text{path}, 1)\}$.

The example parse tree can be annotated with path information thus:

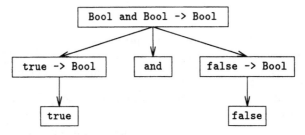

**Fig. 1.** The syntax tree for true and false.

```
appl(prod("Bool and Bool -> Bool"),
    [appl(prod("true -> Bool"),
        [l("true"){path([0,0,0])}]){path([0,0])},
     w(" "),l("and"){path([0,1])},w(" "),
     appl(prod("false -> Bool"),
        [l("false"){path([0,2,0])}]){path([0,2])}
    ]){path([0])}
```

Note that only the application and literal nodes are annotated with path information. The production rules are not annotated since they do not represent nodes in the parse tree for the original input sentence (true and false).

Another example is to use the annotations to store visual information, such as colours, for components that support them. We extend the set $C$ with the constants red, yellow, and blue and the set $F$ with the unary function (colour,1). By adding the annotation colour(red) a tool for visualization knows that the annotated subterm should be printed in the colour red. Other tools will ignore this colour annotation. As an example we annotate in the example parse tree the node l("true").

```
appl(prod("Bool and Bool -> Bool"),
    [appl(prod("true -> Bool"),
        [l("true"){path([0,0,0]),colour(red)}]){path([0,0])},
     w(" "),l("and"){path([0,1])},w(" "),
     appl(prod("false -> Bool"),
        [l("false"){path([0,2,0])}]){path([0,2])}
    ]){path([0])}
```

In a similar way we can define font, font-type, and elision annotations. Fonts can be obtained by extending the set $C$ with the constants like times or helvetica and the set $F$ with the unary function (font,1). Font types are defined analogously (bold and italic are examples of font types). Elision can be obtained by extending $C$ with the constant ... (the common notation for elision of text) and the set $F$ with (elision,1). Elision can be used to suppress (large) parts of program texts.

## 2.3 Discussion

ATF resembles the intermediate tree representations [ASN87, Sno89, Aus90] usually found in compilers and programming environments. It has, however, a number of properties that make it particularly suited for our purpose:

- The term format is straightforward, enabling simple specification, implementation, and use.
- The term format is universal, i.e., all forms of data can be exchanged between components.
- The annotation mechanism permits different components to add their own auxiliary information to data exchanged with other components.
- The term format is language parameterized.

We will see that ATF can be used as a basis for knowledge retrieval (Section 3) and is also suited for exchange of data in heterogeneous, distributed, systems (Section 4.1).

# 3 Knowledge Retrieval

One of the crucial phases in re-engineering a (legacy) system is to obtain, collect, and store relevant knowledge about it. In this phase it is often desirable to first obtain an overall impression of the system and later on to dive into the details of relevant subsystems. The re-engineer can choose to store relevant (inferred) information to be used later on.

Given a specific re-engineering goal (e.g., year 2000 compliance, or language conversion), a re-engineer will have to zoom in and zoom out on the source code in order to increase her understanding and to identify program fragments that are relevant for the re-engineering goal at hand. Tools supporting such an interactive zooming mechanism are important, given the expectation that not all re-engineering tasks can be automated [Cor89] and will require human interaction and intelligence [You89].

Obtaining knowledge about a program is not language specific. Therefore, it is desirable that tools to obtain this knowledge are generic, i.e., can be parameterized with a desired language. An additional advantage of this approach is that a single tool is sufficient to deal with legacy systems implemented in more than one language, since even within one legacy system usually more than one language is used, viz. the combination of COBOL [ANS85] and Job Control Language JCL [Flo71].

## 3.1 Query Algebra: Motivation and Minimal Properties

A natural means for obtaining knowledge about a legacy system is to view it as a special type of data base that can be queried. We will use a parse tree with the possibility of adding annotations (as described in Section 2) as our data base model. Thus, the queries are functions that inspect the parse tree

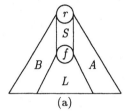 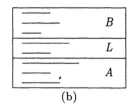

**Fig. 2.** Regions in the syntax tree and program text.

and modify its annotations when appropriate. Often combinations of extracted information yield important new information, therefore, it is natural to have the possibility of combining queries. This implies the existence of basic queries as well as operations to combine them, in other words an algebra of queries.

A query algebra should have at least the following properties:

- It must be generic (i.e., language parameterized).
- It must allow multidirectional propagation of queries through well-defined parts of the trees.
- It must provide random access to tree nodes.
- It must be adjustable.

A query algebra should be language parameterized since obtaining knowledge is not language specific. It can then also effortlessly deal with polylingual legacy systems. In [PP94b] this is identified as an extremely valuable feature.

Zooming in and out on the code is needed in order to locate the code fragments that cause problems or that are related to a specific re-engineering goal.

Random access on tree nodes can be obtained via the *focus*, an interactive pointing mechanism for the re-engineer to locate (sub)trees. A focus divides a tree in regions, such as:

- The region before the path from the root to the focussed tree.
- The region after the path from the root to the focussed tree.
- The region formed by the nodes on the path from the root to the focussed tree.
- The region formed by the focussed tree.

Arbitrary combinations of these four regions are also possible. A syntax tree with these regions is represented in Figure 2(a), where the *B*, *A*, *L*, and *S* stand for *before*, *after*, *local*, and *spine*, respectively. The regions before and after are called this way since in the program text they represent the text before and after the focus (or local), see 2(b). The nodes *r* and *f* in Figure 2(a) represent the root and the focus in the tree, respectively.

A query algebra system for re-engineering should be adjustable in the following ways:

- New parsers can be connected in order to support queries for the languages found in a specific legacy system.

- The results of semantic analysis (e.g., typechecking, data flow analysis) can be attached to the syntax trees constructed by these parsers and this information can be queried.
- New basic queries and query operators can be added.

## 3.2   The Query Algebra of IQAT

The Interactive Query Algebra Tool (IQAT) is a prototype we have developed to experiment with query algebras for system re-engineering to see whether the proposed properties are feasible. The query algebra should, therefore, at least support a multidirectional propagation mechanism of queries over tree regions; it should be language parameterized; and it should be adjustable. We will argue below that the IQAT system satisfies these properties.

The multidirectional propagation mechanism is explicitly available via a number of (basic) queries in IQAT. In Figure 2(a) we have seen that the syntax tree can be divided in a number of regions. An examples of a query that uses these regions is trees(*Region*); selects all nodes in region *Region*, defined by one of the constants before, after, local, spine, discussed in the previous section. Note that this query has the actual tree that is being queried as implicit parameter (see below).

Our query algebra supports a language parameterized mechanism. More precisely, instead of parameterizing it with an entire language definition some queries can be parameterized with elements of a language definition, such as non-terminal names and production rules (we call these in the sequel *Syntactic-Categories*). Each language element in the query is translated to terms in ATF by the query evaluator. The resulting term is used when parse trees of the code of the legacy system are inspected to answer the query. For example, the query has("MOVE" Corr Id-or-lit "TO" Id-or-lit+ -> Stat) checks whether the root of a tree is a move-statement in a COBOL program. Another example is contains(*Region, SyntacticCategory*); it selects all nodes in region *Region* which satisfy property *SyntacticCategory*.

The IQAT system supports a number of (basic) data types, for example booleans, integers, sets, and trees. It supports a number of operations on these types, for example the operations and, or, and not on the booleans and the operations + and - on the integers. We will not further discuss these basic types and their operations, instead, we will focus on the more sophisticated part of the query algebra: queries and operations on them. All queries work implicitly on a set of so-called tree addresses (SetofTrees) each consisting of a syntax tree and a path to a node in the syntax tree. Therefore, the first argument of all query definitions is shown between brackets to emphasize that it is an implicit argument of the query. Note that most (but not all) queries take an implicit SetofTrees argument and yield a SetofTrees as well.

We divide queries in the following conceptual categories and we give some typical examples of each category:

**Topographical queries** select nodes of given trees.
- locate: (SetofTrees ×) Region × SyntacticCategory → SetofTrees
  This query selects the nodes with the property *SyntacticCategory* in the region *Region* for all trees in *SetofTrees*.
- trees: (SetofTrees ×) Region → SetofTrees
  This query selects all nodes in the region *Region* of all trees in *SetofTrees*.
- down,up,left,right: (SetofTrees ×) Int → SetofTrees
  These queries return all nodes that can be reached by going *Int* steps down, up, left, right, respectively, in the trees in SetofTrees.

**Existential queries** check whether a node of a syntactic category exists in given syntax trees.
- exists: (SetofTrees ×) Region × SyntacticCategory → Bool
  This query checks whether one of the trees in *SetofTrees* contains a node with property *SyntacticCategory* and which is located in the region *Region*. In fact, exists is very similar to locate except that a boolean value is returned instead of a *SetofTrees*.
- has: (Tree ×) SyntacticCategory → Bool
  This query checks whether *Tree* has property *SyntacticCategory*.

**Quantitative queries** gather statistics or metrics about a set of trees.
- size: (SetofTrees) → Int
  This query counts the number of trees in *SetofTrees*.

**Attributive queries** manipulate the attributes in syntax trees. These queries are different from the previous ones since they may modify the data structure, whereas the others may only extract data (including the data in attributes).
- add-attribute: (SetofTrees ×) Attribute → SetofTrees
- add-value: (SetofTrees ×) Attribute × Value → SetofTrees
- remove-attribute: (SetofTrees ×) Attribute → SetofTrees
- remove-value: (SetofTrees ×) Attribute → SetofTrees
- get-value: (Tree ×) Attribute → Value

**User-defined queries** are queries to be defined by the user of the IQAT system. For example, a query for calculating the McCabe metric or data flow information.

Next we will discuss a number of composition operations on queries. Note that such operations generally are partial functions. For example, size and exists can not be sensibly composed. Below we list the most important operators.

**Functional composition** is used to apply a query to the results of a previous query and has the form
- Query Query → Query

Consider, e.g., the functional composition trees(local) size. Given an initial (implicit) set of trees $S$, trees(local) will compute a new set of trees $S'$ consisting of all nodes of all subtrees of $S$. Next, size will compute the number of subtrees in $S'$.

**Logical composition** is used to combine queries which have a boolean as result. They have the syntax:

- Query and Query → Query
- Query or Query → Query
- not Query → Query

**Set composition** is used to combine queries which have a set of trees as result. They have the syntax:

- Query intersection Query → Query
- Query union Query → Query

**Hierarchical composition** is used to impose further restrictions on previous query results. It can only eliminate parts of a previous query result but can not generate new ones. Hierarchical composition has the syntax

- Query provided Query → Query

An expression containing this operator returns all the nodes obtained by evaluating the left-hand side that satisfy the criterion of the right-hand side. For example, the provided combinator can be used to locate all while statements that contain if statements:

```
locate(local,"while" Exp "do" Series "od" -> Stat)
provided
contains(local,"if" Exp "then" Series "else" Series "fi" -> Stat)
```

## 3.3 Prototype Implementation

A prototype of the query evaluator has been developed using ASF+SDF [DHK96]. It takes a set of trees and applies the specified query on them. Before the actual evaluation starts the query expression is type-checked. The evaluation function has the following form:

- eval: SetofTrees × Query → Result

The output Result is either a set of trees, a boolean value, or an integer value. The output can be stored for the evaluation of other queries or for visualization.

Based on these experiences an implementation of the IQAT system is being made using the TOOLBUS [BK96a, BK96b], see Section 4.1. Due to the nature of the IQAT system it is crucial that it can be easily modified. This is achieved as follows:

- The TOOLBUS ensures adjustability of the architecture of the IQAT system, e.g., adding new parsers, adding data flow components, or adding graphical components.
- The ASF+SDF Meta-Environment [Kli93] (an interactive programming environment generator) ensures adjustability of those components of the IQAT system that have been developed with it, e.g., creating dialects of COBOL [ANS85] or adding new functionality to the query algebra.
- The annotated term format (ATF) ensures adjustability of data. Annotated terms are used to represent the code of the legacy system and the annotation mechanism is used both to store and visualize the results of queries.

## 3.4 Visualization

A visualization mechanism is necessary to show the results of queries. We separated this mechanism from the query algebra, so it can also be used for the viewing of results of other tools, like a data flow analysis tool. Although we recognize the importance of graphical views, we currently restrict ourselves to textual ones.

We have shown in Section 2 that parse trees in annotated term format can be annotated with `path`, `colour`, `font`, `font-type`, and `elision` information. This information can be used both to give a structured view on legacy code and to visualize the result of query evaluation. These evaluations are either booleans or integers, or sets of trees. We will now only discuss the visualization of trees.

A number of access functions can be defined on annotated parse trees to manipulate the various visual annotations. For example, we can manipulate the `colour` annotation with the functions:

- `set-colour: Tree × SetofTrees × Colour → Tree`
- `reset-colour: Tree × SetofTrees → Tree`

The second argument *SetofTrees* is the set of subtrees (tree addresses) of the *Tree* in the first argument that should be textually visualized with a given colour. For `font`, `font-type` and `elision` we have similar access functions.

The annotations `colour`, `font`, and `font-type` can be used to emphasize parts of the legacy code, whereas `elision` is useful to suppress parts of the legacy code.

The set of trees provided by queries, such as `trees`, serves as input for the access functions of the visualization mechanism. The access functions return a parse tree annotated with `colour`, `font`, `font-type`, and `elision` information. A viewing component traverses the resulting tree and interprets the visual annotations by providing the requested colours, fonts, font-types, and elisions.

## 3.5 Discussion

We have presented a generic approach for querying source code. Although we are currently concentrating on the functionality of the query system itself rather than already applying it in large case studies, we expect the following benefits from this approach:

- During forward engineering, queries can be used to pose *what-if* questions to study the effects of different implementation alternatives.
- During re-engineering queries can be used to explore the structure of a legacy system.

An obvious next step will be to combine queries with program transformations, in order to describe complete conversions of source code.

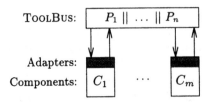

**Fig. 3.** General architecture of the TOOLBUS.

## 4 Structuring and Restructuring

How can a re-engineering tool invoke functionality provided by other tools? How can components of a legacy system call each other's services during incremental renovation?

We will first describe in Section 4.1 an implementation of a software bus, called the TOOLBUS [BK96a, BK96b], that facilitates the construction of software systems consisting of independent, cooperating, components. In Section 4.2 we focus on the creation and modification of systems by means of the TOOL-BUS. In Section 4.3 we emphasize on using the TOOLBUS to re-engineer legacy systems, demonstrated by an example: the re-engineering of the ASF+SDF Meta-Environment[Kli93].

### 4.1 The TOOLBUS Coordination Architecture

The TOOLBUS [BK96a, BK96b] is a component interconnection architecture resembling a hardware communication bus. To control the possible interactions between software components connected to the bus direct inter-component communication is forbidden.

The TOOLBUS serves the purpose of defining the cooperation of a number of *components* $C_i$ $(i = 1, \ldots, m)$ that are to be combined into a complete system as is shown in Figure 3. The internal behaviour or implementation of each component is irrelevant: they may be implemented in different programming languages or be generated from specifications. Components may, or may not, maintain their own internal state. The *parallel process* $P_1 || \ldots || P_n$ in Figure 3 describes the initial behaviour of the interaction of the components $C_1, \ldots, C_m$ and the interaction between the *sequential processes* $P_1, \ldots, P_n$. Where a sequential process $P_i$ can, for example, describe communication between components, communication between processes, creation of new components, or creation of new processes.

To give an idea of the expressive power of the sequential processes $P_s$ we give a simplified BNF definition:

$$P_s ::= \text{send} \mid \text{receive} \mid \text{create} \mid \delta \mid P_s + P_s \mid P_s \cdot P_s \mid P_s * P_s$$

We only give the main operators and we have abstracted from the data part of the atomic actions send, receive, and create. The operators $+$, $\cdot$, and $*$ stand for choice, sequential composition, and iteration, respectively. The constant process $\delta$ stands for the deadlocked process, send and receive are actions for communication, and create is an action for the creation of processes and components. A TOOLBUS process consists of parallel sequential processes: $P_1 \parallel \ldots \parallel P_n$, where $\parallel$ stands for parallel composition. The operators in TOOLBUS processes stem from the algebra of communicating processes (ACP) [BW90, BV95]. In fact, TOOLBUS processes are expressions over a process algebra that also supports relative and absolute time aspects [BB96]. A detailed discussion of TOOLBUS processes is beyond the scope of this paper, and can be found in [BK96a].

The *adapters* in Figure 3 are small pieces of software needed for each component to adapt it to the common data representation (ATF, see Section 2) and the TOOLBUS process expression. A number of adapters are available via TOOLBUS libraries, but for specific components they have to be implemented separately.

## 4.2 Creating and Modifying New Systems

The TOOLBUS provides an architecture to compose systems from (basic) components. Within this architecture there is a mechanism to add and replace components without affecting the rest of the system. The components use a common data format (ATF) to exchange information. The common data format can also be used as internal data structure by the components themselves.

Systems developed with the TOOLBUS can more easily be modified than classical, monolithic, ones. Reasons for modifying an existing system are deleting obsolete components, replacing components by better ones, extending the system with new functionality, and system maintenance. Modifications of a TOOLBUS-based system can take place at various levels:

- Modifications on the level of the TOOLBUS. Examples are creation of a system and alterations of the system by adding or removing components.
- Modifications of the components themselves. Examples are optimizing a component or adding more functionality. Such modifications do not affect the shared data structure of components.
- Modifications of the data structure. An example is adding annotations to parse trees to store position information calculated by a parser, such information will be used by an editor and ignored by a compiler.

In general, the effects of modifications are better localized than in a monolithic system.

## 4.3 Re-engineering Old Systems

If we apply the approach just described in a top-down manner it can also be used to decompose an existing system into (smaller) components. By analyzing a monolithic system one can identify its logic components and their relationships, these are the arrows in Figure 4(a). Having identified these logic components and relationships it may be possible to decompose such a monolithic system. If the

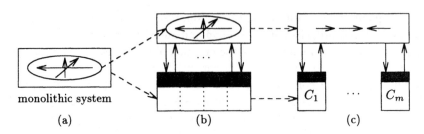

**Fig. 4.** General organization of restructering.

decomposition is feasible, we can implement these relationships in the software bus, see Figure 4(b) where the arrows in the monolithic system have been moved to the software bus. The monolithic system is connected to the software bus via an adapter that redirects the internal communication to the software bus, we call this *communication extraction*. Finally we can decompose the monolithic system by physically decomposing the logic components and connect them to the software bus, see Figure 4(c), we call this *component restructuring*. Furthermore, it is possible to reorganize the communication in the software bus, we call this *communication restructuring*, this is depicted by the reshuffling of the arrows in Figure 4(c). After having identified these components it has to be decided whether the functionality of the components is obsolete or re-usable. Obviously components with obsolete functionality can be thrown away. For components with re-usable functionality it must be decided whether it is possible to re-use existing code and adapt it, to reimplement the entire component, or to use existing third party software. We can now use the techniques described in Section 4.2 to renovate the system in an incremental way. A similar migration strategy for legacy systems is elaborately discussed in [BS95].

There is not necessarily a one-to-one correspondence between the processes and the components. The possibility of controlling a complex component by more than one sequential process frees us from the need to physically split such a component. This is an extremely valuable feature in the communication extraction phase of the decomposition of a legacy system. Namely, communication between the logic components in the legacy system is transferred to communication between the sequential processes in TOOLBUS. It is also possible to have more physical components than sequential processes, e.g., components that operate sequentially can be described by a single sequential process this is a valuable feature in the communication restructuring phase of the decomposition of a legacy system. Even if $n = m$ there is not necessarily a one-to-one correspondence between processes and components.

**Example** The above strategy is used at CWI/UvA to re-engineer the ASF+SDF Meta-Environment, an interactive programming environment generator developed in the mid eighties.

The re-engineering goals of the ASF+SDF Meta-Environment were manifold;

we will enumerate them below:

- Language conversion, from LeLisp [LeL87] to C [KR78].
- Improving maintainability by modularization.
- Using third party software, like Tcl/Tk [Ous94].
- Preparing it for adding external tools in the future without redesign.

Originally this monolithic system was implemented in LeLisp [LeL87], a Lisp dialect, and consisted of 200.000 lines of LeLisp code. No code of the old system could be re-used because of the first reverse engineering goal. Also automatic translation of old code was not feasible because of the costs involved and the desired improvements stated above as the second goal. Automatic conversion would also result in another monolithic and difficult to maintain system. After having identified the main components, it was decided that none of them were obsolete. It was decided which ones could be replaced by third party software and which ones had to be reimplemented.

A first attempt to restructure the ASF+SDF Meta-Environment in order to re-engineer it is described in [KB93]. The main goal of this restructuring was to use third party software for the user interface and the text editor. Those components were successfully separated from the main system and every part worked stand-alone. However, the interaction between those parts failed, since the interaction led to unexpected deadlocks. These problems were studied and described in [VVW94] and gave rise to the development of a more sophisticated coordination archictecture, the TOOLBUS [BK96a, BK96b].

At the time of writing this paper the re-engineering process is still in progress. The relationships between the components are implemented in the TOOLBUS. All components are being reimplemented in parallel by various people.

## 5 Perspective: Software Development using Re-engineering Technology

Interestingly enough, re-engineering techniques can play a useful role during forward engineering as well. Combined with the observation that most systems undergo many forward as well as reverse engineering activities during their life time we argue that a discipline of software engineering should be developed in which both forward and reverse engineering are seemlessly integrated. This approach will improve both the cost effectiveness of the software production and the quality of the resulting software.

One can distinguish the following phases in the life cycle of a software system:

**Creation:** in this phase the system is created using classical engineering, so only forward techniques are used. In Figure 5 this is depicted by a horizontal line: since $r = 0$ we have that $f - r/f + r = 1$, where $r$ and $f$ are a measure for the forward and reverse engineering effort, respectively.

**Maintenance:** in this phase initially minor maintenance is necessary to keep the system running. In Figure 5 this is depicted by small forward engineering

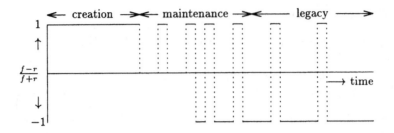

**Fig. 5.** Classical life cycle of a software system.

lines. However, later on it is becoming more difficult to maintain the system. Reverse engineering techniques are then needed. This is visualized by short forward engineering periods, interrupted by reverse engineering periods that are gradually taking longer time.

**Legacy:** in this phase it is hardly possible to maintain the system since maintainers are merely busy trying to understand the system.

The above approach yields a legacy system that can only be re-engineered at high costs. In order to avoid this we propose an alternative scenario that reduces the maintenance effort in the long run and prevents the creation of a legacy system. We distinguish the following two phases:

**Creation:** in this phase reverse engineering techniques are immediately used to influence the design and development of the system: for instance to study the impact of different implementation alternatives. This approach could also be characterized as reverse engineering driven software development. This is depicted in the curve that is presented in Figure 6. The harmonic character of this curve represents the interplay of forward and reverse engineering.

**Maintenance:** in this phase maintenance is necessary to keep the system running. We see a harmonic curve as well, reflecting the reverse and forward engineering activities while maintaining the system and keeping the knowledge about the system up-to-date.

The above approach could be called *harmonic* software engineering.

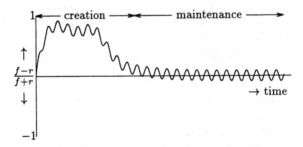

**Fig. 6.** Desired life cycle of a software system.

The core technologies for system renovation that we have briefly reviewed in this paper may thus also contribute to the discipline of software engineering as a whole.

## Acknowledgements

We thank Pieter Olivier for useful comments related to Section 4.1. In addition, we thank all our colleagues in the Resolver project for general discussions on the topic of system renovation.

## References

[ANS85]  *COBOL, ANSI X3.23.* American National Standards Institute, 1985.

[ASN87]  *Specification of Abstract Syntax Notation One (ASN-1).* 1987. ISO 8824.

[Aus90]  D. Austry. The VTP project: modular abstract syntax specification. Rapports de Recherche 1219, INRIA, Sophia-Antipolis, 1990.

[BB96]  J.C.M. Baeten and J.A. Bergstra. Discrete time process algebra. *Formal Aspects of Computing*, 8(2):188–208, 1996.

[BK96a]  J. A. Bergstra and P. Klint. The discrete time toolbus. In M. Wirsing and M. Nivat, editors, *Algebraic Methodology and Software Technology (AMAST '96)*, volume 1101 of *LNCS*, pages 288–305. Springer-Verlag, 1996.

[BK96b]  J.A. Bergstra and P. Klint. The toolbus coordination architecture. In P. Ciancarini and C. Hankin, editors, *Coordination Languages and Models*, volume 1061 of *LNCS*, pages 75–88. Springer-Verlag, 1996.

[BKOV]  M.G.J. van den Brand, P. Klint, P. Olivier, and E. Visser. Aterms: representing structured data for exchange between heterogeneous tools. Unpublished manuscript.

[BKV96]  M.G.J. van den Brand, P. Klint, and C. Verhoef. Reverse engineering and system renovation – an annotated bibliography. Technical Report P9603, University of Amsterdam, Programming Research Group, 1996.

[BS95]  M.L. Brodie and M. Stonebraker. *Migrating Legacy Systems — Gateways, Interfaces & The Incremental Approach.* Morgan Kaufmann Publishers, Inc., 1995.

[BV95]  J.C.M. Baeten and C. Verhoef. Concrete process algebra. In S. Abramsky, D.M. Gabbay, and T.S.E. Maibaum, editors, *Handbook of Logic in Computer Science, Volume IV, Syntactical Methods*, pages 149–268. Oxford University Press, 1995.

[BW90]  J.C.M. Baeten and W.P. Weijland. *Process Algebra.* Cambridge University Press, 1990.

[CC90]  E.J. Chikofsky and J.H. Cross. Reverse engineering and design recovery: A taxonomy. *IEEE Software*, 7(1):13–17, 1990.

[Cor89]  T.A. Corbi. Program understanding: challenge for the 1990s. *IBM System Journal*, 28(2):294–306, 1989.

[DHK96]  A. van Deursen, J. Heering, and P. Klint, editors. *Language Prototyping: An Algebraic Specification Approach*, volume 5 of *AMAST Series in Computing*. World Scientific Publishing Co., 1996.

254

[DRW96]   P.T. Devanbu, D.R. Rosenblum, and A.L. Wolf. Generating testing and analysis tools. *ACM Transactions on Software Engineering and Methodology*, 5(1):42–62, 1996.

[Flo71]   I. Flores. *Job Control Language and File Definition*. Prentice-Hall, Englewood Cliffs, N.J., 1971.

[HHKR92]  J. Heering, P.R.H. Hendriks, P. Klint, and J. Rekers. *The syntax definition formalism SDF - reference manual*, 1992. Earlier version in *SIGPLAN Notices*, 24(11):43-75, 1989.

[KB93]    J.W.C. Koorn and H.C.N. Bakker. Building an editor from existing components: an exercise in software re-use. Report P9312, Programming Research Group, University of Amsterdam, 1993.

[Kli93]   P. Klint. A meta-environment for generating programming environments. *ACM Transactions on Software Engineering and Methodology*, 2(2):176–201, 1993.

[KR78]    B.W. Kernighan and D.M. Ritchie. *The C Programming Language*. Prentice-Hall, 1978.

[LeL87]   INRIA, Rocquencourt. *LeLisp, Version 15.21, le manuel de référence*, 1987.

[Ode93]   M. Odersky. Defining context-dependent syntax without using contexts. *ACM Transactions on Programming Languages and Systems*, 15(3):535–562, 1993.

[Ous94]   J.K. Ousterhout. *Tcl and the Tk Toolkit*. Addison-Wesley, 1994.

[PP94a]   S. Paul and A. Prakash. A framework for source code search using program patterns. *IEEE Transactions on Software Engineering*, 20(6):463–475, 1994.

[PP94b]   S. Paul and A. Prakash. Supporting queries on source code: A formal framework. *International Journal of Software Engineering and Knowledge Engineering*, 4(3):325–348, 1994.

[REQ94]   *REQL Source Code Query Language*. Raleigh, USA, 1994. User Guide and Language Reference — Version 2.0 for Windows.

[RT89]    T. Reps and T. Teitelbaum. *The Synthesizer Generator: a System for Constructing Language-Based Editors*. Springer-Verlag, 1989.

[Sno89]   R. Snodgrass. *The Interface Description Language*. Computer Science Press, 1989.

[VVW94]   S.F.M. van Vlijmen, P.N. Vriend, and A. van Waveren. Control and data transfer in the distributed editor of the ASF+SDF meta-environment. Report P9415, Programming Research Group, University of Amsterdam, 1994.

[You89]   E. Yourdon. RE-3. *American Programmer*, 2(4):3–10, 1989.

# Trends in Game Tree Search

Arie de Bruin and Wim Pijls

Erasmus University, Dept. Comp. Science, H4-29, P.O. Box 1738,
3000 DR The Netherlands
email {adebruin, pijls}@few.eur.nl.

**Abstract.** This paper deals with algorithms searching trees generated by two-person, zero-sum games with perfect information. The standard algorithm in this field is Alpha-Beta. We will discuss this algorithm as well as extensions, like transposition tables, iterative deepening and NegaScout. Special attention is devoted to domain knowledge pertaining to game trees, more specifically to solution trees.
The above mentioned algorithms implement depth first search. The alternative is best first search. The best known algorithm in this area is Stockman's SSS*. We treat a variant equivalent to SSS* called SSS-2. These algorithms are provably better than Alpha-Beta, but it needs a lot of tweaking to show this in practice. A variant of SSS-2, cast in Alpha-Beta terms, will be discussed which does realize this potential. This algorithm is however still worse than NegaScout. On the other hand, applying a similar idea as the one behind NegaScout to this last SSS version yields the best (sequential) game tree searcher known up till now: MTD(f).

## 1  Introduction

In this paper we give an overview on algorithms that search *game trees*, as defined by perfect-information, two-person, zero-sum games like chess, checkers and the like. Let the reader be warned that the presentation is certainly not exhaustive and also rather broad. Most of the algorithms presented here admit refinements, game trees are not so regular as suggested in this paper, many details and all proofs are skipped. The aim of this paper is to give the reader a feeling for what is going on in the field. For more details one should consult the references.

The term 'zero-sum game' indicates that the gain of one player equals the loss of her opponent. This excludes games studied in the field of classical mathematical game theory, such as the prisoner's dilemma. We furthermore exclude random events, the game should proceed completely deterministically. This means that a game like backgammon is not studied here either.

The games in the above described class proceed by the adversaries taking turns in making a move. A move alters the current *position*, e.g. the contents of a chess board, or the number and the size of heaps of matches in Nim-like games. Such games can be represented in abstract terms as *game trees*, the nodes of which correspond to positions, while an edge between two nodes describes the move that transforms the position corresponding to the source node into the position associated with the target node. Because the players take turns, such

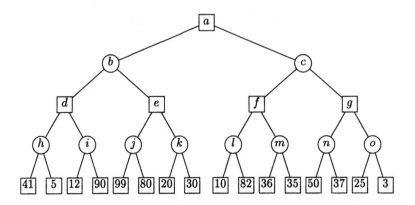

**Fig. 1.** A Game Tree

a tree is layered, in the sense that all nodes at the same depth are of the same type, e.g. MAX nodes (denoted by a square), in which the first player (usually called MAX) has the move. At the next level in the tree we only see MIN nodes, depicted as circles, where the second player (called MIN) should move. The root of the tree corresponds with a given position of the game, and the leaves are nodes from which no move can be made. In these final positions the game is decided, the value of such a position is known, e.g. 'win for MAX', 'loss for MAX', 'draw', or maybe a more subtle score. It is customary to represent a score as an integer which denotes the value that the position has for MAX. For instance, a win for MAX could be denoted by +1, a draw by 0 and a win for MIN by −1. An example of a game tree is given in Fig. 1.

A game tree search algorithm determines the value $f(\text{root})$ of the root node of a game, e.g. 'forced win for MAX' or 'forced win for MIN' or 'one of the players can force a draw'. Moreover the algorithm also determines the best move from the root position.

A few remarks are in order at this moment. First of all one should be aware of the fact that most games do not generate trees but *game graphs* instead. For instance, due to repetitions of moves the game tree for chess is infinite, while the game graph is finite, because there are only finitely many valid positions in chess. For efficiency reasons most game tree algorithms exploit a *transposition table* in which positions already encountered are stored together with relevant information thereof (value, best move, etc.). One gets the impression that transposition tables have been added as an afterthought, or as a coding trick. For instance one still speaks of game tree search instead of game graph search. More importantly, we have the impression that not all information stored in a transposition table is used to good effect by the standard algorithms. In fact, a few of the more recent results discussed in this paper are related to a fuller exploitation of the data hidden there. For other examples the reader is referred to [11, 13].

A second remark is related to the fact that trees for nontrivial games are far too big to be searched fully (which is one of the reasons such games are

257

interesting for us humans). Therefore approximation techniques have to be used. One standard approach is to consider only a finite part of the tree, e.g. only a restricted number of levels (*plies* or half-moves). Notice that Fig. 1 can also be considered as such a partial game tree. This means that not in all leaves of such a reduced tree an exact evaluation of the position is possible (because if we would have such a gadget, there would be no need to search a full tree of variations...). We have to rely on an evaluation function 'eval' that can only approximate the true value of a position. It is hoped however that the inexactness of this approach is leveled by the fact that the tree is searched to a sufficient depth.

The value of a position is determined by the so called *minimax rule*. In a leaf $n$ of the tree the value is given by eval($n$). In non-leaf positions the MAX player will choose the move which leads to the best position, i.e. the position with the highest value. If it is MIN's move then she will choose the move resulting in the best position from her point of view, that is, the one with the smallest value. This mechanism can be applied recursively which yields the following definition.

$$\text{minimax}(n) =$$
$$= \begin{cases} \text{eval}(n) & \text{if } n \text{ is a leaf} \\ \max\{\text{minimax}(c) \mid c \text{ is a child of } n\} & \text{if } n \text{ is a MAX node} \\ \min\{\text{minimax}(c) \mid c \text{ is a child of } n\} & \text{if } n \text{ is a MIN node} \end{cases} \quad (1)$$

This rule straightforwardly translates into the algorithm given in Fig. 2. A few remarks on the 'language' in which the algorithms appearing in this paper are written must be made. The **return** statement is like its C–counterpart, that is, the return value of the function is determined and an exit from the function is performed. Statement grouping is expressed by using indentation, obviating the need for pascal **begin**...**end** pairs or C-like {}-brackets. We will use a genealogical way of expressing relations between nodes in our game trees. For instance, the FirstChild of a node $n$ or the OldestBrother of one of its children $c$ is the leftmost child of $n$ in the tree.

## 2 Alpha-Beta

The Minimax algorithm from the previous section visits all nodes in the game tree. Because this number is exponential in the depth $d$ of the tree, and also because branching factors $w$ can be rather large (for instance in the middle game of chess a node has about 30–40 children), one can be confronted with impressive numbers of nodes to be visited ($O(w^d)$ for *uniform trees*, i.e. trees in which all non-leaf nodes have the same number of children). It is only natural to search for ways to avoid having to visit all nodes. The well known Alpha-Beta algorithm uses, like Minimax, a depth first search but, unlike Minimax, finds a way to *cut off* nodes which are not relevant for the outcome. Alpha-beta has a rich history, a good overview of the early stages is presented in [5].

Suppose the Minimax algorithm of Fig. 2 searches the tree from Fig. 1 and suppose the inner call 'minimax($d$)' executed within the call 'minimax($b$)' has

```
function minimax(n) → g;
    if n is a leaf then g := eval(n);
    else if n is a MAX node then
        g := -∞; c := FirstChild(n);
        while c is well defined do
            g := max(g, minimax(c)); c := NextBrother(c);
    else /* n is a MIN node */
        g := +∞; c := FirstChild(n);
        while c is well defined do
            g := min(g, minimax(c)); c := NextBrother(c);
    return g;
```

**Fig. 2.** The Minimax algorithm

just returned the value 12. The next step is now to determine the minimax value of $e$, a call 'minimax($e$)' is executed which in its turn leads to a call 'miminax($j$)' which delivers the value 80. Therefore we now know that $e$, being a MAX node, will have a minimax value of at least 80. But from this we can already infer the minimax value of $b$, because this will be the minimum of 12 ($d$'s value) and a number not smaller than 80. So the value of $k$ cannot influence $b$'s value any more and there is no need to investigate $k$ or its descendants. This phenomenon, that a node needs not be visited because an older brother (in this case $j$) has a value worse than an uncle (here $d$) is called a *shallow cutoff*.

This is the main idea exploited in Alpha-Beta. It is implemented by giving the recursive search procedure 'alphabeta', apart from the node to be investigated, two other parameters, a lower bound $\alpha$ and an upper bound $\beta$ using which information is transferred about the history of the computation previous to this call. In our case, node $e$ as well as node $j$ will feature in a call 'alphabeta' with parameters $\alpha = -\infty$ and $\beta = 12$. These parameters define the $\alpha\beta$-*window* $(-\infty, 12)$, using which it is communicated to the procedure that only return values within this window matter for the environment. Using this information, in the body of the call 'alphabeta($e$, $-\infty$, 12)' it can *locally* be decided that there is no need to investigate $k$ after $j$'s value has become known.

Let us return to the execution of Minimax and Alpha-Beta on the tree in Fig. 1. Once it is determined that the value of $b$ equals 12, control returns to node $a$, after which the subtree rooted in $c$ should be investigated. Now a similar line of reasoning applies: for node $a$, having already a child with value 12, only values greater than 12 are of interest. This translates into parameter values in the call for node $c$ of $\alpha = 12$ and $\beta = +\infty$. This will lead to an inner call for nodes $f$ and $l$ with the same parameters and once it is determined that the oldest child of $l$ has value smaller than 12 there is no need to visit the other child. Notice however that this cutoff is not of the type discussed earlier, there is no 'older brother – uncle' relationship. This type of cutoff is called a *deep cutoff* and the early versions of Alpha-Beta did not recognize such ones.

```
function alphabeta(n, α, β) → g;
    if n is a leaf then g := eval(n);
    else if n is a MAX node then
        g := −∞; α' := α; c := FirstChild(n);
        while (g < β) and (c is well defined) do
            /* g is max{return values of children seen so far} */
            g := max(g, alphabeta(c, α', β));
            α' := max(g, α'); c := NextBrother(c);
    else /* n is a MIN node */
        g := +∞; β' := β; c := FirstChild(n);
        while (g > α) and (c is well defined) do
            /* g is min{return values of children seen so far} */
            g := min(g, alphabeta(c, α, β'));
            β' := min(g, β'); c := NextBrother(c);
    return g;
```

**Fig. 3.** The Alpha-Beta algorithm

It is also possible to have finite values for both the $\alpha$ and the $\beta$ parameter. Consider node $c$. Once the call 'alphabeta$(f, 12, +\infty)$' has terminated with return value 35, node $g$ will be called with $\alpha\beta$-window $(12, 35)$. There is no need for return values $\leq 12$ because $a$ does not need them (in that case $a$ will choose $b$ instead) and there is no need for a return value $\geq 35$ because $c$ does not need this ($c$ will choose $f$ instead).

The same parameters will feature in the recursive call for $n$. This latter call will return with a *high failure*, i.e. value 37, which will cause a cutoff (a *β-cutoff*) of node $o$.

The mechanism must be clear by now. If a child of a MAX node returns with a high failure, a return value $\geq \beta$, then the remaining younger children can be cut off. Dually, if a child of a MIN node returns with a *low failure*, a return value $\leq \alpha$, then we again have a cutoff, called an *α-cutoff*. Using this explanation the code of Fig. 3 should be clear.

The idea behind the Alpha-Beta function applied to a node $n$ is that it needs only return the right value, the game value $f(n)$, when this value lies within the input $\alpha\beta$-window. It is interesting to see what value is returned if the function returns with a low or a high failure. We first consider the case that $n$ is a MAX node with only leaves as children. From the code in Fig. 3 we see that on low failure all children have been investigated, and the return value is the highest value among the children. Thus in this case also the exact minimax value of $n$ is returned. On the other hand if a high failure occurs, it is not necessary that all children of $n$ have been visited. The procedure returns the value of the oldest child with value $\geq \beta$. This means that now not the exact value $f(n)$ is returned but only a lower bound to the game value of $n$. A dual observation can be made for the case that $n$ is a MIN node.

This again entails that on low failure in a MAX node with height 2 (where 'height' is defined as the distance to the leaves), Alpha-Beta will not return the game value but in general only an upper bound thereof. This is due to the fact that the same holds for all its children. The next lemma states that this observation generalizes.

**Lemma 1.** *Consider a call* alphabeta$(n, \alpha, \beta)$*, returning a value $g$. If on entry to this function the precondition $\alpha < \beta$ holds, then on exit we have the following postcondition*

$$g \leq \alpha \Rightarrow g \geq f(n), \text{ (low failure)} \tag{2}$$

$$\alpha < g < \beta \Rightarrow g = f(n), \text{ (success)} \tag{3}$$

$$g \geq \beta \Rightarrow g \leq f(n), \text{ (high failure)} \tag{4}$$

The proof (cf. [1, 8, 9]) is a formalization of the above line of reasoning, using recursion induction, which is in essence induction on the height of $n$.

It is interesting to notice that the earliest variants of Alpha-Beta would return the input value $\alpha$ on low failure and $\beta$ on high failure, thus discarding information gathered during the call. On first sight the output value is indeed irrelevant on high or low failure because high enough up the game tree it will be discarded anyhow. There are reasons however to state the contrary. The most important ones will surface later when we will discuss Alpha-Beta variants of best first game tree search, but one argument can be given already now. Suppose a transposition table is used in order to apply the results of a previous investigation of a node $n$ when this node turns out to be a transposition. In general, the $\alpha\beta$ input window will not be the same as in the previous call. This suggests that it is useful to store results in the transposition table that are as informative as possible. We return to this issue later.

Earlier we saw that Alpha-Beta searches less nodes than Minimax in essence by exploiting the input $\alpha\beta$-window to prune nodes. It seems that the effect is that making the input window smaller decreases the number of nodes to be visited. Closer examination of the code shows that this is indeed the case. Stated more precisely, we have

**Lemma 2.** *Suppose two calls* alphabeta$(n, \alpha, \beta)$ *and* alphabeta$(n, \alpha', \beta')$ *are executed on the same node in the same game tree and suppose $\alpha \leq \alpha'$ and $\beta \geq \beta'$. Then we have that the set of nodes visited by the second call is a subset of the set of nodes visited by the first call.*

This lemma can be proven by exploiting a characterization of the nodes visited by Alpha-Beta, given in [1, 3] amongst others. It can also be proven straightforwardly using recursion induction. This result will turn out to be very useful in the sequel while comparing the efficiency of Alpha-Beta based game tree search algorithms.

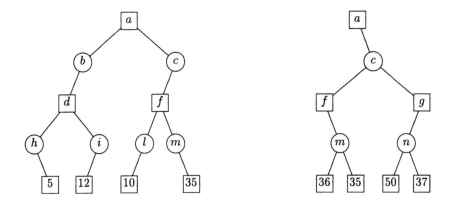

**Fig. 4.** An Optimal Max (left) and Min (right) Solution Tree

## 3   Solution Trees

In the previous section we indeed realized our goal, Alpha-Beta searches less nodes than Minimax (the pathological case that Alpha-Beta searches the whole tree is possible but unlikely). In this section we approach the question whether we can do better from a theoretical point of view, by introducing the notion *solution tree*.

Suppose, for the tree of Fig. 1, we want to find a subtree from which we can derive an upper bound for the game value 35 of the root. We can do so if we have an upper bound for both children, $b$ and $c$. This follows from the minimax rule. So $a$, $b$ and $c$ must be included in the tree to be built. For $b$ and $c$, being MIN nodes, there is a less precious way to establish an upper bound, an upper bound for only one child will do (this follows again from the minimax rule). Let us include $d$ and $f$. Now the story repeats. For these MAX nodes we have to include both children, i.e. $h$, $i$, $l$ and $m$. Finally we have to add one child for each of these 4 nodes and we choose the leaves labeled 5, 12, 10 and 35.

The subtree we have built is the left one in Fig. 4. It is called a *max solution tree*, the shape of which is defined by the rule that the root should be included, all children should be included for a non-leaf MAX node, and exactly one child should be included for a non-leaf MIN node. A max solution tree exhibits a *strategy for the MIN player* because in all possible variations in the tree the choice of MIN is fixed [4, 15].

The minimax value of the tree is an upper bound to the game value of the root. Because in MIN nodes of this tree the minimax rule determines the minimum of a singleton set, there is only maximization left, and we find that the minimax value equals $\max\{l \mid l$ leaf in the tree$\} = 35$. This value is in fact the best we can get, and therefore this solution tree is called *optimal*.

By reversing the 'construction rules' we define the dual notion *min solution tree*. The rightmost tree in Fig. 4 is a min solution tree. It is also optimal because its minimax value, the minimum of the values of its leaves equals $f(a)$.

When we take the union of an optimal min solution tree and an optimal max solution tree we obtain a so called *critical tree*. The intersection of these trees is the *principal variation*, in our example the path from the root to node 35. From the arguments given above we infer that a critical tree establishes both an upper bound and a lower bound equal to the value of the root, that is it establishes the game value. We summarize.

**Lemma 3.** [17] *The minimax value of a min/max solution tree is a lower/upper bound to the game value of the root. Moreover, for each game tree there exists at least one optimal min/max solution tree.*

**Lemma 4.** [3, 5, 10] *In order to establish the game value of the root an algorithm must have visited at least a critical tree.*

The reader is invited to check that both optimal solution trees for the tree of Fig. 1 are unique. Lemma 3 suggest that this need not be so. In fact, assigning to leaf 41 in Fig. 1 the value 11 makes the max solution tree with leaf set $\{11, 12, 10, 35\}$ optimal as well.

It is instructive to study how Alpha-Beta finds the critical tree of Fig. 1. The leaf set visited by Alpha-Beta is $\{41, 5, 12, 90, 99, 80, 10, 36, 35, 50, 37\}$ which is certainly bigger than the critical leaf set $\{5, 12, 10, 36, 35, 50, 37\}$. The overhead is due to the fact that Alpha-Beta determines that 12 is the game value of node $b$, while an upper bound of 12 would have been sufficient. Notice furthermore that on high failure, e.g. in $e$, a min solution tree has been constructed defining the return value 80 which is a lower bound. For these results we will therefore use the notation $f^-$. Similarly a low failure, e.g. in $l$, returns an upper bound $f^+$ defined by a max solution tree.

In [5] it is investigated whether it is possible that Alpha-Beta indeed searches only the critical tree. This will occur if the tree is *perfectly ordered*, i.e. for each node $n$, the oldest child has the best game value (maximal if $n$ is a MAX node, minimal otherwise) of all its children. In that case the optimal solution trees will be the leftmost ones in the game tree. The reader is invited to reorganize the tree of Fig. 1 so that the above property holds, and to check how Alpha-Beta traverses this tree.

Notice that if we are able to organize the search so that we need only to search the critical tree we will have made a big progression because the size of this tree is $O(w^{d/2})$. Or, stated in other words, with the same amount of work we will be able to search trees twice as deep as Minimax can.

## 4  Enhancing Alpha-Beta

In this section we will discuss three reasons why it makes sense to add a transposition table to the Alpha-Beta algorithm [11, 16]. The first one has already appeared in the Introduction, one wants to avoid a recalculation when a transposition is found. Instead, the results stored in the transposition table should

```
function TTalphabeta(n, α, β) → g;
    if n in transposition table then
        if n.f⁻ = n.f⁺ then return n.f⁻;
        if n.f⁻ ≥ β then return n.f⁻;
        if n.f⁺ ≤ α then return n.f⁺;
        /* Info in transposition table did not cause a shortcut */
        α := max(α, n.f⁻); β := min(β, n.f⁺);
    if n is a leaf then g := eval(n);
    else if n is a MAX node then
        g := -∞; α' := α; c := FirstChild(n);
        while (g < β) and (c is well defined) do
            /* g is max{return values of children seen so far} */
            g := max(g, TTalphabeta(c, α', β));
            α' := max(g, α'); c := NextBrother(c);
    else /* n is a MIN node */
        g := +∞; β' := β; c := FirstChild(n);
        while (g > α) and (c is well defined) do
            /* g is min{return values of children seen so far} */
            g := min(g, TTalphabeta(c, α, β'));
            β' := min(g, β'); c := NextBrother(c);
    if n not in transposition table then
        put n into transposition table;
        n.f⁻ := -∞; n.f⁺ := +∞;
    if (g < β) or (n is a leaf) then n.f⁺ := g;
    if (g > α) or (n is a leaf) then n.f⁻ := g;
    return g;
```

**Fig. 5.** Alpha-beta with a transposition table

be used. From Lemma 1 we have that there are three types of outcome possible: high failure yielding a lower bound $f^-$ to the game value, low failure yielding an upper bound $f^+$, and success yielding the game value $f$, combining an upper and a lower bound $f^+ = f^- = f$.

In Fig. 5 the code for Alpha-Beta using a transposition table is given. It is the same as in Fig. 3 except that code has been added that handles the transposition table. At the end of the procedure we store results, and at the beginning we try to profit of them. Information from the transposition table can cause an immediate cutoff, or it can lead to sharper bounds, worthwile to be adopted in view of Lemma 2.

A second advantage of transposition tables is that one can achieve a better move ordering. This is realized for instance by algorithms applying *iterative deepening* (ID). This technique was introduced for another reason though, i.e. to avoid that programs would overstep a time limit. Often only a limited time is available to search a position, and therefore it makes sense to organize the search as an *anytime algorithm*, i.e. one must be able to interrupt it at an arbi-

```
function NegaScout(n, α, β) → g;
    if n is a leaf then g := eval(n);
    else
        c := FirstChild(n); g := NegaScout(c, α, β); c := NextBrother(c);
        if n is a MAX node then
            α' := α;
            while (g < β) and (c is well defined) do
                /* g is max{return values of children seen so far} */
                α' := max(g, α'); t := NegaScout(c, α', α' + 1);
                if (t > α') and (t < β) then t := NegaScout(c, t, β);
                g := max(g, t); c := NextBrother(c);
        else /* n is a MIN node */
            β' := β;
            while (g > α) and (c is well defined) do
                /* g is min{return values of children seen so far} */
                β' := min(g, β'); t := NegaScout(c, β' - 1, β');
                if (t < β') and (t > α) then t := NegaScout(c, α, t);
                g := min(g, t); c := NextBrother(c);
    return g;
```

**Fig. 6.** The NegaScout algorithm

trary moment and still obtain a sensible answer. The idea is to let the program search bigger and bigger trees. One starts with the game tree truncated to a limited depth $d$, which will be searched using an evaluation function defined at the nodes at depth $d$. The tree is then iteratively extended one level deeper, and re-searched. After an interation, the time spent in the earlier iterations will be negligeable to the time spent in the last one because search time grows exponentially with the depth.

The value eval($n$) of a node at depth $d$ shall in general be a good estimate of its minimax value determined by the evaluation function of its children. This means that the best son of an internal node, as calculated by a depth $d$ search, will probably remain so when calculated by a depth $d + 1$ search. It is therefore useful to store the identity of a node's best child in the transposition table. In the next iteration this node can then be searched before the others. This idea turned out to be quite successful, cf. [16], it caused an appreciable speedup, which should not surprise us in the light of the discussion at the end of the previous section.

Having achieved a good move ordering, the Alpha-Beta extension called *NegaScout* [6] tries to make advantage of that. The idea is to search suitable nodes using a *null window*, a window of the form $(f, f+1)$ which cannot contain a game value. This means that a null window call can only end in high or low failure. The NegaScout algorithm, given in Fig. 6 is indeed a more efficient version of Alpha-Beta:

**Lemma 5.** *A call* NegaScout$(n, \alpha, \beta)$ *returns the same value as* alphabeta$(n, \alpha, \beta)$ *and every node it visits must also be visited by* alphabeta.

We give an example of the ideas behind NegaScout, again using the game tree from Fig. 1. Suppose a call NegaScout$(a, -\infty, \infty)$ is performed. First of all the value of $b$ will be determined through NegaScout$(a, -\infty, \infty)$. This returns 12, which it should according to the above lemma. Now Alpha-Beta would proceed with a call alphabeta$(c, 12, \infty)$, but let us try to be smart. If the tree is sufficiently ordered the odds are high that $b$ is better than $c$, meaning that alphabeta$(c, 12, \infty)$ will fail low. But then any window $(12, x)$ will generate a low failure, so why not choose $(12, 13)$ promising the smallest amount of work. This leads to a call NegaScout$(c, 12, 13)$.

Now the risk of gambling is that one might lose, and this is exactly what happens in our case (remember, the tree of Fig. 1 is rather badly ordered.) The NegaScout call returns the value 35, again obeying the above lemma. We now are forced to perform a re-search to obtain the true value of $c$ using a wide window, in our case $(35, \infty)$. Notice the value 35 here, we try to exploit as much information from the previous search as possible. This call will return 35.

Not intimidated by our previous experience, we try to perform the null window trick again. We again assume that $f$ is the better child of $c$, so we do not issue a call with window $(-\infty, 35)$ on $g$ but we do NegaScout$(g, 34, 35)$ instead. Notice that we shifted the window 1 to the left, because we now expect $g$ to have a value $\geq 35$. In this case we are succesful, the return value is 37 and no re-search is needed.

It is instructive to execute manually the recursion chain generated by the call NegaScout$(a, -\infty, \infty)$ on the tree in Fig. 1. A chain of inner calls will lead us to leaf 41, and to the hypothesis that the value of $h$ equals 41. Null window search on leaf 5 immediately refutes this, and a re-search will lead to the conclusion $f(h) = 5$ and the hypothesis $f(d) = 5$. A null window search on $i$ will invalidate this, so again we have to do a re-search on $i$, showing $f(d) = 12$, leading to the hypothesis $f(b) = 12$. The call NegaScout$(e, 11, 12)$ justifies this, leading to the hypothesis $f(a) = 12$, and so on.

The leaf set visited by NegaScout on $a$ is $\{41, 5, 12, 90, 99, 80, 10, 36, 35, 50, 37\}$, unfortunately the same set as visited by Alpha-Beta. In order to show that NegaScout is better than Alpha-Beta the tree should be better ordered. On the other hand, if the tree would be perfectly ordered again NegaScout and Alpha-Beta would search the same subtree, i.e. the critical tree...

Our examples are rather unfortunate. Some of the advantages of NegaScout over Alpha-Beta can be observed by changing the tree of Fig. 1 a little bit: give leaf 10 the value 15, and leaf 50 the value 10. Now Alpha-Beta will generate calls alphabeta$(l, 12, \infty)$ and alphabeta$(m, 15, \infty)$ and it will visit the subtree under $m$. On the other hand, NegaScout will generate a call NegaScout$(l, 12, 13)$ and not visit $m$. Re-search in $f$ will not be needed because NegaScout$(g, 12, 13)$ will fail low.

It turns out in practice that for reasonably well ordered trees NegaScout performs consistently better than Alpha-Beta, cf. [11, 12]. The overhead caused

```
program SSS-2;
    G := {root};
    g := expand(root, ∞);
    repeat
        g' := g;
        g := diminish(root, g');
    until g ≥ g';
```

**Fig. 7.** The SSS-2 algorithm, main loop

by re-searches turns out to be low, especially when the evaluation function is relatively expensive compared to tree traversal. This of course assumes that we store leaf values in a transposition table, which is an indication of the third advantage of transposition tables: it provides useful information for re-searches within the same iteration of iterative deepening. We will return to this issue in a later section.

## 5 The SSS* Family

Because in Alpha-Beta the search is organized in a depth first left to right manner the algorithm easily suffers from bad move orderings in the tree. The SSS* algorithm [17] tries to direct the search to those parts of the tree which are likely to be in the critical tree, in that sense it can be characterized as a best first search. In this section we will not discuss SSS* but SSS-2 instead [7]. The reason is that the latter algorithm is more perspicuous and it is equivalent with SSS* in a rather strong sense: it searches the same nodes in the same order and it shows almost all weaknesses that SSS* has. A similar analysis as given here, but based on SSS* can be found in [11, 12].

The main body of SSS-2 is given in Fig. 7. The idea is to find the best max solution tree. This is realized by first generating the leftmost max solution tree and then successively refining it into a better one until this is no longer possible. The program manipulates a global variable $G$ in which the current max solution tree is stored.

The first max solution tree is generated by the call 'expand$(a, ∞)$'. It finds the leftmost max solution tree, assigns it to $G$ and returns its value $g$. The max solution tree is then refined by a call 'diminish$(a, g')$'. If successful, this procedure returns a sharper upper bound $g$ and stores in $G$ the max solution tree defining this bound. Failure is indicated by a return value $g \geq g'$. When executed on the tree of Fig. 1, the expand call will return the max solution tree with leaf set $\{41, 12, 10, 36\}$, and the leaf sets of the max solution trees built by the diminish calls will be $\{5, 12, 10, 36\}$ and $\{5, 12, 10, 35\}$.

We now give a more detailed description of 'diminish', cf. Fig. 8 and 'expand', cf. Fig. 9. Consider the second time the main body of SSS-2 executes a diminish

**function** diminish$(n, v) \rightarrow g$;
/* may only be called if subtree rooted in $G$ has value $v$ */
    **if** $n$ is a leaf **then**
        /*By virtue of precondition game value of $n$ equals $v$ */
        **return** $v$;
    **else if** $n$ is a MAX node **then**
        /* $n$ has at least one child $c$ with $c.g = v$ */
        **for** $c :=$ FirstChild$(n)$ **to** LastChild$(n)$ **do**
            **if** $c.g = v$ **then** $v' :=$ diminish$(c, v)$;
            **if** $v' \geq v$ **then** /* no tighter upper bound available for $n$ */
                PURGE all descendants of $n$ from $G$;
                **return** $v'$;
        /* loop terminated normally, tighter upper bound available for $n$ */
        $v' := \max\{c.g \mid c$ child of $n\}$;
        $n.g := v'$; **return** $v'$;
    **else** /* $n$ is a MIN node, the only child of $n$ in $G$ has $c.n = v$ */
        $c :=$ the single child of $n$ in $G$;
        $v' :=$ diminish$(c, g)$;
        **if** $v' < v$ **then**
            $n.g := v'$; **return** $v'$;
        /* no tighter bound for $c$ available, children of $c$ in $G$ have already
                been removed */
        remove $c$ from $G$;
        **for** $c :=$ NextBrother$(c)$ **to** LastChild$(n)$ **do**
            add $c$ to $G$; $v' :=$ expand$(c, v)$;
            **if** $v' < v$ **then**
                $n.g := v'$; **return**$(v')$;
            /* arrive here only if $v' \geq v$ */
            remove $c$ from $G$;
        **return** $g$; /* returns the sharpest lower bound, not strictly necessary */

**Fig. 8.** The SSS-2 algorithm, procedure diminish

call. At that moment we have a tree in $G$ with leaf set $\{5, 12, 10, 36\}$. Accordingly, the input parameter $g'$ will be 36. The tree $G$ defines an upper bound of 12 for $b$ and of 36 for $c$. Refining $G$ so that the upper bound of $b$ will become sharper is of no use at this stage as long as we are not able to tighten $g(c)$. Therefore a recursive call 'diminish$(c, 36)$' is generated. In order to efficiently find out which child to choose, the algorithm stores the $g$-value of each node, as defined by $G$, also in $G$. Because $c$ is a MIN node there is only one child, $f$, in $G$. We first try to make the subtree in $f$ better, i.e. we issue a call 'diminish$(f, 36)$'. This generates a call 'diminish$(m, 36)$' and an inner call 'diminish$(36, 36)$' returning 36, i.e. failure. There is one possibility left to make a better $g(m)$, the other child must be investigated. Because this child has not been visited before, a call of 'expand' is in order. However, we will only be satisfied with a return value smaller than 36, and that is why we add this value as a second parameter:

```
function expand(n, v) → g;
      /* G should contain n but no descendants of n */
      if n is a leaf then
            v' := eval(n); n.g := v'; return v';
      else if n is a MAX node then
            for c := FirstChild(n) to LastChild(n) do
                  add c to G; v' := expand(c, v);
                  if v' ≥ v then
                        PURGE all descendants of n from G;
                        return v';
                        /* loop terminated normally; bound for n, tighter than v, available */
            v' := max{c.g | c child of n};
            n.g := v'; return v';
      else /* n is a MIN node */
            v'' := ∞;
            for c := FirstChild(n) to LastChild(n) do
                  add c to G; v' := expand(c, v);
                  if v' < v then
                        n.g := v'; return v';
                  /* arrive here only if v' ≥ v */
                  remove c from G; v'' := min(v', v'');
            /* loop terminated normally, i.e. there is no better bound than v */
            return v''; /* sharpest lower bound, v' would have worked as well */
```

**Fig. 9.** The SSS-2 algorithm, procedure expand

'expand(35, 36)'. This returns successfully, and the whole recursive chain winds up with value 35.

The next call 'diminish($a$, 35)' in the main loop should fail. Recursive calls for $c$, $f$ and $m$ are issued, and the reader is invited to check how failure of the inner call for $m$ is computed. Because $f$ is a MAX node and $m$ has failed there is no way to obtain a better bound for $f$. This means that the subtree of $G$ in $f$ can be destroyed. This is realized by the PURGE operation (notice that $f$ itself will be removed at one level higher). The body of the call for $c$ will now generate a call 'expand($g$, 35)' and this will return the failure value 37 (please check, notice that expand also executes a PURGE). Now $c$ itself fails, $a$ PURGEs all descendants and the computation terminates.

The code given in Figs. 7, 8 and 9 must be clear. Some care has been taken to return on failure the best lower bound which can be deduced for the node. This is not strictly necessary, for the caller any value $\geq g$ will do.

Notice that this computation must have visited the min solution tree with value 35, by virtue of Lemma 4. This is indeed the case because the algorithm has issued a diminish call for nodes $g$ and 36. These nodes are not on the critical path (from $a$ to 35) themselves, but they are children of MIN nodes on the critical path. The second arguments of these diminish calls have been values

$\geq 35$. The calls have reported failure and each of them must therefore have seen a min solution tree with value $\geq 35$.

The SSS-2 algorithm differs in two respects from original SSS*. The first difference is of conceptual nature. SSS* has been set up to find the best *min* solution tree. It achieves this by searching min solution trees from left to right. At each moment more than one tree is under investigation. The search proceeds in an interleaved way. Each tree is characterized by the last node visited, together with the best (minimal) value seen so far in this tree. The algorithm is organized in such a way that at each moment these end nodes form the leaf set of a max solution tree. Because the search of a min solution tree will also visit interior nodes of the game tree, it is possible that the corresponding max solution tree does not descend all the way down to the leaves of the game tree. This corresponds with points in time where SSS-2 is busy expanding new children of a MIN node.

The second difference with SSS* is the data structure used. Where SSS-2 uses a max solution tree, SSS* uses an OPEN list, which is the list of endpoints of this tree. The working of SSS* can roughly be described as a loop with body: search the maximal element in OPEN; perform local operations (like searching younger brothers) until you have found a better value or you recognize failure. This loop is repeated until the search is exhausted. SSS* also needs the PURGE operator, every now and then (corresponding to the points where SSS-2 would do a PURGE) it also discards all descendants from the OPEN list.

The original paper [17] proved that SSS* was more efficient than Alpha-Beta in the sense that the set of nodes visited by SSS* is always a subset of the node set visited by Alpha-Beta. For instance, for Fig. 1 SSS-2 visits the leaves $\{41, 5, 12, 10, 36, 35, 50, 37\}$. Notice that this is more than the critical tree which does not contain 41. SSS-2 suffers here from a left to right effect. On the other hand Alpha-Beta also visits the nodes 90, 99 and 80. This is due to the fact that Alpha-Beta has to evaluate $b$ fully, because there is as yet no indication that another part of the tree is better.

So, SSS* seems to be the better algorithm, but this idea was challenged in the paper [15] which critized the algorithm both on theoretical and on practical grounds. From the theoretical side it was argued that in many cases the superiority of SSS* over Alpha-Beta was not as big as expected. Both algorithms search the same nodes for perfectly ordered trees, for perfectly unordered trees, as well as for trees where 'eval' yields only two values, e.g. 'win' and 'loss'. A statistical analysis indicated that for practical values of the depth of the game tree Alpha-Beta never searches more than 3 times the number of nodes that SSS* would.

From the practical point of view there was the observation that Alpha-Beta hardly needs memory space ($O(d)$ for the stack if the depth of the tree is $d$), while the OPEN list in SSS* would take room $O(w^{\lceil d/2 \rceil})$, i.e. the number of leaves of a max solution tree of depth $d$. A more severe objection is that counting the number of nodes visited is not a good indication for the running time. First of all, nodes are revisited, but more important, visiting a node does not take a constant amount of time: finding the best node in the OPEN list or the PURGE operator needs more than that.

These observations have been justified experimentally in [2]. For random trees (where the evaluation function will just draw a random number) they reported that SSS* was 1.8 to 57 times slower than Alpha-Beta.

It is clear that a more efficient data structure for SSS* (and SSS-2) was needed. The paper [2] came with a proposal which purged the PURGE operator from the scene. Because SSS-2 always manipulates one max solution tree, the algorithm needs only room for one such a tree. The idea was to pre-allocate this room, structured as a max solution tree, but with 'empty nodes'. The first call of 'expand' now fills in the blanks. Purging is not needed because, for instance when the subtree below $f$ has to be purged (in the call 'diminish$(c, 35)$', cf. the discussion above) the algorithm overwrites the entries belonging to the subtree under $f$ with new values from the subtree under $g$. In SSS-2 it is clear when overwriting is allowed, because we go from 'diminish-mode' to 'expand-mode'. With respect to the original SSS* code more care had to be exercised.

This idea proved to be successful, experiments showed that this version of SSS* was competitive with Alpha-Beta, sometimes faster (0.93), sometimes slower (1.38). Moreover, in [14] several optimization tricks have been applied to this idea, leading to relative running times of 40% for unordered random trees to 70% for 60% ordered random trees (i.e. random trees in which the oldest child has 60% chance to be the best one).

However, still SSS* performs best for unordered trees, while game trees tend to be rather well ordered. So the advantage of SSS* is doubtful. Furthermore, we saw already that the ordering in the tree is exploited by algorithms like NegaScout, which makes the algorithm to beat even more efficient. This raises the question whether there is any hope for best first algorithms like SSS*.

## 6 SSS and Alpha-Beta Reconciled

In this section we will elaborate on the similarities between Alpha-Beta and SSS. This will result in an algorithm based on null window search that is equivalent with SSS-2. We will first concentrate on the procedure expand, so let us consider a call 'expand$(n, g)$'. If this call fails it will return a value $\geq g$, a lower bound defined by a min solution tree. This behaviour is similar to that of an Alpha-Beta call with $\beta = g$ failing high. If, on the other hand, the expand call succeeds, it will have built a max solution tree with value $< g$ or, assuming integer game values, a value $\leq g - 1$. This again resembles behaviour of Alpha-Beta, now failing low on input parameter $\alpha = g - 1$. Apparently the calls 'expand$(n, g)$' and 'alphabeta$(n, g - 1, g)$' behave similarly.

We study in more detail the case that $n$ is a MAX node for which the expand call succeeds. In that case the call will generate for all children $c$ of $n$, from left to right, a subcall 'expand$(c, g)$' with the same $g$-parameter. These subcalls all succeed and the call 'expand$(n, g)$' returns the maximum of the return values of the children. Now let us assume that for the children $c$ expand

and alphabeta behave identically. Then Alpha-Beta will also generate a sub-call for each of its children with the same return value as delivered by expand, and 'alphabeta($n, g - 1, g$)' returns the same value as 'expand($n, g$)'. Therefore 'expand($n, g$)' and 'alphabeta($n, g - 1, g$)' behave identically. If one analyzes the other possible cases, and one uses induction, one can prove that the calling tree for 'expand($n, g$)' is completely mirrored by the one for 'alphabeta($n, g - 1, g$)', the same set of nodes is visited in the same order and the same value is returned.

The next step is to extend this result to the calling tree generated by the procedure diminish. However, this procedure expects a max solution tree in $G$ which will guide its search. Therefore, the null window search should generate and use equivalent information. The main result of this section will be that this can be realized by using TTalphabeta instead of Alpha-Beta, i.e. by using a transposition table. This means that we obtain an algorithm equivalent with SSS-2 if we change, in the main body of SSS-2, cf. Fig. 7, the calls 'expand($n, g$)' and 'diminish($n, g$)' by calls 'TTalphabeta($n, g - 1, g$)'. This new version is called 'MTD($\infty$)'.

We will not prove this formally. Instead, we will try to sketch why the flow of control (the calling tree and the return values) will be essentially the same in both versions. We will first show how a call of TTalphabeta builds a structure inside the transposition table which is equivalent with the maximum solution tree a corresponding expand or diminish call would construct in $G$. In this analysis we will use induction-like arguments, like 'earlier calls (or inner calls) do whatever we expect from them'. These assumptions are used only to highlight the essential ideas, not to lay the base for an inductive proof. Such a formal proof can be given but it must be set up with some more care. Furthermore, our analysis will be based on yet another assumption, namely that no entries in the transposition table will be overwritten, i.e. there will be no collisions.

First of all we recall that TTalphabeta stores on low failure its return value in the $f^+$-field of the entry in the transposition table of the node involved. So, assuming that 'expand($n, g$)' or 'diminish($n, g$)' generate the same result value $g'$ as 'TTalphabeta($n, g - 1, g$)' does, we will see in the max solution tree in $G$ $n.g = g'$ and in the transposition table $n.f^+ = g'$. This means that in the transposition table the max solution tree from $G$ can be partially found back by tracing the $f^+$-fields. As it stands we cannot recover the max solution tree completely because it is not yet clear which child should be chosen in a MIN node.

Two observations are relevant here. The first one is that on high failure, TTalphabeta stores its return value in the $f^-$-field of the node involved. The second observation follows from a reconstruction of the way expand and diminish include a node $c$, child of a MIN node $n$, in the max solution tree $G$, say with value $g$. This occurs when a call 'expand($c, g'$)'or 'diminish($c, g'$)' with $g' > g$ ends in success with result value $g$. Again, assuming that there is an equivalent call 'TTalphabeta($c, g' - 1, g'$)' failing low with result $g$, we see that in the transposition table we obtain $c.f^+ = g$. Now what about the other children of $n$? The younger brothers of $c$ have not yet been subjected to an expand or diminish call, so we assume that there has neither been a TTalphabeta call, and therefore they are not in the transposition table. The older brothers $c'$ of $c$ must have been searched earlier by SSS-2 with parameter $g' > g$ and they must have been rejected, i.e. expand or diminish (and we therefore assume TTalphabeta as well) must have ended in a (high) failure with return values $> g'$ and therefore $> g$. This means that for all older brothers $c'$ the transposition table has entries $c'.f^- > g$. Now it is clear how the current max solution tree is encoded in the transposition table. For the children $c$ of a MAX node $n$ which is in the max solution tree we see in the $f^+$-field the same value as in the $g$-field of $G$. The child of a MIN node $n$ is the child with the same $f^+$-value as $n$ itself, while all older children have $f^-$-value bigger than $n.f^+$.

Notice that the line of reasoning from the beginning of this section showing that expand and alphabeta generate equivalent calling trees can be extended. We observe that expand and TTalphabeta generate equivalent calling trees and also that the max solution tree generated in $G$ is encoded in the transposition table. This means that in the sequel we need only compare the behaviour of diminish and TTalphabeta.

So, suppose that we have a call 'diminish$(n, g)$' and 'TTalphabeta$(n, g-1, g)$', where $G$ contains a max solution tree defining the upper bound $g$ for $n$, and where the transposition table encodes this max solution tree. We will now sketch that both procedures generate equivalent subcalls for essentially the same nodes in the same order. We say 'essentially' because TTalphabeta will pay short visits to nodes that will not be visited by diminish. These short visits are needed to determine which node should be the next, say, 'serious' one to be visited, serious nodes being the ones that are also visited by diminish.

Suppose $n$ is a MAX node. By inspecting the code we see that the diminish call will generate subcalls only for children $c$ with $c.g = g$. On the other hand, the code of TTalphabeta specifies that all children $c$ will be visited. However, for all nodes with $n.f^+ < g$, these visits will be short ones, because the test '$n.f^+ \leq \alpha$' in the body of TTalphabeta will be met. So the only serious calls will be for the children with $c.f^+ = g$ and one easily checks that for such a call diminish and TTalphabeta behave in the same way. (Notice that we have $c.f^- = -\infty$ for all non leaf children because all earlier visits to $c$ must have failed low.)

Next, suppose that $n$ is a MIN node. The first node visited by diminish will be its only child $c$ that is in $G$. TTalphabeta has to do some short visits to the older brothers $c'$ of $c$ first, in order to find out which child is the one in the max solution tree. All visits to these brothers will meet a shortcut in the test '$n.f^- \geq \beta$' in the body of TTalphabeta. So the first serious visit will be to $c$ and the reader is again invited to check that from this point on diminish and TTalphabeta exhibit the same behaviour.

In Section 4 we mentioned that a transposition table can provide useful information to speed up re-searches, like the ones done by NegaScout. The analysis given here has elaborated on this, 'short visits' will enable a re-search to efficiently avoid old useless paths. This very mechanism is exploited to good effect in NegaScout as well.

Now that we have reduced SSS to a series of null window searches we can compare this algorithm with Alpha-Beta in a fair way, i.e. in an equal environment. We briefly state some results, the reader is referred to [11, 12] for more details. Experiments have been performed for tournament-quality real-life game playing programs for three different games.

First of all, the idea that SSS* uses too much memory proved to be untrue. The experiments showed that MTD($\infty$) becomes better than Alpha-Beta if the size of the transposition table exceeds roughly $2^{17}$ entries. Assuming that each entry contains 16 bytes, we see that a transposition table of 2 Mbyte is already adequate. The second result is that in general the difference in efficiency of MTD($\infty$) and Alpha-Beta is relatively small, the trend being that MTD($\infty$) is a few percents more efficient. This seems to be in contrast with the results from [14], cf. Section 5. Apparently in real life game trees are so well ordered that the reason why SSS would perform better has almost vanished. Thirdly we found that NegaScout is in general better than both MTD($\infty$) and Alpha-Beta, though the difference is never more than 10

NegaScout improves upon Alpha-Beta by exploiting knowledge gathered from the previous iteration of iterative deepening. For the null window search framework a similar trick is possible. MTD($\infty$) is parameterized with the value $\infty$ and therefore one can view the algorithm as generating it first $g$-value, an upper bound for $f$(root), from the assumption that this value equals $\infty$. However the last iteration of iterative deepening has generated an estimate of $f$(root) that will be much better. It is reasonable to expect that less iterations in the main loop of SSS-2 will be needed if we start from this better estimate. The algorithm which applies this idea is called MTD($f$). We have to be a little careful in the formulation of this algorithm. Starting from $\infty$ we are sure to get an upper bound after all iterations but the last one. This means that we can always re-search using the window $(g - 1, g)$, where $g$ is the result returned previously. In the MTD($f$)-case we have to check whether after the first expand call '$g$ :=TTalphabeta(root, $f - 1, f$);' we obtain a value $g \geq f$ or $g < f$. In the first case we have to approximate the game value from below using calls 'TTalphabeta(root, $g, g + 1$)' while in the second case we can continue using windows $(g - 1, g)$.

Experiments like the one discussed above have shown that MTD($f$) performs (almost) consistently better than NegaScout. We observed margins in the range 1–15%. This shows that the most efficient general purpose game tree searching program that we presently know of is MTD($f$).

**Acknowledgements.** It must have been clear from this paper that many of the newer results reported here have been generated by, or in close collaboration with Aske Plaat and Jonathan Schaeffer. We heartily acknowledge their work, and the pleasant cooperation we enjoyed over the years.

# References

1. G. M. Baudet, *On the branching factor of the alpha-beta pruning algorithm*. Artificial Intelligence 10 (1978), pp 173-199.
2. Subir Bhattacharya and A. Bagchi, *A faster alternative to SSS\* with extension to variable memory*, Information processing letters 47 (1993), 209–214.
3. Toshihide Ibaraki, *Generalization of alpha-beta and SSS\* search procedures*, Artificial Intelligence 29 (1986), 73–117.
4. V. Kumar and L.N. Kanal, *A General Branch and Bound Formulation for Understanding and Synthesizing And/Or Tree Search Procedures*, Artificial Intelligence 21 (1983), 179–198.
5. Donald E. Knuth and Ronald W. Moore, *An analysis of alpha-beta pruning*, Artificial Intelligence 6 (1975), no. 4, 293–326.
6. T. A. Marsland, A. Reineveld, J. Schaeffer, *Low Overhead Alternatives to SSS\**, Artificial Intelligence 31 (1987) pp. 185-199.
7. Wim Pijls and Arie de Bruin, *Another view on the SSS\* algorithm*, Algorithms, International Symposium SIGAL '90, Tokyo, Japan, August 16–18, 1990 Proceedings (T. Asano, T. Ibaraki, H. Imai, and T. Nishizeki, eds.), LNCS, vol. 450, Springer-Verlag, August 1990, pp. 211–220.
8. Wim Pijls. *Shortest Paths and Game Trees*. PhD Thesis, Erasmus University Rotterdam, The Netherlands, November 1991.
9. Wim Pijls and Arie de Bruin, *Searching informed game trees*, In: Algorithms and Computation, ISAAC 92 (T. Ibaraki, ed), pp. 332–341, LNCS 650.
10. Wim Pijls and Arie de Bruin, *A theory of game trees based on solution trees*, Tech.Rep. EUR-CS-96-xxx, Erasmus University Rotterdam, 1996.
11. Aske Plaat. *Research Re:Search & Research*. PhD Thesis, Erasmus University Rotterdam, The Netherlands, June 1996.
12. Aske Plaat, Jonathan Schaeffer, Wim Pijls and Arie de Bruin, *A Minimax Algorithm Better than SSS\**, In: Artificial Intelligence, to appear.
13. Aske Plaat, Jonathan Schaeffer, Wim Pijls and Arie de Bruin, Exploiting graph properties of game trees. In *Proceedings of the 13th National Conference on Artificial Intelligence (AAAI '96)*, Portland, OR, August 1996. American Association for Artificial Intelligence, AAAI Press.
14. Alexander Reinefeld and Peter Ridinger. Time efficient state space search. *Artificial Intelligence*, 71 (2), pp. 397–408, 1994.
15. Igor Roizen and Judea Pearl, *A minimax algorithm better than alpha-beta? yes and no*, Artificial Intelligence 21 (1983), 199–230.
16. Jonathan Schaeffer, *The history heuristic and alpha-beta search enhancements in practice*, IEEE Transactions on Pattern Analysis and Machine Intelligence PAMI-11 (1989), no. 1, 1203–1212.
17. G. Stockman, *A minimax algorithm better than alpha-beta?*, Artificial Intelligence 12 (1979), no. 2, 179–196.

# A Visual Approach to VDM

Jeremy Dick[1], Jérôme Loubersac[2]

[1] 3 Haven Close, Dorchester-on-Thames, UK. Work done whilst at Bull S.A.
[2] Praxis Plc, 20 Manvers Street, Bath, UK. Work done whilst at Bull S.A.

**Abstract.** Two barriers to the widespread industrialisation of formal methods are a lack of methodology, and the use of mathematical notations that are not easily understood by the non-specialist.

The work presented in this paper addresses these problems by defining diagrams which may be used to visualise aspects of formal specifications. The diagrams used are adaptations of classical approaches such as entity-relationship and state-transition diagrams.

The approach described imposes a methodology on the early stages of system specification, and provides the analyst with a choice of notations, visual and non-visual, while maintaining an underlying formality. During the process of analysis, the notation most appropriate for the expression and communication of the concepts required can be selected.

Two sorts of diagram are discussed: Type-Structure Diagrams, and Operation-State Diagrams.

A tool is described that assists the analyst in moving between diagrams and VDM. Each diagram can be mapped onto parts of a common VDM specification, which forms the central underlying system description. Consistency can then be checked by a VDM type-checker.

## 1 Introduction

This paper reports on work carried out by the formal specification group at the Bull Corporate Research Centre near Paris during 1990 to 1992 as part of the ESPRIT project Atmosphere, Ref. #2565 previously reported in [DickLoub91a] [DickLoub91b] [Loub91]. The team created a number of tools for processing the formal notation VDM [Jones90], and integrated them into a PCTE [BGMT88] programming environment for the development of distributed systems.

Amongst these tools was one called "VDM through Pictures", designed for visualising formal specifications.

Formal notations have a reputation in industry for being hermetic. Their terse textual nature, with frequent use of mathematical symbols, does not provide a good medium for communication with the non-mathematician. This creates a barrier to the uptake of formal methods in an industry where 'methodology' is frequently equated with the use of graphical techniques, especially in the early stages of system conception.

Our goal is to combine formality with visual intuition, alleviate the communication problem with non-specialists, and accelerate the uptake and integration of formal methods into industry. It is with this goal in mind that we set about creating a prototype analysis assistant which manages the consistency of a VDM specification and a set of annotated diagrams. The analyst may either

- create a VDM specification from a collection of diagrams
- create a set of diagrams from a specification showing different aspects of the VDM specification
- make changes to the VDM, and have the tool make the appropriate changes to the diagrams, or
- make changes to the diagrams, and have the tool make the appropriate changes to the VDM.

The work involved, in part:

**selecting appropriate diagrams:** Our goal was to find several types of diagram, each giving a significantly different dimension of the problem, and yet which, when taken together, give an as complete as possible formal specification. Where information cannot conveniently be represented diagrammatically, annotations are used to make the meaning of symbols precise.

**defining the well-formedness of diagrams:** A certain level of consistency and completeness will be required in diagrams before successful translation into VDM can be achieved.

**developing appropriate styles of VDM specification:** It is evident that some styles of specification are a great deal easier to represent diagrammatically than others, especially by automatic translation. Without unduly constraining the analyst, these styles should contribute to the methodology imposed by the use of diagrams.

**giving a formal semantics to selected diagrams:** By defining transformations from annotated diagrams to VDM, we are in effect giving the diagrams a formal semantics in VDM. To define these transformations formally, we must provide an abstract syntax for each type of diagram, and functions mapping objects of this syntax to and from the abstract syntax of VDM.

**making a prototype implementation:** Our role in the Atmosphere project was to demonstrate feasibility rather than provide a production quality tool set. Our approach was therefore to specify formally (in VDM) the transformations required, and make a fully working prototype in Prolog and C++. We adopted the diagraming tools of IDE's "Software thru Pictures" for the creation and editing of diagrams, and the Atmosphere editor and type-checker for VDM specifications.

An obvious relationship exists between Entity-Relationship Diagrams and VDM domains. Less obvious is how to represent VDM operations diagrammatically. State-transition diagrams are an immediate choice for examination, and it is here that the style of specification becomes critical. The VDM notation does not have the same notion of state as that usually intended in a state-transition diagram. However, an appropriate methodology surrounding VDM encourages a style in which it is easy to identify states and transitions. Whether such a style is compatible with ease of proof in the later stages of refinement is a question that has not yet been addressed.

In Section 2, we describe our view of the process of analysis, and how the analyst interacts with the tool. In Section 3, we describe an example using Entity Relationship and Operation State diagrams. Section 4 draws conclusions and describes the direction of future work.

# 2   The Process Of Analysis

The process of requirements analysis involves communication and interaction with the commissioners of the system, taking, analysing and presenting information in many different forms, until (in this context) a complete formal specification has been drawn up and agreed.

It is our view that there are advantages in being able concurrently to build diagrams and formal texts during the analysis process. The diagrams assist in communicating the structure of the system in a clear visual manner, and the formal texts encourage the analyst to ask the right questions to remove inconsistencies and ambiguities from the system description.

We envisage, therefore, analysts working alternately on diagrammatic and textual descriptions of the system. They may choose from one of a number of different kinds of diagram, or the formal text, as the most appropriate medium for developing a particular concept. Tool support, then, should enable analysts to move freely from diagram to text and back again, automatically translating changes as required.

Within this scheme also, several analysts may be able simultaneously to work on different diagrams, developing different aspects of a system, and use tools to bring all aspects together in a unified, structured formal text.

Where several diagrams are used to represent different aspect of the same specificaiton, merging is necessary, because there is information contained in both the picture forms and the VDM form, not contained in the abstract form, which we wish to preserve across updates. On the one hand, a VDM text may contain operation definitions, for instance, which are not affected by the content of an entity-relationship diagram. The operation definitions should not be lost. On the other hand, pictures carry implicit information about, for instance, the positioning and size of nodes and arcs which we may wish to retain whilst other details of the diagram are altered.

For translation to be successful, there are various styles of visual or textual notation which must be used. The style arcs marked on the emboldened boxes of Figure 1 represent functions intended to give intelligent assistance in completing the information content of a diagram or text. Not yet implemented, such tools will ask appropriate questions whose answers will supply missing information, lead to the removal of ambiguity or inconsistency, or promote a particular style of specification.

A set of these transformations is required for each kind of picture used. In the following sections of this paper, we shall describe two kinds of picture. One kind, based on entity-relationship diagrams, the other based on states and transitions.

# 3   A Distributer Example

To illustrate the VtP approach, we are now going to apply it to a small example, in order to give a better idea of what we want to represent with diagrams. The meaning of the symbols used is discussed in greater detail in Section 4.

## 3.1   The system requirements

We would like to specify a cash dispenser system. In the normal use of the system, if the distributor is in-service, we insert a card, enter a code, ask for a certain amount of money, and finally get the money and a receipt.

If the card is known as a lost (or stolen) one, or if we have more than two failed attempts to get the right code, then the card is retained by the distributor. Repeated requests for money can be made, so long as the total amount does not exceed the weekly limit for this kind of credit card, and the distributor has sufficient funds. the amount of money asked is not available, or greater than the remaining amount for the week for this type of credit card, we are allowed to ask for another sum until it matches the constraints.

The distributor contains a certain amount of money, dispatched in several kinds of bank notes of fixed value. The amount given to a client is removed from the reserve, and the bank keeps a trace of the transaction. The card itself is updated, with the number of tries for code and the amount already withdrawn for the week.

## 3.2   Type Structure Diagram

First, we are going to focus our attention on the state of the system, and the types. So we are going to define all the components of the distributor. To specify all the requirements of the system, we need at least to represent:

- the in-service indicator,
- the inserted card,
- the bank notes which are contained in the distributor,
- the list of cards reported stolen,
- the retained cards,
- the list of transactions,
- the table indicating the authorised weekly amount for each type of credit card,
- the date and hour,
- the receipt.

The following Type Structure Diagram is proposed:

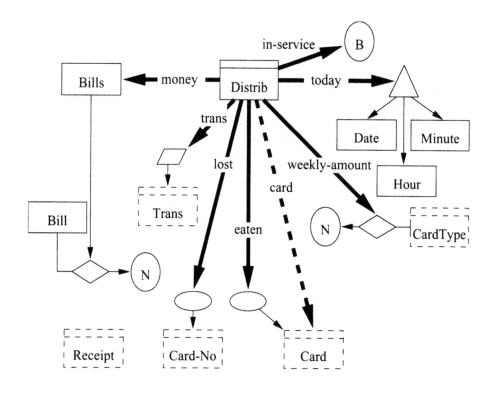

The double-lined box named Distrib at the top centre of the diagram represents the main composite type of the specification, which is exported from the VDM module of the same name. The components of the type are those joined by thick arcs, whose labels specify the component names.

Plain rectangles represent local type definitions, dashed double-lined boxes represent imported types, and circles represent basic VDM types. Other symbols represent type constructors:-

- a oval means "set of";
- a parallelogram means "sequence of";
- a diamond represents a mapping in the sense of the arrow.

Hence, the *money* component of *Distrib* is of type *Bills*, which is turn defined as a mapping from *Bill* to Natural numbers.

Dash lines represent optionality; thus, the *card* component is optional, representing the optional presence of a card in the system.

The VDM equivalent of this diagram is the following module, containing a set of type definitions:

**module** *Distrib*

. . . . . . .

**types**
    *Distrib* ::

| | |
|---|---|
| *money* | : *Bills* |
| *trans* | : *Trans*∗ |
| *lost* | : *Card-No*-set |
| *eaten* | : *Card*-set |
| *in-service* | : $\mathbb{B}$ |
| *today* | : $(Date \times Hour \times Minute)$ |
| *weekly-amount* | : $CardType \xrightarrow{m} \mathbb{N}$ |
| *card* | : $[Card]$ |

$$Bills = Bill \xrightarrow{m} \mathbb{N}$$

*Date* **is not yet defined**

*Hour* **is not yet defined**

*Minute* **is not yet defined**

*Bill* **is not yet defined**

**end** *Distrib*

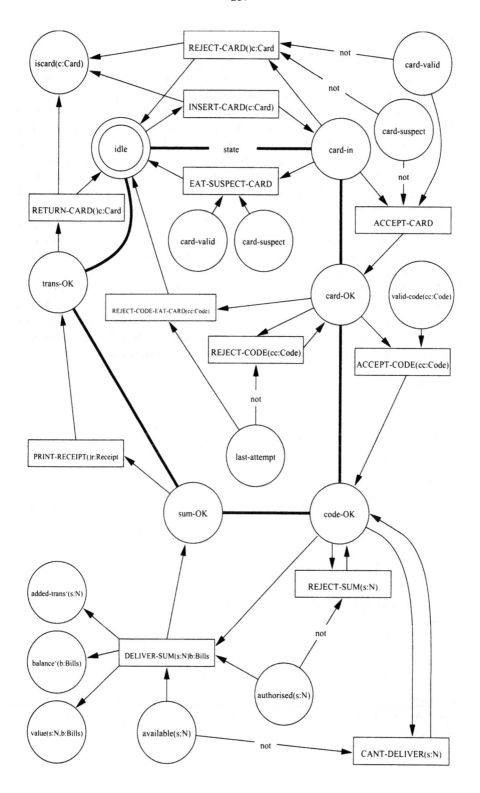

## 3.3 Operation State Diagram

On this diagram, we have represented all the operations (as rectangles) that we want to specify for the distributor. We have also represented some predicates (as circles) which are used to define the pre and post conditions for the operations.

Some predicates will correspond to particular conditions on the elements of the system, conditions that will also be disjoint. They identify system states. The disjointness of these conditions is represented by the bold arcs linking them, one with a label on it which can be considered as a name for the set of disjoint states.

To explain the sense of the diagram a little more, take for example the operation *INSERT-CARD*, which takes as input $c$ of type *Card*. The operation has a precondition, as indicated by the arrow pointing from the state *idle* to the operation box: the operation is only defined for when the system is idle. The double circle round the *idle* state indicates that it is the initial state of the machine.

The operation also has two post conditions: that there is now a card in the machine, and that that card is the card $c$.

The VDM equivalent of this diagram is illustrated by the following extracts, showing some of the function and operation definitions. The functions correspond to the predicates, and will need further textual definition as design proceeds. The main type has a component added to it called *state*, which is an enumeration of state names built from the disjoint state conditions in the diagram.

**module** *Distrib*
**interface**

$\qquad$ . . . . . . .

**definitions**


**types**
$\qquad$ *Distrib* ::
$\qquad\qquad$ *state* : TRANS-OK | IDLE | CARD-IN | CARD-OK | CODE-OK | SUM-OK


**state** *State* **of**
$\qquad$ *distrib* : *Distrib*

$\qquad$ **inv** *mk-State*(*distrib*) $\underline{\Delta}$ **true**
$\qquad$ **init** *mk-State*(*distrib*) $\underline{\Delta}$ *idle*(*distrib*)
**end**


**functions**
*idle* : *Distrib* $\rightarrow$ $\mathbb{B}$
*idle*(*distrib*)
$\qquad$ $\underline{\Delta}$ *distrib.state* = IDLE $\wedge$ **true**

$card\text{-}in : Distrib \rightarrow \mathbb{B}$
$card\text{-}in(distrib)$
  $\Delta$ $distrib.state = $ CARD-IN $\wedge$ **true**

$valid\text{-}code : Distrib \times Code \rightarrow \mathbb{B}$
$valid\text{-}code(distrib, cc)$
  $\Delta$ **true**

$last\text{-}attempt : Distrib \rightarrow \mathbb{B}$
$last\text{-}attempt(distrib)$
  $\Delta$ **true**

$value : Distrib \times \mathbb{N} \times Bills \rightarrow \mathbb{B}$
$value(distrib, s, b)$
  $\Delta$ **true**

. . . . .

**operations**
$REJECT\text{-}CARD()\,c\text{:}Card$
  **wr** $distrib\text{:}Distrib$
**pre** $\neg card\text{-}suspect(distrib) \wedge \neg card\text{-}valid(distrib) \wedge card\text{-}in(distrib)$
**post** $iscard(distrib,c) \wedge idle(distrib)$

$INSERT\text{-}CARD(c\text{:}Card)$
  **wr** $distrib\text{:}Distrib$
**pre** $idle(distrib)$
**post** $iscard(distrib,c) \wedge card\text{-}in(distrib)$

. . . .

$DELIVER\text{-}SUM(s\text{:}\mathbb{N})\,b\text{:}Bills$
  **wr** $distrib\text{:}Distrib$
**pre** $available(distrib,s) \wedge code\text{-}ok(distrib) \wedge authorised(distrib,s)$
**post** $sum\text{-}ok(distrib) \wedge added\text{-}trans(distrib`,distrib,s) \wedge balance(distrib`,distrib,b)$
  $\wedge\ value(distrib,s,b)$

**end** $Distrib$

It is clear that the modules respectively produced from the TSD and the OSD complement one another. By merging them, we obtain a VDM specification of our distributor, which can then be completed by providing VDM definitions for the predicates, and further enrichment of the operation pre and post conditions if necessary.

# 4  Conclusions and Future Work

We have described two visual notations for the expression of aspects of VDM specifications: Type-Structure Diagrams, covered in detail, and Operation-State Diagrams in sketch form. The transformation of TSDs and OSDs to and from VDM are relatively simple to specify, and have been presented in detail elsewhere [DickLoub91a] [DickLoub91b] [Loub91].

We have chosen to depart from the classical entity-relationship and state-transition diagram because neither expressed exactly the kinds of aspects we required for a VDM specification. TSDs allows us to express a containment hierarchy, and OSDs allow us to express non-disjoint states.

Prototype implementations of the TSD and OSD transformations, have been built and tried out on some case studies [BicDickWoods96]

In due course, other diagrams should be considered as alternatives or as complementary to those described here. For instance, it would be interesting to examine a possible role for data-flow diagrams and structure charts.

We are keen also to look at diagrams for other specification languages, such as the RAISE specification language, which has aspects of process, channel, communication and concurrency not present in VDM.

# References

[BicDickWoods96]  *"Quantitative Analysis of an Application of Formal Methods"*, Juan Bicarregui, Jeremy Dick and Eòin Woods, in Proc. Formal Methods Europe'96, LNCS 1051, Springer, Oxford, March 1996.

[BGMT88]  G. Boudier, F. Gallo, R. Minot, I. Thomas, *An Overview of PCTE and PCTE+*, ACM Symposium on Software Development Environments 1988, pp. 248-257

[Chen76]  P. P. Chen, *The Entity-Relationship Model: towards a unified view of data*, ACM Transactions on Database Systems, Vol 1, No 1, March 1976

[DickLoub91a]  J. Dick, J. Loubersac, *A Visual Approach to VDM: Entity-Structure Diagrams*, Bull Research Centre Report, DE/DRPA/DMA/91001, Jan 1991.

[DickLoub91b]  J. Dick, J. Loubersac, *Integrating Structured and Formal Methods: A Visual approach to VDM*, Proc. ESEC'91 LNCS Vol. 550, Springer-Verlag, 1991

[Jones90]  Cliff B. Jones, *Systematic Software Development using VDM*, Second Edition, Prentice Hall Int., 1990

[Loub91]  J. Loubersac, *VtP Users' Guide*, Atmosphere Internal Result I4.1.4.2.3.1, Bull Research Centre, Las Clayes-sous-Bois, France

# Statecharts: Past, Present, Future

David Harel

The Weizmann Institute of Science
Rehovot, Israel
harel@wisdom.weizmann.ac.il

**Abstract.** This will be an informal talk about the graphical specification language of statecharts, and the related STATEMATE tool. Some of the issues that arose in developing the language, its companion formalisms, and the supporting tool will be discussed from both personal and technical points of view. A number of research areas that have evolved from this work in the 13 years since the language was conceived will be discussed. The talk will also describe recent work on a version of statecharts tailored for object-oriented development, and the tool that is being constructed for this.

# Scalable Fault Tolerance

Shay Kutten[1]

Faculty of Industrial Engineering, Technion, Haifa 32000, Israel, and IBM T.J. Watson Research Center, *kutten@ie.technion.ac.il.*

**Abstract.** As communication networks grow, existing fault handling tools become increasingly unaffordable. In many cases the reason is that they involve *global* measures such as global time-outs or reset procedures, and their cost grows with the size of the network. Rather, for a fault handling mechanism to scale to large networks, it should involve local measures, or, at worse, fault local measures, i.e. measures the cost of which depends only on the number of failed nodes (which, thanks to today's technology, grows much slower than the networks). This decreases the recovery time and, moreover, often allows the non-faulty regions of the networks to continue their operation even during the recovery of the faulty parts. We describe several research ideas that lead in this direction.

## 1 Introduction

Computer networks and distributed systems are growing very fast. The Internet [C91] is estimated to double in size every 6 to 12 months. Currently it connects (according to some estimates) about 16,000,000 hosts. Most of them belong to end users, whose involvement in control functions is limited (although they do participate in many distributed computing activities). However, at the rate of 100 to 1000 nodes per router, the number of control nodes is estimated in the tens of thousands. Moreover, the Internet is not the only huge and fast growing network; working hard to realize the celebrated "information super-highway" are all the main telecommunication companies in the world. Phone companies, for example, are planning to invest heavily in the next several years in updating their networks to carry hundreds of video channels and computer information to homes, as well as in wireless networks, to provide computer connection and information (e.g. stock prices, weather reports, etc) to every person on the go.

Another characteristic of the emerging networks is their diversity. Numerous manufacturers are involved in producing the hosts, routers and cables for these networks. Even when equipment of the same source is used, there are significant differences in the ages, sizes, speeds, reliability, and many other attributes of the equipment and software used. Moreover, the Internet is not managed by one single authority, but rather by thousands of organizations, governed by very different policies and considerations. For example, an organization that does not impose strong security measures may face an increase in the number of faults, since its machines are exposed to intruders. Indeed, the parties concerned strive for compatibility, but many differences exist nevertheless.

In such a diverse environment, faults of many different types, leading to information inconsistency, are unavoidable. Indeed, coping with faults, and devising fault-tolerant solutions for various problems, is one of the most active research areas in networking and distributed systems.

However, the speed of growth of the networks out-paces the speed of the developments of the fault tolerance mechanisms, and they do not scale well. It is interesting to note that faults are often called *exceptions*, and their treatment is called *exception handling*. This seems to reflect the approach that faults rarely happen, so a treatment of a fault is really an exceptional case. Thus the treatment did not have to be very efficient, since its amortized cost was very small.

For example, one striking characteristic of this area is that in many of the solutions proposed in the literature, faults are fixed *globally*, i.e., by algorithms involving the entire system. Clearly, using global measures to detect and correct errors is becoming more and more unrealistic as networks grow, and it is essential to develop *scalable* fault-handling tools, that is, solutions that can be applied even in large networks. In particular, the cost of such tools is required to grow slower than the system size. It is also required that the non-faulty parts of the networks will be able to continue operating even while the faulty parts are recovering. Otherwise no meaningful work can be done.

Luckily, technology manages to keep the increase in the number of faults smaller than the increase in the size of the network. Indeed, the damage each fault may cause is amplified by the growing size of the network, but the faults are still very often of extremely *local* nature, and involve only a small number of hosts. For example, the famous ARPANET crash [MRR80] was caused by a single node giving all other nodes wrong routing information. (This node "told" other nodes that it had distance zero from every node.)

In this paper we describe several efforts that were made toward the goal of making fault handling tools more scalable, mostly by emphasizing locality in fault handling.

## 2   Fault Models

Different distributed systems may be designed to withstand faults of different level of severity. The number of models is huge, and we shall only mention a few of them. The model that may be the most common in practice is that of *crash faults*, where the faulty node, or faulty link, stops functioning, and an adjacent node can detect this fact. It may sound odd, but the main difficulties in designing protocols for this model arise when nodes and links are also allowed to recover. Such networks are termed *dynamic networks*.

The case that the fault is not detectable is more severe. This model is used sometimes in the case of asynchronous networks. It is reasoned that in such a network, if a node does not send a message for some time, it is still impossible to distinguish between the case that it stopped functioning, and the case that it is just slow.

A *Byzantine* fault [LSP82] is the most severe one. It is assumed that a faulty node (or a link, in the case of Byzantine edge faults) does not have to even follow the algorithm, and may behave in an arbitrary way. This is modeled by assuming that some adversary took control over the node, and is trying to damage the run of the protocol. The reasoning behind this model is that if a protocol can perform correctly under these assumptions, it can perform correctly in any other environment. In addition, this model may reflect security problems.

The model of *self stabilization*, introduced by Dijkstra [D74], is less extreme. Dijkstra demonstrated the phenomenon of locally legal states forming an inconsistent global picture by using the example of a token ring. Recall that at any given moment exactly one node is supposed to possess a token, which is constantly forwarded from one node to the next. Note that both the local state of possessing a token and the state of not possessing it are legal local states. Hence an inconsistent global state composed of seemingly legal local states could arise as the result of some node accidentally losing the token or generating a new one. Token passing algorithms that overcome this problem (termed *self-stabilizing* algorithms) are proposed in [D74] and in a number of later papers. In [AKY90] the model of self stabilizing dynamic networks, that generalizes both self stabilization and dynamic networks is introduced.

Sometimes the task of recovering from faults is partitioned into two: fault detection, and fault correction. Another task is that of limiting the effect of a fault even before correcting it.

# 3 Global Fault handling

## 3.1 Some early methods

It looks as if distributed fault handling grew out of sequential fault handling, the way distributed systems grew out of sequential systems. In the times that an enterprise had a single computer, when a problem appeared, a common measure was (and still is) to restart the computer, either by turning the power off and on again, or by pressing some "reset" button. Later, when a small number (say two) of machines were connected together, the operator could still walk from one to the other, and restart all (or both) of them. A larger scale distributed system involved machines in several (say two) sites. The operators of those machines could phone each other, and coordinate the "shut down" and the restart of the whole network.

As networks grew and became more complex, these methods were automated. A natural extension of the operation above is that of configuring the network around a central *controller-* one of the nodes to which each node reports and from which each node receives instructions. The controller could monitor the response time of nodes and decide that they failed. In this case, it could perform some correction operation.

For example, in a *token ring* (see e.g. [T81]) only the node that posses the token is allowed to transmit. (Otherwise transmissions of different node can collide, leading to a loss of messages.) The controller could expect to receive the token every $x$ time units for some $x$, termed the *timeout*. If the token is not received, then the controller could generate another token. Note that this method is *global* in several respects. First, the time needed for recovery depends on the size of the network. When determining the size of $x$ the designer had to allow enough time for the token to pass each of the nodes. In addition, the time that was to be allowed per node is closer to the global maximum of time that a node may wish to hold the token. Another global consideration here is that of clock synchronization: the size of $x$ is also influenced by the fact that the clock in some nodes (e.g. the controller) may be faster than the clock in some other nodes. Let us term this kind of a timeout a *global timeout*. In the sequel we mention methods that use *local timeouts* instead.

Another example for the use of a global timeout [P92] is a stabilization of a spanning tree: to make sure that there are no cycles in the tree, the root generates a pulse every time the timeout clock expires. Every node passes the pulse on to its children. A node that receives the pulse twice in too short a time assumes that it is on a cycle, rather than a tree.

Note that another global aspect of the controller solution is the global dependency on a single node that may itself fail. A common solution is to have a *back up* controller that monitors the first one, and replaces the controller when it suspects that the controller failed. Of course, the backup controller itself may fail. A more general solution is that of a *leader election* [L77, G77]. Suppose, for example, that the controller (or the *leader*) failed. The other nodes elect a new leader. Often the election is based on the assumption that each node has a unique identifying, given to it at the time it was manufactured, or at the time it was added to the network. (Indeed, there exist conventions for universal naming schemes.) The nodes compare their identity and the largest "wins". Different studies on this subject differ in the complexity, or in the assumptions about the model (i.e the architecture, technology and environment of the network).

## 3.2 Topology Update

A more scalable solution was used in the ARPANET [MRR80], the previous incarnation of today's Internet. This network was already much more widespread (it was a *wide area network*) than a local area network such as a token ring. The controller method could form a serious bottleneck. In the ARPANET the idea is that every node is responsible of detecting faults (and other changes, e.g. recoveries, changes in the traffic load) in its immediate neighborhood, and of broadcasting this information to the rest of the nodes. This task, is called *topology update*. It maintains, in every (reachable) node, the description of the whole network. Note that when such a description is given, every node can compute locally a way to overcome the faults (if this is possible). In the ARPANET (and the Internet) this was used (among other uses) to compute an alternative routing when faults interrupted the previous route. A similar method is used in other networks, see, e.g. [BGGJP85, CGKK95]. Note that when the network description is given in every node, other tasks can be performed as well. For example, the task of electing the node with the highest identifier as a controller for some limited subtasks (see e.g. [AGKK91]).

Though more scalable than the controller method, the update method suffers from several difficulties. Firstly, it still requires a global computation even for a small number of faults. Secondly, while still rather efficient for a small number of faults, it can be very costly when the number of faults is large. Thirdly, not all the nodes are being updated at the same time. This can introduce inconsistencies in the decisions, or, at least, a waste of effort while the networks descriptions at different nodes converge to the same view. Fourthly, if faults are frequent, then the view of different nodes may never converge to the same view.

The second problem was eased by the results of [CGKK95], implemented in IBM NBBS network, and the results in [ACK90]. However, much before that, a different, very elegant method, that of the *reset*, was introduced. Like the topology update it is a universal method, and its complexity may still be smaller (depending on the specific task) than that of topology update for a large number of faults. However, given the results of [ACK90, CGKK95], the complexity of topology update may be much smaller than that of reset for some other tasks.

## 3.3 Reset

The notion of a global reset was suggested in [F79]. It is intended to imitate virtually, for a network, the restart button of a single computer. Faults are corrected by a global process that "erases" all the results computed before the faults, "deletes" all messages in transit, and restart a global algorithm that recomputes the results. Since the system is distributed, and often even asynchronous, the reset cannot, in fact, be performed everywhere at the same time. However, it simulates this effect. The reset algorithms were improved many times, see e.g. [AAG87, ACK90, AKMPV93]. Algorithms using this method are certainly global, not local. (In [AAG87] there is a notion of local reset; there it refers to the case where not all the network participate in some protocol when that protocol execution is being reset; in this case only the parts of the network that "joined the execution" of the protocol are being reset; still, often the reset may cover the whole network following a single fault.)

The global reset approach to error correction has two major shortcomings. Firstly, it means that even one fault can cause a global computation, that may take a long time to output a legal result. Secondly, the global reset method is mainly suitable for a distributed system that cannot (or is not required to) produce "useful work" when some of its nodes suffer a transient fault. In many cases, however, it seems desirable for the distributed system to correct itself as locally as possible, letting undamaged regions of the system operate as usual in the meantime.

## 3.4 Global Detection

The notion of *snapshot* was suggested in [CL85] to detect a global *stable property*, that is, any property that once it starts holding, continues to hold. The main example was the occurrence of a deadlock (i.e. state were at least two processes depend for their progress on each other, and thus they are waiting for each other forever, doing nothing meanwhile).

The snapshot idea was used later in the context of self stabilization. In this context, the two-step methodology of detection and correction was first suggested in [KP90] using *global detection*, and independently in [AKY90] where the paradigm of *local detection* (called local checking in several later papers) was suggested. *Global* detection is achieved by performing s self stabilizing snapshot that collects the local state information of all nodes to one central node, which is thus able to evaluate the global state and detect any inconsistency.

## 3.5 Faults that are not Contained

In this section we discussed the global nature of the mechanisms for recovering from faults. However, to discuss the global versus local nature of fault handling one needs to discuss also the effect of a fault: is this local, or global. We already mentioned in the Introduction the famous ARPANET crash that resulted from a single fault. Another famous such crash happened to AT&T long distance network several years ago, when a fault of a single switch several years ago propagated to the rest of its network, and caused the crash of a large part of the network. (According to news stories, the switch "shut down" since it was overloaded; this caused other switches to become overloaded, and created a chain reaction.)

Clearly, to have a scalable fault tolerant solution, one needs not only a fast recovery mechanism, but also a mechanism that limits the effect of a small number of faults on the rest of the network.

## 4 Non-Complexity Notions of Locality

A notion of *local correction* was suggested in [APV91] in the context of self stabilization, to complement the notion of local detection [AKY90]. The main meaning of locality in local correction is that each node can act locally to correct a local part of the global state of an algorithm. In fact, the state of a node needs to be consistent with that of its neighbors. For example, if the node "remembers" that it sent some message to the neighbor, either the message must be in transit over the link between the two nodes, or the neighbor should remember that it received the message. Otherwise inconsistent results, or deadlocks, may occur. For that purpose the notion of a "local reset" is introduced in [APV91], which is a reset of a link by its two endpoints. This is done in a way that simulate a simultaneous action (though it is in an asynchronous network) by the two endpoints of the link.

Intuitively, the notion of local correction makes a protocol "more local" in the sense of avoiding the need for synchronization between nodes that act in the correction process. Thus it makes the task of the protocol and the network designers much easier.

Each local correction act actually takes only a constant time. However, once a node corrected its state, its neighbor may notice that now it needs to act too. The effect is that of "correction wave". If the corrected algorithm is global, then the function computed by the corrected algorithm can be output only after $O(n)$ (number of nodes) or $O(Diameter)$ (diameter of the network) time. (It may even be the case that the correction wave needs to traverse some cycles several times.) In fact the example used in in [APV91] for the corrected algorithm is the global reset algorithm.

Another notion of locality is that of "closeness" introduced in [DH95]. The idea is that a fault correction protocol should have as a goal reaching the legal solution which is the "closest" to the faulty one. This means the number of nodes that the protocol needs to change their states for the recovery is the minimum. This seems intuitively appealing: assume that the network nodes are performing some task that depends mostly on the local states (rather than on the global one). It seems that a recovery mechanism that follows the "closeness" paradigm may cause the minimum disruption for the outputs of such tasks, since the outputs of most nodes is not changed, so, intuitively, the part of the task these nodes performed is shielded from both the faults and the mending.

It would be interesting to see the "amount of disruption" in such examples quantified. One example mentioned in [DH95] is that of a spanning tree, one of its edges failed. It is argued that it is desirable to fix the tree just by adding one replacement edge, rather than recomputing a tree. This may hold even if the time for these two alternative recovery approaches is the same. This was observed for example in [ACK90] which presented an algorithm that maintains a spanning tree taking the minimum replacement approach. It argued that otherwise the property of *Path-Preservation* would not have been kept, and that this property is important in virtual circuit-switching environment. For example, suppose that we use edges of a spanning tree for end-to-end communication between a sender and a receiver. If the path is fixed, then the receiver receives the packets exactly in the same order they were sent. However, if the path is changed as a result of changing the tree, then we have to invoke complicated mechanisms to ensure that no packets are lost or duplicated, and that the ordering of the packets is preserved. Thus, we would like to remove tree links only if absolutely necessary, namely in case that they fail.

Note that achieving the goal of [DH95] does not imply locality in the sense of time complexity. For example, the algorithm presented in [DH95] to achieve closeness, performs a global computation even for one change, and thus is not local in the sense of time complexity. Nor is the converse true- a low time complexity mending can be achieved while still changing the state of many nodes. For low time complexity it is only necessary that the time required for changing the state of these nodes is small. For example, this is the case when those many nodes changed are near by to each other.

# 5   Local Detection and Local Timeouts

*Local detection* was introduced in [AKY90] in the context of self stabilization. Informally it means detecting the illegality of the global state in a constant time, either entirely locally or through $O(1)$ communication with neighbors only.

For detection, a legal global state is expressed as a conjunction of conditions, each of which can be checked locally by one node (using only the local states of itself and its neighbors). Thus if the global state is illegal then there must be a node for which the local condition is violated. In [AKY90] the example of a rooted spanning tree was studied. Each node $v$ kept in local variables the identifier of the root node (which was also supposed to be the highest identifier of a node in the network), a pointer to $v$'s parent in the tree, and the distance to the root over the tree. The local conditions at each node $v$ were that (1) the root identities held by its neighbors were smaller than or equal to the identity of its own root (according to the root identifier kept in $v$'s local variable $Root_v$), and that the distance $Dist_v$ of $v$ to the root was larger by one that of its parent. Moreover, if $v$'s distance to the root (according to $Dist_v$ kept in $v$) is zero, then $root_v$ should equal the identifier of $v$ itself (that is, $v$ is the root). Clearly if these conditions hold for every node then there is a spanning tree, rooted at the node with the highest identifier.

The above distance trick was used also in other papers, e.g. [DIM94]. Local detection (renamed *local checking* by [APV91]) has meanwhile been studied further in [APV91, AV91, A94, AO94, APVD94].

Compare this tree stabilization method to the global timeout method mentioned above. Note that the local detection solution too uses a "hidden" timeout- every node needs to compare the values stored in its local variables to those of its neighbors. This means that from time to time the node needs to exchange these values with its neighbors. This is done by the use of a *local* timeout: every time that some local clock expires, the node sends these values to its neighbors. The difference between this method and the global timeout method is in the constraints on the length of the timeout. Firstly, it can be much shorter than the global one, since there is no need to wait for some process to engulf first the whole network. For example, for the maximum time the pulse (generated by the root) exists before it disappears in the leaves of the tree. Secondly, there is no need to coordinate the length of the timeout with the other nodes. For example, there is no need for a clock synchronization.

In fact, one may view the local detection method as one that replaces a global timeout by a local one.

# 6  Fault Proportionality

The term *fault locality* was introduced in [KP95a] in the context of mending outputs that were damaged because of faults. It is intended to capture the following intuitive idea: the fewer are the faults, the faster should the fault handling be performed. Similar motivations for other kinds of fault tolerance were expressed before. The resulting algorithms nevertheless involved the whole network, and were, thus, global. So, maybe they should be called something like *fault proportional* rather than fault local.

In the context of Byzantine agreement (in synchronous networks), the concept of *early stopping* was presented by [DRS90]. In the case that up to $t$ nodes could be faulty, where $t$ is known in advance, the original versions of Byzantine agreement needed $t + 1$ rounds of communication among all the nodes, in order to reach an agreement. (Agreement: all the nodes output the same value, even if their inputs are different.) Assume that actually there are only $f < t$ faults. The idea in [DRS90] was to devise an algorithm that stops in this case in time $f + 2$. An Optimal solution appears in [BGP92].

A different problem is dealt with in [ACKMP96]. It was motivated by the task of topology update, and was concerned with the problem of broadcasting a large message (e.g. the whole local topology of a node) efficiently when each processor has partial prior knowledge about the contents of the broadcast message. The partial information held by the processors might be out of date (e.g. some additional edges failed and some recovered) or otherwise erroneous, and consequently, different processors may hold conflicting information.

It is possible to broadcast the whole long message. However it seems clear that an efficient consistency maintenance strategy should strive to utilize the fact that many processors already have a correct picture of "most" of the object, and need to be informed of relatively few changes. Viewed from this angle, the problem can be thought of as having to broadcast the entire view of the object, while taking advantage of prior partial knowledge available to the processors of the system.

Some previous topology update protocols [SG89, Gaf87, ACK90] accomplished that by the *Incremental Update* strategy. in which only "necessary" information is transmitted. That is, each node $v$ kept an estimate of what is "believed" by its neighbor $u$ regarding the topology. Even if $v$'s "beliefs" are different than those of $u$, $v$ may not send corrections to $u$ if $v$ cannot be certain that $v$'s "beliefs" are more accurate than those of $u$. When $v$ receives an update message, it may increase $v$'s certainty about being more accurate than $u$ regarding certain data items (including, possibly, those in the new update message). In this case it sends updates to $u$. Unfortunately, it was observed that it is not easy to utilize pipelining when sending the messages in this method. This increases the time complexity.

The *Broadcast with Partial Knowledge* problem can be formulated as follows. Consider an asynchronous communication network, consisting of $n+1$ processors, $p_0, \ldots, p_n$, with each processor $p_i$ having an $|E|$-bit *local input* $w_i$, and processor $p_0$ is distinguished as the *broadcaster*. In a correct solution to the problem all the processors write in their local output the value of the broadcaster's input, $w = w_0$.

This formulation of the problem can be interpreted as follows. The input $w_i$ is stored at processor $p_i$ and describes the local representation of the object at processor $p_i$. The correct description of the object is $w = w_0$, held by the broadcaster. The local descriptions $w_i$ may differ from the correct one as a result of changes in the object. In particular, every two processors may have different descriptions due to different sets of messages they got from the broadcaster in the past. This different sets are different as a result of message losses, topology changes and the asynchronous nature of the network. The goal is to inform all the processors throughout the network about the correct view of the object $w$, and to use the processor's local inputs given to each processor in order to minimize the time and communication complexities. The randomized Monte Carlo solution in [ACKMP96] uses $O(\Delta \log |w| + n \log \frac{n}{\epsilon})$ communication (where $\epsilon$ is a parameter of the algorithm and $\Delta$ is the total number of erroneous bits to be corrected in all the nodes) without increasing the time complexity beyond that of the solution that broadcasts all of the long message. Thus, the communication complexity of the algorithm depends on the number of erroneous bits.

Yet another problem is solved in [HK89]. Consider a route of $n$ nodes $v_0, v_1, \ldots v+n$, the first of them is the source of a message, and the last is the destination. If a message is sent by some node $v_i$ to $v_{i+1}$, then, if $v_{i+1}$ is non-faulty then it receives the message and handles it (e.g. forwards it, sends acknowledgments, ...) within some unknown time $\delta << D$ for some known bound $D$. If node $v_{i+1}$ is faulty it may not send an acknowledgment to node $v_i$, then node $v_i$ knows that the message is lost. However, $v_{i+1}$ may send the acknowledgment to $v_i$ and fail only then, or it may even be malicious (i.e. Byzantine).

If $|F|$ nodes are faulty, then there is no algorithm that can prevent either a delay of $O(|F|D)$ in the delivery of the message, or a loss of the message that is only noticed (by a non-faulty node) in time $O(|F|D)$. However, it is desired (and accomplished) to prevent a delay that is larger than that. Notice that the common method, by which the destination sends an acknowledgment to the source upon reception of the message, can run into much longer delays. Assume, for example, that $v_1$ is faulty. The source $v_0$ can expect an acknowledgment from the destination $v_{n-1}$ in order of $|D|n$ time (from the time it sent the original message) at the earliest, though $|F|$ is only $O(1)$. This method of waiting for an acknowledgment from the destination only (an *end to end acknowledgment*) is, in fact, a global timeout. The method used in [HK89] solves this problem by having certain intermediate nodes send acknowledgments (upon reception of the message originated by the source, on its way to the destination) to certain other intermediate nodes. Thus, the intended recipients of such acknowledgments can verify not only the final arrival of the source message to the destination, but also its timely arrival to points on the way.

More than trying to make the complexity depend on the number of faults and thus use a local timeout, rather than a global one, the main aim in [HK89] is to relax the local timeout $D$ itself. Note that the value of $D$ above in one node depends on some global considerations, for example it is defendant on the clock synchronization. The protocols in [HK89] limit the dependency on $D$ to the minimum, and the rest of the time complexity is, instead, a function of $\delta$. In [ADLS91, Pon91] this model was generalized and presented more formally, and an algorithm was presented that bounded the time for the task of agreement to be mostly a function of $\delta$, and depend only minimally on $D$.

# 7  Fault Local Mending

Recall that local detection can help in detecting faults in a constant time. This may suffice if all that is required is to raise an alarm, as is required in the case of [HK89]. However, often an automatic correction of the faults is required.

In [CP87, CK85, NS93, MNS95, DH95]) there are interesting examples of functions that can be checked locally (i.e. by local detection) but also can be mended in a constant time. Clearly, if the time needed to compute a function from scratch is constant then its mending time is trivially depending just on the number of faults, in the sense that it does not grow with the size of the network.

## 7.1  Fault Local Mending of Global Functions

A global function is a function the worst case time complexity of computing it from scratch (as opposed to mending it) is $\Omega(Diameter)$.

The notion of *fault local mending* was suggested in [KP95a] as a paradigm for designing fault tolerant algorithms that scale to large networks. For such algorithms the complexity of recovering is proportional to the number of faults. That paper initiated the study of fault local algorithms by investigating first a very basic (and simple) problem, in a very permissible model. It is also shown how to generalize the solution to any problem (thus showing that any problem can be fault locally mended in that model); however, the solution to a general problem is not very efficient in terms of storage and message sizes.

Consider a problem $X$ on graphs, whose solutions are representable as a function $\mathcal{F}$ on the vertices of the network. The set of legal solutions of $X$ on a given graph $G$ is denoted by $X(G)$. Consider a distributed network, whose nodes collectively store the representation of some solution $\mathcal{F} \in X(G)$ of the problem $X$ on the graph. Suppose that at time $t_0$, the memory contents stored at some subset $F$ of the nodes of the network are distorted due to some transient failures. As a result, while the stored values still look locally legal, the representation of the function stored at the network has changed into some inconsistent function $\tilde{\mathcal{F}}$ that is no longer valid.

It is clear that, assuming the problem $X$ is computable, then investing sufficient computational efforts it is possible to *mend* the function, namely, change the values at some of (or all) the nodes, and reconstruct a valid representation of a (possibly different) solution of the same type, $\mathcal{F}' \in X(G)$. It was shown in [KP95a] that it is possible to distributively mend the function in time complexity dependent on the number of *failed nodes*, rather than on the size of the entire network. This operation (when possible) was termed (in any model) *fault-local mending*.

More formally, problem $X$ is *fault locally $f$-mendable* if, following the occurrence of faults in a set $F$ of nodes, the solution can be mended in $O(f(|F|))$ time. When no confusion arises we may say simply *locally $f$-mendable*, or even just $f$-mendable. A problem $X$ is *fault-locally* mendable if it is fault-locally $f$-mendable for some function $f$.

On the face of it, it is far from clear that locally mendable problems exist. It may be even more surprising if such *global* problems exist. After all, if the input of every node may influence the value of the function (as is the case in global functions), how can the function be mended locally to the faulty area? Yet, it was shown that *any* problem is fault locally mendable.

The first problem solved in [KP95a] is the of a *persistent bit*. in this problem, initially the network stores a bit in a replicated way. That is, all nodes store an identical bit (i.e., each node $v$ has a variable $\mathcal{M}_v$, and initially all bits are set to the same value). As the result of a failure, the values at some of the nodes have flipped. The problem is to restore a legal situation (of all nodes storing a common bit). Of course, if no faults occurred in the network, then it is not allowed to change the values of the bits.

At first glance, it seems that a natural idea for attacking this difficulty would be to require a node in conflict (i.e. with its bit equal to some $b$ and with a neighbor whose bit is equal to $\not{b}$. to consult *all* its neighbors, and adopt the *majority* of their views as its own. For example, in a complete graph, so long as fewer than $n/2$ of the nodes are corrupted, the corrupted nodes can be corrected by using a majority vote. Of course, once the number of corrupted nodes exceeds $n/2$, global mending is necessary, but in this case the extra cost is justified by the size of $F$ (or in other words, the complexity of the mending operation is still well bounded as a function of $|F|$).

However, unlike the case of a complete graph, in a general graph one cannot afford holding the vote among all the nodes, since this requires "global time". Thus one needs to conduct the vote (for the output of each node $v$) in a small locality around this node $v$. Note that even if the majority of the nodes in the graph are non-faulty, some localities of $v$ may have a faulty majority. In fact, [KP95a] contains an example of a graph that has only 2 faulty nodes, but for every non-faulty node, the majority of its neighbors is faulty. (The graph is simple- it contains only edges connecting the two faulty nodes to all the rest of the nodes). In this example two nodes (the faulty ones) have a majority of neighbors that are non-faulty. However, there are even examples where a majority of the nodes are not faulty, but still, for *every* node $v$, the majority of $v$'s neighbors are faulty [LPRS93, P96a].

To overcome this problem, [KP95a] introduces a new technique of controlled voting. We shall not repeat the technical details, but rather try to explain the intuition. Basically, every nodes tries to check whether it is likely that it is faulty, and if so, then it does not vote. To check, a node $v$ guesses the number of faults (increasing the guess gradually) and checks how many "near by " nodes have a different input (different candidate for the common bit) than $v$ has. If the number $C$ of such nodes is large compared to the guess of the number $G$ of faults, node $v$ postpones its vote to a later phase of the algorithm. If the mending succeeds fast (that is, the number of faults is small) then $v$ may never get to vote. Otherwise, the guess on the number of faults is To overcome this problem, [KP95a] introduce a new technique of increased and the new $C$ may not be large now compared to the new $G$. In this case $v$ now may vote, though it avoided voting earlier.

Next, it is demonstrated in [KP95a] how any problem has a fault local mending algorithm. This generic method uses the solution to the common bit problem described above. However, the way it is used is not totally straightforward.

To motivate the solution first consider e.g. the case that all the nodes are faulty, and the function to compute is the highest identity $u$ of a node in the graph. Thus, every node stores as a result an identity $v \neq u$ that is not the highest (since all the nodes are faulty). Clearly an attempted solution of running the persistent bit mending protocol on every bit of the output will not change the wrong value at all, and thus will not mend the output. Consider further the lucky case that the erroneous value $v$ is smaller than $u$. In this case, at least node $u$ can detect locally that there are faults (at least that it itself is faulty), and initiate an execution of a correction algorithm. Of course, we are less lucky in the case that $v$ is larger than $u$, since, in this case, no node posses enough information to detect a fault.

The problem is solved by utilizing an auxiliary data structure that will enable some nodes to detect a fault locally. This uses the idea of *local detection* [AKY90] (termed also *local checking* [APV91]).

Given a problem $X$ whose solutions are functions $\mathcal{F} \in X(G)$, represent the function on $G$ using auxiliary data structures, by storing the entire representation of $\mathcal{F}$ on the whole network, i.e., the vector $\xi = (\mathcal{F}(v_1), \ldots, \mathcal{F}(v_n))$, at every node.

To perform mending, each node, $v_i$, first checks that its own representation of $\mathcal{F}$, i.e. $\mathcal{F}(v)$, matches the value that appears in the auxiliary data structure, that is, matches $\xi_i$. If this is not the case, then $v_i$ considers itself faulty.

Mending is performed by treating each bit of this representation vector $\xi$ separately, and applying to it the common bit algorithm. In case $|F| \geq n/2$, this algorithm as described so far will not do the mending. In this case, however, an inconsistency must be detected for at least some bit $\mathcal{M}$ of the vector $\xi$. In this case, any processor detecting an inconsistency broadcasts a message to this effect throughout the entire network. In response to such a message, the processors collectively employ a global procedure for computing a new solution $\mathcal{F}'$ for the problem $X$. This operation requires at most $O(n)$ time in our model (for instance, by collecting all the inputs to one node, computing a solution locally, and broadcasting the solution to all the nodes in the network). By assumption, this complexity is $O(|F| \log |F| = f(|F|))$.

## 8 Local Mending of Local Functions

Linial and others (cf. [L92, AGLP]) promoted what they call *local* algorithms, namely, algorithms that require the collection of data only from small neighborhoods, even for seemingly global functions such as Maximal Independent Set (MIS). We refer to these algorithms also as *sub-linear*, since their running time is sub-linear in the diameter (or the number of nodes).

the use of local / sub-linear algorithms by itself (when possible) enhances scalability, since when using such an algorithm, even the cost of computing a function from scratch grows more slowly than the growth of the network.

Such functions can be mended by the general method explained in the previous section, but the cost of the mending, in this case, is at least linear in the number of faults, rather than sub-linear. For problems such as MIS its complexity can be exponentially worse than the complexity of known algorithms that recompute the MIS from scratch. In [KP95b] the notion of *tight* fault locality is introduced (versus the notion of *fault locality* in [KP95a]) to capture the performance expected from solutions to problems such as MIS, and it is demonstrated that MIS is tightly fault locally mendable under a reasonable assumption (and *near-tightly fault locally mendable* with no assumption.)

If the cost of computing $X$ from scratch on an $n$-vertex network is $\Omega(f(n))$ and $X$ is fault locally $f$-mendable, then $X$ is termed *tightly locally mendable* (or simply *tightly mendable*). If $X$ is only fault locally $poly(f)$-mendable then $X$ is termed *near-tightly locally mendable*. For randomized algorithms an analogous terminology is used. In particular, if $f(n)$ is the complexity of a randomized algorithm for computing $X$, then $X$ is randomly fault locally $f$-mendable. The notion of tightness is defined similarly.

For the case of MIS, an algorithm with the complexity of $(\log n)$ is known [L86]. In [KP95b] it is shown that MIS is randomly locally $\log |F|$-mendable. That is, if only $|F|$ faults occurred then the expected running time of the randomized mending algorithm is only $O(\log |F|)$ rather than $O(\log n)$. It is not known whether the algorithm of [L86] is optimal. If it is, then MIS is randomly tightly fault locally mendable. For the case that this algorithm is not optimal, it is shown that the existence of any randomized MIS algorithm whose time complexity is a "reasonably nice" function $f$ (defined there) implies that MIS is randomly locally $f$-mendable. This implies, in particular, that if the true randomized complexity of MIS is such a nice function, then MIS is randomly tightly locally mendable. Otherwise MIS is near tightly fault locally mendable.

The work on fault locality leaves many open problems. In particular, while it points at a new direction towards making protocols more scalable, some further hurdles to scalability still need to be removed. In particular, these two papers do not assume any specific bound on the size of the messages. While the messages of the persistent bit protocol are still reasonable in size, those used for a general function may become unrealistically large in the near future. (It is worth mentioning that this approach nevertheless is very similar to the update method mentioned above, that is still widely in use.)

Another research direction is that of devising fault local algorithms for specific practical problems. Such solutions may be more efficient (in terms of space, and length of messages) than the universal method for general functions mentioned above.

The fault local algorithms surveyed above also assumes that a node can process messages from every neighbor at the same time. This is a common assumption in the distributed algorithms literature. However, a newer model ([CGK95], see also [BK92], and a similar model in [1, 20]) defines a spectrum of relations between the time for communication with the neighbors (which indeed can be done in parallel) and the time for the local processing that needs to be done sequentially for each neighbor. It will be interesting to investigate the scalability issues in these models.

# 9 Self Stabilization and Fault Locality

Another direction of research is studying the issues of fault locality in the context of self stabilization, especially in the asynchronous case. Some initial steps along these lines were already taken [KP96, GGHP96, GGP96, GG96, H96].

In [KP96], the universal method of [KP95a] is generalized to be self stabilizing. The mending is started by any node that notices (using local detection) an inconsistency.

A limitation of the solution is that the output is sometimes corrected before the network stabilizes. That is, assume that at some time $t_0$ $|F|$ faults occurred, the output is mended after $O(|F|)$ time, provided that no more faults occur for some time $T$. In fact, $T$ can be much larger than $|F|$. (Self stabilization and mending are obtained even if additional faults do occur within this time, however, the mending time in this case can be longer.)

This kind of a phenomena was investigated and formalized in [GGHP96]. Let $L_f$ be a predicate on the global state of the network (that is, on the collection of the local states of the nodes). The network is self stabilized when $L_f$ holds. However, the output of the system may involve only some of the variables at each node; for example, the common bit mentioned before. Let $L$ be another predicate on the global state, such that $L_f$ implies $L$, and, moreover, the variables of $L$ are only those that are considered the output. Output mending is completed (or, in the terminology of [GGHP96] the fault is *contained*) when $L$ holds. However, the time required for $L_f$ to hold may be much longer. This time is termed the *fault gap*. Moreover, if a second fault occurs after the fault gap, then, a fault local mending algorithm (fault containing, in the terminology of [GGHP96]) is required to mend the output in a constant time ([GGHP96] deals only with a single fault). However, if a second fault occurs before the fault gap ended, even if the output was already mended, it is suggested in [GGHP96] that an algorithm may not be able to guarantee that the mending of the two faults will end within an additional $O(1)$ time. It is shown that optimizing self stabilization time, and optimizing the mending time may be contradicting goals. In particular, there exists a problem (topology update) for which if an algorithm optimizes one of these complexities, it cannot optimize the other. The specific distance shown from the optimum is not large, and it seems interesting to peruse this gap further.

Another result in [GGHP96] is a general method to convert any non-reactive self stabilizing protocol to one that mends the outputs within $O(1)$ time (and with $O(1)$ space overhead) if only one fault occurred. That is, if one assumes that there is a large enough time interval between the occurrence of any two faults, then this algorithm is fault local. Algorithms with a similar property, but for specific functions, appear in [GGP96, GG96, H96].

## 10 Conclusions

A lot of work has been done. However, there is still a lot to be done until distributed systems are reliable enough, and until the fault handling is painless enough.

## Acknowledgments

I would like to thank my coathors, as well as authors of other papers mentioned here, for their help, and for parts of the papers I quoted and summed up here.

## References

[AAG87] Yehuda Afek, Baruch Awerbuch, and Eli Gafni. Applying static network protocols to dynamic networks. In *Proc. 28th IEEE Symp. on Foundations of Computer Science*, October 1987.

[ACKMP96] B. Awerbuch, I. Cidon, S. Kutten, Y. Mansour, and D. Peleg, Broadcasting with Partial Knowledge. to appear in *SIAM Journal on Computing*.

[ADLS91] H. Attiya, C. Dwork, N. Lynch, and L. Stockmeyer. Bounds on the Time to Reach Agreement in the Presence of Timing Uncertainty. In *23rd ACM Symposium on Theory of Computing*, New Orleans, Louisiana, pp. 359-369, May 1991.

[A94] S. Aggarwal. Time optimal self- stabilizing spanning tree algorithms. M.Sc Thesis, MIT, May 1994.

[AGLP] B. Awerbuch, A. Goldberg, M. Luby and S. Plotkin. Network decomposition and locality in distributed computation, *Proc. 30th Symp. on Foundations of Computer Science*, pp. 364–375, October 1989.

[APV91] B. Awerbuch, B. Patt-Shamir, and G. Varghese. Self-stabilization by local checking and correction. In *Proc. 32nd IEEE Symp. on Foundation of Computer Science*, 268–277, 1991.

[AKY90] Y. Afek, S. Kutten, and M. Yung. Memory-efficient self stabilizing protocols for general networks. In *Proc. 4th Int. Workshop on Distributed Algorithms*, S-V LNCS, September 1990.

[AKMPV93] B. Awerbuch, S. Kutten, Y. Mansour, B. Patt-Shamir and G. Varghese, Time-Optimal Self Stabilizing Synchronization, *Proc. 1993 ACM Symp. on Theory of Computing*, San Diego, California, pp. 652–661, May 1993.

[AO94] B. Awerbuch and R. Ostrovsky. Memory efficient and self stabilizing network reset. In *Proc. 14th ACM Symp. on Principles of Distributed Computing (PODC)*, August 1994.

[APVD94] B. Awerbuch, B. Patt-Shamir, G. Varghese, and S. Dolev. Self stabilization by local checking and global reset. in the Proc. of WDAG 94, Springer-Verlag LNCS, pages 226–239, October 1994.

[AV91] B. Awerbuch, , and G. Varghese. Distributed program checking: a paradigm for building self-stabilizing distributed protocols. In *Proc. of the 32nd IEEE Ann. Symp. on Foundation of Computer Science*, pages 258–267, October 1991.

[C91] D. E. Comer. Internetworking with TCP/IP. Prantice Hall, New Jersey, US, 1991.

[BGP92] P. Berman, J. Garay, and K. Perry. Optimal Early Stopping in Distributed Consensus. In *Proceedings of International Workshop on Distributed Algorithms (WDAG)*, Haifa, Israel, LNCS (647), Springer-Verlag, pp. 221-237, November 1992.

[BK92] A. Bar-Noy and S. Kipnis, Designing broadcasting algorithms in the postal model for message-passing systems. invited paper, to appear in *Mathematical Systems Theory*, 1994. Also *Proceedings of the 4th Annual Symposium on Parallel Algorithms and Architectures*, ACM, June 1992, pp. 13–22.

[BP95] J-C. Bermond and D. Peleg. The Power of Small Coalitions in Graphs. *Proc. 2nd Colloq. on Structural Information & Communication Complexity*, Olympia, Greece, June 1995, Carleton Univ. Press, 173–184.

[BBPP96] J-C. Bermond, J. Bond, D. Peleg, and S. Perennes. Tight bounds on the size of 2-monopolies. *Proc. 3rd Colloq. on Structural Information & Communication Complexity*, Siena, Italy, June 1996.

[CGKK95] I. Cidon, I. Gopal, M. Kaplan and S. Kutten. Distributed Control for Fast Networks. *IEEE Trans. on Communications*, Vol. 43(5), pp. 1950–1960, May 1995.

1. D. Culler, R.M. Karp, D. Patterson, A. Sahay, K.E. Schauser, E. Santos, R. Subramonian and T. von Eicken. LogP: towards a realistic model of parallel computation. *Proc. 4th SIGPLAN Symp. on Principles and Practices of Parallel Programming*, ACM, May 1993.

[GG96] S. Ghosh and A. Gupta. An exercise in Fault Containment: Leader Election in a Ring. to appear in *Information Processing Letters*.

[GGHP96] S. Ghosh, A. Gupta, T. Herman, and S.V. Pemmaraju Fault-Containing Self-Stabilizing Algorithms. In Proc. 15th Annual ACM Symposium on Principles of Distributed Computing, Philadelphia, Pennsylvania, USA, May 23-26, 1996, pp. 45-54.

[CL85] M.M. Chandy and L. Lamport. Distributed Snapshots: Determining Global States of Distributed Systems. *Transactions on Computer Systems*, Vol. 3, No. 1, 1985, pp. 63-75.

[GGP96] S. Ghosh, A. Gupta, and S. V. Pemmaraju. A Fault-Containing Self-Stabilizing Spanning Tree Algorithm. *Journal of Computing and Information* Vol. 2, No. 1, 1996, pp. 322-338 (Special issue on the Proceedings of the Eighth International Conference of Computing and Information, Waterloo, Ontario, Canada, June 18-22, 1996.)

[CP87] I. Chlamtac, and S. Pinter. Distributed Node Organization Algorithm for Channel Access in a Multihop Dynamic Radio Network. *IEEE Transactions on Computers*, VOL. C-36, NO 6, June 1987, pp. 728-737.

[CK85] I. Chlamtac and S. Kutten. A Spatial Reuse TDMA/FDMA for Mobile Multihop Radio Networks. *IEEE INFOCOM 85*, Washington, DC, USA, March 1985.

[DH95] S. Dolev and T. Herman. SuperStabilizing Protocols for Dynamic Distributed Systems. In *2nd Workshop on Self-Stabilizing Systems*. Las Vegas, Nevada, May 1995.

[D74] E. W. Dijkstra. Self-stabilizing systems in spite of distributed control. *Communication of the ACM*, 17:643-644, November 1974.

[DIM94] S. Dolev, A. Israeli, and S. Moran. Self-stabilization of dynamic systems assuming only read/write atomicity. *Distributed Computing Journal*, 7, 1994. also In *Proc. 9th ACM Symp. on Principles of Distributed Computing*, August 1990.

[DRS90] D. Dolev, R. Reischuk, and R. Strong, Early Stopping in Byz. Agreement. *JACM* Vol. 37, No. 4 (1990), pp. 720-741.

[F79] Steven G. Finn. Resynch procedures and a fail-safe network protocol. *IEEE Trans. on Communications*, COM-27(6):840-845, June 1979.

[G77] R.E. Gallager. Choosing a Leader in a Network. unpublished memorandum, *M.I.T.*

[Gaf87] Eli Gafni. Topology resynchronization: A new paradigm for fault tolerance in distributed algorithms. In *Proceedings of the Amsterdam Workshop on Distributed Algorithms*. CWI, July 1987.

[H96] T. Herman. Superstabilizing Mutual Exclusion. *International Conference on Parallel and Distributed Systems*, Athens, GA, 1995.

[HK89] A. Herzberg and S. Kutten. Fast Isolation of Faults in Data Transfer. *Proceedings of the 8th Annual ACM Symposium on Principles of Distributed Computing (PODC 89)*, Edmonton, Canada, pp. 349-353, August 1989.

[KP90] S. Katz and K. J. Perry. Self-stabilizing extensions. In *Proc. 9th ACM Symp. on Principles of Distributed Computing*, August 1990.

[KP95a] S. Kutten and D. Peleg. Fault-Local Mending. *Proceedings of the Fourteenth Annual ACM Symposium on Principle of Distributed Computing (PODC 95)*, Ottawa, Canada, pp. 20-27, August 1995.

[KP95b] S. Kutten and D. Peleg. Tight Fault-locality. In *Proc. 36th IEEE Symp. on Foundations of Computer Science*, 1995.

[KP96] S. Kutten and B. Patt-Shamir Fault-Local Self-Stabilization, In preparation.

[20] R.M. Karp, A. Sahay, E. Santos, and K. E. Schauser. Optimal broadcast and summation in the LogP model. *Proc. 5th Symp. on Parallel Algorithms and Architectures*, ACM, June 1993, pp 142-153.

[L77] G. Le-Lann Distributed Systems- towards a Formal Approach. *Information Processing 77 (ed. B. Gilchrist)*. pp. 155-160, North-Holland 1977.

[L86] Michael Luby, A simple parallel algorithm for the maximal independent set problem, *SIAM J. Comput.*, 15(4):1036–1053, November 1986.

[L92] N. Linial, Locality in distributed graph algorithms, *SIAM J. Comput.*, 21:193–201, 1992.

[LPRS93] N. Linial, D. Peleg, Y. Rabinovich and M. Saks, Sphere Packing and Local Majorities in Graphs, *Proc. 2nd Israel Symp. on Theory of Computing and Systems*, Natanya, Israel, June 1993, 141–149.

[LSP82] L. Lamport, R.E. Shostak and M. Pease. The Byzantine Generals Problem. *ACM ToPLaS*, Vol. 4, No. 3, pp. 382-401, July 1982.

[MNS95] A. Mayer, S. Naor, and L. Stockmeyer Local Computations on Static and Dynamic Graphs In *Proceedings of the 3rd Israel Symposium on Theory and Computing Systems (ISTCS)*, 1995.

[MRR80] J. M. McQuillan, I. Richer and E. C. Rosen, The New Routing Algorithm for the ARPANET. *IEEE Trans. on Communications*, COM-28, May 1980, pp. 711-719.

[NS93] M. Naor and L. Stockmeyer, What Can Be Computed Locally? In *Proc. of the 25th ACM Symp. on the Theory of Computing*, San Diego, California, May 1993, pp. 184-193.

[P92] R. Perlman. Interconnections: Bridges and Routers. *Addison Welsley*, 1992.

[P96] D. Peleg. Local Majority Voting, Small Coalitions and Controlling Monopolies in Graphs: A Review. *Proc. 3rd Colloq. on Structural Information & Communication Complexity*, Siena, Italy, June 1996.

[P96a] D. Peleg. Local Majority Voting, Small Coalitions and Controlling Monopolies in Graphs: A Review. *Proc. 3rd Colloq. on Structural Information & Communication Complexity*, June 1996, Siena, Italy.

[Pon91] S. Ponzio. Network Consensus in the Presence of Timing Uncertainty: Omission and Byzantine Failures. In *Proceedings of the 10th Annual ACM Symposium on Principles of Distributed Computing*, Montreal, Quebec, Canada, pp. 125-138, August 1991.

[ACK90] B. Awerbuch, I. Cidon, and S. Kutten, "Optimal Maintenance of Replicated Information", proceedings of the 31st Annual IEEE Symposium on Foundations of Computer Science (FOCS 90), St. Louis, MO, USA, pp. 492–502, October 1990.

[AGKK91] J. Auerbach, P.M. Gopal, M. Kaplan, and S. Kutten, "Multicast Group Membership Management in High Speed Wide Area Networks", Proceedings of the 11th International Conference on Distributed Computing Systems (IC DCS), Arlington, Texas, USA, May 1991.

[BGGJP85] A. E. Baratz, J. P. Gray, P. E. Green Jr., J. M. Jaffe, and D.P. Pozefski. Sna networks of small systems. *IEEE Journal on Selected Areas in Communications*, SAC-3(3):416–426, May 1985.

[CGK95] I. Cidon, I. Gopal, and S. Kutten. New Models and Algorithms for Future Networks. *IEEE Transactions on Information Theory*, Vol. 41, No. 3, pp. 769–780, May 1995.

[SG89] John M. Spinelli and Robert G. Gallager. Broadcasting topology information in computer networks. *IEEE Trans. on Commun.*, May 1989.

[T81] A.S. Tanenbaum. Computer Networks. *Prentice-Hall*, 1981.

# Contributed Papers

*Arranged in alphabetical order
of first author's family name*

# A Deductive Database Support to the Specification of Concurrent Systems [*]

Patrizia Asirelli, Stefania Gnesi and Maria Cristina Rossi

IEI - C.N.R., Pisa, Italy

**Abstract.** We present an approach to the specification of concurrent systems, by means of a deductive database management system. The approach is based on the synthesis of logic formulas: starting from a temporal logic formula, that represents the requirements of a system, a general model for such formula, is derived. From this model, all the concurrent systems satisfying the formula can be generated. A **graphical representation** of the model is given through a deductive database management system GEDBLOG. Moreover, we show that this model can be used to verify when a given system, obtained elsewhere, is in agreement with its requirements expressed by logical specifications.

## 1 Introduction

The specification phase plays a fundamental role in the development of concurrent systems. This is the phase where the properties of systems are expressed and where the use of formal languages and formal methods is strongly recommended. Among formal languages, logic plays an important role, because it provides an abstract specification of concurrent systems.

Indeed, different types of logics have been proposed for this purpose. In particular, modal and temporal logics, due to their ability to deal with notions such as **necessity, possibility** and **eventuality** have been recognised as a suitable formalism for specifying properties of concurrent systems [1]. Among them, we recall the action based version of CTL [2], ACTL[3]. The ACTL logic, being an action_based one, is more suitable than state_based logics such as CTL, to express properties of concurrent systems that are usually defined by the occurrence of actions over time. The models of ACTL formulas are Labelled Transition Systems (LTSs) which in their turn are suitable to formally specify concurrent systems [4].

The work reported in this paper is part of a project whose main purpose is the integration of different tools independently built to support the initial phase of software development. The tools we intend to integrate are NL2ACTL [5] which is a tool to generate ACTL logic formlulas starting from the natural language specification of a reactive system and GEDBLOG [6, 7], which is a Deductive

---

[*] Acknowledgements: This work is partially founded by Progetto Integrato CNR-Comitato 2 and Progetto Coordinato CNR-Comitato 12 : "Programmazione Logica (Logic Progamming)"

database management system. GEDBLOG is based on a logic language extended with the capabilities of handling in a uniform way, graphical and non graphical information, and it has the possibility of defining and verifying integrity constraints. Our aim is to use GEDBLOG to build an environment where a formal specification can be graphically represented, giving the basis on which an animation of the formal specification can be started.

When the specification of a concurrent system is given by means of a set of ACTL formulas, a particular LTS is associated to the conjuction of the set of formulas. This LTS subsumes an infinite set of LTSs each one denoting a more detailed model of the system and it is called the "meta_model" of the formula. The definition of the meta_model is given within GEDBLOG by means of its logical theories handling capability as a set of states, labelled transitions and states constraints. Each state constraint provides the property that every LTS has to satisfy to be a model of the concurrent system under specification. The meta_model can then be used to obtain more refined models, all in agreement with the initial specification, hence giving an animation of the possible implementations of the concurrent systems.

Our approach can be devided into three steps:

  i) **Synthesis Phase**: Given an ACTL formula, its meta_model is generated by GEDBLOG. More precisely, given the specification of a concurrent systems, in terms of ACTL formulas, we deduce its corresponding interpretation in terms of meta_model denotation.

 ii) **Animation Phase**: The meta_model becomes a new input for GEDBLOG to generate more detailed LTSs, each one satisfying the initial ACTL formula, that is, starting from the obtained meta_model we build one LTS model, among the admissible ones;

 This mechanism allows also the analysis of an LTS to be supported. This means that we shall exploit all the deductive capabilities of GEDBLOG, by defining a logic program where the definition of "correctness" for an LTS is given.

iii) **Admissibility Test Phase**: This correctness definition can then be used, to verify the admissibility of other LTS models (generated by means of other tools) with respect to a given formal specification through an ACTL formula.

In the next section we introduce some background knowledge of the ACTL logic and of GEDBLOG. Section 3 describes the approach in more details. Section 4 presents the implementation of the proposed approach using the GEDBLOG environment.

## 2   Background

In the following we present a summary of the basis of our approach. We briefly introduce the ACTL logic and the LTS formalism used to model ACTL formulas, the GEDBLOG system and the definition of meta_models.

## 2.1 ACTL

ACTL is a branching time temporal logic that is suitable for describing the behaviour of systems that perform actions during their working time. In fact, ACTL embeds the idea of "evolution in time by actions" and is suitable for describing the temporal sequences of actions that characterize a system. The syntax and the informal semantics of some of the ACTL operators is shown in Table 1; the grammar in this table has the state formula symbol $\phi$ as initial production. In the table, $\alpha$ is a single observable action belonging to *Act*, which is the set of actions that a given system is assumed to be able to perform. An execution (path) is a (finite or not) sequence of actions. A *state* represents a time in which a single action has been completed and a new next action may be performed. It is possible that there is more than one action that the system can perform, when its execution reaches a state. Each of these actions represents the beginning of an alternative continuation of the execution. A *state formula* gives a characterization about the possible ways an execution could continue after a state has been reached, while a *path formula* states some properties of a *single* execution.

To better explain the ACTL logical modalities, let us parse the formula

`AG (EX{a! | b?} true).`

Unfolding the recursive definition of the ACTL grammar in Table 1 and composing the English sentences on the right of the operators according to the structure of the formula, we get:

| | |
|---|---|
| A | $\equiv$ "for each of the possible executions [of the given system] |
| G | $\equiv$ at each time [of such an execution] |
| E | $\equiv$ there exists an execution in which |
| X{a! \| b?} | $\equiv$ either the observable action *a*! or |
| | the observable action *b*? is immediately |
| | performed and, after that, |
| true | $\equiv$ any behaviour is possible." |

i.e. during its working time the given system *always* has, the possibility to perform either *a*! or *b*?.

The formal semantic of ACTL formulae is given over LTSs, which describe the behaviour of a system in terms of states and labelled transitions relating states.

## 2.2 The Meta_Model

A meta_model is an extention of LTSs in the sense that it denotes all possible LTSs that are models of an ACTL formula. More precisely, a *Meta_model* M is a structure $(MS, MT, MD, ms_0, V_s)$, where MS is a set of states, MT is a set of transition labels, $ms_0 \in$ MS is the initial state, MD $\subseteq$ MS $\times$ MT $\times$ MS is a set of transitions, $V_s$ is a costraint on states, represented by a first order logic formulae. States and transitions of the meta_model are called meta_states and meta_transitions, because they subsume sets of state and sets of transitions respectively.

## Action formulas

| $\Omega$ | $::=$ | $true$ | "any observable action" |
|---|---|---|---|
| | | $false$ | "no observable action" |
| | | $\alpha$ | "the observable action $\alpha$" |
| | | $\neg\Omega$ | "any observable action different from $\Omega$" |
| | | $\Omega \mid \Omega'$ | "either $\Omega$ or $\Omega'$" |
| $\Omega'$ | $::=$ | $\Omega$ | |

## State formulas

| $\mu$ | $::=$ | $true$ | "any·behaviour is possible." |
|---|---|---|---|
| | | $false$ | "no behaviour is possible." |
| | | $\sim \mu$ | " $\mu$ is impossible" |
| | | $\mu \,\&\, \mu'$ | "$\mu$ and $\mu'$" |
| | | $E\theta$ | "there exists a possible execution in which $\theta$" |
| | | $A\theta$ | "for each of the possible executions $\theta$" |
| $\mu'$ | $::=$ | $\mu$ | |

## Path formulas

| $\theta$ | $::=$ | $G\mu$ | "at any time $\mu$" |
|---|---|---|---|
| | | $F\mu$ | "there is a time in which $\mu$" |
| | | $[\mu\{\Omega\}U\{\Omega'\}\mu']$ | "at any time $\Omega$ is performed and *also* $\mu$, *until* $\Omega'$ is performed and then $\mu'$" |
| | | $X\{\tau\}\mu$ | "an unobservable action is immediately performed and, after that, $\mu$" |
| | | $X\{\Omega\}\mu$ | "$\Omega$ is immediately performed and, after that, $\mu$" |

**Table 1.** Some of the ACTL operators

### 2.3 The Gedblog System

The Gedblog system[7], is a uniform environment which supports the fast prototyping of applications that can take benefit from a declarative specification style. For instance, applications which demand for:

- a support for knowledge management (according to the given data-model this knowledge is based on);
- a support for the graphic representation of knowledge;
- a support for the interactions, to make the knowledge manageable at the graphic level.

Gedblog is based on logic databases theory. It is a deductive (logic) database, that can deal with basic knowledge management functionalities (storing, retrieving, quering), and besides it is enriched with several additional features:

– Integrity Constraints and Checks, to define the data model entities must fit in;

- Transactions, to enter the operational framework;
- Input/Output graphic model (declarative, based on prototypes), to define graphics and interactions with graphic objects.

Gedblog can manage logical theories that consist of different kinds of clauses: *Facts, Rules, Integrity Constraints, Checks and Transactions.*

By means of the system-defined predicate *theory*, it is possible to perform inclusion among theories. In this way, given a *starting* theory $Th$, the associated Gedblog theory can be defined as the set-theoretic *union* of all the theories in the inclusion tree rooted in $Th$. Gedblog includes a graphic specification language, integrating the features of Motif and X11 in the Gedblog theories.

# 3   An approach to reactive systems specifications

We now introduce the approach to the specification of reactive systems and in the next section we present its implementation within the GEDBLOG system. From an ACTL formula we derive a finite meta_model M by means of a synthesis algorithm which represents the minimal LTS satisfying the formula.Then this meta_model will be used both for generating more detailed LTSs that represent different implementations of the system under specification (*Animation Phase*) and for analysing already developed implementation of a system against its formal specification *Admissibility Test Phase*).

## 3.1   Synthesis Algorithm

In this paper the synthesis phase is performed only for a subset of the ACTL formulas. In fact, we consider only the path quantifiers (A,E) and the next operators (X). This means that only finite properties can be managed in this subset. An extension to full ACTL is under study. However, we think that the consiedered subst is sufficient to show the potentiality of our approach.

**Synthesis phase** In this phase we associate a possible interpretation, in terms of meta_model, of an ACTL formula $\mu$. This is accomplished by means of the following semantic interpretation functions, one for each syntactic category of the ACTL logic, where:

$F_\mu$ : Meta_model $\times \mu \times$ MS $\longrightarrow$ Meta_model ;

$F_\theta$ : Meta_model $\times \theta \times$ MS $\times$ SI $\longrightarrow$ Meta_model ;

$F_\Omega$: auxiliary function to manage action formulas.

Where SI={ A, E } is the set of quantifiers "forall" and "exist" and MS are meta_states of the meta_model. For sake of semplicity we give here only the ideas of how the meta_model is associated to an ACTL formula, while the complete formal definition can be found in [10].

Let us suppose that we have to construct a meta_model for a generic formula $\mu$; we begin parsing the formula and building the meta_model incrementally, step by step, from an initial state. At each step we produce a new meta_model obtained by expanding the previous one according to the representation defined for the sub_formula $\mu_i$ of $\mu$ that we are analysing. Moreover, during the generation of a Meta_model some constraints, $V_S$, are inserted. They are defined as first order formulas and they give the admissible actions for each system satisfying the formal specification. Thus, let us suppose that for $\mu$ we have produced a meta_model $Met_i$ where the last generated state is $S_i$ and suppose that $\mu_i$ is the sub_formula of $\mu$ that we are incrementally analysing, then we have the following cases:

- a) **if** $\mu_i = True$

In this case we have that from the meta_state $S_i$ any further structural development can take place because the formula true is ever satisfied. This condition is expressed by associating no constraints to $S_i$. Hence:

$$V_{S_i} = \emptyset$$

- b) **if** $\mu_i = EX_{\{\alpha|\tau\}}\mu_{i+1}$

In this case, the following constraints will be introduced:
$V_{S_i} = \forall s \in LTS\_S(S_i).\exists x \in A(s).(F_\Omega(\alpha \vee \tau)) \; \& \; (LAST'(x) \in LTS\_S(S_j));$
where:
* $A(s)$ : denotes all the possible transitions from the state s.
* $LAST'(x)$ : denotes the arrival state of a generic transition x.
* $LTS\_S(S_i)$ : denotes the set of LTSs states subsumed by $S_i$.
This constraint means that all states that are subsumed by the meta_state $S_i$, have at least one transition labelled with the action $F_\Omega(\alpha \vee \tau)$ connecting each one of such states to a state subsumed by the meta_state $S_j$.

- c) **if** $\mu_i = AX_{\{\alpha|\tau\}}\mu_{i+1}$

In this case the constraint is:
$V_{S_i} = \forall s \in LTS\_S(S_i).\forall x \in A(s).(F_\Omega(\alpha \vee \tau)) \; \& \; (LAST'(x) \in LTS\_S(S_j));$
This constraint means that all states that are subsumed by the meta_state $S_i$, have all transitions labelled with the action $F_\Omega(\alpha \vee \tau)$ connecting each one of such states to a state subsumed by the meta_state $S_j$.

**Animation phase** After a meta_model has been obtained for each ACTL formula, a set of LTSs can be derived. Each of these LTSs satisfies the given logic formula. Hence, we introduce a notion of satisfiability of an ACTL formula on a LTS through its derivation from a meta_model.
We say that an LTS satisfies the initial ACTL formula if it is built according to the following steps:

1. From $ms_0$ only one state, $TS_0$, can be derived that represents the initial state of the LTS under construction.

2. Each state of the LTS, TS, is derived by a meta_state MS of the given meta_model.
3. Each transition starting from a state in the LTS is in agreement with the constraint associated to the related meta_state.

**Admissibility test phase**  The meta_model associated to a formula $\mu$, obtained by the previous phases, can also be used to check the satisfiability of $\mu$ on a given LTS independently developed.

# 4  Implementation

We now briefly describe the implementation of the proposed method using GED-BLOG. The environment we have realized is interactive. A graphical interface has been defined to provide a dialog_window, between the ACTL formulas given in input and GEDBLOG.

## 4.1  First step: Synthesis Phase

After the insertion of a formula a button can be pushed. This activates a trans-action, that produces a new window, by which the associate meta_models will be built. The Synthesis Phase can now start. The button allows the meta_model to be visualized step by step during its generation. In order to obtain this meta_model we used the Gedblog transaction mechanism, that allows us to mod-ify the knowledge of the database with graphical and not graphical information according to the semantic rules given by the synthesis mechanism.

## 4.2  Second step: Animation Phase

When a meta_model has been defined a set of LTSs can be derived each one representing a different system that satisfies the initial ACTL formula. Each LTS can be derived from the meta_model interactively by the user, by means of a dialog window. Each meta_state can be splitted into a set of states, each of one sharing the same constraints of the original meta_state. Transitions can be traced between a pair of states of the LTS model according to the constraints of the meta_model. The system forbids the definition of a transition that does not satisfies the constraints.

## 4.3  Third step: Admissibility Test Phase

Given a particular LTS, indipendently developed, it is possible to verify if this is a correct implementation of a specification given by an ACTL formula. The associated meta_model is used to analyse if the structure of the LTS agrees with it, that is, if the constraints in the meta_model are all verified by the LTS. In this case we can say that the LTS is a correct implementation of such specification.

To realize the analysis phase we have used rules and constraints, besides transactions. In this phase two possible answers are provided by the system:
* **check_ok** : if the given LTS is correct;
* **check_failed** : otherwise.

## 5  Conclusions

In this paper we have presented an environment supporting the formal specification of concurrent systems. The environment has been realized implementing a synthesis algorithm that allows the construction of a finite meta_model for each formula of a subset of the ACTL logic. The implementation has been carried out within the deductive database management system, GEDBLOG. We plan, in the next future, to extend this environment in order to manage all the ACTL formulas.

## References

1. Manna, Z. and Pnueli, A. (1989) **The Anchored Version of the Temporal Framework, in Linear Time, Branching Time and Partial Order in Logics and Models for Concurrency**, *Lecture Notes in Computer Science*,**354**, Springer-Verlag, 201-284.
2. Emerson, E. A. and Halpern, J. Y. (1986) **Sometimes and Not Never Revisited: on Branching Time versus Linear Time Temporal Logic.** *Journal of ACM*, **33** (1), 151-178.
3. De Nicola, R. and Vaandrager, F. W. (1990) **Action versus State based Logics for Transition Systems. Proceedings Ecole de Printemps on Semantics of Concurrency.** *Lecture Notes in Computer Science*,**469**, Springer-Verlag, 407-419.
4. R. Milner: **Communication and Concurrency,** *Prentice Hall, 1989.*
5. A. Fantechi, S. Gnesi, G. Ristori, M. Carenini, M. Vanocchi, P. Moreschini: **Assisting Requirement Formalization by Means of Natural Language Translation**\ *Formal Methods in System Design, 4, 243-263 (1994)*
6. P. Asirelli, P. Inverardi, D. Aquilino, D. Apuzzo, G. Bottone, M.C. Rossi: **Gedblog Reference Manual.** *Revised Version: Nota interna B4-18; Aprile 1995.*
7. P. Asirelli, D. Di Grande, P. Inverardi and F. Nicodemi: **Graphics by a logical Database Management System"** *Journal of Visual Languages and Computing (1994),5,365-388.*
8. R. De Nicola, A. Fantechi, S. Gnesi, G. Ristori: **An action-based framework for verifying logical and behavioural properties of concurrent system** *Computer Networks and ISDN Systems,25, (7), pp. 761-778, 1993.*
9. M. C. Rossi: **Sistema logico detuttivo per il supporto allo svilutto di sistemi ed all'analisi di dati telemetrici** *Tesi di Laurea, Scienze dell'informazione, Università di Pisa, Febbraio 1996.*
10. P. Asirelli, S. Gnesi, M.C. Rossi: **Synthesis of temporal logic formulae: an approach to software design** *IEI Internal Report*

# Interprocess Communication in the T4 System

David Bednárek, Petr Merta, David Obdržálek,
Jakub Yaghob, and Filip Zavoral*

Department of Software Engineering,
Faculty of Mathematics and Physics, Charles University Prague, cz

T4 is a microkernel and a distributed operating system built upon it. This paper describes the concepts, goals, and major design features of the T4 system. It provides an overview of the T4 system architecture, communication principles, and support for distributed computation.

## 1.    Introduction

In the past several years, the research of operating systems has shifted from the concept of isolated machines to the notion of a distributed operating system [7][9][10]. At the same time, single-machine operating systems started to use microkernel architecture [1]. This paper describes the T4 project - an attempt to design and to implement a microkernel, suitable for both single-machine and distributed operating systems, and a distributed operating system using this microkernel.

Contemporary implementations of distributed operating systems impose high requirements on hardware [3][10]. Since such hardware is not widely available there was a great emphasis on reduction of hardware requirements in this research project. Another reason for this approach is an intent to use the microkernel as a basis for single-machine operating environment.

Among other important design issues, excluding any special compatibility features from the microkernel allows implementation of arbitrary system interface to user programs. Thus, for example, compatibility with UNIX is obtainable with minimum effort while the microkernel itself is not loaded with any embedded compatibility [5]. Of course this approach probably causes certain loss of performance compared to systems designed with the compatibility in mind, but it was not the performance of UNIX programs that inspired this project.

The authors tried to focus mainly on the following topics:
- kernel speed
- quick message passing
- transparent remote communication
- unified process environment
- transparent object and process migration

---

* http://ulita.ms.mff.cuni.cz
e-mail: {bednarek, merta, obdrz, yaghob, zavoral}@ulita.ms.mff.cuni.cz

## 2.  System Architecture

The architecture of the T4 system consists of the following layers: The hardware, the microkernel, the by-kernel, system and user processes.

### 2.1  Hardware

The authors tried to design the T4 system with minimal dependence on hardware. All hardware-specific parts are strictly separated from the rest of T4 so that porting to any currently used platform would be easy and straightforward. The design allows both single- and multiprocessor machines with minimal restrictions to processor type.

### 2.2  Microkernel

The T4 microkernel deals with these tasks: Process and thread creation and deletion, processor time sharing, local message passing, thread fault handling, physical and virtual memory management, low level hardware operations and hardware interrupt handling.

The level of these services is significantly lower than their analogues in usual operating systems (including many microkernels). For instance, the time sharing algorithm in the T4 microkernel does not recognize any priorities, the virtual memory support does not understand the notion of swapping in and out; it only performs requested page table operations, notifies page faults, and performs a very simple page-discarding algorithm.

This layout enables building different systems based on this microkernel - single machine as well as distributed operating systems with good IPC support. T4 itself is one example of such a system.

### 2.3  By-kernel

Above the microkernel, there is a layer of modules providing basic functionality of operating system This layer is called by-kernel. The difference between the kernel and the by-kernel is in the fact that by-kernel modules run with user privilege level and have only indirect access to kernel entities.

Compared to the user and system modules, by-kernel processes run in a restricted computing environment, because their task is to provide services to form a complete computing environment for the processes. The microkernel provides certain services (e.g. memory allocation) for them in restricted and simplified manner, while the complete range of the same services for the system and user processes is provided by the by-kernel layer. The most important by-kernel modules are: Process manager, virtual memory managers, timer, primary file system, net manager.

## 2.4  System processes

System processes are loaded by by-kernel after its initialization and their use may be categorized into four groups:

- enhancement of by-kernel services (richer access to more media etc.)
- extending interprocess communication to remote machines
- public services (e.g. remote file servers)
- management of user protection domains

The most important system processes are: Remote communicator, secondary file systems, name server, server manager, process loader, user interface managers.

# 3.  Interprocess Communication

In this chapter we will describe basic types of communication between processes. By *interprocess communication* we understand not only communication between two or more separate processes, but communication and synchronisation between any threads, even communication within one thread

It is commonly believed that communication is one of the most important design issues of microkernel based and distributed operating systems with considerable impact on overall system performance [2][3]. Therefore great attention to communication was paid in T4 system design. The main goals of the T4 communication scheme are:

- As fast as possible "short" message passing
- Effective passing of large amount of data - mapping instead of copying whenever possible
- No unpredictable events like exhausting some resources due to the function or malfunction of other processes
- Unifying the expressions of rights to send a message and to use something
- Trusted local objects and services invocation without need of any encryption mechanism or sending long identification bitstreams
- Safe communication with untrusted or unknown counterpart process
- Possibility of transparent extension to remote communication
- Straightforward process and object migration without significant performance degradation

In the T4, a message is not only a piece of data passed between two threads or processes, but an abstract concept which may consist of three parts:

- *synchronisation*, i.e. the fact one thread has sent the message and so another one is able to receive it
- *rights and relations* being handed over to another process
- *information* - the data being sent

The T4 message passing system (as incorporated in the kernel) provides local interprocess communication, but offers no remote communication facilities. On the other hand, the definition of the message passing principles allows transparent extension of the message passing to remote computers by means of non-kernel processes.

In the simplest case, it means that there may be a couple of proxy processes inserted to the communication channel between two processes where each process communicates (through kernel facilities) with the proxy on its side while the proxy processes are connected on their own, e.g. through sending packets over a network. The key issue is that the communication through proxy processes is transparent for the communicating processes, i.e. that the message passing scheme is strong enough to allow emulation and weak enough to be emulated.

## 3.1    Communication Principles

At the bottom of every message-based system, there is the *send/receive* paradigm. If there are only point-to-point messages (i.e. if there are no broadcasts) and if there is no message loss the send/receive model becomes a duality - every message sent is to be received just once and every message received was sent just once.

With client-server model, there comes another duality - *request/reply* dichotomy of messages. In an ideally functioning system, every request message must be sooner or later answered with a reply message and vice versa.

The T4 system introduces the third case of duality between *running* a thread and *passing* a message. This rule is inspired by the observation that real programs usually combine sending a message with waiting for another one - a client program sends a request and waits for an answer, a server sends a reply and waits for another request. In other words, sending a message causes loss of right to run for the sending thread and receiving a message revives the receiving thread. This observation leads to the notion of *logical thread*: A computation that is continuously transferred among communicating processes, switching between the *running* state - executing within a thread - and the *passing* state - waiting for a thread as a message. In the T4, logical threads (and not the physical ones) form the base of the synchronisation and time-sharing system.

The message passing system combines all the three dualities mentioned above:

- The basic message passing primitives (i.e. the kernel calls) always combine sending a message with receiving of another one.
- The implementation of the logical thread relies on the term *stamp*. Stamp is basically a "right to run"; any thread may run only in the case it owns one stamp and any message may be passed only if it is coupled with a stamp. Physically, the stamp is one of the basic kernel entities; the next chapters describe them and their handling from the point of view of a process.
- The message sending operations reflect the request/reply protocol: The most important modes are *push* and *pop* for sending a request and a reply, respectively. The names push/pop come from the fact that the execution of a logical thread in a client-server environment resembles stack operations. The push operation sends a message via a one-way communication channel, typically from a client to a server. The pop operation returns the reply back to the sender of the corresponding push without a need to establish a channel. The message passing system maintains a stack of successive push operations (called envelope

stack) associated with a logical thread and allows replying to a request without specifying any information about the target.

Although both the send/receive and the request/reply dualities are present in the communication primitives, it does not necessarily mean that the message received immediately after sending a request must be the answer to it. This feature is frequently used by servers while simple client processes usually conform to the suspending mode of service calls. These mechanisms allow advanced logically multithreaded servers to be implemented using only one thread.

## 3.2    Vertices

The most basic and most important entity used for interprocess communication is a *vertex*. Vertices help threads to run, send and receive messages, synchronize processes etc. They are maintained by the microkernel and they are *parked* in *slots* which are organised in arrays called *racks*. The racks are attached to processes; a process may access only the vertices parked in its racks. The fact that the vertices are addressed through its position in the process's racks allows transparent process migration.

There are several basic types of vertices:

bag - Bags are used to merge input from different channels: All messages coming through receivers into one bag are queued here and later passed to a thread asking the bag for a message. In the complementary case, threads may be queued in the bag while waiting for messages. The number of messages or threads in a bag is not limited. There may be any number of receivers connected to a bag; on the other hand, every receiver is connected to exactly one bag. To be able to distinguish messages coming through different receivers, the owner process of the bag and the receivers should assign them magic numbers, which are attached to the messages passing through and later returned to the receiving thread.

*transmitter* - This vertex is used for transmitting messages: Every transmitter is connected to exactly one receiver, a receiver may be connected to an unlimited number of transmitters. Transmitters may be created either by attaching to a receiver or by copying existing transmitters (without the owner of the receiver noticing) and they may be easily passed via communication channels. The messages passed through different transmitters to a certain receiver are undistinguishable. Transmitters have attributes which may be used to restrict the set of messages that can be passed through them. With these attributes, it is possible to transfer partial rights to access objects and also to use the transmitters not to pass messages but to prove rights to something.

*stamp* - Stamp is a "right to run". The stamp may be either *active, passive* or *bound*. The active stamp represent the top of an envelope stack and it is attached to a thread. When the active stamp is detached from the thread and waiting for execution, it becomes passive. Bound stamps form the middle of the envelope stack. Stamps are of two kinds - *pure stamps* (forming the bottoms of execution stacks) and stamp ends of *envelopes*. The former is used only to represent the right to run, the latter is also used for message passing.

*envelope* - Envelope is used to represent a message. In its life, the envelope may be used to pass a message repeatedly; there is no need to allocate resources for every message. Some of these envelope states are called *stamped*: Stamped envelopes have two ends, one of which acts as a stamp. A message is sent when it is put into an envelope, the envelope is then stamped and sent through a transmitter.

*receiver* - Receiver is able to receive envelopes, more exactly to pass envelopes to the bag attached to the receiver.

The following figure shows the pictograms used to denote various forms of vertices and entities mentioned in this document:

**Fig. 1.** Basic kernel entities

## 3.3    Basic Communication Scheme

The T4 communication system is based on channels formed by trusted kernel entities, like transmitters, receivers, bags, etc.

Fig. 2 shows a communication channel with some messages already transmitted. With such a channel, every transmitter holder (i.e. *sender*) can send a message through to the receiver holder (i.e. *addressee*). Messages coming to the receiver are passed to the corresponding bag where they form a queue. Every thread asking the bag for a message gets then the first available message in the queue.

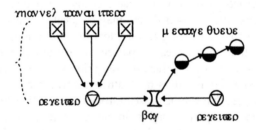

**Fig. 2.** Basic communication scheme

When a thread sends a message, it must use an envelope, fill in the appropriate message data and then ask the system for posting. Since all transmited envelopes must be stamped, the thread's active stamp is used (upon receiving, it becomes the addressee's active stamp). The sender loses it's stamp and to be able to run again, it must obtain another one. Incoming messages have stamps glued to them, so obtaining a new stamp is easy - the thread must receive a message. Therefore the sender must specify a bag from where it expects an answer.

When returning the envelope back to it's previous sender, the destination is known as the message envelope points to its former sender. In the other case, the thread must specify also the message destination (by specifying the transmitter through which the message should be sent).

## 3.4    Message Types

In the T4, there are several message types. The basic message type is the *short message* containing up to 4 words of 32 bits (one machine word) each. To send a longer message, one must use a *vanilla page* or simply *vanilla* (the term was - although slightly modified - borrowed from the SPRING system). It is also possible to add an *attachment* - a set of transmitters. For convenience, the authors have designed message passing so that there is no difference between sending messages of different types.

For purposes where 4 words are not enough, a vanilla page is used. Vanilla messages may store up to 4 KB in this page. The mechanism is the same for both vanilla and non-vanilla messages - there is one virtual page associated with every envelope (non-vanilla messages do not use it). The vanilla is mapped into the process's address space for the process to be able to access it. When sending the message which uses a vanilla, the vanilla page is mapped out of the sender's address space and mapped into the addressee's address space so that the destination process may use it without the data being affected by the sender.

Both short and vanilla messages may contain an attachment representing some rights represented by transmitters, eg. a right to share a memory region, a right to access some object or service, etc. There is no special kernel service for sending messages with attachments; their existence is evident from the envelope being sent. All vertices which are about to be sent out as an attachment, are detached from the sender's rack and "packed" in the message. While sending, no special actions are necessary, the attachment is transferred automatically.

## 4.    Message Passing

For safe and easy use of the communication primitives, the kernel maintains the *envelope stack* of request calls for every virtual thread, so it can be very easily returned back and back to the original request sender either as voluntary response or in case of process crash. There are three different modes of sending a message; they can be distinguished by what logically happens to the envelope stack:

*push* - the message is sent further to a server and a new envelope is added to the envelope stack;

*pop* - the message is returned to the sender of the last push into a bag specified by "return link";

*forward* - the message is forwarded to another destination without any changes in the envelope stack.

As mentioned above, the sending of a message is always coupled with receiving of another one, so the sender thread must always specify a bag from which it wants to receive a new message (and then a new stamp to run on). Note that message reception does not depend on the mode of message sending, for instance the message received after pushing one might be not only the response to the sent one but also another response or message pushed by another thread as well.

In the following sections, the reception phase of message sending primitives is not mentioned and the need to specify the bag for reception is not explicitly stated.

## 4.1    Push

This variant of sending can be viewed as sending a request from a client to a server.

The sending thread must specify *what* (the envelope to be sent) and *where* (the transmitter through which the message should be sent). The system then performs the following actions (Fig. 3a shows relevant information about the situation before the action):

−   A stack link is created for the specified envelope to point back to the stamp the sender was running with. Since the sender's stamp is already linked to another stamp using its stack link, those links form the envelope stack mentioned above. Every stack begins with an active or passive stamped envelope at top and leads through some bound stamped envelopes to a pure stamp forming its bottom

−   The envelope is changed to a stamped one, the stamp will serve as the receiving thread's right to run in the future

−   The envelope is put into the bag denoted by the communication channel

After completing the sending phase, the reception phase of the push primitive is performed as mentioned in the previous section.

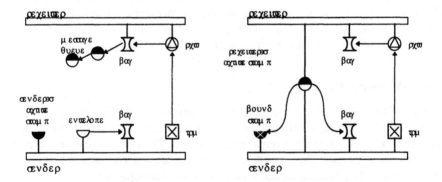

**Fig. 3.** Situation before and after push

So far, we have described the "push" mode of message sending. Now let us concern on receiving a message that has been pushed.

The receiver's thread may ask the destination bag for a message only when it has posted something else out and so it doesn't have any active stamp to run with. When such situation occurs, the first message in the queue is taken out and passed to the receiving thread. The received envelope's stamp end is parked into the receiver's rack (note that the other end of the stamped envelope is still parked in the sender's rack). This stamp becomes the thread's active stamp and the receiver may thus continue running and process the received message. For convenient usage, the thread also gets identification (magic number) of the receiver the message came through. The situation after receiving a pushed message is shown at Fig. 3b.

## 4.2　Pop

This variant is used mainly as an answer from a server back to the client - currently active envelope (the stamp end of which allows the server to run) is sent back to its original sender (i.e. the client).

The thread doesn't need to specify the destination as it is determined by the other end of the active stamp. Neither does it need to specify the envelope to be used to store the message, therefore the pop operation has no parameters other than the message contents (and the bag to receive next message as mentioned earlier).

When the client - the original sender of the push - withdraws the popped message from the bag's queue, it continues to run on the stamp it was running before the push while the message envelope is changed to unstamped one. After receiving the popped message, the situation is exactly the same as before the original push.

## 5.　Process Environment

In this section, we will give the reader an idea about the environment a process lives in. We will describe mainly the situation just after new process is born as it shows all the relevant relations between processes and between process and the system.

Every process has at least one rack. Any vertex must be linked from the rack for the process to be able to access it. It is possible a vertex comes as a part of a message; in that case, the process must explicitly ask the system for unpacking it and linking it to the rack (the system does it as an atomic action).

After being born, a process has the following vertices parked in his rack: one active stamp, one free envelope, one bag and one transmitter; the envelope is tied to the bag and the transmitter is connected through a via to a receiver somewhere else.

The stamp is the active stamp ("right to run") of the main thread. It is this thread the process begins to run with. For the environment to be the same for all new processes, the only way to ask for anything is to send a message using the transmitter; that is also why there is one free envelope created with every new process. For the process to receive anything, it needs also one bag where messages come. The initial transmitter is connected somewhere and it doesn't matter where. The only thing the process must know is that anything it requires must be asked for through that channel (e.g. establishing new connection to any kind of server, other process etc.).

# 6.    Current State and Future Work

Currently, the T4 is an operating prototype. The microkernel (both mono- and multiprocessor versions) is completed by now. Our future work will concentrate on the improvement of system services such as support for process migration, support for distributed memory sharing, etc. The most important (and the most interesting) tasks of future T4 development are:

−    An implementation of a UNIX environment emulator.
−    Fully transparent process migration.
−    Graphical user interface - based on the XWindow system.
− ,  Ports to other platforms.

Although the basic layout of the T4 is uncommon and may seem strange, our project showed that the basic paradigms used in the system design conformed to most of our expectations. Thus, our approach represents an acceptable tradeoff between the complexity of basic primitives and requirements imposed by intended applicability in the area of distributed systems.


# 7.    References

[1]    Acetta M., Baron R., Bolosky W., Golub D., Rashid R., Tevanian A., Young M.: "Mach: A New Kernel Foundation for UNIX Development", Summer USENIX Conference, 1986.

[2]    Bershad B.N., Anderson T.E., Lazowska E.D., Levy H.M.: *"Lightweight Remote Procedure Call"*, ACM Transactions on Computer Systems, 1990.

[3]    Hamilton G., Kougiouris P.: *"The Spring Nucleus: A Microkernel for Objects"*, USENIX Summer Conference, 1993.

[4]    Khalidi Y.A., Nelson M.N.: *"A Flexible External Paging Interface"*, Proceedings of the Usenix conference on Microkernels and Other Architectures, 1993.

[5]    Khalidi Y.A., Nelson M.N.: *"An Implementation of UNIX on an Object-oriented Operating System"*, USENIX Conference, 1993.

[6]    Khalidi Y.A., Nelson M.N.: *"The Spring Virtual Memory System"*, Sun Microsystems Laboratories Technical Report SMLI-93-3, 1993.

[7]    Mitchell J., Gibbons J., Hamilton G., Kessler P., Khalidi Y., Kougiouris P., Madany P., Nelson M., Powell M., Radia S.: *"An Overview of the Spring System"*, Proceedings of Compcon, 1994.

[8]    Rashid R., Tavenian A., Young M., Golub D., Baron R., Black D., Bolosky W., Chew J.: *"Machine-Independent Virtual Memory Management for Paged Uniprocessor and Multiprocessor Architectures"*, IEEE Transactions on Computers, 1988.

[9]    Rozier M., Abrossimov V., Armand F., Boule I., Gien M., Guillermont M., Herrman F., Kaiser C., Langlois S., Leonard P., and Neuhauser W.: *"Overview of the Chorus Distributed Operating System"*, USENIX Workshop on Micro-kernels and Other Kernel Architectures, 1992.

[10]   Tanenbaum A.S., van Renesse R., van Staveren H., Sharp G.J., Mullender S.J., Jansen J., van Rossum G.: *"Experiences with the Amoeba Distributed Operating System"*, Communications of the ACM, 1992.

# A Formal Representation for State Diagrams in the OMT Methodology

Elisa Bertino[1]   Donatella Castelli[2]   Federica Vitale[1]

[1] Dipartimento di Scienze dell'Informazione,
Università degli Studi di Milano (Milano - Italy)
[2] Istituto di Elaborazione dell'Informazione - CNR (Pisa - Italy)

**Abstract.** The paper proposes a formalization of the object and dynamic OMT models in terms of the Abstract Machine model and shows how certain relevant properties, such as whether a state is reachable, there are non-deterministic state transitions or cyclic state transitions, can be detected by using the proof mechanisms provide for Abstract Machine.

## 1 Introduction

Recent years have witnessed the widespread use of object-oriented methodologies for software analysis and development. Most of those methodologies provide "informal", graphical notations by using which designers can model objects, their properties and their behavior. Such notations enable a rapid development of the application model using intuitive user-friendly languages. While such notations are recognized to be useful and have contributed to the wide adoption of these methodologies, they are often ambiguous and not suitable for devising and analyzing useful properties of the specified models. In order to ensure the correctness of the software developed, validation mechanisms and tools must be introduced at every step of the analysis and development process.

Among the existing methodologies, the *Object Modeling Technique*(OMT) [RBP+91] is based on three types of models, each expressing different aspects of objects in a given application environment: the *object model*, the *dynamic model* and the *functional model*. The main qualifying aspect of OMT is thus its *completeness* in describing all aspects related to the application objects. However, the lack of formal foundations for the notations makes it difficult to devise and analyze relevant properties of the developed models. Recently, formalizations for OMT have been proposed in the scientific literature. Some of them either impose very restrictive conditions on the construction of OMT notation [HB94] or are not real formalizations of OMT [JVCH95]. Others are only partial formalizations as they either consider only the object model or the analysis stage (but not the design stage) [BC95, HC91].

In this paper, we propose a formal foundation for OMT in terms of the B-Method formal development method. This method has been chosen because it provides a model, the *Abstract Machine* which is able to represent both static and dynamic aspects of objects[Abr96]. Moreover, it covers not only the functional

*trace* diagrams. This specifies a sequence of events, and the sender and receiver of each event occurring during one particular execution of the system. Figure 1B) shows the event trace for the withdrawal operation in a bank.

Each state diagram consists of a set of states and several events. It describes how an object can change its state when an event occurs. A state change caused by an event is called a *transition*. The name of the event is over the state transition. Consider Figure 2: it shows the state diagrams related to the event trace in the Figure 1 B). If a customer wants to withdraw a certain amount of money from the bank, the operation is possible if there is enough money in the account; otherwise the customer can withdraw only up to the amount in the account. As we can see from the event *send_r* in the example, a transition may have a *condition* -in our example a condition is *[diff > 0]*. A guarded transition fires when its event occurs and the guard condition is true. An event can have some optional attributes -such as *send_r(diff)* in our example-, which can also be the object attributes. These are shown in parentheses after the event name and can appear in conditions. Moreover, an action can be associated with an event; this action is an invocation of a method which is defined in the class of the object -in our example the action *decrement(money)* is associated with the event *send_r(diff)*. Two kinds of action are possible in a state: the *entry* and the *exit* action. For example *check(money)* is the *entry* action within the state *VALUATION* of the *account* object. Another possibility is to have an *activity* in a state which describes the event that the object sends to another object, for example *estimate(money)*.

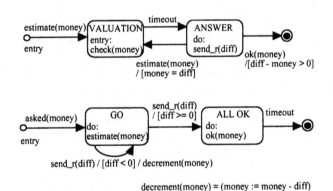

**Fig. 2.** State diagrams for the Account and the Withdrawal classes

In general when defining the state diagram, the designers make assumptions on the object model: on the attributes values by conditions, and on the operations defined in the class by method invocations. As we discussed earlier, the three models represent three different aspects of a given application domain, but they are not completely independent. Therefore problems may arise when the three models are integrated in the Object Design. In our example the value of *diff*, the attribute of the event *send_r*, is the difference between the amount of the account

specification but also the design phase by successive refinement steps. Finally, it provides a number of integrated tools supporting the development.

In our work, we show first how to map the object and dynamic models of OMT onto abstract machines, and then we show how certain relevant properties, such as whether a state is reachable, non-deterministic state transitions, cyclic state transitions, can be detected by using the automatic proof mechanisms on the abstract machines obtained by the mapping. To our knowledge, those properties have never been investigated before and no approaches, thus, exist for detecting them. The remainder of this paper is organized as follows. Section 2 presents a brief survey of OMT. Section 3 recalls notations concerning the B-Method. Section 4 presents our mapping strategy, whereas Section 5 presents our definition of state reachability and discusses the relevant properties.

## 2 Object Modeling Technique

The OMT methodology is based on three models: the *object model*, the *dynamic model* and the *functional model*. Using those models, a system is represented according to three related but different viewpoints, each capturing important aspects of the system, but all required for a complete description. The three models are not completely independent, since they often refer to components of the others. However each model can be examined and understood by itself to a large extent.

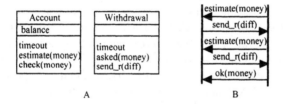

**Fig. 1.** A) Account and Withdrawal classes B) Event trace

In this paper we examine the first and the second models only. The *object model* represents the structural aspects of a system. It consists of a set of objects classes. Figure 1A) illustrates the object model for a BANK domain. This model consists of two classes, *Account* and *Withdrawal*. Each class lists a set of attributes -in our example the first class has attribute *balance* and the second one has no attribute- and a set of operations -in our example *timeout*, *estimate* and *check* in the *Account* class and *timeout*, *asked* and *send_r* in the *Withdrawal* class.

The *dynamic model* represents the control aspects of the modeled system. It consists of a set of state diagrams for each class each specifying the state transitions caused by an event sequence. Before defining the state diagram, the sequence of events and the objects exchanging events can both be specified using *event*

and the money which the customer wants to withdraw. The class *Withdrawal* receives the event *asked(money)* and sends the event *estimate(money)* to the object *account* to verify that the requested amount of money is available in the account. Thus, after the verification, the object *account* sends to the object *withdrawal* the answer through the event *send_r(diff)*. The action *decrement(money)* is the method defined in the class *Withdrawal*, but as we can see in Figure 2, the code of this operation increases the money and, therefore the *account* object is deadlocked because the condition over the event *estimate(money)* is not true and the event *ok(money)* will never arrive to the *account* object. If by contrast, we had not stated such condition over the transition from the state *ANSWER* to the state *VALUATION*, there would have been a loop between these states because the code of the action *decrement(money)* increases the money.

To avoid the above problems, the designers in practice do not very often use some OMT constructs, for example the event conditions. The goal of this work is to allow full use of the OMT notation by providing a tool to check deadlock, cyclic and non-deterministic situations and state reachability. To this aim we will give a formal representation of the object and dynamic models in terms of the Abstract Machine model illustrated briefly in the next Section.

## 3   B-Method

The B-Method is a formal method which supports the specification, the design by successive refinement steps, the integration, the code generation and the maintenance phases of software development. A single notation is used throughout these phases. This notation allows to interpret a software system as collection of interrelated *abstract machines* (AM). An AM comprises a description of a state together with the operations on that state. The machine account in Figure 3, for example, has a state defined by the variables *cc* and *balance* -initialized to zero- which must always satisfy the invariant properties of being, respectively, a subset of a given set ACCOUNT and a function from cc to the given set MONEY. The state of an AM can be modified only by invoking the listed operations -*timeout* in the example-. The operations are specified using the Generalized Substitution Language [Abr96]. The constructs of an AM have an axiomatic definition which renders it possible to prove properties such as, for example, that the given operations always preserve the invariant. AM can be constructed incrementally. To this aim a clause, *include*, can be specified to include in an AM the state of another machine and to make it possible to call to the operations of this machine in the including machine.

The B-Method interprets the software development as the definition of an initial AM, which represents the specification, and a step-wise refinement process which aims at producing an executable module. At each step, the proof of certain refinement proof obligations guarantees that the final code satisfies its initial specification. Integrated tools are currently available to support the B-Method development. These tools assist the designers in formalizing their applications and performing automatically syntax analysis, type checking, generation and demonstration of proof obligations on both the specification and refinements.

# 4 Mapping OMT onto B

Each class of the object model is mapped onto an abstract machine whose state variables and operations represent, respectively, the class attributes and operations. The invariant is the conjunction of the attributes type domain constraints and the constraints on the objects. In the initialization clause, the attribute values of the object are to the state variables of the AM. Each operation of the abstract machine is specified as the most abstract operation that does not break the invariant. Figure 3 shows the abstract machines corresponding to the two objects depicted in Figure 1A).

```
machine account
sets ACCOUNTS, MONEY
variables cc, balance
invariant (cc ⊆ (ACCOUNTS)) ∧
        (balance ∈ cc ⟶ MONEY)
initialization cc,balance:={},{}
operations
timeout(c) ≡ pre (c ∈ cc) ∧ I₁ ∧ I₂
        then ( cc:∈ I₁ ‖ balance :∈ I₂)
    ... end
```

```
machine withdrawal
sets WITHDRAWS
variables pp
invariant pp ⊆ WITHDRAWS
initialization pp:={}
operations
timeout(p) ≡ pre (p ∈ pp) ∧ I₁
        then pp :∈ I end;
    ...
end
```

**Fig. 3.** Account and withdrawal abstract machines

We can see the abstract machine of *Account* and *Withdrawal* classes: the given set $ACCOUNTS$ represents all possible instances of the class *Account* and the variable $cc$ is a subset of $ACCOUNTS$ which models the class *Account* extension. The state variable *balance* represents the attribute *balance*. Figure 3 shows the *timeout* operation only; the parameter $c$ identifies the object of the *Account* class over which the operation is carried out. We can see in the invariant clause the laws which must be always true. The first predicate is for the variable $cc$ -it is abbreviated as $I_1$ in the *timeout* operation- and the second one is for the *balance* variable -it is abbreviated as $I_2$ in the *timeout* operation-. The same applies to the *Withdrawal* class.

A state diagram is mapped onto an abstract machine, where the states of the diagram are represented by a machine state variable. This state variable takes its value from the set $STATUS$ whose elements are constants which name the diagram states. Each event of the diagram is mapped onto an operation which is specified as a before-after state transformation. The condition over the state transition related to the event is represented by a *guarded* substitution of the machine, and each invocation to the method is a *call* to an operation of the machine related to the class. This *call* is possible through the clause *includes* which is added to the abstract machine corresponding to the state diagram.

The Figure 4 shows the abstract machine corresponding to the state diagram depicted in Figure 2. Through the clause *includes*, the machine *dynaccount* can invoke the operation of the machine *account* and can see the variables of the same machine. The event that the *account* object sends to the *withdrawal* object is represented as comment in the *timeout* operation since it has no effects on the state of the sender object.

```
machine dynaccount
includes account
sets STATUS = {valuation, answer, conf}
variables st
invariant st ∈ cc ⟶ STATUS
initialization st:=conf
operations
timeout(c) ≡ pre (st = valuation) ∧ (c ∈ cc) then st := answer {|| send_r(diff)} end;
estimate(c,money) ≡ pre st = answer ∧ c ∈ cc
                    then if money = diff then st := valuation || check(money)
                                         else st := answer end end
       ... end
```

**Fig. 4.** State diagram abstract machine

An important observation is that each construct of the OMT notation is mapped onto one construct of AMN. Therefore, the mapping can be automatically performed. We can define the formal representation of the object model and, then, independently, the formal representation of the dynamic model as in OMT. When we write the machine *dynaccount*, we are only interested in knowing if some attributes or operations are defined in the class, we are not interested to know how the object is internally structured. When we define the state diagram, we make some assumptions on the attribute values and the methods which are defined in the object class; when the models are integrated the definitions must be consistent.

## 5   Proving state reachability

We show in this section how the following properties over the state diagram: (i) state reachability; (ii) non-deterministic state transitions; (iii) cyclic state transitions and (iv) deadlock in a state can be proved using the formal framework given in the previous sections. These properties mainly concern the dynamic model. However, as we have seen in Section 2, they depend on how the object class is structured. We can prove all the above properties as the proof of state reachability. Consider the example of the BANK domain, the object *account* either is deadlocked in the VALUATION state, or it goes from VALUATION to ANSWER state and comes back in a cyclic way. Therefore the object *account* will never reach the final state.

In a state diagram, a state $S_j$ is reachable from a state $S_i$, where $S_i$ is different from the initial state, if there is a state transition from $S_i$ to $S_j$ and the condition over the transition is true. The following definition formalizes this.

**Definition (Reachability)** *Let $S_i$ and $S_j$ be states. $S_j$ is reachable from $S_i$ if an operation $OP_j$ exists which is activated in $S_i$ and produces $S_j$ as output, such that the following condition is verified:*

$$P_j(z) \wedge (st = S_i) \wedge I \implies [OP_j] (st = S_j)$$

*where $P_j(z)$ are the preconditions over the event parameters and st and I are respectively the state variable and the invariant of the machine which represents the diagram.*

The above notion can be generalized to a sequence of states. Consider the diagram in Figure 5A) and suppose we want to determine whether state $S_j$ can be reached from state $S_0$. In the diagram, reachability of state $S_j$ is expressed through an event sequence from $S_0$ to $S_j$. This event sequence on the state diagram is an operation sequence $(SEQ_j)$ on the abstract machine. Therefore, we can define an AM which has only one operation. The specification of this operation carries the AM from state $S_0$ to state $S_j$. The state reachability proof means to prove that $SEQ_j$ is a refinement of the operation specification from $S_0$ to $S_j$. Notice that the goal is to prove the state reachability and the approach we use is a simple proof obligation on the Abstract Machine formal model: the refinement proof obligation.

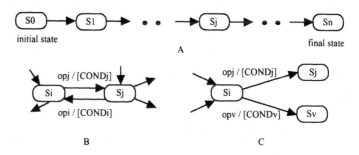

**Fig. 5.** A) A sequence of state B) Loop situation C) Non-deterministic situation

In the following we discuss how all the above properties can be reduced as the proof of state reachability. We refer the interested reader to [Vit96] for the formal definitions of those properties and other theoretical aspects.

**Cyclic state transitions and deadlock situation.** Consider Figure 5B). To determine whether such cycle may actually arise, we use the proof of state reachability. The cyclic situation exists if the following conditions are verified: (1) state $S_i$ is reachable from the initial state; (2) state $S_j$ is the only reachable state from state $S_i$; (3) state $S_i$ is the only reachable state from state $S_j$. All these conditions are proved as reachability proofs.

Consider Figure 2, in the *account* object state diagram there is a loop from the *ANSWER* state to the *VALUATION*, therefore the only possible transition from the *ANSWER* state is labeled *estimate(money)*. This transition brings the object in the *VALUATION* state and the only possible transition from this state is *timeout* which brings in the *ANSWER* state.

Otherwise, if the condition *[money=diff]* is imposed on the transition, the *account* object is deadlocked in the *ANSWER* state. Indeed any state can reached from the *ANSWER* state, because the event *ok(money)* will never arrive to the *account* object.

**Non-deterministic situation**. Consider Figure 5C). Suppose that the object is in state $S_i$, if events $OP_j$ and $OP_v$ arrive and the conditions on the two transitions are true, then it is possible to choose either of the two events. Therefore, a non-deterministic situation is possible. Thus, the non-deterministic situations exist if the following conditions are verified: (1) state $S_i$ is reachable from the initial state; (2) state $S_j$ is reachable from the state $S_i$; (3) state $S_v$ is reachable from the state $S_i$. All these conditions are proved as reachability proofs.

# 6   Concluding remarks

We have experimented our approach also in a University library application. We have first developed the OMT models for our applications by using the Paradigm Plus CASE tool. Then we have mapped the obtained models onto the appropriate abstract machines. These machines have been built using the B-Toolkit. Using this tool we have been able to execute automatically the test of the properties discussed in this paper. In carrying out this experience we have not encountered particular difficulties, this had confirmed the practical applicability of the approach proposed in this paper.

# References

[Abr96]    J. R. Abrial. *The B-Book.* to appear, 1996.

[BC95]     R. H. Bordeau and B. H.C. Cheng. A Formal Semantics for Object Model Diagrams. *IEEE Transaction on Software Engineering, 10,* 1995.

[HB94]     T. C. Hartrum and P. D. Bailor.   In *Teaching Formal Extensions of Informal-Based Object-Oriented Analysis Methodologies*, pages 389–409. Computer Science Education, 1994.

[HC91]     F. Hayes and D. Coleman. Coherent Models for Object-Oriented Analysis. In *Proc. of OOPSLA '91*, pages 171–183, 1991.

[JVCH95]  V. Jonckers, K. Verschaeve, L. Cuypers, and J. Heirbaut. OMT*, Bridging the Gap between Analysis and Design. 1995.

[RBP+91]  J. Rumbaugh, M. Blaha, W. Premerlani, F. Eddy, and W. Lorensen. *Object-Oriented Modeling and Design.* Prentice Hall, Englewood Cliffs, 1991.

[Vit96]    F. Vitale.   Analisi di Proprietà di Modelli Orientati ad Oggetti per lo Sviluppo di Sistemi Informativi. Dip. di Inf., Pisa, Tesi di Laurea, 1996.

# Feasible Real Random Access Machines

Vasco Brattka and Peter Hertling

Theoretische Informatik I, FernUniversität Hagen, D-58084 Hagen, Germany
e-mail: {vasco.brattka,peter.hertling}@fernuni-hagen.de

**Abstract.** We present a modified real RAM model which is equipped
with the usual discrete and real-valued arithmetic operations and with
a finite precision test $<_k$ which allows comparisons of real numbers only
up to a variable uncertainty $\frac{1}{k+1}$. Furthermore our *feasible RAM* has an
extended semantics which allows approximate computations. Using a
logarithmic complexity measure we prove that all functions computable
on a feasible RAM in time $\mathcal{O}(t)$ can be computed on a Turing machine
in time $\mathcal{O}(t^2 \cdot \log(t) \cdot \log\log(t))$. Vice versa all functions computable on
a Turing machine in time $\mathcal{O}(t)$ are computable on a feasible RAM in
time $\mathcal{O}(t)$. Thus our real RAM model does not only express exactly the
computational power of Turing machines on real numbers (in the sense
of Grzegorczyk), but it also yields a high-level tool for realistic time
complexity estimations on real numbers.

## 1  Introduction

The real random access machine (RAM) has a long tradition in computer science.
In computational geometry it is the main model of computability (cf. Preparata
& Shamos [17]) and in numerical analysis it has been used to describe complexity
(cf. Traub, Wasilkowski & Woźniakowski [19], Novak [15]). In the last years a
theory of complexity has been built upon this model (cf. Blum, Shub & Smale
[2], for a modification see Koiran [11]). The main advantage of the RAM model
seems to be that it is easy to describe and easy to handle. Computability is
described on the level of real numbers (which are regarded as entities) in terms
of the arithmetic operations and the order. This level of abstraction is very close
to scientific programming and numerical analysis.

Nevertheless, the model has serious disadvantages which should not be under-
estimated. Real numbers are infinite objects and in the real world we can only
handle finite portions of these objects. Thus one should carefully investigate
where it is admissible to leave the infinite nature of real numbers out of account
and where it is not. A suitable model for such an investigation is the Turing
machine (TM) model which just describes how to handle finite information. The
resulting notion of computability of real-valued functions seems to be the most
natural one (cf. Grzegorczyk [7], Lacombe [12], Pour-El & Richards [16], Ko [10],
Weihrauch [20, 21]). A central result of that investigation is that computable operations are continuous. The reason is that for computing any finite portion of
the output already a finite portion of the input is sufficient. This corresponds to
the well-known fact that tests like "$x = 0$?" are critical in practice (cf. Hertling

& Weihrauch [8]), hence to the problems of numerical stability (compare e.g. Burnikel, Mehlhorn & Schirra [6]). This insight led us to our modified real RAM model which on the one hand can precisely perform the continuous operations but which on the other hand only offers a continuous finite precision version of the discontinuous test $<$ and a continuous finite precision version of the staircase operation $\lfloor\ \rfloor$ which computes the integral part of a non-negative real number. A corresponding characterization of the class of computable real functions can be found in [3]. A prototype of an implementation of the feasible real RAM has been developed by Müller [14]. A different approach to the comparison of real RAMs with Turing machines was given by Hotz, Vierke & Schieffer [9].

Our feasible real RAMs (in the following for short: RAM) can be characterized by the following features: rational constants, arithmetic operations on $\mathbb{N}$ and $\mathbb{R}$, the usual tests $=, <$ on $\mathbb{N}$, a finite precision test $<_k$ with a variable uncertainty $\frac{1}{k+1}$ on $\mathbb{R}$, defined by

$$(x <_k y) \ni \begin{cases} \text{TRUE} : \Longleftrightarrow x < y \\ \text{FALSE} : \Longleftrightarrow x > y - \frac{1}{k+1} \end{cases}$$

for $x, y \in \mathbb{R}$, $k \in \mathbb{N}$, and a finite precision staircase operation, giving one of the values in $\lfloor x \rfloor_k := \{n \in \mathbb{N} \mid n - \frac{1}{k+1} < x < n + 1\} \cup \{0 \mid x < 0\}$ for $x \in \mathbb{R}$ and $k \in \mathbb{N}$, an extended approximative semantics, and a logarithmic cost measure.

One should notice that the cases in the definition of the finite precision test are not disjunct (cf. Figure 1). Similarly the result of the finite precision staircase operations is not always unique. Thus a weak kind of nondeterminism is introduced in our computations. In a realization of the feasible real RAM the result of the test in the uncertainty area and hence the computation path might depend on the precise representations of the real inputs. Nevertheless *each* computation path must lead to a reasonable result. What "reasonable" means is described by our extended semantics where a function $f : \mathbb{R} \to \mathbb{R}$ is *approximated* by a real RAM $M$ if $M$ with input $(x, k)$ yields a result $y$ with $|f(x) - y| < 2^{-k}$.

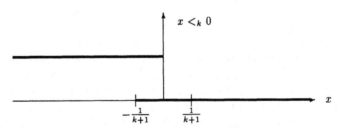

**Fig. 1.** The finite precision test

Our logarithmic time complexity measure will charge each operation with costs depending on the size of the operands. Especially the costs of the finite precision test $<_k$ will tend to infinity if $k$ tends to infinity. We leave out of consideration the fact that in reality (as on Turing machines) the time complexity of an operation does not only depend on the size of the operand $x$ but also on the demanded output precision $k$. This is justified by the fact that the basic arithmetic operations are *online computable* in polynomial time, i.e. there are polynomial-time Turing machine programs for these operations such that the output precision is equal to the input precision minus a certain delay depending on the input size.

The main result of our investigation shows that the logarithmic time complexity of our RAMs is closely related with the time complexity of Turing machines (in the sense of Ko [10], Müller [13] and Weihrauch [23, 21]), i.e. the following inclusions hold for the corresponding time complexity classes of functions (provided that $t$ fulfills some natural regularity properties):

$$\text{TIME}_{\text{TM}}(t) \subseteq \text{TIME}_{\text{RAM}}(t) \subseteq \text{TIME}_{\text{TM}}(t^2 \cdot \log(t) \cdot \log\log(t)).$$

We will start with the definition of our real RAMs and a short introduction of Turing machines in Sections 2 and 3. Section 4 will sketch the results. We will omit the proofs due to lack of space. They can be found in the full version of the paper (cf. [4]), together with an investigation of further topics as indirect addressing, uniform cost measures and extended sets of elementary operations.

## 2 Feasible Real Random Access Machines

We consider random access machines with two different sorts of registers: *natural* registers $n_i$ containing natural numbers (i.e. elements of $\mathbb{N} = \{0, 1, 2, \ldots\}$) and *real* registers $r_i$ containing real numbers where $i \in \mathbb{N}$. For simplicity of notation we usually do not distinguish between a register and its content.

**Definition 1 (RAMs).** A *random access machine (RAM)* is a triple $M = (X, Y, F)$. Here $X$ and $Y$ denote the *input space* and the *output space*, each a finite product of the spaces $\mathbb{N}$ and $\mathbb{R}$. We assume that with each input space and output space there is associated a fixed input mapping from $X$ to the *input registers* and a fixed output mapping from the *output registers* to $Y$. $F$ is a finite *flowchart* labeled by a finite set $Q \subseteq \mathbb{N}$ of nodes containing one initial node 0. With each node $q \in Q$ one operation out of Table 1 and a finite list of successor nodes are associated. If the operation is a test then there is a pair of successor nodes, else there is either one successor node or no successor node (then the node is a *final node*).

A flowchart can be viewed as a finite graph controlling the computations of the machine. In order to define the semantics of a RAM we have to explain the computation process of a RAM. Given an input the machine computes as follows: the machine starts in the initial node with the input in the according input registers. Then a computation path according to the flowchart $F$ is followed. Note that for one input there may be several computation paths, due to the nondeterminism induced by the finite precision tests and the finite precision staircase operation. If a division by zero is tried, then the computation just

| | op | cost(op) | explanation |
|---|---|---|---|
| assignment of constants | $n_i := m$ | 1 | $m \in \mathbb{N}$ |
| | $r_i := q$ | 1 | $q \in \mathbb{Q}$ |
| simple copy instructions | $n_i := n_j$ | $\lg(n_j)$ | |
| | $r_i := r_j$ | $\lg(r_j)$ | |
| mixed copy instructions | $r_i := n_j$ | $\lg(n_j)$ | |
| | $n_i := \lfloor r_j \rfloor_{n_k}$ | $\lg(r_j, n_k)$ | |
| natural arithm. operations | $n_i := n_j \otimes n_k$ | $\lg(n_j, n_k)$ | $\otimes \in \{+, \dot-, *, \mathrm{div}, \mathrm{mod}\}$ |
| real arithmetic operations | $r_i := r_j \otimes r_k$ | $\lg(r_j, r_k)$ | $\otimes \in \{+, -, *\}$ |
| | $r_i := r_j / r_k$ | $\lg(r_j, \frac{1}{r_k})$ | |
| tests | $n_i = n_j$ | $\lg(n_i, n_j)$ | |
| | $n_i < n_j$ | $\lg(n_i, n_j)$ | |
| | $r_i <_{n_k} r_j$ | $\lg(r_i, r_j, n_k)$ | |

**Table 1.** RAM operations and their costs

stops without giving any output. If a final state is reached the computation stops and the output can be read from the output registers.

Since for one input there may be different computation paths leading to different outputs it makes sense to speak of the *computed relation*. Under a *relation* we always understand a subset of a pair of spaces. For a relation $R \subseteq X \times Y$ the *domain* of $R$ is $\mathrm{dom}(R) = \{x \in X \mid (\exists y \in Y)(x, y) \in R\}$, and for $x \in X$ we define $R(x) := \{y \in Y \mid (x, y) \in R\}$.

**Definition 2 (Semantics of RAMs).** A RAM $M = (X, Y, F)$ computes the relation $R_M \subseteq X \times Y$ defined by $R_M := \{(x, y) \mid x \in \mathrm{dom}(R_M)$ and there is a computation path on input $x$ with output $y\}$, where $\mathrm{dom}(R_M) := \{x \in X \mid$ every computation path of $M$ on input $x$ reaches a final node $\}$.

Note that for $x \in \mathrm{dom}(R_M)$ every computation path must lead to a final node. By König's Lemma one can prove:

**Lemma 3 (Finiteness of computation trees).** *Let $M$ be a RAM. For each input $x \in \mathrm{dom}(R_M)$ there are only finitely many computation paths of $M$.*

We introduce two time complexity measures for RAMs. In the uniform time complexity the single operations are just counted. For the logarithmic time complexity we have to define the cost of a single operation. For $x \in \mathbb{N}$ or $x \in \mathbb{R}$ we use $\lg(x) = 1 + \lfloor \log(\max\{|x|, 1\}) \rfloor$. Here log denotes the binary logarithm: $\log(x) := \log_2(x)$. For $x = (x_1, \ldots, x_k)$ we use $\lg(x) = \max\{\lg(x_i) \mid i = 1, \ldots, k\}$. The cost $cost(op)$ of an elementary operation $op$ is defined by the right side of Table 1. In most cases it is essentially the logarithmic size of the operands.

**Definition 4 (Time complexities of a RAM).** Let $M = (X, Y, F)$ be a RAM. The *uniform time complexity*[1] $u_M :\subseteq X \to \mathbb{N}$ is defined by $\mathrm{dom}(u_M) :=$

---

[1] We use the notation $f :\subseteq X \to Y$ for a *partial function* $f$ with domain $\mathrm{dom}(f) \subseteq X$.

$\mathrm{dom}(R_M)$ and $u_M(x) :=$ maximum of the length of all computation paths on input $x$ for $x \in \mathrm{dom}(R_M)$. The *logarithmic time complexity* $t_M :\subseteq X \to \mathbb{N}$ is defined by $\mathrm{dom}(t_M) := \mathrm{dom}(R_M)$ and $t_M(x) := \max_{comp.\ paths\ on\ x}\{\sum_{op} cost(op)\}$ for $x \in \mathrm{dom}(R_M)$ where the last sum is over all operations $op$ in a computation path on input $x$ and the maximum is over all computation paths on input $x$.

Note that in both definitions the maximum exists by Lemma 3. The rational functions with rational coefficients can be computed directly by RAMs but for example $\exp(x)$ can only be approximated (this is true also in the classical real RAM model). Therefore we define the *approximated functions* and their time complexity.

**Definition 5 (Relations approximating functions).** Let $(Y, d)$ be a metric space. A relation $R \subseteq (X \times \mathbb{N}) \times Y$ *approximates* a function $f :\subseteq X \to Y$ if $\mathrm{dom}(f) \times \mathbb{N} \subseteq \mathrm{dom}(R)$ and $d(f(x), y) < 2^{-n}$ for all $x \in \mathrm{dom}(f)$, $n \in \mathbb{N}$ and $y \in R(x, n)$.

In the next two definitions we assume that $X = X_1 \times \ldots \times X_n$ and $Y = Y_1 \times \ldots \times Y_m$ are finite products with $X_i, Y_j \in \{\mathbb{N}, \mathbb{R}\}$. On such product spaces we use the distance induced by the maximum norm: $d(y, y') = |y - y'| := \max\{|y_1 - y_1'|, \ldots, |y_m - y_m'|\}$, for $y, y' \in Y$.

**Definition 6 (RAMs approximating functions).** For $t :\subseteq X \times \mathbb{N} \to \mathbb{N}$ a function $f :\subseteq X \to Y$ is said to be *approximated* by a RAM $M = (X \times \mathbb{N}, Y, F)$ *in time* $t$ if $R_M$ approximates $f$ and $t_M(x, k) \le t(x, k)$ for all $(x, k) \in \mathrm{dom}(f) \times \mathbb{N}$.

**Definition 7 (Time complexity class).** For $t :\subseteq X \times \mathbb{N} \to \mathbb{N}$ we define

$$\mathrm{TIME}_{\mathrm{RAM}}(t) := \{f :\subseteq X \to Y \mid Y \text{ is a finite product of } \mathbb{N} \text{ and } \mathbb{R} \text{ and there is a RAM } M \text{ approximating } f \text{ in time } \mathcal{O}(t)\}.$$

Since the feasible real RAM model contains the classical discrete RAM model (for computations over $\mathbb{N}$) one can hope to obtain a polynomial equivalence between TM time complexity classes and feasible real RAM time complexity classes only for the logarithmic time complexity. This eqivalence will be given in Section 4.

## 3 Turing Machines

In order to compute a function $f :\subseteq \mathbb{R} \to \mathbb{R}$ by a Turing machine one uses suitable representations $\delta :\subseteq \Sigma^\omega \to \mathbb{R}$ of the real numbers. Then one can use a name $p \in \Sigma^\omega$ of an argument $x \in \mathrm{dom}(f)$ as an oracle and for input $k \in \mathbb{N}$ one can compute a prefix of precision $k$ of a name $q \in \Sigma^\omega$ for $f(x)$ (cf. Ko [10]). Or one can use $p$ as an input for a Turing machine which computes without halt a name $q$ (cf. Weihrauch [21]). Here we use a slightly modified version of Ko's approach, which we call *approximation* of real functions.

Our Turing machines have finitely many one-way read only input tapes, finitely many work tapes, and finitely many one-way write only output tapes.

They are controlled by a finite flowchart program. They may have infinite input, but for valid input they must stop after finitely many steps producing finite output. We skip the precise definitions.

We use the *binary notation* for $\mathbb{N}$ and we introduce a *representation* of $\mathbb{R}$. From now on we fix our alphabet to be $\Sigma := \{0, 1, \bar{1}, \cdot\}$. Since the usual binary representation for real numbers is not suitable already by topological reasons (cf. Weihrauch [21]) we use the *signed-digit representation* (cf. Avizienis [1]). This representation has an additional negative digit $-1$ (written as $\bar{1}$). It satisfies all properties necessary for a complexity theory (cf. Schröder [18]).

**Definition 8 (Binary notation).** The *binary notation* $\delta_{\mathbb{N}} :\subseteq \Sigma^* \to \mathbb{N}$ is defined by $\delta_{\mathbb{N}}(a_n...a_0) := \sum_{i=0}^{n} a_i 2^i$ for all $a_n...a_0 \in \{0,1\}^*$, $n \geq 0$ such that $a_n \neq 0$ if $n > 0$. For $k \in \mathbb{N}$ we define $\widehat{k} := \delta_{\mathbb{N}}^{-1}(k)$.

**Definition 9 (Signed-digit representation).** The *signed-digit representation* $\delta_{\mathbb{R}} :\subseteq \Sigma^{\omega} \to \mathbb{R}$ is defined by $\delta_{\mathbb{R}}(a_n...a_0 \cdot a_{-1}a_{-2}...) := \sum_{i=n}^{-\infty} a_i 2^i$ for all $p = a_n...a_0 \cdot a_{-1}a_{-2}... \in \Sigma^{\omega}, n \geq -1$, such that $a_n \neq 0$ if $n \geq 0$, $a_n a_{n-1} \notin \{1\bar{1}, \bar{1}1\}$ if $n \geq 1$, and $a_i \in \{\bar{1}, 0, 1\}$ for $i \leq n$.

For finite words $w$ with $w0^{\omega} \in \mathrm{dom}(\delta_{\mathbb{R}})$ we sometimes use $\delta_{\mathbb{R}}(w) := \delta_{\mathbb{R}}(w0^{\omega})$. If $X = X_1 \times ... \times X_n$ is a finite product of $\{\mathbb{N}, \mathbb{R}\}$, then by $\delta_X$ we denote the representation $\delta_{X_1} \times ... \times \delta_{X_n}$.

Now we can define what it means that a number function is approximated by a Turing machine in a certain time. Since our complexity measures shall be absolute measures we have to ignore the natural parts of numbers while counting the digits. Let $k \in \mathbb{N}$. A word $w$ is called a *k-approximation* of a real number $x$ if it is a prefix of a $\delta_{\mathbb{R}}$-name of $x$ having exactly $k$ digits after the binary point. Let $x = (x_1, ..., x_n)$ be a vector of naturals and reals. A *k-approximation* of $x$ is a vector $w = (w_1, ..., w_n)$ of words such that for each natural number $x_j$ we have $w_j = \widehat{x_j}$ and for each real $x_j$ the word $w_j$ is a $k_j$-approximation of $x_j$ where $k = \min\{k_j \mid x_j \text{ is real}\}$. Thus, if $w$ is a $k$-approximation of an $x \in X$ then $d(\delta_X(w), x) \leq 2^{-k}$. If $q$ is a name for a real or a natural then $q[m]$ is the prefix of $q$ which is an $m$-approximation. If $p = (p_1, ..., p_n) \in \mathrm{dom}(\delta_X)$ then $p[m] := (p_1[m], ..., p_n[m])$.

**Definition 10 (Approximation of number functions by TMs).** Let $f :\subseteq X \to Y$ be a function with $X = X_1 \times ... \times X_n$ and $Y = Y_1 \times ... \times Y_m$, where $X_1, ..., X_n, Y_1, ..., Y_m \in \{\mathbb{N}, \mathbb{R}\}$. Let $M$ be a Turing machine and let $t :\subseteq X \times \mathbb{N} \to \mathbb{N}$ be a function. Then $M$ *approximates* $f$ in *time* $t$ if for any $x \in \mathrm{dom}(f)$, any $p \in \delta_X^{-1}\{x\}$, and any $k \in \mathbb{N}$ the following is true:

1. On input $(p, \widehat{k})$ $M$ stops after at most $t(x, k)$ steps,
2. and $f_M(p, \widehat{k})$ is a $k'$-approximation of $f(x)$ for some $k' \geq k$.

If the output does not contain a real component then we often omit the precision parameter $k$ and speak of a *computation* of the function rather than of an approximation. We are now able to define the time complexity classes for the Turing machine model.

**Definition 11 (Time complexity class).** *Let $X$ be a finite product of $\mathbb{N}$ and $\mathbb{R}$ and $t :\subseteq X \times \mathbb{N} \to \mathbb{N}$ be a function. Then*

$$\text{TIME}_{\text{TM}}(t) := \{f :\subseteq X \to Y \mid Y \text{ is a finite product of } \mathbb{N} \text{ and } \mathbb{R} \text{ and}$$
$$\text{there is a TM approximating } f \text{ in time } \mathcal{O}(t)\}.$$

## 4  Results

In this section we sketch the main results of our investigation. The key result is the following:

**Theorem 12 (Time complexity of RAMs and TMs).** *Let $t :\subseteq X \times \mathbb{N} \to \mathbb{N}$ be a function. Then*

$$\text{TIME}_{\text{TM}}(t) \subseteq \text{TIME}_{\text{RAM}}(t) \subseteq \text{TIME}_{\text{TM}}(t^2 \cdot \log(t) \cdot \log\log(t))$$

*provided that $\lg(x, k) \in \mathcal{O}(t(x, k))$ for the first inclusion and $\lg(x) + k + t(x, k + 1) \in \mathcal{O}(t(x, k))$ for the second inclusion.*

**Proof.** (Idea.) Indeed we prove a slightly stronger result for the second inclusion. Let $F : \mathbb{N} \to \mathbb{N}$ be a function such that the time complexity of the multiplication of two binary $n$-bit integers is in $\mathcal{O}(F(n))$ and such that $F(n)/n$ is nondecreasing and $(\forall c_1, c_2 > 0)(\exists c_3)(\forall n > 0)\, F(c_1 n + c_2) \leq c_3 F(n)$. An example for $F(n)$ is the Schönhage-Strassen-bound $n \cdot \log(n) \cdot \log\log(n)$. Then $\text{TIME}_{\text{RAM}}(t) \subseteq \text{TIME}_{\text{TM}}(t \cdot F(t))$.

The basic idea for the proof is to simulate a computation of the RAM $M$ step by step using finite prefixes of the input with exponentially growing length until the precision of the output is sufficiently large. During the simulation of the elementary operations of the RAM one has to guarantee that the input information is used efficiently, i.e. not too many input digits are wasted. Therefore, in order to simulate the elementary operations we use *online* TMs which have a sufficiently small input lookahead.

The basic idea for the first inclusion is to simulate Turing machine tapes by small real numbers in an enlarged $q$-adic number system. Tape movements are simulated by multiplication and division, where $q$ is sufficiently large such that the read commands on the simulated Turing tapes can be performed by the finite precision staircase operation $\lfloor \rfloor_{q-2}$. Notice that we do not need indirect addressing on the RAM to establish the first inclusion. □

In the full version of the paper (cf. [4]) we have also investigated RAMs with *indirect addressing* and *restricted* RAMs, such that there is a constant $c > 0$ such that at least for one factor $y$ in each multiplication and for the divisor $z$ in each division of the RAM $|y| \leq c$ and $|z| \geq 1/c$ holds. If one replaces RAMs in Theorem 12 by RAMs with indirect adressing or by restricted RAMs with the *uniform time complexity measure* and if one substitutes $t^4 \cdot \log(t)^2 \cdot (\log\log(t))^2$ for $t^2 \cdot \log(t) \cdot \log\log(t)$, then Theorem 12 remains true.

Furthermore, if one equippes RAMs with additional elementary operations, such as the exponential function exp and the logarithm function ln on the real numbers and if one substitutes $t^2 \cdot \log(t)^2 \cdot \log\log(t)$ for $t^2 \cdot \log(t) \cdot \log\log(t)$, then Theorem 12 also remains true.

# References

1. A. Avizienis, Signed–Digit Number Representations for Fast Parallel Arithmetic, *IRE Transactions on Electronic Computers* vol. **EC–10** (1961) 389–400
2. L. Blum, M. Shub & S. Smale, On a theory of computation and complexity over the real numbers: $NP$-completeness, recursive functions and universal machines, *Bull. of the Amer. Math. Soc.* **21** (1989) 1–46
3. V. Brattka, Recursive characterization of computable real-valued functions and relations, *Theoretical Computer Science* **162** (1996) 45–77
4. V. Brattka & P. Hertling, Feasible real random access machines, Informatik Berichte 193, FernUniversität Hagen (1995)
5. R.P. Brent, Fast Multiple-Precision Evaluation of Elementary Functions, *J. of the ACM* **23**, No. 2 (1976) 242–251
6. C. Burnikel, K. Mehlhorn & S. Schirra, On degeneracy in geometric computations, *Proc. of the 5th ACM-SIAM Symp. on Discrete Algorithms* (1994) 16–23
7. A. Grzegorczyk, On the definition of computable real continuous functions, *Fund. Math.* **44** (1957) 61–71
8. P. Hertling & K. Weihrauch, Levels of degeneracy and exact lower complexity bounds for geometric algorithms, *Proc. of the Sixth Can. Conf. on Comp. Geometry* (1994) 237–242
9. G. Hotz, G. Vierke & B. Schieffer, Analytic machines, Electronic Colloquium on Computational Complexity, TR 95-025 (1995)
10. K.-I Ko, *Complexity Theory of Real Functions*, Birkhäuser, Boston (1991)
11. P. Koiran, A weak version of the Blum-Shub-Smale model, *Proc. 34th IEEE Symposium on Foundations of Computer Science* (1993) 486–495
12. D. Lacombe, Extension de la notion de fonction récursive aux fonctions d'une ou plusieurs variables réelles I-III, Comptes Rendus **240/241** (1955) 2478-2480/13-14,151-153,1250-1252
13. N.Th. Müller, Computational complexity of real functions and real numbers, Informatik Berichte 59, FernUniversität Hagen (1986)
14. N.Th. Müller, Towards a real real RAM: a prototype using C++, Proc. of the Workshop on Computability and Complexity in Analysis, Trier (1996) 59–66
15. E. Novak, The real number model in numerical analysis, *Journal of Complexity* **11**, No. 1 (1995) 57–73
16. M.B. Pour-El & J. Richards, *Computability in Analysis and Physics*, Springer, Berlin (1989)
17. F. Preparata & M. Shamos, *Computational Geometry*, Springer, New York (1985)
18. M. Schröder, Topological Spaces Allowing Type 2 Complexity Theory, Proceedings of the Workshop on Computability and Complexity in Analysis 95, Informatik Berichte 190, FernUniversität Hagen (1995)
19. J. Traub, G. Wasilkowski & H. Woźniakowski, *Information-Based Complexity*, Academic Press, New York (1988)
20. K. Weihrauch, *Computability*, Springer, Berlin (1987)
21. K. Weihrauch, A Simple Introduction to Computable Analysis, Informatik Berichte 171, FernUniversität Hagen (1995)
22. K. Weihrauch, On the complexity of online computations of real functions, *Journal of Complexity* **7** (1991) 380–394
23. K. Weihrauch & Ch. Kreitz, Type 2 computational complexity of functions on Cantor's space, *Theoretical Computer Science* **82** (1991) 1–18

# Temporal Conversion Functions
# for Multitemporal Relational Databases

Cristina De Castro

C.S.I.TE. C.N.R. - D.E.I.S.

Italian National Research Council - University of Bologna

Bologna, Italy, 40136

## Abstract

*Most research in the field of algebras for temporal relational databases concerns the study of operations within each of the formats transaction-time, valid-time, bitemporal and snapshot. Nevertheless, data of different temporal format (multitemporal relational data) should be allowed to interact. Two possible scenarios for this problem are: (1) federated databases, where the interaction is required of databases of different temporal format; (2) databases supporting selective versioning, where, due to the different update frequencies, the attributes are maintained in tables of different temporal formats. A solution to this interoperability problem is neither straightforward nor univocal, since the semantics differences among such data are quite deep. As suggested in [DGS94] for the multitemporal natural join, a first step for the definition of a multitemporal relational algebra can be the conversion to a common temporal format for the execution of operations. The semantic criteria at the basis of the temporal conversion functions in [DGS94] have been long debated for their safeness in the deduction or reconstruction of temporal information. In this paper we revise such criteria, discuss their problems and present several alternative solutions.*

**Keywords:** *Multitemporal Relational Data, Temporal Conversion Functions*

## 1 Background on Temporal Semantics

In current bibliography on temporal databases there is a common agreement for the support of at least two different and independent time dimensions: *transaction-time* and *valid-time*. Transaction-time tells when an information is recorded or updated in a database, it is defined by the system and can only grow. Due to such features, transaction-time can be considered the *database time*. Valid-time tells when an event occurs, occurred or is expected to occur in the real world, it is defined by the user and can concern present, past or future events. In this sense, valid time is the *real world time*. According to the temporal dimensions they support, temporal relations can be classified as *monotemporal* (transaction- or valid-time) , *bitemporal* (both time dimensions) or *snapshot* (no time dimension) [TCG$^+$93].

In the following, we introduce the adopted temporal notation and, by means of some examples, show the semantics differences among the temporal formats. As a matter of fact, such differences play a fondamental role in the definition of the temporal conversion functions.

## 1.1 Temporal Notation

In this paper we adopt the *Bitemporal Conceptual Data Model* (BCDM in [TCG$^+$93]) for temporal representation, since it turns out to be an efficient tool for the algebraic definition and the study of temporal conversion functions. In this model, time is represented by disjoint unions [1] of discrete intervals, called *temporal elements*. A temporal element is composed of *chronons*, where a chronon is a non-decomposable interval of time, whose prefixed duration $p$ represents the chosen granularity of time (days, months, years, etc.). Therefore, temporal data are assigned a time they refer to, in terms of temporal elements.

A temporal relational database is an extension of the traditional concept of relational database, to which temporal attributes are added. In a temporal environment, the role of the traditional key, which usually identifies an object (entity or relationship), is assumed by a time-invariant identifier, such as a system defined *surrogate* [TCG$^+$93] [2]. In this case, a time-invariant identifier identifies the collection of the versions of an object. Such collection is called *time-sequence* [TCG$^+$93] or *history* in [GST91]. The temporal attributes identify each version within a history, and thus they become part of the *temporal key* [TCG$^+$93]. In the examples, for the sake of simplicity, the name of a person is assumed to be the time-invariant identifier, even if this is not at all correct. Moreover, for the sake of brevity, the examples refer to only one history.

In order to formally define a temporal relation, we need the following definition: given a time-invariant identifier $k$, a set of non temporal attributes $r$, a temporal format $X$, where $X \in \{s, t, v, b\}$ (snapshot, transaction-time, valid-time, bitemporal), and a temporal element $\mathcal{T}_X$ of format $X$, a version along the temporal dimension $X$ can be defined as $r_X = (k, r, \mathcal{T}_X)$ and a relation of temporal format $X$ can thus be defined as a set $R_X$ of versions $r_X$.

The symbol 0 is used to denote the run-time of the first transaction and the minimum value of valid-time. $NOW$ denotes the current transaction time and the present valid time. The symbol $UC$ (*Until Changed*) refers to transaction-time and means that no further update has occurred yet. The symbol $FOREVER$ refers to valid-time and means that the end of data validity has not been specified. The full temporal domains of transaction-time, valid-time and the bitemporal one are thus:

---

[1]The BCDM representation and other temporal representations are discussed in 1.3. In particular, the problem of time representation atomicity is taken into account.

[2]The concept of surrogate is used and was first defined in other environments, in order to solve the problem of the unique identification of objects

$$\mathcal{U}_t = \{0 .. UC\} \quad \mathcal{U}_v = \{0 .. FOREVER\} \quad \mathcal{U}_b = \mathcal{U}_t \times \mathcal{U}_v$$

We say that: a transaction-time tuple $(k, r, \mathcal{T}_t)$ is *current* if $NOW \in \mathcal{T}_t$; a valid-time tuple $(k, r, \mathcal{T}_v)$ is *present* if $NOW \in \mathcal{T}_v$; a bitemporal tuple $(k, r, \mathcal{T}_b)$ is *current* if $\exists\, t \in \mathcal{U}_v : (NOW, t) \in \mathcal{T}_b$.

## 1.2  Semantics of the Temporal Relations

Suppose that data about the employees are maintained in temporal relations and that John gets his salary raised from 3.000 to 3.500. Let us consider the different results produced in case the data are maintaned in a transaction-time relation or in a valid-time one. The query itself is different in the two cases. If data are stored in a transaction-time relation (see Tab. 1, which represents the history of John), due to the following query $Q_1$:

```
UPDATE T_EMPLOYEE
SET SALARY = 3.500
WHERE NAME = 'John'
```

the relation T_EMPLOYEE is updated as shown in Tab. 2: a new record with the new value of salary is inserted on $\{NOW..UC\}$ and becomes the current version of John; the tuple (John, Engineer, 3.000, $\{92..UC\}$) is *archived* by setting the symbol UC to the finite value $NOW = 1996$ of the update.

In summary, for each history, transaction-time relations maintain all the versions inserted or updated in successive transactions (the current version and the archived versions).

| NAME | JOB | SALARY | $\mathcal{T}_t$ |
|------|-----|--------|-----|
| John | Engineer | 3.000 | $\{92 .. UC\}$ |

Table 1: Transaction-time relation T_EMPLOYEE before update

| NAME | JOB | SALARY | $\mathcal{T}_t$ |
|------|-----|--------|-----|
| John | Engineer | 3.000 | $\{92 .. 96\}$ |
| John | Engineer | 3.500 | $\{96 .. UC\}$ |

Table 2: Transaction-time relation T_EMPLOYEE after update $Q_1$

Let us consider the update of the valid-time relation V_EMPLOYEE in Tab. 3. Due to the following query $Q_2$:

```
UPDATE V_EMLOYEE
SET SALARY = 3.500
WHERE NAME = 'John'
VALID IN [1994 .. 1997]
```

V_EMPLOYEE is updated as shown in Tab. 4: a new record with the new salary is recorded with the specified valid-time pertinence {94..97}. The record (in this particular case only one) whose valid-time temporal element overlaps {94..97} gets its temporal pertinence reduced to the original one {90..$FOREVER$} minus {94..97}. Therefore, let us observe that, in case of valid-time versioning, there can be loss of data. such loss can be total if the validity of the update covers completely the validity of previous data.

In summary, for each history, valid time relations maintain the *most recently inserted* versions, each relative to a distinct valid-time interval (in this sense, valid-time tables maintain current versions only).

As far as the bitemporal and snapshot formats are concerned, bitemporal relations support both transaction and valid-time and thus, for each history, they maintain all the valid-time versions recorded in successive transactions (current and non current versions). Snapshot relations do not support time: for each represented entity, they maintain only the most recently inserted (current) version.

| NAME | JOB | SALARY | $T_v$ |
|------|------|--------|-------|
| John | Engineer | 3.000 | {90 .. FOREVER} |

Table 3: Valid-time relation V_EMPLOYEE before update

| NAME | JOB | SALARY | $T_v$ |
|------|------|--------|-------|
| John | Engineer | 3.000 | {90 .. 94} $\cup$ {97 .. FOREVER} |
| John | Engineer | 3.500 | {94 .. 97} |

Table 4: Valid-time relation V_EMPLOYEE after update $Q_2$

## 1.3  BCDM vs Interval Timestamping

Consider the example of query $Q_2$ (Tabs. 3, 4): the tuple (John, Engineer, 3.000, {90..$FOR.$}) becomes (John, Engineer, 3.000, {90..94} $\cup$ {97..$FOR.$}), that is neither an atomic value, nor a pair of an interval endpoints. As a matter of fact, the BCDM relaxes the atomicity constraint on the time fields. This long dibated feature wants to avoid data duplication as much as possible. This problem is, in fact, intrinsic to temporal databases and causes great problems both in data manipulation, retrieval and storage. Many people in the temporal database community now agree the BCDM can solve these problems and, sometimes mixing the conceptual and the physical level, accept to call the BCDM 1NF, providing that variable-length string can be used. Another time representation (interval timestamping at tuple level [TCG+93]) represents each time dimension by means of two fields, i.e. the endpoints of a time interval. For instance, FROM and TO being the endpoints ov valid-time intervals, the tuple (John, Engineer, 3.000, FROM = 90, TO = FOREVER) would be split in two identical tuples: (John, Engineer, 3.000, 90, 94) and (John, Engineer, 3.000,

97, FOREVER). In general, with such a representation, a valid-time update duplicates each overlapped record; in case of bitemporal data, three tuples are produced; this problem does not exist for transaction-time data due to the semantics of transaction-time itself. In summary, the adoption of the BCDM forces to revise the very concept of temporal atomicity and the related normalization problems.

## 2  Temporal Conversion Functions

The conversion from a temporal format to another is based on four operations: *addition of transaction-time, elimination of transaction-time, addition of valid-time, elimination of valid-time.*

The explicit definition of the temporal conversion from a temporal format to another will be defined as the direct application of one of the following conversion functions or the composition of two of them.

In the figures and in the following, the symbol $\mathcal{T}_s$ is used to denote the snapshot format, the symbols $MAP_{XY}(\mathcal{T}_X)$, $MAP_{XY}(r_X)$ and $MAP_{XY}(R_X)$ denote respectively the translation from the temporal format $X$ to the temporal format $Y$ of the temporal element $\mathcal{T}_X$, of the tuple $r_X$ and of the table $R_X$. Since the temporal functions act on temporal elements, the following definitions concern the temporal elements of tuples and the conversion of a tuple $r_X = (k, r, \mathcal{T}_X)$ and of a table $R_X$ from the temporal format $X$ to the temporal format $Y$ are respectively defined as:

$$MAP_{XY}(r_X) =^{def} (k, r, MAP_{XY}(\mathcal{T}_X))$$
$$MAP_{XY}(R_X) =^{def} \{MAP_{XY}(r_X) \mid r_X \in R_X\}$$

The temporal conversions maps defined in [DGS94] are based on the following four criteria:

**Addition of transaction-time:** snapshot and valid-time data are current, therefore, when transaction-time is added, such data can be associated to the transaction-time element $\{NOW\ ..\ UC\}$. No extension is ever possible along transaction-time beyond the current transaction-time $NOW$. As a matter of fact, any conjecture on the effective instant when data were stored would be definitely arbitrary and unsafe. The conversion is thus formally defined as:

$$ADD_t(\mathcal{T}_X) = \begin{cases} \{NOW\ ..\ UC\} \times \mathcal{T}_v & \text{if } X = v \\ \{NOW\ ..\ UC\} & \text{if } X = s \end{cases}$$

**Elimination of transaction-time:** when transaction-time is dropped, snapshot or valid-time temporal-elements are the target format, thus only the current tuples are retrieved. Thus the map can be formally defined as:

$$DROP_t(\mathcal{T}_X) = \begin{cases} \{t \in \mathcal{T}_v : (NOW, t) \in \mathcal{T}_b\} & \text{if } X = b \\ \mathcal{T}_s & \text{if } X = t \ \wedge \ NOW \in \mathcal{T}_t \end{cases}$$

**Addition of valid-time:** snapshot data are considered valid in the present but can also be considered valid in the future, since it cannot be forecasted if a value will be modified or not. Therefore, when valid time is added, snapshot data can be associated to the valid-time temporal element $\{NOW \ .. \ FOREVER\}$. No conjecture can be made on the effective beginning of their validity, thus no extension beyond the present valid time instant $NOW$ is safe, therefore the map can be defined as:

$$ADD_v(\mathcal{T}_s) = \{NOW \ .. \ FOREVER\}$$

As far as transaction-time data are concerned, as first suggested in [DGS94], suppose you move along the transaction-time axis: *at each transaction-time instant you consider the data you read as valid.* In other words, the data versioning managed by the system along transaction time can also be reflected on the valid-time axis, reconstructing the view a user had throughout the database life, that is the bitemporal data portion seen by a *diagonal user* (for the concept of *user* see [BG93]). The extension to valid-time of a transaction-time temporal element with one component was thus first defined as $ADD_v(\mathcal{T}_t) = \mathcal{T}_b$, where $\mathcal{T}_b$ is:

$$\{min\{\mathcal{T}_t\} \ .. \ UC\} \times \{min\{\mathcal{T}_t\} \ .. \ F.\} - \{max\{\mathcal{T}_t\} \ .. \ UC\} \times \{max\{\mathcal{T}_t\} + 1 \ .. \ F.\}$$

If $\mathcal{T}_t$ is the union of disjoint intervals $\mathcal{T}_t = \cup_i \mathcal{T}_{t_i} = \cup_i \{t_{s_i} \ .. \ t_{e_i}\}$, the above definition must be applied to each component transaction-time temporal element $\mathcal{T}_{t_i}$.

A first alternative is based on the following observation: transaction-time data can be considered *indefinitely valid within their transaction-time period.* In this case, the conversion is defined as:

$$ADD'_v(\mathcal{T}_t) = \mathcal{T}_t \times \{min(\mathcal{T}_t) \ .. \ FOREVER\}$$

A second alternative is based on the following observation: transaction-time data can be considered valid only *within their transaction-time period.* In this case, the conversion is defined as:

$$ADD''_v(\mathcal{T}_t) = \mathcal{T}_t \times \mathcal{T}_t$$

Note that also these alternatives are safer than $ADD_v(\mathcal{T}_t)$. In all the three solutions, the beginning of the inferred validity is the ingres value. The difference is in how much the inferred validity spans along the valid-time axis. Note also that the alternative solutions do not reconstruct any current portion from an archived version.

**Elimination of valid-time:** when valid-time is dropped from a bitemporal relation, only one valid-time chronon per transaction-time chronon must be chosen. Again, as suggested in [DGS94], suppose you move along the diagonal: at each bitemporal instant, the present value of valid-time is the current one, thus a natural choice is the selection of that version which is *present with respect to its transaction-time period.* This leads to the selection of those pairs whose valid-time chronon equals the transaction-time chronon.

The elimination of valid-time from a valid-time table follows the same criterion and only the tuples whose temporal element contains the present chronon are retrieved:

$$DROP_v(\mathcal{T}_X) = \begin{cases} \{t : (t,t) \in \mathcal{T}_b\} & \text{if } X = b \\ \mathcal{T}_s & X = v \quad \wedge \quad NOW \in \mathcal{T}_v \end{cases}$$

As far as the translation from the bitemporal format to the transaction-time one is concerned, note that the risk of the solution above depends on at least two factors: the first is that fictious values of *transaction-time* can be produced; the second is the above solution selects also records whose validity is future with respect to the ingres transaction-time value. This means that data can be retrieved that were only a forecast with respect to when they were recorded. A first possible alternative can be to retrieve all and only those records whose validity contains the transaction-time pertinence. Such solution solves both the above problems and, since $\mathcal{T}_b = \mathcal{T}_t \times \mathcal{T}_v$, the conversion can be defined as:

$$DROP_v'(\mathcal{T}_b) = \{t : t \in \mathcal{T}_b \wedge t \leq max(\mathcal{T}_b)\}$$

A second possibility, completely safe, selects the only present and current record of each history:

$$DROP_v''(\mathcal{T}_b) = \{\mathcal{T}_t : NOW \in \mathcal{T}_t \wedge NOW \in \mathcal{T}_v\}$$

Note that the first alternative allows to retrieve also a portion of the archived data, whereas the second prevents from doing this.

## 3 Summary

In this paper the problem of the conversion from a temporal format to another was revised and alternative solutions were proposed to the most critical maps defined in [DGS94]. Such solutions are important in the definition of a suitable basis for an extended relational algebra which allows the manipulation of data of different temporal format. Further work will be devoted to the study of the different results produced by the use of differnt type of conversions: as a matter of fact, each set of temporal conversion functions generates a multitemporal algebra with specific features.

## References

[BG93]      BHARGAVA G., GADIA S.K.: "Relational Database Systems with Zero Information Loss," IEEE Trans. on Knowledge and Data Engineering, Vol. 5, No. 1, Feb. 1993.

[DGS94]    DE CASTRO C., GRANDI F., SCALAS M.R.: "Interoperabil-
           ity of Heterogeneous Temporal Relational Databases", Proc. of
           $12^{th}$ *International Conference on Entity-Relationship Approach
           (ER '93)*, 460-473, also in Lecture Notes in Computer Science,
           Springer-Verlag 1994, Vol. 823, 463-474.

[GST91]    GRANDI F., SCALAS M.R., TIBERIO P.: "A History Ori-
           ented Data View and Operation Semantics for Temporal Rela-
           tional Databases", C.I.O.C.-C.N.R. Tech. Rep. No. 76, Bologna,
           Jan. 1991.

[JW93]     JAJODIA S., WANG X.S.: "Temporal Mediators: Support-
           ing Uniform Access to Heterogeneous Temporal Databases,"
           Proc. of *Workshop on Interoperability of Database Systems and
           Database Applications*, Fribourg, 1993.

[TCG⁺93]   TANSEL A., CLIFFORD J., GADIA V. et al.: *Temporal
           Databases: Theory, Design and Implementation*, The Ben-
           jamin/Cummings Publishing Company, Redwood city, Califor-
           nia, 1993.

# An Output Sensitive Solution to the Set Union and Intersection Problem

Carlo Gaibisso[1], Enrico Nardelli[1,2], Guido Proietti[2]

1: Istituto di Analisi dei Sistemi ed Informatica, C.N.R., 00185 Roma, Italy
2: Dipartimento di Matematica Pura ed Applicata, Università di L'Aquila, 67100 Italy

### Abstract

In this paper we propose an alternative approaches for the efficient solution of the set union and intersection problem, a variant of the classical disjoint set union problem, in which two distinct sequences of unions are simultaneously performed on two distinct collections of $n$ singletons. In this context, it makes sense to introduce a new operation, named $findint(x)$, that, given an element $x$, returns the intersection of the two sets containing $x$ in both collections. We use a new data structures called *intersection lists* that reaches the optimal $\Theta(p)$ worst case time for executing a *findint* operation, where $p$ is the size of the output, and spends $O(n)$ worst case time for a *union* and $O(1)$ worst case time for a *find* operation.

## 1 Introduction

Given a collection of $n$ disjoint singletons $S_1, S_2, ..., S_n$, the *disjoint set union problem* [4] consists of efficiently performing an intermixed sequence of the following operations:

$union(S_i,S_j)$: combine the disjoint sets named $S_i$ and $S_j$ into a new set named $S_i$;
$find(x)$: return the name of the unique set containing the element $x$.

The *set union and intersection problem* [2] is a natural extension of the disjoint set union problem. It can be formulated in the following way: given two collections of $n$ disjoint singletons:

$S=\{S_1, S_2, ..., S_n\}$
$T=\{T_1, T_2, ..., T_n\}$

such that initially $S_i$ contains the same element of $T_i$ for $i=1, ...,n$, perform an intermixed sequence of the following operations:

$union(S,S_i,S_j)$: combine disjoint sets of the collection $S$ named $S_i$ and $S_j$ into a new set named $S_i$;
$union(T,T_i,T_j)$: combine disjoint sets of the collection $T$ named $T_i$ and $T_j$ into a new set named $T_i$;
$find(S,x)$: return the name of the set in collection $S$ containing the element $x$;
$find(T,x)$: return the name of the set in collection $T$ containing the element $x$;
$findint(x)$: return the intersection of the two sets containing $x$ in $S$ and $T$.

As an example of application of the set union and intersection problem consider the incremental maintenance of constraints in a concurrent environment. Here, concurrent agents working on different sets of constraints define different partitions into equivalence classes over the universe of feasible values. When it needs to know which is the equivalence class of a given value with respect to two different agents, a set union and intersection problem has to be solved.

The known algorithms for the set union and intersection problem make use of classical data structures employed to efficiently solve the set union problem.

Furthermore, in [3], a new quick-find data structure, called *binary list*, having the same performances of the well-known quick-find trees, has been introduced and analysed. The model of computation considered is the *pointer machine* [5], and the known upper bounds for the set union and intersection problem apply to the class of algorithms (called *separable algorithms*) which satisfy the following rules:

(i) The operations are presented on-line, i.e., each operation must be completed before the next one is known.

(ii) Each set element of each collection is separate node of the data structure.

(iii) (*Separability*) After any operation, the data structure can be partitioned into subgraphs such that each subgraph corresponds exactly to a current set. There exists no edge from a node in such a subgraph to a node outside the subgraph.

(iv) For executing a *find(S,x)* (*find(T,x)*) operation the algorithm obtains the node $v$ containing the requested element in the collection $S$ ($T$). The algorithm follows paths with start node $v$ until it reaches the node which contains the name of the corresponding set.

(v) For executing a *find*, a *union* or a *findint* operation the algorithm may insert or delete any edge as long as rule (iii) is satisfied.

All of these algorithms perform a *findint* operation, in the best cases, in $O(n)$ time. Unfortunately, this time is far from the optimal, corresponding to $O(p)$ time, where $p$ is the size of the output. In this paper we propose an output sensitive approach that allows to decrease the cost for a *findint* operation to the optimal, without using any additional storage. Thus, in a highly dynamic context, when the number of *findint* operations becomes higher and higher, the saving in terms of global charged time will be larger.

# 2 A gallery of known algorithms

In this section we recall how to solve the set union and intersection problem using classical data structures, that is quick-find trees, quick-union trees [5], k-UF trees [1] and binary lists [3]. All of them are linked structures. The way subgraphs representing sets are built during *union* operations determines the complexity of various approaches. Figure 1 shows the general schema we use to satisfy a *findint* operation. Procedure *FIND(X,x)* returns the pointer to the representative element of the set containing $x$ in the collection $X$, while procedure *OUTPUT(x)* outputs element $x$:

**procedure** *FINDINT(x)*; /\*return the intersection of sets $find(S,x)$ and $find(T,x)$;
**begin**
**if** ( $|FIND(S,x)| \geq |FIND(T,x)|$ ) **then** *INTERSECT(FIND(T,x),FIND(S,x),S)*
    **else** *INTERSECT(FIND(S,x), FIND(T,x), T)*
**end**;

**procedure** *INTERSECT(A,B,Z)*;
    /\*return the intersection of elements pointed by $A$ and $B$, where elements
    /\*pointed by $B$ belong to collection $Z$;
**begin**
**for** (each element $x$ contained in the set whose representative element is $A$) **do**
    **if** ($B=FIND(Z,x)$) **then** *OUTPUT(x)*
**end**;

**Fig. 1**: Procedure *FINDINT(x)*

Note that the efficient execution of the loop in the procedure INTERSECT(), requires elements in each set be circularly linked together. In this way, from anyone of them, all the elements in the same set can be reached in time proportional to the number of elements in the set itself. Details on how to manage these circular lists for the various classical data structures we are going to study are straightforward and left to the reader.

## 2.1 Weighted quick-find trees

In quick-find trees, a *union* is performed by making all the element of one set children of the tree root of the other. Thus a *union* costs $O(n)$ and, since every element points to the root, a *find* costs $O(1)$. Using the freedom implicit in each *union* operation, we make the children of the smaller tree point to the root of the larger. This improves to $O(\log n)$ the amortized complexity of a *union*.

**Proposition 1:** Using weighted quick-find trees, a single *findint* operation can be executed in $O(n)$ worst-case time.

**Proof:** Trivial. □

## 2.2 Weighted quick-union trees

In quick-union trees a *union* is performed by making the tree root of one set children of the tree root of the other. Thus a *union* costs $O(1)$. A *find* is performed by starting from the node representing the requested element and following the pointer to the parent until the tree root is reached, and thus a *find* costs $O(n)$. This time, making weighted unions (on the basis of the size or the rank of the involved trees), we can improve to $O(\log n)$ the worst case complexity of a *find*. The best possible solution for the worst case time of a sequence of operations can be achieved by applying one of the known *compaction rules* [6]. This leads to $O(n+m\alpha(m+n,n))$ amortized time complexity on a sequence of $n$ *union* and $m$ *find* operations, where $\alpha$ is the functional inverse of the Ackermann's function.

**Proposition 2:** Using weighted quick-union trees, a single *findint* operation can be executed in $O(n\log n)$ worst-case time.

**Proof:** Trivial. □

## 2.3 k-UF trees

k-UF trees [1] support each *union* and each *find* in $O(\log n/\log\log n)$ time in the worst case, so balancing the cost of the two operations. No better bound is possible for any separable pointer algorithm.

**Proposition 3:** k-UF trees support a *findint* operation in $O(n\log n/\log\log n)$ time in the worst case.

**Proof:** Trivial. □

## 2.4 Binary lists

Binary lists [3] have the same performances of the well-known quick-find trees. In addition, they allow to sort each set in $O(n\log\log n)$ time, while quick-find trees need $\Omega(n\log n)$ time. This means, for example, that the new structure is able to produce sorted output to a *findint* request in a better time than the classical approaches. Such a property can be useful every time that a priority is attached to an element of the universe.

We briefly describe the binary list data structure. Given an integer $p \geq 0$, let $L_p$ be a list with exactly $2^p$ nodes sorted in decreasing order: we say that $L_p$ is a *bit list* (*b-list* for short) of order $p$. In order to use b-lists for representing sets whose number $k$ of elements is not a power of two, we consider the binary representation of $k = \Sigma_{i \geq 0} b_i 2^i$, with $b_i \in \{0,1\}$, and we define a *binary list* $C_k$ of order $k$ as the concatenation (linking) of b-lists, one for each 1 in the binary representation of $k$. Therefore the $i$-th component of $C_k$ is $L_i$ if $b_i=1$ and empty otherwise. With respect to classical quick-find trees, an element of a binary lists makes use of an additive pointer field containing the pointer to the next element in the binary list (in the representative element, this pointer points to the first element of the binary list representing the set).

In [3] it has been proved that using binary lists to represent sets it is possible to execute a *union* operation in $O(n)$ time in the worst case and in $O(\log n)$ amortized time. Of course, the standard *find* operation in $S$ or $T$ can be executed in constant time, since each element points to the representative element, and then it follows:

**Proposition 4:** Using binary lists to represent sets it is possible to execute a *findint* operation in $O(n)$ worst case time.

**Proof:** Trivial.  $\square$

We resume in Table 1 below worst case performances for each operation of the proposed approaches:

| Data Structure | *find* | *union* | *findint* |
|---|---|---|---|
| *Quick-Find Trees* | $O(1)$ | $O(n)$ | $O(n)$ |
| *Quick-Union Trees* | $O(\log n)$ | $O(1)$ | $O(n\log n)$ |
| *k-UF Trees* | $O\left(\frac{\log n}{\log\log n}\right)$ | $O\left(\frac{\log n}{\log\log n}\right)$ | $O\left(\frac{n\log n}{\log\log n}\right)$ |
| *Binary Lists* | $O(1)$ | $O(n)$ | $O(n)$ |

**Table 1:** Worst case time bounds for each operation

The following Table 2 resumes the worst case bounds on a sequence of $2n-2$ union, $m$ *find* and $k$ *findint* operations for all the considered structures:

| Data Structure | Time |
|---|---|
| *Quick-Find Trees* | $O(n\log n+m+kn)$ |
| *Quick-Union Trees* | $O(n+m\alpha(m+n,n)+kn\log n)$ |
| *k-UF Trees* | $O\left((n+m)\left(\frac{\log n}{\log\log n}\right)+kn\frac{\log n}{\log\log n}\right)$ |
| *Binary Lists* | $O(n\log n+m+kn)$ |

**Table 2:** Worst case time bounds on a sequence of operations

# 3 An output sensitive approach

Solving the set union and intersection problem using classical approaches allows to perform a *findint* operation, in the best cases, in $O(n)$ time. Unfortunately, this time is far from the optimal, corresponding to $O(p)$ time, where $p$ is the size of the output. In this section we propose an approach that allows to decrease the cost for a *findint* operation to the optimal, without using any additional storage. Thus, in a highly dynamic context, when the number of *findint* operations becomes higher and higher, the saving in terms of global charged time will be larger.

Let assume for simplicity that it is initially $S_i=T_i=\{i\}$. The *universe* of elements over which the two collections are defined is then $U=\{1, 2, ...,n\}$. Let $Q=U/\mathcal{R}$ be the quotient set of $U$ by the equivalence relation $\mathcal{R}$:

$$x,y \in U, x\mathcal{R}y \Leftrightarrow x,y \in S_i \text{ and } x,y \in T_j$$

We improve the cost of a *findint* operation by dynamically maintaining up-to-date the set (of sets) $Q$. Remember that, for the assumptions we made on the model, no additional nodes can be used to maintain $Q$. Then we have to represent $Q$ implicitily, inside the sets of the two collections. To do that, we note that, on the basis of $\mathcal{R}$, every set in one of the collections is partitioned in subsets made up of those elements belonging at a same set into the other collection. If we update this subsets at each *union* operation executed on $S$ or $T$, then a *findint(x)* can be executed in $O(find(S,x)+p)$ time, where $p$ corresponds to the output size; this implies that if we can execute a *find* operation in constant time, then a *findint* operation is performed in optimal time. To obtain this, we represent sets in the collections using trees in which each element points to the root, so that a *find* operation can be executed in $O(1)$ time and we add to the record structure the following field:

INT: this is a pointer field containing the pointer to the next element in the intersection list; initially, this pointer points to itself.

We call *intersection list* the structure resulting from this modification. To update $Q$ at each *union*, we use the procedure given in Figure 2.

The collection where most recently has occurred a *union* operation contains the updated status of $Q$. Thus, when a *findint(x)* occurs, we focus on the most recently collection interested by a *union* operation (which can be determined in $O(1)$ time) and then we output the intersection list attached to $x$. Resuming, the following can be easily proved:

**Theorem 1:** Performing a *union* operation on $S$ or $T$ and maintaining the intersection lists costs $O(n)$ operations.

**Proof:** The analysis of the worst case is given in the comments of the procedure *UNION()* given above. □

This bound is tight, since there can be *union* operations on $S$ or $T$ producing $\Omega(n)$ merging in $Q$. Consider, for example, the following case: assume, without loss of generality, that $n$ is even; suppose that after $n-2$ *union* operations on $S$, this is made up by two sets (the set of odd numbers and the set of even numbers) and that after $n/2$ *union* operations on $T$, this is made up by $n/2$ sets, each containing two consecutive numbers. At the next *union* on $S$, the two residual sets are unified, and

```
procedure UNION(S,A,B);
        /*combine the sets named A and B of the collection S into a new set
        /*named A and update the intersection subsets of A;
    begin
    WEIGHTED_UNION(A,B);
        /*make the children of the root of the smaller tree point to root of the
        /*larger; this has a worst-case time complexity of
        /*O(min(|A|,|B|))=O(n) and an amortized cost of O(logn);
    for (each element x contained in A) do
        begin
            /*this loops costs Σ∀x∈AO(|Bx|), where Bx is the generic set in T containing
            /*x; since each set in T is examined exactly once, summation is limited by n;
        Bx=FIND(T, x);    /*this costs O(1) time;
        if (Bx is unmarked) then
            begin
                MARK_SET(Bx); /* Bx is marked, to be examined only once;
                for (each element y other than x contained in Bx) do
                    begin    /*this loop costs O(|Bx|)
                        Ay=FIND(S, y)      /*this costs O(1) time;
                        if (Ay=A) then
                            begin    /*update the intersection lists in S and T;
                                APPEND(S,x,y) ;
                                APPEND(T,x,y);
                            end
                    end
            end
        end
    end;
```

**Fig. 2:** Procedure $UNION(S,A,B)$

there will be $n/2$ merging among the $n$ singletons in $Q$. This means that the lower bound for operation is in the worst-case $\Omega(n)$ and then we have in any case to pay $\Omega(n)$ to perform a *union* operation and simultaneously to update $Q$. On the other hand, what it happens on a sequence of *union* operations? The following proposition characterizes the problem of maintaining up-to-date the status of $Q$ at each *union* operation; for the sake of clarity, we will assume the existence of a third collection $C$ maintaining on-line the intersections among sets in $S$ and in $T$:

**Theorem 2:** Given a complete sequence of $2n-2$ unions on two collections $S$ and $T$, any algorithm based on comparisons requires $\Omega(nlogn)$ comparisons to maintain up-to-date the intersection collection $C$ at each *union* operation.

**Proof:** Without loss of generality, suppose that $S$ and $T$ contain $n=m^2=2^k$ elements. At the beginning we have:

$$S=\{S_1, S_2, ..., S_n\}$$
$$T=\{T_1, T_2, ..., T_n\}$$
$$C=\{C_1, C_2, ..., C_n\}$$

where $S_i=T_i=C_i=\{i\}$. Consider now the following situation, where $(n-m-1)$ unions on $S$ and $(n-m-1)$ unions on $T$ have been done but $C$ is still made up by singletons:

$$S=\{A_1, A_2, ..., A_m\} \quad T=\{B_1, B_2, ..., B_m\}$$

with:

$$A_1=\{a_{1,1}, a_{1,2}, ..., a_{1,m}\}, A_2=\{a_{2,1}, a_{2,2}, ..., a_{2,m}\}, .., A_m=\{a_{m,1}, a_{m,2}, ..., a_{m,m}\}$$
with $a_{i,j} \in [1..n]$
$$B_k=\{a_{i,k} \mid i=1,2, ...,m\} \text{ for } k=1,2, ..., m.$$

To complete the union sequence, $(m-1)$ unions on $S$ and $(m-1)$ unions on $T$ are needed. We now show a particular sequence of unions on $S$ and $T$ that requires $\Omega(n\log n)$ comparisons to maintain up-to-date $C$. We divide such a sequence in *steps*; one step is a sequence of unions on the same collection which halves the number of contained sets. The first step manipulates $S$ executing $m/2$ unions. The $i$-th union in this step merges sets $A_{2i-1}$ and $A_{2i}$, $i=1, 2, ..., \frac{m}{2}$. Each merging of two sets in $S$ generates $m$ couples in $C$. This set of $m$ couples belongs to a universe of $m(m-1)(m-2)...1=m!$ possible sets of $m$ couples[1]. The size of the universe implies that we have to do at least $\log(m!)$ comparisons, that is (by the Stirling's approximation) at least $m\log m$ comparisons. Since we execute $\frac{m}{2}$ unions in the first step (generating $\frac{n}{2}$ couples in $C$), we spend a total of:

$$C_1 \geq \frac{m}{2} m \log m = \frac{m^2 \log m}{2} = \frac{n \log \sqrt{n}}{2} = \frac{n}{4} \log n$$

The second step manipulates $T$. The $i$-th union in this step merges sets $B_{2i-1}$ and $B_{2i}$, $i=1, 2, ..., \frac{m}{2}$. Each merging of two sets in $T$ at this step generates $\frac{n}{4}$ quadruples in $C$. This set of $\frac{m}{2}$ quadruples belongs to a universe of $\left(\frac{m}{2}\right)!$ possible sets of $\frac{m}{2}$ quadruples. In fact, now in $S$ there are sets of $2m$ elements each, so when unions are executed on $T$, quadruples result in $C$.

This means that we have to do at least $\log\left(\left(\frac{m}{2}\right)!\right)$ comparisons, that is (by the Stirling's approximation) at least $\frac{m}{2}\log\frac{m}{2}$ comparisons. Since we execute $\frac{m}{2}$ unions in the second step (generating $\frac{n}{4}$ quadruples in $C$), we spend a total of:

---

[1] In fact, given two disjoint sets $X$ and $Y$ of $m$ distinct elements each, there exist $m!$ different sets of exactly $m$ couples $\{x, y\}$ where $x \in X$ and $y \in Y$. To see why, consider that each element in the universe can be obtained in the following way: take the first element in $X$; this element can be coupled with any of the $m$ elements contained in $Y$; then, take the second element in $X$; this element can be coupled with any of the $(m-1)$ remaining elements contained in $Y$; following this procedure, at the $m$-th coupling, we are forced to take the residual elements in the two merging sets.

$$C_2 \geq \frac{m}{2} \frac{m}{2} \log\frac{m}{2} = \frac{n}{8} \log\frac{n}{2}$$

By iterating the process, we have that at the last step on $T$ (i.e., the $(2\log m)$-th=$k$-th step) we merge two sets of cardinality $\frac{n}{2}$, producing $C=\{U\}$ without any comparison. The total cost $C_{TOT}$ is therefore:

$$C_{TOT} = \sum_{i=1}^{k-1} C_i \geq \sum_{i=1}^{k-1} \frac{n}{2^{i+1}} \log\frac{n}{2^{i-1}} = \sum_{i=1}^{k-1} \frac{n}{2^{i+1}} \left(\log n - \log 2^{i-1}\right) =$$

$$= \sum_{i=1}^{k-1} \frac{n \log n}{2^{i+1}} - \sum_{i=1}^{k-1} n \frac{i-1}{2^{i+1}} = n \log n \left(\frac{1}{2} - \frac{1}{2^k}\right) - n\left(\frac{1}{2} - \frac{k}{2^k}\right) = \frac{1}{2}n \log n - \frac{1}{2}n$$

from which the thesis. □

Finally, the following corollary immediately descends by the previous results:

**Corollary 1:** The set union and intersection problem can be solved dynamically by maintaining the intersection lists spending $O(n^2+m+P)$ time in the worst case on a sequence of $2n-2$ *union* operations, $m$ *find* operations and $k$ *findint* operations, where $P$ is the output size over all the $k$ *findint* operations. □

# 4 Conclusions

In this paper we have proposed an output sensitive approach to the set union and intersection problem that allows to perform a *findint* operation in optimal time.

Future work will be focused in the direction of determining lower bounds for a sequence of *find*, *union* and *findint* operations in the context of separable algorithms.

# References

[1] N. Blum, On the Single Operation Worst-case Time Complexity of Disjoint Set Union Problems, in *SIAM Journal on Computing*, 15, 1986, pp. 1021-1024.
[2] C.Gaibisso, E.Nardelli and G.Proietti, Algorithms for the Set Union and Intersection Problem, Technical Report nº 83 April 1995 of the Department of Pure and Applied Mathematics of the University of L'Aquila.
[3] C.Gaibisso, E.Nardelli and G.Proietti, Intersection Reporting on two Collection of Disjoint Sets, submitted to *Information Processing Letters*, April 1996.
[4] Z. Galil and G.F. Italiano, Data Structures and Algorithms for Disjoint Set Union Problems, in *ACM Computing Surveys*, 23 (3), 1991, pp. 319-344.
[5] R.E. Tarjan, A Class of Algorithms which Require Nonlinear Time to Maintain Disjoint Sets, in *Journal of Computer and System Sciences*, 18, 1979, pp. 110-127.
[6] R.E. Tarjan and J. Van Leeuwen, Worst-Case Analysis of Set Union Algorithms, in *Journal of the Association for Computing Machinery*, 31 (2), 1984, pp. 245-281.

# On the Semantics of Multistage Interconnection Networks*

Anna Gambin** and Sławomir Lasota

Fachbereich Informatik LS-2, Dortmund Universität, D-44221 Dortmund 50, Germany.
Instytut Informatyki, Uniwersytet Warszawski, Banacha 2, Warszawa 02-097, Poland.
{aniag,sl}@mimuw.edu.pl

**Abstract.** Multistage interconnection networks (MINs) have a number of applications in many areas, for example in communication networks or parallel computer systems. While several performance analyses have been done, as far as we know a formal description of the behaviour of such networks is lacking. In the paper we define Markov chains describing the behaviour of the buffered MIN with a butterfly interconnection structure and $2 \times 2$ switching elements. We study several models of packet flow, which appear in the literature and develop technical mathematical tools which allow us to compare them. We prove some equivalence results regarding the models.

## 1 Introduction

Multistage interconnection networks (MIN) have been widely used for connecting processors in parallel computing systems and in constructing communication networks [7]. It consists (in general) of $(k \times k)$-switching elements (*switches*), which are grouped into several stages. In this paper we are concerned with MINs having the butterfly interconnection structure containing $(2 \times 2)$-switches with input buffers of capacity one (see fig. 1). They belong to the broader class of *banyan networks* [1].

A number of papers studied the behaviour of MINs, aiming mainly at evaluation of their performance [1] [3, 5, 9]. In most of these papers some crucial assumptions (relaxations) are made, simplifying the analysis of the network. The reason is that the behaviour of MIN, arising from the dependencies between neighbour switches, is very complex.

In this paper we propose the formal definition of the dynamic behaviour of MIN without making any simplifying assumptions, i.e. in the *full blocking model*. As far as we know, no such definitions have been proposed by now. We describe the network by means of Markov chain, as its behaviour is history-independent. We develop some mathematical machinery which allows us to define

---

* This work was performed at the University of Dortmund.
** Research supported by DAAD (Deutscher Akademischer Austauschdienst).
[1] The most frequently evaluated performance measure is *throughput* (expected number of packets reaching their destinations per time step).

the semantics of several models of packet flow (including also some relaxed ones [6]). Such a formal approach helps to express differences between models – it appears to us, that so precise comparison was not possible before. Using proposed notation we are able to prove certain equivalence of models.

## 1.1 Models of a packet flow

MINs are used to route packets appearing in the switches at the first stage (input switches) to appropriate output switches (addresses) at the last stage (see fig. 1). There is exactly one path from every input switch to every output switch, and every packet visits all the stages along its way through the network. We assume, following many related papers ([4, 8]) that an address of a packet is random (it is usually done to make a performance analysis possible), – it means that a packet after entering into each switch chooses its direction randomly. The computation of the network proceeds in synchronized steps more or less simultaneously by all the switches. One step consists of the flow of packets between every pair of neighbour stages. Locally, in one switch, such a step consists of two half-steps:

1) *Flow-out phase*: some packets leave the switch (after resolving conflicts), but only if there is a place in the appropriate buffer of the switch at the next stage.

2) *Input phase*: packets from the previous stage enter to the empty buffers of the switch.

The *ripple model* is the most frequently used in the literature [5, 8, 9]. It has the property that the flow-out phase at the stage happens after the flow-out phase at the next stage has been completed. We can effectively simulate such a model (switches need not to wait). There is an equivalent *odd-even model* (pipelining implementation of the ripple model): the flow-out phases occur simultaneously at the odd stages (while even stages are idle), followed by input phases at the even stages, then in every consecutive step the odd and even stages change their roles. Another natural possibility is offered by the *simultaneous model*, in which the flow-out phase occurs simultaneously at all the stages (similarly input phase which follows flow-out one). In this model switches are never idle.

The paper is organized as follows. In section 2 we define three Markov chains corresponding to the models mentioned above. We start by defining the local behaviour of one switch in section 2.1, then in section 2.2 we define the global-state Markov chains. To this end some mathematical tools are developed – the properties of them are discused in the appendix, which contains also some general theorems regarding these tools. In section 3 we prove the main result of this paper, giving the equivalence of simultaneous and odd-even models. The formal proof of the key lemma is moved to the appendix. We finish with conclusions and a sketch of some directions for the further work in the area in section 4.

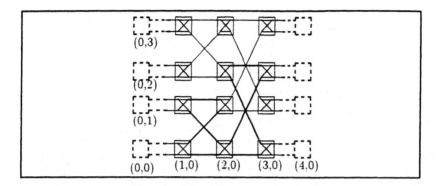

**Fig. 1.** Butterfly network for $H = 3$ with border stages (dashed line).

## 2  Semantics of MIN

Throughout the rest of the paper let $H$ denote the number of stages of the butterfly network. The structure of the network can be represented by the graph $G = (I, E)$. The sets of nodes and edges are defined as follows:

$$I = \{1, 2, \ldots, H\} \times \{0, 1, \ldots, W\}, \quad W = 2^{H-1} - 1,$$

$$E = \{((r, c), (r + 1, c')) : 1 \le r \le H - 1, \quad 0 \le c \le W, \quad c' = c \text{ or } c' = \bar{c}^r\}$$

where $\bar{c}^i$ is a number c with its $i$-th bit negated, $0 \le c \le W$, $1 \le i \le H - 1$. Nodes $(r, c)$ and $(r, \bar{c}^r)$ have common neighbours $(r + 1, c)$ and $(r + 1, \bar{c}^r)$ at the next $(r + 1)$-th stage. In further definitions we will need the notion of c-map :

**Definition 1.** For finite sets $A, B$, c-map $\quad P : A \leadsto B$ is a function $P : A \to [0, 1]^B$ such that for every $a \in A$, $P(a)$ is a probabilistic distribution, i.e. $\sum_{b \in B} P(a)(b) = 1$.

**Note:** C-map is precisely the conditional probabilistic distribution. For $A = B$, $P$ defines a transition matrix of a Markov chain.

### 2.1  Local description of one switch

As a single switching element cannot be described by a Markov chain $S \leadsto S$ (because its behaviour depends on states of its neighbours), we encode the behaviour of it by means of two c-maps :

$$\sigma : S \times \{0, 1\}^2 \leadsto S \times \{0, 1\}^2, \quad \tau : S \times \{0, 1\}^2 \leadsto S$$

(see tables 1, 2). Such a description of one switch is in the spirit of probabilistic automaton from [6]. Elements of $S = B \times B$ represent states of both buffers of a switch, $B = \{\circ, \downarrow, \searrow\}$. Element "$\circ$" represents empty buffer, and two other elements of $B$ represent two possible directions of a packet staying in the buffer. We introduce "$\swarrow$"="$\searrow$" only to improve a readability. $\sigma(s, (b_1, b_2))$ "returns"

| S | in:1, 1 | out | in: 0, 1 | out | in: 1, 0 | out | in: 0, 0 | out |
|---|---|---|---|---|---|---|---|---|
| ○ ○ | ○ ○ | 0, 0 | ○ ○ | 0, 0 | ○ ○ | 0, 0 | ○ ○ | 0, 0 |
| ↓ ○ | ↓ ○ | 0, 0 | ○ ○ | 1, 0 | ↓ ○ | 0, 0 | ○ ○ | 1, 0 |
| ↘○ | ↘○ | 0, 0 | ↘○ | 0, 0 | ○ ○ | 0, 1 | ○ ○ | 0, 1 |
| ○ ↓ | ○ ↓ | 0, 0 | ○ ↓ | 0, 0 | ○ ○ | 0, 1 | ○ ○ | 0, 1 |
| ○↗ | ○↗ | 0, 0 | ○ ○ | 1, 0 | ○↗ | 0, 0 | ○ ○ | 1, 0 |
| ↓↗ | ↓↗ | 0, 0 | $\frac{1}{2}$↓○, $\frac{1}{2}$○↗ | 1, 0 | ↓↗ | 0, 0 | $\frac{1}{2}$↓○, $\frac{1}{2}$○↗ | 1, 0 |
| ↘↓ | ↘↓ | 0, 0 | ↘↓ | 0, 0 | $\frac{1}{2}$○↓, $\frac{1}{2}$↘○ | 0, 1 | $\frac{1}{2}$○↓, $\frac{1}{2}$↘○ | 0, 1 |
| ✕ | ✕ | 0, 0 | ↘○ | 1, 0 | ○↗ | 0, 1 | ○ ○ | 1, 1 |
| ↓ ↓ | ↓ ↓ | 0, 0 | ○ ↓ | 1, 0 | ↓ ○ | 0, 1 | ○ ○ | 1, 1 |

**Table 1.** Definition of $\sigma$: the first half of the step (flow out of packets)

| S | in: 0, 0 | in: 1, 0 | in: 0, 1 | in: 1, 1 |
|---|---|---|---|---|
| ○ ○ | ○ ○ | $\frac{1}{2}$↓○, $\frac{1}{2}$○↗ | $\frac{1}{2}$○↓, $\frac{1}{2}$○↗ | $\frac{1}{4}$↓↗, $\frac{1}{4}$↘↓, $\frac{1}{4}$✕, $\frac{1}{4}$↓↓ |
| ↓ ○ | ↓ ○ | | $\frac{1}{2}$↓↗, $\frac{1}{2}$↓↓ | |
| ↘○ | ↘○ | | $\frac{1}{2}$↘↓, $\frac{1}{2}$✕ | |
| ○ ↓ | ○ ↓ | $\frac{1}{2}$↘↓, $\frac{1}{2}$↓↓ | | |
| ○↗ | ○↗ | $\frac{1}{2}$↓↗, $\frac{1}{2}$✕ | | |
| ↓↗ | ↓↗ | | | |
| ↘↓ | ↘↓ | | | |
| ✕ | ✕ | | | |
| ↓ ↓ | ↓ ↓ | | | |

**Table 2.** Definition of $\tau$: the second half of the step: (input of packets). In empty fields $\tau$ can be arbitrarily defined

an output of packets from a switch in a state $s$ (together with a new state) when $(b_1, b_2)$ describes whether two buffers of neighbours at the next stage are empty, i.e. $b_j = 0$ denotes a free buffer. $\tau(s, (i_1, i_2))$ describes an input of packets into a switch in a state $s$, assuming that $i_j = 1$ means that a packet is comming into a buffer.

For convenience let us introduce sets $I_r = \{(r, c) : 0 \le c \le W\}$, for $0 \le r \le H + 1$. It represents nodes at the r-th stage. In the next section we will define Markov chains $V \rightsquigarrow V$, describing one step of the computation of the network, where $V = S^{I \cup I_{H+1}}$ is a set of its states, $I = \bigcup_{1 \le r \le H} I_r$. We will also need a set $V'$ of states in a half-step defined as $V' = (S \times \{0, 1\}^2)^{I_0 \cup I \cup I_{H+1}}$. Stages 0 and $H + 1$ are introduced only for technical convenience. The stage 0 intuitively represents input of packets into the network. Symmetrically stage $(H + 1)$ receives packets which flow out from the network. For further definitions we need two families of auxiliary functions:

$$IN^{r,c} : V \rightarrow \{0, 1\}^2, \quad \text{for} \quad (r, c) \in I \cup I_0$$

$$in^{r,c} : V' \to \{0,1\}^2, \quad \text{for} \quad (r,c) \in I \cup I_{H+1}$$

$IN^{r,c}(v)$ simply returns an information about buffers of neighbours at the next stage for a switch at node $(r,c)$ (the pair $(b_1, b_2)$ above); similarly $in^{r,c}(v)$ returns an information about packets comming into the switch $((i_1, i_2)$ above). In the definition of these functions we are "looking through" the edges of graph $G$:

$$IN^{r,c}(v) = \begin{cases} (is(s\downarrow_1), is(\bar{s}\downarrow_1)) & \text{if } c < \bar{c}^r \\ (is(\bar{s}\downarrow_2), is(s\downarrow_2)) & \text{otherwise} \end{cases} \quad \text{for } 0 < r < H$$

where $s = v(r+1, c) \in B^2$, $\bar{s} = v(r+1, \bar{c}^r) \in B^2$. $(a,b)\downarrow_1 = a$, $(a,b)\downarrow_2 = b$ denote usual projections. Auxiliary function $is$ tells us whether the buffer is occupied; $is : B \to \{0,1\}$, $is(\circ) = 0$, $is(\downarrow) = is(\searrow) = 1$.

$$in^{r,c}(v') = \begin{cases} (o\downarrow_1, \bar{o}\downarrow_1) & \text{if } c < \bar{c}^{(r-1)} \\ (\bar{o}\downarrow_2, o\downarrow_2) & \text{otherwise} \end{cases} \quad \text{for } 1 < r < H+1$$

where $o = v'(r-1, c)\downarrow_2 \in \{0,1\}^2$, $\bar{o} = v'(r-1, \bar{c}^{(r-1)})\downarrow_2 \in \{0,1\}^2$. The definitions of $IN^{0,c}, in^{1,c}$, $IN^{H,c}$ and $in^{H+1,c}$ are slightly different, as they describe the "border" of the network:

$$IN^{r,c}(v) = (is(v(r+1, c)\downarrow_1), is(v(r+1, c)\downarrow_2)), \quad \text{for } r = 0, H$$

$$in^{r+1,c}(v') = v'(r, c)\downarrow_2 \in \{0,1\}^2, \quad \text{for } r = 0, H$$

We define four families of c-maps $\sigma^{r,c}, \tau^{r,c}$, $\pi^{r,c}, \Omega^{r,c}$, indexed by $(r,c) \in I$, which will be the atomic elements of proper Markov chains in the next section. The c-maps

$$\sigma^{r,c} : V \rightsquigarrow S \times \{0,1\}^2, \quad \tau^{r,c} : V' \rightsquigarrow S$$

simply apply $\sigma, \tau$ to the switch at node $(r,c)$:

$$\sigma^{r,c}(v)(s,o) = \sigma(v(r,c), IN^{r,c}(v))(s,o), \quad \tau^{r,c}(v')(s) = \tau(v'(r,c), in^{r,c}(v'))(s)$$

On the other hand $\pi^{r,c} : V \rightsquigarrow S \times \{0,1\}^2$, $\Omega^{r,c} : V' \rightsquigarrow S$ describe idle phase of a switch at node $(r,c)$ and are defined by:

$$\pi^{r,c}(v)(v(r,c), (0,0)) = 1, \quad \Omega^{r,c}(v')(v'(r,c)\downarrow_1) = 1$$

To unify our notation we will also need some "border" c-maps describing input and output of packets into/from the network:

$$\sigma^{0,c}, \pi^{0,c}, \sigma^{H+1,c}, \pi^{H+1,c}, : V \rightsquigarrow S \times \{0,1\}^2, \quad \tau^{H+1,c}, \Omega^{H+1,c} : V' \rightsquigarrow S$$

defined as follows:

$$\sigma^{0,c}(v)(s,o) = \sigma((\downarrow,\downarrow), IN^{0,c}(v))(s,o), \quad \pi^{0,c}(v)((\downarrow,\downarrow), (0,0)) = 1,$$

$$\sigma^{H+1,c}(v)((\circ,\circ), (0,0)) = 1, \quad \pi^{H+1,c}(v)(v(r,c), (0,0)) = 1,$$

$$\tau^{H+1,c}(v')(s) = \tau(v'(H+1,c), in^{H+1,c}(v'))(s), \quad \Omega^{H+1,c}(v')(v'(H+1,c)\downarrow_1) = 1$$

## 2.2 Semantics of the network

In this section we define three Markov chains $\Gamma_{\text{ripple}}, \Gamma_{\text{sim}}, \Gamma_{\text{odd-even}} : V \rightsquigarrow V$, which correspond to the described models of a packet flow. The Markov chains will be composed of c-maps $\sigma^{r,c}, \tau^{r,c}, \pi^{r,c}, \Omega^{r,c}$ defined in the previous section by means of the following two operations on c-maps :

**Definition 2.** For $P : A \rightsquigarrow B$ and $Q : B \rightsquigarrow C$, we define a **sequential composition of $P$ and $Q$**, $P;Q : A \rightsquigarrow C$ as follows: $(P;Q)(a,c) = \sum_{b \in B} P(a,b) \cdot Q(b,c)$.
For $P : A \rightsquigarrow B$ and $Q : A \rightsquigarrow C$, a **parallel composition of $P$ and $Q$**, $P \parallel Q : A \rightsquigarrow B \times C$, is defined as $(P \parallel Q)(a)(b,c) = P(a)(b) \cdot Q(a)(c)$.

**Note:** Essentially ";" corresponds to matrix multiplication, while "$\parallel$" gives a product distribution. Both operations are associative and "$\parallel$" is also commutative. While defining them we were inspired by the operators of CSP ([2]) – for example "$\parallel$" enforces component c-maps to "proceed" simultaneously like the operator of synchronized parallel composition in CSP. In the following "$\parallel$" has a higher priority than ";". We sometimes write $\binom{P;}{Q}$ instead of $(P;Q)$ for the sake of simplicity (this allows us to better recognize c-maps concerned with certain stages of the network).
We group c-maps $\sigma^{r,c}$ from the $r$-th stage into $\sigma^r : V \rightsquigarrow (S \times \{0,1\}^2)^{I_r}$

$$\sigma^r = \parallel_{0 \le c \le W} \sigma^{r,c}, \text{ for } r = 0, 1, \ldots H+1$$

Analogously we define $\tau^r, \pi^r, \Omega^r$ as a parallel composition of appropriate components.
In the following we ignore the subtle difference between sets $A^{B \cup C}$ and $A^B \times A^C$, for example by treating a c-map with a domain equal to the former as if it has a domain equal to the latter. It is useful in definitions below as well as in the appendix.
The three Markov chains are as follows:

$$\Gamma_{\text{sim}} = (\sigma^0 \parallel \sigma^1 \parallel \sigma^2 \parallel \sigma^3 \parallel \ldots \parallel \sigma^{H-2} \parallel \sigma^{H-1} \parallel \sigma^H \parallel \sigma^{H+1});$$
$$(\tau^1 \parallel \tau^2 \parallel \tau^3 \parallel \ldots \parallel \tau^{H-2} \parallel \tau^{H-1} \parallel \tau^H \parallel \tau^{H+1})$$

$$\Gamma_{\text{ripple}} = (\pi^0 \parallel \pi^1 \parallel \pi^2 \parallel \ldots \parallel \pi^{H-1} \parallel \pi^H \parallel \sigma^{H+1});$$
$$(\Omega^1 \parallel \Omega^2 \parallel \ldots \parallel \Omega^{H-1} \parallel \Omega^H \parallel \Omega^{H+1});$$
$$(\pi^0 \parallel \pi^1 \parallel \pi^2 \parallel \ldots \parallel \pi^{H-1} \parallel \sigma^H \parallel \pi^{H+1});$$
$$(\Omega^1 \parallel \Omega^2 \parallel \ldots \parallel \Omega^{H-1} \parallel \Omega^H \parallel \tau^{H+1});$$
$$(\pi^0 \parallel \pi^1 \parallel \pi^2 \parallel \ldots \parallel \sigma^{H-1} \parallel \pi^H \parallel \pi^{H+1});$$
$$(\Omega^1 \parallel \Omega^2 \parallel \ldots \parallel \Omega^{H-1} \parallel \tau^H \parallel \Omega^{H+1});$$

$$\ldots$$

$$(\sigma^0 \parallel \pi^1 \parallel \pi^2 \parallel \ldots \parallel \pi^{H-1} \parallel \pi^H \parallel \pi^{H+1});$$
$$(\tau^1 \parallel \Omega^2 \parallel \ldots \parallel \Omega^{H-1} \parallel \Omega^H \parallel \Omega^{H+1})$$

$$\Gamma_{\text{odd-even}} = (\sigma^0 \parallel \pi^1 \parallel \sigma^2 \parallel \pi^3 \parallel \ldots \parallel \sigma^{H-2} \parallel \pi^{H-1} \parallel \sigma^H \parallel \pi^{H+1});$$
$$(\tau^1 \parallel \Omega^2 \parallel \tau^3 \parallel \ldots \parallel \Omega^{H-2} \parallel \tau^{H-1} \parallel \Omega^H \parallel \tau^{H+1});$$
$$(\pi^0 \parallel \sigma^1 \parallel \pi^2 \parallel \sigma^3 \parallel \ldots \parallel \pi^{H-2} \parallel \sigma^{H-1} \parallel \pi^H \parallel \sigma^{H+1});$$
$$(\Omega^1 \parallel \tau^2 \parallel \Omega^3 \parallel \ldots \parallel \tau^{H-2} \parallel \Omega^{H-1} \parallel \tau^H \parallel \Omega^{H+1})$$

Let $\Gamma_1 : V \leadsto V$ denote the c-map consisting of two first lines of the definition of $\Gamma_{\text{odd-even}}$, $\Gamma_2^1 : V \leadsto V'$ denote the third line, $\Gamma_2^2 : V' \leadsto V$ denote the fourth, and $\Gamma_2 = \Gamma_2^1 ; \Gamma_2^2$. Analogously $\Gamma_{\text{sim}} = \Gamma_{\text{sim}}^1 ; \Gamma_{\text{sim}}^2$.

**Note:** The definition of $\Gamma_{\text{odd-even}}$ assumes that $H$ is even (for $H$ odd one should exchange the beginning parts of $\Gamma_1$ and $\Gamma_2$).

## 3   Equivalence results

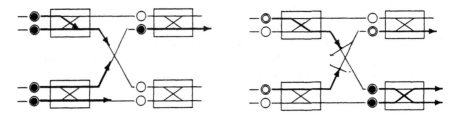

**Fig. 2.** One even group of switches before and after $\Gamma_1$; on the right side black packet moved during $\Gamma_1$, while doubled ones did not move.

**Lemma 3.** $\Gamma_1 ; \Gamma_{sim} = \Gamma_1 ; \Gamma_2$.

The formal proof, which is involved, can be found in the appendix. Here we present some intuitive arguments. All the switches can be divided into groups of four (nodes $(r, c)$, $(r, \bar{c}^r)$, $(r + 1, c)$, $(r + 1, \bar{c}^r)$). We call a group *even* or *odd*, depending on parity of $r$. Each switch belongs to precisely two groups (fig. 2 shows an even group). During $\Gamma_1$ even groups make their work, while odd ones stay idle. During $\Gamma_2$ role changes: only odd groups perform their actions. Odd groups during $\Gamma_{\text{sim}}$ do precisely the same as during $\Gamma_2$. We only should observe that even groups after $\Gamma_1$, during $\Gamma_{\text{sim}}$ do nothing more. This can be established by careful analysis of possible cases. As in $\Gamma_1$ groups operate independently, we will consider one group. We should only think about non-empty buffers at $r$-th stage switch. Let us consider one such a buffer. The packet staying in it could not have come during $\Gamma_1$ as odd groups were idle. There are two possible causes why it did not move forward during $\Gamma_1$. If the reason was stage blocking, i.e. another packet staying in the appropriate buffer at the next stage, then this packet still remains in its buffer (the argument as before). If the reason was a collision in the switch, then our packet is now blocked by the winner. In both cases our packet can not move forward.

The proof of the following lemma is analogous to the proof of lemma 3.

**Lemma 4.** $\Gamma_2; \Gamma_{sim} = \Gamma_2; \Gamma_1$.

**Theorem 5.** $\Gamma^k_{odd-even} = \Gamma_1; \Gamma^{2k-1}_{sim}$.

*Proof.* We apply interchangeably lemmas 3 and 4 to obtain the required equality.
$$\Gamma^k_{odd-even} = (\Gamma_1; \Gamma_2)^k \overset{L.3}{=} (\Gamma_1; \Gamma_2)^{k-1}; \Gamma_1; \Gamma_{sim} \overset{L.4}{=} \ldots \overset{L.4}{=} \Gamma_1; \Gamma^{2k-1}_{sim}$$

## 4  Conclusions

In this paper we have presented the formal description of several models of packet flow in the butterfly MINs. By varying the definitions of c-maps $\sigma$ and $\tau$ one can obtain the number of different models, without introducing any changes in the main definitions. For example the relaxed model of [6] can be easily obtained in this way. It is interesting to observe how the correspondence between ripple, odd-even and simultaneous changes when we modify $\sigma$ and $\tau$.

The other possible continuation of the work is to examine the usefulness of the presented notation in the analysis of the performance of MIN, what is a challenging problem, because there are no results in this field for the full blocking MIN model with finite buffers.

**Acknowledgement.** Thanks are due to Martin Dietzfelbinger for helpful discussions and his comments which helped to improve the exposition of the paper.

## References

1. G.F. Goke, G.J. Lipovski, *Banyan Network for Partitioning Multiprocessor Systems*, Proc. 1st Ann. Symp. on Computer Architecture, 1973, pp. 21-28
2. C.A.R. Hoare, "Communicating Sequential Processes," Prentice – Hall, 1985.
3. R.R. Koch, *Increasing the Size of a Network by a Constant Factor Can Increase Performance by More Than a Constant Factor*, Proc. 28th Ann. Symposium on Foundations of Computer Science (1988), 221-231.
4. T.F. Leighton, "Parallel Algorithms and Architectures: Arrays, Trees, Hypercubes," Morgan Kaufmann, 1992.
5. Y. Mun, H. Yong, *Performance Analysis of Finite Buffered Multistage Interconnection Networks*, IEEE Trans. on Computers, vol. C-43, 1994, pp. 152-162
6. R. Rehrmann, B. Monien, R. Lüling, R. Diekmann, *On the Communication Throughput of Buffered Multistage Interconnection Networks*, Proc. 8th ACM Symposium on Parallel Algorithms and Architectures, 1996.
7. R. Rooholaminiight, *Finding the Right ATM Switch for the Market*, IEEE J. Comp., 1994, pp. 16-28
8. T.H. Theimer, E.P. Rathgeb, M.N. Huber, *Performance Analysis of Buffered Banyan Networks* IEEE Trans. on Communication, vol. C-39, 1991, pp. 269-277

9. H.Y. Yoon, K.Y. Lee, M.T. Liu, *Performance Analysis of Multibuffered Packet-switching Networks in Multiprocessor Systems*, IEEE Trans. on Computers, vol. C-39, 1990, pp. 319-327

## Appendix

We present here some definitions and theorems which facilitate the proof of lemma 3. In the following let $P : A \rightsquigarrow B_1$, $Q, Q' : B_1 \times B_2 \rightsquigarrow C$ be arbitrary c-maps.

**Definition 6.**
$Q$ **is equal to** $Q'$ **after** $P$, denoted by $Q = Q'(\triangleleft P)$, iff $\forall a, c, (b_1, b_2) :$ $P(a, b_1) > 0$ implies $Q((b_1, b_2), c) = Q'((b_1, b_2), c)$.
$Q$ **is independent of** $B_2$, (denoted by $Q \dashv B_2$) iff $\forall (b_1, b_2), (b_1, b_2') \in B_1 \times B_2 :$ $Q((b_1, b_2)) = Q((b_1, b_2'))$.
For $Q \dashv B_2$ we define a **generalized sequential composition** $P; Q : A \rightsquigarrow C$ as follows: $(P; Q)(a, c) = \sum_{b_1 \in B_1} P(a)(b_1) \cdot Q((b_1, b_2))(c)$ where $b_2 \in B_2$ is arbitrarily chosen.

Theorem 7 below compares both sequential compositions. It allows to remove some sub-components of c-map , what we do implicitly in the proof of lemma 3. Theorem 8 reduces the equality of c-maps to the equality of their small sub-components after a common predecessor. In definition 9 we slightly generalize the notion of the independence of a set. Theorem 11 essentially allows to decompose a c-map into independent fragments. Lemma 12 regards some preservation properties of "$\|$".

**Theorem 7.** *For each* $R : A \rightsquigarrow B_2$, $Q \dashv B_2$ *holds:* $P; Q = (P \| R); Q$.

**Theorem 8.** *For any* $R : B_1 \times B_2 \rightsquigarrow D$ *holds:* $Q = Q'(\triangleleft P)$ *implies* $\binom{P;}{Q \| R} = \binom{P;}{Q' \| R}$.

**Definition 9.** Let $P(\{a\}) = \{b_1 \in B_1 : P(a, b_1) > 0\}$. We say that $Q$ is **independent of** $P$ (denoted $Q \dashv P$) iff

$$\forall a \in A, c \in C, b_1, b_1' \in P(\{a\}), b_2 \in B_2 \text{ holds } Q((b_1, b_2), c) = Q((b_1', b_2), c)$$

**Lemma 10.** $Q \dashv B_1$ *implies* $Q \dashv P$.

**Theorem 11.** *Let* $P_i : A \rightsquigarrow B_i$, $Q_i : B_1 \times B_2 \rightsquigarrow C_i$, *for* $i = 1, 2$, *such that* $Q_1 \dashv P_2$, $Q_2 \dashv P_1$. *Then*

$$\binom{P_1 \| P_2;}{Q_1 \| Q_2} = \binom{P_1 \| P_2;}{Q_1} \| \binom{P_1 \| P_2;}{Q_2}$$

**Lemma 12.** *Let* $Q_i, Q_i' : B_1 \times B_2 \rightsquigarrow C_i$, *for* $i = 1, 2$ *Then*
$Q_1 = Q_1'(\triangleleft P)$ *and* $Q_2 = Q_2'(\triangleleft P)$ *implies* $(Q_1 \| Q_2) = (Q_1' \| Q_2')(\triangleleft P)$.
$Q_1 \dashv B_1$ *and* $Q_2 \dashv B_1$ *implies* $(Q_1 \| Q_2) \dashv B_1$.
$Q_1 \dashv P$ *and* $Q_2 \dashv P$ *implies* $(Q_1 \| Q_2) \dashv P$.

**Proof of the lemma 3:** In the proof the assumption is done that $H$ is even (in the odd case proof runs analogously).

1) First we prove that $\Gamma_1;\Gamma_{\text{sim}}^1 = \Gamma_1;\Gamma_2^1$. From theorem 8 we conclude that it is enough to prove that $\sigma^r = \pi^r(\lhd\Gamma_1)$, for any even $r$. The principal idea now is to carefully separate the fragments of both c-maps of which $\sigma^r$, $\tau^r$, $\pi^r$ and $\Omega^r$ are independent. It is easy to see that: $\tau^{r,c} \dashv S^{D'_{r,c}}$, where $D'_{r,c} = (I \cup I_0) \setminus \{(r,c),(r-1,c),(r-1,\bar{c}^{(r-1)})\}$ and $\Omega^{r,c} \dashv S^{(I \cup I_0) \setminus \{(r,c)\}}$. There holds also $\tau^{r,c} \dashv \sigma^{r-1,c}$, $\tau^{r,c} \dashv \sigma^{r-1,\bar{c}^{(r-1)}}$. Now from lemma 12 we have: $\tau^r \dashv S^{(I \cup I_0) \setminus (I_r \cup I_{r-1})}$. From lemma 10 we have $\tau^r \dashv \sigma^q$, when $q \neq r$. We have also $\tau^r \dashv \pi^q$, $\Omega^r \dashv \pi^q$ (as $\pi^q$ is deterministic), for any $q$ and $\Omega^r \dashv \sigma^q$, for $q \neq r$. Quite analogously the analysis proceeds for $\sigma^{r,c} \dashv \ldots$ and $\pi^{r,c} \dashv \ldots$.

Now we are prepared to use theorem 11 together with lemmas 10 and 12 to divide $\Gamma_1$ into independent parts. We obtain:

$$\Gamma_1 = \begin{pmatrix} \sigma^0 \parallel \pi^1; \\ \tau^1 \end{pmatrix} \parallel \begin{pmatrix} \sigma^2 \parallel \pi^3; \\ \Omega^2 \parallel \tau^3 \end{pmatrix} \parallel \cdots \parallel \begin{pmatrix} \sigma^r \parallel \pi^{r+1}; \\ \Omega^r \parallel \tau^{r+1} \end{pmatrix} \parallel \cdots$$

It is enough to prove: $\sigma^r = \pi^r(\lhd\begin{pmatrix} \sigma^r \parallel \pi^{r+1}; \\ \Omega^r \parallel \tau^{r+1} \end{pmatrix})$. We want to consider as small pieces of the network as possible. Once more we use theorem 11 together with the lemmas and conclude that, what remains to show is:

$$\sigma^{r,c} = \pi^{r,c}\left(\lhd\begin{pmatrix} \sigma^{r,c} \parallel \sigma^{r,\bar{c}} \parallel \pi^{r+1,c} \parallel \pi^{r+1,\bar{c}}; \\ \Omega^{r,c} \parallel \Omega^{r,\bar{c}} \parallel \tau^{r+1,c} \parallel \tau^{r+1,\bar{c}} \end{pmatrix}\right), \text{ where } \bar{c} = \bar{c}^{(r)}. \text{ This can be}$$

easy observed by carefully looking at the definitions of $\sigma$ and $\tau$.

**Remark:** a slight difference arises for $r = 0$ or $r = H$, but the argument rests the same.

2) Second, we prove that $\Gamma_2^1;\Gamma_{\text{sim}}^2 = \Gamma_2$. By the analogous decomposition it is enough to show: $\begin{pmatrix} \pi^r \parallel \sigma^{r+1}; \\ \tau^{r+1} \end{pmatrix} = \begin{pmatrix} \pi^r \parallel \sigma^{r+1}; \\ \Omega^{r+1} \end{pmatrix}$, for even $r$, and after further decomposition:

$$\begin{pmatrix} \pi^{r,c} \parallel \pi^{r,\bar{c}} \parallel \sigma^{r+1,c}; \\ \tau^{r+1,c} \end{pmatrix} = \begin{pmatrix} \pi^{r,c} \parallel \pi^{r,\bar{c}} \parallel \sigma^{r+1,c}; \\ \Omega^{r+1,c} \end{pmatrix}, \text{ for even } r \text{ and any } c,$$

what can be verified from definitions.

From 1) and 2) we have $\Gamma_1;\Gamma_{\text{sim}} = \Gamma_1;\Gamma_2^1;\Gamma_{\text{sim}}^2 = \Gamma_1;\Gamma_2$. $\qquad\square$

# Decision Trees, Knowledge Rules and Some Related Data Mining Algorithms

Jia Liang Han

University of Southern Queensland, Toowoomba, Queensland 4350 AUSTRALIA

## Abstract

We show that the decision tree representation and the knowledge rules representation for data mining are semantically equivalent. Quinlan's production rule generators use attribute removal functions that are more powerful than ID3. The HCC-algorithm uses both attribute removal and concept tree ascension in its generalization function. The HCC-algorithm usually has more generalization power than the other ones. On computational efficiency, ID3 and the HCC-algorithm are efficient while Quinlan's production rule generators are less efficient. We also point out some disadvantages of the HCC-algorithm.

We propose a hybrid algorithm that combines all the above generalization functions and at the same time avoids over-generalization carefully. It is stable, complete, and non-local and is about as efficient as Quinlan's rule generators.

## 1 Introduction

Data mining (knowledge discovery in databases) [7] extracts implicit, previously unknown, useful information from large databases. Today's technology automatically generates huge amounts of data that are often not directly useful to applications and the size of data is so large that it is impossible, time consuming, or too costly to analyze data manually. Data mining has wide applications.

In this paper, we show that two of the knowledge representations for data mining, *decision trees* and *knowledge rules*, are semantically equivalent. We compare three data mining methods given in [8, 9, 3]. Quinlan's rule generators are strictly more powerful than ID3. The HCC-algorithm often has more generalization power than the other methods. Disadvantages of the HCC-algorithm are (a) its output may be incomplete, i.e., it may miss out some legitimate knowledge rules; (b) its output may be unstable, i.e., the output may depend on the ordering of data and implementation details; (c) the generalization decision is done locally instead of globally as in the other two methods.

We estimate computation costs of these methods assuming that the database size is no larger than main memory, known as *main memory data mining*. Let $|D|$ be the cardinality of the database, $\|D\|$ the database size, $|A|$ the arity of the relevant relation. We denote $\max(O(T_1), O(T_2), \ldots)$ by $O(T_1, T_2, \ldots)$. ID3 costs $O(|A||D|, c_d\|D\|)$, where $c_d$ is the unit cost of disk I/O. Quinlan's rule generators cost $O(\sum_i k_i|A||D|, c_d\|D\|)$. The HCC-algorithm costs approximately $O(|A||R||D|, c_d\|D\|)$, where $|R|$ is the cardinality of the concept hierarchy.

Practical applications may have various requirements on efficiency, completeness, stability, etc. Our analysis provides means to combine generalization functions and evaluation strategies to obtain many hybrid algorithms. As an example,
we give a stable, complete, non-local hybrid algorithm that incorporates many
generalization functions and avoids over-generalization carefully. The proposed
algorithm costs $O(\sum_i k_i|A||D|, d_t|A||D|, c_d\|D\|)$, where $d_t$ is the difference be-
tween the size of the concept hierarchy and the output threshold.

The rest is organized as follows. Section 2 introduces the background. Section 3 is on knowledge representations. Section 4 analyzes ID3. Quinlan's rule
generators are studied in section 5. The HCC-algorithm is examined in section
6. Section 7 introduces a hybrid algorithm. We conclude in section 8.

## 2  Background

From the viewpoint of semantics, data mining may be regarded as a subclass of
machine learning [2, 4, 5]. This paper belongs to *conceptual inductive learning*.
A general formalism for machine learning by Mitchell [5] is:

- *Given:*
    1. A language in which to describe data.
    2. A language in which to describe generalizations.
    3. A generalization function that matches data to generalizations.
    4. A set of positive and negative training data.
- *Determine:*
    - Generalizations within the provided language that are consistent with
      the presented training data.

The positiveness/negativeness of data is regarded as the *class*.

For this paper, input data for each problem consists of only one relation,
either a universal relation [6] or the relevant relation constructed from stored
relations [3]. The arguments of the relation are known as *attributes*. The input language is first order logic. The outputs here are either decision trees or
knowledge rules, also first order logic.

We use $A_i$ for attribute names, $a_i$ for attribute values or constants. Like in
[4], we use $\Rightarrow$ for implication instead of $\rightarrow$. A typical knowledge rule is

$$(A_1 = a_1)\&\ldots\&(A_k = a_k) \Rightarrow b, \quad [c]. \tag{1}$$

where $b$ represents a class. The optional $c$ stands for confidence (related to certainty factor in production rules [9], quantities in quantitative rules [3] or confidence in association rules [1]).

A knowledge rule might also be written in the form:

$$p(X_1,\ldots,X_n) \Rightarrow b, \quad [c], \tag{2}$$

where $p$ is a predicate symbol and $X_i$ can be either (anonymous) variables or constants. Because each problem has only one predicate symbol, it may be dropped

in (2). Since a variable does not restrict the data, it may be removed. Thus, although quite different looking, (2) is (1) in a different form.

*Generalization functions* are known as *generalization rules* in [4] or *matching predicates* in [5]. We use the term function to avoid possible confusion with knowledge rules. A generalization function maps a set of data into a more general formula. Suppose $g, f$ are two generalization functions. A generalization function $f$ has *strictly more generalization power* than $g$ if for any $D$ we can find another generalization function $h$ such that $h(g(D)) = f(D)$. In a weaker form, $f$ is *more powerful* than $g$ if for some $D$, $|f(D)| \leq |g(D)|$.

## 3 Equivalence of Two Representations

A decision tree is a tree in which each leaf is labeled by a class while the inner nodes are labeled by attributes. Any attribute may be chosen as the root. We may construct nodes and edges recursively starting from the root until all attributes have been considered. Finally, we assign classes to leaves. A decision tree thus constructed is known as a *complete decision tree*.

If all the leaves of a subtree belong to the same class, we may replace the whole subtree by one leaf node. This results in a *simplified decision tree*, which is more efficient to construct and to classify unknown tuples.

The following states equivalence of decision trees and knowledge rules.

**Theorem 1.** *For a decision tree, we can obtain a set of equivalent knowledge rules. For a set of knowledge rules, we can construct an equivalent decision tree.*

For the purpose to obtain confidence of a rule, we may record the number of training tuples that satisfy a rule as the *vote* of the rule [3] (on the leaf).

## 4 ID3 Algorithm

It is desirable to construct the simplest decision tree. However, such a goal is computation expensive. ID3 (Fig. 1) [8] uses information theory to construct a simple decision tree. Each step it chooses the attribute whose test gains the most information as the next node. This is a mean field approach that does not guarantee to find the simplest decision tree but significantly reduces cost.

The generalization function for ID3 replaces a subtree in a complete decision tree by one node to form a simplified decision tree. It is a *partial attribute removal type*, corresponding to dropping condition rule [4]. ID3 costs

$$O(|A||D|, c_d\|D\|). \tag{3}$$

## 5 Quinlan's Rule Generators

Quinlan proposed two rule generators [9] to extract knowledge rules from a decision tree. Both Quinlan's methods compare the original data with the knowledge

call function($S_0$)     // $S_0$ is the initial data
function($S$)     // $S$ is a set of tuples
(1)    **if** all tuples in $S$ belong to a single class $b$
(2)        **then** construct leaf $= b$;
(3)    **else begin**
(4)        **for** each remaining attribute **do**
(5)            find the information gain from testing this attribute;
(6)        select the attribute that gains most information;
(7)        draw a node labeled with this attribute;
(8)        partition $S$ into $\{S_i\}$ according to values of the attribute;
(9)        draw edges according to the values and nodes for $\{S_i\}$;
(10)       **for** each $S_i$ **do**
(11)           call function($S_i$); **end**

**Fig. 1.** Algorithm 1. The ID3 Algorithm.

rules generated from the decision tree. Quinlan's Rule Generator 1 (Fig. 2) considers effects of removing each condition in turn from each rule on $c$, the certainty factor (initially being 1), using a contingency table. If the removal does not reduce $c$ noticeably (a small threshold given by the problem), then this condition is removed. Finally, redundant rules are removed.

(1) **for** each tuple $r$ in $R$ **do**    // $R$ a decision tree
(2)    **for** each condition of $r$ **do begin**
(3)        construct a contingency table;
(4)        determine $c$ before/after removing condition $r$;
(5)        **if** its removal does not reduce $c$ significantly
(6)            **then** remove the condition;
(7)    **end**
(8) remove redundant tuples if any;

**Fig. 2.** Algorithm 2. Rule Generator 1 (partial attribute removal).

The total cost for Rule Generator 1 is in the order

$$O(\sum_i k_i |A||D|, c_d ||D||). \tag{4}$$

Quinlan's Rule Generator 2 (Fig. 3) is a *winnowing* process. A simple mechanism based on certainty factors was used in [9] to find a matching rule for a tuple to be classified. *Misclassification rate* is the ratio of the number of misclassified tuples versus the number of total tuples. For every rule $r$ in $R$, we examine the misclassification rates for both $R - \{r\}$ and $R$. If deleting $r$ does not increase the misclassification rate noticeably, then $r$ is removed from $R$. In Fig. 3, $t_m$ is the threshold for misclassification rate, which should be determined by the problem.

(1) **for** each rule $r$ in $R$ **do**
(2)     compute misclassification rate for $R$: $m_R$;
(3)     compute misclassification rate for $R - r$: $m_r$;
(4)     **if** $m_r - m_R \leq t_m$    // threshold test
(5)         **then** remove this rule;

**Fig. 3.** Algorithm 3. Rule Generator 2 (winnowing).

The cost of Fig. 3 using the method specified in [9] is again

$$O(\sum_i k_i |A||D|, c_d ||D||). \tag{5}$$

Both Quinlan's rule generators first use ID3 to construct a decision tree then apply the rule generators. This is unnecessary, as mentioned in [9]. It is possible to show that both Quinlan's rule generators may have strictly more generalization power than ID3. Thus, if they are applied to data directly, they may generate the same set of knowledge rules. However, applying ID3 first creates $R$. $\|R\|$ can be significantly less than $\|D\|$. This reduces computation cost. ID3 should be applied before the rule generators.

## 6   HCC-Algorithm

The HCC-algorithm [3] adapts a subset of well-known machine learning strategies to discover knowledge rules (characteristic rules, discriminant rules, and quantitative rules) from a large database.

Generalization functions in [3] are the *attribute removal* (*dropping condition rule* [4]) and the *concept tree ascension* (*climbing generalization trees* [4]). The attribute removal here is total not partial as in ID3 or [9].

Other strategies used in [3] include the following. (1) *Vote propagation.* (2) Attribute threshold, $t_a$. (3) Rule threshold, $t_r$. The number of knowledge rules, $|R|$, is restricted by $t_r$. The thresholds, $t_a, t_r$, either supplied by the user or system default, control the complexity of output.

The HCC-algorithm [3] (Fig. 4) has two phases (the original description does not state lines 1–5 explicitly). First, it generalizes a tuple according to $R$ and $H$ (line 3). $R$ contains the information on generalization used so far. Then, $t$ and $R$ are combined and generalized further in function *gen*. After *gen*, the number of rules in $R$ is $\leq t_r$ and the number of values for any attribute $|A_i| \leq t_a$. $R$ is then used for the next generalization step until all tuples in $D$ are processed.

Input: $D$: database; $H$: concept hierarchy;
Output: $R$: set of rules

(1)   initialize $R$ to the first tuple;
(2)   **for** each tuple $t$ in $D$ **do begin**
(3)      generalize $t$ according to $R$ and $H$;
(4)      call $gen(t, R)$; **end**

function $gen(t, R)$:    // $t$ : new tuple;
(6)   combine $t$ and $R$;    // $R$ : temporary results
(7)   **for** each attribute $A_i (1 \leq i \leq n)$ **do**
(8)      **while** $|A_i| > t_a$ **do**    // threshold test
(9)         **if** no higher level concept for $A_i$
(10)           **then** remove $A_i$;    // attribute removal
(11)        **else begin** perform concept tree ascension;
(12)           merge duplicate tuples; **end**
(13)     **while** $|R| > t_r$ **do begin**
(14)        selectively generalize attributes;
(15)        merge duplicate tuples; **end**

**Fig. 4.** Algorithm 4. The HCC-algorithm.

The cost of the HCC-algorithm is bound by

$$O(|A||R||D|, c_d\|D\|). \tag{6}$$

Generally speaking, the generalization functions of HCC are more powerful than ID3 or Quinlan's rule generators but they are not directly comparable. The output complexity of HCC is low, guaranteed by the thresholds.

There are certain disadvantages of the HCC-algorithm. (1) It may be incomplete. (2) It is unstable. (3) Generalization decisions are done locally. Local generalization is undesirable with respect to global generalization since it might over-generalize some attributes or rules while under-generalize others. To understand the first two points, let us view the output of generalization as a final decision tree. Given an initial decision tree (i.e., data), domain knowledge, and output requirements, there are usually a number of possible final decision trees. The HCC-algorithm gives one of these potential solutions and may miss out other legitimate solutions. The HCC-algorithm is unstable because a different solution may result if the ordering of data and implementation details are changed.

Unstability is not necessarily unacceptable. Many machine learning algorithms are unstable. For data mining, however, stability is desirable since the output is supposed to generalize all tuples in the database.

# 7 Hybrid Algorithms

Since data mining may be applied in diverse areas, it is likely that different applications may require different efficiency, generalization types, output complexity, etc. We may combine generalization functions and strategies to form hybrid algorithms. One may choose a suitable algorithm for a particular application.

ID3 may be used as the first stage of data mining. Its output may be used as the input of Quinlan's rule generators or HCC. Neither has to use ID3. ID3 + HCC may improve the stability but incur extra computation cost.

Generalization functions in [9] and in [3] are incompatible. We may combine them into hybrid algorithms. Furthermore, they may be modified (not considered in this paper) to reflect applications or domain knowledge.

Algorithm 5 in Fig. 5 is an example of hybrid algorithms. It utilizes domain knowledge in the form of primary keys (optional) and concept hierarchy. Algorithm 5 first removes an attribute(s) if it is a primary key since otherwise generalization will be difficult. Line 3 applies ID3. This step is optional. Since ID3 reduces the number of rules, sometimes significantly, and there is no risk of over-generalization, this step is recommended. Line 4 applies Quinlan's generalization functions. This step is somewhat expensive. The advantage of this step is that it risks little over-generalization. Like the HCC-algorithm, termination of Algorithm 5 is determined by the threshold, $t_r$. The main loop performs the concept tree ascension incrementally. In each iteration it examines the effect of various one concept tree ascensions. It chooses the ascension that has the most generalization power with the minimum misclassification as the next generalization step. Other choices might also be considered.

Algorithm 5 is complete and stable. Its generalization is non-local. To estimate computational cost of Algorithm 5, we note that line 4 dominates line 3 and costs $O(\sum_i k_i |A||D|)$. The loop iterates $d_t$ times, $d_t = d - t_r$, where $d$ is the size (the number of nodes) of the concept hierarchy. The computational cost of Algorithm 5, thus, is $O(\sum_i k_i |A||D|, d_t |A||D|, c_d ||D||)$.

(1)  **if** there is an uninteresting primary key
(2)      **then** remove the attribute(s);
(3)      apply ID3 (optional);
(4)      remove attributes using certainty factors;    // Quinlan's rule generators
(5)  **while** $|R_G| > t_r$ **begin**    // threshold test
(6)      **for** each concept tree ascension **do**
(7)          estimate the generalization gain and misclassification;
(8)      select the step which gains most and has least misclassification; **end**

**Fig. 5.** Algorithm 5. A stable hybrid data mining algorithm

# 8   Conclusion

In this paper, we show that the two knowledge representations in data mining: decision trees and knowledge rules, are semantically equivalent. We compare three data mining methods [8, 9, 3] in generalization functions, output complexity, computation costs, and stability. ID3 reorganizes data to find removable subtrees. It may output too many knowledge rules. ID3 costs $O(|A||D|, c_d||D||)$.

Quinlan's production rule generators uses partial attribute removal or a winnowing process. Quinlan's rule generators are more powerful than ID3. Their outputs have fewer knowledge rules. Their costs are $O(\sum_i k_i|A||D|, c_d||D||)$.

The HCC-algorithm uses both the attribute removal and the concept tree ascension. HCC normally has more generalization power than ID3 and Quinlan's rule generators. Its output complexity is restricted by user-supplied or system-default thresholds. It outputs a small number of knowledge rules. HCC is efficient, $O(|A||R||D|, c_d||D||)$. However, it may be incomplete, unstable, and local.

Many hybrid algorithms are possible. Algorithm 5 uses both the attribute removal and concept tree ascension. For the attribute removal, we argue that from semantics the first removal should be the primary key. The generalization function based on certainty factors (Quinlan's rule generators) is used. We then perform the concept tree ascension one step at a time based on the generalization gain and misclassification. Algorithm 5 costs $O(\sum_i k_i|A||D|, d_t|A||D|, c_k||D||)$. In comparison with HCC, Algorithm 5 is complete, stable, and nonlocal but is less efficient and more complex to implement.

Further research may conduct empirical studies on these algorithms and compare strong rules [6] and association rules [1] with knowledge rules.

# References

1. R. Agrawal, T. Imielinski, and A. Swami. Mining association rules between sets of items in large databases. In *Proc. 1993 ACM-SIGMOD*, pages 207–216, May 1993.
2. T. G. Dietterich and R. S. Michalski. A comparative review of selected methods for learning from examples. In Michalski et al., editor, *Machine Learning: An Artificial Intelligence Approach, Vol. 1*, pages 41–82. Morgan Kaufmann, 1983.
3. J. Han, Y. Cai, and N. Cercone. Knowledge discovery in databases: An attribute-oriented approach. In *Proc. 18th VLDB*, pages 547–559, August 1992.
4. R. S. Michalski. A theory and methodology of inductive learning. In Michalski et al., editor, *Machine Learning: An Artificial Intelligence Approach, Vol. 1*, pages 83–134. Morgan Kaufmann, 1983.
5. T. M. Mitchell. Generalization as search. *Artificial Intelligence*, 18:203–226, 1982.
6. G. Piatetsky-Shapiro. Discovery, analysis, and presentation of strong rules. In [7] pages 229–238. 1991.
7. G. Piatetsky-Shapiro and W. J. Frawley. *Knowledge Discovery in Databases*. AAAI/MIT Press, 1991.
8. J. R. Quinlan. Induction of decision trees. *Machine Learning*, 1:81–106, 1986.
9. J. R. Quinlan. Generating production rules from decision trees. In *Proc. 10th Int. Joint Conf. Artificial Intelligence*, pages 304–307, Milan, Italy, August 1987.

# Regularity is Decidable for Normed BPA and Normed BPP Processes in Polynomial Time

Antonín Kučera

e-mail: tony@fi.muni.cz

Faculty of Informatics, Masaryk University
Botanická 68a, 60200 Brno
Czech Republic

**Abstract.** We consider the problem of deciding regularity of normed BPP and normed BPA processes. A process is regular if it is bisimilar to a process with finitely many states. We show that regularity of normed BPP and normed BPA processes is decidable in polynomial time and we present constructive regularity tests. Combining these two results we obtain a rich subclass of normed PA processes (called sPA) where the regularity is also decidable. Moreover, constructiveness of this result implies decidability of bisimilarity for pairs of processes such that one process of this pair is sPA and the other has finitely many states.

## 1 Introduction

One of the most popular models for concurrency are process algebras like CCS, CSP or ACP. Various properties of these models have beed studied in the last decades. This paper belongs to the bunch which could be labelled "decidability results".

We consider the problem of deciding regularity in several process algebras. A process is regular if it is bisimilar to a process with finitely many states. Almost all interesting properties are decidable for finite-state processes and designed algorithms are practically usable.

This is no more true if one moves to process classes which contain also processes with infinitely many states (up to bisimilarity). Some problems can remain decidable—for example, bisimilarity is known to be decidable for BPA (see [1, 3, 10, 8, 6]) and BPP (see [5, 4]) processes. The same problem becomes undecidable for labelled Petri nets (see [11]). But even if a given property is decidable, the algorithm is usually not interesting from the practical point of view due to its complexity. Before running a complex algorithm, it is a good idea to ask whether the process we are dealing with can be replaced with some equivalent (bisimilar) process with finitely many states. If so, we can usually run a much more efficient algorithm. Natural questions are, whether the regularity is decidable for a given class of processes and whether the equivalent finite-state process can be effectively constructed.

This natural problem is generally undecidable (see [17]), but Mauw and Mulder showed in [14], that "regularity" is decidable in the class of BPA processes.

The quotes are important here because Mauw and Mulder used the word regularity in a different sense.

A recent result of Esparza and Jančar [7] says that regularity is decidable for labelled Petri nets. The algorithm is obtained by a combination of two semi-decidability results and hence there are no complexity estimations.

In this paper we prove that regularity is decidable in classes of normed BPA and normed BPP processes. Presented algorithms are polynomial (and practically usable). As normed BPP processes form a proper subclass of labelled Petri nets, this part of our result can be seen as a refinement of [7].

Combining decision algorithms for normed BPA and normed BPP we can even prove that regularity is decidable in quite a large subclass of normed PA processes (PA processes have both sequential and parallel compositions and were introduced in [2]). We denote this subclass sPA ("s" stands for simple). The class sPA is strictly greater then the union of normed BPA and normed BPP processes. Moreover, if the tested sPA process $\Delta$ is regular then a process $\Delta'$ with finitely many states such that $\Delta \sim \Delta'$ can be effectively constructed.

An interesting related problem is decidability of various behavioural equivalences and preorders for pairs of processes such that one process of this pair has finitely many states. For example, Jančar and Moller proved in [12] that bisimilarity is decidable for a pair of labelled Petri nets provided one net of this pair is bounded (a net is bounded iff it has finitely many states). The same result holds for trace equivalence and simulation equivalence.

The constructiveness of our decidability result for sPA allows us to conclude that bisimilarity is decidable for pairs of processes, such that one process is sPA and the other has finitely many states (decidabilility of bisimilarity for PA and even for sPA processes are open questions).

## 2 Basic definitions

### 2.1 BPA and BPP processes

Let $Act = \{a, b, c, \ldots\}$ be a countably infinite set of *atomic actions*. Let $Var = \{X, Y, Z, \ldots\}$ be a countably infinite set of *variables* such that $Var \cap Act = \emptyset$. The classes of recursive BPA and BPP expressions are defined by the following abstract syntax equations:

$$E_{BPA} ::= a \mid X \mid E_{BPA}.E_{BPA} \mid E_{BPA} + E_{BPA}$$
$$E_{BPP} ::= a \mid X \mid aE_{BPP} \mid E_{BPP}\|E_{BPP} \mid E_{BPP} + E_{BPP}$$

Here $a$ ranges over $Act$ and $X$ ranges over $Var$. The symbol $Act^*$ denotes the set of all finite strings over $Act$.

As usual, we restrict our attention to guarded expressions. A BPA or BPP expression $E$ is *guarded* if every variable occurence in $E$ is within the scope of an atomic action.

A *guarded BPA (or BPP) process* is defined by a finite family $\Delta$ of recursive process equations

$$\Delta = \{X_i \stackrel{def}{=} E_i \mid 1 \leq i \leq n\}$$

where $X_i$ are distinct elements of *Var* and $E_i$ are guarded BPA (or BPP) expressions, containing variables from $\{X_1, \ldots, X_n\}$. The set of variables which appear in $\Delta$ is denoted by $Var(\Delta)$.

The variable $X_1$ plays a special role ($X_1$ is sometimes called *the leading variable*—it is a root of a labelled transition system, defined by the process $\Delta$ and following rules:

$$\frac{}{a \xrightarrow{a} \epsilon} \qquad \frac{E \xrightarrow{a} E'}{E.F \xrightarrow{a} E'.F} \qquad \frac{E \xrightarrow{a} E'}{E + F \xrightarrow{a} E'} \qquad \frac{F \xrightarrow{a} F'}{E + F \xrightarrow{a} F'}$$

$$\frac{E \xrightarrow{a} E'}{E \| F \xrightarrow{a} E' \| F} \qquad \frac{F \xrightarrow{a} F'}{E \| F \xrightarrow{a} E \| F'} \qquad \frac{E \xrightarrow{a} E'}{X \xrightarrow{a} E'} \; (X \overset{def}{=} E \in \Delta)$$

The symbol $\epsilon$ denotes the empty expression with usual conventions: $\epsilon \| E = E$, $E \| \epsilon = E$ and $\epsilon.E = E$. Nodes of the transition system generated by $\Delta$ are BPA (or BPP) expressions, which are often called *states of $\Delta$*, or just "states" when $\Delta$ is understood from the context. We also define the relation $\xrightarrow{w}*$, where $w \in Act^*$, as the reflexive and transitive closure of $\xrightarrow{a}$ (we often write $E \rightarrow^* F$ instead of $E \xrightarrow{w}* F$ if $w$ is irrelevant). Given two states $E, F$, we say that $F$ is *reachable from $E$*, if $E \rightarrow^* F$. States of $\Delta$ which are reachable from $X_1$ are said to be *reachable*.

*Remark.* Processes are often identified with their leading variables. Furthermore, if we assume a fixed process $\Delta$, we can view any process expression $E$ (not necessarily guarded) whose variables are defined in $\Delta$ as a process too; we simply add a new leading equation $X \overset{def}{=} E'$ to $\Delta$, where $X$ is a variable from *Var* such that $X \notin Var(\Delta)$ and $E'$ is a process expression which is obtained from $E$ by substituting each variable in $E$ with the right-hand side of its corresponding defining equation in $\Delta$ ($E'$ must be guarded now). All notions originally defined for processes can be used for process expressions in this sense too.

**Bisimulation** The equivalence between process expressions (states) we are interested in here is *bisimilarity* [16], defined as follows:

**Definition 1.** A binary relation R over process expressions is a *bisimulation* if whenever $(E, F) \in R$ then for each $a \in Act$

- if $E \xrightarrow{a} E'$, then $F \xrightarrow{a} F'$ for some $F'$ such that $(E', F') \in R$
- if $F \xrightarrow{a} F'$, then $E \xrightarrow{a} E'$ for some $E'$ such that $(E', F') \in R$

Processes $\Delta$ and $\Delta'$ are *bisimilar*, written $\Delta \sim \Delta'$, if their leading variables are related by some bisimulation.

**Normed processes** Important subclasses of BPA and BPP processes can be obtained by an extra restriction of *normedness*. A variable $X \in Var(\Delta)$ is *normed* if there is $w \in Act^*$ such that $X \xrightarrow{w}* \epsilon$. In that case we define the *norm* of $X$, written $|X|$, to be the length of the shortest such $w$. Thus $|X| = \min\{Length(w) \mid X \xrightarrow{w}* \epsilon\}$. A process $\Delta$ is *normed* if all variables of $Var(\Delta)$ are normed. The norm of $\Delta$ is then defined to be the norm of $X_1$.

**Greibach normal form** Any BPA or BPP process $\Delta$ can be effectively presented in so-called 3-Greibach normal form (see [1] and [4]). Before the definition we need to introduce the set $Var(\Delta)^*$ of all finite sequences of variables from $Var(\Delta)$, and the set $Var(\Delta)^\otimes$ of all finite multisets over $Var(\Delta)$. Each multiset of $Var(\Delta)^\otimes$ denotes a BPP expression by combining its elements in parallel using the '$\|$' operator.

**Definition 2.** A BPA (resp. BPP) process $\Delta$ is said to be in *Greibach normal form (GNF)* if all its equations are of the form

$$X \stackrel{def}{=} \sum_{j=1}^{n} a_j \alpha_j$$

where $n \in N$, $a_j \in Act$ and $\alpha_j \in Var(\Delta)^*$ (resp. $\alpha_j \in Var(\Delta)^\otimes$). We also require that for each $X \in Var(\Delta)$ there is reachable state $\alpha$ of $\Delta$ such that $X \in \alpha$. If $Length(\alpha_j) \leq 2$ (resp. $card(\alpha_j) \leq 2$) for each $j$, $1 \leq j \leq n$, then $\Delta$ is said to be in 3-GNF.

From now on we assume that all BPA and BPP processes we are working with are presented in GNF. This justifies also the assumption that all reachable states of a BPA process $\Delta$ are elements of $Var(\Delta)^*$ and all reachable states of a BPP process $\Delta'$ are elements of $Var(\Delta')^\otimes$.

**sPA processes** To be able to define the class of sPA processes we first need the notion of *VPA expression*. VPA expressions are defined as follows:

$$E_{VPA} ::= X \mid E_{VPA} \| E_{VPA} \mid E_{VPA}.E_{VPA}$$

The set of variables, which apper in a VPA expression $\alpha$ is denoted $Var(\alpha)$. The class of sPA processes is composed of VPA expresions whose variables are normed BPA or normed BPP processes (see remark in Section 2.1). An sPA process $\alpha$ generates a labelled trasition system using SOS rules mentioned above. The root of this transition system is $\alpha$.

sPA processes form a subclass of PA processes (defined in [2]). The main restriction is the form of recursion which is allowed in sPA (the variables of $Var(\alpha)$ can be defined recursively, but using only BPA or only BPP operators). In spite of this restriction, sPA class is strictly greater then the union of normed BPA and normed BPP processes. This is demonstrated by the following example:

*Example 1.* Let $\Delta_1, \Delta_2$ be normed BPA processes given by the following equations:

$$\Delta_1 : X \stackrel{def}{=} aY + bZ \qquad\qquad \Delta_2 : A \stackrel{def}{=} cB + dC$$
$$Y \stackrel{def}{=} a(Y.Y) + bX + b \qquad\qquad B \stackrel{def}{=} c(B.B) + dA + d$$
$$Z \stackrel{def}{=} aX + b(Z.Z) + a \qquad\qquad C \stackrel{def}{=} cA + d(C.C) + c$$

Then there is no normed BPA or BPP process bisimilar to the sPA process $X\|A$ (it can be proved using pumping lemmas for context-free languages and for BPP languages—see [4]).

## 2.2 Regular processes

The main question considered in this paper is, whether the behaviour of a given process is regular, i.e. whether it is bisimilar to a process with finitely many states.

**Definition 3.** A process $\Delta$ is *regular* if there is a process $\Delta'$ with finitely many states such that $\Delta \sim \Delta'$.

It is easy to show that a process is regular iff it can reach only finitely many states up to bisimilarity. In [15] it is shown, that regular processes can be represented in the following normal form:

**Definition 4.** A regular process $\Delta$ is said to be in normal form if all its equations are of the form

$$X_i \stackrel{def}{=} \sum_{j=1}^{n_i} a_{ij} X_{ij}$$

where $1 \leq i \leq n$, $n_i \in N$, $a_{ij} \in Act$ and $X_{ij} \in Var(\Delta)$.

Thus a process $\Delta$ is regular iff there is a regular process $\Delta'$ in normal form such that $\Delta \sim \Delta'$.

## 3 Constructive regularity tests for normed BPA, normed BPP and sPA processes

In this section we show that regularity is decidable for normed BPA, normed BPP and sPA processes. Proofs are mostly omitted due to the lack of space and can be found in [13].

**Definition 5.** Let $\Delta$ be a normed BPA (resp. BPP) process. A variable $X \in Var(\Delta)$ is *growing* if $X \rightarrow^* X.\alpha$ (resp. $X \rightarrow^* X\|\alpha$) where $\alpha \neq \epsilon$.

**Lemma 6.** *Let $\Delta$ be a normed BPA (resp. BPP) process in 3-GNF. It is decidable, whether $Var(\Delta)$ contains a growing variable.*

*Proof.* We define the binary relation *Grow* on $Var(\Delta)$ in the following way:

$$(X,Y) \in Grow \stackrel{def}{\Longleftrightarrow} X \rightarrow^* Y.\alpha \text{ (resp. } X \rightarrow^* Y\|\alpha) \text{ where } \alpha \neq \epsilon.$$

Clearly $Var(\Delta)$ contains a growing variable iff there is $X \in Var(\Delta)$ such that $(X,X) \in Grow$. We show that the relation *Grow* can be effectively constructed. We need two auxiliary binary relations on $Var(\Delta)$:

$\leadsto$:     $X \leadsto Y \stackrel{def}{\Longleftrightarrow}$ there is a summand $a\alpha$ in the defining equation for $X$ in $\Delta$ such that $\alpha = Y.Z$ (resp. $\alpha = Y\|Z$ or $\alpha = Z\|Y$) where $Z \in Var(\Delta)$

$\hookrightarrow$:     $X \hookrightarrow Y \stackrel{def}{\Longleftrightarrow}$ there is a summand $a\alpha$ in the defining equation for $X$ in $\Delta$ such that $Y \in Var(\alpha)$.

It is easy to prove that $Grow = \hookrightarrow^* . \rightsquigarrow . \hookrightarrow^*$, where $\hookrightarrow^*$ denotes the reflexive and transitive closure of $\hookrightarrow$. Moreover, the composition $\hookrightarrow^* . \rightsquigarrow . \hookrightarrow^*$ can be effectively constructed.

Let $\Delta$ be a normed BPA or BPP process in GNF. Let $n$ denote the number of summands which are contained in defining equations of $\Delta$. Relations $\rightsquigarrow$ and $\hookrightarrow$ can be computed in $n$ steps. As relations can be represented as boolean matrices and closure as well as product of boolean matrices can be computed in polynomial time, we can conclude that the relation $Grow$ can be computed in polynomial time.

**Proposition 7.** *Let $\Delta$ be a normed BPA or BPP process in 3-GNF. $\Delta$ is regular iff $Var(\Delta)$ does not contain any growing variable.*

*Proof.* It can be found in [13].

**Proposition 8.** *Let $\Delta$ be a normed BPA or BPP process. If $\Delta$ is regular, then a regular process $\Delta'$ in normal form such that $\Delta \sim \Delta'$ can be effectively constructed.*

*Proof.* It can be found in [13].

Propositions 7 and 8 together say that there are constructive regularity tests for normed BPA and BPP processes.

It is interesting to compare this result with decidability issues of context-free languages. For any normed BPA or BPP process $\Delta$ we can define its associated language over the alphabet $Act$ in the following way:

$$Language(\Delta) = \{w \in Act^* \mid X_1 \xrightarrow{w}{}^* \epsilon\}$$

The variable $X_1$ is the leading variable of $\Delta$. Normed BPA processes in 3-GNF can be seen as context-free grammars in 3-GNF and hence the class of languages generated by normed BPA processes is exactly the class of context-free languages. It is well-known that a CF language $L$ is not regular iff each CF grammar generating $L$ contains a self-embedding nonterminal. Self-embedding nonterminals are in some sense related to growing variables (see Definition 5). Growing variables and self-embedding nonterminals can be effectively recognised. However, an existence of a self-embedding nonterminal in a given CF grammar $G$ does not allow to conclude that $L(G)$ is not regular. There can still be an equivalent grammar which does not contain any self-embedding nonterminal. Bisimulation equivalence is a finer relation—if a given normed BPA process $\Delta$ contains a growing variable, then each bisimilar normed BPA process $\Delta'$ has this property. We could also speak about "regularity w.r.t. language equivalence" (a process $\Delta$ is regular w.r.t. language equivalence if there is a process $\Delta'$ with finitely many states such that $Language(\Delta) = Language(\Delta')$). Hence regularity (w.r.t. bisimulation equivalence) is decidable for normed BPA processes, while regularity w.r.t. language equivalence is not.

Normed BPP processes generate a class of languages which is incomparable with context-free languages but it forms a proper subclass of context-sensitive languages.

Now we show that we can combine these two results and obtain a positive decidability result also for sPA processes:

**Proposition 9.** *Regularity is decidable for sPA processes in polynomial time.*

*Proof.* (sketch) It suffices to prove that an sPA process $\alpha$ is regular iff all its variables from $Var(\alpha)$ are regular (see remark in Section 2.1). The proof is easy to complete by induction on the structure of $\alpha$. The only subcase which is not immediate is $\alpha = \beta_1.\beta_2$. It can be proved using a cancelation lemma for normed processes (see [3]).

Moreover, if the tested sPA process is regular then the regular process $\Delta'$ in normal form such that $\alpha \sim \Delta'$ can be effectively constructed. It implies the following proposition:

**Proposition 10.** *Bisimilarity is decidable for pairs of processes such that one process of this pair is sPA and the other is a regular process in normal form.*

## 4 Conclusions, future work

If we compare the decidability results, obtained for classes of normed BPP and normed BPA processes, we can observe that they are of a similar form. This is not surprising if fact—the only difference between BPP and BPA algebras is the form of binary composition they provide—the parallel composition in the case of BPP and the sequential composition in the case of BPA. But these two operators have similar algebraic properties and it reflects in many things—processes of BPP and BPA can be represented in similar normal forms (GNF), there are similar cancelation properties, the notion of self-bisimulation, introduced in [3], can be defined in a uniform way (see [9]) and so on.

Presented regularity tests are of polynomial time complexity (all what has to be done is the computation of the *Grow* relation). But if we want to *construct* a bisimilar process with finitely many states in normal form, we are faced to the problem of exponential state explosion—hence the space complexity is exponential because we need a special variable (and a special defining equation) for each such state.

An open problem still remains the question of deciding regularity in the class of PA processes and this is the area we would like to examine in the future.

## Acknowledgement

All presented results were obtained during my stay at BRICS (Basic Research in Computer Science), Department of Computer Science, University of Aarhus.

I would like to thank Mogens Nielsen for his support and encouragement. He was always willing to listen to my ideas, commenting them in a very inspiring way. Thanks are also due to Mojmír Křetínský for reading the first draft of this paper and providing me with various helpful information.

# References

1. J. C. M. Baeten, J. A. Bergstra, and J. W. Klop. Decidability of bisimulation equivalence for processes generating context-free languages. In *Proceedings of PARLE 87*, volume 259 of *LNCS*, pages 93–114. Springer-Verlag, 1987.
2. J. C. M. Baeten and W. P. Weijland. *Process Algebra*. Number 18 in Cambridge Tracts in Theoretical Computer Science. Cambridge University Press, 1990.
3. D. Caucal. Graphes canoniques de graphes algebriques. Rapport de Recherche 872, INRIA, 1988.
4. S. Christensen. *Decidability and Decomposition in Process Algebras*. PhD thesis, The University of Edinburgh, 1993.
5. S. Christensen, Y. Hirsfeld, and F. Moller. Bisimulation is decidable for all basic parallel processes. In *Proceedings of CONCUR 93*, volume 715 of *LNCS*, pages 143–157. Springer-Verlag, 1993.
6. S. Christensen, H. Hüttel, and C. Stirling. Bisimulation equivalence is decidable for all context-free processes. In *Proceedings of CONCUR 92*, volume 630 of *LNCS*, pages 138–147. Springer-Verlag, 1992.
7. J. Esparza and P. Jančar. Deciding finiteness of Petri nets up to bisimilarity. In *Proceedings of ICALP 96*, volume 1099 of *LNCS*, pages 478–489. Springer-Verlag, 1996.
8. J. F. Groote. A short proof of the decidability of bisimulation for normed BPA processes. *Information Processing Letters*, 42:167–171, 1991.
9. Y. Hirsfeld. Deciding equivalences in simple process algebras. Technical report ECS-LFCS-94-294, Department of Computer Science, University of Edinburgh, 1994.
10. H. Hüttel and C. Stirling. Actions speak louder than words: Proving bisimilarity for context-free processes. In *Proceedings of LICS 91*, pages 376–386. IEEE Computer Society Press, 1991.
11. P. Jančar. Decidability questions for bisimilarity of Petri nets and some related problems. In *Proceedings of STACS 94*, volume 775 of *LNCS*, pages 581–592. Springer-Verlag, 1994.
12. P. Jančar and F. Moller. Checking regular properties of Petri nets. In *Proceedings of CONCUR 95*, volume 962 of *LNCS*, pages 348–362. Springer-Verlag, 1995.
13. A. Kučera. Deciding regularity in process algebras. BRICS Report Series RS-95-52, Department of Computer Science, University of Aarhus, October 1995.
14. S. Mauw and H. Mulder. Regularity of BPA-systems is decidable. In *Proceedings of CONCUR 94*, volume 836 of *LNCS*, pages 34–47. Springer-Verlag, 1994.
15. R. Milner. *Communication and Concurrency*. Prentice-Hall International, 1989.
16. D.M.R. Park. Concurrency and automata on infinite sequences. In *Proceedings 5th GI Conference*, volume 104 of *LNCS*, pages 167–183. Springer-Verlag, 1981.
17. D. Taubner. *Finite Representations of CCS and TCSP Programs by Automata and Petri Nets*. Number 369 in LNCS. Springer-Verlag, 1989.

# A New Proposal of Concurrent Process Calculus *

Salvador Lucas and Javier Oliver

Departamento de Sistemas Informáticos y Computación
Universidad Politécnica de Valencia
Camino de Vera s/n, Apdo. 22012, 46020 Valencia, Spain.
e.mail:{slucas,joliver}@dsic.upv.es

**Abstract.** In this paper, we present a new calculus to model concurrent systems, the Parallel Label-Selective λ-calculus. This calculus integrates the (functional) expressiveness of the λ-calculus in a unified framework with some powerful features for expressing communication actions and supporting the independence of processes which can be a main source of improvement when performing parallel computations.

**Keywords:** Concurrency, Extensions of λ-calculus, Functional Programming, Process Algebra.

## 1 Introduction

A computational model *links* the software and hardware description levels of computer systems, in order to analyze the correctness, completeness or efficiency of programs which we want to run on a given machine. General agreement seems to exist on the main features that a model of concurrency should include: a concurrent system is *a community of sequential processes which can work in an independent or interdependent fashion* [3]. Concurrency and communication express *independency* and *interdependency*: concurrent processes (independently) deal with their respective tasks until a cooperation (i.e., a communication) is needed. Functional languages provide an excellent tool for parallel computation because there are no side-effects. Functional programs can be evaluated sequentially or in parallel without changing their denotational or declarative semantics. Nevertheless, the inclusion of constructs for explicit concurrency enhances the expressiveness of executable specification languages as there are programs which can best be described as a composition of parallel processes [8]. Sequential (*functional*) computation is traditionally captured by the λ-calculus [2] as Berry showed in [4]. Function declarations and their application to data (which can eventually be other functions) is supported by the language. Thus, an important challenge for researchers was to find a framework for the concurrency and the communication between processes similar to the λ-calculus, [1, 5, 7, 10, 11].

We introduce the Parallel Label-Selective λ-calculus, LCEP², to model concurrency and communication from a functional perspective. The expressiveness of the λ-calculus is integrated within a unified framework with powerful features to explicitly express the communication actions and the independence of processes, which are the main source of improvements when performing parallel computations. Since our framework originates from the λ-calculus, we chose a

---

* This work has been partially supported by CICYT, TIC 95-0433-C03-03.
² λ-Cálculo Etiquetado Paralelo.

*functional* point of view to describe concurrency. The basic feature of functional programming is the application of functions to values. In this setting, *communication* can be viewed as *argument instantiation*, if we embed the adequate means to provide 'remote' instantiation of parameters. The formal parameter takes the role of a communication channel. The need for an ordered matching of the formal and actual parameters is also relaxed to bring up the necessary independence of parallel systems. This allows us to speak of the *sequential* application of a function to its parameters instead of the standard application, and the *parallel* application of a function to remote, possibly committing parameters which in this case models the standard communication. The idea of *how long* and *to what extent* a remote parameter can be instantiated in a function call is captured by means of the notion of *tunnel*, which is novel in the literature.

This paper is organized as follows: Section 2 describes the language and the reduction system of the calculus. Section 3 gives a general idea of using LCEP as a target language to mechanize functional concurrent languages. The last section offers some conclusions and suggestions for future work.

## 2 The calculus

LCEP is a calculus which originated from a previous proposal by H. Aït-Kaci, the *Label-Selective $\lambda$-calculus* [1], an extension of the $\lambda$-calculus in which function arguments are selected by labels. Symbolic and numeric labels can be used to name the communication channels. This has not been possible in other proposals and permits the use of currying and labeled specification of parameters. It makes the ordering of the actual parameters in a function call independent of the presentation order of the formal parameters in the definition.

**Example 1** Let $f = \lambda x y . x - y$ be a $\lambda$-term. In LCEP, we can define the function $f$ as $f(p, q) = \lambda_p x . \lambda_q y . x - y$. We name the formal parameters of $f$ by means of labels $p, q$. We can specify the application of $f$ to parameters $a, b$ by giving its destination in two ways: by explicitly indicating either the *number* of the formal parameters, $f(b — 2, a — 1) = f(a, b)$, or the *name* of the formal parameters, $f(b — \mathbf{q}, a — \mathbf{p}) = f(a, b)$.

However, the *Label-Selective $\lambda$-calculus* is not very appropriate for concurrency: it lacks both a non-deterministic choice and explicit parallelism operators. The calculus supports concurrency among different channels, but it is not able to describe, for example, alternative choices over the *same* channel. For instance, the *dining philosophers problem*, cannot be modeled using Label-Selective $\lambda$-calculus because non-deterministic choice and parallelism operators are both needed [12]. They are introduced by following Milner's $\pi$-calculus [11].

### 2.1 Description of LCEP

Let $\mathcal{V} = \{x, y, z, \ldots\}$ be a set of variables, and $\mathcal{C} = \{a, b, c, \ldots\}$ be a set of constants. $P$ represents a channel name from a set of labels $\mathcal{L} = \mathbb{N} \cup \mathcal{S}$, where $m, n, \ldots$ denote numerical labels taken from $\mathbb{N}$ (the set of natural numbers), $\mathcal{S} = \{p, q, \ldots\}$ is a set of symbolic labels, and $\mathbb{N} \cap \mathcal{S} = \emptyset$. Constants, variables and the null process (denoted by 0) form the *atomic* elements of the language. The language of the formal system that we present is $\mathcal{M}$. It is defined as follows:

$M ::= 0 \mid a \mid x \mid \lambda p x . M \mid \widehat{p} M \mid (M \parallel M) \mid (M \circ M) \mid (M + M) \mid !M$

$P ::= number \mid symbol$

In concurrent programming, the terms $M \in \mathcal{M}$ represent *processes*. Symbols o (*sequential* composition), $\|$ (*parallel* composition), $+$ (*nondeterministic choice*) and ! (*replication*) are considered as *process constructors*. The operators $\lambda_P x$ (abstraction or *input*) and $\hat{P}$ (parameter passing or *output*) are also considered as *process constructors*, whose effect over a process $M$ is to define processes ($\lambda_P x.M$ and $\hat{P}M$, respectively) which are involved in functional applications under certain given conditions. We consider a *partial order* relation, $\preceq_{\mathcal{L}}$ on $\mathcal{L}$. The numerical label 0 is the minimum of this *poset*. By analogy with $\lambda$-calculus, the process constructors can be viewed as symbols of a signature [9], that is, a set of function symbols, each of which has a fixed arity. Symbols o, $\|$, $+$ are binary operations, !, $\lambda_P x$ and $\hat{P}$ are unary operations for all $P \in \mathcal{L}$ and $x \in \mathcal{V}$, $x, 0$ are 0-ary operations for all $x \in \mathcal{V}$ and we let $\mathcal{P} = \{\hat{P} : P \in \mathcal{L}\}$ and $\Lambda = \{\lambda_P x : (P \in \mathcal{L}) \wedge (x \in \mathcal{V})\}$ be the set of output and input operations, respectively. The terms of this signature are called $\lambda_\|$-terms.

We use the habitual notions of *occurrence, set of occurrences, subterm*, etc. (see [6] for complete definitions). Terms are viewed as labeled trees in the usual way. Occurrences $u, v, \ldots$ are chains of positive natural numbers used to address subterms of $t$. They are ordered by: $u \leq v$. if $\exists w. u.w = v$. We let $u \mid v$ iff $u \not\leq v$ and $v \not\leq u$. $O(t)$ denotes the set of occurrences of a term $t$. $t|_u$ is the subterm at an occurrence $u$ of $t$. $t[s]_u$ is the term $t$ with the subterm at the occurrence $u$ replaced with $s$. $t[u]$ denotes the symbol which labels the root of $t|_u$.

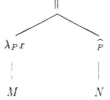

**Fig. 1.** Syntactical tree of the process $\lambda_P x.M \parallel \hat{P}N$

In the tree representation of a $\lambda_\|$-term $A$, a tuple $\gamma = \langle u_1, \ldots, u_n \rangle$, $u_i \in O(A)$ for $1 \leq i \leq n$ is a *path between the subprocesses* $M = A|_u$ and $N = A|_v$ ($u.v$ disjoint occurrences), if $\gamma$ is the shortest path in $A$ verifying $u_1 = u'$ and $u_n = v'$ whenever $u = u'.i$ and $v = v'.j$ for some $i, j \in \mathbb{N}$. We associate to the path of occurrences $\gamma$ the path $\gamma^s = \langle s_1, \ldots, s_n \rangle$ of symbols $s_i = A[u_i]$ rooted at these occurrences. For the sake of expressiveness, we usually identify $\gamma^s$ and $\gamma$. For example, in Figure 1 the path between the processes $M$ and $N$ is $\langle \lambda_P x, \|, \hat{P} \rangle$.

The symbol $\equiv$ represents the least congruence over $\mathcal{M}$, satisfying the following properties [11]: $(\mathcal{M}/ \equiv, \|, 0)$ and $(\mathcal{M}/ \equiv, +, 0)$ are commutative monoids, $M \circ 0 = 0 \circ M \equiv M$ (identity), $!M \equiv M \parallel !M$, and $\hat{0}M \equiv M$.

## 2.2  Reduction system

Reductions between processes are defined by an Inference System.

**Axioms:** First, $\beta_{sec}$ and $\beta_P$ model the different kinds of application.
1. $\beta_{sec}$: $\beta$ sequential application:
   $$(\ldots + \lambda_P x.M) \circ (\hat{P}N \circ L + \ldots) \longrightarrow_{\beta_{sec}} M[N/x] \circ L \text{ where } P \in \mathcal{L} - \{0\}$$
2. $\beta_P$: $\beta$ parallel application, through the argument labeled with channel $P$:
   $$(\ldots + \lambda_P x.M) \parallel (\hat{P}N \circ L + \ldots) \longrightarrow_{\beta_P} M[N/x] \parallel L \text{ where } P \in \mathcal{L} - \{0\} \text{ and }$$
   $\beta_P$ is a family of rules indexed by $\mathcal{L} - \{0\}$.

$\beta_{sec}$ models the standard *side-by-side* application of a function to its arguments. A $\beta_P$ rule expresses the 'parallel' application of a function to (possibly many) committing arguments (on the same *channel* or *name-of-formal-parameter*). Therefore, $\beta_P$ expresses the classical communication process on a channel $P$, which can also be viewed from a functional perspective.

Now the *reordering* rules extend the corresponding rules of the Label-Selective $\lambda$-calculus. They manage currying and unordered specification of arguments to a function (Example 1).

1. Reordering with numeric labels. Let $m, n \in \mathbb{N} - \{0\}$, $L, M, N \in \mathcal{M}$, $x, y \in \mathcal{V}$:

$\eta_1 : (\lambda_m x.\lambda_n y.M) \to_{\eta_1} (\lambda_n y.\lambda_{m-1} x.M)$      if $m \succ_{\mathcal{L}} n$

$\eta_2 : \widehat{m}M \circ \widehat{n}N \to_{\eta_2} \widehat{n}N \circ \widehat{m-1}M$      if $m \succ_{\mathcal{L}} n$

$\eta_{sec_3} : (\dots + \lambda_m x.M) \circ (\widehat{n}N \circ L + \dots) \to_{\eta_{sec_3}} \lambda_{m-1}x.(M \circ \widehat{n}N) \circ L$ if $m \succ_{\mathcal{L}} n$

$\eta_{sec_4} : (\dots + \lambda_m x.M) \circ (\widehat{n}N \circ L + \dots) \to_{\eta_{sec_4}} \lambda_m x.(M \circ \widehat{n-1}N) \circ L$ if $m \prec_{\mathcal{L}} n$

2. Reordering with symbolic labels. Let $p, q \in \mathcal{S}$, $L, M, N \in \mathcal{M}$, $x, y \in \mathcal{V}$:

$\rho_1 : (\lambda_p x.\lambda_q y.M) \to_{\rho_1} (\lambda_q y.\lambda_p x.M)$      if $p \succ_{\mathcal{L}} q$

$\rho_2 : \widehat{p}M \circ \widehat{q}N \to_{\rho_2} \widehat{q}N \circ \widehat{p}M$      if $p \succ_{\mathcal{L}} q$

$\rho_{sec_3} : (\dots + \lambda_p x.M) \circ (\widehat{q}N \circ L + \dots) \to_{\rho_{sec_3}} \lambda_p x.(M \circ \widehat{q}N) \circ L$ if $(p \succ_{\mathcal{L}} q) \vee (p \prec_{\mathcal{L}} q)$

**Rules:** The structural inference rules are the following:

$$\mu_{\circ_1} : \frac{M \to M'}{M \circ N \to M' \circ N} \qquad \mu_{\circ_2} : \frac{M \to M'}{N \circ M \to N \circ M'}$$

$$\mu_\lambda : \frac{M \to M'}{\lambda_P x.M \to \lambda_P x.M'} \qquad \mu_{\widehat{}} : \frac{M \to M'}{\widehat{p}M \to \widehat{p}M'}$$

$$\mu_{\|} : \frac{M \to M'}{M \parallel N \to M' \parallel N} \qquad \mu_{Congr} : \frac{M \equiv N \quad N \to N' \quad N' \equiv M'}{M \to M'}$$

## 2.3 The concept of tunnel

We interpret the *syntactical structure of the process* as *the 'physical' means within which communication among the subprocesses is established*. From this point of view, $\beta_P$ application describes the communication between two communicating processes, $\lambda_P x.M$ and $\widehat{p}N$, on channel $P$ linked by a single constructor of parallelism ($\|$). From the functional point of view, this can be thought of as the remote instantiation of the actual parameter $N$ in the body $M$ of a function through the formal parameter $P$. We extend the scope of this simplest 'remote' binding by our notion of *tunnel*. For example, in Figure 1, $\lambda_P x.M$ and $\widehat{p}N$ communicate (using channel $P$) through the (shortest) tunnel $\langle \parallel \rangle$. We extend the scope of $\beta_P$ communication by means of the *tunnel rule*:

$$\mu_T : \frac{M \parallel N \to_{\beta_P} M' \parallel N'}{\widehat{Q_1}M \parallel \widehat{Q_2}N \to_{\beta_P} \widehat{Q_1}M' \parallel \widehat{Q_2}N'} \text{ for } Q_1, Q_2 \in \mathcal{L} \text{ if } P \succ_{\mathcal{L}} Q_1, Q_2$$

$\mu_T$ expresses the possibility of $\beta_P$ communication between processes $M$ and $N$, provided the following conditions are met: **[T1]** $M$ and $N$ are able to establish a $\beta_P$ communication, **[T2]** $\widehat{Q_1}M$ and $\widehat{Q_2}N$ are compound in parallel, and **[T3]** the label $P \in \mathcal{L}$ is *greater* than labels $Q_1$ and $Q_2$.

**T1** is obviously necessary to make any communication feasible. **T2** motivates the definition of a syntactic object, namely the *tunnel*. It is possible to formalize it as *a (special kind of) path in the syntactical tree of a process*.

**Definition 2.1 (Tunnel)** *Let $A$ be a $\lambda_{\|}$-term. An elemental path in the syntactical tree of $A$, $\gamma = \langle u_1, \ldots, u_n \rangle$, $u_i \in O(A)$, for $1 \leq i \leq n$ is a tunnel iff. $n > 1 \Rightarrow u_1 \mid u_n$ and, being $\gamma^s = \langle s_1, \ldots, s_n \rangle$, $s_i \in \{\|\} \cup \mathcal{P}$ for $i$ $1 \leq i \leq n$, and there is $j$, $1 \leq j \leq n$ such that $s_j = \|$.*

**Definition 2.2 (Tunnel location)** *Given a tunnel $\gamma = \langle u_1, \ldots, u_n \rangle$ in a $\lambda_{\|}$-term $A$, the tunnel location $\nu_\gamma$ is the least occurrence of the elemental path of the tunnel: $\nu_\gamma = \min\{u_i \mid 1 \leq i \leq n\}$. Note that $A[\nu_\gamma] = \|$.*

**Example 2** In the syntactical tree of $C \equiv \widehat{Q_1} A \parallel \widehat{Q_2}(A_1 \parallel B)$, we identify a tunnel.

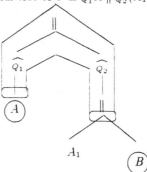

**Fig. 2.** Tunnel between processes $A$ and $B$

We are going to verify that, if $A \equiv \lambda_P x.M$ and $B \equiv \widehat{P} N$, then a $\beta_P$ communication is possible between $A$ and $B$, in $C$. We assume that $P \succ Q_i$ for $i = 1, 2$.

$$(1) \quad A \parallel B \; -_{\beta_P} \; A' \parallel B' \qquad\qquad A \text{ and } B \text{ definition}$$
$$(2) \quad A \parallel A_1 \parallel B \; -_{\beta_P} \; A' \parallel A_1 \parallel B' \qquad\qquad \mu_{\|_1}$$
$$(3) \quad \widehat{Q_1} A \parallel \widehat{Q_2}(A_1 \parallel B) \; -_{\beta_P} \; \widehat{Q_1} A' \parallel \widehat{Q_2}(A_1 \parallel B') \qquad \mu_T$$

In the syntactical tree of process $C$, $\langle \widehat{Q_1}, \|, \widehat{Q_2}, \| \rangle$ is a tunnel between nodes $A$ and $B$.

Having a tunnel between a sender and a receiver is not sufficient to get communication. Condition **T3** motivates the definition of transparency of a tunnel.

**Definition 2.3 ($P$-transparent tunnel)** *Given a label $P \in \mathcal{L}$, a tunnel $\gamma = \langle u_1, \ldots, u_n \rangle$ is $P$-transparent if, being $\gamma^s = \langle s_1, \ldots, s_n \rangle$, for all $i$, $1 \leq i \leq n$. $s_i \neq \| \; \Rightarrow \; P \succ_{\mathcal{L}} Q_i$, where $s_i = \widehat{Q_i}$.*

**Definition 2.4 ($T$-communicability)** *Let $A$ be a $\lambda_{\|}$-term, $M = A|_u$ be a sender and $N = A|_v$ be a receiver on a channel $P$. They are $T$-communicable on $P$ if:*

*1. There exists a $P$-transparent tunnel $\gamma$ between $M$ and $N$.*

*2. Let $\nu_\gamma$ the location of $\gamma$. Then, $\forall w \in O(A) : w \leq \nu_\gamma \; \Rightarrow \; A[w] \in \{\|, \circ\} \cup \Lambda \cup \mathcal{P}$.*

Thus, parallel communication is a particular $T$-communication in which the tunnel between the communicating processes is the simplest one: $\gamma = \langle \| \rangle$. From the definition of tunnel transparency, it follows that, for all $P \in \mathcal{L}$, $\gamma$ is always $P$-transparent.

# 3 Mechanizing functional concurrent languages using LCEP

In this section, we illustrate the ability of LCEP for mechanizing a functional concurrent language. A functional program $\mathcal{F}$ is a set of function definitions. Its execution is the evaluation of an expression $E$. Thus, the two main challenges are the modelling of function definitions and the modelling of the evaluation of expressions[3].

**Modelling function definitions.** In a functional program, a $k$-ary (user-defined) function $F$ can be specified as follows: **def** $F(x_1, \ldots, x_k) = E_F$. Formal parameters are named $x_1, \ldots, x_k$ and the expression $E_F$ describes the 'actions' performed by $F$. $E_F$ is an expression in which calls to other functions can be found: *basic* functions from $B_1, \ldots, B_m$ (for instance, $if, +, *$), user-defined functions from $F_1, \ldots, F_n$ (even the same $F$ function in recursive definitions).

A program with a goal expression $E$ is translated into a $\lambda_{\parallel}$-term $M = M_{\mathcal{B}} \parallel M_{\mathcal{F}} \parallel M_E$. It contains the representation of the basic functions $M_{\mathcal{B}}$, the program representation $M_{\mathcal{F}}$ and the representation of the expression to be evaluated $M_E$. The process $M_{\mathcal{B}}$ is $M_{\mathcal{B}} = M_{B_1} \parallel \cdots \parallel M_{B_m}$, where $M_{B_i}$ corresponds to the basic function $B_i$. $M_{\mathcal{F}}$ is $M_{\mathcal{F}} = M_{F_1} \parallel \cdots \parallel M_{F_n}$, where $M_{F_i}$ corresponds to the user-defined function $F_i$. $M_E$ is $\tau[E]$, where the *translation function* $\tau$, mapping sentences of the language into $\lambda_{\parallel}$-expressions is defined below.

The structures of $M_{B_i}$, $1 \leq i \leq m$ and $M_{F_j}$, $1 \leq j \leq n$ are similar. We translate a (general) function definition **def** $H(x_1, \ldots, x_k) = E_H$, where $H$ can be a basic or user-defined function, into a $\lambda_{\parallel}$-term $M_H$ as follows:
- $M_H = !\widehat{H} A_H$. $A_H$ is the *abstraction* of the function $H$. By using the function name $H$ as a communication channel, we enable the communication mechanism to 'send' the abstraction of $H$ to the place where it is needed. By prefixing with the ! operator, we are able to obtain as many copies of $A_H$ as necessary.
- $A_H = \lambda_1 x_1'. \cdots . \lambda_1 x_k'. S_H$ has two parts. The first one $(\lambda_1 x_1'. \cdots . \lambda_1 x_k'.)$ is devoted to *receiving* the arguments for the second one, $S_H$, which translates the expresion $E_H$.
- Basic and user-defined functions differ in the way that the process $S_H$ is defined. A basic function $B$ is *predefined*: we let $S_B = C_B \circ x_1' \circ \cdots \circ x_k'$, where $C_B \in \mathcal{C}$ is a constant expressing the basic function. The evaluation of LCEP expressions involving these constants is managed in a special manner as we show below.
- On the other hand, $S_F = \tau[E_F]$ for user-defined functions $F$. Therefore, $S_F$ only represents the process which evaluates the expression $E_F$ defining $F$.

We complete the definition of the translation function $\tau$ as follows[4]:

**Translation of expressions.** An expression $E$ is always viewed as a function call $E = F(E_1 \rightarrow \mathbf{j_1}, \ldots, E_k \rightarrow \mathbf{j_k})$. $E_i \rightarrow \mathbf{j_i}$ means that the $i$-th real parameter $E_i$ corresponds to the $\mathbf{j_i}$-th formal parameter of $F$. Since the calculus expresses concurrency, the evaluation of a function call starts with the *parallel* evaluation of the *actual* parameters:
- $\tau[E] = M_{Arg} \parallel M_{Ap}$. The evaluation of $E$ splits up into two parts: the process evaluating the arguments, $M_{Arg}$, and the process which performs the application of the function to the (evaluated) arguments, $M_{Ap}$.
- $M_{Ap} = \lambda_{\sigma_1} \sigma_1'. \cdots . \lambda_{\sigma_k} \sigma_k'. \lambda_F F'. F' \circ \widehat{1} \sigma_1' \circ \cdots \circ \widehat{1} \sigma_k'$. Application of the function $F$ consists in first receiving the (evaluated) arguments $E_1, \ldots, E_k$ through channels $\sigma_1, \ldots, \sigma_k$, next, receiving the abstraction of $F$ through the channel $F$ and then,

---

[3] For reasons of brevity, the development is somewhat informal. We do not start from a real language, but rather from general sentences which have a syntax which is similar to almost every functional language.

[4] In a more complete treatment, we would be able to introduce many other features to increase parallelism.

applying it to the arguments. The labels $\sigma_i$ are considered to be *fresh*.

- $M_{Arg} = \widehat{\sigma_1}\tau[E_1] \parallel \cdots \parallel \widehat{\sigma_k}\tau[E_k]$. For each real parameter $E_i$, we build an *evaluation environment*[5] $\widehat{\sigma_i}\tau[E_i]$ for the process $\tau[E_i]$ that represents the expression to evaluate. They are transparent for global scope processes but they are not transparent for the local processes.

Therefore, the activation mechanism begins building an execution environment for each formal parameter and then communicates the final result through the channels $\sigma_i$. When the function arguments are evaluated, the execution continues applying the function definition over them.

The ordering of labels is essential in this scheme. We define the ordering $\preceq_{\mathcal{L}}$ adequately to deal with these requirements. In the set of symbolic labels, we state $\sigma \mid_{\mathcal{L}} \sigma'$, $H \mid_{\mathcal{L}} H'$ and $\sigma \preceq_{\mathcal{L}} H$ for all labels $\sigma, \sigma'$ used in evaluation environments and basic or user-defined functions $H, H'$. The set of numeric labels inherits the standard ordering on $\mathbb{N}$. This definition of the order $\preceq_{\mathcal{L}}$ is also essential in managing recursivity.

**Modelling the evaluation of expressions.** Similar to the usual practice in implementing pure functional languages [13], the execution of the process $M$ on LCEP is composed of mixed steps. The different reduction rules apply in this precedence order:

1. Evaluation rules defined for the basic functions: $+$, $-$, etc.[6]
2. Reordering rules,
3. Sequential application and
4. Extended parallel $\beta$-application, i.e. $\mathcal{T}$-communication. $\beta_H$ communications are (equally) priority for all basic or user-defined function $H$. Tunnels located at outermost positions are (equally) priority.

Evaluation rules are associated to basic functions. For example, denote as $PLUS$ and $MINUS$ the LCEP constants associated to the functions $+$ and $-$. Assuming that $A, B$ are numbers, we have the following built-in *evaluation* rules: $PLUS \circ A \circ B \, -_{eval_{PLUS}} \, A + B$ and $MINUS \circ A \circ B \, -_{eval_{MINUS}} \, A - B$.

**Example 3** Let $F$ be defined by **def** $F(x, y) = x - y$ (as in Example 1). The associated process is $M_F = ! \, \widehat{F}\lambda_1 x.\lambda_1 y.\lambda_{MINUS}MINUS'.MINUS' \circ \widehat{1}x \circ \widehat{1}y$. Processes $M_{PLUS}$ and $M_{MINUS}$ are: $M_{PLUS} = ! \, \widehat{PLUS}(\lambda_1 r_1.\lambda_1 r_2.PLUS \circ r_1 \circ r_2)$, and $M_{MINUS} = ! \, \widehat{MINUS}(\lambda_1 r_1.\lambda_1 r_2.MINUS \circ r_1 \circ r_2)$. Since $!M \equiv M \parallel !M$ (see Section 2.1), we have the necessary copies of the processes.

The evaluation of $E = F(1 + 1 - 2, 3 + 3 - 1)$ is the execution of:

$$M_E = \tau[F(1 + 1 - 2, 3 + 3 - 1)] = \lambda_{\sigma_1}\sigma_1'.\lambda_{\sigma_2}\sigma_2'.\lambda_F F'.(F' \circ \widehat{2}\sigma_1' \circ \widehat{1}\sigma_2') \parallel$$
$$\parallel \widehat{\sigma_1}(\lambda_{PLUS}PLUS'.(PLUS' \circ \widehat{1}1 \circ \widehat{1}1)) \parallel$$
$$\parallel \widehat{\sigma_2}(\lambda_{PLUS}PLUS'.(PLUS' \circ \widehat{1}3 \circ \widehat{1}3))$$

as follows: $M_{PLUS} \parallel M_{MINUS} \parallel M_F \parallel M_E$

In contrast to the $\lambda$-calculus where the abstractions must be kept in an environment for use when they are needed, in LCEP it is possible to completely express the program as a term of the calculus.

---

[5] In some cases, we simplify the expression of $M_{Ap}$ and $M_{Arg}$ by avoiding useless evaluations of the basic expressions: variables and constants (see below).

[6] Since LCEP includes the $\lambda$-calculus, it would be possible to express these operations as $\lambda_{\parallel}$-expressions, by defining the natural numbers and operations as $\lambda$-terms. However, this is not used in real implementations and so we follow this standard approach.

# 4 Conclusions and future work

LCEP has been presented in this paper. It is an extension of the $\lambda$-calculus to model concurrent systems. In our framework, communication is viewed as a special kind of function application. We distinguish between sequential and parallel application of functions to arguments. The tunnel concept is introduced to relate remote arguments and function abstractions. Also, one of the new features in relation to previous proposals is to allow the function arguments to be selected by means of both symbolic and numerical labels, which permits the use of currying. We are building a prototype of an abstract machine based on the formal system described here to execute programs written in a high-level language that allows us to express explicit parallelism.

# References

1. H. Aït-Kaci and J. Garrigue. Label-Selective $\lambda$-Calculus: Syntax and Confluence. In R. K. Shyamasundar, editor, *Foundations of Software Technology and Theoretical Computer Science*, volume 761 of *LNCS*, pages 24–40. Springer-Verlag, Berlin, 1993.
2. H.P. Barendregt. *The $\lambda$-calculus, its Syntax and Semantics*, volume 103 of *Studies in Logic and the Foundations of Mathematics*. Elsevier Science Publishers, 1984 edition, Amsterdam, 1991.
3. M. Ben-Ari. *Principles of Concurrent Programming*. Englewood Cliffs: Prentice Hall, 1982.
4. G. Berry. Séquentialité de l'évaluation formelle des $\lambda$-expressions. *In Proc. of 3-e Colloque International sur la Programmation*, Dunod, Paris 1978.
5. G. Berry and G. Boudol. The Chemical Abstract Machine. *In Proc. of 20'th ACM Annual Symp. on Principles of Programming Languages*, pages 81–93, ACM Press, 1993.
6. N. Dershowitz and J.P. Jouannaud. Rewrite Systems. In J. van Leeuwen, editor, *Handbook of Theoretical Computer Science*, volume B: Formal Models and Semantics, pages 243–320. Elsevier, Amsterdam and the MIT Press, Cambridge, MA., 1990.
7. C.A.R. Hoare. *Communicating Sequential Processes*. Prentice Hall International, Great Britain, 1985.
8. M.P. Jones and P. Hudak. Implicit and explicit parallel programming in Haskell. Technical report, YALEU/DCS/RR-982, Yale University, New Haven, Connecticut, USA, August 1993.
9. R. Lalement. *Computation as Logic*. Prentice Hall International, Great Britain, 1993.
10. R. Milner. A Calculus of Communicating Systems. *LNCS 92*, 1980. Springer Verlag.
11. R. Milner. The polyadic $\pi$-calculus: A tutorial. In F.L. Brauer, W. Bauer, and H. Schwichtenberg, editors, *Logic and Algebra of Specifications*. Springer-Verlag, Berlin, 1993.
12. J. Oliver and S. Lucas. Survey of concurrent calculi. In M.A. Fernández, J.M. García, J.A. Guerrero, and G. Moreno, editors, *Nuevas tendencias en la Informática: Arquitecturas Paralelas y Programación Declarativa*, pages 267–289, 1994.
13. S.L. Peyton-Jones. *The implementation of functional programming languages*. Prentice Hall International, Great Britain, 1987.

# On the Specification of Visual Languages: Multisets as First-Class Citizens

Massimo Marchiori

Dept. of Pure and Applied Mathematics, University of Padova
Via Belzoni 7, 35131 Padova, Italy
max@math.unipd.it

### Abstract

We propose a new paradigm for the specification of the syntax and semantics of visual languages, where multisets, contrary to so far existing works, are integrated as first-class citizens, in the sense that they can be manipulated without any limitation. We show that the resulting systems, called multiset rewriting systems, are extremely expressive for reasoning about multidimensional objects. Moreover, we provide a thorough analysis of their properties, like confluence and termination, and of their possible extensions.

## 1  Introduction

The importance of multisets for the specification of visual languages is well-known. This stems from the fact that the usual ordering proper of textual languages, like the sequence, corresponds to spatial limitations on the syntax, which is inherently one-dimensional. In visual languages, instead, the considered objects are usually two or three-dimensional, and in general there is no prefixed ordering which is better to assume. Hence it is somehow natural that multisets, that mathematically formalize an unordered collection of elements, have been introduced in formalisms for the specification of visual languages (see e.g. [6, 5, 4, 17, 16]). All the so far developed approaches, however, integrate multisets like a special structure, with heavy limitations on the syntax. The general idea in common to all these works is to extend grammars with special features tailored for visual languages, like for instance multisets. Roughly speaking, the underlying idea is that the input of a visual language is encoded into a multiset. Then, such 'extended grammars' select some objects from this multiset and rewrite them into other objects. However, in this approach multisets are treated as *different* objects than the other ones. More precisely, there is *a* multiset, which encodes *the* objects. Then, rewriting acts on objects, extracted and inserted from the multiset. Thus, multisets are introduced as neatly separated entities, and their behaviour is static: there is one multiset of objects which is rewritten by modifying its inner components. In this paper, we present a new approach to the integration of multisets: multisets are treated just like any other object, and there is no limitation from the rewriting point of view between multisets and other terms. This way, multisets are not a simple add-on 'on top' of a grammar, but become *first-class citizens* in the rewriting process. Another choice is that we do not use grammars any more, but we employ the more expressive tool of term rewriting. This approach presents several advantages. First, the syntax becomes much neater and clean. Second, the expressive power increases by far, being especially suited for the treatment of multi-dimensional objects. Third, it allows a nice mathematical treatment, since most of the work developed for term rewriting can be automatically restated in this new setting.

## 2  Flat Multisets

We assume familiarity with the basic notions of term rewriting (see e.g. [12]). From what said in the introduction, a natural idea is so to introduce in the language of term rewriting the multiset symbol. This way, we can express rewriting rules just in the usual way, only that the interpretation of the multiset symbol, as expected, should be that of a semantical multiset (i.e. it doesn't matter in what order terms are written inside the multisets). Anyway, this naïve approach presents some serious problems. Adding the multiset symbol to the signature, we should also provide an *arity* for it. But the multiset is intrinsically a varyadic operator. One could wonder why we don't simply allow the multiset symbol to be varyadic. For instance, a rule of the form $\{\!\{a,b\}\!\} \rightarrow \{\!\{c,d,e\}\!\}$ would simply rewrite the multiset $\{\!\{a,b\}\!\}$ into the multiset $\{\!\{c,d,e\}\!\}$. This, of course, can be done, but there is a serious problem of *expressive power*. Once we write down the $\{\!\{\ \}\!\}$ symbol in a rewrite rule, we necessarily have to specify its arity. For instance, in the above rewrite rule $\{\!\{a,b\}\!\} \rightarrow \{\!\{c,d,e\}\!\}$ the first multiset symbol has arity 2 and the second has arity 3. But this means we cannot cope any more with multisets of arbitrary length: every rule applies only to multisets of length determined in advance. This is an untolerable limitation: the sense of rewriting is just that *a part* of a term can be rewritten to another; using the above approach, instead, leads to the unpleasant (and practically unuseful) situation that in order to modify a multiset we have to rewrite it as a whole, i.e. fully specifying its structure.

There is, however, a nice mathematical solution to this serious problem: we will use not multisets, but the novel tool of *flat multisets*. Flat multisets are just like multisets, only that they satisfy the additional property:

$$\{\!\{s_1,\ldots,s_\ell,\{\!\{t_1,\ldots,t_m\}\!\},u_1,\ldots,u_n\}\!\} = \{\!\{s_1,\ldots,s_\ell,t_1,\ldots,t_m,u_1,\ldots,u_n\}\!\}$$

The meaning is that 'nested' multisets are just equivalent to the 'flattened' multiset containing all its objects. For example, the multiset $\{\!\{a,\{\!\{b,c\}\!\},d\}\!\}$ is equivalent to the 'flattened' multiset $\{\!\{a,b,c,d\}\!\}$. The intuition is that a multiset $\{\!\{t_1,\ldots,t_l\}\!\}$ only specifies the information that the relative ordering of $t_1,\ldots,t_k$ does not matter. Hence, this should hold for every part of it (i.e., every part of it should be a multiset). Note that we do not lose the capacity of having the usual multisets as 'closed boxes'. What we do is simply to introduce multisets in the weak form given by flat multisets; then, one can add more structure to multisets using other symbols: for instance, one can recover usual multisets by employing a distinguished unary symbol (say $M$), and writing a 'closed box' multiset like $M(\{\!\{t_1,\ldots,t_k\}\!\})$.

So, how can flat multisets avoid the expressibility problem that we have seen before? The fact is that now a term of the form $\{\!\{a,b\}\!\}$ can be applied not only to a multiset of two elements containing $a$ and $b$, but also to a multiset of greater length containing them: if $\{\!\{\cdots,a,b,\cdots\}\!\}$ is such a multiset, then it is equivalent to $\{\!\{a,b,\cdots,\cdots\}\!\}$, which is equivalent by the flat axiom to $\{\!\{\{\!\{a,b\}\!\},\cdots,\cdots\}\!\}$, and so the term $\{\!\{a,b\}\!\}$ matches with it. This way, for instance, we can express rules of the form 'rewrite the elements $s_1\ldots,s_k$ from a multiset into $t_1,\ldots,t_m$': they can be simply written as $\{\!\{s_1,\ldots,s_k\}\!\} \rightarrow \{\!\{t_1,\ldots,t_m\}\!\}$.

*Assumption:* This construct is so common that we will employ the following syntactic convention: $s_1,\ldots,s_k \rightarrow t_1,\ldots,t_m$ (with $k > 1$ and $m \geq 0$) is the same as writing $\{\!\{s_1,\ldots,s_k\}\!\} \rightarrow \{\!\{t_1,\ldots,t_m\}\!\}$.

In the sequel, we will add the following harmless axiom to the definition of flat multisets: $\{\!\{t\}\!\} = t$ (i.e. a multiset of one object is just the object itself). The intuition is that if we have only one element, then the information provided by the multiset that the relative ordering of its elements does not matter is superfluous.

## 2.1  The $\mathcal{FM}$ theory

We now give a formal description of the concepts illustrated so far. As said, term rewriting should behave as usual, but for the fact the properties of flat multisets should be respected. In order to achieve this, we employ the notion of rewriting modulo a system of equation (see e.g. [12]). Recall that an equational theory $E$ is a set of equational axioms of the form $s = t$. Every equational theory induces a corresponding equality relation $\underset{E}{=}$, such that $t_1 \underset{E}{=} t_2$ if and only if $t_1$ and $t_2$ are provably equal using the axioms of the theory (this can be rigorously formalized, see e.g. [12]).

**Definition 2.1** The *equational rewriting system* $T/E$ ("$T$ modulo $E$") is a couple $(T, E)$, where $T$ is a term rewriting system and $E$ is an equational theory (defined on the same signature of $T$). The corresponding reduction relation is: a term $s$ rewrites to $t$ in $T/E$ (notation $s \underset{T/E}{\longrightarrow} t$) if there are two terms $s'$ and $t'$ such that $s \underset{E}{=} s' \underset{T}{\longrightarrow} t' \underset{E}{=} t$. $\Box$

Now, we only have to provide a formal theory stating what properties flat multisets enjoy, and use rewriting modulo it.

**Definition 2.2** The (varyadic) theory $\mathcal{FM}$ of *flat multisets* is defined by the following three axioms schemata:
1. $\forall n, \forall$ permutation $\pi$ of $\{1, \ldots, n\}$: $\{\!\{t_1, \ldots, t_n\}\!\} = \{\!\{t_{\pi(1)}, \ldots, t_{\pi(n)}\}\!\}$
2. $\forall \ell, m, n : \{\!\{s_1, \ldots, s_\ell, \{\!\{t_1, \ldots, t_m\}\!\}, u_1, \ldots, u_n\}\!\} = \{\!\{s_1, \ldots, s_\ell, t_1, \ldots, t_m, u_1, \ldots, u_n\}\!\}$
3. $\{\!\{t\}\!\} = t$ $\Box$

**Definition 2.3** A *Multiset Rewriting System* (MRS) is an equational term rewriting system of the form $(T, \mathcal{FM})$. $\Box$

## 2.2 Varyadic is not a problem

We have formally defined rewriting modulo (flat) multisets; therefore, one could naturally ask whether some existing results on equational rewriting carry over to MRSs as well. The interesting point is that, despite $\mathcal{FM}$ is a *varyadic* theory, it can be simulated via a non-varyadic equational theory: that of associative and commutative rewriting. Call $AC$ the theory stating the associative and commutative axioms for a binary operator. Then, we have the following result:

**Theorem 2.4 (Simulation)** *There are two maps $\alpha$ and $\beta$ such that for every multiset rewriting system $M$ and for every term rewriting system $T$ we have:*

- $s \underset{M/\mathcal{FM}}{\longrightarrow}^* t \Rightarrow \alpha(s) \underset{\alpha(M)/AC}{\longrightarrow}^* \alpha(t)$
- $s \underset{T/AC}{\longrightarrow}^* t \Rightarrow \beta(s) \underset{\beta(T)/\mathcal{FM}}{\longrightarrow}^* \beta(t)$
- $t \underset{\mathcal{FM}}{=} \beta(\alpha(t))$
- $t \underset{AC}{=} \alpha(\beta(t))$

This way, many results on equational rewriting can be automatically restated in the MRS setting. Also, from the decidability of $AC$-equational rewriting we obtain that MRSs are computationally feasible (provided they have finitely many rules). Another important fact is that the theory $AC$ is a so-called *permutative* theory, cf. [19] (roughly, it preserves the length of terms). For these nice kinds of theories, many results have been developed (for instance, [19, 11] provide methods to pass from a possibly non-confluent equational rewriting system to an equivalent confluent one): hence, all of these results can be applied to MRSs as well. The fact $AC$ is permutative is important also for the study of termination of MRSs, as we will see in Section 6.

# 3 Multidimensional Objects

The great flexibility of using multisets as first-class citizens is particularly well-suited when manipulating multi-dimensional geometrical objects (i.e. the major domain of application of visual languages).

For instance, consider the following example after [17], describing a 2D language where legal pictures contain only triangles[1]. The specification of a triangle contains a 'rewrite rules' part

$line(U, V), line(W, X), line(Y, Z) \to tri(A, B, C)$ **if** $connected(line(U, V), line(W, X), A)$
$\wedge\ connected(line(U, V), line(Y, Z), B) \wedge\ connected(line(W, X), line(Y, Z), C)$

---

[1] Actually, this specification is even *faulty*, as it is not difficult to see. This is somehow symptomatic of the difficulties that weakly expressive paradigms can give in developing correct code.

and a 'predicate definitions' part

$connected(line(X,Y), line(X,Z), X)$        $connected(line(Y,X), line(X,Z), X)$
$connected(line(X,Y), line(Z,X), X)$        $connected(line(Y,X), line(Z,X), X)$

Observe how all the possible cases have to be exploited, due to the symmetry of lines. In general, just to define from lines a $k$-polygon the number of rules grows *exponentially* w.r.t. $k$. This is not a feature proper only of the specification of [17], but it is a feature common to all the specifications of visual languages so far introduced.

The problem is that when defining a line, we only need two points, *no matter in what order they are*: that is to say, we just need a multiset. However, since in all the existing paradigms the multiset structure cannot be freely used as any other structure (but only, so to say, at 'outer level', cf. the discussion in the introduction), we have that we are forced to express the points defining a line in a fixed textual order.

Instead, using MRSs, we can define triangles in the natural way:

$$line\{\!\{U,V\}\!\}, line\{\!\{V,W\}\!\}, line\{\!\{W,U\}\!\} \rightarrow tri\{\!\{U,V,W\}\!\}$$

Note that now the two points defining a line are not imposed the artificial textual ordering: they are an unordered couple.

When multidimensional environments are considered, like for instance 3-dimensional reasoning, the situation gets even worse. For instance, consider the simplest example of tridimensional structure, a tetrahedron defined via terms of the form $tetr(v_1, v_2, v_3, v_4)$ (where $v_1, v_2, v_3, v_4$ are the four vertices). Just to check that two tetrahedra are equal, with the usual approaches one needs to check something like $4! = 24$ cases. Instead, using the multisets as first-class citizens approach, one can check equality just via the natural specification $eq(X, X) \rightarrow true$. Moreover, while with the other approaches one has to define a different ad-hoc specification of equality for every considered object (triangles, tetrahedra, lines etc.), the above specification works for all of them. We remark that the above examples are not particular cases: almost every other example so far presented in the literature can be given a much simpler and natural specification using a (possibly extended, cf. Section 5) MRS.

A concrete important application of the flexibility of MRSs is the Virtual Reality Modeling Language (see e.g. [1]). In VRML, the so-called 'group nodes' are essentially multiset-like separators. More important, in *every* node the 'field structure' is order-independent: that is to say, all the informative fields inside each node enjoy a multiset structure. Using MRSs, it is almost straightforward to provide a syntax definition of VRML, or manipulation rules of VRML objects (think for instance of the equality problem seen above), something which is extremely cumbersome to do in other existing formalisms.

## 4  Confluence

Confluence is one of the most important properties of a specification, since it says that no matter in what order reductions are applied, the obtained result is still the same (i.e. we do not have different ambiguous meanings for the same object). On the other hand, the field of modular analysis is of fundamental importance in software engineering, and is nowadays attracting increasing interest by the scientific community. In essence, modularity allows to study a complex object by studying his smaller subparts: given a 'big' object composed by the union of smaller subparts, we want to state that it enjoys a certain property by simply investigating its smaller subcomponents. Hence, modular analysis allows to develop correct complex objects 'bottom-up', just building correct smaller submodules, and even dually to verify the correctness of a complex object by decomposing it into its submodules and verifying them. As far as TRSs are concerned, modularity is a well-developed field (see e.g. [12]). However, no results have been developed for equational rewriting. In this section we develop a powerful modular methodology to analyze confluence of MRSs.

**Definition 4.1** Two terms $s$ and $t$ are $\mathcal{FM}$-*unifiable* if there is a substitution $\sigma$ such that $s\sigma \underset{\mathcal{FM}}{=} t\sigma$. A term $s$ $\mathcal{FM}$-*overlaps* a term $t$ if $s$ is $\mathcal{FM}$-unifiable with a non-variable subterm of $t$. A rewrite rule $l \rightarrow r$ $\mathcal{FM}$-overlaps a rewrite rule $l' \rightarrow r'$ if there is a renaming of $l' \rightarrow r'$, say $l'' \rightarrow r''$, that has no variables in common with $l \rightarrow r$, and such that $l$ $\mathcal{FM}$-overlaps $l''$. □

**Definition 4.2** Two multiset rewriting systems $R_1$ and $R_2$ are *orthogonal to each other* if no rule of $R_1$ $\mathcal{FM}$-overlaps with a rule of $R_2$ and vice versa. □

Now we can state the following modular result on confluence of MRSs:

**Theorem 4.3** *If two left-linear MRSs are orthogonal to each other, then their union is confluent.*

Hence via this theorem, as said, we can infer confluence of a complex MRS just by splitting it into its smaller submodules (provided they are orthogonal to each other) and study separately their confluence. In the best case, we end with MRSs composed of a single rule. It is therefore important to have a criterion enabling to state that a one-rule MRS is confluent:

**Definition 4.4** A rule $l \rightarrow r$ is *self-$\mathcal{FM}$-overlapping* if $l$ $\mathcal{FM}$-overlaps a proper subterm of $l$. □

**Theorem 4.5** *If $l \rightarrow r$ is left-linear and not self-$\mathcal{FM}$-overlapping, then the associated multiset rewriting system is confluent.*

Also, as said, modularity is useful for program development: if the user writes specifications that are left-linear and *unambiguous* in the sense that each rule is non self-$\mathcal{FM}$-overlapping and orthogonal to each other, then the specification is automatically confluent.

One could ask why in the above results we imposed left-linearity on the rules. The fact is that, rather subtly, without left-linearity they do not hold, as the following example reveals.

**Example 4.6** Suppose in a visual system the user is allowed to draw elements on the screen and also to specify commands to delete them. An easy way to specify a 'delete' command is via the rule $X, delete(X) \rightarrow$ that says that if an object $X$ is present, and also the command to delete it $(delete(X))$, then the object is removed. Another natural feature of the system could be that drawing the same object on the screen more than once is the same as drawing it once. This can be expressed by the rule $X, X \rightarrow X$. The MRS corresponding to these two rules (say $R_1$) is confluent (this can be formally proved, as we will see later). Now, suppose drawing points on some parts of the screen is not allowed, for instance on the x axis (points with second coordinate 0). A (not very smart, in fact, but semantically correct) way to express this is by the rule $point(X, 0) \rightarrow delete(point(X, 0))$ that removes the point and also produces a corresponding delete command. The MRS corresponding to this rule (say $R_2$) is confluent by Theorem 4.5, since the rule is readily non self-$\mathcal{FM}$-overlapping. $R_1$ and $R_2$ are orthogonal to each other, as it is trivial to check. However, their combined system *is not confluent*. Suppose the user has put two points on the same location in the x axis (say $(20, 0)$), so that the representation of the screen status is $\{\!\{point(20, 0), point(20, 0)\}\!\}$. In the combined system we have the two reductions

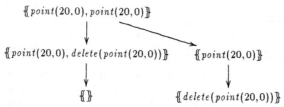

Now, $\{\!\{\}\!\}$ is a normal form, and $\{\!\{delete(point(20, 0))\}\!\}$ does not rewrite to it. □

This means that, for instance, we cannot apply the above modular analysis of confluence to MRSs containing rules like the one specifying triangles, as seen in Section 3, since it is non left-linear. There is, however, a way to drop the left-linearity assumption: when the specification is correct in the sense that it is *terminating*. In this case we have

**Theorem 4.7** *If two terminating confluent MRSs are orthogonal to each other, then their union is confluent.*

**Theorem 4.8** *If $l \to r$ is terminating and not self-$\mathcal{FM}$-overlapping, then the associated multiset rewriting system is confluent.*

So, for instance, via the above two theorems we can formally prove that the MRS $R_1$ of Example 4.6 is confluent. And, in fact, note that in the above Example 4.6 the MRS $R_2$ is non terminating, since $point(20,0) \to delete(point(20,0)) \to delete(delete(point(20,0))) \to \ldots$.

Note that all the results stated in this section readily hold, by Theorem 2.4, for the confluence of $AC$-equational rewriting. As far as proving termination of MRSs is concerned, we will examine this topic in Section 6.

# 5 Extending MRSs

Multiset Rewriting Systems are a powerful tool for the specification of visual languages. However, one might wish to increase their expressive power, just like in the existing works on specification of visual languages, grammars have been extended via attributes, conditions and so on. In this section we see that the basic theory of MRSs can be easily extended in order to incorporate more flexible constructs like conditional tests and logic programming features. These extensions are not arbitrary, but rely on the solid existing paradigms of conditional rewriting and logic programming, which makes possible to reuse existing tools from these two fields.

## 5.1 Conditional Multiset Rewriting

The idea of extending the expressive power of term rewriting systems led to the concept of Conditional Term Rewriting System (CTRS). This paradigm is now a well established field (cf. [12]). So, just like multiset rewriting can be seen as term rewriting integrated with (flat) multisets, we can naturally define conditional multiset rewriting like conditional rewriting integrated with multisets. This way we gain all the advantages seen in the MRS case: we do not develop a new ad hoc theory, but rely on a solid existing paradigm, and so the extensive amount of theory and results developed in the CTRS field can be lifted to CMRSs. Therefore, we can analogously define a *conditional multiset rewriting system* (CMRS) simply considering an equational CTRS modulo $\mathcal{FM}$. It can be proved that the same maps $\alpha$ and $\beta$ of the Simulation Theorem 2.4 can be used in this new setting to provide a corresponding simulation theorem for CMRSs. This way, all the existing results concerning semantics of equational CTRSs, completion procedures and so on can be automatically lifted to CMRSs.

## 5.2 Multiset Logic Programming

One of the most expressive languages nowadays available is logic programming (and its various extensions, like constraint logic programming, cf. [10]). Usage of this paradigm to enhance expressibility of visual languages specifications was introduced by Helm and Marriott (see e.g. [8]), and subsequently employed in Multiset Constraint Grammars ([16]). Limited form of logic programming inferences (often hidden in the formalism) can be found also in almost all the other approaches to the specification of visual languages (e.g. [6, 5, 4, 17, 16]). Analogously, MRSs and CMRSs can be extended allowing in the conditions predicates defined via ($\mathcal{FM}$-equational) logic programs (the definition of the corresponding denotational and operational semantics is a routine matter, cf. [9]). This gives without doubt an extremely expressive paradigm, but a disadvantage is that we have a new paradigm to be studied almost from the scratch. A nice solution is not to add logic programming as a whole, but instead to add the class of *functionally moded* or the class of *regularly typed* (normal) logic programs. The main interest of these classes, introduced respectively in [13] and [15], is that they can be translated respectively into functional programs and TRSs. Again, it can be proved that their properties remain the same when considering their $\mathcal{FM}$-equational version. Hence, while the user is allowed with a much more expressive paradigm, the theoretical foundation still remains within the realm of MRSs. Another aspect which should not be undertaken is that these kinds of programs have been shown to have extremely *fast* implementations (cf. [13]), so that this extra expressive power is not affected by the well known problem of efficiency of logic programming.

# 6 Termination

Another important topic is the study of termination of the specifications provided by MRSs (for instance, this affects decidability of visual parsing, and total correctness of visual programs). Using the Simulation Theorem 2.4, we can prove that the powerful techniques so far developed to prove termination of $AC$-equational rewriting (e.g. [20]) can be also applied to prove termination of MRSs. Note that an interesting problem is to obtain results on the modularity of termination for MRSs like those obtained for confluence in Section 4; this would also allow to perform a correctness analysis of confluence and termination in parallel by using Theorem 4.7. No results are known on the modularity of termination for equational term rewriting, hence an interesting open problem is to see to what extent the best-so-far results on the modularity of termination for TRSs (cf. [18, 14, 21]) extends to MRSs. The last case to be considered is then the extension of (C)MRSs with ($\mathcal{FM}$-equational) constraint logic programming. If the extension, as previously advocated, stays within functionally moded programs, all the above mentioned techniques can still be used. If, instead, the whole class of ($\mathcal{FM}$-equational) constraint logic programs is used (e.g. the $\mathcal{FM}$-equational version of $CLP(\mathcal{R})$, similarly to [8, 16]), then one can employ an integration of the aforementioned techniques with the techniques of [3] in the following way. Given a CMRS $R$ extended with an $\mathcal{FM}$-equational constraint logic program $C$, let $\hat{R}$ denote the CMRS obtained by deleting from the conditions all the terms that are predicates of the constraint logic program. Then we have the following result:

**Theorem 6.1** *A CMRS $R$ extended with an $\mathcal{FM}$-equational constraint logic program $C$ terminates if $\hat{R}$ terminates and $C$ strongly terminates.*

It can be shown that the results of [3] can be easily extended to $\mathcal{FM}$-equational constraint logic programs. Hence, we can apply the aforementioned techniques on termination of CMRSs to $\hat{R}$, and the techniques of [3] to $C$.

# 7 Conclusion

As seen, MRSs can be given a nice mathematical treatment, since most of the works developed for term rewriting can be automatically restated in this new setting. Moreover, we have provided a new modular analysis for the study of their confluence. Another feature of MRSs and their extensions is that they are extremely expressive when compared to other existing formalism based on grammars, especially as far as reasoning about multidimensional objects is concerned. This can be explained by a combination of two effects. The first is the introduction of multisets as first-class citizens in the language, as seen for instance in Section 3. The second is due to the choice of term rewriting. Indeed, term rewriting has been successfully used for analysis and implementation of abstract data types specifications, and for implementing computations (e.g. functional languages). The same situation occurs in multiset rewriting: besides the use of MRSs for the parsing of visual languages (and this, for instance, raises the interesting problem of finding effective translations of MRSs specifications into existing visual grammars formalisms), the high degree of expressibility of MRSs makes them a unique prototype for the *specification* of the semantics of visual languages and for their *implementation*, just like TRSs are for functional programming and have successfully been used as executable specifications in languages like OBJ3 (cf. [12]). The most relevant works trying to shed some light on semantics specification for visual languages are [2] and [7]. These works, although interesting, are intrinsically different from our approach, since they resort on predicate or spatial logic; moreover, they are less general than MRSs, since (besides the fact they are not meant to deal with parsing), they rely on a fixed graphical logic representation, unlike MRSs. Finally, MRSs do not need the development of a new ad-hoc engine, since they can be directly run on any of the many existing system implementing $AC$-equational rewriting (e.g. OBJ3, ReDuX, etc.).

# References

[1] A. Ames, D. Nadeau, and J.L. Moreland. *The VRML Sourcebook*. Wiley & Sons, 1996.

[2] A.G. Cohn and J.M. Gooday. Defining the syntax and the semantics of a visual programming language in a spatial logic. In *AAAI'94 Workshop on Spatial and Temporal Reasoning*, 1994.

[3] L. Colussi, E. Marchiori, and M. Marchiori. On termination of constraint logic programs. In *Int. Conf. on Principles and Practice of Constraint Programming*, vol. 976 of *LNCS*, pp. 431–448. Springer, 1995.

[4] C. Crimi, A. Guercio, G. Nota, G. Pacini, G. Tortora, and M. Tucci. Relation grammars and their application to multi-dimensional languages. *JVLC*, 2:333–346, 1991.

[5] E.J. Golin. Parsing visual languages with picture layout grammars. *Journal of Visual Languages and Computing*, 2:371–393, 1991.

[6] E.J. Golin and S.P. Reiss. The specification of visual language syntax. *Journal of Visual Languages and Computing*, 1:141–157, 1990.

[7] V. Haarslev. Formal semantics of visual languages using spatial reasoning. In *IEEE Symposium on Visual Languages*, pages 156–163. IEEE Press, 1995.

[8] R. Helm and K. Marriott. A declarative specification and semantics of visual languages. *Journal of Visual Languages and Computing*, 2:311–331, 1991.

[9] S. Hölldobler. *Foundations of Equational Logic Programming*, vol. 353 of *LNCS*. 1989.

[10] J. Jaffar and M.J. Maher. Constraint logic programming: A survey. *Journal of Logic Programming*, 19,20:503–581, 1994.

[11] J.-P. Jouannaud and H. Kirchner. Completion of a set of rules modulo a set of equations. *SIAM Journal on Computing*, 15:1155–1194, 1986.

[12] J.W. Klop. Term rewriting systems. *Handbook of Logic in Computer Science*, vol. 2, chapter 1, pp. 1–116. Clarendon Press, Oxford, 1992.

[13] M. Marchiori. The functional side of logic programming. *ACM Int. Conf. on Functional Programming Languages and Computer Architecture*, pp. 55–65. ACM Press, 1995.

[14] M. Marchiori. Modularity of completeness revisited. In J. Hsiang, editor, *Int. Conf. on Rewriting Techniques and Applications*, vol. 914 of *LNCS*, pp. 2–10. Springer, 1995.

[15] M. Marchiori. Proving Existential Termination of Normal Logic Programs. *Int. Conf. on Algebraic Methodology and Software Technology*, vol. 1101 of *LNCS*, pp. 375–390, 1996.

[16] K. Marriott. Constraint multiset grammars. In *IEEE Symposium on Visual Languages*, pages 118–125. IEEE Press, 1994.

[17] M.A. Najork and S.M. Kaplan. Specifying visual languages with conditional set rewrite systems. In *IEEE Symposium on Visual Languages*. IEEE Press, 1993.

[18] E. Ohlebusch. On the modularity of termination of term rewriting systems. *Theoretical Comp. Science*, 136(2):333–360, 1994.

[19] G.E. Peterson and M.E. Stickel. Complete sets of reductions for some equational theories. *Journal of the ACM*, 28(2):233–264, 1981.

[20] A. Rubio and R. Nieuwenhuis. A total AC-compatible ordering based on RPO. *Theoretical Comp. Science*, 142(2):209–227, 1995.

[21] M. Schmidt-Schauß, M. Marchiori, and S.E. Panitz. Modular termination of r-consistent and left-linear term rewriting systems. *Theoretical Comp. Science*, 149(2):361–374, 1995.

# Restarting Automata with Rewriting*

František Mráz[1] and Martin Plátek[1] and Jörg Vogel[2]

[1] Charles University, Department of Computer Science,
Malostranské nám. 25, 118 00 PRAHA 1, Czech Republic
e-mail: mraz,platek@kki.mff.cuni.cz
[2] Friedrich Schiller University, Computer Science Institute,
07740 JENA, Germany
e-mail: vogel@minet.uni-jena.de

**Abstract.** We introduce restarting automata with rewriting (*RW*-automata) as a generalization of restarting automata (*R*-automata). Their computation proceeds in certain cycles; in each cycle, a (bounded) substring of the input word is rewritten by a shorter string, and the computation restarts on the arising shorter word. Nondeterministic, deterministic, rewriting, and nonrewriting versions are considered and a natural property of monotonicity is introduced in a similar way as for *R*-automata. Monotonic *RW*-automata recognize a proper subset of *CFL*. A new characterization of deterministic context-free languages is given by deterministic monotonic *RW*-automata. Further different classes of *RW*-automata and the class of *CFL* are compared.

## 1 Introduction

We are going out from our FCT'95 contribution [1], where we introduced the notion of restarting automata. We discuss here generalized restarting automata which are able to rewrite.

Our motivation comes from the area of natural language analysis and resembles the motivation for Marcus contextual grammars ([3] – the nonrewriting (deleting only) versions of restarting automata), and for "pure generalized grammars" studied in Novotny's book [4] (the rewriting versions of restarting automata).

Another part of motivation comes from the area of grammar checking of natural as well as programming languages. See e.g. [5].

We define the restarting automaton with rewriting (*RW*-automaton) which can be roughly described as follows. It has a finite control unit, a head with a lookahead window, and it works in certain cycles. In a cycle, it moves the head from left to right along the word; according to its instructions, it can at some point "cut off" some symbols out of the lookahead, replace them by some shorter sequence of symbols and "restart" – i.e. reset the control unit to the initial state and place the head on the left end of the shortened word. The computation halts in an accepting or a rejecting state. The older version of

* Supported by the Grant Agency of the Czech Republic, Grant-No. 201/96/0195

restarting automata without rewriting are $RW$-automata by which the replacing string can be obtained from the "cut-off" string by removing some symbols (at least one).

As usual, we define nondeterministic and deterministic versions of the automata. Similarly as in [1] we consider monotonic $RW$-automata (during any computation, "the places of restarting do not increase their distances from the right end") and show that all monotonic $RW$-automata recognize a subset of the class of context-free languages ($CFL$) and deterministic monotonic $RW$-automata recognize only deterministic $CFL$ ($DCFL$). From this result we get a new characterization of $DCFL$. The paper continues with separation theorems for rewriting and nonrewriting classes of automata and some related results.

## 2   Definitions and Results

We present the definitions informally; the formal technical details could be added in a standard way of the automata theory.

A *restarting automaton with rewriting*, or an *RW-automaton*, $M$ (with bounded lookahead) is a device with a finite state control unit and one head moving on a finite linear (doubly linked) list of items (cells). The first item always contains a special symbol ¢, the last one another special symbol \$, and each other item contains a symbol from a finite alphabet (not containing ¢, \$). The head has a lookahead "window" of length $k$ (for some $k \geq 0$) – besides the current item, $M$ also scans the next $k$ right neighbour items (or simply the end of the word when the distance to \$ is less than $k$). In the *initial configuration*, the control unit is in a fixed, initial, state and the head is attached to the item with the left sentinel ¢ (scanning also the first $k$ symbols of the input word).

The *computation* of $M$ is controlled by a finite set of *instructions* of the following two types:

(1) $(q, au) \rightarrow (q', MVR)$
(2) $(q, au) \rightarrow RESTART(v)$

The left-hand side of an instruction determines when it is applicable – $q$ means the current state (of the control unit), $a$ the symbol being scanned by the head, and $u$ means the contents of the lookahead window ($u$ being a string of length $k$ or less if it ends with \$). The right-hand side describes the activity to be performed. In case (1), $M$ changes the current state to $q'$ and moves the head to the right neighbour item. In case (2), $au$ is replaced with $v$, where $v$ must be shorter than $au$), and $M$ restarts – i.e. it enters the initial state and places the head on the first item of the list (containing ¢).

We say that $M$ is a *restarting automaton (R-automaton)* if in each instruction of the form $(q, au) \rightarrow RESTART(v)$ the word $v$ can be obtained only by deleting some (nonzero) number of symbols out of the word $au$.

We will suppose that the control unit states are divided into two groups: the *nonhalting states* (an instruction is always applicable when the unit is in such a state) and the *halting states* (a computation finishes by entering such a state);

the halting states are further divided into the *accepting states* and the *rejecting states*.

In general, an *RW*-automaton is *nondeterministic*, i.e. there can be two or more instructions with the same left-hand side $(q, au)$. If it is not the case, the automaton is *deterministic* (*det-RW*-automaton).

An input *word w is accepted by M* if there is a computation which starts in the initial configuration with $w$ (bounded by sentinels ¢,$) on the list and finishes in an *accepting configuration* where the control unit is in one of the accepting states. $L(M)$ denotes the language consisting of all words accepted by $M$; we say that *M recognizes the language $L(M)$*.

It is natural to divide any computation of an *RW*-automaton into certain phases or *cycles*: in one cycle, the head moves right along the input list (with a bounded lookahead) until a halting state is entered or something in a bounded space is rewritten – in that case the computation is resumed in the initial configuration on the shortened word (thus a new cycle starts). It immediately implies that any computation of any *RW*-automaton is finite (finishing in a halting state).

The next three claims (with obvious, and hence omitted, proofs) express certain lucidness of computations of *RW*-automata. The notation $u \longrightarrow_M v$ means that there is a cycle of $M$ starting in the initial configuration with the word $u$ and finishing in the initial configuration with the word $v$; the relation $\longrightarrow_M^*$ is the reflexive and transitive closure of $\longrightarrow_M$.

**Claim 1 (The error preserving property (for all *RW*-automata))** *Let M be an RW-automaton, and $u \longrightarrow_M^* v$ for some words $u$, $v$. If $u \notin L(M)$, then $v \notin L(M)$.*

**Claim 2 (The correctness preserving property (for *det-RW*-automata))** *Let M be a deterministic R-automaton and $u \longrightarrow_M^* v$ for some words $u$, $v$. If $u \in L(M)$, then $v \in L(M)$.*

**Claim 3** *Let M be a deterministic R-automaton and $u \longrightarrow_M^* v$ for some words $u$, $v$. Then $v \in L(M)$ if and only if $u \in L(M)$.*

In [1] we introduced a natural property of monotonicity for *R*-automata. By a *monotonic RW-automaton* we mean an *RW*-automaton where the following holds for all computations: all items which appeared in the lookahead window (and were not deleted) during one cycle will appear in the lookahead in the next cycle as well – if it does not finish in a halting state (during any computation, "the places of deleting do not increase their distances from the right endmarker $"). Considering a deterministic *RW*-automaton $M$, it is sometimes convenient to suppose it to be in the *strong cyclic form*; it means that the words of length less than $k$, $k$ being the length of lookahead, are immediately (hence in the first cycle) accepted or rejected, and that $M$ performs at least two cycles (at least one restarting) for any longer word.

For a nondeterministic $RW$-automaton $M$, we can suppose the *weak cyclic form* – any word from $L(M)$ longer than $k$ (the length of lookahead) can be only accepted by performing two cycles at least. The cyclic forms are justified by the following claim.

**Claim 4** *For any $RW$-automaton $M$, with lookahead $k$, there exists an $RW$-automaton $M'$, with some lookahead $n$, $n \geq k$, such that $M'$ is in the weak cyclic form and $L(M) = L(M')$. Moreover, if $M$ is deterministic then $M'$ is deterministic and in strong cyclic form.*

**Proof:** To prove this claim we can proceed in the same way as for $R$-automata. See [2]. $\square$

For brevity, we use the following obvious notation. $RW$ denotes the class of all (nondeterministic) restarting automata with rewriting (with some lookahead). $R$ denotes the class of all (nondeterministic) restarting automata without rewriting. Prefix *det-* denotes the deterministic version, similarly *mon-* the monotonic version. $\mathcal{L}(A)$, where $A$ is some class of automata, denotes the class of languages recognizable by automata from $A$. E.g. the class of languages recognizable by deterministic monotonic $R$-automata is denoted by $\mathcal{L}(det\text{-}mon\text{-}R)$.

**Theorem 5.** $\mathcal{L}(mon\text{-}RW) \subseteq CFL$ and $\mathcal{L}(det\text{-}mon\text{-}RW) \subseteq DCFL$

**Proof:** At first we show that $\mathcal{L}(mon\text{-}RW)$ is a subclass of $CFL$. Let $L$ be a language recognized by $mon\text{-}RW$-automaton $M$, with lookahead of length $k$. We show how to construct a pushdown automaton $P$ which simulates $M$. The construction is similar to the construction of a deterministic pushdown automaton which should simulate a given $det\text{-}mon\text{-}R$-automaton (see [1]). The difference is the following: Instead of one step simulation of a single $MVR$-step, $P$ will simulate in one step all possible "nondeterministic" $MVR$-steps performed on the simulated scanned item simultaneously, and the simulation of a restart without rewriting is replaced by a simulation of a restart with rewriting.

$P$ is able to store in its control unit in a component $CSt$ the set of possible current states of $M$ (i.e. any subset of the set of states of $M$) and in a component $B$ a word of length at most $1 + 2k$. $P$ starts by storing $\{q_0\}$, where $q_0$ is the initial state of $M$, in $CSt$ and pushing $\phi$ (the left endmarker of $M$) into the first cell of the buffer $B$ and the first $k$ symbols of the input word of $M$ into the next $k$ cells of the buffer $B$ (cells $2, 3, \ldots, k + 1$).

During the simulation, the following conditions will hold invariantly:
– $CSt$ contains the set of all states of $M$, in which can be $M$ visiting the simulated (currently scanned) item, with the current left-hand side, and the current lookahead,
– the first cell of $B$ contains the current symbol of $M$ (scanned by the head) and the rest of $B$ contains $m$ right neighbour symbols of the current one (lookahead of length $m$) where $m$ varies between $k$ and $2k$,
– the pushdown contains the left-hand side (w.r.t. the head) of the list, the leftmost symbol ($\phi$) being at the bottom. In fact, any pushdown symbol will be

composed – it will contain the relevant symbol of the input list and the set of states of $M$ in which this symbol (this item) could be entered (from the left) by the situation, which corresponds to the last simulated visit.

The mentioned invariant will be maintained by the following simulation of instructions of $M$; the left-hand side $(q, au)$ of the instruction to be simulated is determined by the information stored in the control unit. The activity to be performed depends on the right-hand sides of applicable instructions of $M$. $P$ can

> either (1)  nondeterministically simulate one of *RESTART* instructions of $M$,
>
> or (2)  simulate all possible *MVR* instructions in one step.

(1) $RESTART(v)$ is simulated by deleting and rewriting in the buffer $B$ (some of the first $k+1$ symbols are deleted and the rest is pushed to the left and possibly rewritten). Then $k+1$ (composed) symbols are successively taken from the pushdown and the relevant symbols are added from the left to $B$ (shifting the rest to the right). The state parts of $k$ (composed) symbols are forgotten, the state part of the $(k+1)$-th symbol (the leftmost in the buffer) is stored in $CSt$. Thus not only the $RESTART(v)$ - operation is simulated but also the beginning part of the next cycle, the part which was prepared in the previous cycle.

(2) $P$ puts the contents of the first cell of $B$ and $CSt$ as a composed symbol on the top of the pushdown, stores the set $\{q' \mid (q, au) \rightarrow_M (q', MVR), q \in CSt\}$ of simulated new states which can be entered after $MVR$-step from some state in the original $CSt$ with the lookahead $au$, and shifts the contents of $B$ one symbol to the left; if the $(k+1)$-th cell of $B$ is then empty, then $P$ reads the next input symbol into it.

It should be clear that due to monotonicity of $M$ the second half of $B$ (cells $k+2, k+3, \ldots, 2k$) is empty at the time of simulating a $RESTART(v)$–operation. Hence the described construction is correct which proves the first part of the proposition. It is clear that the previous construction applied to a *det-mon-R*-automaton yields a deterministic push-down automaton. This proves the second part of the proposition. □

The following theorem is a consequence of the previous theorem, the trivial inclusion $\mathcal{L}(det\text{-}mon\text{-}R) \subseteq \mathcal{L}(det\text{-}mon\text{-}RW)$ and the following lemma.

**Lemma 6.** $DCFL \subseteq \mathcal{L}(det\text{-}mon\text{-}R)$

**Proof:** This lemma was proved in [1]. We omit the proof here. □

**Theorem 7.** $\mathcal{L}(det\text{-}mon\text{-}RW) = DCFL = \mathcal{L}(det\text{-}mon\text{-}R)$

**Theorem 8.** *There is an algorithm which for any RW-automaton $M$ decides whether $M$ is monotonic or not.*

**Proof:** The proof is almost the same as for $R$-automata in [1]. □

The next theorem shows, that restarting automata with rewriting are stronger than restarting automata (without rewriting).

**Theorem 9.** $\mathcal{L}(R)$ *is a proper subclass of* $\mathcal{L}(RW)$.

**Proof:** Obviously $\mathcal{L}(R)$ is a subclass of $\mathcal{L}(RW)$.

At first, we will show that the language

$$L_A = \{ww^R \mid w \in \{a, b\}^*\} \cup \{wcw^R \mid w \in \{a, b\}^*\}$$

can be recognized by a $RW$-automaton $M_A$. $M_A$ can be constructed in such a way that the following properties holds:

($i_1$) $xaay \longrightarrow_{M_A} xcy$, for any words $x, y \in \{a, b\}^*$.
($i_2$) $xbby \longrightarrow_{M_A} xcy$, for any words $x, y \in \{a, b\}^*$.
($i_3$) $xacay \longrightarrow_{M_A} xcy$, for any words $x, y \in \{a, b\}^*$.
($i_4$) $xbcby \longrightarrow_{M_A} xcy$, for any words $x, y \in \{a, b\}^*$.
($i_5$) $M_A$ accepts the one-symbol-word $c$ in a cycle.
($i_6$) $M_A$ rejects in a cycle any word of the form $cy$ or $yc$, where $y$ is any nonempty word.
($i_7$) Any cycle performed by $M_A$ is one of the types $i_1, .., i_6$.

Secondly, we will show that $L_A$ cannot be recognized by any $R$-automaton by a contradiction. W.l.o.g. let us suppose that $L_A$ is recognized by some $R$-automaton $M$ in the weak cyclic form. Let us consider an accepting computation on a sufficiently long word $a^l b^m b^m a^l$, where $l, n > 0$. In the first cycle of the accepting computation, $M$ can only shorten the segment of $b$'s. We will get a word of the form $a^l b^{2m'} a^l$, for some $m' < m$, after the first cycle. But $M$ can make the same first cycle in the computation on the word $a^l b^{2m} a^l a^l b^{2m'} a^l$, which is not in $L(M)$ and get the word $a^l b^{2m'} a^l a^l b^{2m'} a^l$ which is from $L(M)$. This is a contradiction to the "error preserving" property of $RW$-automata (and $R$-automata are a special type of $RW$-automata). □

The language $L_A$ used in the previous proof is a context-free language. Thus we have proved that $RW$-automata are stronger than $R$-automata even in the class *CFL*. The next theorem shows that deterministic $RW$-automata are stronger than deterministic $R$-automata.

**Theorem 10.** $\mathcal{L}(det RW) - (\mathcal{L}(R) \cup CFL) \neq \emptyset$

**Proof:** We will construct a deterministic $RW$-automaton $M$ such, that $L(M)$ is not a context-free language and cannot be recognized by any $R$-automaton. Let us describe the automaton $M$: $M$ has lookahead of the length 3, and three states only – the initial state $q_0$, the accepting state $q_a$, the rejecting state $q_r$. The working alphabet of $M$ is $\{a, b\}$ and $M$ has the following instructions:

1. $(q_0, \text{¢}a\$) \rightarrow_M (q_a, MVR)$,       4. $(q_0, aaaa) \rightarrow_M (q_0, MVR)$,
2. $(q_0, \text{¢}aaa) \rightarrow_M (q_0, MVR)$,       5. $(q_0, aaab) \rightarrow_M RESTART(ba)$,
3. $(q_0, \text{¢}baa) \rightarrow_M RESTART(\text{¢}a)$,       6. $(q_0, aaa\$) \rightarrow_M RESTART(ba\$)$,

and $(q_0, u) \rightarrow_M (q_r, MVR)$ for any other $u$ of the lenght four not covered in the previous cases.

Actually

$$L(M) \cap \{a^i \mid i \geq 1\} = \{a^{3^n} \mid n \geq 0\} \tag{1}$$

i.e. an intersection of $L(M)$ and the regular language $a^*$ is a non context-free language, thus $L(M)$ cannot be from $CFL$. We can show that:

$$a^{3i+j} \longrightarrow_M^* a^j ba^i \text{ for } i > 0 \text{ and } 2 \geq j \geq 0$$

The automaton $M$ makes cycles (using instructions 2–6) until the symbol $b$ appears in the lookahead window in the initial configuration. If it is the first symbol after $\phi$ then $b$ is deleted otherwise the current word is rejected. From this observation (1) directly follows.

$L(M)$ cannot be recognized by any $R$-automaton $M_R$ in the weak cyclic form. Let the length of the lookahead of $M_R$ be $k$. Then for a sufficiently large $m$ (e.g. greater then $k$) such automaton accepts the word $a^{3^m}$ and let $a^{3^m} \longrightarrow_{M_R} a^l$ be the first cycle of an accepting computation on the word $a^{3^m}$. But $l$ cannot be a power of 3 ($3^m - k - 1 \leq l < 3^m$), this contradicts the error preserving property (Claim 1). $\qquad \square$

Moreover the previous theorem shows, that $RW$-automata are stronger than $R$-automata also outside $CFL$. Next we will show that also monotonic $RW$-automata are stronger that monotonic $R$-automata by giving a language $L$ which cannot be recognized by any $R$-automaton, but is recognized by a monotonic $RW$-automaton.

**Theorem 11.** $\mathcal{L}(mon\text{-}R)$ *is a proper subclass of* $\mathcal{L}(mon\text{-}RW)$.

**Proof:** Let $L_1 = \{a^n b^n \mid n \geq 0\}$, $L_2 = \{a^n b^{2n} \mid n \geq 0\}$ and $L = \{c, ee\}.L_1 \cup \{d, ee\}.L_2$. The language $L$ is a context-free language and can be recognized by a nondeterministic $RW$-automaton $M$ in the following way:

- if the word starts by $c$ then $M$ simply deletes $ab$ "in the middle" of the word and restarts,
- if the word starts by $d$ then $M$ deletes $abb$ "in the middle" of the word and restarts,
- if the word starts by $ee$ then $M$ nondeterministically rewrites $ee$ by $c$ or $d$,
- $M$ immediately accepts the words $c$ and $d$.

It is easy to show that $M$ is monotonic and $L(M) = L$.

$L$ cannot be recognized by any $R$-automaton. For a contradiction let us suppose that $L$ is recognized by some $R$-automaton $M$ in a cyclic form with the size of lookahead $k$. That means that any $eea^i b^i$ for $i \geq k$ is accepted by $M$ in at least two cycles.

In the first cycle of an accepting computation on this word $M$ can only shorten the both segments of $a'$s and $b'$s in the same way. After the first cycle, we will get a word of the form $eea^{i-n}b^{i-n}$, for some $n < i$. But $M$ can make the same first cycle in the computation on the word $eea^i b^{2i-n}$, which is not in $L(M)$ and get the word $eea^{i-n}b^{2i-2n}$ which is from $L(M)$. This is a contradiction to the "error preserving" property of $R$-automata. $\qquad \square$

**Theorem 12.** $\mathcal{L}(mon\text{-}RW)$ *is a proper subclass of CFL.*

**Proof:** The Theorem 5 says that $\mathcal{L}(mon\text{-}RW)$ is a subclass of *CFL*.
It is sufficient to show that the context-free language

$$L_1 = \{ww^R \mid w \in \{a, b\}^*\}$$

cannot be recognized by any $RW$-automaton $M_A$.
The full proof is left out, but a quite similar one for $R$-automata could be found in [1].

$\square$

## 3   Additional remarks

In the previous section we showed some typical results concerning $RW$-automata and $R$-automata. On one side we have shown that the deterministic monotonic $RW$-automata have the same power as deterministic monotonic $R$-automata, i.e. in deterministic monotonic case the rewriting does not increase the power of restarting automata. On the other side we have shown that $det\text{-}RW$-automata ($mon\text{-}RW$-automata, resp.) are stronger than $det\text{-}R$-automata ($mon\text{-}R$-automata, resp.).

One direction of our further research will be in detailed comparisons of classes of languages recognized by different classes of $RW$- and $R$-automata.

We propose to study in the future connections between restarting automata with rewriting and "pure grammars" studied in Novotny's book [4].

Further we propose to take $RW$-automata as the theoretical background for a program simulating 'pure' developments, and reductions of Czech sentences. This can be a nice tool for a natural learning of syntax of Czech.

## References

1. P. Jančar, F. Mráz, M. Plátek, J. Vogel: *Restarting Automata;*, in Proc. FCT'95, Dresden, Germany, August 1995, LNCS 965, Springer Verlag 1995, pp. 283 - 292
2. P. Jančar, F. Mráz, M. Plátek, M. Procházka, J. Vogel: *Restarting Automata and Marcus Grammars*, TR Math/95/1, Friedrich-Schiller-University, Jena, Germany, January 1995
3. S. Marcus: *Contextual grammars*, Revue Roum. Math. Pures Appl.,14, 10, 1969, pp.1525-1534
4. M.Novotný: *S algebrou od jazyka ke gramatice a zpět*, Academia, Praha, 1988, (*in Czech*)
5. M. Procházka: *Syntax Errors and Their Detection*, Diploma Work on MFF UK (*in Czech*), Prague, 1994

# On the Role of Orthogonality in the GMRES Method

M. ROZLOŽNÍK, Z. STRAKOŠ, M. TŮMA * **

*Institute of Computer Science, Academy of Sciences of the Czech Republic*
*Pod vodárenskou věží 2, 182 07 Praha 8, Czech Republic*
*e-mail: miro@uivt.cas.cz, strakos@uivt.cas.cz, tuma@uivt.cas.cz*

**Abstract.** In the paper we deal with some computational aspects of the Generalized minimal residual method (GMRES) for solving systems of linear algebraic equations. The key question of the paper is the importance of the orthogonality of computed vectors and its influence on the rate of convergence, numerical stability and accuracy of different implementations of the method. Practical impact on the efficiency in the parallel computer environment is considered.

## 1  Introduction

Scientific and engineering research is becoming increasingly dependent upon development and implementation of efficient parallel algorithms on modern high-performance computers. Numerical linear algebra is an important part of such research and numerical linear algebra algorithms represent the most widely used computational tools in science and engineering. Matrix computations, including the solution of systems of linear equations, least squares problems, and algebraic eigenvalue problems, govern the performance of many applications on vector and parallel computers.

In recent years there has been a surge of interest for numerical solving of partial differential equations in numerous application fields. The major obstacle arising in solving the corresponding linear algebraic systems is the fact that these problems are usually very large and ill-conditioned. On the other hand, the resulting systems have often some special structure and they are usually sparse. These properties can be naturally exploited in the development of the efficient numerical algorithms for solving these problems.

This paper concentrates on the special important question in the solution of large sparse systems of linear algebraic equations. We consider the Generalized Minimal Residual Method (GMRES) [7], most widely known and used representative of the class of Krylov subspace methods, presented in recent years (for a deep survey we refer to [5]). In particular, we consider the preconditioned GMRES method and its possible implementations based on different orthogonalization techniques. We will examine the level of orthogonality among the

---

\* Part of this work was performed while the second author visited Department of Mathematics and Computer Science, Emory University, Atlanta, USA

\*\* This work was supported by the GA AS CR under grant 230401 and by the NSF grant Int 921824

computed basis vectors produced by these schemes in connection to the decrease of the norm of the GMRES residual. Presented results will lead to important conclusions about the parallel implementation and application of the method.

The organization of this paper is as follows. Section 2 briefly introduces the GMRES method, discusses some of its basic algorithmic aspects and its preconditioning. In Section 3 we give a description of practical application and preconditioning technique used in the numerical experiments presented in this paper. Section 4 concerns three important implementations of the GMRES method based on different orthogonalization schemes, namely the Householder orthogonalization, classical and modified variant of the Gram-Schmidt orthogonalization.

## 2 The Generalized Minimal Residual Method

Let $Ax = b$ be a system of linear algebraic equations, where $A$ is a real nonsingular $N$ by $N$ matrix and $b$ an $N$-dimensional real vector. The Generalized minimal residual method (GMRES) for solving this system starts with an initial guess $x_0$ and seeks the $n$-th approximate solution $x_n$ of the form

$$(2.\,1) \qquad x_n \in x_0 + K_n(A, r_0),$$

where $r_0 = b - Ax_0$ is the initial residual and $K_n(A, r_0)$ is the $n$-th Krylov subspace generated by the matrix $A$ and vector $r_0$,

$$(2.\,2) \qquad K_n(A, r_0) = span\{r_0, Ar_0, \ldots, A^{n-1}r_0\}.$$

The approximate solution of the GMRES method minimizes the Euclidean norm of the residual, i.e.

$$(2.\,3) \qquad \|b - Ax_n\| = \min_{u \in x_0 + K_n(A, r_0)} \|b - Au\|.$$

The classical variant of the Generalized Minimal Residual Method consists of constructing the Arnoldi basis of the Krylov subspaces and then solving the transformed least squares problem at each individual iteration step.
The orthonormal basis $V_{n+1} = [v_1, \ldots, v_{n+1}]$ of the Krylov subspace $K_n(A, r_0)$, called the Arnoldi basis, is computed via the recurrences

$$(2.\,4) \quad v_1 = r_0/\rho, \; \rho = \|r_0\|, \; AV_n = V_{n+1}H_{n+1,n}, \; V_{n+1}^T V_{n+1} = I_{n+1}.$$

The approximate solution $x_n$ is then given by

$$x_n = x_0 + V_n y_n,$$

where $y_n$ is chosen as the solution of the transformed least squares problem

$$(2.\,5) \qquad \|\varrho e_1 - H_{n+1,n} y_n\| = \min_{y \in R^n} \|\varrho e_1 - H_{n+1,n} y\|.$$

For more detailed description of the algorithm we refer to [7], [4].

In practice, preconditioning is the essential ingredient in the success of projection type methods like GMRES. It consists of transforming the original system in such a way that the resulting system would be easier to solve. For example, when the preconditioner is applied, we will solve the preconditioned linear system

$$(2.\ 6) \qquad AM^{-1}z = b, \text{ where } x = M^{-1}z,$$

where the matrix $M^{-1}$ is some approximation to the matrix $A^{-1}$. The relation (2. 6) represents so-called *explicit* preconditioning (see, e.g., [1]). Its application in the iteration cycle of GMRES reduces to matrix-vector products. On the contrary, a preconditioner is *implicit* if its application requires a solution of the special linear system within each step of the iterative method. It was realized that straightforward implementation of implicit preconditioning in conjugate gradient-like methods could lead to severe degradation of the performance on supercomputers. In particular, the sparse triangular solves involved in the ILU-type preconditioning were found to be a serial bottleneck (due to the recursive nature of the computation), thus limiting the effectiveness of this approach on vector and parallel computers. Perhaps the most important examples are provided by preconditioners based on an incomplete LU (ILU) decomposition. Here $M = \bar{L}\bar{U}$ where $\bar{L}$ and $\bar{U}$ are sparse triangular matrices which approximate the exact $L$ and $U$ factors of $A$. Applying the preconditioner requires the solution of two sparse triangular systems (the forward and backward solves). Other notable examples of preconditioners include the ILQ, SSOR and ADI preconditioners (an initial information can be found, e.g., in [1]).

## 3 Numerical experiment - description

We show the behaviour of the preconditioned GMRES method on a real-world problem. We have chosen a typical matrix which arises in the circuit simulation (in our case we used the matrix from the 32-bit adder design (see [3])). Its structural pattern is shown in Figure 1.

We have chosen explicit preconditioning technique based on a direct approximation of $A^{-1}$. We used a preconditioner AIBC (see [2]) with drop tolerance 0.6. Structural pattern of the preconditioner is shown in figure 2. It is worth to note how close is the structure of the preconditioner to the structure of the original nonsymmetric matrix although the complete inverse of $A$ should in this case contain much more nonzero elements than shown on Figure 2. Numerical experiments were performed on the SGI workstation with the machine precision $\varepsilon = 2.2.10^{-16}$.

## 4 Implementations of GMRES with different orthogonalization schemes

Several algorithms for computing the Arnoldi basis exist. They differ in the way in which the orthogonalization in the Arnoldi process is carried out. Utilizing

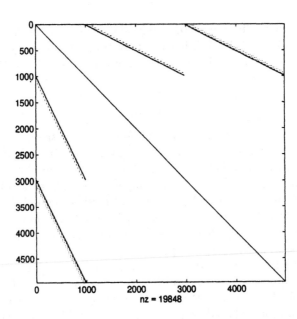

**Fig. 1.** Structural pattern of the matrix ADD1(4960). Dots (lines) represent positions of nonzero elements in the matrix.

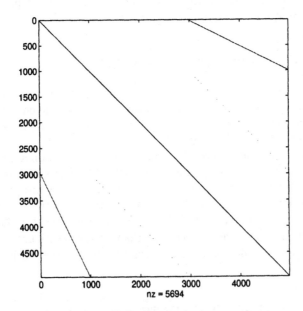

**Fig. 2.** Structural pattern of the approximate inverse preconditioner for the matrix ADD1(4960). Dots (lines) represent positions of nonzero elements in the matrix.

[7], [8], we will consider classical and modified Gram-Schmidt (MGS) and House-holder (HH) orthogonalizations.

In exact arithmetic the Arnoldi vectors are orthogonal. However, in finite precision computation the orthogonality is lost, which may potentially affect both the convergence rate and the ultimate attainable accuracy of the computed approximate solution. In figure 3 we have plotted the loss of orthogonality of computed vectors of different implementations of the GMRES method. Solid line represents the loss of orthogonality $\|I - V_n^T V_n\|_F$ for the Householder implementation, dotted line and dashed lines, the loss of orthogonality for the modified and classical Gram-Schmidt implementations, respectively.

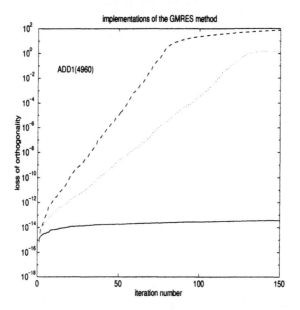

**Fig. 3.** The loss of orthogonality for different orthogonalization schemes. Solid line represents loss of orthogonality of the Householder orthogonalization. Dotted and dash-dotted lines represent loss of orthogonality of the MGS and CGS orthogonalization, respectively.

If we want to keep the computed orthogonality as close to the machine precision as possible, we need to use the proper orthogonal scheme, namely Householder orthogonalizations. It was shown in [4], that for the Householder implementation the loss of orthogonality of the computed vectors $\bar{V}_{n+1}$ is bounded independently of the system parameters,

$$(4.\ 7) \qquad \|I - \bar{V}_{n+1}^T \bar{V}_{n+1}\| \leq \zeta_1 n^{3/2} N \varepsilon.$$

where $\zeta_1$ is a moderate constant independent of $n, N, \varepsilon$ and of other system parameters. Moreover, under obvious assumption on the numerical nonsingularity of the system matrix, the Householder implementation of GMRES is proved backward stable.

In Figure 4 we have plotted the norm of the relative true residual $\|b - A\bar{x}_n\|/\rho$ (solid line), norm of the relative Arnoldi residual, which is given as $\|\, \|r_0\|e_1 - \bar{H}_{n+1,n}\bar{y}_n\|/\rho$ (dashed line). As we can see these two quantities may differ in the finite precision arithmetic. The dash-dotted line represents the smallest singular value of the matrix $\bar{V}_n$ (here it is almost equal to 1 for any value of $N$) and the dotted line represents the loss of orthogonality of computed vectors.

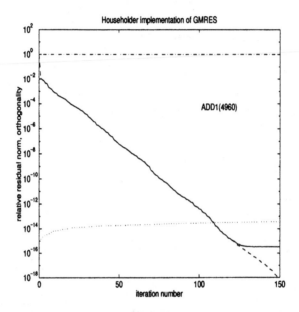

**Fig. 4.** Householder implementation of GMRES for matrix ADD1(4960). Solid line represents the norm of the relative true residual. Dashed line represents the norm of the relative Arnoldi residual. Dashed-dotted line represents the smallest singular value of the smallest singular value of the matrix $\bar{V}_n$.

The price for preserving of orthogonality near the machine precision is, unfortunately, too high for most of the applications. Moreover, the Householder implementation is less amenable to parallel computer architectures. The Gram-Schmidt process is a cheaper alternative and its modified version represents the most frequently used compromise. In the parallel computational environment, however, the classical Gram-Schmidt would be preferable, but it is not trusted. The loss of orthogonality in the classical Gram-Schmidt is much worse then in the modified version (Figure 3). The loss of orthogonality would be a crucial thing if the computed basis was a primary goal of our computation. But we are not interested in the basis itself – our goal is to solve the linear system. As we will explain, the emphasis on the orthogonality of the computed basis can lead to a completely wrong judgement about the numerical stability and applicability of the GMRES implementations.

In the GMRES context, there is a very important relation between the loss of orthogonality among the Arnoldi vectors and the decrease of the residual of the computed approximation. This relation has been described in [6]. It was shown that, the loss of orthogonality for the modified Gram-Schmidt implementation of GMRES is bounded by

$$(4.\,8) \qquad \|I - \bar{V}_{n+1}^T \bar{V}_{n+1}\| \leq \zeta_2 n^{3/2} N \frac{\varepsilon \kappa(A)}{\|\hat{r}_n\|/\rho},$$

where $\kappa(A)$ is the condition number of the matrix $A$ and the quantity $\|\hat{r}_n\|/\rho$ is close to the relative residual norm of the approximate solution in the $n$-th iteration step, $\zeta_2$ is a moderate constant. Consequently, it can be shown that the Arnoldi vectors will loose their orthogonality completely *only after* the residual of the computed approximation is reduced close to its final level, which is proportional to the machine precision multiplied by the condition number of the system matrix. Until the orthogonality is completely lost, the modified Gram-Schmidt GMRES performs almost exactly as well as the Householder implementation. This suggests that unless the system matrix is extremely ill-conditioned, the use of the modified Gram-Schmidt GMRES is theoretically well justified. These results are illustrated on Figure 5. The proof of (4. 8) is far from trivial and its explanation is beyond the scope of this contribution.

In other words, despite the fact that the Arnoldi basis computed via the modified Gram-Schmidt is much worse than that one computed via the Householder reflections, in the GMRES context it does not really matter. This rises a question about the classical Gram-Schmidt GMRES. For the classical Gram-Schmidt GMRES implementation an analogous statement can be formulated (the final accuracy is, however, different). Although the theoretical analysis has not been finished yet and would need more work [6], we believe that it will lead to reinstating of the classical Gram-Schmidt as a suitable alternative for the parallel implementation of the preconditioned GMRES method.

# References

1. R. Barret, M. Berry, T. Chan, J. Demmel, J. Donato, J. Dongarra, V. Eijkhout, R. Pozo, C. Romine and H. van der Vorst. Templates for the Solution of Linear Systems. SIAM, Philadelphia, 1994.
2. M. Benzi, M. Tůma: A sparse approximate inverse preconditioner for nonsymmetric linear systems. to appear in SIAM J. Sci. Comput..
3. T. Davis: Sparse matrix collection. *NA Digest*, Volume 94, Issue 42, October 1994.
4. J. Drkošová, A. Greenbaum, M. Rozložník, Z. Strakoš, *Numerical Stability of the GMRES Method*, BIT 3, pp. 309-330, 1995

416

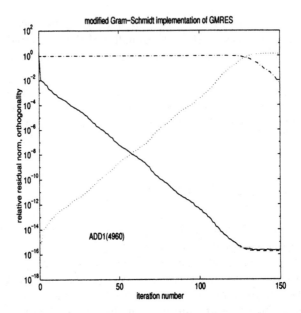

**Fig. 5.** modified Gram-Schmidt implementation of GMRES. Lines show the same quantities as on Figure 4.

5. R.W. Freund, G.H. Golub, N.M. Nachtigal, *Iterative Solution of Linear Systems*, Acta Numerica 1, pp. 1-44, 1992
6. A. Greenbaum, M. Rozložník, Z. Strakoš, *Numerical Behaviour of the Modified Gram Schmidt GMRES Method*, (submitted to BIT)
7. Y. Saad, M.H. Schultz, *GMRES: A Generalized Minimal Residual Algorithm for Solving Nonsymmetric Linear Systems*, SIAM J. Sci. Stat. Comput. 7, pp. 856-869, 1986
8. H. F. Walker, *Implementation of the GMRES method using Householder transformations*, SIAM J. Sci. Stat. Comput. 9, 1 (1988), pp. 152-163.

# Efficient Tree Pattern Unification *

Peter Ružička

Institute of Informatics
Faculty of Mathematics and Physics
Comenius University
Mlynská dolina, 842 15 Bratislava
Slovak Republic

**Abstract:** The problem of many–to–one unification, i.e. a simultaneous weak unification of pattern terms against all subterms of a target term, is studied for linear terms. Two algorithms proposed in [10] generalize either the many–to–one tree pattern matching algorithm [5] based on the path counting principle or the rooted many–to–one tree pattern unification algorithm [11] based on the pattern elimination principle. In both cases, the asymptotical worst–case time complexity of tree pattern unification is quadratic as in the special case of tree pattern matching. However, the expected time complexity of the "pattern–eliminating" algorithm is linear according to the size of the input. In this paper we improve the worst–case time bound result by designing an $O(nm^{0.75} \log^k m)$ algorithm for finding all occurrences of a pattern term–tree of the size $m$ in a target term–tree of the size $n$, for some fixed $k$. The algorithm is extensible to many–to–one version of tree pattern unification problem and is also suitable for applications with dynamically changing set of patterns.

## 1 Motivation

Various variants of pattern matching have been extensively studied in computer science for well over two decades. Much of this study has been motivated by and has found applications in many diverse fields ranging from bibliographic database searching, compiler construction technology, artificial intelligence systems to molecular biology. In recent years, interest in the area of tree matching has grown even further due to the computational needs of functional, logic and equational programming [7].

Our work has been primally motivated by various applications of term rewriting, including rewriting based equational programming and narrowing based equational solving. In these applications a goal (a term or an equational formula) is rewritten according to a set of term rewriting rules. A rewriting step is based on matching a goal against a set of patterns (i.e. the left–hand sides of rewrite rules) or on unification of a goal with a set of patterns.

---

* This research has been partially supported by the EC Cooperative Action IC 1000 (project ALTEC: Algorithms for Future Technologies) and by the Slovak GAV project 1/1447/94.

From the theoretical point of view time and space complexity of tree pattern matching/unification algorithms is of interest. However, in the context of term rewriting applications additional requirements are emphasized on the selection of usable tree pattern matching/unification algorithms. Some of these requirements are dynamization, adaptability to various reduction strategies, compactness, adaptability to various (required) traversal orders and adaptability to local changes in the goal.

The first results solving many–to–one matching of linear terms (both patterns and goals) have been summarized in [5]. An asymptotical improvement of the bottom–up technique in both time and space is given in [3]. This solution is adaptable to the dynamic version of the problem. The efficient top–down algorithm for non–linear pattern matching in trees is given in [8]. However, it is not easily adaptable for dynamic pattern matching. Recently, the asymptotical time improvements of the top–down matching have been achieved by [6, 4]. As for the unification, there was only one known result [11] solving the rooted many–to–one unification of linear terms. It means that the set of patterns is weakly unified with the whole goal (target term) but not with its subterms.

In our previous paper [10] the problem of many–to–one (non–rooted) unification for linear terms has been studied. Two top–down algorithms solving the studied problem were proposed generalizing either the known many–to–one tree pattern matching algorithm based on the path counting principle or the rooted many–to–one tree pattern unification algorithm based on the pattern elimination principle. In both cases, the asymptotical worst–case time complexity of tree pattern unification was the same as in the special case of tree pattern matching. Moreover, the expected time complexity of the "pattern–eliminating" algorithm was linear according to the size of input. A possibility of dynamization of the set of input pattern terms was discussed, too. While the "path–counting" algorithm was not adaptable to the dynamic version of the problem, it turned out that the "pattern–eliminating" algorithm was effective enough also in the case when the set of input pattern terms is changed during the computation.

The fundamental problem remained unsolved, namely whether the quadratic time complexity of naive one–to–one tree pattern unification algorithm can be asymptoticaly improved. We present an $O(nm^{0.75} \log^k m)$ algorithm to solve the problem, based on techniques due to Kosaraju [6]. The algorithm is extensible also for many–to–one version of tree pattern unification problem using techniques presented in [10] and it is also suitable for applications requiring dynamically changing set of patterns.

## 2 Tree pattern unification problems

The matching and unification problems are defined and studied in various formalisms. In this paper the tree notation is preferred since we concentrate on the problems concerning the design of suitable term representations and of efficient algorithms on them.

*2.1. Terms.* Let $V$ be a countable set of variable symbols and $F = \{F_n\}_{n=0}^{\infty}$ be a ranked alphabet of function symbols. A set $F_n$ contains the function symbols of the arity $n$. The constants of $F_0$ and the variables of $V$ are the nullary symbols, i.e., the symbols of arity $0$.

Denote $T$ the set of all well–formed *terms* over an alphabet of function symbols $F$ and variables $V$. The *size of a term* $t \in T$ (denoted as $|t|$) is equal to the number of function symbols occurring in the term $t$. A *term is linear* if each variable occurs in it at most once.

*2.2. Term–trees.* The terms can be considered as ordered labelled trees, called *term–trees.* Each interior vertex of a term–tree is labelled by a non–constant function symbol from $F - F_0$ and each leaf by a symbol from $F_0 \cup V$, i.e., either by a constant symbol or by a variable symbol. The out–degree of a vertex labelled by $f \in F$ is equal to the *arity* of $f$. The outgoing edges of each vertex are ordered. Their ordering corresponds to the ordering of arguments of $f$.

The *size of a term–tree* $T$ (denoted as $|T|$) is equal to the number of vertices. We use the same notation as in the case of terms because there is one–to–one correspondence between the symbols of terms and the vertices in term–trees. To reference the $k$–th successor of a vertex $v$ in a term–tree $T$ we use the notation $suc(v, k)$.

In a term–tree $T$ for any vertex $v$ by $\sigma_{T,v}$ we denote a sequence of labels from the root of $T$ to $v$. For a set $S$ of vertices, the set of all $\sigma_{T,v}$, where $v$ is in $S$, is denoted by $\sigma_{T,S}$. A *suffix number* of a string $w$ in a set of strings $A$ is the number of strings in $A$ such that they are suffixes of $w$. The *suffix index* of $A$ is the maximum among all suffix numbers of the strings in $A$.

*2.3. Tree pattern unification problems.* A pattern term–tree $P$ *unifies* with a non–variable *target* term–tree $T$ at a vertex $v$ from $T$ if there is a mapping from the vertices of $P$ into the vertices of $T$ such that

- the root $r$ of $P$ maps to the vertex $v$ of $T$;
- if $u$ maps to $w$ and $u, w$ are not variable leaves, then vertices $u, w$ have the same label, equal out–degrees, and the $k$-th successor of $u$ maps to the $k$-th successor of $w$;
- if $u$ maps to $w$ and $w$ is a variable leaf in $T$, then also each successor of $u$ maps to $w$.

The *(one–to–one) tree pattern unification problem* for a pattern term–tree $P$ and a target term–tree $T$ is to find all occurrences of a given pattern term–tree $P$ in a given target term–tree $T$, i.e. to determine the set of all vertices of $T$ at which $P$ unifies with $T$.

The *many-to-one tree pattern unification problem* for "many" pattern term–trees $\{P_1, \cdots, P_k\}$ and "one" target term–tree $T$ is for each vertex $v$ in $T$ to determine a subset of pattern term–trees which unify with $T$ at $v$.

In *the dynamic version of the many-to-one tree pattern unification* an additional condition is required: a pattern term–tree is inserted to or deleted from the set of pattern term–trees $\{P_1, \cdots, P_k\}$ in time $o(|P_1, \cdots, P_k|)$.

# 3 Basic techniques

We start with three basic techniques introduced by Kosaraju [6], adapted to term–trees.

*3.1. Convolution of a term–tree and a string* The *convolution* of linear sequences $a_0, ..., a_{n-1}$ and $b_0, ..., b_{m-1}$, $n \geq m$, is the convolution sequence $c_0, ..., c_{n-1}$ such that for $0 \leq i \leq n-1$

$$c_i = \sum_{j=0}^{m-1} a_{i-j} b_j.$$

We assume that $a_{i-j} = 0$ for $i < j$. If $a_i, b_i$ are values from $\{0, 1, ..., m\}$, then the resulting convolution sequence can be computed in time $O(n \log^k m)$ for some fixed $k$.

If, in addition, we are given a function $h : \{0, 1, ..., n-1\} \mapsto \{0, 1, ..., m-1\}$, then *the truncated convolution* for $0 \leq i \leq n-1$ is

$$c_i = \sum_{0 \leq j \leq m-1, h(i-j) \geq j} a_{i-j} b_j.$$

If $a_i, b_i$ are values from $\{0, 1, ..., m\}$, then the truncated convolution can be computed in time $O(n \sqrt{m} \log^k m)$ for some fixed $k$.

Now, replace the sequence $a_0, ..., a_{n-1}$ by an $n$–vertex term–tree $T$, where $a(u)$ denotes the label $a$ of a vertex $u$. Then the convolution of the tree $T$ and the sequence $b_0, ..., b_{m-1}$ determines a value $c(u)$ to each vertex $u$ of $T$ in the following manner

$$c(u) = \sum_{j=0}^{m-1} \sum_{pred^j(v)=u} a(v) b_j$$

where $pred^j(v)$ is the $j$-th predecessor of $v$ ($pred^j(v) = v$ for $j \leq 0$).

Moreover, for a given function $h$ defined for each vertex in $T$ we have for each vertex $u$ in $T$

$$c(u) = \sum_{j=0}^{m-1} \sum_{pred^j(v)=u, h(v) \geq j} a(v) b_j.$$

When $a(v)$ and $b_j$ are values from $\{0, 1\}$, then the truncated term–tree convolution can be computed in time $O(|T| \sqrt{m} \log^k m)$ for some fixed $k$.

*3.2. A suffix tree of a term–tree* A *suffix tree* for a string $a_0 a_1 ... a_{n-1}$ is a trie of suffixes of $a_0 a_1 ... a_{n-1}\$$. The *compact suffix tree* is obtained by condensing the information such that every interior vertex has at least two successors.

The *suffix tree* of a term–tree $T$ is a trie of the set

$$\{\sigma_{T,v}^R \$ \mid v \text{ is not a variable leaf in } T\}.$$

Analogously, we define the compact suffix tree of a term–tree. In the following, by a suffix tree we mean the compact suffix tree after removing the symbol $\$$. We denote the suffix tree of $T$ by $\Sigma_T$. The suffix tree of a term–tree $T$ can be computed in time $O(|T| \log |T|)$.

*3.3. Partition of term–trees into chains and anti–chains* A set of vertices $S$ in a term–tree $T$ has the *suffix property* if $\sigma_{T,S}$ can be ordered in a sequence $x_1, ..., x_l$ such that for $i = 1, ..., l - 1$ each $x_i$ is a suffix of $x_{i+1}$. The set of vertices $S$ in a term–tree $T$ has *anti–suffix property* if $\sigma_{T,S}$ has the property that no string in it is a suffix of any other string in it.

A set of vertices $S$ in a term–tree $T$ is a *chain* if $S$ can be ordered as $v_1, ..., v_l$ such that for $i = 1, ..., l - 1$ each $v_i$ is a predecessor of $v_{i+1}$. The set of vertices $S$ is an *anti–chain* if no vertex in $S$ is a predecessor of any other vertex in $S$.

A set of vertices $S$ in a term–tree $T$ has the suffix (resp. anti–suffix) property iff the set $S$ is a chain (resp. anti–chain) in its suffix tree $\Sigma_T$.

A partition of the suffix tree $\Sigma_T$ into chains and anti–chains is called $(\alpha, \beta)$–*partition*, if the vertex set of $T$ can be partitioned into at most $\alpha + \beta$ sets such that at most $\alpha$ sets are chains and at most $\beta$ sets are anti–chains.

# 4 Fast term–tree pattern unification algorithm

First, we give the overall design of the term–tree pattern unification algorithm.

1. Construct the suffix tree $\Sigma_P$ for the pattern term–tree $P$.
2. Partition the vertex set of the suffix tree $\Sigma_P$ into chains and anti–chains.
3. For every vertex set $S$ having anti–suffix property compute a set of vertices in the target term–tree $T$ at which $P$ (restricted to leaves in $S$) unifies with $T$.
4. For every vertex set $S$ having suffix property compute a set of vertices in $T$ at which $P$ (restricted to leaves in $S$) unifies with $T$.
5. Compute the intersection of two sets obtained in Step 3 and Step 4.

Further, we specify the details of individual steps of the algorithm along with their complexity analysis.

*4.1.* The time complexity of Step 1 is $O(|P| \log |P|)$. It follows from an extension of Weiner's construction for strings [12] and it is also the consequence of the parallel suffix construction algorithm of [2] for strings, which translates into an $O(|P| \log |P|)$ sequential algorithm for term–trees and strings.

*4.2.* In Step 2, we choose $(\alpha, \beta)$–partition of the vertex set of suffix tree $\Sigma_P$ for $\alpha = |P|^{0.25}$. Thus $O(|P|^{0.25})$ sets of the partition are chains and $O(|P|^{0.75})$ sets of the partition are anti–chains. Such a partition can be computed in time $O(|P|)$. Traverse the tree $P$ using depth–first–search strategy and remove from $P$ all chains of the size at least $\beta$. There are at most $\alpha$ such chains, as $\alpha\beta = |P|$. The remaining fragments of $|P|$ are a forest, in which each tree has the hight lower than $\beta$. Therefore this forest can be partitioned into at most $\beta - 1$ anti–chains. This specifies the partition of the vertex set of $\Sigma_P$ into $O(|P|^{0.25} + |P|^{0.75})$ sets, in which there are $O(|P|^{0.25})$ sets having suffix property and $O(|P|^{0.75})$ sets having anti–suffix property.

*4.3.* For Step 3, we show the following proposition: if a set of leaves of $P$ has the anti–suffix property, then we can find the set of all vertices of $T$ at each of which $P$ unifies with $T$ in time $O(|P| + |T|)$.

We outline the idea of the proof of this proposition. The proof is based on the modification of the failure function in Aho & Corasick many–to–one string pattern matching algorithm [1] in a manner similar to the failure function designed for many–to–one tree pattern unification algorithm based on the path counting principle in [10]. The definition of the failure–transition function $f$ is the following: (assume vertices $v, u$ in $P$ and a label $a$)

$$f(v, a) = u \; if \; \sigma_{P,u} \; is \; the \; longest \; proper \; suffix \; of \; \sigma_{P,v} a$$

The function $f$ can be computed in time $O(|P|)$. As in [10] by traversing the target tree $T$ in top–down manner and by using function $f$, we can mark every vertex of $T$ which either specifies the termination of a leaf–to–root path string match or specifies a path substring match due to a variable leaf in $T$. With respect to anti–suffix property of $P$, no vertex in $T$ can be the terminating vertex of more than one leaf–to–root path string of $P$. Following [10], for each vertex of $T$ we count the number of leaf–to–root path strings of $P$ that match at that vertex in $T$ plus the number of path substrings of $P$ that match (due to the variable leaf) at that vertex in $T$. From Theorem 1 in [10] (as for leaf–to–root path strings of $P$ with anti–suffix property we have the suffix index equal to $O(1)$) the time complexity of computing the set of vertices of $T$ at each of which $P$ unifies with $T$ is $O(|P| + |T|)$.

To conclude Step 3, we repeat the above procedure for each of the $O(|P|^{0.75})$ sets having anti–suffix property. The resulting set of vertices of $T$ is obtained as the intersection of sets of vertices of $T$ computed in the $O(|P|^{0.75})$ iterations. Hence, the complete computation of Step 3 can be performed in time $O((|P| + |T|)|P|^{0.75})$.

*4.4.* For Step 4, we show the following proposition: if the set of leaves of $P$ has the suffix property, then we can find the set of vertices of $T$ at each of which $P$ unifies with $T$ in time $O(|T|\sqrt{|P|}\log^k |P|)$ for some fixed $k$.

We outline the idea of the proof of this proposition.

- As the set of leaves of the pattern term–tree $P$ has the suffix property, it is on a chain of $\Sigma_P$. Denote this chain as $u_0, u_1, ..., u_{l-1}$ and the corresponding path strings in $\Sigma_P$ as $x_0, x_0x_1, ..., x_0x_1...x_{l-1}$. Thus $\sigma_{P,u_i} = (x_0x_1...x_i)^R$.
- For the target term-tree $T$ construct its suffix tree $\Sigma_T$ in time $O(|T| \log |T|)$.
- Determine the "truncation" function $h$ in the following manner. Trace the $x_0x_1...x_{l-1}$ path in $\Sigma_T$, starting at the root, and mark the termination of each substring $x_i$ on this path. Using these markings we can compute for each vertex $v$ in $T$ the length $h(v)$ of the longest common suffix of $\sigma_{T,v}$ and $(x_0x_1...x_{l-1})^R$ in time $O(|T|)$.
- Determine $\{0, 1\}$–valued sequence $b_0, ..., b_{m-1}$, $m = |x_0...x_{l-1}| + 1$, in the following way. Let $b_j$ be of value 1 for $j = |x_0|, |x_0x_1|, ..., |x_0...x_{l-1}|$ and of value 0 otherwise.

- Assign value 1 to each non-variable vertex in $T$. Compute truncated convolution of the term-tree $T$, the sequence $b_0, ..., b_{m-1}$ and the function $h$ for every non-variable vertex in $T$. The resulting convolution value is the number of strings from $\{x_0...x_i \mid i = 0, ..., l-1\}$ that matches at that vertex.
- Let $T_{var}$ be a subtree of the term–tree $T$ restricted to variable leaves. For each variable $v$ in $T_{var}$ compute the length $h(v)$ of the longest suffix of $x_0 x_1...x_{l-1}$ such that its proper prefix $\gamma$ is also a suffix of $\sigma_{\Sigma_{T_{var}},v}$. It can be computed in time $O(|T_{var}|)$. Denote the difference $d(v) = h(v) - |\gamma|$. Compute the truncated convolution $c(u)$ of the term–tree $T$, the sequence $b_0, ..., b_{m-1}$ and the function $h$ for every variable vertex $u$ in $T_{var}$ as

$$c(u) = \sum_{j=0}^{m-1} \sum_{pred^{j-d(v)}(v)=u, h(v) \geq j} a(v).b_j .$$

The resulting convolution value is the number of strings from $\{x_0 x_1...x_i \mid i = 0, 1, ..., l-1\}$ that matches at variable vertices in $T_{var}$.
- Output the set of vertices where the count is equal to $l$.
- Time complexity of the above computation is

$$O(|T| \log |T| + |T| \sqrt{|P|} \log^k |P|)$$

for some fixed $k$. To eliminate the term $|T| \log |T|$, we can split $T$ into $O(|T|/|P|)$ subtrees, each of the size $O(|P|)$ and solve a problem for each subtree separately.

The above procedure in Step 4 is repeated $O(|P|^{0.25})$ times, once for each set of leaves of $P$ having the suffix property. The intersection of the sets of vertices of $T$ computed in $O(|P|^{0.25})$ repetitions is the set of vertices in $T$ at each of which $P$ restricted to the set of leaves in the union of sets having suffix property unifies with $T$. The complete computation requires time $O(|T||P|^{0.75} \log^k |P|)$ for some fixed $k$.

4.5. In Step 5 we compute the intersection of two sets determined in Step 3 and Step 4. Each vertex in this intersection is a vertex at which $P$ unifies with $T$. Time complexity of this step is $O(|T|)$.

4.6. To put the analysis together, we have the following result.

**Theorem 1** *The algorithm constructing the set of vertices of the target term–tree $T$, at each of which the pattern term–tree $P$ unifies with $T$, can be computed in time complexity $O(|T||P|^{0.75} \log^k |P|)$ for some fixed $k$.*

# 5 Conclusions

We have made an improvement in asymptotical time complexity of (non–rooted) weak unification problem for linear terms, in breaking $O(|T||P|)$ barrier for the linear pattern term (represented as the term–tree $P$) and the linear target term (represented as the term–tree $T$). We conjecture that a time bound $O(|T|\sqrt{|P|})$ is achievable.

Proposed algorithm was analyzed from the viewpoint of certain special requirements posed by term rewriting applications. It turns out that the algorithm is extensible for many–to–one tree pattern unification problem, is suitable for applications with dynamically changing set of patterns, is adaptable to local changes in target tree and compact representation of patterns (the ideas similar to [9]) and that the data structures representing a set of pattern terms can be used for both matching and unification (This is important for applications performing rewriting and narrowing simultaneously, e.g. in equation solving).

# References

1. Aho, A.V. – Corasick, M.J.: *Efficient string matching: an aid to bibliographic search.* CACM 16, 1975, pp. 333–340.
2. Apostolico, A. – Iliopoulos, C. – Landau, C.M. – Schieber, B. – Vishkin, U.: *Parallel Construction of a Suffix Tree with Applications.* Algorithmica, 1988, pp. 347–365.
3. Cai, J. – Paige, R. – Tarjan, R.: *More efficient bottom–up pattern matching.* In Proc. of the CAAP, LNCS 577, Springer–Verlag, 1992, pp. 72–86.
4. Dubiner, M. – Galil, Z. – Magen, M.: *Faster tree pattern matching.* In Proc. of the 31–st FOCS, 1991, pp. 145–150.
5. Hoffmann, C.M. – O'Donnell, M.J.: *Pattern matching in trees.* JACM 29, 1982, pp. 68–95.
6. Kosaraju, S.R.: *Efficient tree pattern matching.* In Proc. of the 30–th FOCS, 1989, pp. 178–183.
7. O'Donnell, M.J.: *Equational logic as a programming language.* MIT Press, 1985.
8. Ramesh, R. – Ramakrishnan, I.V.: *Nonlinear pattern matching in trees.* JACM 39, 1992, pp. 295–316.
9. Ružička, P. – Prívara, I.: *An almost linear Robinson unification algorithm.* Acta Informatica 27, 1989, pp. 61–71.
10. Ružička, P. – Prívara, I.: *On tree pattern unification problems.* In Proc. of the 9–th FCT, LNCS 710, Springer–Verlag, 1993, pp. 418–429.
11. Vittek, M.: *Many–to–one unification for linear terms* (in Slovak). In Proc. of the 2–nd LOP, 1989, pp. 47–56.
12. Weiner, P.: *Linear Pattern Matching Algorithm.* In Proc. of the 14–th IEEE SWAT (FOCS), 1973, pp. 1–11.

# A Light-Weight Formalism for the Specification of Reactive Systems *

Peter Scholz

scholzp@informatik.tu-muenchen.de

Technische Universität München, Institut für Informatik
D-80290 München

**Abstract.** Statecharts are a visual specification mechanism for reactive, embedded systems. They are implemented in commercial tools like Statemate. However, some syntactic constructs impede the modular system specification and have a confusing semantics. We have developed Mini-Statecharts, a lean version of Statecharts. Mini-Statecharts are restricted to the most important syntactic elements of Statecharts but are nevertheless powerful enough to specify complex systems. In this contribution, we extend the core language with local variables and integer-valued signals to avoid state explosion. We show that the formal semantics of the core language smoothly carries over to the semantics of the extended language.

## 1 Introduction

Statecharts [2] are a visual specification language for reactive systems. They extend conventional state transition diagrams with structuring and communication mechanisms. These mechanisms allow the description of large and complex systems. Due to this fact Statecharts have become quite successful in industry. The full Statecharts language however contains many mechanisms that cause ambiguities concerning both syntax and semantics [11].

In this paper, we describe a dialect of Statecharts, called *Mini-Statecharts*. In contrast to traditional Statecharts [2], Mini-Statecharts can be clearly decomposed into Subcharts. Thus, they can be developed in a fully modular way by simply sticking them together. Mini-Statecharts are restricted to the essential constructs. They do not contain superfluous syntax with complicated semantics and can be described graphically or textually. While [7] and [5] already provided steps in the right direction, our work extends their approaches by local variables, integer-valued signals, and the concept of explicit feedback operators for communication.

Although Mini-Statecharts are powerful enough to describe large and complex reactive systems, we assign a concise, formal semantics to them. It is given in

---

* This work is partially funded by the German Federal Ministry of Education and Research (BMBF) as part of the compound project "KorSys".

a fully functional way. Therefore, we can mix purely functional specifications of interactive systems [1] with Mini-Statecharts.

Furthermore, the semantics can be immediately executed by a suitable interpreter. Thus, we do not only define a theoretical semantics, but in addition provide a simple program for simulating and prototyping Mini-Statecharts. This is in contrast to existing tools like *Statemate* [3], where the semantic behavior of the prototyping tool sometimes differs from published Statecharts semantics. Even the authors of Statemate admit that Statemate's simulation and dynamic tests tools and its various code generators have a slightly different semantics [4]. In our approach there exists exactly one semantics. It can be used to prototype and simulate reactive systems as well as to reason about systems with a suitable theorem prover. For the deductive development of correct systems, the availability of a compositional semantics is urgently necessary to get manageable proofs.

This paper is organized as follows. In Section 2 we outline the core language of Mini-Statecharts and present a concise, abstract syntax for it. In Section 3 we extend the core language by the concept of local variables and integer-valued signals. Finally, Section 4 gives a brief summary.

## 2 The Core Language

Our formalism assumes a global, discrete time. Every single transition takes place in exactly one time unit. Informally speaking, every Mini-Statechart consumes and yields a sequence of sets of signals. Each element of the sequence exactly denotes the set of signals that are present at one time unit. All other signals that are not contained in this set are assumed to be absent. Subsequent sets denote subsequent instants of time. Signals that occur between two consecutive time ticks are considered to arrive simultaneously.

In this section we propose an abstract, inductively defined textual syntax for Mini-Statecharts $S$. It consists of sequential automata, parallel composition, several feedback operators with different timings for broadcast communication, hierarchical decomposition, and hiding; [8] and [9] provide a detailed introduction. Due to space limitations we only give a short overview. Let $M$ denote a (potentially infinite) set of signal names, *States* a nonempty (potentially infinite) set of state-names, and $\wp(X)$ the set of finite subsets of some set $X$. Our core language contains the following syntactic notations:

- *Sequential Automaton:* $(\Sigma, \sigma, \delta)$, where:

  1. $\Sigma \in \wp(States)$: the finite set of all states of the automaton.
  2. $\sigma \in \Sigma$: the current state of the automaton. In addition, our core language also contains a default state $\sigma_d$, which is needed to define the formal semantics of hierarchically decomposed charts [8, 10]. In this contribution, however, we only consider flat charts and therefore omit $\sigma_d$.

3. $\delta : \Sigma \times \wp(M) \to \Sigma \times \wp(M)$ is the total state transition function that takes a state and a finite set of signals and yields the subsequent state together with a finite set of output signals. In our concrete syntax, we use a Boolean term instead of a set of signals $x \in \wp(M)$ as trigger. It is however a straightforward step to translate a partial transition function that deals with arbitrary Boolean terms as trigger condition into the set-valued total function $\delta$ (see for example [10]).

At each instant of time, $(\Sigma, \sigma, \delta)$ consumes a set of signals $x$ and instantaneously produces a set of signals $y$. Otherwise it performs an idle step, i.e., remains in its current state and produces $\emptyset$ as output.

- *Parallel Composition:* Parallel composition is used to denote independent, concurrent charts $S_1$ and $S_2$: And $(S_1, S_2)$. Notice that this construct does not contain any communication mechanism.
- *Broadcast Communication:* To denote interaction of such components, our language provides a broadcast communication mechanism. In [8, 9, 10] we have discussed different communication operators with different timings. Here we only present the delayed communication of signals $L \in \wp(M)$ in chart $S$: D-Feedback $(S, L)$.

Though in our language there are still further syntactic notations that are useful from the pragmatic and methodical point of view, they are not technically necessary to model parallel systems and therefore, for brevity, omitted.

# 3 The Extended Language

In spite of parallel composition and hierarchy, state explosion can occur. An example is given in [9]. Therefore, we decided to extend Mini-Statecharts by the concept of local variables to avoid state explosion. Traditional Statecharts allow to declare global variables. However, global variables impede the definition of a compositional semantics. Moreover, there exist two basic concepts for communication: message passing and global variables. Traditional Statecharts incorporate both. In our opinion, there is no need to use both concepts together in one language.

In this section we propose a syntactic notation for Mini-Statecharts that is extended by the concept of local integer variables and integer-valued signals. In contrast to a pure signal, an integer-valued signal incorporates, in addition to the information about its presence, an integer number denoting its value.

## 3.1 Signals, Variables, Expressions, and Commands

In contrast to Section 2, $M$ is here disjointly partitioned in $M_p$ and $M_v$, representing the set of *pure* and *integer-valued* signals, respectively. Furthermore, we assume a set $V$ of local integer-valued variables. $V$ has to be disjoint from the sets introduced so far. The other syntactic sets associated with $\mathcal{T}$, a simple language for transitions (borrowed from [12] and adapted for our purposes) are: integers $Int$, truth values $Bool = \{\text{true}, \text{false}\}$, arithmetic expressions $Aexp$, Boolean expressions $Bexp$, and commands $Com$. In presenting the syntax of $\mathcal{T}$ we will follow the convention that $n \in Int$, $X \in V$, $E_v \in M_v$, $E_p \in M_p$, $a \in Aexp$, $b \in Bexp$, and $c \in Com$. Note that expressions are only used in commands and not as trigger conditions. Arithmetic/Boolean expressions and commands are formed by:

$$a ::= n \mid X \mid E_v \mid a_1 + a_2 \mid a_1 - a_2 \mid a_1 * a_2$$
$$b ::= \text{true} \mid \text{false} \mid a_1 = a_2 \mid a_1 \leq a_2 \mid \neg b \mid b_1 \wedge b_2$$
$$c ::= \text{skip} \mid X := a \mid E_v := a \mid E_p \mid \text{if } b \text{ then } c_1 \text{ else } c_2 \text{ fi} \mid c_1 ; c_2 \mid \text{while } b \text{ do } c \text{ od}.$$

The meaning of these expressions and commands is straightforward. In contrast to [6, 4], we use the semicolon as sequential and not as parallel composition. To see the difference, we take a look at the following example. Suppose that the command $c$ of a transition is defined as $X := X + 1; Y := X$ and that $X = 2$ is the value $X$ had before executing this command. Executing $c$ in our setting yields $Y = 3$. In [6, 4], however, this results in $Y = 2$ but when two or more commands want to change the same variable in the same step so-called race conditions [4] can occur, which have to be detected by Statemate's simulation and dynamic test tools because the values of the variables are unknown before runtime. To us, this seems complicated and superfluous. As a consequence, we have chosen the sequential execution order to get a non-ambiguous meaning and to avoid dynamic analysis.

The command $E_p$ generates a pure signal whereas $E_v := a$ generates an integer-valued signal; its value is calculated by evaluating $a$. Applying the delayed communication concept both kind of signals are only present in the very next instant of time but are absent in all subsequent steps unless they are explicitly emitted again (see Section 3.4).

To define the denotational semantics of $\mathcal{T}$ we firstly need a partial function $\gamma : M_v \to \mathbb{Z}$ that holds the value for present integer-valued signals. Here, we often interpret $\gamma$ as a set in $\wp(M_v \times \mathbb{Z})$. We abbreviate $M_v \to \mathbb{Z}$ to $\Gamma$. Secondly, we define the evaluation of local variables as a total function $\varepsilon : V \to \mathbb{Z}$. Also $\varepsilon$ is here interpreted as a set in $\wp(V \times \mathbb{Z})$. The set of all evaluations is denoted by $\mathcal{E}$. Note that $\mathcal{E}$ contains total functions whereas $\Gamma$ only contains partial functions: variables have a defined value at every single time point, whereas signals only do when they are present. With this background we are able to define the semantic functions:

$$\mathcal{A}[\![.]\!] : Aexp \to (\Gamma \to (\mathcal{E} \to \mathbb{Z})), \quad \mathcal{B}[\![.]\!] : Bexp \to (\Gamma \to (\mathcal{E} \to \mathbb{B})),$$
$$\mathcal{C}[\![.]\!] : Com \to (\wp(M) \times \Gamma \times \mathcal{E} \to \wp(M) \times \Gamma \times \mathcal{E}).$$

Due to space limitations, we only define the denotation of a selection of expres-

429

sions and commands, by structural induction, using the $\lambda$-notation:

$$\mathcal{A}[\![X]\!]\gamma = \lambda\varepsilon \in \mathcal{E}.\varepsilon(X)$$
$$\mathcal{A}[\![E_v]\!]\gamma = \lambda\varepsilon \in \mathcal{E}.\gamma(E_v)$$
$$\mathcal{C}[\![X := a]\!] = \lambda(x,\gamma,\varepsilon) \in \wp(M) \times \Gamma \times \mathcal{E}. \text{ let } n = \mathcal{A}[\![a]\!]\gamma\varepsilon \text{ in } (x,\gamma,\varepsilon[n/X])$$
$$\mathcal{C}[\![E_v := a]\!] = \lambda(x,\gamma,\varepsilon) \in \wp(M) \times \Gamma \times \mathcal{E}. \text{ let } n = \mathcal{A}[\![a]\!]\gamma\varepsilon \text{ in } (x \cup \{E_v\},\gamma[n/E_v],\varepsilon)$$
$$\mathcal{C}[\![E_p]\!] = \lambda(x,\gamma,\varepsilon) \in \wp(M) \times \Gamma \times \mathcal{E}.(x \cup \{E_p\},\gamma,\varepsilon)$$
$$\mathcal{C}[\![c_1;c_2]\!] = \mathcal{C}[\![c_2]\!] \circ \mathcal{C}[\![c_1]\!].$$

The assignment $X := a$ to a local variable $X$ induces an update of the evaluation $\varepsilon$, and the statement $E_p$ outputs a pure signal and adds it to the set of signals generated so far. If we assign an arithmetic expression $a$ to an integer-valued signal $E_p$, we get a more complicated effect. Like a pure signal, $E_v$ is added to the set of generated signals. In addition, $\gamma$ has to be updated with the current value of $a$. Notice that multiple occurances of $E_p$ in a sequential composition have the same effect as one single occurance. Slightly more subtle is the handling of integer-valued signals. For example, the command $E_v := 1; X := E_v; E_v := 2$ yields the following result: having executed this command, $X$ holds the value 1. However, because $E_v$ only can be sent once from every sequential automaton at every instant of time, the second assignment updates $\gamma$. Thus, supposing $E_v$ is broadcasted, the emitted value is 2.

## 3.2  Extended Sequential Automata

Applying the concepts introduced before, we have to modify the syntactic notation for sequential automata to $(V_l, \beta_d, \Sigma, \sigma, \delta)$, where $\Sigma$ and $\sigma$ are as in Section 2. The following additional syntactic constraints must hold:

1. $V_l \in \wp(V)$ denotes the set of local, i.e., private read/write variables. These variables can be only read and/or written by the automaton itself. They have to be initialized:
2. $\beta_d : V_l \to Int$ is a finite, total function that describes the initial values of the local variables.

Furthermore, $\delta$ has to be modified to $\delta : \Sigma \times \wp(M) \to \Sigma \times Com$. It is now a total state transition function that takes a state and a set of stimuli and yields the subsequent state together with a command, describing the modification of the internal variables and the generation of pure or integer-valued signals. Each transitions between two states $\sigma, \sigma'$ with $\delta(\sigma, x) = (\sigma', c)$ is labeled with $x/c$. There is a further syntactic restriction on $\delta$. For every transition with label $x/c$ the following must be valid: each integer-valued signal $E_v$ that occurs on the right-hand-side of an assignment in $c$ also has to be a member of $x$, i.e., has to be present. As in the core language, we assume that every transition, i.e., every command can be computed in exactly one instant of time.

Note that also for integer-valued signals, we only check absence or presence but not their values. As a consequence, even the determinism of the extended automata is easily decidable by static analysis and we can avoid dynamic analysis. Moreover, for a nondeterministic version of Mini-Statecharts, the fact that only the presence of events can be checked in a trigger, but not their values, is essential: by abstracting from the integer values, they can be reduced to a *finite* counterpart.

## 3.3 Resolution of Conflicts

Using integer-valued signals some problems can occur. Let us assume that each of two parallel components $S_1$, $S_2$ tries to broadcast the integer-valued signal $E_v$. Furthermore, we suppose that $S_1$ assigns 21 to $E_v$ and $S_2$ 42 both at the same instant of time. In this case, we get a conflict. However, the parallel composed Mini-Statechart And $(S_1, S_2)$ must produce the signal $E_v$ with a unique value. Hence, we introduce a total *resolution* function $\varphi$, which resolves this conflict and produces a unique value:

$$\varphi : \wp(\mathbb{Z}) \to \mathbb{Z}.$$

For every set of conflicting integers $Z$, $\varphi(Z)$ yields the integer that will be calculated when a conflict occurs. We include $\varphi$ in the syntactic notation of the parallel composition and get And $(S_1, S_2, \varphi)$.

In addition, contradictory integer-valued signals also can emerge when using the communication operator. Though in this case we do not have two parallel, conflicting Mini-Statecharts, we can get conflicts between signals from the environment and signals that are fed back for communication. Thus, the feedback operator must also to be adapted: D-Feedback $(S, L, \varphi)$.

## 3.4 The Formal Semantics

Reactive systems have to interact continuously with their environment. Thus, to define their semantics, their complete input/output behavior has to be described. This can be done by communication histories. We model the communication history of Mini-Statecharts by streams carrying tuples of sets of (pure and integer-valued) signals together with values of integer-valued signals. Mathematically, we describe the behavior of Mini-Statecharts by stream processing functions. Hence, we briefly discuss the notion of streams and stream processing functions. For a detailed description we refer to [1].

Given a set $X$ of signals a stream over $X$, denoted by $X^\omega$, is an infinite sequence of elements from $X$. Our notation for the concatenation operator is &. Given an element $x$ of type $X$ and a stream $s$ over $X$, the term $x \& s$ denotes the stream that starts with the element $x$ followed by the stream $s$. The destructor *ft* selects the first element of a stream. A stream processing function is a function with type $X^\omega \to X^\omega$. The functionality of the denotational semantics is:

$$D[\![.]\!] : \mathcal{S} \to ((\wp(M) \times \Gamma)^\omega \to (\wp(M) \times \Gamma)^\omega).$$

This semantics is defined as a higher order function. For its definition, we use an auxiliary higher order function of type

$$[\![.]\!] : S \rightarrow \mathcal{E} \rightarrow ((\wp(M) \times \Gamma)^\omega \rightarrow (\wp(M) \times \Gamma \times \mathcal{E} \times S)^\omega)$$

to take into account current/successor evaluation and successor chart. For $S \in \mathcal{S}$ and $s \in (\wp(M) \times \Gamma)^\omega$, $D[\![S]\!]s$ is defined by $map\ \pi_{1,2}\ ([\![S]\!]\ (init\ S)\ s)$, where $\pi_{1,2}$ denotes the tuple of first and second projection and $map\ \pi_{1,2}\ (w, x, y, z)\&s = (w, x)\&(map\ \pi_{1,2}\ s)$; $init$ initializes the evaluation according to the initialization functions $\beta_d$. We now exemplarily define the stream semantics for some syntactic constructs of Mini-Statecharts. A detailed formal definition of all syntactic notations can be found in [9].

The sequential automaton takes the current evaluation $\varepsilon$ together with the tuple $(x, \gamma)$ in every time point. $x$ represents the set of all (pure and integer-valued) signals that are currently present. $\gamma$ is defined for all integer-valued signals that are contained in $x$. The semantics instantaneously yields the quadruple $(y, \gamma', \varepsilon', S')$. Here $y$ denotes the set of generated output signals, $\gamma'$, $\varepsilon'$, and $S'$ the successors for $\gamma$, $\varepsilon$, and $S$, respectively. After that, the automaton behaves like the automaton with – should the occasion arise – modified current state $\sigma'$:

$$[\![(V_l, \beta_d, \Sigma, \sigma, \delta)]\!]\varepsilon\ (x, \gamma)\&s = \text{let } (\sigma', c) = \delta(\sigma, x);$$
$$(y, \gamma', \varepsilon') = \mathcal{C}[\![c]\!](x, \varepsilon, \gamma);$$
$$S' = (V_l, \beta_d, \Sigma, \sigma', \delta)$$
$$\text{in } (y, \gamma', \varepsilon', S')\&([\![S']\!]\varepsilon'\ s).$$

The parallel composition of And $(S_1, S_2, \varphi)$ behaves as $S_1$ and $S_2$ synchronously together. Generated signals of the parallel components are unified, denoted by $y_1 \cup y_2$ and $\gamma_1 \cup_\varphi \gamma_2$, where $\cup$ denotes the standard union and $\cup_\varphi$ the union of integer-valued signals w.r.t. the resolution function $\varphi$. Their evaluations also can be simply unified because they represent disjoint sets of variables. The formal semantics of And $(S_1, S_2, \varphi)$ demonstrates the advantage of our compositional semantics: to define $[\![$And $(S_1, S_2, \varphi)]\!]$ we just have to calculate $[\![S_1]\!]$ and $[\![S_2]\!]$ and then put the results together:

$$[\![\text{And } (S_1, S_2, \varphi)]\!]\varepsilon\ (x, \gamma)\&s = \text{let } (y_1, \gamma_1, \varepsilon_1, S_1') = ft([\![S_1]\!]\varepsilon\ (x, \gamma)\&s);$$
$$(y_2, \gamma_2, \varepsilon_2, S_2') = ft([\![S_2]\!]\varepsilon\ (x, \gamma)\&s);$$
$$y' = y_1 \cup y_2;\ \gamma' = \gamma_1 \cup_\varphi \gamma_2;\ \varepsilon' = \varepsilon_1 \cup \varepsilon_2;$$
$$S' = \text{And } (S_1', S_2', \varphi)$$
$$\text{in } (y', \gamma', \varepsilon', S')\&([\![S']\!]\varepsilon'\ s).$$

Defining the delayed broadcast communication, the tuples $(x_1, \gamma_1)$ and $(x_2, \gamma_2)$ denote the input signals of the current and the next instant, respectively. Signals $(y, \gamma')$ that are instantaneously generated, are fed back as additional input in the next time point, provided that they are included in $L$: $(x_2 \cup (y \cap L), \gamma_2 \cup_\varphi \gamma'|_{M_v \cap L})$, where $\gamma|_{M_v \cap L}$ denotes the restriction of $\gamma$ on signals in $M_v \cap L$:

$[\![$D-Feedback $(S, L, \varphi)]\!]\varepsilon\, (x_1, \gamma_1)\&(x_2, \gamma_2)\&s =$
$\quad$ let $(y, \gamma', \varepsilon', S') = ft([\![S]\!]\varepsilon\, (x_1, \gamma_1)\&(x_2, \gamma_2)\&s);$
$\qquad S'' = $ D-Feedback $(S', L, \varphi)$
$\quad$ in $(y, \gamma', \varepsilon', S'')\&([\![S'']\!]\varepsilon'\, (x_2 \cup (y \cap L), \gamma_2 \cup_\varphi \gamma'|_{M_v \cap L})\&s).$

## 4 Conclusion

We presented an algebraic notation for Mini-Statecharts, a dialect of Statecharts, where we restricted ourselves to the most essential syntactic constructs. Mini-Statecharts are well-suited for the modular development of parallel, reactive systems. Broadcast communication, which is a basic concept of Statecharts, was in contrast to related approaches explicitly realized by a special feedback operator. We presented a compositional and well-defined semantics for our language. We demonstrated that the core language only has to be slightly modified in order to include local variables and integer-valued signals. For a full version of this paper the interested reader is referred to [9]. Further research is necessary in the areas of formal verification and code generation.

## References

1. M. Broy. Interaction Refinement - The Easy Way. In *Program Design Calculi*, volume 118 of *NATO ASI Series F: Computer & System Sciences*. Springer, 1993.
2. D. Harel. Statecharts: A Visual Formalism for Complex Systems. *Science of Computer Programming*, 8:231 – 274, 1987.
3. D. Harel. Statemate: A working environment for the development of complex reactive systems. *IEEE Transactions on Software Engineering*, 16:403 – 413, 1990.
4. D. Harel and A. Naamad. The STATEMATE Semantics of Statecharts. Submitted to: ACM Transations Software Engineering Methods, 1995.
5. J.J.M. Hooman, S. Ramesh, and W.P. de Roever. A compositional axiomatization of statecharts. *Theoretical Computer Science*, 101:289 – 335, 1992.
6. i-Logix Inc. *Languages of Statemate*. i-Logix Inc., 22 Third Avenue, Burlington, Mass. 01803, U.S.A., January 1990.
7. F. Maraninchi. Operational and compositional semantics of synchronous automaton compositions. volume 630 of *Lecture Notes in Computer Science*, pages 550 – 564. Springer-Verlag, 1992.
8. D. Nazareth, F. Regensburger, and P. Scholz. Mini-Statecharts: A Lean Version of Statecharts. Technical Report TUM-I9610, Technische Universität München, D-80290 München, 1996. Also available in the WWW: http://www4.informatik.tu-muenchen.de/reports/TUM-I9610.html.
9. P. Scholz. An Extended Version of Mini-Statecharts. Technical Report TUM-I9628, Technische Universität München, D-80290 München, 1996. Also available in the WWW: http://www4.informatik.tu-muenchen.de/reports/TUM-I9628.html.
10. P. Scholz, D. Nazareth, and F. Regensburger. Mini-Statecharts: A Compositional Way to Model Parallel Systems. 1996. To Appear in: PDCS'96.
11. M. von der Beeck. A comparison of statecharts variants. volume 863 of *Lecture Notes in Computer Science*, pages 128 – 148. Springer, 1994.
12. G. Winskel. *The Formal Semantics of Programming Languages*. The MIT Press, 1993.

# Knowledge Discovery in Alarm Data Analysis

J Shao

Department of Computer Science
University of Wales College Cardiff
Cardiff, United Kingdom
e-mail j.shao@cs.cf.ac.uk

**Abstract.** *In this paper we consider the discovery of knowledge from telecommunication alarm data. We use rough sets theory to analyse the possible dependencies existing among alarm data and express such dependencies as a belief network. The discovered knowledge helps system engineers to understand the overall behaviour of the telecommunication network, to filter some non-critical alarms and to predict possible occurrence of faults in future.*

## 1 Introduction

Knowledge discovery in databases (KDD) has emerged as an important area of research. The general goal of KDD is to extract non-trivial and potentially useful information from data [3]. It is widely recognised that KDD methods and techniques are application specific. Different applications require different methods or techniques to be designed.

In this paper we consider the problem of discovering knowledge from telecommunication network alarm databases. A telecommunication network, when tested or in operation, can produce large amounts of alarm data which describe various events occurred in the network.[1] These alarms contain valuable knowledge about the behaviour of the network. However, alarm analysis is complex because

- the occurrence of faults is time variant and non-deterministic; and
- faults can produce a cascade of other faults.

There are a number of methods that have been proposed for alarm management. With the *alarm filtering and correlation* method [4], each component in the network is equipted with some knowledge provided by system engineers. This knowledge is then used to eliminate non-critical alarms so that only the critical ones will be dealt with. While this does reduce the amount of alarms for engineers, it cannot predict the behaviour of the network. The *TASA system* [5], on the other hand, has certain predictive power. With this system, users specify roughly what are of interest, and the system will discover, with some confidence, the following form of knowledge: if a certain combination of alarms occurs within a time period, then an alarm of a given type will occur within a

---

[1] Note that the occurrence of an alarm does not necessarily indicate that there is actually a visible problem to the users.

time period. This is useful if we know how to specify patterns that are potentially useful. But if we are interested in behaviours that are unknown to us, for example when a telecommunication network is still at testing stage, then TASA is less useful. Finally, if we are only interested in the predictive power, the use of neural networks may be considered. However, if we also wish to comprehend what has caused those predicted events or alarms, then they are less desirable.

In this paper, we consider the analysis of alarm data generated from the testing of a telecommunication network whose behaviour is unknown to us. We use rough sets theory to analyse the causal dependencies that may exist among the observed alarms and use belief networks to express the discovered dependencies. Rough sets theory has the advantage that dependency analysis can be performed completely within the data available; no external assumptions on data distribution is required. On the other hand, belief networks allow probabilistic inference to be carried out, but deriving an accurate belief network from a given database can be difficult. We show in this paper that the use of two methods together is desirable for alarm management. The knowledge extracted this way helps system engineers to understand the overall behaviour of the network, to filter some non-critical alarms and to predict possible occurrence of faults in future.

The rest of this paper is organised as follows. In Sect. 2, we describe telecommunication network alarm data. In Sect. 3 we show how knowledge may be extracted from an alarm database by using rough sets theory and belief networks. Finally, in Sect. 4 we draw conclusions.

## 2 Alarm Data

Suppose that a telecommunication network with a fixed topology is tested with a single input (often a purposely introduced fault). Running the network for a fixed period of time we may observe an alarm sequence $< A_1, A_2, \ldots, A_n >$ where each $A_j = \{a_{j1}, a_{j2}, \ldots, a_{jk_j}\}$ is a set of alarms observed at time $t_j$. The system is *non-deterministic*. Thus, if we repeat the same test $m$ times, we may observe the following sequences:

$$
\begin{aligned}
\mathcal{T}_1 &= < A_{11}, \ A_{12}, \ \cdots, \ A_{1n} > \\
\mathcal{T}_2 &= < A_{21}, \ A_{22}, \ \cdots, \ A_{2n} > \\
&\vdots \\
\mathcal{T}_m &= < A_{m1}, \ A_{m2}, \ \cdots, \ A_{mn} >
\end{aligned}
$$

where $A_{ij} = \{a_{j1}^i, a_{j2}^i, \ldots, a_{jk_j}^i\}$ is the set of alarms observed at time $t_j$ during test $\mathcal{T}_i$. An example of such alarm data is given in Table 1. Note that a particular alarm may be observed several times at different points of time (e.g. $a_1$ at both $t_1$ and $t_2$). This is because some of the alarms are persistent if no action is taken. This model of alarm data assumes that:

- The alarms are observed at the same points of time for all the tests. That is, we assume, for example, for both $\mathcal{T}_1$ and $\mathcal{T}_2$, the first sets of alarms ($A_{11}$ and $A_{21}$) are observed at the same point of time $t_1$.

**Table 1.** Alarm Data

| test | $t_1$ | $t_2$ | $t_3$ |
|------|-------|-------|-------|
| $T_1$ | $a_1, a_3$ | $a_1, a_4, a_5$ | $a_7, a_8$ |
| $T_2$ | $a_1, a_2$ | $a_1$ | $a_7, a_9$ |
| $T_3$ | $a_1, a_3$ | $a_1, a_6$ | |
| $T_4$ | $a_1, a_3$ | $a_1$ | |
| $T_5$ | $a_2, a_3$ | $a_4, a_5$ | $a_7, a_8, a_9$ |
| $T_6$ | $a_1, a_3$ | $a_1, a_4, a_5, a_6$ | $a_7, a_8$ |
| $T_7$ | $a_2$ | | $a_8, a_9$ |
| $T_8$ | $a_1, a_3$ | $a_1, a_4, a_5$ | $a_8$ |
| $T_9$ | $a_1, a_3$ | $a_1, a_4, a_5$ | $a_7, a_8$ |
| $T_{10}$ | $a_3$ | $a_4, a_5$ | |

- There exist direct causal dependencies among the adjacent sets of alarms, but not among the non-adjacent ones. That is, we assume that $A_{ij}$ may cause $A_{ij+1}$, but not $A_{ik}, k > j + 1$.

Both assumptions can be removed by a careful *grouping* and a *backtracking* based on information theory [10]. Due to space limit, we will not discuss them here. Our objective is to extract knowledge from this alarm database, so that users can ask queries such as *Given $a_4$ at $t_2$, how likely that $a_9$ is going to happen at $t_9$*.

## 3   Discovering Knowledge from Alarm Databases

We now describe how rough sets theory and belief networks are used to extract and model knowledge from alarm databases. To make this paper self-contained, we also introduce very briefly the basics of belief networks and rough sets theory.

### 3.1   Belief Networks

A belief network is defined by $B = (B_S, B_P)$, where $B_S$ is a directed acyclic graph in which nodes represent domain variables and arcs between nodes probabilistic dependencies, and $B_P$ is a set of conditional probabilities associated with each node. Figure 1 shows an example of a belief network.

The arc from $x_1$ to $x_2$ indicates that these two variables are probabilistically dependent, but the absence of an arc from $x_1$ to $x_3$ implies that there is no direct probabilistic dependency between these two variables. The probabilistic dependencies between the nodes are detailed in the probability tables associated with the nodes. If a node has no parent nodes, then a prior probability is given.

Learning a belief network is thus to learn both $B_S$ and $B_P$. For some applications, $B_S$ can be derived easily from human experts, and one only needs to learn $B_P$. This is relatively simple [9]. Learning a belief network without a known

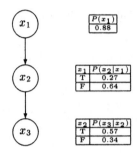

**Fig. 1.** A simple belief network

$B_S$ is usually difficult as the number of possible structures is super-exponential in the number of variables, and there is no clear way of effectively pruning the search space [1].

In learning belief networks from alarm databases, $B_S$ is clearly not derivable from human experts because the behaviour of a telecommunication network is unknown. However, we are fortunate that $B_S$ is *semi-known*. This is due to a simple observation: *only the alarms occurred at time $t_i$ can lead to those occurred at $t_j, j > i$.* Based on this observation and our assumption that there are no direct causal dependencies between non-adjacent alarm sets, we can have a *layered* belief network structure immediately. For example, for the alarm data given in Table 1, we have the following layered belief network structure:

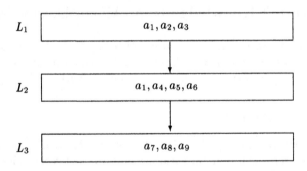

**Fig. 2.** A layered belief network structure for Table 1

That is, we know roughly which set of alarms have caused which set, but we do not know which one in particular. The remaining task is to find more detailed knowledge about which alarms at level $L_j$ have caused which alarms at level $L_{j+1}$ and the probability of that. This may be achieved by performing the following: for any $L'_j \subseteq L_j$ and $a \in L_{j+1}$, calculate $p(a|L'_j)$, the probability of $a$ given $L'_j$. However, by calculating all $n_{j+1} \times 2^{n_j}$ relationships, where $n_j$ and

$n_{j+1}$ are the cardinalities of $L_j$ and $L_{j+1}$, this approach is likely to introduce the *overfitting* problem, because alarm databases can contain noise data due to the dynamic and non-deterministic nature of telecommunication networks. Furthermore, this approach may also cause some *redundant* dependencies to be modelled. For example, if $L_j'' \subset L_j'$ and $p(a \in L_{j+1}|L_j') = p(a \in L_{j+1}|L_j'')$, then clearly there is no need for $L_j'$ to be considered as a cause for $a \in L_{j+1}$. To avoid these problems, we use rough sets theory.

## 3.2 Rough Sets Analysis

The basic rough sets theory was introduced in [7]. Let $U = \{x_1, x_2, \ldots, x_n\}$ be a finite set of objects, and each $x_i \in U$ is described by a set of attributes $R = \{R_1, R_2, \ldots, R_k\}$. Clearly, the values of $R$ partition $U$. We call $A = (U, R)$ an *approximation space*.

Let $R^* = \{X_1, X_2, \ldots, X_n\}$ denote the partition of $U$ induced by $R$, where $X_i$ is an equivalence class of $R$. Suppose that $X \subseteq U$ represents a certain *concept* of interest, and we wish to characterise $X$ with $A = (U, R)$. In rough sets theory, this is achieved by defining an appropriate approximation of $X$ using $A$. There are various ways in which such an approximation may be defined. For example, the *lower approximation* $\underline{A}(X) = \bigcup_{X_i \subseteq X} X_i$ allows one to conclude what definitely characterises $X$, and the *upper approximation* $\overline{A}(X) = \bigcup_{X_i \cap X \neq \phi} X_i$ allows one to conclude what possibly characterises $X$.

In the following, we introduce a $\theta$-*approximation* [2] which is particularly suitable for analysing our alarm data.

$$A_\theta(X) = \bigcup_{\frac{|X_i \cap X|}{|X_i|} > \theta} X_i \quad \text{where} \quad 0 \leq \theta < 1 .$$

This approximation is useful in handling uncertain data. The set $A_\theta(X)$ includes the objects of $U$ which have a probability greater than $\theta$ to be in $X$. The threshold value $\theta$ is determined by the user. Throughout this paper, we set $\theta = 0.5$.

To measure how well $X$ is approximated by $A_\theta$, we define the following

$$\gamma_\theta(R, X) = \frac{|A_\theta(X) \cap X|}{|A_\theta(X)|}$$

We say that $R' \subset R$ is $\theta$-superfluous in $R$ if $\gamma_\theta(R, X) = \gamma_\theta(R - R', X)$. Similarly, we say that $P$ is a $\theta$-reduct of $R$ if $R - P$ is superfluous in $R$ and no $P' \subset P$ such that $P'$ is superfluous. Clearly, it is advantageous to use the reducts of $R$ in characterising $X$.

We now turn our attention to using rough sets theory to analyse alarm data. The basic idea is as follows. For each alarm observed at level $L_{j+1}$, we carry out rough sets analysis to decide what are the likely causes at level $L_j$. For example, to determine what has possibly caused $a_4$ at $L_2$ in Table 1, we perform rough sets analysis on the data shown in Table 2. For convenience, we have expressed the alarms in a binary table with a 1 denoting an occurrence of an alarm.

**Table 2.** Analysing the causes for $a_4$ at $L_2$

| test | $T_1$ | $T_2$ | $T_3$ | $T_4$ | $T_5$ | $T_6$ | $T_7$ | $T_8$ | $T_9$ | $T_{10}$ |
|------|-------|-------|-------|-------|-------|-------|-------|-------|-------|----------|
| $a_1$ | 1 | 1 | 1 | 1 | 0 | 1 | 0 | 1 | 1 | 0 |
| $a_2$ | 0 | 1 | 0 | 0 | 1 | 0 | 1 | 0 | 0 | 0 |
| $a_3$ | 1 | 0 | 1 | 1 | 1 | 1 | 0 | 1 | 1 | 1 |
| $a_4$ | 1 | 0 | 0 | 0 | 1 | 1 | 0 | 1 | 1 | 1 |

Here we have $U = \{T_1, T_2, \ldots T_{10}\}$, $a_1, a_2$ and $a_3$ at $L_1$ are the attributes that describe the objects in $U$, and $a_4$ at $L_2$ represents a concept of interest. From this table, we have $A_\theta(a_4) = \{T_1, T_3, T_4, T_5, T_6, T_8, T_9, T_{10}\}$, and $\gamma_\theta(\{a_1, a_2, a_3\}, a_4) = 6/8$. Since $\gamma_\theta(\{a_1, a_2, a_3\}, a_4) = \gamma_\theta(\{a_1, a_3\}, a_4)$, we have a reduct $\{a_1, a_3\}$. Finally, we obtain two probabilistic causal dependencies: $a_1, a_3 \xrightarrow{0.67} a_4$ and $\neg a_1, a_3 \xrightarrow{1.00} a_4$ from the reduct. The detailed computation is omitted here, as it is rather standard [7].

The algorithm for carrying out the rough sets analysis is outlined below, where $D$ is a set of discovered probabilistic causal dependencies and $rs$ is a procedure for performing the required rough sets computation. Note that this algorithm only derives *many-to-one* causal dependencies. That is, we only derive $p(a \in L_{j+1}|L_j)$. Other dependencies such as $p(a, b \in L_{j+1}|L_j)$ can be obtained by performing appropriate probabilistic inferences on the derived belief network.

> **Algorithm** *RS*-analysis;
>     **input** $L = \{L_1, L_2, \ldots, L_n\}$;
>     **output** $D$;
>     **for** $j = 1$ **to** $n - 1$ **do**
>         **for** every $a \in L_{j+1}$ **do**
>             $D := D \cup rs(a, L_j)$
>         **endfor**
>         $PostProcessing(L_{j+1}, D)$
>     **endfor**

Again, the detailed computation involved in $rs$, e.g. to decide reducts, is omitted here as it is rather standard. The reader is referred to [8, 7] for explanation. One difference, however, is that when there are multiple reducts available, $rs$ uses all of them as they are all possible causes, but the standard rough sets analysis will only use one of them as that is enough to discern the objects.

The *post processing* at the end of each level's analysis is required for two reasons. Firstly, there may be some alarms left at level $L_{j+1}$ that are unconnected to any alarm at $L_j$. These are considered to be insignificant or noises and hence their occurrence in $L_{j+1}$ is discarded before processing the following level. Secondly, there are two types of causal dependencies discovered by $rs$ that are not useful in our alarm analysis:

- Causal dependencies with negative causes only, e.g. $\neg a_1 \to a_2$. These are not useful because the alarm management system usually mornitors the occurrence of alarms and acts upon them, not upon the absence of alarms.
- Causal dependencies with negative consequences only, e.g. $a_1 \to \neg a_2$. Since we are only interested in what will happen, these dependencies are considered to be irrelevant.

The *post processing* will discard these unwanted dependencies in order to derive a most relevant and simple belief network.

Apply the algorithm to Table 1, we derive the belief network as shown in Fig. 3. Note that conditional probability tables are listed separately in Fig. 3.

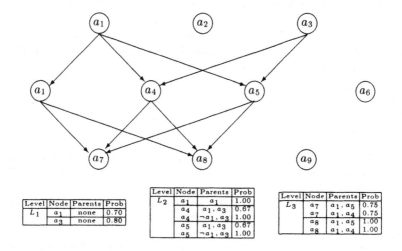

**Fig. 3.** The belief network for Table 1

$a_1$, $a_2$ and $a_3$ at $L_1$ are assigned with prior probabilities. Some alarms have more than one cause (e.g. $a_1, a_3 \xrightarrow{0.67} a_4$ and $\neg a_1, a_3 \xrightarrow{1.00} a_4$ at $L_2$). $a_2$ at $L_1$, $a_6$ at $L_2$ and $a_9$ at $L_3$ are unconnected to other nodes and hence are considered to be irrelevant and discarded. Note that if a particular combination of parent nodes is not present in the conditional probability table (e.g. $a_1, \neg a_3$ for $a_4 \in L_2$), then a probability value 0 is assumed.

Finally, it is worth pointing out that with our rough sets analysis, we discover only the dependencies with probability greater than a specified threshold. All lower probability dependencies are ignored. This can be seen as a *hueristic* used in searching for a simple $B_S$ that covers most probable and relevant causal dependencies supported by the given database. It will be also interesting to consider an *iterative* implementation, where the threshold is decreased gradually and the quality of the overall belief network is measured. Further discussion on this issue is beyond the scope of this paper.

# 4 Conclusions

In this paper, we briefly discussed how to discover knowledge from alarm data using rough sets theory and belief networks. The work reported here was originated from an alarm data analysis problem from a local telecommunication company [6]. By focusing on a specific problem and on the most probable causal dependencies, our approach does seem to be practical. Note that although we discussed our method exclusively in this paper within the domain of alarm data analysis, it is applicable to a class of similar problems, i.e. the problems that are related to the analysis of testing data obtained from time-variant and non-deterministic systems.

We plan to continue our study in the following two directions. Firstly, an incremental learning system will be considered, so that more accurate model of a telecommunication network may be derived step by step. Secondly, the algorithms proposed in this paper only derive belief networks for alarm data that is generated from tests with a fixed single input and a fixed network topology. The construction/integration of belief networks from tests with different inputs/topologies should also be investigated.

# References

1. G.F. Cooper and E. Herskovits. A bayesian method for constructing bayesian belief networks from databases. In *Proceedings of Uncertainty in Artificial Intelligence*, pages 86–94, 1991.
2. J.S. Deogun, V.V. Raghavan, and H.Sever. Exploiting Upper approximation in the rough set methodology. In *International Conference on Knowledge Discovery and Data Mining*, pages 69–74, 1995.
3. W.J. Frawley, G. Piatetsky-Shapiro, and C.J. Matheus. Knowledge discovery in databases: An overview. In G. Piatetsky-Shapiro and W.J. Frawley, editors, *Knowledge Discovery in Databases*, pages 1–27. AAAI/MIT Press, 1991.
4. G. Jakobson and M.D. Weissman. Alarm correlation. *IEEE Network*, 7(6):52–59, 1993.
5. K. Hätönen and M. Clemettinen and H. Mannila and P. Ronkainen and H Toivonen. Knowledge Discovery from Telecommunication Network Alarm Databases. In *Proceedings of International Conference on Data Engineering*, 1996.
6. P. Moore, J. Shao, K. Adamson, M.E.C. Hull, D.A. Bell, and M. Shapcott. An Architecture for Modelling Non-Deterministic Systems using Bayesian Belief Networks. In *Proceedings of Applied Informatics Conference*, 1996.
7. Z. Pawlak. *Rough Sets: Theoretical Aspects of Reasoning About Data*. Kluwer Academic Publishers, 1991.
8. Z. Pawlak, S.K.M. Wong, and W. Ziarko. Rough Sets: Probabilistic versus Deterministic. In B.R. Gaines and J.H. Boose, editors, *Machine Learning and Uncertain Reasoning*, pages 227–241. Academic Press, 1990.
9. S.J. Russell and P. Norvig. *Artificial Intelligence: A Mordern Appraoch*. Prentice-Hall, 1995.
10. J. Shao. Knowledge Discovery from Telecommunication Alarm Databases. technical report, 1996.

# Aunt's Problem: Table Rounding

Jiří Šíma [*]

Department of Theoretical Informatics
Institute of Computer Science
Academy of Sciences of the Czech Republic
Pod vodárenskou věží 2, 182 07 Prague 8
Czech Republic
e-mail: sima@uivt.cas.cz

## 1 Introduction

One day I met with my aunt. She asked me to help her with a computational problem because she knows I work at the institute of computer science. She is employed by an accounting department of one company where she faces the following table rounding problem. They process tables with numerical values corresponding to some economical factors. These tables contain the check sums of rows and columns. For a very simple example of such scheme see table 1.

| | | | |
|---|---|---|---|
| 1.5 | 5.5 | 1.6 | 8.6 |
| 2.6 | 0.6 | 3.6 | 6.8 |
| 4.1 | 6.1 | 5.2 | 15.4 |

**Table 1.** Example of a table with check sums.

It is required that all non-integer numbers in the resulting arrangement of the table should be rounded off[1]. However, the usage of the *classical rounding procedure* in which a number is rounded down if its fraction is less than 0.5 and it is rounded up otherwise, can generally violate the validity of the check sums. This is the case of table 1 in which rounding does not preserve almost any row or column sum as it is shown in table 2. For large tables the error in the check sums can even be arbitrarily large. Clearly, if sums are required to agree after rounding, we must generally not insist on the classical rounding approach.

| | | | |
|---|---|---|---|
| 2 | 6 | 2 | 9 |
| 3 | 1 | 4 | 7 |
| 4 | 6 | 5 | 15 |

**Table 2.** Table 1 after rounding.

The above-described situation led my aunt to round several numbers in the table inconsistently by hand with respect to the classical rounding so that the check sums agree. She wants me to find a way to round the table automatically. When I was sharing this problem with several people from a commercial area,

---

[*] This research was supported by GA ČR Grant No. 201/95/0976.
[1] For notation simplicity we consider rounding to integers but all ideas in this paper can be straightforwardly generalized for rounding to the given number of valid digits.

they confirmed that they had encountered the same problem in their accounting. That is why I found this problem to be important from a practical point of view.

As my aunt has mentioned, it is possible to weaken the rounding condition in order to preserve the validity of check sums. Instead of rounding to the nearest integer as the classical approach suggests, she generally rounded off to an adjacent integer either up or down independently on the fraction. There is a natural question whether this modified rounding procedure can always preserve the row and column sums.

Sometimes the rounding of check sums is prescribed because, for example, these sums can represent important economical results. In this case the rounding of numbers in the table which is consistent with the given check sums may not exist. In Section 4 we will formulate a necessary and sufficient condition stating when such rounding exists. For this purpose the table rounding problem is reduced to a maximum flow problem and its correspondence with minimum cut is exploited. Therefore, in Section 3 some basic notions and properties concerning the maximum flow problem are mentioned. On the other hand, it is proved in Section 5 that the relevant rounding always exists when the check sums are not prescribed as an input and are allowed to be rounded off to adjacent integers as well.

Using the maximum flow algorithm the table rounding can be found in polynomial time $O((m+n)^3)$ where $m$ is the number of rows and $n$ is the number of columns, provided that it exists. Moreover, it is shown that a adjacent integer rounding with minimal sum of absolute round-errors can be computed within $O(mn(m+n)^2)$ time using an algorithm for the so-called minimum cost flow problem.

## 2 Table Rounding Problem

In this section two types of the table rounding problem are formulated. We introduce the following notation. Let $c_{ij}$ for $i = 1, \ldots, m$, $j = 1, \ldots, n$ be the *common numbers* in the table and $a_i = \sum_{j=1}^{n} c_{ij}$ $(i = 1, \ldots, m)$, $b_j = \sum_{i=1}^{m} c_{ij}$ $(j = 1, \ldots, n)$ are the corresponding *row* and *column check sums*. Furthermore, denote by $\sigma = \sum_{i=1}^{m} a_i = \sum_{j=1}^{n} b_j = \sum_{i=1}^{m} \sum_{j=1}^{n} c_{ij}$ the *total sum* of all common numbers. We will also use the notation $\lfloor x \rfloor$ for rounding-down a real number $x$ to a smaller or equal adjacent integer and $\lceil x \rceil$ for rounding-up to a greater or equal adjacent integer. This means $\lceil x \rceil - \lfloor x \rfloor = 1$ for non-integer $x$ and $\lceil x \rceil = \lfloor x \rfloor = x$ for integer $x$.

Without loss of generality, assume $0 \leq c_{ij} < 1$ because the adjacent integer rounding of a common number in the table can cause a change of at most 1 and the tables with general values can easily be *normalized* to satisfy this condition as it is shown for table 1 in table 3. It is clear that the resulting *adjacent integer rounding* (i.e., whether round-down or round-up) for the normalized form which preserves the check sums is also a consistent rounding for the original table.

| 0.5 | 0.5 | 0.6 | 1.6 |
|-----|-----|-----|-----|
| 0.6 | 0.6 | 0.6 | 1.8 |
| 1.1 | 1.1 | 1.2 | 3.4 |

**Table 3.** Table 1 after normalization.

At first the total sum $\sigma$ of all common numbers is rounded off to integer $\bar{\sigma} \in \mathcal{Z}$ (for example, using the classical rounding procedure) because this number has the greatest significance. Then we will distinguish two variants of the table rounding problem. First the *table rounding problem with prescribed sums* (TRPS) can be formulated in the following way. Given the prescribed integer rounding $\bar{a}_i \in \mathcal{Z}$, $\bar{b}_j \in \mathcal{Z}$ of the row and column check sums $a_i$ $(i = 1, \ldots, m)$, $b_j$ $(j = 1, \ldots, n)$ such that their sums $\sum_{i=1}^{m} \bar{a}_i = \sum_{j=1}^{n} \bar{b}_j = \bar{\sigma}$ equal the rounded total sum, find the rounding $\bar{c}_{ij} \in \{0, 1\}$ of common numbers $c_{ij}$ $(i = 1, \ldots, m$, $j = 1, \ldots, n)$, so that $\bar{a}_i = \sum_{j=1}^{n} \bar{c}_{ij}$ $(i = 1, \ldots, m)$, $\bar{b}_j = \sum_{i=1}^{m} \bar{c}_{ij}$ $(j = 1, \ldots, n)$. Table 4 is an example of the input of this problem for table 3.

| 0.5 | 0.5 | 0.6 | 1 |
|-----|-----|-----|---|
| 0.6 | 0.6 | 0.6 | 2 |
| 1 | 1 | 1 | 3 |

**Table 4.** Table 3 as an example of input for TRPS.

The second type of the *table rounding problem* (TRP) does not have prescribed rounding of check sums and can be formulated as follows. Given the table of common numbers $0 \leq c_{ij} < 1$ $(i = 1, \ldots, m$, $j = 1, \ldots, n)$ and the rounded total sum $\bar{\sigma} \in \{\lfloor \sigma \rfloor, \lceil \sigma \rceil\}$ find the rounding $\bar{c}_{ij} \in \{0, 1\}$ and the rounding of the row and column check sums $a_i$, $b_j$ to the adjacent integer $\bar{a}_i \in \{\lfloor a_i \rfloor, \lceil a_i \rceil\}$, $\bar{b}_j \in \{\lfloor b_j \rfloor, \lceil b_j \rceil\}$ such that $\bar{a}_i = \sum_{j=1}^{n} \bar{c}_{ij}$ $(i = 1, \ldots, m)$, $\bar{b}_j = \sum_{i=1}^{m} \bar{c}_{ij}$ $(j = 1, \ldots, n)$, and $\bar{\sigma} = \sum_{i=1}^{m} \bar{a}_i = \sum_{j=1}^{n} \bar{b}_j$.

Considering both types of table rounding problem we will look for the rounding with a minimal error. A *round-error* $\varepsilon(x)$ of the number $x$ from the table (i.e. $c_{ij}$, $a_i$ or $b_j$) is defined as an absolute error $\varepsilon(x) = |x - \bar{x}|$. The *total rounding error* $E_S = \sum_{i=1}^{m} \sum_{j=1}^{n} \varepsilon(c_{ij})$ for the TRPS and $E = E_S + \sum_{i=1}^{m} \varepsilon(a_i) + \sum_{j=1}^{n} \varepsilon(b_j)$ for the TRP is a sum of round-errors of the relevant numbers in the table.

## 3 Maximum Flow Problem

We recall the definition of maximum flow problem [2]. A *network* is a 4-tuple $S = (G, z, s, c)$, where $G = (V, E)$ is an oriented graph with the set of vertices $V$ and the set of edges $E \subseteq V \times V$, $z \in V$ is a *source*, $s \in V$ is a *sink* and $c : E \longrightarrow \Re_0^+$ is a *capacity* which associates each edge $(u, v) \in E$ with a non-negative real number $c(u, v)$. A function $t : E \longrightarrow \Re_0^+$ is said to be a *flow* of the network $S$, if $0 \leq t(u, v) \leq c(u, v)$ for any edge $(u, v) \in E$ and for each vertex $v \in V - \{z, s\}$ the *conservation law* holds:

$$\sum_{(u,v) \in E} t(u, v) = \sum_{(v,u) \in E} t(v, u). \tag{1}$$

In addition the *flow size* is defined

$$|t| = \sum_{(z,v) \in E} t(z, v) - \sum_{(v,z) \in E} t(v, z) \tag{2}$$

and $t$ is said to be the *maximum flow* if for any flow $t_1$ of $S$ holds $|t_1| \leq |t|$. The *maximum flow problem* (MFP) is to determine the maximum flow for a given network. We will confine ourselves to a special case in which the edge capacity of the network is an integer function. Then it can be shown [2] that there exits a maximum flow which assigns each edge with an integer and can be found in a polynomial time:

**Theorem 1.** *Given a network with integer edge capacity then the integer maximum flow can be found within $O(|V|^3)$ time, in which $|V|$ is the number of network vertices.*

Furthermore, the *cut* $z \in C \subseteq V - \{s\}$ of the network $S$ is defined as a subset of vertices including the source and excluding the sink and the *cut size* is determined:

$$|C| = \sum_{\substack{(u, v) \in E \\ u \in C, v \notin C}} c(u, v). \tag{3}$$

The following theorem recalls the known relationship between the maximum flow and the minimum cut:

**Theorem 2.** *In any network the size of a flow is smaller or equal to the size of a cut. Especially, the maximum flow size equals the minimum cut size.*

Finally, we introduce a so-called *edge cost* [1], [3], which is a function $h : E \longrightarrow \Re$ which associates each edge $(u, v) \in E$ with a real number $h(u, v)$. Using this notion the *cost* $h(t)$ of the flow $t$ is defined as

$$h(t) = \sum_{(u,v) \in E} h(u, v) t(u, v). \tag{4}$$

Then given the flow size $T$ the *minimum cost flow problem* (MCFP) is to determine the flow $t$ of the size $|t| \geq T$ with minimal $h(t)$. This problem can be solved in a polynomial time [3] as well. We will use the following theorem:

**Theorem 3.** *Given an integer $T$ and a network with integer edge capacity and with non-negative edge cost $h$, then the integer flow $t$ of the size $|t| \geq T$ with minimal $h(t)$ can be found within $O(T \cdot |V|^2)$ time, where $|V|$ is the number of network vertices.*

## 4 Table Rounding with Prescribed Sums

In this section we will deal with the TRPS. At first the TRPS is reduced to the MFP:

**Definition 4.** Let $\bar{a}_i$ $(i = 1, \ldots, m)$, $\bar{b}_j$ $(j = 1, \ldots, n)$ be the prescribed rounding of check sums from the TRPS. We define the network $S(\bar{a}_i, \bar{b}_j) = (G = (V, E), z, s, c)$ of the corresponding MFP as follows:

$$V = \{A_i \mid i = 1, \ldots, m\} \cup \{B_j \mid j = 1, \ldots, n\} \cup \{z, s\},$$
$$E = \{(A_i, B_j) \mid i = 1, \ldots, m; \, j = 1, \ldots, n\} \cup$$
$$\{(z, A_i) \mid i = 1, \ldots, m\} \cup \{(B_j, s) \mid j = 1, \ldots, n\},$$
$$c(A_i, B_j) = \begin{cases} 0 & c_{ij} = 0 \\ 1 & c_{ij} > 0 \end{cases} \quad i = 1, \ldots, m; \, j = 1, \ldots, n,$$
$$c(z, A_i) = \bar{a}_i \quad i = 1, \ldots, m,$$
$$c(B_j, s) = \bar{b}_j \quad j = 1, \ldots, n.$$

The correctness of the previous reduction is expressed in the following theorem:

**Theorem 5.** *A solution of the TRPS $\bar{a}_i$, $\bar{b}_j$ exists iff there is an integer flow $t$ in the network $S(\bar{a}_i, \bar{b}_j)$ of the size $|t| = \sum_{i=1}^{m} \bar{a}_i = \sum_{j=1}^{n} \bar{b}_j$.*

*Proof.* Let $t$ be the integer flow of the desired size. Consider the cut $C_z = \{z\}$ of the size $|C_z| = \sum_{i=1}^{m} c(z, A_i) = \sum_{i=1}^{m} \bar{a}_i$ which is equal to $|t| = \sum_{i=1}^{m} t(z, A_i) = \sum_{i=1}^{m} \bar{a}_i$ and this implies $t(z, A_i) = c(z, A_i)$ for $i = 1, \ldots, m$, due to Theorem 2. Similarly, $t(B_j, s) = c(B_j, s)$ for $j = 1, \ldots, n$ using $C_s = V - \{s\}$. Then define the adjacent integer rounding $\bar{c}_{ij} = t(A_i, B_j) \in \{0, 1\}$ of the common numbers in the table. From the conservation law (1) for $A_i$, $B_j$ it follows that this rounding preserves the check sums:

$$\bar{a}_i = c(z, A_i) = t(z, A_i) = \sum_{j=1}^{n} t(A_i, B_j) = \sum_{j=1}^{n} \bar{c}_{ij} \quad i = 1, \ldots, m \qquad (5)$$

$$\bar{b}_j = c(B_j, s) = t(B_j, s) = \sum_{i=1}^{m} t(A_i, B_j) = \sum_{i=1}^{m} \bar{c}_{ij} \quad j = 1, \ldots, n. \qquad (6)$$

The opposite implication is similar. $\qquad\qquad\qquad\qquad\qquad\qquad\qquad\qquad\square$

Using the reduction to the MFP and its relationship with the minimum cut, we formulate a necessary and sufficient condition when the adjacent integer table rounding, preserving the prescribed check sums, exits.

**Theorem 6.** *A solution for the TRPS $\bar{a}_i$ $(i = 1, \ldots, m)$, $\bar{b}_j$ $(j = 1, \ldots, n)$ exists iff for any choice of $p$ rows $P \subseteq \{1, \ldots, m\}$ and of $q$ columns $Q \subseteq \{1, \ldots, n\}$ it holds*

$$\sum_{i \in P} \bar{a}_i - \sum_{i \in Q} \bar{b}_j \leq p(n - q) - z_{PQ} \qquad (7)$$

*where $z_{PQ} = |\{c_{ij} = 0 \mid i \in P, j \notin Q\}|$ is the number of zero elements situated in the rows from $P$ which are not in the columns from $Q$ at the same time.*

*Proof.* Reduce the TRPS $\bar{a}_i$, $\bar{b}_j$ to the MFP $S(\bar{a}_i, \bar{b}_j)$. All possible cuts $C_{PQ}$ ($P \subseteq \{1, \ldots, m\}$, $Q \subseteq \{1, \ldots, n\}$) in the network $S(\bar{a}_i, \bar{b}_j)$ have the following form:

$$C_{PQ} = \{z\} \cup \{A_i \mid i \in P\} \cup \{B_j \mid j \in Q\}. \tag{8}$$

Thus, the size of any cut $C_{PQ}$ can be expressed:

$$|C_{PQ}| = \sum_{i \notin P} c(z, A_i) + \sum_{i \in P} \sum_{j \notin Q} c(A_i, B_j) + \sum_{j \in Q} c(B_j, s) =$$

$$\sum_{i=1}^{m} \bar{a}_i - \sum_{i \in P} \bar{a}_i + p(n - q) - z_{PQ} + \sum_{j \in Q} \bar{b}_j. \tag{9}$$

From Theorem 5 a solution of the TRPS exists iff there is an integer flow $t$ in the network $S(\bar{a}_i, \bar{b}_j)$ of the size $|t| = \sum_{i=1}^{m} \bar{a}_i$, i.e. iff the size of any cut in this network is greater or equal to this flow, due to Theorem 2. This means $|C_{PQ}| \geq \sum_{i=1}^{m} \bar{a}_i$ for any $P \subseteq \{1, \ldots, m\}$, $Q \subseteq \{1, \ldots, n\}$. Substituting for $|C_{PQ}|$ we obtain

$$\sum_{i=1}^{m} \bar{a}_i - \sum_{i \in P} \bar{a}_i + p(n - q) - z_{PQ} + \sum_{j \in Q} \bar{b}_j \geq \sum_{i=1}^{m} \bar{a}_i \tag{10}$$

from which the proposition follows:

$$\sum_{i \in P} \bar{a}_i - \sum_{i \in Q} \bar{b}_j \leq p(n - q) - z_{PQ}. \tag{11}$$

$\square$

An example of the TRPS instance for which the condition (7) is not satisfied is in table 6 (consider first two rows and first column), which means that the required rounding does not exist, due to Theorem 6.

|     |     |     |   |
|-----|-----|-----|---|
| 0.7 | 0.9 | 0.9 | 3 |
| 0.6 | 0.9 | 0.9 | 3 |
| 0.1 | 0.7 | 0.6 | 1 |
| 1   | 3   | 3   | 7 |

**Table 5.** An example of TRPS which does not have a solution.

On the other hand the table adjacent integer rounding, consistent with the prescribed check sums, can be found in a polynomial time when it exists.

**Corollary 7.** *The TRPS for the table which consists of $m$ rows and of $n$ columns can be solved in $O((m+n)^3)$ time and the corresponding rounding with minimal total rounding error can be computed within $O(mn(m + n)^2)$ time.*

*Proof.* Using Definition 4 reduce the TRPS $\bar{a}_i$, $\bar{b}_j$ to the MFP with the network $S(\bar{a}_i, \bar{b}_j)$ having $m + n + 2$ vertices. Then employ the algorithm from Theorem 1 to find the integer maximum flow $t$ within $O((m+n)^3)$ time. Check whether the flow size achieves $|t| = \sum_{i=1}^{m} \bar{a}_i = \sum_{j=1}^{n} \bar{b}_j$. If it does the relevant table rounding exists due to Theorem 5 and can be determined as $\bar{c}_{ij} = t(A_i, B_j) \in \{0,1\}$ from the proof of Theorem 5.

Moreover, the rounding with minimal total rounding error $E_S$ can be computed using the algorithm for the minimum cost flow problem from Theorem 3, in which the prescribed size of the integer flow $t$ is set to $T = \sum_{i=1}^{m} \bar{a}_i$ and the edge cost is defined as follows: $h(A_i, B_j) = \lceil c_{ij} \rceil - c_{ij}$, $h(z, A_i) = h(B_j, s) = 0$ $(i = 1, \ldots, m, \ j = 1, \ldots, n)$. The inequality $T \le \sum_{i=1}^{m} \sum_{j=1}^{n} \lceil c_{ij} \rceil \le mn$ implies that this algorithm ends in polynomial time $O(mn(m+n)^2)$ with the minimal flow cost which can be expressed as follows:

$$h(t) = \sum_{i=1}^{m} \sum_{j=1}^{n} h(A_i, B_j) t(A_i, B_j) = \sum_{i=1}^{m} \sum_{j=1}^{n} \left( \lceil c_{ij} \rceil - c_{ij} \right) \bar{c}_{ij}. \tag{12}$$

Denote by $U = \{ c_{ij} \mid \bar{c}_{ij} = \lceil c_{ij} \rceil = 1, \ i = 1, \ldots, m, \ j = 1, \ldots, n \}$ the set of non-integer common numbers which are rounded up and $\bar{U}$ is the complement of $U$. The minimal flow cost can be further rewritten as

$$h(t) = \sum_{U} \left( \lceil c_{ij} \rceil - c_{ij} \right). \tag{13}$$

We prove that the minimal flow cost $h(t)$ minimizes the total rounding error $E_S$. Let $U$ correspond to the minimal flow cost which means that for any other $U' \ne U$ holds:

$$\sum_{U} \left( \lceil c_{ij} \rceil - c_{ij} \right) \le \sum_{U'} \left( \lceil c_{ij} \rceil - c_{ij} \right). \tag{14}$$

Adding $\sum_{\bar{U} \cap \bar{U}'} \left( \lceil c_{ij} \rceil - c_{ij} \right) - \sum_{U \cap U'} \left( \lceil c_{ij} \rceil - c_{ij} \right)$ to (14) we obtain:

$$\sum_{\bar{U}'} \left( \lceil c_{ij} \rceil - c_{ij} \right) \le \sum_{\bar{U}} \left( \lceil c_{ij} \rceil - c_{ij} \right). \tag{15}$$

We realize that the numbers of elements in $U$, $U'$ are the same, i.e. $|U| = |U'|$ because of the prescribed total sum. Thus, $|\bar{U}|$ is added to (15) multiplied by -1:

$$\sum_{\bar{U}} \left( 1 - \lceil c_{ij} \rceil + c_{ij} \right) \le \sum_{\bar{U}'} \left( 1 - \lceil c_{ij} \rceil + c_{ij} \right) \tag{16}$$

which implies

$$\sum_{\bar{U}} \left( c_{ij} - \lfloor c_{ij} \rfloor \right) \le \sum_{\bar{U}'} \left( c_{ij} - \lfloor c_{ij} \rfloor \right) \tag{17}$$

Adding (14) and (17) the total rounding error $E_S$ for $U$ is proved to be minimal, i.e. for any other $U' \ne U$ holds:

$$E_S = \sum_{U} \left( \lceil c_{ij} \rceil - c_{ij} \right) + \sum_{\bar{U}} \left( c_{ij} - \lfloor c_{ij} \rfloor \right) \le \sum_{U'} \left( \lceil c_{ij} \rceil - c_{ij} \right) + \sum_{\bar{U}'} \left( c_{ij} - \lfloor c_{ij} \rfloor \right).$$

$\square$

# 5 Table Rounding Always Exists

In this section we will generalize the results from Section 4 for the TRP using the same technique. The corresponding reduction to the MFP follows:

**Definition 8.** Let $a_i$ $(i = 1,\ldots,m)$, $b_j$ $(j = 1,\ldots,n)$ be the row and column check sums and $\bar{\sigma} \in \{\lfloor \sigma \rfloor, \lceil \sigma \rceil\}$ be the rounded total sum from the TRP. We define a network $S(\bar{\sigma}) = (G = (V,E), z, s, c)$ of the corresponding MFP as follows:

$$V = \{A_i \mid i = 1,\ldots,m\} \cup \{B_j \mid j = 1,\ldots,n\} \cup \{z, s, X, Y\},$$
$$E = \{(A_i, B_j) \mid i = 1,\ldots,m; \; j = 1,\ldots,n\} \cup \{(z, X), (Y, s)\} \cup$$
$$\{(z, A_i) \mid i = 1,\ldots,m\} \cup \{(B_j, s) \mid j = 1,\ldots,n\} \cup$$
$$\{(X, A_i) \mid i = 1,\ldots,m\} \cup \{(B_j, Y) \mid j = 1,\ldots,n\},$$

$$c(A_i, B_j) = \begin{cases} 0 & c_{ij} = 0 \\ 1 & c_{ij} > 0 \end{cases} \quad i = 1,\ldots,m; \; j = 1,\ldots,n,$$

$$c(z, A_i) = \lfloor a_i \rfloor, \quad c(X, A_i) = \begin{cases} 0 & a_i = \lfloor a_i \rfloor \\ 1 & a_i > \lfloor a_i \rfloor \end{cases} \quad i = 1,\ldots,m,$$

$$c(B_j, s) = \lfloor b_j \rfloor, \quad c(B_j, Y) = \begin{cases} 0 & b_j = \lfloor b_j \rfloor \\ 1 & b_j > \lfloor b_j \rfloor \end{cases} \quad j = 1,\ldots,n,$$

$$c(z, X) = \bar{\sigma} - \sum_{i=1}^{m} \lfloor a_i \rfloor, \quad c(Y, s) = \bar{\sigma} - \sum_{j=1}^{n} \lfloor b_j \rfloor.$$

An example of this generalized reduction for table 5 is in picture 1.

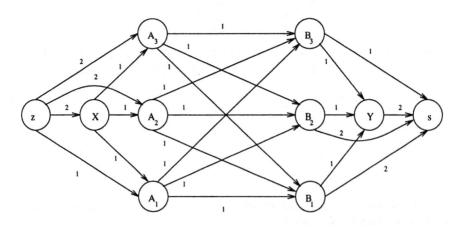

**Fig. 1.** An example of TRP reduction of table 5 to MFP.

**Theorem 9.** *A solution of the TRP with $\bar{\sigma} \in \{\lfloor \sigma \rfloor, \lceil \sigma \rceil\}$ exists iff there is an integer flow $t$ in the network $S(\bar{\sigma})$ of the size $|t| = \bar{\sigma}$.*

*Proof.* Let $t$ be the integer flow of the size $|t| = \bar{\sigma}$. Then define the rounding $\bar{c}_{ij} = t(A_i, B_j) \in \{0, 1\}$ $(i = 1, \ldots, m, j = 1, \ldots, n)$ of the common numbers and $\bar{a}_i = t(z, A_i) + t(X, A_i)$, $\bar{b}_j = t(B_j, s) + t(B_j, Y)$ of the corresponding check sums. First we prove that this is an adjacent integer rounding, i.e. $\bar{a}_i \in \{\lfloor a_i \rfloor, \lceil a_i \rceil\}$, $\bar{b}_j \in \{\lfloor b_j \rfloor, \lceil b_j \rceil\}$. Furthermore, we will confine ourselves on the row sums $\bar{a}_i$, while the proof for $\bar{b}_j$ is similar. It is clear that $\bar{a}_i = t(z, A_i) + t(X, A_i) \leq c(z, A_i) + c(X, A_i) \leq \lceil a_i \rceil$. It even holds $t(z, A_i) = c(z, A_i) = \lfloor a_i \rfloor$ from $\bar{\sigma} = |t| = \sum_{i=1}^{m} t(z, A_i) + t(z, X) \leq \sum_{i=1}^{m} c(z, A_i) + c(z, X) = \bar{\sigma}$, which implies $\bar{a}_i \geq \lfloor a_i \rfloor$. Now we check whether the relevant rounded sums agree. From the conservation law (1) for the vertex $X$ we obtain $t(z, X) = \sum_{i=1}^{m} t(X, A_i)$. This implies

$$\bar{\sigma} = |t| = \sum_{i=1}^{m} t(z, A_i) + t(z, X) = \sum_{i=1}^{m} (t(z, A_i) + t(X, A_i)) = \sum_{i=1}^{m} \bar{a}_i. \quad (18)$$

Using (1) for the vertices $A_i$ we obtain

$$\bar{a}_i = t(z, A_i) + t(X, A_i) = \sum_{j=1}^{n} t(A_i, B_j) = \bar{c}_{ij} \quad i = 1, \ldots, m. \quad (19)$$

The opposite implication is similar. $\qquad\square$

Now we prove that the adjacent integer table rounding always exits.

**Theorem 10.** *A solution for the TRP with the given $\bar{\sigma} \in \{\lfloor \sigma \rfloor, \lceil \sigma \rceil\}$ always exists.*

*Proof.* Reduce the TRP with $\bar{\sigma}$ to the MFP $S(\bar{\sigma})$. From Theorems 2, 9 it is sufficient to prove that any cut size in $S(\bar{\sigma})$ is greater or equal to the size $|C_z| = \bar{\sigma}$ of the cut $C_z = \{z\}$. All possible cuts $C_{PQ}^H$ in $S(\bar{\sigma})$ have the following form:

$$C_{PQ}^H = \{z\} \cup \{A_i \mid i \in P\} \cup \{B_j \mid j \in Q\} \cup H, \quad (20)$$

where $P \subseteq \{1, \ldots, m\}$ contains $p$ rows, $Q \subseteq \{1, \ldots, n\}$ consists of $q$ columns and $H \subseteq \{X, Y\}$. Remember that $z_{PQ} = |\{c_{ij} = 0 \mid i \in P, j \notin Q\}|$. We will distinguish four cases according to four possible $H$:

1. $X \in H, Y \in H$:

$$|C_{PQ}^H| = \sum_{i \notin P} \lceil a_i \rceil + p(n - q) - z_{PQ} + \sum_{j \in Q} \lfloor b_j \rfloor + \bar{\sigma} - \sum_{j=1}^{n} \lfloor b_j \rfloor = \quad (21)$$

$$= \sum_{i \notin P} \lceil a_i \rceil + p(n - q) - z_{PQ} - \sum_{j \notin Q} \lfloor b_j \rfloor + \bar{\sigma} \geq$$

$$\geq \sum_{i \notin P} \sum_{j=1}^{n} c_{ij} + \sum_{i \in P} \sum_{j \notin Q} c_{ij} - \sum_{i=1}^{m} \sum_{j \notin Q} c_{ij} + \bar{\sigma} = \sum_{i \notin P} \sum_{j \in Q} c_{ij} + \bar{\sigma} \geq \bar{\sigma}.$$

2. $X \in H, Y \notin H$:

$$|C_{PQ}^H| = \sum_{i \notin P} \lceil a_i \rceil + p(n-q) - z_{PQ} + \sum_{j \in Q} \lceil b_j \rceil \geq \sum_{i=1}^{m} \bar{a}_i = \bar{\sigma}. \qquad (22)$$

3. $X \notin H, Y \in H$:

$$|C_{PQ}^H| = \bar{\sigma} - \sum_{i \in P} \lfloor a_i \rfloor + p(n-q) - z_{PQ} - \sum_{j \notin Q} \lfloor b_j \rfloor + \bar{\sigma} \geq \qquad (23)$$

$$\geq \bar{\sigma} - \sum_{i \in P} \sum_{j=1}^{n} c_{ij} + \sum_{i \in P} \sum_{j \notin Q} c_{ij} - \sum_{i=1}^{m} \sum_{j \notin Q} c_{ij} + \bar{\sigma} =$$

$$= \sum_{i \notin P} \sum_{j \in Q} c_{ij} + \bar{\sigma} \geq \bar{\sigma}.$$

4. $X \notin H, Y \notin H$:

$$|C_{PQ}^H| = \bar{\sigma} - \sum_{i \in P} \lfloor a_i \rfloor + p(n-q) - z_{PQ} + \sum_{j \in Q} \lceil b_j \rceil \geq \qquad (24)$$

$$\geq \bar{\sigma} - \sum_{i \in P} \sum_{j=1}^{n} c_{ij} + \sum_{i \in P} \sum_{j \notin Q} c_{ij} + \sum_{i=1}^{m} \sum_{j \in Q} c_{ij} = \bar{\sigma} + \sum_{i \notin P} \sum_{j \in Q} c_{ij} \geq \bar{\sigma}.$$

$\square$

**Corollary 11.** *The TRP for the table containing m rows and n columns can be solved in $O((m+n)^3)$ time and the corresponding rounding with minimal total rounding error can be computed within $O(mn(m+n)^2)$ time.*

*Proof.* The proof is analogous to Corollary 7. In addition, the total rounding error $E$ takes into account rounding errors of check sums which are represented as the edge costs $h(X, A_i) = \lceil a_i \rceil - a_i$ $(i = 1, \ldots, m)$, $h(B_j, Y) = \lceil b_j \rceil - b_j$ $(j = 1, \ldots, n)$. $\square$

## Acknowledgement

I am grateful to my aunt Marta Kyslíková who asked me to solve the table rounding problem which has resulted in writing this paper. Further, I thank my colleagues Arnošt Štědrý for the preliminary discussions related to this problem and Tereza Vavříková who has created the picture in a computer form.

## References

1. Jensen, P. A., Barnes, J. W. 1980. Network Flow Programming. John Wiley & Sons, New York.
2. Kučera, L. 1983. Combinatorial Algorithms. (in czech) MS 18, SNTL, Prague.
3. Lawler, E. L. 1976. Combinatorial Optimization: Networks and Matroids. Holt, Rinehart and Winston, New York.

# A Seven-Head Dragon for Optimal Pattern Searching

Ivana Vovsová [*]

Department of Computer Science
Faculty of Mathematics and Physics of Charles University
Malostranské náměstí 25
118 00 Prague 1
Czech Republic

**Abstract.** We present an implementation of a variant of the Knuth–Morris–Pratt pattern matching algorithm that runs in time $O(n+m)$ on a seven–tape Turing machine, where $n$ is the length of the text and $m$ is the length of the pattern.

## 1  Introduction

Pattern searching is one of the oldest problems studied in computer science. Many variants of this problem have been investigated [2]. There are several linear–time algorithms for pattern searching on the RAM with the unit cost but under different complexity assumptions (RAM with logarithmic cost, Turing machine) this problem has not been investigated so much.

When one straightforwardly translates the standard unit–cost linear–time RAM pattern matching algorithm into a logarithmic–cost RAM program, the resulting program will have the time complexity $O(n \log n)$ (assuming $n = \Theta(m)$). Nevertheless, it appears that for these machines, and also for multi–tape Turing machines, faster pattern matching algorithms exist.

In this paper we shall study the asymptotic complexity of pattern matching on multi–tape Turing machines. For these machines we shall present an algorithm of time complexity that is linear both in the length of the text as well as in that of the pattern. Clearly, it is impossible to achieve a better result, because in the worst case the Turing machine has to read the whole text and the whole pattern.

## 2  Preliminaries

*Problem definition:* Let $t = t_1, \ldots, t_n$ be an input text over some alphabet and let $p = p_1, \ldots, p_m$ be a pattern (over the same alphabet), for some $m \geq 1, n \geq 1$. Both text and pattern are stored on two extra input tapes of a Turing machine. We say that the pattern $p$ has an occurrence in the text $t$ iff there exists such $i$ that $p_j = t_{i+j}$, for $j = 1, \ldots, m$. Given $t$ and $p$, our task is to design a Turing machine that decide whether there is an occurrence of $p$ in $t$.

[*] This research was partially supported by GA ČR Grant No. 201/95/0976

*The KMP Algorithm:* As our method is based on the ideas of the KMP (Knuth–Morris–Pratt) algorithm [1], we shall briefly review the KMP algorithm.

The KMP algorithm works in two phases. In the first one, it builds some data structures based on the input pattern. To be exact, it computes a representation of a finite automaton. In the second phase, it uses the automaton for searching.

There are several versions of the KMP algorithm. For our case we shall take the simplest one. The finite automaton from the first phase will be very simple. It will have $m + 1$ states. Let the automaton be in the state $x$ iff the first $x$ characters of the pattern match the last $x$ characters of the already processed part of the text (states are non-negative integers). Then, when comparing the next character of the pattern with the next piece of the text, two cases can occur.

If these two characters are identical, the automaton makes a forward step and goes into the state $x + 1$.

Otherwise, the automaton enters some state $y < x$. The state $y$ must also fulfil the condition that the last $y$ characters of the text must match the first $y$ characters of the pattern. As we do not want to miss any occurrence of the pattern, the new state $y$ must be the biggest one fulfilling this condition.

After our automaton enters the state $y$, it will again compare the same character of the text with the next character of the pattern. This "loop back" continues until the automaton makes a forward step or reaches the state 0.

```
abcacabcacabaabxxx    text
| | | | | | | |↗
abcacabaab            pattern
   | |
   abcacabaab         pattern after shift
```

Fig. 1. A KMP–automaton

The KMP–algorithm can be briefly described as follows (in the formalism of C++):

```
preprocessing;
state = 0; pos = 1;
while (pos <= n) {
        while (p[state]! = t[pos] && state! = 0) state = fail(state);
        if (state == m) return found;
        pos + +; state + +;
}
return not_found;
```

This algorithm has a linear–time complexity (we do not consider preprocessing for now). The outer loop goes $n$ times and the variable *state* is increased $n$ times. As $fail(state) < state$, the inner loop decreases the variable *state* and hence it can be performed maximally $n$ times, too.

# 3 A TM implementation of a KMP–algorithm

*The Basic Algorithm:* The most important part of the TM–algorithm is the implementation of the function *fail*. It must be implemented in such a way that the Turing machine can compute its values and move its head to the computed place (state) very quickly. Note that the range of the *fail* function is from 0 to $m-2$ but in any linear-time algorithm the complexity of making backward steps can not depend on $m$.

It appears that on the Turing machine it is easier to realize moves of a specific length than moves to some specified state. Therefore, we will consider a new function $\delta(x) := x - fail(x)$ instead of *fail*. This function says how many moves to the left we should make. Its range is from 1 to $m-1$.

Our goal is to ensure that any move of length $x$ (for both left and right directions) takes $O(x)$ steps. This implies that we can not store values of the $\delta$ function directly because it would need $\Omega(\log m)$ bits to store its values.

In other words, for storing its values for all possible arguments from 1 to $m-1$ the $\delta$ function should occupy only $O(m)$ cells on the tape. To achieve this, we should devote more care to the implementation of this function. Note the following three important features of this function:

1. $\delta(x) \leq x$. This is trivial: we can not jump before the beginning of the pattern.
2. $\delta(x) \leq \delta(x+1)$. Values of the $\delta$ function never decrease because the *fail* function must return the biggest prefix of the pattern which can be a suffix of the text. The opposite would mean, for example, that the first ten characters of the pattern match with the text but the first five do not, but this is nonsense.
3. $0 < \delta(x) < m$

The typical graph of the $\delta$ function is shown in Fig. 2.

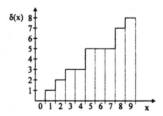

**Fig. 2.** The typical graph of the $\delta$ function

We can find out that we need not remember values of the $\delta$ function for all arguments. It is enough to remember differences of values. If we use these differences (we use unary coding and separators between values) the property (3) implies that the whole $\delta$ function (for all arguments) will need only $2m$ tape cells.

The next question is whether we can effectively compute values of the $\delta$ function being coded in this way. The answer is yes and it will become clear from the following description of the searching machine.

*The Searching Machine:* We will suppose that we have already done preprocessing (which will be described later). The searching machine is a five–tape Turing machine. The first two tapes are read–only tapes containing the pattern and the text, respectively. The third tape contains differences of the $\delta$ function. On the fourth tape we compute the actual value of the $\delta$ function. The fifth tape serves as a counter for jumps toward the left end. (see Fig. 3).

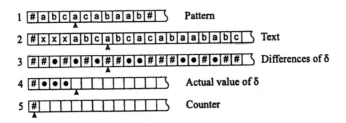

**Fig. 3.** A searching machine

At the beginning all heads are on the left end of their respective tapes. There are separators under all heads. Then the machine scans the text and for each of its character it makes several steps (we say that the machine processes the character). Now we will describe these steps in detail.

Let us suppose that the automaton finds itself is in the state $x$. This means that the first $x$ characters of the pattern match the last $x$ characters of the text. In such a case the following invariant is maintained in the searching machine.

The first head is on the $x$-th character of the pattern. The second head is on the last processed character of the text. The third head is on the separator on the right of the $x$-th value of the difference of the $\delta$ function. The actual value of the $\delta$ function is recorded by the position of the fourth head. This position corresponds to the number of markers (denoted by black spots in our figures) from the fourth head toward the left end of the tape. The fifth head is on the separator.

Then, the first two heads make one step to the right, and the machine compares characters under these two heads. There are three possible cases:

1. If the two characters are identical, the third head will go to the right to the next separator. Meanwhile, whenever the third head goes over a spot, the fourth head writes the spot and moves to the right. This ensures that after this step finishes the actual value of the $\delta$ function will be written on the fourth tape. If the first head reaches the end of the pattern, we have found an occurrence of the pattern and we can finish. Otherwise, this action is finished and we will continue with the next character of the text.

2. If the two compared characters are different and the automaton is in the state 0 (there is a separator left of the first head), then this particular character of the text has been processed and the machine will proceed to the next one.

3. If the characters under the first and the second heads are different and the machine is not in the state 0, the heads will move to the left according to the actual value of the $\delta$ function. At first, the machine will copy the actual value of the $\delta$ function from the fourth tape to the fifth one. Then it moves in the pattern (the first head) and in the differences of the $\delta$ function (the third head) toward left. The number of steps is recorded on the fifth tape. For the third head, one step means its move to the next separator toward the left. Whenever the third head goes over a spot, the fourth head deletes one spot thus adjusting the actual value of the $\delta$ function.

Then, the characters under the first two heads are again compared. Again there are three possible cases and the whole "inner loop" repeats. Whenever case (3) happens, the first head goes to the left. Thus after a finite number of steps case (1) or (2) must happen. This will stop the processing of this character.

*Complexity Analysis:* Now we can analyze the time complexity of the searching phase. We will analyze all three above mentioned cases. The complexity of case (2) is constant, so it takes $O(n)$ steps for the whole text. As the total number of backward steps is less or equal to the total number of forward steps, we also need not analyze the complexity of case (3). If we compare forward and backward steps, the backward steps only add some overhead with the copying of the actual value of the $\delta$ function from the fourth tape to the fifth one. But this overhead is linear in the size of the jump and its time is not bigger than the time of the jump. To sum up, we only have to prove that the time complexity of case (1) (forward steps) is linear in the length of the text.

Clearly, some forward steps can be relatively time–consuming but such steps occur only rarely. The only problem is when the third head goes over some large number (the difference of the $\delta$ function can be as high as $m - 1$). But when the third head moves right over some place where the number $x$ is written, then it will not move over there toward right at least for the next $x$ steps (toward left the head can move earlier but now we are analyzing forward steps). This means that time expensive steps occur only rarely and the whole complexity is linear.

# 4  Preprocessing

*The Basic Algorithm:* On a RAM with the unit cost the preprocessing of the KMP algorithm has a time complexity $O(m)$. Now we shall show the implementation of the preprocessing with the same complexity on the Turing machine.

The preprocessing will use a similar machine as the searching. The difference will be that we will not use the second tape (the text), two tapes will have a different meaning and two more tapes will be added to this machine.

First, we will show a "classical" version of the preprocessing, where the whole *fail* function is defined in $O(m)$ steps. We will prove neither its correctness nor its time complexity. This can be found for example in [1].

```
1.    state = 1; pos = 0; fail(0) = -1;
2.    while (state < m) {
3.        while (pos >= 0 && p[state]! = p[pos]) {
4.            pos = fail(pos);          // same as 'pos- = δ(pos)'
5.        }
6.        state + +; pos + +;
7.        fail(state) = pos;           // same as 'δ(state) = state - pos'
8.    }
```

We will not compute values of the *fail* function on our Turing machine. Rather we will directly compute the differences of the $\delta$ function. When one wants to rewrite the above algorithm to the Turing machine, he must solve the problem of direct access to values of the *fail* function at two different positions. This algorithm defines a new value for the position *state* and, nearly at the same time, it needs the value for the position *pos*. Therefore we must use two tapes and synchronize their contents. To ensure the linear-time complexity we used the "lazy computing" technique: the new values are copied only when they are necessary. Moreover, the classical algorithm also requires direct access to the pattern at two different locations. But this problem was solved very easily. We copied the pattern onto another tape.

The tapes of the preprocessing machine have the following meaning. The first three tapes are similar to the corresponding tapes of the searching machine. They contain the pattern, the text and the already defined differences of the $\delta$ function, respectively. On the fourth tape we will copy the pattern. The fifth and the sixth tape will be used for holding already computed values of the $\delta$ function (we will need them in line 4 of the above algorithm). To the fifth tape we will sometimes copy the actually computed differences of the $\delta$ function and the sixth tape will contain the actual value of the $\delta$ function for the fifth head. The seventh head will serve as a counter for backward steps in line 4.

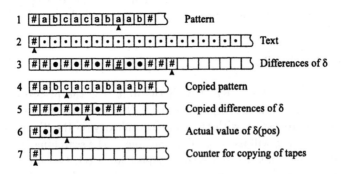

**Fig. 4.** The preprocessing machine

Now we will explain the meaning of some heads in the context of the above mentioned "classical" version of preprocessing. The position of the first head corresponds to the variable *state*. The third head is at the place where a new difference of the $\delta$ function will be defined. The position of the fourth head corresponds to the variable *pos*. The fifth and the sixth heads together give the value of $\delta(pos)$.

Our preprocessing algorithm works as follows. At the beginning, all heads are on the separators on the left side of the tapes. At first, we will copy the pattern from the first to the fourth tape. Let us suppose that we have already defined differences of the $\delta$ function for several first characters of the pattern. Now, we will define the difference for the next character. The evaluation of the condition in line 3 is easy. The fourth head checks whether it is on the separator and if it is not then the characters under the first and the fourth head will be compared.

If the condition in line 3 is true, the fourth head will go toward the left end of the tape (i.e., backwards). The number of steps is recorded on the sixth tape. Since we must maintain its contents, we will copy the contents of the sixth tape to the seventh one which will serve as a counter. These "backward steps" are ones of the most difficult parts of our preprocessing. Therefore, we will describe them in more detail.

When the fourth head moves one step toward the left, the other heads make the following actions. The fifth head moves to the next separator toward the left. Whenever the fifth head goes over a spot, the sixth head deletes a spot. At the same time, the third head adds a spot to its tape for each step of the fourth head. Note that this correctly defines the new difference of the $\delta$ function (when the fourth head makes one move toward the left, we must increase by one the actual value of the $\delta$ function).

Now, the condition in line 3 is evaluated again and if it is again true then the machine will again "go back". As soon as the condition is false, the third head writes the separator. This means that the new difference of the delta function is already defined.

Finally, the machine makes a "forward step". The first and the fourth head make one step toward the right. The fifth head goes to the next separator toward the right and whenever it goes over a spot, the sixth head adds one spot. This ensures that we can use values of $\delta(pos)$ also in the next step.

As the fifth head goes to the right, it sometimes reaches the right end of the tape (if the condition in line 3 is false). This is possible because we define new differences of the $\delta$ function only on the third tape and only a part of this tape has been already copied onto the fifth one. Therefore, as soon as the fifth head reaches the right end of this copied part, we must copy another difference from the third to the fifth tape.

To achieve a linear–time complexity, we will copy the whole uncopied part of the third tape at once. This will be done as follows. The third head returns to the position above the fifth head. Then both heads go toward the right and the third tape is copied onto the fifth one. Finally, the fifth head returns. The third head has to know how far it should go, because it does not understand the term "above the fifth head". Therefore, it has to mark the end of the already copied part of its tape by a special separator. Similarly, before copying, the fifth head marks the actual end of its tape, so it can return then.

*Time complexity of the preprocessing:* In such a way we define the differences of the $\delta$ function for all characters of the pattern. The time complexity of this algorithm is $O(m)$. For each "backward step" the third head adds one spot and as we know that the total number of spots is $m$, there can not be more than $m$ backward steps. The more difficult problem is showing that the fifth head also makes only $O(m)$ moves altogether (one step of the fourth head means that the fifth head must go to the next separator). But when the fifth head goes toward the right over some place on the tape where the difference $x$ is written, it will not go there toward the right until at least the next $x$ characters of the pattern are processed (the $x$ new differences of the $\delta$ function are defined). The number of steps toward the left is not bigger than the number of steps toward the right. (The function of the fifth head is similar to the function of the fourth head for the searching machine, so the argumentation is very similar.)

The last problem is copying the contents of the third tape to the fifth one. But it takes $O(x)$ steps to copy $x$ characters of the tape and the whole tape has only $2m$ characters. Therefore, the total time complexity of the copying is $O(m)$.

**Theorem 1.** *There exists a seven–tape Turing machine that solves the pattern matching problem in linear time.*

## 5 Conclusions

Our Turing machine algorithm shows that the asymptotic complexity of pattern matching is linear. By using standard simulation techniques between Turing machines and RAMs (cf. [3]) one can show that there is a RAM realizing pattern matching in time $O(n \log \log n)$ under the logarithmic cost criterion.

By simulating the respective Turing machine by a unit cost RAM with the word size $O(\log n)$ it seems that a pattern matching algorithms of the worst case time complexity $O(n/\log n)$ would be possible to achieve. The design of the respective algorithm is under development.

**Acknowledgement.** The author thanks her PhD advisor J. Wiedermann for suggesting the investigation of pattern matching on Turing machines and his idea of efficient realization of the next–move function with the help of differences.

## References

1. Knuth, D. E. – Morris J. H. – Pratt V. B.: Fast pattern matching in string. In: SIAM J. Comput., Vol. 6, June 1977, pp. 323–350
2. Baeza–Yates, R.: A Unified View to Pattern Matching Problems
3. Katajainen, J. – van Leeuwen, J. – Penttonen, M.: Fast Simulation of Turing Machines by Random Access Machines. In: SIAM J. Comput., Vol. 17, No.1, February 1988, pp. 77–88

# Choosing Reference Views for Image-Based Representation*

Tomáš Werner, Václav Hlaváč, Aleš Leonardis[†], Tomáš Pajdla

Czech Technical University, Faculty of Electrical Engineering
Center for Machine Perception
12135 Prague 2, Karlovo náměstí 13, Czech Republic
hlavac@vision.felk.cvut.cz
[†]Technical University of Vienna
Institute for Image Processing and Pattern Recognition
A-1040 Wien, Treitlstrasse 3, Austria
(also University of Ljubljana, Slovenia)

**Abstract.** Recently, much attention has been devoted to image-based scene representations. They allow to construct an arbitrary view of a 3-D scene by the interpolation (transfer) from a sparse set of real 2-D (*reference*) images, rather than by rendering an explicit 3-D model. While many authors address mainly the purely geometrical aspect of the task, we focus on the problem, how to select the optimal set of reference views. Selection of reference views from a dense set of real primary views is posed as a selection and fitting of parametric models. The selected set must minimize a weighted sum of the number of reference views and the total fit error. We propose two different algorithms solving this optimization problem. The experimental results on synthetic and real data indicate the feasibility of the approach for 1-DOF camera movement. We discuss the possibility to extend one of the algorithms for more general case.

## 1 Task Formulation and Concepts

It is known that given several *reference* images of a rigid scene and their correspondences, any other image can virtually be reconstructed by *image interpolation* (transfer) [SA90, Sha94, LF94]. Yet, due to occlusions and noise, different images can be reconstructed with different accuracy. The problem we address is, how to find the set of reference views such that their number is small and the accuracy of the reconstructed images is high.

We assume the image-based representation of a scene to be obtained and used as follows: (i) A large set of *primary views* of the scene is captured. (ii)

* We are indebted to Prof. Roger Hersch from the EPFL Lausanne in Switzerland who gave the initial idea, to the Swiss National Fund grant 83H-036863, grants GACR 102/95/1378, and the EU Copernicus No. 1068/1994. A. Leonardis' work was supported by the Austrian FWF grant S7002MAT and Slovenian grants J2-6187, #95-158.

A small subset of them is selected and stored as *reference views*. These form the scene representation. (iii) Any of the primary views can be reconstructed from some subset of reference views by interpolation (e.g.,[SD95, WHH95]). We call the views resulting from this process *interpolated views*. We will denote primary views by $P$, reference views by $R$, and interpolated views by $I$.

We assume that *neighborhood* is defined on the primary view set. The neighboring primary views were taken with similar camera positions and/or parameters. If each primary view has two neighbors, we talk about 1-DOF camera movement (the views form a line). Similarly, we can talk about 2-DOF camera movement (the views form a surface), etc.

In this paper, we will consider mainly 1-DOF camera movement. In this case, the primary views $P_k$ can be ordered, and numbered with a scalar index $k$ so that $P_k$ and $P_{k+1}$ are neighbors. The construction of an interpolated view $I_k$ from the primary views $P_m$ and $P_n$, considered as reference ones, can be written as

$$I(m, n; k) = interpolate(P_m, P_n; k) , \qquad (1)$$

where $m, n = 1, \ldots, N_P$ and, without loss of generality since the interpolation process is symmetric, $m < n$. We are thus assuming that a new view is in this 1-DOF case interpolated from *two* reference views. Moreover, we will make the restriction $m \leq k \leq n$, meaning that the interpolation procedure reconstructs only views *between* the reference views.

To estimate the accuracy of the reconstruction, we are able to measure difference $d(P, I)$ between a primary and an interpolated view. Then the *interpolation error* is $\epsilon(m, n; k) = d[P_k, I(m, n; k)]$. Obviously, it is $\epsilon(m, m+1; k) = 0$ as no interpolation is necessary. More about $d(P, I)$ will be said in Section 4.

## 2  Main Idea

The main idea consists in posing the problem of the optimal reference views selection as the *selection and fitting of parametric models* [SL95]. In our case of selecting the optimal set of reference views, we let

- the *model* be our interpolation method, *interpolate*$(m, n; k)$,
- the *model domain* be the set of primary views replaced by interpolated views, $\{P_k \mid m \leq k \leq n\}$,
- the *fit error* be the interpolation error, $\epsilon(m, n; k)$.

Being inspired by *Minimum Description Length Principle* (e.g., [Ris89]), we formalize the requirement "both the number of reference views and the total fit error must be small" as:

$$C = a_R N_R + a_\epsilon \sum \epsilon , \qquad (2)$$

where $N_R$ is the number of the reference views and $a_R$, $a_\epsilon$ are weights.

We used two approaches to minimizing (2). The first one (Section 3) is based on dynamic programming, the second one is based on growing and selecting viewing intervals. Due to lack of space we do not describe it here, please refer to [HLW96].

# 3   Dynamic Programming Solution

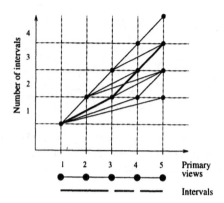

**Fig. 1.** Dynamic programming selects the path with the minimum cost.

The global minimum of (2) can be found by dynamic programming. Let us denote the minimum of the cost function (2) by $C_n$ provided that we consider only primary views $P_1, \ldots, P_n$. The minimum $C^* = C_{N_P}$ of (2) can be computed from recurrent formulas:

$$C_1 = a_R \qquad (3)$$
$$C_n = \min_{m=1,\ldots,n-1} \{C_m + c(m,n)\}$$

$c(m,n)$ is the cost of the interval bounded by views $P_m$, $P_n$ (i.e., the cost of the primitive path $(m,n)$):

$$c(m,n) = a_R + a_\epsilon \sum_{k=m}^{n} \epsilon(m,n;k) \qquad (4)$$

The optimal set of reference views can easily be obtained by storing the index $m$ for each minimum of $C_m + c(m,n)$ and backtracking these indices.

Figure 1 shows all possible selections and an example of the best selection for $N_P = 5$. Here, any possible selection of reference views can be denoted by a path connecting the node $(1,1)$ with the vertical line crossing the horizontal axis in $N_P$. Path is a concatenation of primitive paths (line segments). Any valid path must be *monotonic* and each of the primitive paths it consists of must connect *neighboring* horizontal lines.

When extending to 2-DOF or a more general case, we obviously lose simple ordering. Therefore, the dynamic programming solution *cannot* be used when the primary views are the result of 2-DOF camera movement.

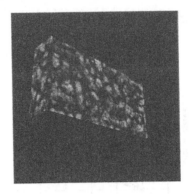

**Fig. 2.** 3-D synthetic object was a prism with a granite-like random texture warped. Lambertian reflectance model of the object's surface and four point light sources evenly distributed around the object were used.

## 4 Interpolation Error

So far, we have not discussed the specific form of the difference $d(P, I)$ between primary and corresponding interpolated view, which is used in the interpolation error $\epsilon(m, n; k)$. There is no solid background for deriving the "correct" difference function. It must be defined *ad hoc*, considering the purpose the interpolated images are to serve.

## 5 Experiments

We applied both algorithms on two kinds of data: (i) synthetic images of one simple object, taken by a virtual single-line camera (see Fig. 2), (ii) real images of one complex object. In both cases, the objects were rotated around a vertical axis and were viewed by a static camera. The objects were rotated 360° and the neighboring primary views were separated by 2°, resulting thus in 180 primary views. The rotation angle was used to order the primary views.

### 5.1 Synthetic Data, Single-Line Camera

A ray-tracer was used for synthesizing primary views. Compared to a corresponding real situation, we made the geometry one dimension simpler—a 2-D object (an intersection of the 3-D object in Figure 2 and a horizontal plane) was viewed by a 1-D (single-line) camera. The size of the images was 300 pixels.

For constructing interpolated views, transfer via the trifocal tensor [Har95] was used[2]. Dense correspondence was generated also synthetically by the ray-tracer. Therefore, the correspondence was error-free except for the sampling and quantization noise.

---

[2] It can be shown that the trifocal tensor and the corresponding trilinear relations exist not only for 3-D world and 2-D camera, but for $N$-D world and $(N-1)$-D camera, $N > 1$.

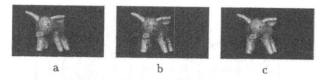

a          b          c

**Fig. 3.** A pair of reference views and the interpolated view. $(a, c)$ are the reference views ($8°$ and $16°$ in the captured sequence), $(b)$ is the interpolated view (corresponding to $12°$ in the sequence).

We designed a simple image difference function $d(P, I)$ in order to evaluate the interpolation error $\epsilon(m, n; k)$: Absolute value of the smoothed pixelwise difference of the primary view $P$ and the interpolated view $I$ was computed, and the sum of these values which were larger than a threshold was taken as $d(P, I)$.

## 5.2 Real Data

The object (a clay sculpture of a small pig) was placed on a rotating table and viewed by a static camera. The size of images was $150 \times 80$ pixels. Simple linear interpolation of positions and intensities of corresponding pixels [WHH95] was used to construct interpolated views. The binocular stereo matcher [CHMR92] was used to find a dense correspondence of neighboring reference views. An example of reference and interpolated views is shown in Figure 3.

As $d(P, I)$, we used the number of pixels in the interpolated view $I$ that could not be reconstructed due to occlusions in reference views or different sampling frequencies of reference and interpolated views[3]. These pixels are visible in Figure 3b as black points. Figure 4 shows the selected reference views/PVIs for both algorithms and kinds of data. Table 1 surveys the adjustable parameters of the algorithms[4], invested computational effort, and the numbers of selected views.

## 6 Summary

Two different algorithms for the selection of the optimal set of reference views has been presented. The optimal set has been defined as the set minimizing the objective function (2). The first algorithm, using dynamic programming, finds global minimum of (2), requires large computational effort (see Table 1) and can

---

[3] Thus, $d(P, I)$ does not explicitly depend on the primary view $P$. We made this simplification because we could not directly compute the pixelwise differences of $P$ and $I$. The reason was that the interpolation method [WHH95] yields the interpolated views geometrically distorted.

[4] The interpolation error was kept below $\epsilon_{max}$ (by letting $\epsilon(m, n; k) = +\infty$ if $\epsilon(m, n; k) > \epsilon_{max}$) also in the dynamic programming algorithm. That is the reason why $\epsilon_{max}$ is present in all columns of Table 1.

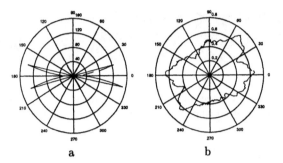

**Fig. 4.** Plot of the interpolation error for the synthetic data $(a)$ and real data $(b)$. The angle in the polar plot corresponds to $(m + n)/2$ and the radius corresponds to $\sum_{k=m}^{n} \epsilon(m, n; k)$. The distance of the reference views $m$ and $n$ is fixed and equal to $20°$.

| data | synthetic | | real | |
|---|---|---|---|---|
| $\epsilon_{max}$ | 2.5 | | 0.05 | |
| $a_R$ | 1 | | 1.0 | |
| $a_P$ | 1 | | 1.0 | |
| $a_\epsilon$ | 0.05 | | 1.0 | |
| algorithm | **DP** | **G-S** | **DP** | **G-S** |
| calls of matcher | 7065 | 372 | 2580 | 570 |
| calls of $d(P,I)$ | 161970 | 6121 | 22940 | 3944 |
| No. of sel. views | 14 | 14 | 36 | 35 |

**Table 1.** Some numerical characteristics related to the experiments. **DP** is an abbreviation for dynamic programming, **G-S** for grow-and-select. By *calls of matcher*, the number of different pairs of reference views (for which the correspondence had to be found) is meant. By *calls of $d(P,I)$*, the number of different image pairs for which $d(P,I)$ was evaluated is meant.

be used only for 1-DOF case. It is appropriate for, e.g., selecting reference views from a video sequence.

The second algorithm, based on growing and selecting plausible viewing intervals, finds suboptimum of the objective function by a heuristic optimization. It needs no ordering of primary views and thus is open for extension to 2-DOF camera movement. In that case, we would have patches instead of intervals. Yet, the crucial question is the design of the growing part with acceptable computational effort needed.

The main drawback of the whole approach is the assumption of the restricted form (1) of the interpolation procedure. Currently, interpolated views are constructed from only two reference views and only in-between them. More sophisticated interpolation procedure is needed to eliminate the influence of the

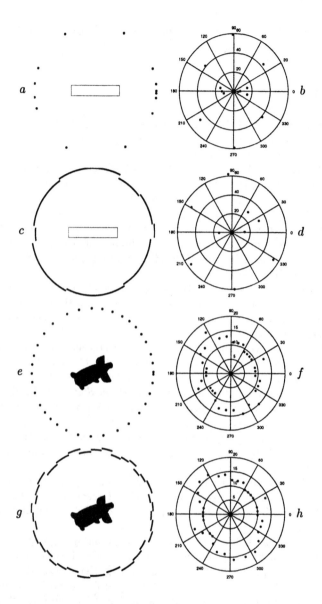

**Fig. 5.** The results of experiments. Subfigures (a, b, c, d) and (e, f, g, h) apply for synthetic and real data, respectively. Subfigures (a, c, e, g) and (b, d, f, h) show the selected reference views/PVIs and the distances between neighboring reference views, resp. Subfigures (a, b, e, f) and (c, d, g, h) apply for the algorithm from Section 3 and region growing algorithm, resp. Top views of the experimental objects were superimposed to (a, c, e, g).

occlusions more effectivelly, however, our current algorithms cannot be directly extended to this more general case.

# References

[GL93]     F. Glover and M. Laguna. Tabu search. In C. R. Reeves, editor, *Modern heuristic techniques for combinatorial problems*, pages 70–150. Blackwell Scientific Publications, 1993.

[Har95]    R.I. Hartley. A linear method for reconstruction from lines and points. In *Proceedings of the 5th International Conference on Computer Vision*, pages 882–887, Boston, USA, June 1995. IEEE.

[HLW96]    V. Hlaváč, A. Leonardis, and T. Werner. Automatic selection of reference views for image-based scene representations. In *Proceedings of the European Conference in Computer Vision*, volume 1 of *Lecture Notes in Computer Science, No. 1064*, pages 526–535, Cambridge, U.K., April 1996. Springer-Verlag, Heidelberg, Germany.

[CHMR92]   Ingemar J. Cox, Sunita Hingorani, Bruce M. Maggs, and Satish B. Rao. Stereo without disparity gradient smoothing: a Bayesian sensor fusion solution. In *British Machine Vision Conference*, pages 337–346, Berlin, 1992. Springer-Verlag.

[LF94]     Stéphane Laveau and Olivier Faugeras. 3-D scene representation as a collection of images. In *Proc. of 12th International Conf. on Pattern Recognition, Jerusalem, Israel*, pages 689–691, October 9–13 1994.

[Ris89]    Jorma Rissanen. *Stochastic Complexity in Statistical Inquiry*. World Scientific Publishing Co., Series in Computer Science, IBM Almaden Research Center, San Jose, California U.S.A, 1989.

[SA90]     M. Spetsakis and J. Alomoinos. A unified theory of structure from motion. In *Proceedigs ARPA Image Understanding Workshop*, pages 271–283, Pittsburg, PA, USA, 1990.

[SD95]     S.M. Seitz and C.R. Dyer. Physically-valid view synthesis by image interpolation. In *Proceedings of the Visual Scene Representation Workshop, Boston, MA., USA, June 24*, pages 18–27. IEEE Computer Society Press, 1995.

[Sha94]    A. Shashua. Trilinearity in visual recognition by alignment. In *Proceedings of the 3rd European Conference on Computer Vision, Stockholm, Sweden*, volume 1, pages 479–484. Springer-Verlag, Heidelberg, 1994.

[SL95]     M. Stricker and A. Leonardis. ExSel++: A general framework to extract parametric models. In V. Hlaváč and R. Šára, editors, *6th International Conference on Computer Analysis of Images and Patterns, CAIP'95*, number 970 in Lecture Notes in Computer Science, pages 90–97, Prague, Czech Republic, September 1995. Springer-Verlag, Heidelberg.

[WHH95]    T. Werner, R.D. Hersch, and V. Hlaváč. Rendering real-world objects using view interpolation. In *Proceedings of the 5th International Conference on Computer Vision*, pages 957–962, Boston, USA, June 1995. IEEE Press.

# Recognizing Graph Products and Bundles

Janez Žerovnik

[1] FME, University of Maribor, Smetanova 17, 2000 Maribor, Slovenia
[2] IMFM/TCS, Jadranska 19, 1111 Ljubljana, Slovenia.

**Abstract.** Problems of recognition of product graphs and graph bundles with respect to Cartesian, categorical, strong and lexicographic product are considered. A short survey of results and open problems is given.

## 1 Introduction

Knowledge of the structure of a graph often leads to faster algorithms for solving combinatorial problems on these graphs. In general, an efficient algorithm for recognizing a special class of graphs may allow us to compute certain graph invariants faster. For example, the chromatic number of a Cartesian product is the maximum of the chromatic numbers of the factors. Computing the chromatic number is in general an NP–hard problem, but factoring can be done in polynomial time. Hence, if the graph is a Cartesian product, we can save computation time by first factoring and then computing the chromatic numbers of the factors.

In this paper a short survey of algorithmic results on recognition of product graphs (Section 3) and graph bundles (Section 4) is given.

## 2 Definitions

We now give some definitions, in particular we define certain relations on the edge set of a graph which proved to be useful in studies of products and bundles. Another important notion is convexity. We define convex and $k$-convex subgraphs and also convex and weakly convex relations. (We need this definitions to give more details on the results for Cartesian and for strong product.)

Although some of the results mentioned can be generalized to infinite graphs, we study here only finite undirected graphs without loops or multiple edges since we are mainly interested in algorithmic problems. If $G$ is a graph, we shall write $V(G)$ or $V$ for its vertex set and $E(G)$ or $E$ for its edge set. $E(G)$ shall be considered as a set of unordered pairs $\{x, y\} = xy = yx$ of distinct vertices of $G$. Considering $G$ as $V(G) \cup E(G)$, we often write $x \in G$ for $x \in V(G)$ and $e \in G$ for $e \in E(G)$. We say that two edges are *adjacent* if they have a common vertex. Furthermore, $G \cong H$ denotes graph isomorphism, i.e. the existence of a bijection $b : V(G) \to V(H)$ such that vertices $v_1, v_2$ are adjacent in $G$ exactly if $b(v_1), b(v_2)$ are adjacent in $H$. A *walk* between vertices $x$ and $y$ is a sequence of vertices $P = v_0, v_1, \ldots, v_\ell$ such that each pair $v_{i-1}v_i$ is an edge of $G$. If all vertices of $P$ are distinct, then $P$ is a *path*. The *length* of $P$ is the number of edges, $|P| = \ell$. Graph is *connected,* if there is a path of finite length between every pair of vertices. If not stated otherwise, we will always assume that graphs are connected.

Of the numerous possible products of graphs the Cartesian product, the categorical (weak, cardinal) product, the strong product and the lexicographic product (also called composition of graphs) are most important ones. All these products are associative (for a classification of all possible associative products, see [11]). Cartesian, categorical and strong products are also commutative. The graph on one vertex is the unit for Cartesian, strong and lexicographic product.

The *Cartesian product* $G \Box H$ of graphs $G$ and $H$ has as vertices the pairs $(v, w)$ where $v \in V(G)$ and $w \in V(H)$. $(v_1, w_1)$ and $(v_2, w_2)$ are connected if $\{v_1, v_2\}$ is an edge of $G$ and $w_1 = w_2$, or if $v_1 = v_2$ and $\{w_1, w_2\}$ is an edge of $H$.

Cartesian product graph is up to isomorphism determined by its factors, the order being unimportant. For product of more than two factors, we write $G = \Box_{\iota \in I}^{a} G_{\iota}$.

Common examples of Cartesian products are squares, hypercubes, prisms (Cartesian products of $n$–gons by an edge) or the square lattice as the product of two infinite paths.

Here are simple examples of a Cartesian product and of a strong product.

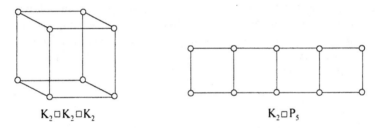

$$K_2 \Box K_2 \Box K_2 \qquad\qquad K_2 \Box P_5$$

All products are defined on the Cartesian product of sets of vertices of their factors. The edges for the *categorical product* $G \times H$ are defined as follows: $(v_1, w_1)$ and $(v_2, w_2)$ are connected if $\{v_1, v_2\}$ is an edge of $G$ and $\{w_1, w_2\}$ is an edge of $H$.

Edges of the *strong product* $G \boxtimes H$ are the union of the set of Cartesian edges and the set of categorical product edges (i.e. $E(G \boxtimes H) = E(G \Box H) \cup E(G \times H)$.)

The Cartesian, the categorical and the strong product of two edges gives $\Box$, $\times$ and $\boxtimes$, respectively. Hence the notation, which was proposed by Nešetril.

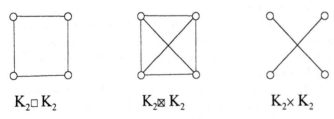

$$K_2 \Box K_2 \qquad\qquad K_2 \boxtimes K_2 \qquad\qquad K_2 \times K_2$$

The lexicographic product $G \circ H$ has edges defined with: $(v_1, w_1)$ and $(v_2, w_2)$ are connected if either $\{v_1, v_2\}$ is an edge of $G$ or if $v_1 = v_2$ and $\{w_1, w_2\}$ is an edge of $H$.

Now we define relations $\sigma$, $\delta$ and $\Theta$ on $E(G)$ and state some of their properties.

**Definition.** Let $G = \square^a_{\iota \in I} G_\iota$. Call $e = \{u, v\}$ a $G_\kappa$-edge if $e$ connects vertices $u$ and $v$ such that $u_\iota = v_\iota$ for all $\iota \neq \kappa$ and $\{v_\kappa, u_\kappa\} \in E(G_\kappa)$. We say that two edges $e, f$ are in the relation $\sigma(\square^a_{\iota \in I} G_\iota)$ if there is an $\iota$ such that both $e$ and $f$ are $G_\iota$ edges.

Clearly $\sigma(\square^a_{\iota \in I} G_\iota)$ is an equivalence relation. Because of the unique factorization theorem there exists a finest relation induced by a Cartesian product representation of $G$. This relation is denoted by $\sigma_G$ or simply $\sigma$.

**Definition.** Let $e, f \in E(G)$. We say $e$ and $f$ are in the relation $\delta$ if one of the following two conditions is satisfied

(1) $e$ and $f$ are opposite edges of a chordless square.
(2) $e$ and $f$ are adjacent and there is no chordless square containing $e$ and $f$ or $e = f$.

Clearly $\delta$ is reflexive and symmetric, hence its transitive closure $\delta^\star$ is an equivalence relation.

By the definition of $\delta$ any pair of adjacent edges which belong to distinct $\delta$ equivalence classes span a square without a diagonal. Furthermore, if these edges are in different classes with respect to $\delta^\star$, then there is exactly one such square. We say that the relation $\delta^\star$ has the *square property*. It is easy to see that the square property also holds for any equivalence relation containing $\delta^\star$. Note that every product relation $\sigma(\square^a_{\iota \in I} G_\iota)$ contains $\delta$ and thus has the square property.

**Definition.** Let $e = \{x, y\} \in E(G)$ and $f = \{x', y'\} \in E(G)$ be two edges of $G$. We say that $e$ and $f$ are in the relation $\Theta$ if $d(x, x') + d(y, y') \neq d(x, y') + d(x', y)$.

In the strong and the categorical product, although the graph is up to isomorphism uniquely factorable, some vertices may be interchangeable. We define two relations on the vertex set of a graph as follows. $uRv$ if every vertex of $G$ is either connected with both $u$ and $v$ or with none of them. $uSv$ if $uv \in E(G)$ and if every vertex of $G$ is either connected with both $u$ and $v$ or with none of them. When interested in categorical product, we call $G$ *thin* if it has trivial relation $R$. If we study strong product, we call $G$ *thin* if it has trivial relation $S$.

Let $H$ be a subgraph of $G$. Then $H$ is *convex* (in $G$) if all shortest $G$–paths between two vertices of $H$ are already in $H$.

Let $H$ be a connected subgraph of $G$. We say that $H$ is *k-convex in $G$* if for any pair of vertices $u, v \in V(H)$ of distance $d_G(u, v) \leq k$ the set of all shortest paths $I_G(u, v)$ from $u$ to $v$ in $G$ is also contained in $H$: $I_G(u, v) \subseteq I_H(u, v)$. The usual convexity is the same as $\infty$-convexity and a subgraph is induced if and only if it is 1-convex. If graph $H$ is not connected, we define: $H$ is *k-convex in $G$* if and only if each of its connected components is $k$-convex.

A natural way for defining convexity of relations is to call a relation convex if the graphs induced by its equivalence classes are convex. It turns out, however, that such a definition is not strong enough for our purpose. Therefore the following definition was proposed in [13]:

**Definition.** Let $\gamma$ be an equivalence relation with equivalence classes $E_\iota$, $\iota \in I$. We say $\gamma$ is *convex* if for any $K \subseteq I$ every connected component of the graph induced on $\cup_{\iota \in K} E_\iota$ is convex.

Examples of convex relations considered here are the Cartesian product relation $\sigma(\square_{\iota \in I}^a G_\iota)$ and relation $\Theta$.

It is not obvious from the above definition whether the intersection of convex relations is convex. It can be shown that it is true for equivalence relations containing $\delta$. Hence, for the relations of interest in this paper we can define the *convex hull* $C(\rho)$ of a relation $\rho$ to be the minimal convex equivalence relation containing $\rho$. More precisely, $\gamma = C(\rho)$ if $\gamma$ is convex, contains $\delta$ and $\rho$ and if for any convex relation $\gamma' \supseteq \rho$ we have $\gamma \subseteq \gamma'$.

Let $B$ and $F$ be graphs. A graph $G$ is a *(Cartesian) graph bundle* with fibre $F$ over the base graph $B$ if there is a mapping $p: G \to B$ which satisfies the following conditions:

1. It maps adjacent vertices of $G$ to adjacent or identical vertices in $B$.
2. The edges are mapped to edges or collapsed to a vertex.
3. For each vertex $v \in V(B)$, $p^{-1}(v) \cong F$, and for each edge $e \in E(B)$, $p^{-1}(e) \cong K_2 \square F$.

Graph bundles can be seen as 'twisted product'. A small example of a Cartesian graph bundle is $K_{3,3}$ below. It is a discrete nalog of the well-known Möbious band, which is a topological bundle (base is a circle, fibres are lines).

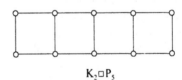

$K_2 \square K_2 \square K_2$

$K_2 \square P_5$

To get definitions of graph bundles with respect to other products just replace $\square$ with some other product.

For a given graph $G$ there may be several mappings $p_\iota : G \to B_\iota$ with the above properties. In such cases we write $(G, p_\iota, B_\iota)$ to avoid confusion. We say an edge $e$ is *degenerate* (with respect to $\iota$) if $p(e)$ is a vertex. Otherwise we call it *nondegenerate*. A factorization of a graph $G$ is a collection of spanning subgraphs $H_i$ of $G$ such that the edge set of $G$ is partitioned into the edge sets of the graphs $H_i$. In other words, the set $E(G)$ can be written as a disjoint union of the sets $E(H_i)$. The projection $p$ induces a factorization of $G$ into the graph consisting of isomorphic copies of the fibre $F$ and the graph $\tilde{G}$ consisting of all nondegenerate edges. This factorization is called the *fundamental factorization*. It can be shown that the restriction of $p$ to $\tilde{G}$ is a covering projection of graphs; see for instance [17], [18] for details.

# 3   Products

Products of graphs were first studied by Sabidussi [19]. In eighties, interest for products of graphs rised again, mainly because of some algorithmic problems and some applications in computer science.

It is well known that all finite connected graphs have unique prime factorizations [19, 20]. Based on Sabidussi's method Feigenbaum, Herschberger and Schäffer [5] developed a decomposition algorithm with running time $O(n^{4.5})$, where $n$ is the number of vertices of the graph. Independently, Winkler [21] presented an $O(n^4)$ algorithm which is based on a method of isometrically embedding graphs into Cartesian products by Graham and Winkler [9]. The product relation which defines the prime factorization is the transitive closure of the union of the starting relations of the algorithms by Feigenbaum et al. and by Winkler [4, 22, 13]. More formally,

$$\sigma = (\theta \cup \delta)^{\star}.$$

As Feder already remarks, this leads to a simple algorithm with running time $O(nm)$. Due to its simplicity, this algorithm has high inherent parallelism and is efficient on the P-RAM parallel model of computation. In other words, it has polylogarithmic time complexity on a polynomial number of processors.

We should recall that the best known algorithm for decomposing a connected graph into prime factors with respect to the Cartesian product is due to Aurenhammer, Hagauer and Imrich [2]. It has time complexity $O(m \log n)$ and is based on an entirely different approach. Their method does not seem to be easily parallelizable.

**Problem 1** *Is the $O(m \log n)$ complexity the best possible for recognition of Cartesian product graphs?*

Another characterization of $\sigma$ is $\sigma = \mathcal{C}(\delta)$ i.e. the convex hull of the local product relation [13]. This result does not seem to give a fast algorithm, since we do not know

**Problem 2** *What is the complexity of a good (the best) algorithm for computing the convex closure of a relation? (or at least closure of the relation $\delta$)*

Cartesian product graphs can be found in many applications. For example Hamming graphs are used in coding theory. It may be interesting to recall that Hamming graphs and median graphs are isometric subgraphs of Cartesian products. There are $O(mn)$ [12] and $O(D + n^2)$ [3] algorithms for recognition of

Hamming graphs. ($D$ is time neeeded to compute the distance matrix of $G$.) Median graphs can be recognized in time $O(n^{3/2} \log n)$ [10].

Another application is in design of interconnection networks, hypercubes being only the most well known example. For a given network, it may be of interest to known how many nodes and connections have to be added to obtain a product graph topology. The problem is NP-hard [6]. But if we restrict to question whether it is possible to construct a Cartesian product graph by adding only one vertex and only edges connecting the new vertex to the rest of the graph, the problem is polynomial [14].

The categorical product of two graphs is connected if and only if both factors are connected and at least one is not bipartite. Lovász has shown that for any three graphs $G, H, C$

$$G \times C \simeq H \times C \quad \text{implies} \quad G \simeq H$$

if $C$ contains at least one loop [16].

**Problem 3** *Find a polynomial algorithm for recognition of categorical product graphs?*

According to Sandi Klavžar, Problem 3 was recently solved by Imrich.

The set of edges of the strong product is the union of edges of Cartesian product and edges of categorical product. Cartesian edges can be recognized in polynomial time. Together with the observation that a graph can be reduced to a thin one in polynomial time by forming the quotient with respect to $S$ this is the basis of the polynomial decomposition algorithm by Feigenbaum and Schäffer [8]

**Problem 4** *What is the complexity of best possible algorithm for recognition of strong product graphs?*

Feigenbaum and Schäffer [7] showed that the problem of recognizing composite graphs with respect to the lexicographic product is equivalent to testing graph isomorphism, which is well known to be one of the few candidates for membership in $NP - P$ which is not NP-complete.

# 4  Bundles

Graph bundles [18, 17] generalize the notion of covering graphs and graph products. While at least for some products there are polynomial algorithms, it is known that recognition of covering graphs is NP-hard [1].

In contrast to the unique factorization property of product graphs, a graph may have more than one presentation as a graph bundle. Natural questions therefore are to find all possible presentations of a graph as a graph bundle or to decide whether a graph has at least one presentation as a nontrivial graph bundle.

It is known that Cartesian and strong bundles with totally disconnected fibre are covering graphs. A bundle with respect to categorical product with totally disconnected fibre is a trivial graph without any edge. We will therefore restrict our attention to cases where fibres are connected.

In [15] it is shown

**Lemma 1** *Let G be a graph bundle whose base graph contains no triangles and let $\varphi$ be any equivalence class of $\delta^{\star}$ containing only degenerate edges. If $\rho := C_2(\varphi, \delta^{\star}) \neq E(G)$, then $G$ is a graph bundle with fibres being the connected components of $G_\rho$.*

Here, $C_2(\varphi, \delta^{\star})$ is a certain closure of the relation $\delta$.

**Problem 5** *Find an optimal algorithm for recognition of Cartesian bundles over triangle free base?*

**Problem 6** *Is there a polynomial algorithm for recognition of Cartesian bundles over arbitrary base?*

**Problem 7** *Is there a polynomial algorithm for recognition of strong bundles?*

The answer to Problem 7 seem to be positive [24].

**Problem 8** *Is there a polynomial algorithm for recognition of categorical bundles?*

**Acknowledgement:** The author wishes to thank Sandi Klavžar for helpful comments on the manuscript.

# References

1. J.Abello, M.R.Fellows and J.C.Stillwell: On the Complexity and Combinatorics of Covering Finite Complexes, Australasian Journal of Combinatorics **4** (1991) 103-112.

2. F.Aurenhammer, J.Hagauer and W.Imrich: Cartesian Graph Factorization at Logarithmic Cost per Edge, Computational Complexity **2** (1992) 331-349.

3. F.Aurenhammer, M.Formann, R.Idury, A.Schäffer and F.Wagner: Faster Isometric Embedding in Products of Complete Graphs, Discrete Applied Mathematics **52** (1994) 17-28.

4. T.Feder: Product Graph Representations, Journal of Graph Theory **16** (1992) 467-488.

5. J.Feigenbaum, J.Hershberger and A.A.Schäffer: A Polynomial Time Algorithm for Finding the Prime Factors of Cartesian-Product Graphs, Discrete Applied Mathematics **12** (1985) 123-138.

6. J. Feigenbaum, R. Haddad: On Factorable Extensions and Subgraphs of Prime Graphs, SIAM J. Disc. Math **2** (1989) 197-218.

7. J.Feigenbaum and A.A.Schäffer: Recognizing composite graphs is equivalent to testing graph isomorphism, SIAM J.Comp. **15** (1986) 619-627.

8. J.Feigenbaum and A.A.Schäffer: Finding the Prime Factors of Strong Direct Product Graphs in Polynomial Time, Discrete Math. **109** (1992) 77-102.

9. R.L.Graham and P.M.Winkler: On Isometric Embeddings of Graphs, Transactions of the American Mathematical Society **288** (1985) 527-536.

10. J. Hagauer, W. Imrich and S. Klavžar: Recognizing graphs of windex 2, Preprint, 1993.

11. W.Imrich and H.Izbicki: Associative Products of Graphs, Monat. für Math. **80** (1975) 277-281.

12. W.Imrich and S.Klavžar: A simple $O(mn)$ algorithm for recognizing Hamming graphs, Bull. Inst. Combin. Appl. **9** (1993) 45-56.

13. W.Imrich and J.Žerovnik: Factoring Cartesian-product Graphs, Journal of Graph Theory **18** (1994) 557-567.

14. W.Imrich and J.Žerovnik: On the weak reconstruction of Cartesian-product graphs, Discrete Mathematics, vol.150 (1996) 167-178.

15. W.Imrich, T.Pisanski and J.Žerovnik, Recognizing Cartesian graph bundles, to appear in Discrete Mathematics.

16. L.Lovasz: Operations with structures, Acta Math. Acad. Sci. Hungaricae **18** (1967) 321-328.

17. T.Pisanski, J. Shawe–Taylor and J.Vrabec, Edge–colorability of graph bundles, Journal of Combinatorial Theory Series B **35** (1983) 12-19.

18. T.Pisanski and J.Vrabec, Graph bundles, unpublished manuscript, 1982.

19. G.Sabidussi: Graph Multiplication, Mathematische Zeitschrift **72** (1960) 446-457.

20. V.G.Vizing: The Cartesian Product of Graphs (in Russian), Vyčisl.Syst. 9 (1963) 30-43, (English translation: Comp.El.Syst. 2 (1966) 352-365).

21. P.M.Winkler: Factoring a Graph in Polynomial Time, European Journal of Combinatorics **8** (1987) 209-212.

22. J.Žerovnik, A simple algorithm for factoring Cartesian product graphs, Arbeitsbericht 5/1991, Montanuniversitaet Leoben.

23. J.Hagauer and J.Žerovnik, An algorithm for the weak reconstruction of Cartesian-product graphs, submitted. (also in Preprint Series Vol.33 (1995) 470, Department of Mathematics, University of Ljubljana.)

24. J.Žerovnik, Recognizing strong bundles, in preparation.

# Genetic Algorithms-Based Creation of Fuzzy-Rule Bases for the Car Control

Jan Žižka and Zdeněk Kratochvíl

Department of Automation and Instrumentation, Technical University of Brno
Božetěchova 2, 612 66 Brno, Czech Republic
E-mail: zizka@dame.fee.vutbr.cz

**Abstract.** This paper presents an application of genetic algorithms (GA) to the automated generation of fuzzy-rule bases. The evolved fuzzy-rule bases are used for the fuzzy control of a simulated car when the drive is influenced by side-wind effects. GA generate and optimize the number of state variables with their respective values defined as fuzzy sets and the number and composition of fuzzy control-rules. The method used in this paper strongly reduces the number of rules (the rules simulate actions of a driver and are needed for the successful control of the car), and provides better results in comparison with fuzzy controllers created by human designers.

## 1 Introduction

One of the very successful applications of fuzzy logic is process control. The idea is quite simple: for many nonlinear systems, it is very difficult or impossible to create a good mathematical model and to apply the classical control theory. However, such systems can be controlled by experienced human operators very well. Using the extracted human knowledge represented as rules, these systems may be also controlled by intelligent automatic controllers. During his or her control actions, the human operator thinks usually in approximate notions rather than in exact crisp values. Such notions can be modeled by fuzzy sets distributed in their corresponding universes where systems' state variables take their values. Designers of fuzzy control systems determine the input and output state variables, then for each typical combination of the input values set up the output values, or, in other words, the control actions. Many industrial and other applications of fuzzy logic were described in literature, see, e.g., (Dubois et al, 1993). Even if the idea itself is so simple, its realization is often a difficult and tedious process. The design of an efficient and optimal – or nearly optimal – control system is often problematic because there is no clear way how to distribute and combine too many possible input and output values. The designer must face the problem of very high combinatorial complexity. In this paper, we suggest a general automatic method how to select values of the state variables and how to combine them so that the result is (nearly) optimal from the control criterions' point of view. In addition, the method presented here automatically generates – even from the scratch – rules and determines their number and composition. Our method is based on the application of the nowadays popular Artificial Intelligence tool called Genetic Algorithms, inspired in biological genetics.

　　To demonstrate the abilities of automatically generated fuzzy rule-bases, we chose the problem of a car driving on a road and being deflected from the ideal direction by side-wind effects. This is a situation known to many drivers: a sudden gust of wind can move the car aside. The deflection depends on several factors, mainly on the velocity of the car and on the speed and angle of the wind. It would be very favorable if the side-wind effect could be automatically compensated, at least to a certain degree. Under normal conditions, every experienced driver can keep his or her car on the road within the given lane. Human drivers behave quite well, however, it is unfortunately not known how to model their behavior mathematically. The driver subconsciously compensates the car's deflection, following the general rules like this: if the deflection is fast and strongly to the right then the control action is turning the steering wheel strongly to the left. Drivers do not care what the exact values are; they simply think in approximate terms as "strongly to the right," "big turning angle of the steering wheel," and so like. Therefore, having no suitable model of the driver, the alternative knowledge-based approach is considered. The model of the driver can be created using a set of rules, which describe the driver's actions depending actual situations. Taking into account the actual change of the car's direction, it is possible to decide the change of the steering-wheel turning-angle to obtain again the correct position of the car on the road. The control action may be inferred from the rules using appropriate mechanisms, which in our case is fuzzy logic in its broader sense (Hájek, 1995).

## 2 Fuzzy Rule-Based Control

A fuzzy rule consists of the conditional part (antecedent) and the consequent connected by a specific implementation of the logical connective *THEN*. The antecedent part may consist of a set of partial fuzzy goals to be fulfilled; the goals are connected by a specific implementation of the logical connective *AND*: IF $x_1 = A_{1j}$ AND ... AND $x_m = A_{mj}$ THEN $y = B_j$ OR *next_rule*. Here $x_i \in X_i$ is an $i$-th input state-variable defined in its corresponding universe $X_i$, $y \in Y$ is the output state-variable in the universe $Y$, $A_{ij} \subseteq X_i$ is a fuzzy set (an approximate value) defined in its corresponding universe $X_i$, $B_j \subseteq Y$ is the output fuzzy set in $Y$, where $j$ is the rule index ($j=1, \ldots, n$, $n$ is the number of rules), and $i$ is the input variable index ($i=1, \ldots, m$, $m$ is the number of input variables). All rules are aggregated in the rule base by the logical connective *OR*, which must be implemented in a specific way. In our experiments, we implemented the *AND* connective by the operator $\wedge$ (minimum) and sometimes (extreme velocities of the car) by the operator * (the algebraic product). The connective *THEN* was always implemented by $\wedge$ [i.e., we used the compositional rule of inference, cf., e.g., (Kruse et al, 1994)], and the connective *OR* was realized by $\vee$ (maximum). So, we employed two kinds of fuzzy inference: *Min-Max* and *Prod-Max*, see, e.g., (Žižka and Pivoňka, 1995) for details.

For the description of the driver's situation, we chose four input variables: the car's side shift from the middle of the lane, the time change of this shift, the car's turn angle, and the time change of the turn. For the output variable we used the steering-wheel turn-angle compensating the car's deflection. This selection enabled us to model the driver's behavior using a set of rules where each rule had the form similar to the following example:

```
IF car_angle=BIG+ AND car_angle_change=ZERO AND car_shift=MEDIUM_LEFT
AND car_shift_change=SMALL+ THEN steering-wheel_turn=BIG-
```

The interpretation of the given rule is that the car is substantially turned to the left, the angle does not change, the car is somehow shifted to the left and the shift increases slightly; consequently, the driver's control action is a big turn of the steering wheel to the right. Values such as *BIG+, ZERO, MEDIUM_LEFT, SMALL+, BIG-* etc. are labels of fuzzy sets, which model approximate values. Each fuzzy set is represented by its membership function $\mu_A(x)$ defined within the real unit interval $(0.0 \leq \mu_A(x) \leq 1.0)$ that expresses to what degree a specific point $x \in X$ matches a certain approximate value $A$, cf. (Dubois et al, 1993). For example, *angle=BIG+* can denote "a big positive angle value," which may be an angle greater than $60°$ with no sharp boundaries with adjacent overlapped values. As its result, fuzzy reasoning provides an approximate value, too, which has the form of a composed fuzzy set. During the inference process, more than one rule can fire; therefore, more rules contribute partially – to a lesser or greater degree – to the overall result. All the partial solutions (fuzzy sets defined in rules' consequents) are aggregated using the *OR* operator, which is usually the set union implemented as *maximum*. The crisp control action (steering-wheel turn-angle) is obtained by defuzzification of the aggregated fuzzy set.

# 3  Genetic Algorithms

Genetic Algorithms (GA) have recently become an often applied Artificial Intelligence tool. The main reason is that GA enable its users to perform a search within a solution space in those cases when no analytical/algorithmic solution is available or the problem has exponential complexity. While using straightforward enumerative schemes (i.e., looking at objective function values at every point in the space) is simple, it suffers from the lack of efficiency. Many practical spaces are simply too large. GA are an example of search procedures that use random choice as a tool to guide a highly exploitative search through a coding of a parameter space. A good introduction to GA can be found in Goldberg's book (Goldberg, 1989). GA are inspired in the mechanics of natural selection and natural genetics. They combine survival of the fittest among string structures with a structured yet randomized information exchange to form a search algorithm with some innovative flair of a human search. In every generation, a new set of artificial creatures (strings) is created using bits and pieces of the fittest of the old. Essentially, an application of GA to searching for an optimal (or for nearly optimal) solution consists of the following five steps:

  (1) generate the initial population
  (2) perform genetic operations (e.g., a crossover, mutation, reproduction)
  (3) evaluate individual solutions by calculating their scores
  (4) select the best solutions with the highest scores
  (5) if the requested goal is not reached repeat again from the step. No. 2

The expression "requested goal" usually means a minimized error (or cost) function. A population is a generation of individual entities whose features are encoded usually into bit strings called *chromosomes*. Each feature in a chromosome is called a *gene*. Combinations of genes determine the quality of a solution. Therefore, GA look for chromosomes having the best fitness for a requested task. This paper describes the application of GA to automatic generation of rule bases where rules consist of values modeled as fuzzy sets.

The concrete realization of GA for a given task requires specific implementation of genetic operators. Our system was supposed to produce fuzzy rules with fuzzy sets having a general trapezoidal shape both in the conditional and in the consequent part of a rule. Positions and base lengths of trapezoids distributed as fuzzy values in corresponding universes were encoded into bit strings. A trapezoid can be described by four numerical coordinates on its universe. Regardless of the actual ranges of values, every number was normalized by linear transformation into the interval [0, 255], i.e., into a string consisting of 8 bits. These strings were concatenated into one long bit string where the meaning of each substring was given by its position (positional encoding). Each rule can be seen as a string consisting of fuzzy-set coordinate values. Concatenated rule strings created individual controllers (chromosomes). The reason for this transformation is that such a representation allows highly efficient bit-like coding and processing of values. When an actual value is needed, it is re-mapped from the normalized interval into the original range. For the crossover of chromosome couples, where each chromosome represented a set of fuzzy rules (i.e., a fuzzy controller), the crossover point was chosen randomly within the bit string; the position of the crossover could be anywhere, even inside the encoded numbers, which resulted in creation of new genes. Because all the chromosomes were of the same length, the crossover point was the same for each pair. Chromosome couples were selected randomly, however, with respect to their survival probability. The survival probability $p_{qi}$ of an individual depended on its quality $q_i$ ($i=1, \ldots, N$, where $N$ is the number of individuals) and on its difference from the rest of population. Using general requirements needed for determination of $p_{qi}$ (see, e.g., Winston, 1992), we developed the following formula:

$$p_{qi} = \frac{1}{N}\left(1 - \ln\prod_{i=1}^{N}\left(1 + \frac{q'_{max} - q'_i}{Q'}\right)\right) + \ln\left(1 + \frac{q'_{max} - q'_i}{Q'}\right) \tag{1}$$

where

$$q'_i = \ln(1+q_i), \quad q'_{max} = \max_{i=1}^{N}(q'_i), \quad Q' = \sum_{i=1}^{N}(q'_{max} - q'_i) \tag{2}$$

In **Equation (1)** and **(2)**, the quality $q_i$ (see also **Equation (3)**) of an individual never equals zero because the car always changes its position and angle on the road owing to the sidewind. A chromosome quality function depended on the relative significance of individual controller parameters. Usually, this function is formulated as the sum of integrals of selected variable deviations from their desired values. In our case, we defined the following quality function (the error quadratic measure) to evaluate evolved fuzzy controllers, where $t$ means the testing time:

$$q = 1000(160 - t) + K_c\left(\int e^2\, dt + 1000\int\left(\frac{d\alpha}{dt}\right)^2 dt + \int\left(\frac{d\beta}{dt}\right)^2 dt\right) \tag{3}$$

In **Equation (3)**, the first integral represents the accumulated car's shift from the middle of the lane, the second integral represents the car's turn angle, and the third integral expresses the amount of steering-wheel changes – the lesser is this value the smaller is the car's "swivelling" on the road. Each controller was tested either during the whole testing interval (160 seconds) or until the moment when the car's shift from the middle of the lane exceeded

1.5 m. So the expression $1000(160-t)$ guarantees the absolute priority of the car's position within the lane. The constant $K_c$ influences the number of fuzzy sets because smaller number of fuzzy sets means a more simple controller:

$$K_c = \sqrt[3]{(n_1'+1)\cdots(n_N'+1)}, \quad n_i' = n_i \; div \; 2 \tag{4}$$

where $n_i$ is the number of actually used fuzzy sets for the $i$-th variable and $N$ is the number of the input variables. The goal was to reduce the overall error in the car's position so lower $q$ corresponded to higher quality.

To prevent irrecoverable loss of some potentially useful genetic material, the *mutation* operator was applied. Mutation inverts randomly selected bit values in strings. In our case, we chose the probability of mutation so that on average four bits of each string were inverted. Under normal conditions, mutation is applied only to new individuals. However, in the case of population degradation (all individuals have very similar features and there is almost no difference between the quality of the best individual and the average one), mutation was applied to the parent chromosomes. The measure of the degradation was given by the ratio $(q_{average}-q_{best})/q_{best}$. If the ratio was less than $1/500$, the population was mutated normally. When the ratio was less than $1/10000$, the probability was increased 10 times, however, the best chromosome was never changed.

## 4 The Car Model

As we were interested in a car's behavior when it drives on a road under the side-wind influence, which makes the vehicle change its position, we developed the corresponding mathematical model to verify solutions generated by GA. The plane dynamical model assumes that the car's center of gravity is in the road plane which means that the car's body leaning (e.g., in curves) is neglected. The drive of the car is described by the following two linear nonhomogeneous differential **Equations (5)** and **(6)**, which can be solved – after the substitution of symbolic values with the real ones – e.g., by the Runge-Kutta method:

$$mv\dot\alpha + (C_{\alpha p} + C_{\alpha z})\alpha + [mv^2 - (C_{\alpha z}l_z - C_{\alpha p}l_p)]\frac{\dot\varepsilon}{v} = C_{\alpha p}\frac{\beta_v}{i_g} - k_N v_r^2 \tau \tag{5}$$

$$J_z\dot\varepsilon + (C_{\alpha p}l_p^2 + C_{\alpha z}l_z^2)\frac{\dot\varepsilon}{v} - (C_{\alpha z}l_z - C_{\alpha p}l_p)\alpha = C_{\alpha p}l_p\frac{\beta_v}{i_g} - k_N v_r^2 \tau \tag{6}$$

where the individual symbols stand for the following:

$C_{\alpha p}$ .... the directional rigidity of the front axle [N·rad⁻¹]
$C_{\alpha z}$ .... the directional rigidity of the rear axle [N·rad⁻¹]
$l_p$ ..... the gravity center distance from the front axle [m]
$l_z$ ...... the gravity center distance from the rear axle [m]
$k_N$ ..... the side-wind force coefficient [kg·m⁻¹]
$i_g$ ..... the driving system gear [–]

τ . . . . . . the air-slope angle [rad]
$v_r$ . . . . . the total wind-gust velocity [m·s⁻¹]
$v$ . . . . . . the car velocity [m·s⁻¹]
$β_v$ . . . . . the steering-wheel turn-angle [rad]
$J_z$ . . . . . the car momentum with respect to the vertical axis in the gravity center
ε . . . . . . the car lengthwise-axis turn-angle [rad]
α . . . . . the angle between the car lengthwise-axis and the velocity vector [rad]
$m$ . . . . . the mass of the car [kg]

With respect to **Equations (5)** and **(6)**, the car's position coordinates $(x_0, y_0)$ at a certain time $t$ was calculated in the following way:

$$x_0 = \int_0^t v_{x_0}\, dt = \int_0^t v\cos(α + ε)\, dt \ , \quad y_0 = \int_0^t v_{y_0}\, dt = \int_0^t v\sin(α + ε)\, dt \qquad (7)$$

To decide the effect of the air environment on the car, it was necessary to calculate the relative direction and speed of the air flow toward the car. Because the relative wind direction was generally oblique and much less than 90°, the car's body was not only shifted aside but also turned around the vertical axis due to the aerodynamic moment, see also (Wallentowitz, 1981) and (Vlk, 1982). Let us remark that the aerodynamical effects are more significant for fast and light vehicles because the aerodynamical forces increase with $v^2$ and the side leading-wheel-forces are limited for lower adhesive forces of light cars.


## 5 Results

In the initial situation, the system randomly distributed seven fuzzy sets for each state variable. The fuzzy sets were labeled *NB* (negative big), *NM* (negative medium), *NS* (negative small), *ZO* (zero), *PS* (positive small), *PM* (positive medium), *PB* (positive big). These fuzzy sets represented approximate values, e.g., *negative_small_angle, zero_shift*, etc. For four input and 1 output variables, there were $7^5=16807$ possible combinations (i.e., rules) of the values. This number was too high to be processed manually; moreover, it was not known in advance which values should have been combined and which should have not. Also, the shape and position of each fuzzy set in its universe were not known as well and there was no clear guide how to distribute the fuzzy sets so that the control would be (nearly) optimal. The concrete composition and number of rules must be usually determined experimentally, which is tedious work and the result is not guaranteed. Obviously, testing all combinations of values and, simultaneously, tuning specific membership functions is impossible for a designer. GA can do it because they are based on a guided search. During the search, the best distribution of fuzzy sets is looked for and the number of rules (and even variables!) decreases. The results, provided by GA, depended on the specific definition of the fitness function. During experiments with our system, we revealed that the desired quality of control was obtained not later than after the first 100 generations. In some situations, we tried 1000 generations, however, there was no further improvement (actually, we did not expect that the system would improve because the control quality under the given

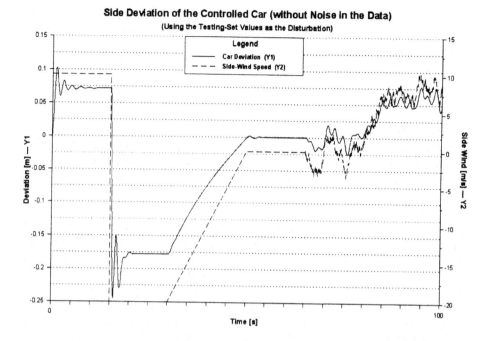

**Fig. 1.** The deviation of the car from the ideal road position due to the side-wind

conditions was perfect around the 100th generation). At the beginning, the quality converged quickly; usually, between the 20th and 30th generation, the improvement slowed significantly. During evolution of the controllers, the number of fuzzy sets and rules was dramatically decreased which resulted in small and compact knowledge bases. For example, one of the best controllers was based on 189 rules, i.e., 1.13% of the original number. What was of a really great interest it was the fact that the best controllers did not use all the input variables. Typically, the result did not consider the car's turn angle – only the shift, the shift change and the turn angle change were enough. Such a result is very surprising for a human designer. Generally, the controllers evolved by GA differed from what people would usually create, however, the functionality of artificially generated controllers outperformed their "human" counterparts. We compared the GA results with a few good controllers set up by human designers; the "artificial" product provided at least 10 times lower deviation from the desired course with almost no oscillation. An example of the control quality illustrates **Fig. 1**. From the fuzzy logic point of view, the choice of the specific implementation of the *AND* connective played an important role in extreme situations, i.e., for high velocities of the car and wind. In those cases, the choice of the algebraic product gave better results than minimum. The application of the algebraic product enabled the inference system to calculate the overall truth degree of antecedents using *all* subgoals, while minimum selected only one subgoal per antecedent with the least truth degree. Using the minimum connective resulted in higher robustness of the control, however, the control quality in extreme situations was inferior.

To visualize the results, we also developed the graphical output to the computer screen so the user could easily watch how the driving process was controlled when interactive testing data were used.


# 6 Conclusions

The results of our experiments showed that the application of GA to the automatic generation of fuzzy rule bases was very successful. Reliable and good controllers evolved during the first 100 generations and always significantly outperformed controllers designed by humans. Sets of fuzzy rules, developed with evaluation data, proved their excellent control capabilities even when tested with quite different data and also with random data. The fuzzy controllers obtained by our experiments simulated control actions of human drivers very well. In situations when we used input noisy data, the control quality deteriorated, especially for the noise > 5% of the original data magnitude. This effect was caused by the fact that the fuzzy controller itself did not assume any noise and therefore it would be desirable to evolve controllers where the input data would not be crisp numbers but, instead, fuzzy sets, too. The sensitivity to noise may present a serious problem in some applications.

Among the positive features of generating fuzzy rule bases by GA, it is necessary to stress the ability to produce rule bases of very reasonable sizes, which are easy to be maintained. Even if the GA's results differed from the "human" ones, the evolved controllers were quite transparent. Perhaps, a certain disadvantage was the need of extensive computations, however, this problem can be solved with faster hardware.


# References

1. Dubois, D., Prade, H. and Yager, R. R.: Readings in Fuzzy Sets for Intelligent Systems. Morgan Kaufmann Publishers Inc., 1993.
2. Goldberg, D. E.: Genetic Algorithms in Search, Optimization, and Machine Learning. Addison-Wesley Publishing Inc., 1989.
3. Hájek, P.: Fuzzy Logic From the Logical Point of View. Proceedings of SOFSEM'95, November/December 1995, Milovy, Czech Republic, Springer-Verlag, pp. 31-49.
4. Kruse, R., Gebhardt, J. and Klawonn, F.: Foundations of Fuzzy Systems. J. Wiley & Sons, 1994.
5. Vlk, F.: Theory of Vehicles: Cars. SNTL, 1982 (in Czech).
6. Wallentowitz, H.: Fahren bei Seitenwind. Automobil Industrie, 2, 1981 (in German).
7. Winston, P.: Artificial Intelligence. 3rd Edition. Addison-Wesley Publishing Inc., 1992.
8. Žižka, J. and Pivoňka, P.: The Influence of Selected Inference Operators on the Design of Fuzzy Controllers. Proc. of the 2nd International Workshop on Artificial Intelligence Techniques AIT'95, September 18-20, 1995, Brno, Czech Republic, pp. 127-139.
9. Žižka, J.: Side-Wind Compensation Using Fuzzy-Logic Based Inference. Proc. of the 6th Intl. DAAAM Symposium, 26-28th October 1995, Kraków, Poland, pp. 375-376.

# A Transaction Model for Mobile and Active Database Systems

Olaf Zukunft

Universität Oldenburg, Fachbereich Informatik
Escherweg 2, D-26121 Oldenburg
zukunft@informatik.uni-oldenburg.de

**Abstract.** Recent development in hardware and network technology has lead to the availability of portable computers and ubiquitous wireless networks. The new research area of mobile computing is concerned with the handling of problems and opportunities arising in this new environment. As one part of this research area, mobile database systems are developed for handling large amounts of data in mobile systems.

In this paper we focus on the use of active database systems in a mobile environment. We propose for the first time a transaction model suitable for mobile and active database systems. It combines reduced consistency as required in mobile systems with the dimensions of active rules regarding their transactional binding. This transaction model is described at both an intuitive and a formal level.

## 1 Introduction

Mobile Computing is concerned with the use of portable computers and wireless networks in a ubiquitous computing environment. This allows to access databases everywhere and anytime. However, current database technology can not always be used in mobile environments because existing solutions for database processing in distributed environments make a number of assumptions not valid in mobile systems. Opposed to conventional distributed database systems, mobile ones are not always connected to other computers either due to a missing network coverage of the area the mobile user operates in or due to the high cost charged for use of the limited wireless network bandwidth. Furthermore, the network connection between mobile and stationary computers is slow and error prune compared to wired networks. Similar problems exist regarding the power–consumption of mobile computers. Supplying energy in a mobile environment means to carry batteries. Despite their limited capacity, they are still heavy units. Hence, current research looks for techniques to limit the power–consumption of the mobile unit without sacrificing functionality. Traditional algorithms require applications to query the database for interesting information. This is not feasible for mobile computers because it wastes both energy and bandwidth. Instead, the idea of using triggers to initiate a network connection was first raised in [8]. There, the authors propose to use triggers to notify the mobile user of interesting events happening outside his current domain. The motivation behind this is to limit connections to cases where a connection is useful.

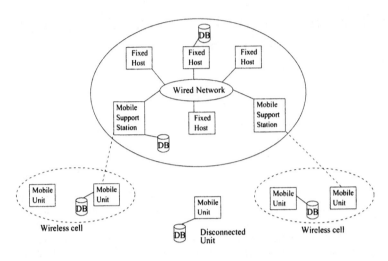

**Fig. 1.** The mobile database scenario

In this paper, we present a transaction model supporting the use of active database systems operating in mobile environments. Existing transaction models for active database systems use global serialisability as a correctness criterion. This is not suited for a mobile environment where long periods of disconnection and network partitioning are not rare errors, but frequent and desired features.

Since it is beyond the scope of this paper to propose yet another model for mobile computing, we will use a model from the literature. Our understanding of mobile computing follows the models as given in [8] and [1], i.e. we assume the availability of a wireless network able to connect mobile units to stationary hosts. As depicted in figure 1, some stationary hosts are called mobile support station (MSS) and provide an interface to the wired network. We further assume that the mobile units are full fledged computers capable of running advanced and demanding applications such as active database clients. In contrast to conventional distributed database systems, mobile systems require the ability to adjust to changes in the mobile environment and to operate in disconnected and low–bandwidth networks.

Active database systems [7] augment the passive database functionality with an event based rule system. Triggers as available in commercial database systems offer the most primitive active database functionality. On signalling of an event, a condition is evaluated and if this evaluation yields true, an action is performed. More sophisticated levels of active behaviour can be defined. The most common ones are complex events including conjunction and sequence operators and the introduction of coupling modes describing the interconnection of the rule executing with rule triggering transactions.

In the next section, we describe a unifying transaction model supporting the special needs of mobile and active database systems. Related work is described in section 3, and finally we give our conclusions and discuss some future work.

# 2  A Transaction Model for Mobile Active DBS

When we want to use active database system functionality in mobile environments, we can not simply reuse existing transaction models proposed for active database systems. The reason is that they are designed with global serialisability, mutual isolation of users and full network connectivity between network nodes in mind. In contrast, mobile users work often disconnected, with the goal of releasing limited information to co–workers during periods of low–connectivity and performing as much work as possible in the rare fully connected periods. Hence, they use different consistency criteria and different transaction models compared to active database systems. Our goal is to describe a transaction model offering support for the execution of rules in a mobile environment while limiting the modifications to the largest extend possible.

## 2.1  Structure

The structure of a transaction model defines the different kind of transactions available in the model. Typically, active database systems support a nested model where rules can be executed as subtransactions of rule triggering transactions. In a mobile environment, we need an open nested transaction model where some subtransactions can share their results with other transactions without waiting for their ancestors to commit. Open nested transaction models allow to release the results of a subtransaction if it has an associated compensating transaction. Additionally, we allow rule executions that are nested within other transactions but form their own top–level transaction. Different intertransactional dependencies between these top–level transactions can be specified through coupling modes as described in subsection 2.3. In the structural model, we distinguish between rule executions triggered in disconnected and in connected state.

## 2.2  Consistency

While nonmobile active database systems assume a globally consistent database state, this is not feasible in mobile environments. There, access to replicated data on disconnected units might trigger rules that must be either executed without connection to other nodes or be deferred until a reconnection. Hence, we use a different consistency model with a system controlled degree of global inconsistency. The basic idea follows [10] by defining different clusters of consistent data composed of strongly connected computers. Within these clusters, strong consistency and a conventional transaction execution as in nonmobile active database systems is enforced. The effect of rule executions performed in the state of disconnection may conflict with transactions performed at different clusters. For their reconciliation we extend the notion of rules to include a flag that describes the connectivity–requirement of the rule. It may be either deferrable or autonomous. Rules are autonomous if they can be executed in isolated clusters. Examples are business rules that initiate a business process at a specific point of time. Deferrable rules are those that are triggered by operations executed in disconnected clusters but require access to the globally consistent database. They are executed only during or after a reconciliation. However, they carry an additional transaction executed upon their triggering within the disconnected cluster. Here, a typical reaction might be to try to initiate a connection to the MSS or to inform the mobile user about the occurrence of the triggering event. The handling of conflicts depends on the consistency model employed by the mobile database system and is hence orthogonal to the additional semantics introduced through active DBS.

## 2.3   Coupling Modes

Coupling modes describe the transactional interdependencies between rule triggering and rule executing transactions. Different coupling modes are required in order to provide the expected semantics for rules used for specific applications. The six coupling modes depicted in the middle of table 1 are well known [3].

| Coupling mode | Example of application area | Problem in disconnected state |
|---|---|---|
| Immediate | Retrieval of derived data | Retrieval might require connection |
| Deferred | Secondary integrity constraints | Discrepancy between global/local constraints |
| Detached | Auditing | Might initiate connection |
| Causally dependant parallel | Business rules | Split between single- and multi-user |
| Causally dependant sequential | Execution of non-compensatable actions | Deferred until reconnection |
| Causally dependant exclusive | Contingency Rules | Used for delegating to different MSS |
| Critical dependent sequential | Delegation of vital tasks | — |

Table 1. Coupling modes in mobile environments

However, their use in a mobile environment raises the following questions:

**Immediate** rules are used e.g. to retrieve derived data. In mobile environments, we have to distinguish between strategies for locally replicated and remote data. For access to remote data, a connection is required which can only be provided in certain situations.

**Deferred** rules are mainly used to check consistency constraints before committing a transaction. In mobile environments, some constraints can only be checked in a fully connected state and their execution needs to be further deferred until a reconnection.

**Detached** rules have been introduced to support an auditing of transactions. Since mobile computers are considered error prune, they can not always fulfil their task locally but might require to store the data resulting from rule execution on stable stationary storage.

**Causally dependent parallel** rules implement the automatic initiation of logical consequences in the form of business rules. They are serialised after the rule triggering transaction and are aborted if that one aborts. In a mobile environment, we distinguish between three different kinds of causally dependent parallel rules:

1. autonomous rules can be completely executed on the mobile unit. They typically process data generated by the rule triggering transaction and involve only the owner of the mobile unit.
2. deferrable rules require access to globally consistent data or interactions from users other than the owner of the mobile unit. They may initiate a connection to the MSS or inform the user of their execution.
3. rules left by the mobile user on his MSS to inform him on the occurrence of certain events. Here, the active rule system is used to control the forwarding of events to mobile units. This is a significant task since an implicit event distribution to the mobile computer is not feasible and a system controlled optimisation of event distribution is not adequate without incorporating knowledge about the intention of the mobile user.

**Causally dependent sequential** rules are used in nonmobile active database systems to replace those causally dependent parallel rules that are not compensatable. In a mobile environment, the commit of a rule triggering transaction does not necessarily mean that it has finally succeeded. Instead, the open nested transaction model together with the possibility of conflicts during a reconciliation might result in a later compensation of a committed transaction. Hence, the triggered transaction can only be executed after both the commit and the reconciliation has been performed.

**Causally dependent exclusive** rules were originally intended to spawn alternative actions in time constrained database systems. They gain additional importance in mobile database systems, because they are useful to support the movement of mobile users. While in nonmobile environments a different algorithm is used by the spawned transaction, we execute the same transaction on different computers in a mobile environment. This includes different MSS for anticipating movements of the mobile unit or the execution of a transaction on a stationary computer as a backup of a mobile transaction.

In addition to the well known coupling modes, we have to introduce a new one for mobile environments. This coupling mode is called "critical dependent sequential". It is used to support an execution of transactions serialised before the rule triggering one, where the rule triggering is dependent on the triggered transaction. This coupling mode is employed in situation where the triggering transaction relies on data stored in a different cluster. When such data is accessed, a rule is triggered that checks the validity of the local data. Its failure results in an abort of the triggering transaction. Due to the used open nested transaction model, the rule triggering does not defer the execution or the commit of the triggering transaction since it can be compensated afterwards. Hence, this coupling mode is generally useful for performing system related critical task that requiring access to the database state before a modification is performed.

## 2.4 Formalisation

We use this subsection to define the presented transaction model using the ACTA–formalism. Due to space limitations, we restrict the presentation to the newly defined coupling mode and exemplary describe modifications of existing coupling modes[1].

In the following definition of the "critical dependent sequential" coupling mode let $t_0$ be a root transaction, $t_p$ be a parent transaction, and $t_{cds}$ a transaction spawned in the "critical dependent sequential" coupling mode:

1. $SE_{t_0} = \{$Begin, Spawn$^{cds}$, Commit, Abort$\}$.
   A new transaction using this coupling mode is spawned by Spawn$^{cds}$.
2. $IE_{t_0} = \{$Begin$\}$.
3. $TE_{t_0} = \{$Commit, Abort$\}$.
4. $SE_{t_{cds}} = \{$Spawn$^{cds}$, Commit, Abort$\}$.
5. $IE_{t_{cds}} = \{$Spawn$^{cds}\}$.
6. $TE_{t_{cds}} = \{$Commit, Abort$\}$.
   Together, the axioms 1–6 define the operations of the coupling mode.
7. $t_{cds}$ fulfils the four fundamental axioms of transactions.
8. $t_{cds}$ is failure atomic.
9. $($Commit$_{t_{cds}} \in H) \Rightarrow \neg(t_{cds}C^*t_{cds})$.
   Only transactions that are free of conflicts may commit.
10. $($Spawn$_{t_p}^{cds}[t_{cds}] \in H) \Rightarrow (\neg($Commit$_{t_p} \to$ Spawn$_{t_p}^{cds}[t_{cds}]) \wedge \neg($Abort$_{t_p} \to$ Spawn$_{t_p}^{cds}[t_{cds}]) \wedge ($Begin$_{t_p} \to$ Spawn$_{t_p}^{cds}[t_{cds}]) \wedge ($cdsParent$(t_{cds}) = t_p))$.
    Only active transactions spawn new transactions.
11. $($Spawn$_{t_p}^{cds}[t_{cds}] \in H) \Rightarrow (($Abort$_{t_{cds}} \in H) \Rightarrow ($Abort$_{t_p} \in H)) \vee ($Commit$_{Compensate_{t_p}} \in H)$.
    Aborting a spawned transactions either aborts the spawning transaction or commits of its compensating transaction (Abort dependency AD).
12. $\forall t_a, t_{cds}(t_{cds} AD^* t_a) \wedge \forall ob \forall p(p_{t_{cds}}[ob] \in H) \Rightarrow \neg \exists q((p_{t_{cds}}[ob] \to q_{t_a}[ob]) \wedge$ conflict$(p, q))$.
    A transaction $t_a$ can not execute a conflicting operation on a data item previously executed by a spawned transaction.
13. $\forall t \forall ob \exists p(p_t[ob] \in H) \Rightarrow ($ob is atomic$)$.
14. ViewSet$_{t_{cds}} = H_{ct}$.
    Spawned transaction can see the whole history of operations performed by committed transactions (ct).

---

[1] For a survey of the ACTA–formalism as well as a basic description of the used transaction model in nonmobile environments see [6] and [4].

15. $\text{ConflictSet}_{t_{cds}} = \{p_t[ob] \mid t \neq t_{cds}, \text{Inprogress}(p_t[ob])\}$.
    Spawned transactions may conflict with other executing transactions.

16. $\exists ob \exists t \exists q(\text{Abort}_{t_{cds}}[q_t[ob]] \in H) \Rightarrow (\text{Abort}_{t_{cds}} \in H)$.

17. $(\text{Abort}_{t_{cds}} \in H) \Rightarrow \forall t \forall ob \forall q((q_t[ob] \in \text{AccessSet}_{t_{cds}}) \Rightarrow (\text{Abort}_{t_{cds}}[q_t[ob]] \in H))$.

    Axioms 16 and 17 together define spawned transactions as atomic w.r.t. the abort operation.

18. $(\text{Commit}_{t_{cds}} \in Hi) \Rightarrow (\forall ob \forall t \forall p([p_t[ob]] \in \text{AccessSet}_{t_{cds}}) \Rightarrow (\text{Commit}_{t_{cds}}[p_t[ob]] \in H))$.

    If a spawned transaction commits, all operations of its AccessSet are also committed.

19. $(\text{Spawn}_{t_p}^{cds}[t_{cds}] \in H) \wedge (\text{Commit}_{t_p} \in H) \Rightarrow (\text{Commit}_{t_{cds}} \in H) \wedge (\text{Commit}_{t_{cds}} \to \text{Commit}_{t_p})$.

    If a spawning transaction $t_p$ commits, so do their spawned transactions and they are serialised before the spawning one.

The features specific to this coupling mode are found in axioms 11 (an abort of the spawned transaction triggers an abort of the spawning transaction) and 19 (the spawning transaction is commit dependent on the spawned one and will be serialised before the spawning one). In axiom 9, consistency is defined as the absence of a conflict w.r.t. the conflict relation $C$. This relation is well defined in the ACTA–publications for serialisability, which is the correctness criterion used within the clusters. After reconciliation, the same conflict relation is used to check for possible conflicts.

# 3   Related Work

Other work related to the one presented here can be categorised by their origin. From the area of active database systems, we have reused the six coupling modes proposed for the REACH system [3]. No work specific to mobile computing is known to the author from this community. The only article describing the processing of active rules in a distributed nonmobile environment is the work by Ceri and Widom [5]. In contrast to the work described here, they limited themselves to the immediate coupling mode, simple events and propose algorithms assuming global serialisability as a consistency model.

Existing work on transaction models for mobile and other disconnected environments has not offered support for active rules. They are mentioned as a supporting technique in [2] but no details are given. The idea of clusters of lower consistency is shared with [10]. However, they use only a closed nested transaction model. Walborn and Chrysanthis propose in [11] a transaction model for mobile clients that exploits the semantics of fragmentable objects. This is orthogonal to the approach presented in this paper. The transaction model presented in [9] focuses on providing the traditional UNIX–semantics to mobile users and is therefore more restricted than our model.

# 4 Conclusion

The usage of active rules has been proposed by various authors in order to solve problems inherent in mobile computing. To allow a processing of rules in mobile environments, we need to check if the well known concepts of active database systems are still usable. In this paper, we have investigated this for the transaction model. A merging of transaction models proposed for mobile and active database systems has been proposed. This transaction model owes its structure to the requirements from the active part, while its consistency model is imposed by the nature of mobile environments. Semantical requirements of active rules have been examined regarding their suitability for mobile environments. A new coupling mode has been proposed and formally specified. In future work we plan to test the proposed transaction model in a workflow management scenario where the mobile users take part in transactional workflows. This scenario is typical for mobile users and allows easy access to explicit semantic information provided in the workflow descriptions.

# References

1. R. Alonso and H. Korth. Database system issues in nomadic computing. In *Proc. Intl. Conf. on Management of Data (SIGMOD 93)*, pages 388–392, 1993.
2. N. S. Barghouti and G. E. Kaiser. Concurrency control in advanced database applications. *Computing Surveys*, 23:269–318, 1991.
3. H. Branding, A. Buchmann, T. Kudrass, and J. Zimmermann. Rules in an open system: The REACH rule system. In *First Intl. Workshop on Rules in Database Systems*, Edinburgh, 1993.
4. A. Buchmann, M. T. Özsu, M. Hornick, D. Georgakopoulos, and F. A. Manola. A transaction model for active distributed object systems. In A. K. Elmagarmid, editor, *Database Transaction Models for Advanced Applications*, 1992.
5. S. Ceri and J. Widom. Production rules in parallel and distributed database environments. In *Proc. Intl. Conf. on Very Large Data Bases*, pages 339–350, 1992.
6. P. K. Chrysanthis and K. Ramamritham. ACTA: A framework for specifying and reasoning about transaction structure and behavior. In *Proc. Intl. Conf. on Management of Data (SIGMOD 90)*, pages 194–203, Atlantic City, NJ, 1990.
7. K. R. Dittrich, S. Gatziu, and A. Geppert. The active database management systems manifesto. In *Proc. 2nd. Intl. Workshop on Rules in Database Systems. LNCS 985*, pages 3–17, Athens, Greece, 1995. Springer.
8. T. Imielinski and B. R. Badrinath. Wireless mobile computing: Solutions and challenges in data management. Technical Report DCS-TR-296, Rutgers University (Short Version appeared in CACM 10:37, 1994), 1992.
9. Q. Lu and M. Satyanaranyanan. Isolation-only transactions for mobile computing. *Operating Systems Review*, 28:81–87, 1994.
10. E. Pitoura and B. Bhargava. Maintaining consistency of data in mobile distributed environments. In *Proc. 15th Intl. Conf. on Distributed Computing Systems (ICDCS95)*, 1995.
11. G. D. Walborn and P. K. Chrysanthis. Supporting semantics-based transaction processing in mobile database applications. In *14th Symposium on reliable distributed systems*, Bad Neuenahr, Germany, 1995.

# Author Index

\* invited speaker

# Springer
# and the
# environment

At Springer we firmly believe that an international science publisher has a special obligation to the environment, and our corporate policies consistently reflect this conviction.
We also expect our business partners – paper mills, printers, packaging manufacturers, etc. – to commit themselves to using materials and production processes that do not harm the environment. The paper in this book is made from low- or no-chlorine pulp and is acid free, in conformance with international standards for paper permanency.

Springer

# Lecture Notes in Computer Science

For information about Vols. 1–1091

please contact your bookseller or Springer-Verlag